P9-DDM-102

Francis Ford Coppola

Francis Ford Coppola

A
Filmmaker's
Life

Michael Schumacher

Crown Publishers

NEW YORK

Photo credits for insert following page 248: American Zoetrope/United Artists, courtesy Kobal Collection: page 8 top, page 9 bottom; American Zoetrope/United Artists, courtesy Photofest: page 8 bottom; American Zoetrope/Warner Bros., courtesy Photofest: page 11 top; Archive Photos/AGIP: page 9 top; Archive Photos: page 2 bottom; Columbia Pictures, courtesy Photofest: page 14 bottom; Fotos International/Archive Photos: page 16 top; Kobal Collection: page 4 top, page 16 bottom; Max Miller/Fotos International/Archive Photos: page 6 bottom; Merrick Morton/Hollywood Pictures, courtesy Photofest: page 15 top; Paramount Pictures, courtesy Archive Photos: page 7 bottom; Paramount Pictures, courtesy Kobal Collection: page 6 top, page 10 top and bottom; Paramount Pictures, courtesy Photofest: page 5 top, page 7 top, page 13 top and bottom; Phillip V. Caruso/Paramount Pictures, courtesy Kobal Collection: page 15 bottom; Photofest: page 1, page 2 top, page 5 bottom; 7Arts, courtesy Photofest: page 3 top; Steve Schapiro/Paramount Pictures, courtesy Kobal Collection: page 14 top; Tristar Pictures, courtesy Kobal Collection: page 11 bottom, Twentieth Century-Fox, courtesy Kobal Collection: page 12 bottom; Vinnie Zuffante, courtesy Star File: page 12 top; Warner Bros., courtesy Photofest: page 4 bottom; Warner Bros./7Arts, courtesy Photofest: page 3 bottom

Published by Crown Publishers, 201 East 50th Street, New York, New York 10022. Member of the Crown Publishing Group.

Random House, Inc. New York, Toronto, London, Sydney, Auckland www.randomhouse.com

CROWN is a trademark and Crown colophon is a registered trademark of Random House, Inc.

Printed in the United States of America

Design by Lynne Amft

Library of Congress Cataloging-in-Publication Data
Schumacher, Michael.
Francis Ford Coppola: a filmmaker's life /
Michael Schumacher. – 1st ed.
Filmography: p.
Includes bibliographical references and index.
1. Coppola, Francis Ford, 1939– . 2. Motion picture producers
and directors–United States–Biography. I. Title.
PN1998.3.C67S38   1999
791.43'0233'092–dc21
[h]   99-12750
CIP

ISBN 0 517 70445 5

10 9 8 7 6 5 4 3 2 1

First Edition

To Simma Holt
Brave Heart, Precious Friend

Contents

Prologue

One warm summer evening in 1972, Francis Ford Coppola, director William Friedkin, and actress Ellen Burstyn were being driven to downtown Los Angeles in Coppola's limousine. A short time earlier, Coppola had christened the brand-new Mercedes 600 stretch limo with a spray of champagne, the gesture an outrageous, yet somehow appropriate, symbol of the filmmaker's status as the hottest young director in Hollywood. Coppola had recently turned thirty-three, but he seemed to have been in and around the industry for a long time. He had worked on a couple of "nudie" flicks and several Roger Corman B movies; he had established himself as a first-rate screenwriter, winning an Oscar for his script for *Patton*. The feature-length movies that he had directed himself—five in all—had sealed his reputation as an artist and auteur, but none of the pictures, except the most recent one, had made a dent at the box office. Coppola himself had been wondering if he would wind up being a screenwriter who directed an occasional film.

His latest picture, *The Godfather*, not only changed his career but also the attitudes, if not the structure, of Hollywood itself. Young filmmakers, often the products of the UCLA or Southern Cal film schools, had been flooding the industry for the better part of a decade, learning their craft and searching for a breakthrough in a business that, by tradition, was slow to welcome newcomers. Coppola, easily the brightest star to rise out of the UCLA back lots, had begun directing at a very early age and, consequently, became a model for every putative director or screenwriter trying to piece together a decent student film or script. To industry observers, Coppola seemed to have earned his reputation for equal parts talent and bombast. He certainly had been blessed with an abundance of both.

The Godfather had been a phenomenal success at the box office, inching its way toward becoming the most successful motion picture in history and sowing the seeds for a new blockbuster mentality that would hold Hollywood in its grip for a decade. Paramount Pictures, the studio that had produced *The Godfather*, had rewarded Coppola with the Mercedes limo after the picture had taken in $50 million.

It was no wonder that Coppola was in an ebullient mood as he, Friedkin, and Burstyn were ushered down Sunset Boulevard. The group sang "Hooray for Hollywood"—a bit cornball perhaps, but forgivable under the circumstances. Friedkin was a huge name in his own right; the director of the highly acclaimed cop action drama *The French Connection*, he would soon direct the film adaptation of the best-selling novel *The Exorcist*, in which Burstyn would play a starring role. Friedkin was only thirty-six.

The limo stopped for a red light, and as the group waited for it to change, they watched a Volvo station wagon pull up beside them. The car's passenger was Peter Bogdanovich, another of Hollywood's highly respected young directors. Almost exactly Coppola's age, Bogdanovich had felt intense competition toward Coppola and the others, particularly in the late sixties, when he was scrambling around and looking for work while Coppola was directing his early pictures. Bogdanovich's breakthrough movie, *The Last Picture Show*, had been released in 1971, the same year as *The French Connection*.

Seeing Bogdanovich in the car next to them, Friedkin could not resist the temptation to razz the other director with a little competitive banter. He stuck his head out of the limo's sunroof and called out to Bogdanovich, offering him a line from a review of *The French Connection*.

"'The most exciting American film in twenty-five years!'" he shouted. Then, to underscore his point, he held up a hand with all five fingers extended. "Eight nominations and five Oscars, including Best Picture!"

Bogdanovich responded in kind. "'*The Last Picture Show*, a film that will revolutionize film history,'" he shot back, quoting from one of *his* reviews. "Eight nominations, and my movie's better than yours."

As would be the case throughout much of his career, Coppola got in the last word. He stood up, poked his head through the sunroof, and roared, "*The Godfather*, a hundred and fifty million dollars!"

The following winter, *The Godfather* would earn more Oscar nominations than either *The French Connection* or *The Last Picture Show*, but for the moment, Coppola had proven that, even in those early, heady days, he understood the real language of Hollywood.

Chapter One

From Puppet Shows to *Dementia:* A Filmmaker's Beginnings

"Dear Mommy. I want to be rich and famous. I'm so discouraged. I don't think it will come true."

—FRANCIS FORD COPPOLA, in a letter to his mother

1.

FRANCIS FORD COPPOLA, the second of Carmine and Italia Coppola's three children, was born in the Henry Ford Hospital in Detroit, Michigan, on April 7, 1939. Francis's older brother, August, an enormous influence in Francis's life, had been born five years earlier, on February 16, 1934, and his sister, Talia, who, as Talia Shire, would become a successful actress, would arrive in 1946. Francis received his name from his maternal grandfather, Francesco Pennino, and from the sponsor of the "Ford Sunday Evening Hour," a radio program that employed Carmine Coppola as an assistant conductor and musical arranger. After her son had become an internationally known film director, Italia Coppola would remark that she had slight regrets about Americanizing Francis's name because he seemed the most deeply connected to his Italian heritage.

Both of Coppola's parents were first-generation Italian-Americans, the children of immigrants who left Italy for the United States around the turn of the century. Great ambition and artistic talent ran on both sides of the family. Francesco Pennino, a musician and songwriter, worked for a time as Enrico Caruso's pianist; his grandson would eventually honor him by using a fragment of one of his musical plays, a melodrama called *Senza Mama,* in a scene in *The Godfather, Part II.* But Pennino's biggest contribution to Francis Ford Coppola's life and career could be traced to his enthusiasm for movies: He operated several movie theaters in the New York area, and he was responsible for bringing a number of silent Italian films to the United States. He had connections to Paramount Pictures, which led to his being offered a job writing scores for the company's silent films, but Pennino, for all of his love of the movies, wanted nothing to do with Hollywood.

Augustino Coppola, Francis's paternal grandfather, while not a musician himself, encouraged his large family to study music, and two of his sons, Anton and Carmine, went on to have careers in music. Augustino worked as a tool-and-die maker, and he could boast of building the first Vitaphone sound system for Warner Bros. He, too, was immortalized in a scene in *Godfather II:* A group of Mafia hoods enter and demand that a gunsmith oil their machine guns, which he does while his young son plays the flute nearby. In real life, Augustino Coppola was similarly approached by neighborhood toughs; he oiled their guns while little Carmine stood nearby. "Who's this?" the gunmen wanted to know. "It's all right," Augustino Coppola assured them. "That's my son. Don't worry. He is studying the flute." When Augustino had finished working on the guns, the men gave him money for Carmine's musical education.

Evidently, the Coppola side of the family had a number of colorful characters in its ranks. As an adult, Francis would remember hearing all kinds of stories about his Italian ancestors—tales of robberies and "honor" slayings and the kind of mayhem that might have fit perfectly into one of his *Godfather* movies.

Mostly, however, there were stories of poverty, of the classic struggles that Italian immigrants went through to gain a foothold in the new country.

Carmine Coppola's youth had been anything but easy. He was left-handed and, like many left-handed kids at that time, he had to endure the rappings on the hand administered by well-intentioned teachers and adults trying to "convert" the youngsters to right-handedness. In addition, Carmine stuttered—a condition that led him to humiliating experiences in the classroom. Learning to play the flute became an urgent means of self-expression.

It also led to the most moving moment of his young life.

"My father was very attached to his older brother, Archimedes," Talia Shire remembered. "They were about a year or so apart, and my father loved his brother beyond belief. When Archimedes started kindergarten, my father became so uncontrollable that they couldn't be separated, so the teacher was kind enough to let Carmine Coppola sit in his diapers in the back of the class and go through the kindergarten with his older brother.

"When, at the age of seventeen, Archimedes was in the hospital and dying, my father desperately played the flute to make a couple of bucks for blood transfusions. My father visited his brother in the hospital, and Archimedes said, 'Carmine, you have a gift. Would you play for me?' So my father brought his flute and played for him. It was devastating for him."

Carmine studied flute on a Julliard scholarship, and he was accomplished enough to be offered jobs with prestigious orchestras, including the Detroit Symphony Orchestra. Not long after Francis's birth, Carmine was hired by the NBC Symphony Orchestra in New York City, where he played as first flautist for Arturo Toscanini—a position that would have thrilled any musician in the country. Carmine, however, had great aspirations. He wanted to write every kind of music conceivable—songs and serious music, perhaps even a Broadway musical or two—and his ten years with the NBC Symphony Orchestra were tinged with his own dissatisfaction over his inability to strike out on his own. He studiously worked to establish the kind of connections that he hoped would prove helpful, but nothing was forthcoming. Every night when the Coppola children said their prayers, they added a final adjoinder, imploring God to "give Daddy his break."

Life in the Coppola household revolved around Carmine's tempestuous career. The family moved often, even in the New York area—so much so that Francis soon lost track of the number of schools he had attended. He was always the new kid in school, always struggling to catch up with the curriculum in his new school, always the outsider—at least until he told his schoolmates that his father was a soloist for Toscanini; then he became a kind of schoolyard celebrity, a status he clearly relished.

According to August Coppola, Carmine Coppola's career in music had a subtle but very important influence on his children's development.

"We were raised with a sense of musical time and technique and discipline —a musical structure," he recalled. "Most people are raised to be mainly aware of space. We were aware of time. So when a person would, say, take life day by day, we took life note by note. There had to be a phrase, a melody—something. We were fundamentally raised on the technique of music. That's all we ever heard."

For Carmine Coppola, life around Radio City Music Hall might have been a matter of work, but for Francis, the occasional forays to this revered

Manhattan landmark, with its backstage bustle, the presence of the famed Rockettes, and the crescendos of heart-stopping music, were magic. On a day-to-day basis, times around the Coppola house were good. While certainly not wealthy by anyone's definition, the Coppolas lived a comfortable middle-class life that contrasted significantly with the much more modest existence that Carmine had seen as a boy. Whenever he could, Carmine showered his children with toys and gifts, and as an adult, Francis would look back on the family's post–World War II years in New York as some of the happiest days of his life.

Carmine harbored ambivalent feelings about success, similar to the ones that his son would confront many years later as a filmmaker. As a hired musician, Carmine could carve out a decent living, but he would never develop into the kind of artist he aspired to be; if he abandoned the safe route to pursue his dream, he faced financial ruin—the ultimate failure in a country where success was measured in dollars and cents and earthly possessions. Carmine's feelings, of course, were no different from those of any serious artist trying to balance art and commerce, but Carmine, like so many sons of recent immigrants, had been schooled in the American dream and how success served as an indication of one's self-worth.

It was a complex issue, and one not easily resolved, for while he honored those who achieved fame and fortune through hard work, he also had the deepest respect for the risk takers and innovators. Maverick automaker Preston Tucker, with his bold designs for a safer, more efficient car than those being built by the big three in Detroit, was one of his heroes.

"My father was the kind who bought a Motorola television in 1946 and an Eicor tape recorder," Francis recalled. "He heard about the Tucker project and it appealed to him. . . . He began to follow Tucker, and he showed us magazine stories about the car, and finally he invested $5000. He got his two brothers to invest as well, and then he ordered a Tucker."

Carmine's excitement rubbed off on his son, and Francis was thrilled when his father took him to an auto show where a Tucker was being featured. He kept waiting for the family's own Tucker car to arrive, but it never happened. "I was eight years old and kept asking him, 'When are we going to get it?' I'd seen the Tucker and thought it was a beautiful rocket ship, I couldn't believe that it wouldn't be made."

Neither could Carmine. Not only had he lost a sizable investment, he had also received a brutal lesson in the American dream rejected.

In time, Carmine became increasingly embittered over what he felt was a lack of progress in his career, and resentful of those he deemed to be less talented but who had become more successful than he had. Life wasn't fair. According to one story, he grew so frustrated that he ran into his backyard one day and threatened to finish his career by running his hand into the blade of a power mower. Decades later, his son disputed this story, although he admitted that he was intrigued by the symbolism of what he said really happened.

"My father was heartbroken over how he felt his career was going," Francis said. "He was trying to give up the flute and concentrate on composition, conducting, arranging–anything but the flute. One day, he was mowing the lawn with a power mower, and it got away from him. He ran after it, finally leaping toward it before it hit his car, but in doing so, he caught his hand in the blades. Fortunately, they only removed the tips of two or three fingers. Obviously, this was a tragedy for a flutist. However, a plastic surgeon worked on his hand all night, and repaired it as best he could. My father was still able to play after that, by having some extensions put on his instrument's keys. It was strange, I remember thinking, that such an accident happened after knowing how much he felt the instrument held him back. It was an accident, but it did seem portentious."

Francis's deep-seated hopes of seeing his father overcome what he later called "the tragedy of his career" led to one of the most bizarre episodes of his youth. He was fourteen years old and working for the summer at Western Union when he concocted a telegram, supposedly written by the musical director at Paramount Studios, informing Carmine that he had been chosen to write the musical score for one of the studio's forthcoming movies. All Francis wanted was to see his father happy–and for a brief moment, he got his wish. "It's my break! It's my break!" Carmine shouted when he received the bogus telegram, waving it in the air. A short time later, he was crushed when his son told him the truth.

2.

EVEN AT A VERY EARLY AGE, FRANCIS had problems of his own in measuring up to his parents' definition of success. His older brother was proving to be a parent's dream. Augie was intelligent, good-looking, and popular, and he seemed destined to achieve great things. Italia Coppola made a point of comparing her two sons, which might have been devastating to someone like Francis, who disliked his name (which he felt was a girl's name), who felt he was gangly and homely and cursed by an oversized lower lip, and who struggled to make the grade in school. To Italia, "Francie," as she called him, was "the affectionate one in the family," whereas Tally was "the beautiful one" and Augie was "the brilliant one." However, rather than resent Augie and grow competitive in what might easily have evolved into a classic sibling rivalry, Francis yearned to be just like his brother.

"He was the star of the family," he recalled, "and I did most of what I did to imitate him. Tried to look like him, tried to be like him. I even took his short stories and handed them in under my name when I went to writing class in high school. . . . I would say that my love for my older brother formed the majority of aspects of what I am."

"Augie was blazing an interesting trail," added Talia Shire, "but he was sharing that trail with the rest of us. Francis did benefit from that."

Fortunately for Francis, Augie didn't resent having a brother five years his junior hanging around and pestering him. In fact, it was quite the opposite. Augie took Francis under his wing, not only allowing him to tag along when he and his friends were out on the town but also taking him along to the movies, helping him with his homework, advising him on how to dress in a way that would attract girls, and, in almost every respect, encouraging him to blossom on his own; the two even shared the same room for years. Francis, a sensitive child, was deeply touched by his brother's kindness, and throughout his life, he would speak almost reverentially of him.

The profound family ties would have a strong effect on Francis as an adult, when he had achieved great wealth and acclaim, leaving him with mixed feelings about his achievements in comparison with those of his father and brother. Francis could—and did—use his position to secure work for his father—usually writing scores for his movies—but the reversal in status, a delicate point in Italian-American families such as the Coppolas, must have been trying at times. Carmine Coppola, a proud man with an encyclopedic knowledge of music, was, in essence, riding on the coattails of his son's reputation, and while both Carmine and Francis would have vehemently denied, with good cause, cynical charges of nepotism, Francis would always have to address, at least in his own private thoughts, the unsettling truth that his talented, frustrated father had reached his goals only after he, Francis, had met his own—a situation underscored at the Academy Awards ceremony in early 1975, when Francis took home three Oscars for *Godfather II*. On that same evening, Carmine Coppola was awarded an Oscar for his score in *Godfather II*, an honor that his grateful son noted during one of his acceptance speeches. "Thanks for giving my dad an Oscar," Francis said to the voting members of the Academy, meaning every word of it, no doubt unaware that his remarks sounded perhaps more patronizing than prideful. "After I'd spent a lifetime with a frustrated and often unemployed man who hated anybody who was successful," he later commented, "to see him get an Oscar, it added twenty years to his lifetime."

With his brother, it was a slightly different story. Augie did not aspire to the kind of career path taken by his father and younger brother, and he went on to achieve his own highly respected position, earned on his own terms, as a writer and professor of comparative literature. Francis was extremely pleased with Augie's success, and he would talk him up in his interviews with the press, yet by his own admission, he also felt very protective of the man who had been so good to him as a child—a feeling that he could trace back to his boyhood.

"I had a dream once as a kid that scared me to death," he recalled. "I was in one of those kinds of streets and there was an enormous manhole, big manhole cover, and these tough kids were getting my brother and putting him in there and were going to cover him in this manhole. And I ran to the different houses to get a phone to call the cops. I never forgot that dream."

3·

The turning point in Francis Ford Coppola's early life occurred when he was nine years old, when he was struck down with polio. He had been on a weekend Cub Scout camping outing, where it had rained a deluge, soaking the tents and everything in them. The following morning, after sleeping in the dampness, Francis awoke with a stiffness in his neck. On his father's orders, he tried to attend classes, but the school nurse, alarmed by his condition, sent him home. A short time later, he was delivered by ambulance to Jamaica Hospital in Queens, where it was determined that he had contracted the deadly disease.

"The hospital was incredible," Coppola told biographer and film critic Peter Cowie. "The epidemic was such that they had kids stashed in the bathrooms, three high on these racks, and in the hallways. . . . The first night was pretty painful, and I kept calling out for my mother, but I was more frightened by the cries of the other kids."

At first, Francis had no idea what lay in store for him, and, by his own account, he felt sorry for the other children. That changed soon enough, when he tried to get out of his hospital bed and found himself in a heap on the floor. His left arm, leg, and side were paralyzed, as was his entire back. "My parents, of course, were hysterical," he remembered. "I was taken to this doctor who said I was paralyzed. He told me that I was not going to be able to walk again and that I had to be a soldier. They took me home and put me in the bedroom. They pinned me to the bedsheet so I wouldn't fall out. It was then that I realized what was going on."

For the better part of the next year, Francis was confined to his bed, working with a physical therapist and slowly regaining his health. It was a terribly lonely time. Since polio was so contagious, Francis was not allowed to receive visitors—especially children—outside of his immediate family, and for a kid who already felt like an outsider, the isolation was difficult and painful. However, when reflecting on the experience three decades later, Coppola depicted the ordeal as a growing experience. "I think any tough time you go through, any real crisis where you break down, then survive, leaves you in a far different place from where you were," he explained. "Generally, I feel that people who have been traumatized tend to develop levels and wrinkles that really add something to them."

For Francis, this meant adding to an already active imagination. The Coppolas had a television set, which Francis watched from his bed, his favorite program being the Horn and Hardart's *Children's Hour* on Sunday mornings. He also had a record player and radio to entertain him, and as he gained back the use of his arm, he experimented with a tape recorder and 16-mm movie projector given to him by his Grandpa Pennino, beginning a lifelong obsession with electronic gadgets. Much of the early fascination, Coppola later explained, was born out of the need to find a pragmatic solution to problems arising from his physical disability. "I lived in a bed, unable to walk, with a television across the room," he said. "My frustration at not being able to change the channels led to [my wanting to find a way of] putting wires across the room for remote control."

Since he could not see anyone outside of his family, Francis created his own set of friends out of puppets, inventing stories and conversations. Over the months, he became a decent puppeteer. He had an autographed picture of Paul Winchell and Jerry Mahoney nearby, and a Jerry Mahoney ventriloquist's dummy that he learned to manipulate. It helped pass time and stave off his loneliness, but it also gave him his first rudimentary experiences with directing his own little stories. When he was finally allowed to receive outside visitors, he entertained them with puppet shows and, later, screenings of his homemade movies. Said Coppola: "I am sure that from those shows came the idea of my studio—a place where we could work together like children, with music, puppets, scenery, lights, dramatic action, whatever we wanted to do."

Using the tape recorder that his father had given him, Francis tried to find ways to synchronize sound and dialogue for his family's home movies. He cut up some of the movies and created new stories, usually finding himself the hero of his own adventures. "I was really just fooling around," he remembered, "and was more involved in the exhibition end. I was also very interested in physics, and gadgetry, and what have you, and then another side of me became involved in theater, for my father [was] a conductor of musical comedies. So the two interests—the technical thing for gadgetry and the interest in plays and puppets and theater and musical comedy—sort of came together in film, which was like a playground for all those things."

Although few of Coppola's film experimentations from this period survive, none is anything more than child's play—early indications of a fertile mind at work.

One experience from Coppola's fight with polio—a nightmarish episode that occurred while he was still paralyzed—did find its way into a fragment of dialogue in his movie *The Conversation*. Italia Coppola, who usually had to help Francis with his bath, had lowered him into the hot water one day, only to leave the room for a brief period to answer the doorbell. Unable to stay seated in the tub, Francis began to slide downward in the water, which soon reached his chin and began to work its way up to his nose. Italia returned at the last moment. *The Conversation*'s protagonist, Harry Caul, had an identical experience in his youth, and he tells the story at one point during the movie. When he has finished, he expresses disappointment that he hadn't drowned, speaking volumes about the isolation and despair that Francis felt when he lay in bed, disabled by polio, listening to the sounds of children playing outside.

Francis recovered, almost miraculously and entirely, from his battle with polio, retaining only the slightest hint of a limp to remind him of the ordeal. He continued to build crude moviemaking equipment out of household items, and over the ensuing months he designed a makeshift television studio—complete with fake television cameras and a boom mike—in the basement of his parents' home. He even tried to build his own television set.

Unfortunately, more disruption lay ahead. Carmine Coppola ended his tenure with the NBC Symphony Orchestra, and after a stint with Radio City Music Hall, arranging the music for the Rockettes, he was on the move again, working with theater road companies and searching for the kind of job that, at long last, might offer him some satisfaction.

4.

CARMINE COPPOLA HAD BIG PLANS for his sons. August, he declared, was going to be a doctor, and Francis would be an engineer. There was no way his children were going to have careers in the arts. The boys, however, had other ideas. By the time Francis entered high school, he was considering a career as a scientist, perhaps as a nuclear physicist, while Augie, studying philosophy at UCLA, decided that he wanted to be a writer.

Not surprisingly, when it came time to address Carmine Coppola's designs for his children's futures, it was Augie who paved the way, though he took a blow to the ego in the process.

"I was to be a doctor," he remembered, "and all my life I received doctor's kits every Christmas, as the parental incentive to steer me in the right direction. I was actually in pre-med. But I said to my father, 'Why can't I be an artist? You are.' He said, 'Yeah, but there can only be one genius in the family, and since I'm already it, what chance do you have?'"

By now, Francis's fascination with science and technology had developed into a full-blown obsession. He hid microphones throughout his house, so he could listen in on conversations; he bugged the family telephone. He squirreled away his money until he had saved the fifty dollars needed to purchase an A. C. Gilbert atomic energy lab, equipped with a Geiger counter and a cloud chamber with a radioactive needle. He learned how to concoct small explosive devices, which he placed in his backyard and set off by remote control. Years later, when he wrote *The Conversation*, he based the background of Harry Caul on some of his boyhood experiences.

"Somewhere along the way, [Caul] must have been one of those kids who's sort of a weirdo in high school," Coppola said. "You know, the kind of technical freak who's president of the radio club. When I was a kid, I was one of those guys. . . . In fact, my nickname was 'Science.' You know, 'Hey, Science, come over here and tell him about induction coils.' And I was president of the radio club. I became attracted to the theater because it fulfilled the two poles in my life: one was stories and the other was science."

High school, for Francis, was rough. Ever the nerdy outsider, he found it impossible to fit into the usual high school cliques and activities. He had never been very athletic to begin with, but polio had limited him even more, leaving him with one leg slightly shorter than the other, cutting off even the slightest chance of his being accepted by the popular jock crowd.* He was still very shy around girls, and more inclined to see them as unattainable fantasies than as classmates. He tried running with a small gang for a while, but he no more belonged to this group than to any of the others. In the end, he was the skinny, bespectacled egghead who knew all the stuff that no one else was interested in, and who, fittingly enough, played the tuba, perhaps the least glamorous instrument in the orchestra, designed to blend in and complement but never stand out on its own.

---

*As an adult, Coppola would become quite rotund, but he was actually very thin in high school. While in military school, he wrestled in the 140-pound weight class.

The instrument, in fact, was responsible for Francis's enrollment in the school he loathed the most—the boys-only New York Military Academy at Cornwall-on-Hudson. He had won a tuba scholarship to the school, and for the better part of a year and a half, he endured the macho environment that found upperclassmen picking on underclassmen, athletes treated like gods, and bookish kids like him being discarded as misfits. Francis might have been miserable, but he was also resourceful, putting his already considerable writing skills to work for him, composing love letters to the tune of a dollar per page. Classmates would provide him with photographs of their girlfriends, and Francis would be off in his own creative fantasyland, letting his imagination guide him to the kind of pronouncements certain to score points with girls he would never meet.

He was reading a great deal now, leafing through the pages of *Ulysses* and other classics, trying to follow the path of his older brother. Francis was attempting some writing of his own, mostly in the form of sketches and short stories, but by the time he reached the end of his junior year in high school, his interests were tilting toward the theater. This could not have been the best of news for his parents, who were still contending with the ups and downs of Carmine's career, and who worried that their son might be heading for a similarly difficult life if he didn't pursue a more stable line of work.

Francis's new interests received an important boost the summer after his junior year of high school, when he went to California to live with Augie. His brother, three other guys, and, occasionally, a couple of girls were living in a tiny house in Westwood, not far from the UCLA campus, their days occupied by reading and writing and impassioned intellectual discussions. To his delight, Francis was included in the group's activities, and, in turn, he began to write more seriously. It was, he later declared, a "wonderful summer."

August remembered his brother's visit a little differently, and with some humor.

"To be honest, he was kind of a pain in the ass," August stated. "He had to go to summer school, and he would wake me up to drive him there. I really wanted to sleep and he had to go to school. It was my responsibility. He knew all the girls that I knew, and he would promise them that if he ever became famous, he would buy them a sports car. I don't know how many he scored with, but he promised."

This only removed him that much more from military school. When he returned in the fall, he found himself as disenchanted as ever, and he reached the end of his patience when he wrote the book and lyrics for a school musical, only to see his work rewritten by the faculty. With his parents out of town, due to Carmine's work as the orchestra conductor for a road production of *Kismet,* Francis fled the military school's campus, and knocked around in New York City for several days, "sleeping where I could and having certain crazy adventures," as he recalled.

"When I got home," Coppola said, "my brother gave me a book and said, 'Read this.' It was *Catcher in the Rye.* I had just lived it."

The Coppola family settled in Great Neck, New York, where Francis enrolled in high school. He graduated in the spring of 1956.

5.

AFTER ALL HIS PERIPATETIC WANDERINGS, Francis was ready to settle into college life and pursue what was shaping up to be a career in theater. Before heading out to UCLA, Augie had attended Hofstra University on Long Island, and he had highly recommended that his younger brother do the same. This was all Francis needed to hear. He showed samples of his writings to Hofstra officials, and on the basis of his potential and talent, he was offered a partial scholarship to the university.

He wasted little time in establishing himself on campus. He was bright and energetic, rather pretentious and occasionally arrogant, friendly, eager to learn, and, above all else, not at all afraid of asserting himself. Movies remained his real love, and he had barely settled into college life when he started a club called the Hofstra Cinema Workshop and set up screenings of classic films. As he would later recall, the films of Sergei Eisenstein, particularly *Ten Days That Shook the World,* had made all the difference in his decision to pursue a career as a filmmaker. The year he entered Hofstra, he attended a screening of *Ten Days That Shook the World,* and was shaken to the roots by what he saw. "On Monday," he said, "I was in the theater. On Tuesday I wanted to be a filmmaker."

Hofstra's theater arts department was rich in talent, with members who would go on to distinguish themselves in the performing arts. James Caan, whom Coppola would cast a decade later in *The Rain People,* and who would break through to stardom in his featured role in *The Godfather,* attended Hofstra, as did Lainie Kazan, who would become a successful singer and actress, and who would work for Coppola in *One from the Heart.* Joel Oliansky, a future award-winning director and screenwriter for both television and motion pictures, was a drama major who also edited *The Word,* the campus student magazine to which Coppola contributed articles and short stories.

Oliansky, a transfer student a year ahead of Coppola, liked the spirit of adventure in the university's drama department, which, compared to other colleges, gave the students a fair amount of freedom.

"They had an *eager* drama department," he explained, "and the faculty was good. They were a little tradition-bound in those days, but they were eager to let you try things. You could always make mistakes. They cherished people like Francis and me; they thought we were different, and they liked the idea. They were interested in anybody that could contribute something fresh."

Oliansky and Coppola became friends, and Oliansky eventually appointed Coppola to the position of drama-music editor of *The Word*.

"My take on him then," Oliansky said of Coppola in a 1999 interview, "was exactly what my take on him is today: He's incredibly talented and incredibly pretentious; he doesn't know what he's doing half the time, and the other half of the time he's brilliant. What I love about Francis is that he hasn't changed. He's consistent. I had an early appreciation of him. I published his short stories in the college magazine. I had a column in the college paper, and I profiled him in 1958. I said he was going to go all the way or burn himself out—there would be no middle ground. It was a column predicting that he was going to do great things, and people said to me, 'What are you? Nuts? He's all talk.'"

Coppola was eager to direct a student play, but Hofstra rarely allowed its students to direct major productions. Instead, he absorbed everything he could learn about theater production, acquiring much of his knowledge from hands-on experience. He worked with lighting and technical crews; he built scenery. He watched the way others directed their actors. He took small roles in several plays. All the while, he continued to write short stories and short plays, perfecting his skills in narration, dialogue, and plot development.

People took notice, particularly of Coppola's technical skills, which were augmented by his ability to improvise when the going got tough. He sought solutions when fellow students were frozen by the problem. Oliansky recalled a time when he was asked to direct a television production of *Julius Caesar* for a new, experimental television station at a local high school; he was ready to begin shooting, only to realize that he had only one microphone to work with.

"Francis was playing Casca for me in that production," Oliansky recalled, "and thank God he was with us. All he did was look around at gadgets—'What's this? What's that? How does this work?'—exactly as he always was. I, on the other hand, pretended not to see any of the stuff. They had no microphone except the one hand mike, and they were so amateurish that the teacher said, 'Oh, we thought you'd just pass it back and forth between you.' It was Francis, of course, who rigged a boom. He figured out a way to put the hand mike on a fishing pole. That's the way he was, from the beginning."

By his sophomore year, Coppola was deemed ready to take the reins of his own production—Eugene O'Neill's one-act play *The Rope*. Coppola threw himself into the project, pushing himself and his crew to the limit and adding his own creative spin to a production that would have challenged far more experienced directors. The play, Coppola decided, was not going to be your run-of-the-mill student production, simply staged and, more likely than not, quickly forgotten; this production would have interesting sets, a musical score, and complicated lighting. Students complained that their dictatorial leader knew nothing about what he was doing, but when the curtains closed on the play, Hofstra's drama department chairman proclaimed *The Rope* to be the best student-directed show that he could remember. Coppola was given the Dan H. Lawrence Award—the first of three that he would win at Hofstra—for outstanding direction and production. Coppola had established his name.

This was only the beginning. Over the following two years, Coppola sprinted ahead of the rest of his class, staging plays, reorganizing the school's drama department, and, in general, distinguishing himself to such an extent that he was ultimately honored with Hofstra's Beckerman Award for student directing. ("It carried a two-hundred-dollar reward, which is what I was *really* interested in," he quipped, years later.) He was known throughout the university for his enormous ambition, his plays becoming gigantic, complex productions that defied the traditional fare.

Such was the case with *Inertia,* an elaborate musical staged during Coppola's junior year at Hofstra—the first production in the university's history to be entirely written, produced, and directed by students. Coppola came up with the story for the play, directed it and wrote its songs' lyrics. Based on H. G. Wells's story "The Man Who Could Work Miracles," *Inertia* featured numerous set changes and production numbers that would have challenged a much more experienced director, but Coppola managed to pull it off. The play was a huge success and a glowing testament to Coppola's creative gifts.

His ability to organize was equally impressive. While in his junior year, Coppola was elected president of both the Green Wig—Hofstra's drama society—and the Kaleidoscopians, the school's musical comedy club. He combined the two groups into a single organization called the Spectrum Players and announced that the new group would be staging a play every Wednesday. He, of course, would be directing them all. By using extracurricular funds, he was able to put together enough money to support the productions, and, to his delight, the plays were well attended. No one seemed to mind Coppola's taking over the theater arts department except some of the faculty, who ultimately set up a new rule, whereby a student could direct only two shows per year.

For all his involvement in theater, Coppola still hoped to work in the movies. He sold his car and used the money to purchase a 16-mm camera, which he used to put together a student film—a short about a woman who takes her children on an outing to the countryside. After playing with the children, the mother falls asleep, only to awaken and find them gone. In her frantic search for the missing children, the mother begins to see the country-side, once so beautiful and inviting, as threatening to her children's safety. "I wanted to experiment with this duality," Coppola recalled of the film, "but I only filmed one part of it and never finished the project. I had no technical experience then."

His first production of his senior year, a musical comedy entitled *A Delicate Touch,* for which he wrote the book and lyrics, was even larger in scope than *Inertia.* This time, however, Coppola watched his grand plans wiped out by a string of mishaps, including the collapse of a set facade, which would have crashed down on the front rows had it not been for the split-second thinking of an alert stagehand, who managed to pull it back at the last instant. Coppola had envisioned an event rivaling a Broadway production, complete with a huge cast, thirty-piece orchestra, and full slate of musical numbers, but for all his vision and ambition, neither Coppola nor his fellow students had the expertise or experience to pull it off.

"When I was watching, in horror, all the stuff that was going on in *One from the Heart,*" Joel Oliansky remarked, referring to Coppola's disastrous 1981 film, "I said, 'There's nothing new about this. This is *A Delicate Touch.*' It was absolutely the same thing."

Coppola's other senior production, Tennessee Williams's *A Streetcar Named Desire,* was much more memorable. Ironically, two of his future business associates—Robert Spiotta, who would become the head of Coppola's Zoetrope Studios in the early 1980s, and Ron Colby, who would appear as an actor in *Finian's Rainbow* and produce *The Rain People*—competed for the role of Stanley Kowalski. Spiotta, a football player, won the lead, and his perfor-mance assured Coppola that his exit from Hofstra would be on a high note.

6.

COPPOLA GRADUATED FROM HOFSTRA in the spring of 1960. He was, as he related, "the central figure of the drama department," a student who "commanded as much power [at Hofstra] as I might on the outside." During his time at the university, he had applied himself to learning as much as possible about the theater, modeling his studies after Eisenstein, who had taken a similar approach before setting out to establish a career as a filmmaker. "Eisenstein, who was my god in those days, said a theatrical foundation was essential," Coppola explained, "so I stayed away from film until later."

There was little question that, by the end of his four years at Hofstra, Coppola had every intention of devoting his life to the movies. Nor was there any question as to where he would be continuing his education. Not only had his older brother attended UCLA; the university had the reputation of housing one of the finest film schools in the country.

Coppola's timing could not have been better. He was entering UCLA during a period when film schools were about to explode in a proliferation of talent that, within a decade, would change the face of the motion picture industry. As film writer Dale Pollock noted, "By happy coincidence or predetermination, a group of filmmakers emerged from the film schools in the mid-1960s that is the cinematic equivalent of the Paris writers' group of the 1920s." In just a few years' time, George Lucas, John Milius, Caleb Deschanel, Randal Kleiser, Robert Zemeckis, and John Carpenter, among others, would pass through the film school at the University of Southern California, while Martin Scorsese and Brian De Palma would make their marks at New York University and Columbia, respectively. UCLA would produce Coppola, Carroll Ballard, Steve Burum, Frank Zuniga, and Jack Hill.

While remarkable in retrospect, the impressive roster of students at UCLA, Southern Cal, NYU, and elsewhere was largely the result of a new attitude toward these schools as training grounds for future filmmakers. In the past, an aspiring director wouldn't have dreamed of attending classes to learn the business. He would have worked his way up the industry ladder—the industry at the time was most definitely an old boys' network—beginning with a menial job and advancing through the ranks over the years. Prior to the early 1960s, film students were scorned by an industry that believed it was a waste of time to study how to make a movie when you could learn through experience.

"For a while, film schools seemed to have a stigma," observed Martin Scorsese, who pointed out that even after he and his colleagues had broken through, there was still some critical snobbery aimed at the new filmmakers. "A few reviewers would write, 'His work is full of student pretensions,' But there are too many of us now. Actually, film school is a microcosm of the industry."

When glancing back at his time at UCLA, Coppola, too, was inclined to sing the praises of the film school environment. "They provide a terrific stimulus, a chance for young people to meet someone—a teacher or another student—who can influence them," he remarked. "And secondly, they let you get your hands on real movie equipment. You can't do that anywhere unless you're rich enough to go out and buy your own."

In theory, students entering a two-year program would be exposed to what usually took many years to learn through on-the-job experience. Beside receiving a heavy dose of film history, students studied directing and, to a much lesser extent, acting, as well as the technical aspects of animation and film and sound editing. They actually worked with 8-mm or 16-mm cameras; they learned the basics of setting up and working within the framework of a budget. Perhaps most significantly, students operated in a creatively fertile environment where they could work with and encourage one another on projects and engage in spirited late-night discussions and arguments about film and their eventual place in it.

When Coppola arrived at UCLA in 1960, things were much less exciting than they would become a few years later, when some of his younger colleagues attended film school. In fact, Coppola was quite disappointed by the film school, and for a while he considered going back into theater. The UCLA film school was located in a wooded area behind the university, isolated from the rest of the student body. Most of the students were older than Coppola, and he was depressed by what he felt was an aura of negativity emanating from the group.

"There was none of the camaraderie I had imagined while I was in college," he said of his first impressions of UCLA. "All they knew was how to criticize the lazy ways of Hollywood film producers, implying that only they could be capable of directing great films."

Carroll Ballard, who would eventually direct *The Black Stallion* for Coppola, agreed.

"It was highly competitive and ego-driven," he recalled. "Everybody thought of themselves as the next Kurosawa. I don't remember it being all that congenial. What was good about film school was not the school itself; it was the enthusiasm of so many young people who had the same dreams, and how that kind of cross-fertilized. The academic aspects of it were a snore and a waste, as far as I was concerned. I felt that film school should be run like a body shop: you had to learn how to bang out those fenders and do all this stuff. No amount of talk is really going to do it."

Very few fenders were being pounded out at UCLA. For someone of Coppola's talent and ambition, the program moved at a painfully slow pace. Only two student films were funded each year by the university, and the day-to-day workings of the film school seemed woefully inadequate. As Coppola remembered, students were handed a minuscule amount of 16-mm film, for which they were to create a short movie; equipment was hard to come by. He did manage to put together a film entitled *The Two Christophers*—a brief exercise about a murderous boy who wants to kill another boy with the same name—and, the following semester, a longer work, *Aymonn the Terrible,* which told the story of a narcissistic sculptor interested in creating sculptures only of himself.

Aymonn the Terrible went a long way toward establishing Coppola's reputation at UCLA. The script was light-years ahead of the average fare turned out by students, and Coppola displayed, as he had at Hofstra, a remarkable ability to do whatever was necessary to get the job done. For one scene, he needed to film the movie's main character standing near Michelangelo's *David.* Forest Lawn Cemetery had a full-scale replica of the statue, but the cemetery also had a strict policy of allowing no one to shoot a film on its premises. Undeterred, Coppola contacted a cemetery official and, after explaining that he was a student making a modest, noncommercial film, he was given permission to shoot in the cemetery. He then contacted the Chapman Company, builder of the biggest and best camera crane in existence. After running through the film-school spiel with one of the company's officials, he promised to provide Chapman with a high-quality photograph of one of its cranes posed next to Michelangelo's *David* in exchange for a brief loan of the crane. Once he had secured use of the crane, Coppola headed over to Forest Lawn, where he shocked groundskeepers by turning up not with the expected small, amateur film crew, but with a sixty-man crew and a Chapman crane.

"He was unbelievable," remembered Carroll Ballard, who worked as a grip on the film. "At the time, I was very bitter about it. Francis showed up at UCLA, and within a very short period of time, he seemed to have the whole department wrapped around his little finger. Who *was* this guy? He got everything he wanted and had everybody working for him like a bunch of slaves. What qualified him for this? I have since come to realize that the qualities that he had—and chutzpah, to a large degree—were the most important qualities for making it in the movie business. It was incredible, what an operator he was."

7·

THE STUDENT FILMS ONLY WHET Coppola's appetite for more work. Others might have been content to sit in darkened rooms and watch classic films, or discuss theory and technique, but Coppola was far from satisfied.

"They talked a lot but nothing seemed to happen much," he complained. "I had this overwhelming urge to make films; not to read about them or see them, just to make them. All I lacked was the opportunity."

When he finally got his chance, it came from a totally unpredictable source. Russ Meyer, who would build a profitable career out of sexploitation films, had recently released *The Immoral Mr. Teas,* a nudie flick that somehow managed to escape obscenity busts while earning a lot of money. Before long, everybody wanted to make one of these low-budget pictures, and film school students were ideal candidates to work on the productions. Some of Coppola's classmates scorned the opportunity to engage in what they felt were sleazy ventures beneath their talents, but Coppola had no such reservations. All he wanted was the chance to work behind the camera, and though nudies were about as far removed from Eisenstein or Kurosawa as one could have imagined, they did offer the opportunity to pick up some badly needed experience. When a small group of investors approached Coppola and asked him to produce a script along the line of *The Immoral Mr. Teas,* Coppola went right to work.

The investors liked his script and were willing to buy it, but, unfortunately for Coppola, they were not interested in hiring him to direct the picture—"which," Coppola later remarked, "was the only thing I was interested in." He showed the script to other potential investors and was able to raise two thousand dollars to shoot the film himself.

By today's standards, *The Peeper,* shot in an abandoned Venice, California, department store and using sets that Coppola built himself, is far less provocative than a great percentage of the adult material found on today's video store shelves. Coppola himself would compare it to a Tom and Jerry cartoon—a description not as far-fetched as it might seem, given the comical nature of the film's plot, which is little more than a series of funny scenes depicting the main character's exercise in futility. In *The Peeper,* the main character, a Peeping Tom, discovers that pinup photo sessions are taking place in a nearby apartment, and the movie's story is an account of his comical attempts to catch a glimpse of the women being photographed. He fumbles around, trying to hoist himself into a better viewing position, only to take a fall; he gets a huge telescope that is so powerful that he can see only small parts of the women.

Ironically, Coppola would never be comfortable directing nude scenes at any point in his career, even after he was well established.

"I have great trepidations about approaching erotic scenes in movies," he admitted nearly two decades later. "My mother was sort of a fanatic about having to respect women, and I was brought up believing that if you like a girl, if you make some kind of little pass at her, you'll be disrespecting her. So if the actress said, 'Oh, I'm going to do it,' that's okay, but if I have to ask her, I feel like I'm some dirty old man or something."

True to form, Coppola tried to make *The Peeper* something more than a cheap skin flick, and as a result, he had no takers when he tried to find someone to distribute the finished film. He eventually connected with another group of filmmakers who had made a comic nudie of their own—this one involving a preposterous Western setting and a plot in which a drunken cowboy hits his head and begins to see cows as naked women; Coppola agreed to splice the two films together with a slightly different plot. In *Tonight for Sure*, the new permutation of the two pictures, the two main characters, supposedly moral crusaders out to shut down the local strip joints, meet and compare notes, the Coppola-created character talking about his life as a Peeping Tom, the other telling a tale about a cowboy friend who hit his head and now sees nothing but naked women when he looks at his cows. In combining the two films, Coppola was able to work in enough nudity to satisfy the market at the time, and he made certain that he received sole credit for directing the film, although, by his own estimation, roughly 80 percent of the new movie was someone else's work.

Whatever his reservations about shooting nude scenes, Coppola knew one thing for certain: He was actually working as a filmmaker—as opposed to just studying about it in school—and he was being paid for it to boot. Shortly after completing *Tonight for Sure,* he was offered another opportunity, this time to fill in a 1958 German movie called *Mit Eva Fing die Sunde* (later retitled *The Playgirls and the Bellboy*). Once again, the film was lighthearted and voyeuristic, involving a bellhop who dresses in a number of disguises in an effort to gain admittance to a room occupied by lingerie models. In this movie, Coppola got to work with June Wilkinson, a popular *Playboy* model, and his job involved shooting a number of 3-D color scenes to insert into the original black-and-white German footage.

As Coppola remembered it, his mixed feelings about shooting nude scenes became an issue during the filming.

"There was a 3-D scene where we had to have five girls sitting at their dressers, and they were hired and paid to do this. One of the girls came to me and said, 'I'm only seventeen and my father is going to kill me.' So I said, 'Well, okay, leave your brassiere on.' So there were these four girls, plus one who had a bra on, and I got fired because they [the producers] were complaining they paid the girls $500."

In years to come, Coppola's nudies would be packaged and repackaged, sometimes under different titles. In essence, he had passed his first practical course in filmmaking. He was on his way.

8.

As Coppola was about to discover, there was an even better way to learn the ropes of filmmaking. Roger Corman, the undisputed king of the B movies, loved to employ film students as cheap labor, and Coppola would soon become the first in a long line of distinguished Corman apprentices.

In 1961, there was no one in the business quite like Corman—nor, arguably, would there ever be. At a time when young American filmmakers aspired to follow in the footsteps of John Ford or Orson Welles, Corman chose another path. The 1950s had seen the rapid growth of drive-in movie theaters in the United States and over the years, these overgrown parking lots, with their huge screens, tacky concession booths, and little microphone stands became a haven for teenaged baby boomers looking for an inexpensive place to congregate or, better yet, make out. The motion picture industry was evolving into a youth market, and the kids attending the drive-ins were most assuredly *not* interested in movies with complex characters and long, involved plotlines. Television was already shrinking attention spans, and that, along with the many built-in distractions that seemed to be de rigueur elements of the drive-in, made the simple, action-packed genre picture an ideal offering. The more sensational the picture, the better.

Born in Detroit on April 5, 1926, Roger Corman had moved to Beverly Hills with his family when he was about fourteen years old. He attended Stanford University, where he earned a degree in industrial engineering, his education interrupted by a stint in the navy during World War II. After graduating from Stanford, he found a job with Twentieth Century–Fox, beginning as a messenger and working his way up to story analyst. Dissatisfied with the direction that his career was taking, he left the business and attended Oxford University on the GI Bill, studying modern English literature. From there, it was on to Paris, where he lived for a while before returning to the States and the movie business. In 1955, he directed his first films, *Five Guns West* and *Apache Woman*, both low-budget Westerns. He had an uncanny ability to work inexpensively and quickly—some of his films took only a few days to shoot—and he soon established himself as the top producer-director of Hollywood exploitation films, churning out movies at an amazing clip, the pictures bearing such dubious titles as *Attack of the Crab Monsters*, *The Viking Women and the Sea Serpent*, *Machine Gun Kelly*, *The Wasp Woman*, and *The Little Shop of Horrors*. These and other titles might not have sprung to people's minds when the Academy Award nominations were being announced every year, but the movies always seemed to make money. When he met Coppola, Corman was embarking on a series of more ambitious projects, including adaptations of Edgar Allan Poe classics—films such as *The House of Usher, The Pit and the Pendulum, The Premature Burial, Tower of London,* and *The Raven.*

Corman learned of Coppola through director Dorothy Arzner, a teacher at UCLA and one of Coppola's early supporters. Corman asked Arzner if she had any students whom she might recommend for work as an editor on one of his pictures, and she immediately named Coppola. The timing, Coppola noted later, was fortuitous. He was running out of money and was so broke that he literally feared that his telephone would be disconnected before he heard from Corman. Not that he was going to become wealthy working for the producer-director: For the six months' work that he put into his first Corman project, Coppola was paid a whopping $250.

For what it meant to his budding career, Coppola probably would have paid Corman for a shot at working for him. "At the time, I had no complaints," Coppola said of the meager payment for his work. "He had a little office and a couple of cutting rooms. It was very exciting. It felt as if I had got started at last."

The first project, a B movie called *Battle Beyond the Sun,* was in a sense an extension of the kind of work that Coppola had done on *Mit Eva Fing die Sunde.* Corman had purchased some Russian science fiction pictures, which he intended to rework and distribute to American audiences. Doing so, however, required some fancy footwork, since in 1961 Cold War America, anything remotely Russian was frowned upon. ("Monsters play well at the drive-in," Corman wryly noted. "Communism does not.") Coppola's main task was to rewrite the dialogue, which would be dubbed into the movie in English. He would also be shooting a few scenes and inserts.

Coppola secured the assignment by telling Corman that he spoke Russian—a lie that in the long run bore very little consequence. All Coppola had to do was watch the movie and invent dialogue that fit the action. Most of the dialogue in the finished film was so generic that it would have fit into any of Corman's science fiction films.

Coppola proved to be as ingenious when shooting his scenes for *Battle Beyond the Sun* as he had been when working on low-budget college plays and his early UCLA student films. One of the new scenes required a crowd of flag-waving people. With no money to pay extras, Coppola had to come up with a cheap way to accomplish the task. He and Jack Hill, a classmate who was working as a cameraman on the project, drove to Pasadena just before the Rose Bowl Parade was to begin, and after announcing that he was making a student film, Coppola distributed tiny flags to the people waiting for the parade to begin. "When I signal," Coppola instructed the throng of extras, "wave the flag and cheer." The scene wound up costing next to nothing.

Of all the work that he did on the movie, Coppola would remember one particular scene, both for what it meant to him in actual work and for the way it symbolized Roger Corman's method of retooling a movie.

"There is a scene on a planet where an astronaut sees the image of a golden astronaut holding a golden torch of hope and humanity," Coppola recalled. "Roger had me matte that out and matte in two monsters fighting, with one devouring the other. Difference in translation between Russian and American science fiction?"

Corman was looking for a battle between a good-looking, sexy female monster and a good-looking, sexy male opponent, with the female winning the fight and devouring her vanquished foe, and he instructed Coppola to create monsters that were "subtly male and female." Working in his bathtub, Coppola and a friend designed the monsters out of foam rubber, one looking like a thinly disguised giant vagina, the other like a giant penis, complete with a single hideous eyeball. Corman was surprised by Coppola's creations—"I was surprised by what he considered subtle, but not shocked"—and he worried that they would never slip by the censors. Coppola argued that no one would ever know the difference—a prediction that turned out to be true enough.

Coppola wanted to impress his mentor, going to extremes to see that Corman appreciated his efforts. "I'd deliberately work all night so when he'd arrive in the morning, he'd see me slumped over the Moviola," Coppola recalled. "He started to see me as an all-purpose guy."

Corman rewarded Coppola by giving him as much work as he could handle. There were other Russian space flicks to dub and edit, as well as a string of new movies that needed Coppola's various skills. He served as the dialogue director on *Tower of London* and as an assistant on *The Premature Burial*. To a twenty-two-year-old film school student looking for entrée into the movie business, the prospects of working on the set with such an established veteran as Vincent Price was a dream come true, a learning experience that Coppola later characterized as "just exhilarating."

9.

HIS UCLA CLASSMATES WERE LESS enthusiastic about his connection to Roger Corman. Coppola, they felt, had sold out his talent. He was becoming just another cheap Hollywood hack.

Some of these sentiments were undoubtedly weighted by envy, for Coppola was turning out to be as gifted as he was resourceful. This much was evident when one of his student scripts claimed the prestigious Samuel Goldwyn Award, a prize normally awarded to novels or plays. According to Coppola, his entry, entitled *Pilma, Pilma* and loosely patterned after *The Two Christophers,* his earlier student movie, was written in a single marathon session. Coppola had been scheduled to take a physical examination for the army, and on the night before his appointment, hoping to find a way to flunk the physical and avoid the draft, he stayed up all night, plying himself with pot after pot of coffee and filling his hours by writing *Pilma, Pilma.* The following morning, a completely exhausted Coppola passed his physical (though he was never drafted), but he had a completed script to show for his efforts. "I won $2000 for the screenplay," Coppola said of his prizewinning entry, "and then I sold it later for $5000. All that money for one night of passionate writing. . . ."

Corman, for one, was thrilled by all the recognition bestowed upon his protégé, and he took out ads in the trade papers announcing the Samuel Goldwyn Award. Coppola was touched. Corman had a new picture in the works, a film called *The Young Racers,* to be shot in Europe, which would integrate actual Grand Prix footage into another cut-rate quickie destined for the drive-ins. Corman asked Coppola if he knew anyone who could work on the film's sound, and, undaunted by the fact that he knew virtually nothing about sound recording, Coppola volunteered for the job. As soon as he had been hired, he rushed home and read through *The 'Perfectone' Sound Recorder* manual, giving himself a crash course in working the equipment.

By all accounts, the experience was a mixed bag. Corman, Coppola, and the rest of the small crew traveled from race to race in a Volkswagen minibus. Coppola's inexperience in sound recording infuriated Floyd Crosby, the movie's main cameraman, who complained that you could hear camera noise on the sound track, meaning the picture would have to be reduped. Coppola steadfastly maintained that the problem was not his doing. In any event, he was much more successful when he doubled as the film's second-unit director, raising eyebrows when he took a handheld camera right down to the trackside and, laying on the ground, filmed the cars zooming past within only a few feet of him.

The group concluded the shooting in England and Ireland. The film had been extremely inexpensive, even by Corman's standards. Knowing that Corman liked to cut costs by shooting two movies back-to-back, using the same crew and many of the same actors in both movies, Coppola suggested that he would be able to make a movie on the leftover money from *The Young Racers*.

"I knew that whenever Roger takes a crew on location he can't resist the temptation of doing a second picture, having already paid the crew's expenses there," noted Coppola. "I played on this, managing to convince him that I should direct it. At the time, Roger wanted to make a movie molded on the success of *Psycho,* so I told him a zesty horror scene which more or less turned him on."

"When we were shooting *The Young Racers,*" Corman remembered, "I realized we would have some money left over to make another feature. We had all our equipment in a Volkswagen Microbus, which could be used to make a quick film with the extra money. Francis seized the opportunity. He stayed up all night to write an entire treatment.* It was smart, well written, and extremely demented. Appropriately, it developed into *Dementia 13,* his first feature."

Coppola's scene was a natural for the Roger Corman oeuvre: It's late at night, and a man is standing alone at the side of a pond. He takes five dolls out of a bag and ties them together with string. He then removes all his clothing and dives into the pond, swimming deeper and deeper with the dolls, which he intends to weigh down on the floor of the pond. Just as he has completed the task and is about to return to the surface, he sees the preserved body of a seven-year-old girl at the bottom of the pond.

Corman loved the idea. "Change the man to a woman," he told Coppola, "and you can do it."

Once again, Coppola's chutzpah had paid off. There was, however, one important detail that Coppola had to address: He had no script or any idea where his story was going—only the scene that he had contrived in order to talk Corman into letting him do the movie. Coppola wasn't worried. As he would point out later, his willingness to seize the moment was one of the main characteristics separating him from some of his fellow students and aspiring filmmakers.

"We were in Ireland with a movie crew that was just begging to be utilized," he said. "I was dreaming up an idea for a story while everybody else just talked about making a film. The secret of all my getting things off the ground is that I've always taken big chances with personal investments. While

---

*According to Coppola and published accounts elsewhere, it was actually one scene, not an entire treatment.

the other guys my age were all pleading, 'Roger, let me make a film,' I simply sat down and wrote a script."

Corman liked *Dementia* as a film title, and that, along with Coppola's scene at the pond, became the backbone of the script. Today, when watching *Dementia 13*, one sees a strange combination of influences and talents, part Coppola and part Corman, owing heavily to both *Psycho* and the drive-in horror flicks of the day. Coppola's lifelong obsession with the dynamics of the family lies at the heart of the story, with its telling of the dysfunctional Haloran family, run by a half-mad matriarch and haunted by the drowning death of one of the children.

At the opening of the story, the family has gathered to commemorate the anniversary of Kathleen Haloran's death. It's late in the evening, and John Haloran and his wife, Louise, are rowing a boat on the estate's large pond, discussing the disposition of Lady Haloran's will. Lady Haloran, it seems, wants to leave the bulk of her family's wealth to charity—a decision that does not sit well with Louise, who, in all likelihood, married her husband for his money. John Haloran, we learn, has a heart condition, and while rowing the boat and arguing with his wife, he suffers a fatal heart attack. Realizing that she will no longer be considered a member of the family, Louise dumps Haloran's body in the pond, then, upon returning unnoticed to the estate, fabricates a tale about his absence. She types and signs a letter, supposedly written by her husband, in which he states that he had to return suddenly to New York and will be unable to attend Kathleen's memorial. Louise slips the letter under Lady Haloran's door and returns to the pond, where she disposes of the typewriter and her husband's suitcase.

The next morning, we meet the rest of the Haloran clan. They are, to say the least, an odd bunch. After seven years, Lady Haloran continues to mourn the death of her only daughter—to such an extent that Justin Caleb, the family physician, worries for her sanity. Richard Haloran, a renowned sculptor, is a brooding presence who always seems to be a split second away from erupting; his fiancée, Kane, who arrives on the morning of the memorial, appears to be a stabilizing force in his life. Billy Haloran, the youngest son, who was playing with his sister at the time of her drowning, is haunted by horrible nightmares and feelings of guilt. Simon, a friend of the family, roams around the estate, hunting and, in general, getting on people's nerves.

The memorial service gives us our first look at the way Coppola handles rituals—one of his strongest points as a director—and he doesn't disappoint: All family members hold identical black umbrellas and, at the end of the service, place a single flower on Kathleen's grave—a simple enough service, yet somehow it is oozing with hidden meaning and implication. As the memorial ends, Lady Haloran faints and Louise offers to take care of her. No one in the family suspects that Louise's motives are to get the woman alone and try to drive her mad.

That evening, while wandering around "Castle Haloran," Louise comes across Kathleen's old room, which, we suspect, is exactly the way it was at the time of the young girl's death. Louise steals some of Kathleen's dolls and takes them to the pond. She ties the dolls together with string, slips into the pond, and is about to weigh them down on the floor of the pond when she sees what appears to be the body of a young girl—Kathleen—floating in an underwater monument nearby. Terrified, she rushes to the surface. As she reaches the shore, she is attacked by a man wielding an ax. He murders her before she can escape.

Unaware of the murder, the family speculates about Louise's sudden disappearance. While eating lunch on the lawn, the family is horrified by the sight of the dolls floating on the surface of the pond. Robert Haloran is willing to write it off as a cruel prank, but the others are not as convinced. Justin Caleb, suspicious of the goings-on at the Haloran estate, and conducting his own private investigation into the events, suggests that the pond be drained.

At this point, the mayhem is coming fast and furious—a nod, no doubt, to Corman. While hunting, Simon stumbles upon Louise's body, hidden in a small cave, but he is attacked and decapitated by the (still-unknown) ax murderer before he can defend himself or call out for help. Lady Haloran is similarly attacked when she visits Kathleen's old play area, but she manages to escape.

The next day, the pool is drained and the family finds an eerie artifact—a headstone, made for Kathleen—in the muck. Richard is immediately suspected as being the one who made the headstone, but he denies having anything to do with it. After finding Louise's body hanging on a hook, Justin Caleb decides to try to flush the killer out of hiding. He succeeds by placing a lifelike doll of Kathleen in a fountain near the estate, and when the murderer—Billy Haloran—appears with an ax, ready to take out another family member, the doctor shoots him. As Billy dies, his long-kept secret is revealed: He had pushed Kathleen into the pond, and then had been driven mad by his feelings of guilt.

10.

ROGER CORMAN WAS DUE BACK in the States, so he left Coppola on his own to shoot his movie. Before taking off, Corman assigned the twenty-thousand-dollar production money to a secretary, who was required to cosign any checks being written for the movie's expenses. Coppola quickly found a way around the dictum: He had the secretary give him a blank check, which he filled in for the full twenty thousand. He then used the money to open a new, separate account.

Thinking that he might need more money to finance his movie, Coppola met with Raymond Stross, a British film producer, who offered a matching twenty thousand dollars for the British rights to the film. As a perk, Coppola would be allowed to shoot at the Ardmore Studio in Dublin. Coppola was thrilled. "We were young and making a feature film!" he remarked. "I think that kind of enthusiasm has a lot to do with the fact that when you're young your standards are low. If you shoot something that looks like a real movie, that puts you into euphoria."

With forty thousand dollars at his disposal, Coppola had all the money he needed to shoot for two weeks in the countryside and nine days at Ardmore. He had a number of people left over from *The Young Racers,* including art director Al Locatelli, who had been with Coppola since his work on the nudies, and actor William Campbell, who was given the role of Richard Haloran. Luana Anders, another Corman veteran, took the important part of Louise Haloran, while Bart Patton, a Coppola friend from UCLA, handled the role of Billy Haloran. Coppola filled out his cast with local actors who were willing to work for cut-rate salaries or, in some cases, a tiny percentage of the picture's future profits—if there proved to be any.

"When I was about to film *Dementia 13* in Ireland," Coppola recalled, "I sent word to many of my UCLA film student friends that I was about to make a feature—magic words—and asked some to come over to be on my crew, obviously for very little money. I had hoped that one of them, John Vicario, would be the camera operator. He mentioned that he hoped his girlfriend, Ellie Neil, could come as well."

Three years Coppola's senior, Eleanor Neil was a talented artist in her own right. A native of Los Angeles, she had attended UCLA, graduating from its art department with an applied design degree, and she had traveled extensively, visiting Mexico and Peru, as well as hitchhiking and driving around Europe. She had come to Ireland thinking that the movie business was a big, glamorous profession, but, as she would recall, the first time she set eyes on Coppola in a farmhouse that was serving as a production headquarters, she saw a rather frumpy, disheveled character, shirtless and wearing only pajama bottoms, hammering out the screenplay for *Dementia* on mimeograph sheets. She knew instantly that he was a leader, and she found herself immensely attracted to him.

"I was struck by his intensity and energy," she remembered. "Everyone was running around, prepping to shoot per his directions, and I was impressed with his command of the situation. In low budget chaos, he had control and everyone working for him." Besides being attracted to Francis's obvious intelligence and powerful air of authority, Eleanor was taken by what she felt was his exotic Italian personality. "I had never known an Italian-American before," she admitted. "He was fun, affectionate, and emotionally very expressive, compared to the reserved, mostly English family that I'd come from. I found him thrilling."

At the time, Coppola was seeing a young Irish woman on weekends, and he and Ellie started their relationship as friends. However, by the time Coppola had wrapped the shooting of his film, both he and Ellie had ended their respective relationships and were prepared to move their friendship into something more romantic. In no time, they were constant companions.

Throughout his stay in Ireland, Coppola received messages from Roger Corman, who kept urging him to slip more sex and violence into his picture; he certainly had no use for an artsy psychological thriller. Corman, as it turned out, had more work for Coppola, and as soon as he had completed the principal photography for *Dementia*, Coppola was dispatched to Yugoslavia, where he was to work as a script supervisor on a mystery entitled *Operation Titian*. Ellie accompanied Coppola to Dubrovnik, but she was due back at UCLA, where she was teaching a course, and what had turned into a romantic interlude came to an end. Ellie returned to the States and Coppola remained in Yugoslavia to finish work on the Corman film.

When he returned home, Coppola assembled a rough cut of *Dementia* and showed it to Corman. The producer found the film confusing in spots, and he wanted more violence—most notably, another ax murder—but he was generally "happy" with Coppola's efforts.

"It was a little short," Corman recalled. "We needed to give it an extra scene to make it the proper length, but Francis was busy, so we hired Jack Hill to shoot the additional scene. Francis wasn't pleased with it, but he understood that it had to be added in order for the film to be the right length. In the end, the film was very good—an extremely impressive first effort."

Coppola's tutelage under Corman was clearly drawing to a conclusion, although Coppola did agree to help Corman with a messy bit of work eventually released as *The Terror*. Corman had recently wrapped the shooting of *The Raven*, one of his better Edgar Allan Poe adaptations, and realizing that Boris Karloff, the picture's star, was still in Big Sur, where *The Raven* had been filmed, he decided to try to knock off another quick picture. Since he had no script for the picture—or even an idea of what the story was going to be about—he enlisted a screenwriter to throw together a few scenes that could be shot while Karloff was still on location. That none of it made sense was of little immediate concern to Corman: He still had his star UCLA filmmaker in his employ, and he could find a way to bring the plot together.

Coppola did his best, but the movie was laughably bad—too horrible to be anything but perhaps a poor parody of one of Corman's own movies. The dialogue was incomprehensible, and the action meandered aimlessly. However, *The Terror* afforded Coppola the opportunity to work with an unknown actor named Jack Nicholson, who was putting in his own time under Roger Corman. To someone as inexperienced as Coppola, Nicholson could be a challenge.

"I was really a theater student type," Coppola allowed, "and many of the people Roger had assembled for *The Terror*—Dick Miller and Jack Nicholson, to name two—were veterans of some of his previous low-budget movies. When I first arrived, I suggested that we all meet that night to rehearse. Jack thought that was very funny: How can you rehearse a movie, especially one that takes place in the woods? These folks were a little older than me, and were not above utilizing a strange herb they were always smoking.

"I think Jack took some delight in ribbing me. One day, we were about to shoot a scene where he's supposed to look into a brook and see fish swimming, and say, 'Look, there must be thousands of them.' But he refused to say the line. When I asked him why, he said, 'Well, once Roger had me come into a scene where Vincent Price was strumming a lute, which was going *twang-twang-twang*. I was supposed to say, "That's very lovely, did you compose it yourself?" Roger told me that he was going to replace the *twang* with beautiful lute-playing. Of course, in the finished movie, I walk in and say, "That's very lovely, did you compose it yourself?" and there was still this horrible *twang-twang-twang*. I felt like an idiot. So if you ask me to say, "Look, there must be thousands of them," I know when you cut there's going to be three goddamn goldfish swimming around.'"

Indeed, Nicholson had worked for Corman long enough to know his methods, and he was somewhat amused by Coppola's treating *The Terror* as seriously as he was, when the movie was really intended to be a low-budget flick. "I think Roger went wild with Francis," Nicholson speculated, "because no one ever went over budget and he was supposed to be up there for three days and we stayed eleven or something like that. We all thought we'd be machine-gunned or fired forever out of the business."

Nicholson recalled one particular scene—which Coppola, when asked years later, denied any memory of—in which he, Nicholson, had nearly drowned in the Big Sur surf. According to Nicholson, Coppola had asked him to wade into the water, supposedly to search for one of the film's characters. Nicholson, wearing a heavy military uniform from the Napoleonic era, was to walk a substantial distance into the surf, but when he did, he found himself in a terrifying situation.

"The water never [got] deep," he explained, "so in order to look disappeared—I made this up as I was going out there—I sort of crouched down to my knees. When the first white-water waves hit me, the water knocked me under. When I went under with Lieutenant Duvalier's huge Chasseur uniform on, I felt I couldn't stand up. I was pinned to the ground from the weight of this uniform. I had that split-second panic because I was out a ways already. I came flying out of there and just threw that fucking uniform off while I ran, freezing to death."

("I really don't remember anything in the least like that happening," Coppola said when disputing the account, although he admitted to shooting scenes of Nicholson in Big Sur. "Jack was a pretty bright, cynical guy—I can't imagine him letting me get him into a spot anything like that.")

Considering the fame that both men would attain within a few years, *The Terror* shoot proved to be a revealing glimpse of one of Hollywood's bad-boy actors contending with an ambitious and determined young director. Coppola's story of Nicholson by the brook constituted only one of his memories of the brief shoot.

"Another time," he remembered, "I found a spot where there were thousands of butterflies. I guess they had just emerged as butterflies. I sent some helpers out for three or four hours to collect them into baskets. I then set up a spot where Jack and his then wife, Sandra Knight [who was appearing in the movie], were to come lovingly down a path and kiss in the midst of thousands of butterflies. We got ready and rolled. When Jack and Sandra came down the path, I signaled to release the butterflies. Jack walked right up to the camera and stuck his tongue out at it. Then, as the butterflies all disappeared, he said, 'Oh, were you rolling?'"

After two weeks, Coppola decided that he'd had enough. He returned to Los Angeles and told Roger Corman that he was moving on.

In retrospect, Coppola's time with Corman represented the best education he could have hoped to receive, and while three years would pass before he would direct another feature or have that kind of hands-on experience again, Coppola had been primed for his work as a filmmaker. In future interviews, he would always express his gratitude and debt to Corman for the chances he had given him.

For a first film, *Dementia 13* (renamed because the title *Dementia* was already taken, and because Corman believed that with the *13* in the title, the film might be shown in theaters on the thirteenth of each month) was derivative but far from embarrassing. At times, the black-and-white photography was creative and beautiful, and if the story seemed weak, some of the shortcomings could be attributed to Coppola's being very young and very much under the influence of Roger Corman, and to his having written the script in a mere three days.

The movie, however, didn't play well at the drive-ins—or with the critics—when it was released in September 1963. As a rule, critics for the major newspapers and magazines passed on reviewing Corman's teen drive-in fare, and *Dementia 13* was no exception. The *New York Times* ran a review, but it was not the kind of notice that Coppola could brag about. "Don't ask what *Dementia 13* means—or whatever happened to the first 12 dementias. One is enough," wrote critic Howard Thompson, who called Coppola's direction "stolid." ("At first, I thought it said 'solid,'" Coppola later remarked, "but my brother corrected me.") Across town, at the *New York Herald Tribune,* the reaction to the movie was a little kinder, but not by much: "*Dementia 13* is a gory little mystery shocker that horror-and-whodunit fans won't mind."

The movie's reception was of little consequence to Coppola. By the time his first legitimate picture was hitting screens, he had moved on, with no way of knowing when—or if—he would be directing another movie.

Chapter Two

Big Boy

"If Francis Ford Coppola had not existed, Hollywood would never have bothered to invent him. He would have gotten in the way. . . . He comes from a long, honorable line of rule breakers and system buckers. The family name is Artist."

—JOSEPH MORGENSTERN, *Newsweek*

1.

ON FEBRUARY 2, 1963, ONE WEEK after leaving Roger Corman, Francis Ford Coppola married Eleanor Neil in a small ceremony in Las Vegas, capping off a whirlwind romance that had begun less than a year earlier. For Coppola, the timing of the wedding was more a practical issue than a matter of his having an overwhelming desire to get married at that very moment. He was once again hearing noises about the draft, and being married was one way to avoid conscription. Not that he and Ellie wouldn't have married in any event: The two were deeply in love and, as Ellie joked years later, she was beginning to feel, at twenty-six, like an old maid, especially since most of her friends had already tied the knot.

Francis was also eager to get married. "I very much wanted a wife, a family, and children when I was young," he later remarked.

35

The Las Vegas location for the ceremony was also largely a matter of practicality. Ellie, a tapestry maker, created her murals for businesses, and she had recently sold one to the Las Vegas airport. She and Francis, along with ten family members, took a train to Las Vegas, giving all the chance for a brief, intimate vacation while Ellie took care of business.

"I had been in—and to—a zillion weddings, and had no desire for a big one," Ellie remembered. "We got married in the most attractive little wedding chapel we could find, and we stayed at the Dunes. The next day, my mother treated us to a helicopter ride that went up in front of the hotel. I thought about that when I was up in all those helicopters during *Apocalypse Now:* I wondered if it had been an omen."

Coppola's fortunes were changing dramatically. As a result of his Samuel Goldwyn Award, he was hearing from studios eager to tap into his screenwriting talent. Universal Studios made a tentative job offer, but Coppola, fearing that his employment with the company would find him working more on television than in the movies, turned down the offer. He also heard from Seven Arts Productions, which offered him $375 per week to create a script for Carson McCullers's controversial novel *Reflections in a Golden Eye.* Coppola accepted the offer.

Reflections was a project in serious trouble. Seven Arts had paid McCullers a substantial fifty thousand dollars for the screen rights to her book and had sunk additional money in trying to get a workable script, but no one seemed to be up to the task. With the option due to expire, Seven Arts was in danger of watching its investment amount to nothing. As Coppola put it, "They figured they'd hire some young shlump for six weeks and see if he could do anything."

Coppola's screenplay, written over a six-week stretch, was a big hit with the studio executives—too much so, according to Coppola, who was embarrassed by the studio's fawning over what he considered to be a decent, although hardly noteworthy, script. ("The reaction was such a load of baloney," he stated.) Still, the work had its rewards. Seven Arts immediately offered him a full-time position on its writing staff at $450 per week. Taking the job required Coppola's departure from UCLA, but the decision wasn't especially difficult. Coppola had grown annoyed with all the criticism aimed at him by fellow students—somebody had even tacked a sign reading SELLOUT to the school's bulletin board—and as a newlywed, he felt a responsibility to bring home some money. He withdrew from the university and signed on with Seven Arts.

Ironically, *Reflections in a Golden Eye* was not made into a movie just then, and when it was, the Coppola script would not be used. John Huston liked the screenplay, but he had other commitments and was unable to make the picture at that time. When he did get around to directing the movie a few years later, in 1967, it was with someone else's script.

Reflections in a Golden Eye was merely the beginning of a long string of frustrations that Coppola would contend with during his tenure with Seven Arts. Much of his work never made it to the screen, and other scripts suffered the indignity of being reworked by others to such an extent that Coppola barely recognized his work when it did appear on-screen. He was learning what nearly everyone else in the business already knew: As a general rule, screenwriters are near the bottom of the Hollywood food chain, despite their great importance to the filmmaking process. "The position of the screenwriter is an absurd, ridiculous one," he'd say later. "He earns a great deal of money but has no say whatsoever about the film, unless he is one of the more famous screenwriters. This is particularly true for young authors."

Coppola would be largely responsible for a shift in the prevailing system when he, along with a number of other talented new directors, began writing the scripts for the movies they were directing, taking an auteur approach to filmmaking, a theory already popular in France. The approach, controversial in the industry, even among other directors, afforded filmmakers much more control over their films, from the original concept of a story through postproduction, allowing the directors to preserve the integrity of their material.

Those days, however, were years away, and for the time being, Coppola was just another new kid in a very old system. Given his work on *Reflections,* his bosses at Seven Arts decided that he was an expert in writing about the South—a notion that amused Coppola, who at that point had never been farther south than New Jersey—so for his second job with the studio he was assigned the scriptwriting tasks for the screen adaptation of Tennessee Williams's play *This Property Is Condemned.* Coppola knew the material well, having directed the one-act play while he was at Hofstra, but he was concerned about how the compact, tightly written play would translate to the screen. At first, the movie was to be a vehicle for Elizabeth Taylor, slotted to play the female lead, and her husband, Richard Burton, who had agreed to direct, but when Seven Arts refused to hire Montgomery Clift, Taylor's selection for the picture's leading man, Taylor and Burton were off the project. Other directors came and went. Coppola would meet with each new prospect, trying to determine the approach that each director wanted to take in his film, but nothing productive came out of their conferences. "It was very Alice in Wonderland," Coppola said of the meetings. "Eventually, we got a script of sorts."

"Fred Coe was the producer of *This Property*," Coppola pointed out, "and he was the one that I worked with the most intensely on this project—adapting a full-length movie out of a four-page Tennessee Williams one-act play about a little girl and a boy on a railroad track. When we had a draft of the script, I heard that we were going to deliver it to Williams, who was staying at a hotel in Beverly Hills or somewhere. I thought if I delivered it myself, I could meet him: I certainly idolized him. So I went and knocked on the door, and he answered in a bathrobe to okay the script. He disappeared before I got the chance to shake his hand and introduce myself.

"Years later, after *The Godfather*, I did get to meet him. He visited the library at our winery, and said to me, 'By the way, could you cash a hundred-dollar check for me?' I said, 'Sure.' He took out a beautifully printed check that said *Tennessee Williams, Special Account*, and in a firm hand, he filled it out to me, and I gave him the cash. Of course, I never cashed that check, and I'm sure he had done this many times, which is why it was called a special account. I had that check framed, and it's hanging in our library. I wouldn't sell it for ten thousand dollars—I admire his work so much."

The Coppola version of *This Property Is Condemned*, like his script for *Reflections in a Golden Eye*, never made the final cut. By the time the Natalie Wood–Robert Redford film was released in 1966, it was an entirely different movie.

Other scripts followed—about a dozen within a two-year period, by Coppola's estimation—but very few were produced, and of the handful that made it to the screen, none would earn him any kind of reputation other than the one he already had at Seven Arts, that of someone who could grind out decent scripts in short order. There was an original comedy entitled *My Last Duchess*, as well as dramas called *The Fifth Coin* and *The Disenchanted*. *My Last Duchess* was eventually filmed by Ken Hughes, under the new title of *Drop Dead, Darling*, but the Hughes movie, based on the *prologue* of Coppola's script, was so different from the original that Coppola didn't receive on-screen credit for his contribution.

"What's a real pity is I've seen scripts of Francis's that never got made—scripts that were some of the best stuff that he ever did," offered Joel Oliansky, Coppola's old Hofstra buddy who, at Coppola's recommendation, had been hired as a scriptwriter at Seven Arts. "He did an adaptation of *The Disenchanted*—a Budd Schulburg book about F. Scott Fitzgerald—that was the best screenplay I've ever read. He was romantically attached to the whole Fitzgerald story. He used to talk about it in college."

Coppola, Oliansky continued, was full of ideas, some of which turned out to be remarkably prophetic. "When I came out here, he had a bunch of things in his quiver. He said, 'You know what would really work today? Somebody should make a big, expensive Batman movie.' That was even before the television show. He had other projects. He had one that he called *The Star Spangled Banana*, which was a sort of *Easy Rider*–type of movie, and I don't know what happened to it. *The Rain People* had some elements of it, I guess. Back in college, he used to talk about making a movie about Tucker, and he still had that in his head."

Whatever his feelings about the motion picture industry's version of the sausage factory, Coppola was being paid handsomely for his work. After a year on the job, he was given a raise in pay to one thousand dollars a week–the kind of money that would have kept any young scriptwriter happy. And, for a while, he was. He bought an A-frame in Mandeville Canyon; he purchased a Jaguar. He and Ellie had their first child, Gian-Carlo (born on September 17, 1963), and the family was living a nice, upper-middle-class existence.

Coppola, however, still desperately wanted to direct a movie of his own, and since Seven Arts kept stalling whenever he badgered them for a chance, he figured that he would have to come up with the financing himself. He had put away about twenty thousand dollars of his earnings, but such savings were nowhere near what he needed to make even a low-budget film like *Dementia 13*. Hoping to come up with some quick cash, he invested his entire savings in a company that produced the Scopitone, a jukebox that showed short movies on a tiny built-in screen. The investment turned out to be a miserable failure. "I decided I was going to make it all on the stock market and either have $100,000 to make a film, or have nothing," he remembered. "I lost it, every penny of it. In one stock."

Coppola's first big gamble was a prelude to things to come. In time, he would establish himself as the biggest risk taker in film history, a man willing to stake his personal wealth on projects he believed in.

2.

PRODUCER RAY STARK, COPPOLA'S boss at Seven Arts, had watched his young screenwriter develop over a two-year stretch with the company, and he decided to "reward" Coppola with an all-expenses-paid trip to Paris. He could take his wife and young son, escape the daily grind in Los Angeles, and do the whole tourist bit.

Naturally, there was one small catch: Seven Arts was putting together a war film, *Is Paris Burning?*, to be directed by René Clement. The scriptwriter on the project was very ill, and Stark feared that he would die before he finished his screenplay. Coppola was to be Seven Arts' insurance policy. "When the pencil falls out of his hand," Stark told Coppola, "we want you to pick it up."

When Coppola arrived in Paris, he discovered that the writer had no idea why the young screenwriter was there. Their working relationship was, in turns, tense and awkward. "This nice, sick old man didn't know the arrangement and thought I was his assistant," Coppola recalled. "He would criticize and say my scenes were no good, and just as I was about to quit and get out of there, he *did* die! Suddenly I inherited this enormous project."

What followed was, in Coppola's words, "an insane mess." Paul Graetz, the film's French producer, had cut a deal with the French government whereby the production company would have run of the city if the movie presented history in a way favorable to Charles de Gaulle. As Coppola saw it, the white-hot center of the film's plot focused on the struggle between the Communists and the Gaullists for control of Paris when the Germans were driven out, but since de Gaulle refused to acknowledge publicly the existence of the Communists, that part of the plot had to be left out. To see that the general's position was adhered to in the script, a number of French writers were installed as writer/advisers.

Coppola seethed. Appeals to Graetz and Clement went nowhere, and story meetings turned into shouting matches. Coppola, always under fire and one step from being kicked off the project, was ready to pack his bags and head home. "Nobody would speak up," he groused. "They were all terrified. They just wouldn't admit that there were any Communists in France during the war. Or if there were, we were never to use their names." Nor was he to use the word "Communist" in the script.

Seven Arts, perhaps sensing that Coppola was in over his head, dispatched novelist Gore Vidal to France to help with the screenplay, and Vidal persuaded Coppola to stay on the picture. Vidal, who had come from an illustrious political family and knew the value of calm negotiating and compromise better than an obstinent young film student with no interest in politics, French or otherwise, brought a stabilizing influence to the project, even if he fared no better, in the long run, than Coppola. In the end, *Is Paris Burning?*, like so many of Coppola's Seven Arts scripts, had been manhandled by so many writers that Coppola lost count of them. This time, however, the film was produced, and because of Writers Guild rules, Coppola's and Vidal's names appeared in the credits as the coscreenwriters—an honor that neither of them wanted or, given the terrible state of the final product, deserved. Coppola would always refer to the *Is Paris Burning?* experience as one of the biggest disasters of his career, though he was glad to have met and worked with Vidal.

To keep his sanity during these turbulent times, Coppola began work on yet another screenplay—a film adaptation of British novelist David Benedictus's *You're a Big Boy Now*. Coppola had spent one thousand dollars of his own money to purchase the option on the book, and he worked on the script in the evenings, during his off-hours from *Is Paris Burning?* In Coppola's mind, this was his own personal screen property, independent of his association with Seven Arts, and he would find a way to write and direct the movie— the sooner the better, preferably while he was still in Europe. He could shoot the film inexpensively, using unknown actors and shooting in black and white.

Seven Arts had other ideas. The company had no interest in the project and a disappointed Coppola returned to the States as soon as he had finished working on *Is Paris Burning?* Dispirited, Coppola gave up his plans for *Big Boy*—for the time being.

He and Seven Arts had reached the point of no return, each party feeling betrayed by the other. Coppola wanted to direct a film so badly that, at one point, he had written and submitted a script about an aspiring filmmaker driven crazy by his inability to direct a movie, but the not-so-subtle hint netted him nothing. Seven Arts, on the other hand, was not pleased by Coppola's trying to circumvent the company in developing *Big Boy*. As far as Ray Stark was concerned, Coppola should have been grateful for his high-paying job and all that it bought him; there would be plenty of time for directing pictures in the future. A confrontation was inevitable, and it took place as soon as Coppola returned to Los Angeles. Somehow, Coppola managed to quit and be fired during the course of the same meeting.

His timing could have been better. Beside losing all his savings in the Scopitone misadventure, he owed a bank for the money he had borrowed to buy the rights to *Big Boy*. To make matters worse, Seven Arts was claiming ownership of the *Big Boy* script, which, it correctly asserted, had been written during Coppola's employment there. Coppola countered that he owned the screen rights—a fact that Seven Arts could not contest, but which did Coppola little good: Coppola, after all, was in a bigger hurry to make the picture than Seven Arts. He was going nowhere.

Depressed, Coppola now had another mouth to feed—a second son, Roman. Named after director Roman Polanski, he had been born on April 17,

1966, during their stay in Paris. And Coppola had no immediate job prospects. His friends, he claimed, had all abandoned him, jealous of his success. Completely overwhelmed, he fled with his family to Denmark, but he found no answers there.

Fortunately, his agent had encouraging news when he returned. Twentieth Century–Fox had purchased the film rights to Ladislas Farago's *Patton: Ordeal and Triumph*, a biography of George S. Patton, and the studio was looking for someone to write a screenplay about the controversial American general. Fox, aware of Coppola's work on *Is Paris Burning?*, had categorized him as a war writer, and though the closest he had ever been to war was his earlier attendance at military school (where he had been armed with a tuba), Coppola decided to give the script a shot—his motivation, no doubt, boosted by the huge fifty-thousand-dollar writing fee that Fox was offering. At the time of his hiring, he had only vaguely heard of Patton.

In a way, Coppola's ignorance served him well. In knowing nothing about his subject, he was not bound to honor the mythology that surrounded the legendary but eccentric war hero. Coppola immersed himself into a study of Patton, and the more he learned, the more convinced he became that Patton needed to be treated as a quixotic figure, complete with heroic and villainous traits. "I said, 'Wait a minute, this guy was obviously nuts,'" he remembered. "'If they want to make a film glorifying him as a great American hero, it will be laughed at. And if I write a film that condemns him, it won't be made at all.'"

Coppola wisely chose to show the conflicting sides of the man's personality—an approach that pleased both the people who despised Patton as a crazy, egotistical warmonger willing to sacrifice his men for his own honor and glory *and* those who believed he was a hard-boiled but brilliant commander.

Coppola worked on the script for six months, creating a character that would capture Americans' imaginations when the film was eventually released, after a lengthy delay, in 1970. By then, another scriptwriter, Edmund North, had been brought in to revise the Coppola screenplay after years on the shelf. Coppola's major contribution to the movie was his stunning opening scene, in which George C. Scott, playing General Patton, stands on a stage in front of an enormous flag, addressing an audience never shown on-screen.

"I wrote that first scene by combining several of Patton's speeches," Coppola recalled. "At first, some of the executives at Fox thought the script was too 'strange,' and they objected to that opening, among other things."

The problem, Coppola explained, was that some of the executives felt that there would be some confusion concerning the speech, which was being delivered after all the action in the movie had taken place, when Patton was a three-star general, whereas at the beginning of the actual film narrative he was presented as a four-star general. Coppola, however, was anything but prepared to buy into these objections.

"That's one of the things that made me realize that things that get you in trouble are usually the things you are remembered for. They brought in another writer—a fine screenwriter named Edmund North—but he pretty much added some additional battle scenes and didn't change the strange parts that *Patton* is remembered for, such as the beginning and the ending."

The movie was definitely more Coppola than his earlier efforts in *Reflections in a Golden Eye*, *This Property Is Condemned*, or even *Is Paris Burning?* Still, when watching the finished version of the film, Coppola credited George C. Scott for contributing enormously to the way his character appeared in the movie.

"I had nothing to do with evolving the character the way George C. Scott played him," he admitted. "The script I wrote was very much like *parts* of the film. You know the beginning, which was sort of more stylized with this character way out in the foreground. That was the opening of the original script, but *more* of my script was that way."

3.

COPPOLA WANTED TO INVEST the money he earned from writing *Patton* into *You're a Big Boy Now*, but before he could go off and make the picture, he had to clear a number of obstacles involving Seven Arts.

It wasn't easy. He had been negotiating with the company for some time, making very little headway. It was tough enough bickering with Seven Arts over the dual ownership of the property and script, but now, with Seven Arts in the process of merging with Warner Bros., there was a possibility of new players and attitudes in the dispute. Fortunately, Coppola had a strong ally in Phil Feldman, Seven Arts' business manager, who decided that it would be in his own best interests to break away from the company and work as an independent producer. Feldman wanted to make *You're a Big Boy Now*, and he managed to persuade Ray Stark and Seven Arts that he should produce the picture and Coppola should direct it.

The persuasion involved the kind of razzle-dazzle for which Coppola would become well known. Rather than simply approach Seven Arts with hats in their hands, Coppola and Feldman flew to New York at their own expense and prepared a package that they hoped would be irresistible to the company. Knowing that Seven Arts would never give them the kind of money needed to attract marquee names to the film, Coppola and Feldman carefully assembled an affordable cast that would also be appealing to the studio. According to the strategy, they would place unknowns in the main roles and try to attract gifted but minor (by Hollywood standards) stars for the film's supporting roles. Even this was going to require some fast talking, since established actors, including lesser-known ones, came with a price tag. Coppola hoped to entice them by appealing to their artistic sensibilities, and by casting them against type.

It was all a big bluff. Coppola approached the actors as if he already had big studio financing behind him, and then he approached the studio as if he had already set up the production and was prepared to go forward, with or without the studio's help. Somehow, it worked, and he was given the green light on the project. As Coppola boasted afterward, "If there's one thing I've found out, it's don't ask. Just go ahead and force the issue. That way you get a momentum going with everybody wanting to jump on the bandwagon."

The cast was excellent—far better than anyone could have expected, given Coppola's lack of directorial experience and the film's budget. For the leads, he signed Canadian actor Peter Kastner, who had made all of one film (*Nobody Waved Goodbye,* the previous year), and Karen Black, a stage actress who had received favorable notices for her role in *The Playroom.* To sign his supporting cast, Coppola took an audacious approach: Rather than follow procedure and approach the actors' individual agents, he contacted Julie Harris, Rip Torn, and Michael Dunn directly and asked if they would be willing to look at his script. All read the screenplay and agreed to appear in the film, as did Geraldine Page, Torn's wife, who later said that she was attracted to the script because it made her laugh. "I had never met this young man," she said of Coppola, "but I trusted him implicitly."

The addition of these actors was significant—more than enough to impress the studio officials at Seven Arts. Michael Dunn had recently turned in a standout performance in *Ship of Fools,* for which he received an Oscar nomination. Julie Harris, a fourteen-year film veteran and former Academy Award nominee, had appeared in such films as *I Am a Camera, East of Eden,* and *Requiem for a Heavyweight.* Rip Torn and Geraldine Page were both highly regarded stage actors, and Page had secured a solid reputation in the movies as well, receiving two Oscar nominations and winning two Golden Globes for her roles in film adaptations of Tennessee Williams's *Summer and Smoke* and *Sweet Bird of Youth.*

Of all of Coppola's casting decisions, the one going the most against type was his selection of Elizabeth Hartman for the role of Barbara Darling, the sexy, sadistic go-go dancer in *Big Boy.* The twenty-four-year-old Hartman had received an Oscar nomination for her first major film appearance, as a blind girl in *A Patch of Blue,* and she had recently appeared as a similarly mousy character, Priss Hartshorn, in *The Group.* She couldn't believe Coppola wanted her to play Barbara Darling in the new film. "I read the script," she said at the time, "and I thought, 'Has he ever *seen* me?'"

Coppola assured the painfully shy actress not only that he had seen her but that she would be perfect for the part. "I could have gotten the usual pretty girl," he noted, "but that would be putting a ceiling on the part. With Elizabeth, there'd be no limits."

Seven Arts liked Coppola's package enough to raise its original $250,000 budget to $800,000. Coppola would receive only $8,000 for writing and directing the picture—a concession that, in the wake of his earlier squabbles over the property's ownership, he was happy to make; he would also receive 10 percent of the film's profits. He would have fourteen days to shoot the feature. The Seven Arts offer, ridiculously weak by today's standards, represented a breakthrough at the time: No one had ever offered someone as young and inexperienced as Coppola the opportunity to direct a mainstream feature-length picture.

"You should have seen it," said one witness of the Coppola–Seven Arts meetings. "Typical conference-table session, with all these stuffy executives sitting around, offering the moon to this funny-looking guy with a beard in bluejeans."

Coppola quickly discovered that the logistics of making a picture in New York City differed substantially from his experiences with Roger Corman. No one, it seemed, was especially impressed that a film was being made in the city, despite efforts by city officials to convince filmmakers that New York was friendly to location shooting. For openers, Coppola had to contend with unions with stringent, inflexible ways of doing business. Then there was the issue of the locations themselves. The New York Public Library, the setting for much of the action, refused to permit Coppola to shoot at its main branch; officials remembered unpleasant experiences with film crews in the past, and they were less than thrilled with the script's call for a collection of pornography to be hidden in its vaults. Coppola appealed to Mayor John Lindsay, who overruled the library and allowed Coppola to use the facility in his movie. Coppola needed his powers of persuasion elsewhere as well, but somehow he was able to win the day. He persuaded May's Department Store to allow him to shoot a frantic chase scene in the store during its noontime rush hour and, perhaps even more impressive, he convinced the powers that be to permit him to interrupt the news headlines flashing in the Times Square

Accutron sign so he could flash the name Barbara Darling on the sign during one of his night shots.

Before going into production, Coppola assembled his actors for three weeks of rehearsals, including extensive improvisation—a practice almost unheard of in the movie industry at the time, but one that Coppola would employ, in various forms, throughout his career. Much of Coppola's philosophy dated back to his days of directing plays at Hofstra, when actors would rehearse exhaustively and, through repetition and adjustment, grow into their characters. Applying these same principles, Coppola reasoned, would allow the actors to be better prepared by the time they were standing in front of the camera. For *Big Boy,* Coppola rehearsed his actors on a bare stage in a Manhattan warehouse, videotaping some of the action to use as a reference. During the rehearsals, Coppola used a script different from the shooting script—the rehearsal script, containing additional dialogue and fewer images, all intended to encourage the actors to develop their characters. As critic Rex Reed, present during some of the rehearsals, would comment, some of the discussions between Coppola and his actors looked more like a group therapy session than traditional moviemaking.

The rehearsals also afforded the director and cast the opportunity to get to know one another prior to the actual shoot, establishing a level of trust that would prove useful later on. Elizabeth Hartman recalled how Coppola would coax her into character, often in unconventional ways. Sometimes, after rehearsals, he would drive her around Manhattan on the back of his motorcycle, shouting, "YOU'RE SEXY, BEAUTIFUL BARBARA DARLING" at the top of his lungs. Other times, he would take her shopping in fashionable clothing stores, only to deliver her later to Ellie, who would trim the purchased miniskirts even shorter than they already were.

For all his preparation, Coppola was nervous when he finally began to shoot. This was *real,* there was a lot of money on the line, and he didn't want to blow his big chance at direction.

"The first day on the set, you could feel the panic," he confessed. "I was pacing back and forth across a stage I had never seen before. Nine actors and a crew of forty technicians waited for me to tell them what to do. The cameraman asked me where to position the first camera. I had to tell him that I did not know."

He tried to shoot his first scene, but after some fumbling around, he shut down the works and asked the crew and actors to take a half-hour break—time that he used to compose himself.

Coppola had originally intended to shoot the film in sequence—another rarity in the business—but he abandoned the idea early in the proceedings.

With such a brief production schedule, he had to work more hastily than he would have preferred, shooting day and night, scampering from one location to another, trying his best to bring the picture in on time and on budget. He wanted a zany, controlled-frenzy look to the film, similar to what he had seen in *A Hard Day's Night,* Richard Lester's Beatles movie, and at times he achieved it simply because the film *was* barely under control. For the chase scene in the department store, Coppola filmed without telling anyone other than his crew what was going on. Concealing the cameras in shopping bags and delivery carts, the crew stormed into the store during one of its busiest hours, the startled patrons witnessing a young man, brandishing a Bible, being chased up and down the aisles by fourteen people and a dog with a wooden leg.

"It was terrific," Coppola said of the chase scene. "It started a riot. Little old ladies were having heart attacks. One guy grabbed Peter and started a fight with him—which Peter won. Some kids started ripping Peter's clothes off him. My only regret is that we didn't have thirty cameras to get everything down on film."

In all likelihood, Peter Kastner was much less enthusiastic about all the mayhem. His role was demanding, involving a lot of physical comedy, and to see that his young actor stayed in shape, Coppola insisted that Kastner run for an hour at seven each morning through Riverside Park—often after the actor had been working late the evening before. Quipped Kastner during the shoot: "I think when it's over, I'll check into a hospital for a while and get some sleep."

4.

WHILE PRAISING *YOU'RE A BIG BOY NOW* in the *Los Angeles Times,* critic Charles Champlin referred to the film as "one of those rare American things, what the Europeans call the *auteur* film"—a particularly astute observation because *Big Boy,* to Coppola, was much more a personal film than an adaptation. When he had begun writing the script in Paris, he was writing an original screenplay largely based on the events of his life, but he immediately realized that, as an employee of Seven Arts, he would be obligated to turn the script over to the company—a prospect he did not relish. He figured he had found a loophole when he read David Benedictus's novel and noticed the similarities between his script and Benedictus's book. He purchased the film rights to the book and began to adapt portions of the work into his screenplay. The result was a strange sort of hybrid, only vaguely resembling the literary source.*

---

*The following plot synopsis, and all the others to follow in this book, will reflect the plot of the *finished* movie, and not necessarily the original source material.

Bernard Chanticleer, the film's protagonist, is the product of a suffocating mother who refuses to allow him to grow up, and a self-absorbed, authoritarian father who believes that Bernard, at nineteen, has a lot of growing up to do. He is absolutely correct: Bernard is as naïve and klutzy as a boy just reaching puberty, with an obsession with sex that finds him hanging around Manhattan's lingerie stores, strip clubs, adult bookstores, and sex parlors. To help his son break away, Bernard's father installs him in an apartment occupied by, among others, an ever-suspicious policeman, a rooster that hates and attacks women, and a spinster landlady with the unlikely name of Miss Thing. Bernard's mother gives Miss Thing three dimes and orders her to call whenever she sees Bernard going into the apartment with a girl.

Bernard's father works as a librarian in the rare books division of the New York Public Library, and he has secured his son a job that involves roller-skating through the basement stacks in search of books for the patrons upstairs. One of Bernard's coworkers, a sweet, attractive librarian named Amy, has a crush on him and flirts with him, but he keeps his distance. By his own admission, he is "dying to grow up," but he is reluctant to go through the process. "Pain is part of it all," he tells Raef, a friend and coworker at the library. "[Part] of what?" Raef inquires. "Freedom," Bernard replies.

This becomes the theme of the story. Bernard finally asks Amy out, but their date is far from perfect. They go to a New York club, where Bernard frustrates Amy to no end by gawking at a go-go dancer he'd seen earlier in the library. He is so smitten that he barely pays attention to anything Amy is saying, and it only gets worse when they head back to Bernard's apartment, where, in a series of comical mishaps, Amy is attacked by the resident rooster, Bernard is confronted by the cop, and Miss Thing, while trying to restore order, is knocked down a flight of stairs, breaking her arm in the process.

Miss Thing dutifully reports the entire episode to Bernard's parents, who insist that Bernard join them once a week for a "family night" of dinner, talk, and maybe a play or movie. During one of these punishing evenings, the three attend an Off-Broadway play called *The Department Store,* a dreadful production that, to Bernard's delight, stars Barbara Darling, the go-go girl he'd seen in the club. Bernard writes her a gushing fan letter, and she responds by inviting him to join her in her dressing room after one of the performances.

Barbara is Bernard's complete opposite—a sadistic, self-centered, and totally neurotic young woman who hates all men. (She claims that one time she was sexually assaulted by an albino hypnotherapist with a wooden leg.) Sensing Bernard's naïveté, she invites him to her apartment for a night of fun and games—at his expense. After teasing him relentlessly, she rolls over in her pull-out bed and goes to sleep, leaving a frustrated Bernard to contemplate his failures with women.

Noting that Bernard had spent a night away from his apartment, Miss Thing visits the library to report his behavior to his father. In yet another funny scene, she finds herself locked in a timed vault with him, and, in her hysteria, she misinterprets his actions as his trying to make a pass at her. For Mr. Chanticleer, the accusation is ironic, since only a short time earlier, he actually had make a pass at Amy.

Bernard hears from Amy about his father's actions, but he has other things on his mind. An angry Miss Thing has evicted him from his apartment, and, at Barbara Darling's invitation, he moves in with the actress/dancer—a decision that turns out to be a predictable fiasco. Barbara turns on him as soon as he has moved in, then begs him to stay when he threatens to leave.

In an expanded, hilarious conclusion owing much to Richard Lester, all the loose threads of the story are neatly tied together. While visiting Miss Thing to ask about Bernard, Mrs. Chanticleer learns of her husband's so-called transgression in the library vault, and she immediately heads to the library to confront him. Bernard, meanwhile, has returned to Barbara's apartment, ready to announce that he's leaving, only to discover that she is now shacked up with his friend Raef. He, too, takes off for the library.

At the library, Bernard's parents and Amy sort out the truth. Barbara Darling, wanting to talk to Bernard, turns up, as do Miss Thing and the policeman, who is bent on arresting Mr. Chanticleer. A wild chase ensues, begun by Bernard, who steals the library's priceless Gutenberg Bible. The entire group races down Fifth Avenue, chasing one another for different reasons, weaving its way through a marching band and parade, and eventually winding up in May's Department Store.

Bernard is captured, arrested, and taken to jail. His bail, however, is paid by Amy, who is waiting for him with his dog. Amy and Bernard, now new lovers, frolic through the streets of New York City, both feeling the flight of freedom. Although he has taken a circuitous route, Bernard has become the "big boy" his father wanted him to be.

5·

YOU'RE A BIG BOY NOW PREMIERED in New York on March 21, 1967, and would be featured as the only American film entry at that year's Cannes Film Festival, but, with only limited distribution, it was destined for failure at the box office. Coppola would remember the reviews for *Big Boy* as being "terrific," both in the United States and overseas, with the exception of a scathing notice printed in *Life* magazine. His memory, however, was selective. The reviews, in fact, were largely mixed. Critics were willing to award Coppola with high marks for his ambition and effort, but many were unimpressed with the story itself. *Time* magazine, in a mixed but generally favorable review, frowned on *Big Boy*'s "custard-pie plot" but predicted that Coppola "will make a major movie once he learns not to trip over the line separating dafiness with deftness." After conceding that "Francis Ford Coppola is a gifted young man," the *New York Times* reviewer Howard Thompson, unamused by characters that he deemed to be more mean-spirited than funny, lashed out against what he called "a magnetically exasperating comic strip of a movie." *Life* magazine's Richard Schickel, in the review that Coppola would remember for its negativity, dismissed *Big Boy* outright: "It makes one very tired, as self-admiring brattiness always does."

The positive notices, on the other hand, were real scrapbook material, offering the kind of praise that would give a young director encouragement even as he watched his film bomb at the box office. Judith Crist, one of the most influential reviewers of her time, praised *Big Boy* as "a director's delicious debut . . . youthful in the best sense, in its imaginative irreverence, its compassionate ego, its earnest confusion and its offbeat inspiration. . . . *You're a Big Boy Now* is almost unmitigated delight—and a harbinger of good things its creator will do as he himself grows and grows." *Newsweek*'s Joseph Morgenstern, while conceding that the picture was "no masterpiece," predicted that the movie—"a national anthem" for kids—would be a whopping success at drive-ins, art houses, and film festivals alike. "Not since Welles was a boy wonder or Kubrick a kid," wrote Morgenstern, "has any young American made a film as original, spunky or just plain funny as this one."

The national exposure in such publications as *Time, Newsweek, Life,* and *The Saturday Review,* along with notices published in such newspapers as the *New York Times* and the *Los Angeles Times,* was the kind of publicity that any filmmaker would have cherished at the beginning of a career, but in Coppola's case, the first rush of attention was tainted by a remark that would reverberate for years to come. The Morgenstern piece in *Newsweek* was accompanied by a profile of Coppola—his first in a national publication—and during the course of his interview with Coppola, Morgenstern asked how a young filmmaker such as Coppola had managed to break through Hollywood's old-boy network and obtain financing for his movie.

Coppola responded with words that would set off a firestorm of criticism.

"I pattern my life on Hitler in this respect," he said. "He didn't take over the country. He worked his way into the existing fabric first."

This type of remark was nothing new to Coppola—a few years earlier, he had outraged students and faculty members at Hofstra by spouting off about how he had read a biography of Lenin and was modeling his life after that of the Communist leader—and though it was difficult to misinterpret Coppola's meaning when his most recent remarks were placed in the context of the discussion, he had nevertheless set himself up, in his naïve, poorly drawn example, for charges of insensitivity or, worse yet, megalomania. Whether Coppola liked it or not, intelligent people did not go around comparing themselves to Hitler or Lenin.

In years to come, interviewers would trot out the Hitler quote, and Coppola's responses, never repentant, are revealing. In an April 1968 interview with Richard Koszarski, conducted over Hofstra University's WVHC radio station, Coppola, when questioned about the statement, insisted that he had used the shocking comparison to make a point.

"My allusion to Hitler," he told Koszarski, "was simply that, contrary to what a lot of people think, he wasn't a revolutionary who came down from the hills and took the government over. He worked his way into government, became a part of it, and then used that to take it over. . . . The way to come to power is not always to merely challenge the Establishment, but first make a place in it and then challenge, and double-cross, the Establishment. Which is essentially what I've done."

A few years later, in early 1975, now an established director and internationally known for his work on *The Godfather*, Coppola mentioned Hitler again, this time while addressing the criticism that he had romanticized the Mafia in *The Godfather*.

"If you were taken inside Adolf Hitler's home, went to his parties and heard his stories, you'd probably have liked him," Coppola stated. "If I make a film of Hitler and get some charismatic actor to play him, people would say I was trying to make him a good human being. He wasn't, of course, but the greatest evil on earth is done by sane human beings who are miserable in themselves."

His statements continued to dog him and, in 1990, shortly after completing *The Godfather, Part III*, he tried again to clarify his position in an interview with *Rolling Stone*'s David Breskin.

"You learn from these people," he said of Hitler and Napoleon. "When I talk about the fact that Napoleon was a person who understood that artillery was power in his time, and communications is power in our time, it's because I was the kind of person that read all those stories of Napoleon, Caesar, those people. I tried to learn. It doesn't mean that I'm Napoleon or Hitler by any means, but we can use the people who are the prime movers in the culture to inspire us."

The statements spoke volumes, not only about Coppola's powerful ego and unwillingness (or inability) to admit that he might have chosen poor examples in his illustrations but also of the contradictions in the way he tried to pass himself off to the public. Throughout his career, Coppola has tried to present himself as the perennial Hollywood outsider, but in his early statements to Morgenstern and Koszarski, he indicated that he was working within the system—at least for the time being. In fact, he would never be a true outsider, not in the strictest sense of the word, nor would he be the megalomaniac that some of the press presented him to be. He would, however, have a difficult time with the press, which was more than happy to report his more outrageous statements, infuriating a man who might have learned, somewhere along the way, how to choose his words more judiciously.

6.

IN A MOVE UNPRECEDENTED IN film school history, Coppola submitted *You're a Big Boy Now* to UCLA as his master's thesis, a gesture that not only earned him his degree but also delivered a final word to anyone at the university who still wanted to make noises about his compromising or selling out. *Big Boy* might have been viewed from a number of differing perspectives, but it was not a slick commercial venture.

It did, however, boost Coppola's reputation in Hollywood, and he soon had a flood of job offers pouring in—thirty, by his estimation. Coppola was reluctant to jump. Although the money was good, he wanted to write *and* direct his future pictures, and he feared that he might lose the opportunity if he gained the reputation as strictly a writer or director for hire. It would be better, he reasoned, to hold out for an offer that gave him more control of his destiny. "If I don't have the guts to do it now, I might never have the guts to do it ever," he told *Variety*.

He was pleased, then, when Seven Arts offered him a three-film contract, which, while not giving him everything he hoped for, at least represented his best offer to date. By terms of the agreement, Coppola would write three screenplays—two originals and an adaptation of Nathaniel Hawthorne's classic novel *The Scarlet Letter*—one of which he would be allowed to direct. For the two originals, Coppola offered two ideas that he had been kicking around in his head for a long time: a film about surveillance and privacy that he was calling *The Conversation*, and *The Rain People*, a screen adaptation of one of his early short stories, which was about three women who leave their husbands and take off together on a road adventure. He had begun work on the *The Conversation* while wrapping up postproduction on *Big Boy* in December 1966, and he had hinted in interviews that he would be making this his next film.

The Seven Arts deal proved to be short-lived, and Coppola never did produce the three scripts for the company. Instead, less than two weeks after the announcement of the agreement in *Variety*, Abe Greenberg reported in his *Hollywood Citizen-News* column that Coppola had signed on to direct the screen version of the 1947 Broadway musical *Finian's Rainbow*. Coppola's abrupt change in plans came as a result of a number of factors, including the Warner Bros.–Seven Arts merger, Coppola's love of musicals, and his desire to please his father. In addition, he would be getting the chance to direct the great song-and-dance actor Fred Astaire in a musical.

Time had not been all that kind to the venerable musical. When it had played on Broadway nearly two decades earlier, *Finian's Rainbow*, with its commentary on racial bigotry, had seemed very progressive—too much so, in fact, for Hollywood, which, in the era of McCarthyism and blacklisting, passed on bringing it to the big screen. By the time it was safe to make a film adaptation of *Finian's Rainbow*, the civil rights movement, with all its incendiary rhetoric and victories and defeats, had made the musical's charming idealism seem sophomoric and dated.

Coppola was completely put off when producer Joseph Landon showed him a script. The musical had been overhauled and updated. Woody Mahoney, one of the main characters, was now a hippie folksinger from San Francisco. To Coppola, never a fan of hippies to begin with, the changes were ineffective, and one of his first orders of business was to restore the script to the original story. "It can only be treated successfully now as a sort of period piece," he explained. "In its period it has its own coherence, and its comment on color, for instance, was perfectly acceptable, but now it would be completely inadequate. So I decided that it had to be handled as what it is, a fantasy without time or place."

That was only part of the problem. When Landon initially approached Coppola about *Finian's Rainbow*, he was actually just seeking Coppola's advice on who might be best to direct the picture. When Coppola himself was offered the job, he immediately had visions of making a big-budget Hollywood musical, perhaps along the lines of *The Sound of Music* or, more recently, *Camelot*, which had just been completed for Warner Bros. This was not to be the case. The merger of Warner Bros. and Seven Arts was bringing about a number of changes, and *Finian's Rainbow* was to be the last movie made on the old Warner's lot. The new company officials wanted him to shoot the movie as quickly and inexpensively as possible, and, to save expenses, Warner Bros.–Seven Arts (as the company was now called) officials demanded that the picture be shot entirely on location, using the leftover forest set from *Camelot*.

As far as Coppola could see, he had been asked to direct the movie not because of his skills as a filmmaker, but for all the wrong reasons. "The only reason I got the job," he said, "was because I was young. Warner's had this creaky old property lying around, and they wanted a young director to modernize it. It was between me and Billy Friedkin."

Despite what should have been some heavy-duty warning signals, Coppola decided to go forward with the project. As he now planned it, he would put aside his screenplay for *The Conversation*, shoot *Finian's Rainbow*, and, if all went well, make *The Rain People* immediately afterward, using the money he earned from *Finian's Rainbow* to finance his personal film.

He later admitted that he might have been less willing to take on the project if it hadn't been for his father. Francis saw *You're a Big Boy Now*, with its music by John Sebastian and songs by Sebastian's band, the Lovin' Spoonful, as largely a musical picture, but in much the same sense that *A Hard Day's Night* or the Monkees' television show was a musical production. *Finian's Rainbow* was a musical in the grand Broadway tradition, and Coppola relished the notion of being able to prove to his father that he could handle that kind of material on the big screen.

Carmine Coppola couldn't have been happier. When his son was offered the job directing *Finian's Rainbow*, Carmine Coppola was out on the road, conducting the orchestra in a production of *Half a Sixpence*. When Francis called and offered him a similar position on his new film, he left the theater production, packed up all of his possessions, and moved with his wife to Los Angeles. Thanks to his son, his dream of working in the movies was coming true.

7.

IT DIDN'T TAKE LONG FOR COPPOLA to see that he was going to have some serious problems with his film. As a rule, movie musicals carried larger than-average budgets and required extra time to work on the big production numbers; Coppola was allotted $3.5 million to make his movie—about one-third the budget assigned to *Funny Girl* and *Star!*, the Barbra Streisand and Julie Andrews musicals currently in production elsewhere—and Warner's decided that the picture had to be shot quickly, so it could be released while the public's renewed interest in musicals, spurred on by the enormous popularity of *The Sound of Music,* was still at a peak. Coppola tried to convince the studio to allow him to shoot his movie in Kentucky, but the company remained adamant: The picture would be filmed on the company lot, and if Coppola had half the talent of his reputation, he would see to it that it *looked* as if it had been shot on location.

The cast was a strange assortment, and not an especially good match to the material. Fred Astaire, indisputably one of the greatest dancers in show business history, was now sixty-eight years old and decades removed from his historic dance partnerships with Ginger Rogers, Rita Hayworth, Lucille Bremer, and Cyd Charisse. Petula Clark, who began her career as a child actress in England, had not appeared before cameras in years, and she was presently known more as a pop singer, renowned for such hits as "Downtown," "I Know a Place," and "My Love." Although Coppola liked Clark for the role of Sharon, the female lead in *Finian's Rainbow,* her involvement was clearly more the result of her being under contract to Warner's record division than for what she promised to bring to the picture. Tommy Steele, slotted to play the pivotal role of Og, the leprechaun, was another pop singer working his way into theater, most recently the London production of *Half a Sixpence.* Don Francks, a Canadian television star and lounge singer, was assigned the role of Woody Mahoney, the hard-luck farmer who winds up in a partnership with Finian McLonergan, and who falls in love with his daughter, Sharon.

It's doubtful that Coppola could have gotten much more from the cast if he'd had a year to prepare, but with only three and a half weeks' rehearsal time, he was in trouble as soon as the cameras rolled on June 26, 1967. During rehearsals, he had taken his actors through their paces, and he had actually staged rehearsals before live audiences, seated in a theater-in-the-round, with Carmine conducting a small combo as musical accompaniment. The performances began to come together, but not nearly as well as Coppola had hoped. He was unhappy with Don Francks's acting from the beginning, and once the shooting began and time went on, he grew disenchanted with Tommy Steele, as well. Coppola wanted Steele to play a leprechaun as a soft-spoken introvert, but Steele, a stage actor, had a way of exaggerating his performances. Coppola, shooting the picture hurriedly and out of sequence, didn't notice Steele's deviation from the way he had rehearsed his part until it was too late. By then, he had much greater concerns to address. Several weeks into the shooting, Coppola fired choreographer Hermes Pan, who had worked with Fred Astaire on some of his most unforgettable screen performances. With no time to find and break in a replacement, Coppola had no choice but to stage the dance numbers himself.

The results, as Coppola was quick to admit, were "disappointing." Coppola had ideas for the look and effect that he wanted in each production, but he knew little about choreography other than what he'd learned as a result of his directing plays at Hofstra. As a result, he tried to wing it as he went along, inviting disaster every step of the way. The process more resembled the kind of work Coppola had done during his Roger Corman days than a Hollywood musical, with each scene shot as quickly and cheaply as possible, only in this case, as Coppola recalled, there were more people standing around and waiting for his instructions. "There was no planning, no set choreography," he said. "It was a matter of doing what seemed right at the time."

One can only imagine what Fred Astaire thought of the situation. After contributing to some of the most memorable song-and-dance pictures of all time, and working closely with choreographers who meticulously mapped out each dance routine, Astaire was working for a director who would give him such orders as "Fred, go over there and do a thing. Then let's get two girls to block in this space." Fortunately, Astaire was gifted enough to improvise convincingly. Other scenes were just preposterous, and they were damaged even further during postproduction of the film. Coppola would shoot seven or eight takes of a scene, but since each take was largely improvised and different from the others, nothing fit together during the editing process.

Some of Coppola's innovations, however, saved the picture from being a total loss. He continued to badger Warner officials until he was granted permission to shoot away from the soundstages—on the condition that he choose nearby locations. Encouraged by this little window of opportunity, Coppola had Carroll Ballard spend eight days shooting scenes in and around San Francisco, Modesto, Carmel, and Monterey, which he judiciously mixed into the film and its titles, giving the picture a more natural, and less claustrophobic, look. As he later complained, it might not have been like shooting *The Sound of Music* in the Alps, but it beat trying to replicate nature's grandeur on a Hollywood lot.

Nor did his efforts go unnoticed. In his review of *Finian's Rainbow*, *Sight and Sound*'s Tom Milne praised what he called "a demonstration of the naturalness of the musical as a means of expression, with barely an interior visible throughout the entire film, with dancers pounding rough grass and muddy earth instead of carefully prepared surfaces." Although not as effusive in its praise, *Variety* also noted Coppola's skills in staging his musical. "The fact that Rainbow Valley was created on a studio backlot is not apparent," wrote the publication's reviewer, "and technical credits are excellent."

Working on the picture might have been intolerable for Coppola had he not struck up a new friendship during the shoot—a friendship that would survive great highs and lows and would seem as improbable, in many respects, as the great differences between the two men.

Not long after filming began on *Finian's Rainbow,* Coppola noticed a young bearded man, barely more than a kid, standing at the edges of the production company, silently watching the proceedings. Every day, the young man wore a white T-shirt, black chinos, and white sneakers, and he rarely said a word to anyone. Although he did nothing to disrupt the shoot, Coppola found his presence a little unnerving. "You always feel uncomfortable when there's a stranger watching you," Coppola explained, "so I went up to him and asked him who he was."

The kid's name was George Lucas, and he, like Coppola a few years earlier, was hoping to find a way to break into the movie business.

8.

GEORGE LUCAS, THE FUTURE FILM MOGUL and director of such enduring films as *Star Wars* and *American Graffiti,* was born in Modesto, California, on May 14, 1944, and, as the largely autobiographical *American Graffiti* indicated, he had lived a quiet, small-town life. His adolescence was devoted to fast cars, which he dreamed of racing professionally some day, until a near-fatal accident changed his thinking. After attending Modesto Junior College for two years, Lucas transferred to the Southern Cal film school, distinguishing himself by making several prizewinning short films, including the futuristic fantasy *THX-1138: 4EB (Electronic Labyrinth),* which captured first prize at the 1967 National Student Film Festival. He subsequently won a Samuel Warner Memorial Scholarship from Warner Bros., which he could use to observe the filmmaking process at the studio for a period of six months. Lucas hoped to work in animation, but unfortunately, the studio was in the process of being sold, and that department, along with every other department in the studio, was already shut down. The lot was virtually empty when Lucas arrived in Hollywood, leaving him with no alternative but to watch the making of Warner's last picture, a musical called *Finian's Rainbow.*

Lucas had been well aware of Francis Ford Coppola prior to hooking up with him on the Warners lot in the summer of 1967. The two had met at a film school function, and Coppola was a legendary figure at the Southern Cal and UCLA film schools—living proof that one could break through into the system without generations of family connections—and Lucas was eager to watch the man in action.

"I was in admiration of him because he was the first film student to break into the film industry," Lucas remembered. "At that point, film students just didn't make it into the film industry. You had to be related to somebody or know somebody; the idea that you could get there with an education and knowledge and skill and talent was unheard of. Francis was the first one to break through, so all of us students were very much in awe of him. When I first saw him on the set, we rekindled our acquaintance."

The two hit it off immediately. Coppola enjoyed having someone approximately his age for company—someone with whom he could commiserate on the trials and tribulations of filmmaking—and Lucas was happy to establish what he hoped would be a useful connection to the film business. However, after observing Coppola for several days, watching him hack away at a film that seemed more of a struggle than the creation of art, Lucas was beginning to have second thoughts about Hollywood. Maybe, he thought, it would be better if he returned to Southern Cal, obtained his master's degree, and moved somewhere far away from all the madness—a place, perhaps, like San Francisco—where he could earn a living by making commercials or educational films. He had never been all that enamored with the prospects of commercial filmmaking, and after seeing Coppola on the job, he wasn't sure he ever would be. "I was not that interested in making theatrical films," Lucas explained, "but when I met him I was on a scholarship, so I had to sit there and watch him make the kind of movie I wasn't interested in making. I was more interested in trying to get over to the animation department, to try to see if I could steal some film and make a movie."

Coppola exploded when Lucas told him that he was going to go his own way.

"What do you mean, you're leaving?" he teased his new friend. "Aren't I entertaining enough? Have you learned everything you're going to learn watching me direct?"

"There's nothing to do over here," Lucas replied.

If that was the case, Coppola countered, he would find something for Lucas to do. After finishing *Finian's Rainbow*, he told Lucas, he intended to make *The Rain People*, a picture that Lucas might find more to his liking. In addition, he could help Lucas with *THX-1138*, a full-length feature of his earlier prizewinning student film, which Lucas hoped to make. Lucas would help Coppola in all facets of work on *Finian's Rainbow* and then move on with him.

Other than their youth and mutual interest in making movies, Coppola and Lucas could not have been more different. The huge, bearlike Coppola, always talking and gesturing wildly, attacking his goals with a singular purpose, which impressed even those who disliked him personally, cut a striking contrast to the quiet, bone-thin Lucas, who took a measured approach to the business, sizing up a project or problem before addressing it. In time, Lucas would see the two of them as opposite halves of the same whole. Coppola would view Lucas as a "brother."

9.

THE SUMMER OF 1967 WOULD BE forever remembered as the Summer of Love, particularly on the West Coast, where be-ins and festivals, set against a sound track provided by the Grateful Dead, the Beatles' *Sgt. Pepper's Lonely Hearts Club Band,* and psychedelic music, pushed hard against the violence of Vietnam. Ironically, *Finian's Rainbow* possessed the kind of idealism that the hippies might have found appealing had Coppola decided to aim his film at the youth market, but he was looking more to the past, to the old tradition of musicals like *The Wizard of Oz,* than to the politically charged future and the anthems and bombast of *Hair.*

Finian's Rainbow is packed with optimism, its story playing off equal parts of whimsy, idealism, and magic, all staged in the fictitious Appalachian burg of Rainbow Valley, Missitucky. Finian McLonergan, an Irish scamp who believes that he can earn countless riches by burying a pot of gold near Fort Knox, steals a leprechaun's pot of gold and moves, with his daughter, Sharon, to Missitucky. Once an ideal land where people of all color lived together harmoniously, Missitucky is now under the control of Senator "Billboard" Rawkins, a racist lout who is trying to foreclose on Woody Mahoney's tobacco farm. Mahoney has been working with a black scientist named Howard on a new, mint-flavored tobacco plant, but somehow they can't get the dried plant to burn. Woody is spared the worst when Finian comes to his aid and pays the interest on his back taxes, thwarting Rawkins's attempts to seize his land. Woody meets and immediately falls in love with Sharon.

Finian, however, has problems of his own. His stolen pot does indeed have magical powers, not in terms of its increasing wealth but in maintaining the magical powers of Og, its leprechaun owner. Without the pot of gold, he will become a mortal. Og follows Finian and Sharon to Missitucky, where he hopes to locate and recover the pot without giving away its secret.

Unfortunately, geologists have detected the presence of gold in the area, and the race is on. Rawkins, smelling wealth, again tries to find a way to get his hands on Woody's land, and Og scurries to find the gold, which, as it turns out, has another magic power—the power to grant three wishes. The first is granted when Sharon, infuriated by Rawkins's racism, wishes that he were black, so he would know how it feels to be a poor sharecropper in the valley. When Rawkins subsequently turns black and goes into hiding in the woods, Sharon is first accused of kidnapping, and then of being a witch, and she is sentenced to burn at the stake. Og, however, rescues her by wishing that Rawkins would turn white again.

Time is running out on Og, who finds himself in the throes of a major dilemma. He has fallen in love with Woody's sister, Susan the Silent, but she, of course, is mortal. Deciding to live with her as a mortal, Og uses his final wish in giving Susan the power of speech.

In a story of happy endings, Woody and Sharon marry, and Woody becomes wealthy when he learns that his mint tobacco plants will burn after all. Finian's stolen treasure has ultimately brought riches to the people of Rainbow Valley—just not in a way he could ever have predicted.

10.

COPPOLA SPENT TWELVE WEEKS SHOOTING *Finian's Rainbow,* and by the time he had wrapped principal photography, he was so tired of the project that he was more than willing to turn postproduction over to the studio and move on to making *The Rain People.*

This turned out to be a terrible mistake. For all of the flaws in the movie, Coppola had his own vision of how he wanted the picture to turn out. Warner Bros., on the other hand, had its eye on the box office and a head-on competition with *Funny Girl* and *Star!* Of all its decisions, the most damaging was the company's decision to blow the picture up from 35 mm to 70 mm. With the format change, the top and bottom of the original 35-mm frames were cropped—the worst possible scenario for a film with a lot of dancing.

"Everyone at Warners thought *Finian's Rainbow* was going to be a big hit; they were just wild about it," Coppola explained. "They decided to blow the picture up to 70 and make it a roadshow picture. And when they did that, they blew the feet off Fred Astaire when he was dancing. No one had calculated the top and bottom of the frame. I just wanted to be done with it, but I was upset thinking that this thing might be an enormous success. I remember telling my wife, 'God, why should I become rich and famous because of this?'"

Such concerns, it turned out, were unfounded. *Finian's Rainbow,* when released in October 1968, dropped like a boulder at the box office. Apparently, older audiences, familiar with the play and its great musical numbers

("Old Devil Moon," "Look to the Rainbow," "If This Isn't Love," "How Are Things in Glocca Morra?") had little interest in seeing the production resurrected for the big screen; younger audiences had no interest at all. However, despite Coppola's problems with the film and his dissatisfaction with the way it turned out, *Finian's Rainbow* collected a number of respectable reviews. The notices were brutal around New York City, where memories of the Broadway play were nostalgic, and feelings about its message were oh so politically correct ("It has been done listlessly and even tastelessly, with quick updatings of Negro personalities to match what people who have lived in Beverly Hills too long must imagine modern black sensibilities are"); they were equally dismal in *Time* ("The movie might have survived were it not for the ham-handed direction of Francis Ford Coppola") and *Newsweek* ("*Finian's Rainbow* is a shuffling relic that tried valiantly to be modern. It is the right show at the wrong time").

Coppola fared much better elsewhere, and he even picked up several raves. "*Finian's Rainbow* is a stunning piece of cinema," reported *Sight and Sound*'s Tom Milne, who "loved every minute of it." Milne was so enthralled with the picture that he even found a way to reconcile Coppola's makeshift choreography, as well as the unfortunate cutting of Astaire's footwork in the dance numbers: "[Coppola's] secret seems to lie partly in the way he choreographed the action beyond the limits of the frame, and partly in the impeccable rhythms of his curiously fragmented technique."

Arthur Knight of *The Saturday Review*, in another glowing review, was especially pleased by the decision to keep the musical true to its period. "They have kept it just the lovely show it was—tuneful, well-intended, occasionally funny, always appealing," he wrote. "By staging completely in its period, and doing everything supremely well, this *Finian's Rainbow* transcends time. Like Astaire himself, it seems ageless."

Immediately after wrapping the filming of *Finian's Rainbow*, Coppola was offered nearly $400,000 to direct the movie version of *Mame*, another enormously successful Broadway musical. Coppola wisely demurred. It was time to make his personal film.

Chapter Three

American Zoetrope

"In Los Angeles, you talk about deals. Here you talk about film."

—Francis Ford Coppola,
discussing his move to San Francisco

1.

WHILE MAKING *FINIAN'S RAINBOW*, Francis Ford Coppola had assured George Lucas that the success of the picture would be the meal ticket for their future films. Coppola would use his influence to secure financing for future projects, and all Lucas needed to do was ride on Coppola's coattails. Coppola's self-assurance, however, had begun to erode by the time he'd finished *Finian's Rainbow*, despite Warner Bros.–Seven Arts' predictions of a box-office smash. Coppola recognized that if *Finian's Rainbow* performed poorly, it could sink future projects as surely as success could help them, and rather than wait to see how the film fared with critics and the public, he decided that it was imperative to secure a deal for *The Rain People* as soon as possible.

He already had a rough partial script, done while he was still shooting *Finian's Rainbow*. It was based on his short story "The Old Gray Station Wagon" (later changed to "Echoes"), written for a creative writing class at UCLA. In the story, three women—a young housewife, married for only a few weeks; a middle-aged woman with several children; and another older woman—leave their husbands and take off together in a station wagon. Coppola based his tale on a childhood incident: His mother, after a quarrel with his father, left the family for two days. When Italia returned, she told her family that she had stayed in a motel, even though she had actually passed the time at her sister's house. But the idea of his mother, off on her own, alone and frightened in a motel room, was a powerful image for young Francis. Although begun at Hofstra, the story had never been completed to his satisfaction.

When he wrote the film adaptation of the story, now called *The Rain People*, Coppola decided to focus on only one woman—a very young housewife who learns that she is pregnant—and he specifically tailored the character to fit actress Shirley Knight, whom he had met earlier in the year at the Cannes Film Festival. He admired Knight's work a great deal—the thirty-year-old actress had already been nominated for two Academy Awards, for *The Dark at the Top of the Stairs*, in 1960, and for *Sweet Bird of Youth*, in 1962—and she had recently turned in a powerful performance in the British feature *Dutchman*. Coppola had met her after the screening of *Dutchman* at Cannes.

"She was crying because someone had been rude to her," he remembered. "I went up to her and said, 'Don't cry, I'll write you a movie.' And she said, 'You will? That's sweet.' I went back and I took out this old college draft and decided to make it just one character."

The idea of writing a screenplay for one actress, Coppola admitted, appealed to his "romantic preconceptions." As he saw it, he would be like Michelangelo Antonioni writing scripts for Monica Vitti. *The Rain People* would be a film about self-discovery. Natalie, the movie's main character, would just leave her husband, without any idea of where she was going or if she was going to return. Somewhere along the way, she would pick up a former college football star. This brain-damaged young man would become very dependent upon her. Coppola had written a script for the film, but a portion of the action, as well as the settings, he decided, would be determined as they went along. He, his actors, and a skeletal production company would hit the road, filming wherever they went, and let the different locations help determine the action in the movie. The idea was daring and bold, but it was not the kind of idea that one could easily propose to potential backers, who tended to want specifics about both the movie's plot and the project's ultimate cost.

Coppola, however, had learned a few things from his experiences in Hollywood. From Roger Corman, he had discovered how to work quickly and inexpensively, improvising whenever necessary. From his days as a scriptwriter, he had learned how to hammer out a screenplay on extremely short notice. He had also had enough experience with the studios to know some of the ins and outs of getting a picture approved. He had managed to obtain financing for *You're a Big Boy Now* by convincing a studio that he had every intention of making the film, with or without the studio's help; he would take the same approach, with a slightly different spin, with *The Rain People.*

Realizing that he could make the rumor mill work to his advantage, Coppola dropped a few well-placed hints at Warner Bros.–Seven Arts that he was developing a new, secret project—one that he was already beginning to shoot. He then took George Lucas, actor James Caan, and a small film crew to Hofstra, where he shot some very rough footage of a football game, intended for use as flashbacks in *The Rain People.* The studio knew only the sketchiest of details about Coppola's activities, but from what they knew, officials concluded that Coppola had every intention of making the film independently, if necessary.

It was a shrewd move—and another successful bluff. Coppola had invested eighty thousand dollars of his earnings from *Finian's Rainbow* in state-of-the-art equipment needed to create the mobile filming and editing unit that he would take on his road trip, and he had nowhere near the kind of money that would be necessary to make *The Rain People.* The studio, of course, had no way of knowing what kind of money Coppola had, or if he had another investor ready to back him if they refused.

Coppola kept his best poker face. He had little money, no completed shooting script, or even a solid budget, but when studio officials questioned him about the rumors they had been hearing about his activities, he acted as if the movie were a done deal.

"Look," he told them one Friday in the late fall of 1967, "I'm starting to shoot on Monday and I need some money and if you don't give it to me, I'll get it from someone else."

Warner Bros.–Seven Arts, unwilling to call his bluff and risk losing a talented young director, decided to make at least a minimal offer. The studio promised Coppola three-quarters of a million dollars—a far from generous offer, but enough to get the movie off and running.

2.

OVER THE COURSE OF HIS CAREER, Coppola would have a prickly relationship with the labor unions, which, he correctly charged, drove up the costs of a film's production and restricted spontaneity. For someone like Coppola, who still harbored a film school student's mentality and who, as a rule, had little sympathy for unions to begin with, dealing with labor unions was a necessary evil, a fact of life that he could hate but not ignore.

The Rain People posed special challenges to Coppola. He had been given very little money to work with, but he had hoped that, with any luck, he could hold his expenses to a minimum. The production was to be a modest enterprise, involving a very small company of actors and technicians traveling from city to city, caravan-style, connected by two-way radios. Stops were not planned far in advance. People would be staying in inexpensive motels and would be prohibited from bringing spouses, lovers, or family members along. Making the movie was going to be an adventure.

The trade unions saw it differently. For decades, their leadership had worked diligently to establish favorable, long-standing agreements with the film industry, and someone like Coppola posed a threat to the established order. As Coppola himself admitted, he'd always had between fifty and one hundred people on hand during the making of *Finian's Rainbow;* by traveling with a small troupe of a dozen or so people for *The Rain People,* he was eliminating dozens of jobs.

In addition, because he would be moving his company from state to state, Coppola would have to deal with a number of local unions, each wanting a cut of the action—a situation that the financially limited director could ill afford. After some negotiating, an agreement was reached.

"We made a very creative deal with the locals," Coppola recalled. "We had a nine-man crew, and they allowed that if we would take three men from New York, three from Chicago, and three from Los Angeles, we could travel all over the country and work in any jurisdiction. I thought that was really helpful and very creative."

Coppola's crew for *The Rain People* was an excellent one. George Lucas helped in a number of ways, assisting with the camera work and sound and, in general, acting as an overall man Friday. Cinematographer Bill Butler, who would shoot dozens of movies in the future, including several of the *Rocky* pictures, *Jaws,* and *One Flew Over the Cuckoo's Nest* (for which he would receive, along with Haskell Wexler, an Oscar nomination), was director of photography. Barry Malkin, a Coppola friend for over a decade, climbed aboard as the film's editor.

Although Shirley Knight was the best known of the principal cast members, Coppola assigned major roles to two actors who, within just a few years, would become huge names in the film industry. James Caan, a Hofstra alumnus, who had played mostly very small parts in the past, was given his first starring role, playing Jimmie "Killer" Kilgannon, the former football player.

Robert Duvall, another character actor, remembered theretofore mostly for his role as Boo Radley in *To Kill a Mockingbird,* was given the picture's other substantial male role, as a troubled motorcycle cop named Gordon.

The *Rain People* journey began in early April 1968 in Long Island, New York, and lasted for the next eighteen weeks, taking the small seven-vehicle caravan through eighteen states and 105 shooting days. Coppola adjusted his script as he went along, custom-fitting some of the scenes to the locations that they stumbled upon. While in Kentucky, the company ran into a snag when a ferry operator refused to allow them to shoot the movie on board the vessel; Coppola appealed to state officials and was eventually permitted to film. In Chattanooga, Tennessee, the group witnessed an Armed Forces Day parade, which Coppola filmed and ingeniously worked into the picture. ("I was kind of embarrassed," James Caan said of the parade experience, "but Francis had more guts than anything. Of course," Caan quipped, "it's easy to have guts when you tell your actor to go in the middle of the parade.") When they hit the Southwest, Coppola, Lucas, and others shaved their beards and tried to make themselves more presentable to the local townspeople, who tended to be distrustful of anyone looking like a hippie. "Coppola was unrecognizable without his beard," Lucas recalled with some amusement, "and no one would listen to him."

Lucas would eventually compare the making of *The Rain People* to the kind of experience he'd been through in film school.

"The crew for *The Rain People* was very, very small, and it was very anti-establishment," he said. "I think there were only about thirteen or fourteen people in the whole crew. I became the general assistant to everybody. I was the third assistant director, the third assistant art director, the third camera assistant—the third assistant everything. I sort of filled in when we were short, because we had so few people on the crew. It was fun. We all pitched in and worked together, and we really had a ball."

Barry Malkin would call the making of *The Rain People* "one of the most interesting experiences that I've had in the business"—and for good reason. Everything seemed to be done by the seat of the pants, and on the most stringent of budgets and in the most nontraditional fashion, but for the company of young filmmakers, it all added to the spirit of adventure.

"I worked in a motor home that served many purposes on the film," Malkin remembered. "It was a cutting room of sorts. It carried the wardrobe and makeup and film stock. We did the transferring of our sound in the back of it. We would send our film to New York for processing, and it would be sent back to us, via Greyhound—these were the pre-FedEx days. We occasionally would get to a city and rent a movie theater late at night, where we would try to run our dailies within ten seconds of sync. We would have a radio in the orchestra, where we would be sitting, and another radio set up in the projection booth. We would tell our sound man to stop the machine for a couple of seconds—or we'd tell him to speed it up—and this was our hokey way of looking at dailies up on the big screen. It was an unforgettable experience, but we had a lot of fun doing it, and you can't often say that about moviemaking."

Much of the company's journey was captured on film by Lucas, who was shooting a short cinema verité documentary about the making of *The Rain People*. Early on, Lucas had approached Coppola with the idea of making such a documentary, and Coppola gave him the go-ahead, along with a spare camera and twelve thousand dollars taken from the production's photography budget. Lucas's documentary, *Filmmaker*, caught the essence of the ups and downs of making *The Rain People*, from the exuberance of working on a risky yet fulfilling project that flew in the face of the way movies were normally made in Hollywood to Coppola's angry telephone confrontation with a Warner Bros.–Seven Arts official, during which he openly challenged the system he had grown to dislike so intensely. "The system will fall by its own weight," Coppola shouted into the telephone receiver. "It can't fail to!"

For George Lucas, *The Rain People* shoot would be remembered as a time when the seeds for much of his future were being germinated. He was gaining practical experience in filmmaking and, through some of his discussions with Coppola and others, he was forming the ideas for the creation of his own studio—ideas that would evolve, first, into American Zoetrope and, later, into the Lucasfilm enterprises. In addition, it was while he was with *The Rain People* company in Nebraska that he began to plan the movie that would be most often associated with his name.

"George came up with the idea for *Star Wars* while we were making *The Rain People*," remembered Mona Skager, who served as a production associate on the Coppola picture. "We were sitting in the motel lobby, waiting for Francis and Ellie to arrive, and George was watching *Flash Gordon* on the television. All of a sudden, he started talking about how he should make a movie like that, with holograms and everything. I didn't even know what a hologram was. But that's when he vocalized that he wanted to do *Star Wars*."

Although most of the people working on *The Rain People* would remember the experience fondly, there was plenty of tension to go around, both on and off the set. The daily uncertainty left Coppola emotionally drained. He struggled, as he had during the making of his two earlier pictures, with the responsibilities that burdened him as a director. He was expected to be a leader, but every time he stepped behind the camera, he had to grapple with his own feelings of insecurity, fearing that he might not be measuring up to the task. "I'm tired of being the anchor when I see my world crumbling," he moaned during the making of *The Rain People*, his complaint registered by Lucas's camera.

For the most part, he got along well with his cast and crew, although there was some grumbling when, after issuing his edict that spouses, lovers, and family members were not allowed on the shoot, Coppola exempted himself and brought Ellie, Gio, and Roman along, his family following the caravan in a Volkswagen minivan.

The dispute was minor in comparison to the problems that Coppola was having with Shirley Knight. The actress, accustomed to working within a more structured framework, disliked Coppola's improvisational approach, which, she claimed, found him moving away from the character she thought she was going to portray. She hated watching the other cast and crew members cater to Coppola's every whim as if he were the next Orson Welles in the making, and she resented the working conditions that found her in a different motel every night, eating lousy road food and wandering about trying to find the film's story. She and Coppola argued frequently about the movie and her character, but little was resolved to her liking. "If he had done everything he said he was going to do, it would have been a marvelous movie," she said afterward.

Coppola felt badly about the way things were working out, but there was little that he could do. He and Knight had reached an impasse.

"She's very talented, but she's the only actor I really haven't gotten along with," Coppola told film writer Stephen Farber several years later, explaining that, in his view, the heart of their problems was a basic distrust on Knight's part, and an unwillingness to allow him to guide her as a director. "As I look back on it now," he stated, "I feel that the real problem was that she had a bad taste in her mouth from her experience in Hollywood; she prefers the theatre. I came along and promised this wonderful, idealistic kind of filmmaking. When we started to work, she realized that it had some realities to it as well, and perhaps she started to feel that this was just another Hollywood movie."

The differences in opinion marred the character of Natalie in the final film. As developed by Coppola, Natalie was to be a decent, compassionate woman driven to the brink of despair by the fear and uncertainty of having a child. Some of her less savory actions were supposed to be looked upon as the result of the intense pressure brought on by pregnancy and her relationship with the childlike Kilgannon. However, as portrayed by Knight, Natalie came across at times as very unsympathetic—distant, selfish, and even cruel—and viewers found it difficult to see her point of view.

"The character that Francis was searching for was a little more sympathetic," James Caan remarked afterward, when questioned about the problems Coppola had with his leading actress. "But there was something a little mean about her, and it kind of put the audience on another road. There's a scene where I was pulling the wires out of the telephone in a phone booth. Shirley was supposed to come out of the phone booth and reprimand me. But the next thing I knew, she slapped me in the face and kind of grabbed me and dug her nails in my cheek; she dragged them down my face and literally cut me. I was so into this character that I yelled, 'You hurt me,' even though it wasn't written in the script. Francis liked it and left it in the film. She had this kind of evil shit going on."

The failings of the character, Coppola would eventually intimate, were at least partially his fault. The more angered he became by his confrontations with Knight, the more emphasis he began to place on the Kilgannon character. Greater substance was assigned to other characters as well, particularly the cop and a roadside zookeeper who briefly employs Kilgannon. The Knight character shrank and, in the process, her actions and motivations became less clear. Coppola's solution to his problems with Knight might have spared him more grief on the set, but it ultimately damaged his movie. "I chickened out," he would eventually confess, adding that he would have liked the chance to rewrite the film.

3.

BUT FILMS, AS COPPOLA KNEW all too well, are not rewritten or necessarily revisited. "Movies are like old girlfriends," he remarked in 1974, dredging up a simile that he might wince at decades later, when reminded of it. "Once you've done them and you're finished with them, you don't go back."

Yet, for all its flaws—most notably an ending that feels uncomfortably contrived—The Rain People was easily Coppola's most accomplished work to that point and, viewed as part of his overall body of work three decades later, stands as a well-intended, often brilliant, and generally favorable movie, with a story that is still compelling today.

The story opens in a quiet neighborhood on Long Island. It is early in the morning, barely daylight, and as a soft rain falls on the street outside, Natalie Ravenna awakens and moves quietly about her bedroom, hoping not to disturb her husband Vinny. After dressing, she goes to the dining room, where she sets one place at the table and writes her husband a brief note telling him that she is leaving for a short time and that he should not worry about her.

Natalie has no plan, other than she will drive around the country in her station wagon and try to sort through her thoughts. She loves her husband and hates to cause him grief, but she has also just learned that she is pregnant, and she has mixed feelings about the responsibilities of being a parent. She has barely had time to grow up herself. Before she knows it, she has driven out of New York and is moving along the turnpike in Pennsylvania. On her first night away, in a lonely motel room, she remembers her honeymoon and reflects on her married life.

The next day, she picks up a youthful hitchhiker, and as they travel, Jimmie "Killer" Kilgannon tells her his story. Not long ago, he had been a star football player in college, but now he is on his own and no longer attending school. His girlfriend's father has promised him a job in West Virginia, and he was on his way there when Natalie picked him up.

That evening, they take separate rooms in a motel. Natalie, attracted to Kilgannon, invites him to her room, where she plans to seduce him, but after they dance and talk for a while, she realizes that something is not quite right about this young man: Despite the fact that he has attended college and has an athlete's body, he is little more than a child. She invites him to play Simon Says, which quickly takes a cruel turn when Natalie demands that he kneel down and bow to her. When he does, Natalie notices a scar on his head. He has a metal plate in his head—the result, he tells her, of a terrible injury sustained during one of his games. Kilgannon goes on to explain that, after the injury, he raked leaves for the college, but officials there had eventually given him an envelope with a thousand dollars enclosed, on the condition that he go away.

Moved by the story, Natalie takes Kilgannon to West Virginia, but he is rejected there, as well. His girlfriend, Ellen, wants nothing to do with him in his present condition. Natalie, who wanted nothing more than to dump this overgrown responsibility on someone else, feels trapped, but she refuses to abandon him.

The two travel from town to town, from one expanse of highway to another, until they find themselves in Nebraska. Natalie stops at a small animal farm and manages to talk its owner into hiring Kilgannon to clean cages and look after the animals. The owner, however, is more interested in Kilgannon's money than in giving him a job. Feeling as confined as the animals around her, Natalie speeds away from the farm, but she has not driven far before she is stopped by a highway patrolman named Gordon, who issues her a speeding ticket and insists that she accompany him to town to pay the fine. They wind up back at the animal farm, checking on Kilgannon and seeing how he's doing.

Not surprisingly, things have gone poorly for Kilgannon. He has liberated all the animals from their cages, and the angry farm owner wants Kilgannon's money as compensation. Natalie bails him out again, but now, with no job, no home, and no money, Kilgannon is more dependent upon her than ever. To make matters worse, he has become as possessive as a small child. Wanting Natalie only for himself, he rips the phone out of the wall when she tries to call her husband. Infuriated, Natalie slaps him and leaves him to fend for himself–this time for good.

Earlier in the day, Natalie had agreed to go on a date with Gordon, who lives in a trailer court with Rosalie, his precocious young daughter. The date goes smoothly enough, but later in the evening, after they return to Gordon's trailer, Natalie is put off when Gordon tries to send his daughter away for the night. Rosalie leaves and Natalie, against her better judgment, decides to stay.

While walking around the trailer park, Rosalie runs into Kilgannon. He has somehow managed to follow Natalie and Gordon, but with no plan of action, he is delighted to have company. They wander from trailer to trailer, looking in windows and talking.

Meanwhile, back at Gordon's, Natalie has decided that she's had enough of the policeman. Gordon has his own tortured past, including the horror of watching his wife burn to death in a house fire, but he is too needy and aggressive for Natalie. When he tries to force himself on her, Natalie reaches for his gun, but he is too powerful for her. At the last instant, Kilgannon bursts into the camper and begins to beat Gordon. Fearing for her father's safety, Rosalie snatches the gun and shoots Kilgannon. Natalie weeps over her fallen rescuer, vowing to take care of him forever, but he dies before she can call for help.

4.

BY THE END OF THE *RAIN PEOPLE* shoot, Coppola was confident enough of the film to announce that he would be writing all of his future movies. He told the *The Hollywood Reporter* that he had four projects in mind, each costing under a million dollars to make, though he had yet to reach a final decision on which project he would be pursuing next. "The reason I haven't made up my mind," he offered as an official explanation, "is because I want to spend the next six months with editor Barry Malkin on *Rain*."

He also wanted time to weigh his options. *The Rain People*, filmed entirely in sequence, had been a relatively easy project. In all likelihood, the next picture would be more difficult, requiring, for one, a completed script prior to shooting, and while he prided himself on his ability to write good screenplays, Coppola admitted that he would feel more pressure if he intended to write all of his future movies. "I'm really trying to make it as a writer working on original screenplays," he said. "Writing is a more formidable problem for me now than directing."

Still, he had reason to feel confident. He had brought *The Rain People* in under budget, at $740,000, and he'd had a better time making his small personal movie than he'd had with the much larger-scaled *Finian's Rainbow. The Rain People,* he was convinced, was going to be a better all-around film than any of his previous efforts—a thought that gave him pause. Maybe it would be better to go off on his own and make the kind of films that he wanted to make, rather than work for big studios on movies that gave him less satisfaction.

He was by no means alone in his thinking. Carroll Ballard, his old UCLA colleague, who had shot the excellent title sequence for *Finian's Rainbow,* was one of several people who had suggested to Coppola that they might be better off in finding a place outside of Hollywood to make their movies.

"I remember Francis calling me one day," Ballard recalled. "He'd bought a sailboat and, knowing that I was interested in sailing, he wanted to know if I wanted to go sailing with him. While we were out, he talked about how we could take over the world, how we could finally make the movies that we wanted to make and gain this little upper hand on Hollywood. I suggested that the route to take might be sort of like Caesar's going to Gaul: Caesar consolidated his power by going away and putting together this gigantic army and then returning home when things were not so good there. That's where we sort of got the idea to get out of L.A."

George Lucas, who hated Hollywood, agreed. While he and Coppola were holed up in Nebraska during the *Rain People* shoot, they had discussed the prospects of working out of San Francisco. They could operate a low-key moviemaking facility, pursue modest film projects such as Lucas's *THX-1138,* and live a far less hectic existence than the one they encountered in Los Angeles. Coppola loved the idea. San Francisco would be a great place to raise a family, he decided, and the city's bohemian community offered just the kind of artistic environment that he could thrive in. "We thought that we could go to San Francisco and produce a new cinema of contemporary stories, with more ambitious themes, shot with tiny and mobile crews, and making use of the new film technology," Coppola remarked.

"Francis just didn't want to be part of that Hollywood scene," added Lucas. "He wanted to be more independent. We were more antiestablishment than ever because it was the sixties. We didn't want to be part of the establishment. Francis wanted to be doing more artistic films, and not be forced to make commercial films. I was still interested in doing avant-garde, nonstory, noncharacter films. I grew up knowing the underground of Scott Bartlett and Bruce Connor and the whole gang of underground filmmakers in San Francisco. So, for me, it was great. That was the sort of world I wanted to come back to."

The idea seemed all the more appealing when, a short time later, Lucas told Coppola of a chance meeting he'd had with John Korty, a Bay Area resident who was actually carving out a decent living as an independent filmmaker. At Lucas's urging, Coppola spoke with Korty and explained his plans, and they agreed to meet after Coppola had wrapped principal photography on *The Rain People*. When Coppola, along with Lucas and Ron Colby, producer of *The Rain People*, rolled into Korty's Stinson Beach studio, they were amazed by what they saw. There, lodged inside a gray barn, was a fully equipped studio, modest but totally functional. It was just the kind of facility that Coppola and Lucas had envisioned.

Their studio idea gained momentum—and supporters—over the ensuing months. Colby wanted in, as did Mona Skager, one of Coppola's production assistants (and one of the director's most loyal associates in years to come). Coppola began to research the prospects seriously. Late in the year, he traveled to Denmark, to check out Lanterna Film, housed in a lovely mansion in Klampenborg, a seaside town about fifty miles from Copenhagen. He was utterly charmed. Bedrooms had been converted into editing rooms, and a nearby barn contained a state-of-the-art sound-mixing facility. Laterna also boasted an impressive collection of antique moviemaking equipment, magic lanterns and zoetropes. He was especially fascinated by the zoetrope, a cylinder-shaped gadget that, when spun, projected a moving image. In Greek, *zoetrope* means "life movement"—an apt description, Coppola felt, for the kind of company he had in mind.

To Coppola, Lanterna Film preserved the spirit of *La Bohème* that he and Lucas wanted for their new San Francisco studio. The mansion and its beautiful surroundings, the low-key working environment, the feeling of adventure and creativity, the high-tech equipment—all had a very seductive effect on Coppola. He was ready to return to California, purchase a mansion of his own, and get started.

After visiting Lanterna, Coppola stopped off at the Photokina film trade show in Cologne, Germany, where, in a moment of impulse, fueled by his excitement over all he'd seen at Lanterna, Coppola ordered eighty thousand dollars' worth of equipment, including a high-tech sound-mixing system. It didn't seem to matter that he had neither the money to pay for the equipment nor a place in which to store it; in characteristic fashion, Coppola was forging ahead, strangely confident that somehow everything would work out.

Upon his return to the United States, Coppola put his Los Angeles house on the market and tried to consolidate his financial resources. The new company was going to cost a bundle, and very few of Coppola's enthusiastic associates had significant money to invest. Lucas, having seen John Korty's facility, and having heard Coppola talk about the facility in Denmark, was still keen on finding a mansion in Marin County and setting up a nice small enterprise capable of supporting modest art films made by a handful of filmmakers. The studio, he thought, should be given a whimsical name—something like Transamerican Sprocket Works.

Coppola's ambitions were expanding by the day. He, too, wanted to create a studio that encouraged creative young talent to make the kind of movies that were regularly passed over by Hollywood, but his plans for the studio, considerably larger in scope than Lucas's, now involved the creation of a full-blown facility, complete with a helipad and a large parking lot for the company's mobile studios. The company, he maintained, should be called American Zoetrope, largely because, when it came time to sell public stock, it would be listed early on the New York Stock Exchange's board.

Coppola, Lucas, Ron Colby, and Mona Skager searched Marin Country for the kind of house that Lucas wanted. They located three homes that suited their needs, but in each case, their bids for the property fell through. They then looked around San Francisco for a Victorian house, but this, too, proved futile. Coppola was growing edgy. His equipment was due to arrive from Germany at any time, and he had no place for it. Finally, he heard of an available warehouse at 827 Folson Street in San Francisco—a three-story loft with plenty of room, even if it was located in one of the city's declining business districts. American Zoetrope had found its home.

5.

THE RAIN PEOPLE PREMIERED on August 27, 1969. Coppola, busy with his plans for American Zoetrope, hoped the movie would realize at least a little profit, which he could then apply to the studio, but it was not to be. Even with the surprising success of *Easy Rider,* a low-budget road film that had exceeded all expectations in ticket sales, *The Rain People* was a box-office flop.

The reviews indicated that the press was now prepared to view Coppola as a major filmmaker—as opposed to a precocious film school graduate lucky to get *anything* to direct—but as such, he was walked on a much shorter and tighter chain than in the past. To make matters worse, he was not only being measured against his own talent and history; in many reviews, his movie was compared to *Easy Rider*, which, in its earlier release, had caught critics by surprise. Reviewers that had once smirked at *Easy Rider*'s hippie ideology, labeling it as being "forced," now had to reassess the value of a movie that had obviously captured the imaginations, if not the approval, of so many viewers. For Coppola and his film, this was not good news.

The majority of critics found *The Rain People* to be a well-meaning experiment that ultimately came up a little short of the mark. "*The Rain People* is a minor failure by a major young talent," reported the *Washington Post*, "but it's the sort of failure that has interesting implications for the future of American films." The *San Francisco Chronicle* was harsher in its assessment. "*The Rain People* is a film that promises a great deal but delivers very little," wrote John L. Wasserman, adding that the film had "an interesting non-plot, and endeavors to get in some good insights along the way, [but] it disappears when it ends." *Newsweek*'s Joseph Morgenstern, author of very favorable reviews of *You're a Big Boy Now* and *Finian's Rainbow*, including the often-quoted comparison of Coppola to Orson Welles, attacked Coppola's script. "It might have been an enjoyable movie," wrote Morgenstern, "if Coppola had been a worse traveler and a better thinker, if he spent less time on the road and more time in a quiet room, sitting in front of a typewriter and letting his fingers do the driving."

Most reviewers pointed to Coppola's ending as the film's most serious weakness. "It is the worst thing in the movie, heavy with meaning and giddy in execution," protested *New York Times* critic Roger Greenspun, "and for all its freakishness it tends almost fatally to tame an otherwise wayward, tactful, compassionate film." Gary Arnold of the *Washington Post* agreed. "Coppola can't end this film," he wrote, "and [he] merely kisses it off with the sort of violent finale that seems to be very popular this year." Arnold's reference to the bloody ending to *Easy Rider* was an objection posted by other critics.

As always, Coppola could fall back on one rave review for comfort and inspiration. Charles Champlin, writing for the *Los Angeles Times*, took issue with Coppola's "disappointing" ending, but otherwise judged the movie to be "gentle, sentimental, traditional." Champlin, like other critics, was intrigued by the way Coppola made his picture, and, like other colleagues, he was pleasantly surprised by the way Coppola captured life in America: "It is a superbly acted private drama, saturated with the look and the feel of a large swatch of this country in the 60s. . . . The middle America strung out along a transcontinental highway is a real presence in *The Rain People:* the America of neon incarnadine and soul-bleaching fluorescence, of access roads and the staring storefronts of decaying small cities, tawdry sprawl and sudden glorious vistas of green hills and chimney smoke."

Of all the notices, Stephen Farber's may have come closest to detecting the true significance of *The Rain People*. In a lengthy essay for *Film Quarterly*, Farber found a ray of hope even in a flawed production like *The Rain People*. "The chance to fail with material too complex and urgent to sort it out all at once is a luxury that filmmakers in Hollywood have never been able to afford," he stated. "And if the fragmentation of the industry leads to more low-budget, independently made films, filmmakers may have that luxury again."

Farber's point was an important one. As he noted in his essay, *Easy Rider*, *Alice's Restaurant*, and *Medium Cool*—all small, independently produced personal films—were released the same year as *The Rain People*, indicating a subtle but extremely important shift in the motion picture industry. The "New Hollywood" was about to be born.

6.

FOR A FEW GLORIOUS MONTHS at the end of 1969, American Zoetrope was the proverbial snowball moving downhill, gaining in size and momentum until it no longer seemed like a utopian dream. The San Francisco warehouse was besieged by carpenters, electricians, and other construction specialists, all feverishly working to convert the building into a maze of offices and production rooms. The equipment arrived from Germany, only to be temporarily stored in the hallway until construction on some of the rooms was completed. George Lucas invited a number of his Southern Cal cronies—John Milius, Willard Huyck, Matthew Robbins, Walter Murch, Hal Barwood, and Gloria Katz—to enter into the new adventure, while Coppola took calls from such established directors as Stanley Kubrick, John Schlesinger, and Mike Nichols—all interested in what American Zoetrope had to offer. Orson Welles shocked Coppola by calling with the proposal of shooting a 16-mm movie at the facility. For a while, it looked as if Coppola and his company were in the process of creating the film equivalent of the arts explosion in New York's Greenwich Village during the 1950s. They had the vision, the technology, the creative minds—but, sadly, not the necessary money. As Coppola would regretfully admit, the young filmmakers pouring into American Zoetrope were, almost to the individual, rebelling against the old Hollywood system, but in their idealism, they neglected to appreciate fully the fact that even small studios and films require capital to survive.

"My enthusiasm and my imagination far outpaced any kind of financial logic," Coppola confessed. "I wasn't associated with anyone who was the businessman of the group. It was all me, and I was forging ahead without looking back and seeing whether we could afford this or that."

He did manage to put together a multipicture deal with Warner Bros.–Seven Arts, which, had it worked, might have helped immensely. According to the agreement, American Zoetrope would develop seven pictures, each to be budgeted under $1 million. Included in the deal were Coppola's *The Conversation*, George Lucas's *THX-1138*, Carroll Ballard's *Vesuvio*, and a project being developed by Lucas and scriptwriter John Milius, a film about Vietnam entitled *Apocalypse Now*. Warner Bros.–Seven Arts production head Ted Ashley, far less interested in creating art than in creating profits, agreed to lend Coppola $300,000, plus put up an additional $300,000 for script development for the seven pictures, but the money was to be considered a loan, and had to be repaid if the studio ever decided that it wanted out of the deal. If the young filmmakers came through, and even one or two pictures proved to be profitable, everyone would be happy. If not, Coppola would be responsible for repaying the $300,000 loan. From the studio's perspective, the deal not only made sense, it was warranted: None of the filmmakers at American Zoetrope, with the exceptions of Coppola and John Korty, had made a feature film.

Coppola invested the bulk of the money in the Zoetrope facility—on the construction and new equipment—and in no time, the studio could boast of being one of the most up-to-date facilities in the business. As a gadget lover, Coppola had always been irked by Hollywood's reluctance to embrace the new technology, which, he felt, would revitalize the industry and make films easier, cheaper, and quicker to produce. In less than two years' time, beginning with his purchase of the equipment for *The Rain People*, Coppola had amassed an impressive array of modern equipment, including a Keller three-screen editing table—the only one of its kind in the states—and Steenbeck editing machines, Ariflex cameras, and the sound system he had ordered at the fair in Germany. Newspapers and trade publications began to take notice, and Coppola soon found himself with a forum to spread his new gospel on filmmaking and technology.

"I became a sort of minor expert on this stuff by really trying to find out about it," he explained. "If someone told me of a new way of doing something, I often checked it out. Maybe I didn't like it, but at least I inquired." The problem, Coppola insisted, was Hollywood's resistance to change.

Rather than explore new technology, traditionalists rejected it outright. "You go to a Hollywood editor," Coppola said, "and ask him about a Steenbeck, and he'll say, 'Aw, you can't cut film on that.' It's true you can't cut on a Steenbeck the way you cut on a Moviola, but if you adapt yourself, you can do it faster. It's like taking a guy who flies a biplane and showing him the controls of a 707. He's going to say, 'Aw, I can't fly this.'"

Christopher Pearce, Zoetrope's general manager, pointed out the practical reasons for Coppola's seemingly large investment in the new technology.

"One of the reasons for having such a complete installation," he explained, "is that, despite the incredible insecurity of this industry, you know that, whatever happens, you can go on making films. You need relatively little money if you have all of that equipment sitting there. You know, for example, that you can mix your own film for nothing, because the equipment is there—it's paid for. I think that's the basic philosophy behind why it was set up in this way."

The founding of American Zoetrope symbolized a further split in the industry—between the new and old filmmakers. Coppola, a true visionary, was leading the way, defying a time-tested system and its economic laws, charging ahead with new theories of filmmaking like a brilliantly eccentric hare pacing the plodding yet wizened tortoise. Hollywood, of course, could afford to smirk at the young idealist and humor him as he issued his proclamations: After all, what, *really*, had he done? He had made a B-grade suspense movie, a charming yet unsuccessful coming-of-age flick, an outdated musical, and an interesting, if self-indulgent, road picture. None had fared well where the minds meet—at the bottom line—and while there was no denying that the kid had talent, at the rate he was going, he was likely to be hard-pressed to find someone to finance his future films, let alone lead the industry to another new, exciting level.

Indeed, Coppola would see his dream falter, not for a lack of ambition, but because he outran his own intentions. Like Preston Tucker, his old idol, he would have the design but lack the wherewithal to bring it to fruition.

But he would leave his mark.

7.

THE RAIN PEOPLE HAD BEEN the first film released under the American Zoetrope banner, but George Lucas's *THX-1138*, which went into production on September 22, 1969, had the distinction of becoming the first picture officially begun under the aegis of the new company.

THX had been in the works for a long time. Lucas had spoken to Coppola about making a feature-length movie based on his prizewinning student short when the two had met on the set of *Finian's Rainbow*. Coppola had encouraged him to work on a script for the film, but Lucas found it tough going.

"When we were working on *The Rain People*," Lucas recalled, "I got an offer to do a screenplay for Columbia. Francis said, 'No, stay here. Do it here and you'll have more freedom.' So he got me a job writing *THX*, and I was writing the script for *THX* while we were doing *The Rain People*. I worked on *THX* from four in the morning until six in the morning, and then I'd work on the picture." Lucas, however, for all his ambitions to make a film, was a reluctant screenwriter, and he needed a nudge from Coppola to get rolling on his script. "Francis forced me to write the screenplay. I wanted somebody else to do it, but he said, 'Look, if you're going to become a good director, you're going to have to learn to become a writer.' So he coached me on writing and forced me through a few drafts of the screenplay."

Lucas showed Coppola an early draft, but they agreed that it was nowhere near ready to film. After discussing the script with Lucas and offering his suggestions, Coppola turned it over to screenwriter Oliver Hailey. This time, it was Lucas who was dissatisfied with the results. Lucas finally teamed up with Walter Murch, a Southern Cal classmate who had worked on the sound on *The Rain People,* and the two put together a quirky, esoteric script that met with everyone's approval.

Everyone, that is, except the officials at Warner Bros.–Seven Arts. Coppola had personally pitched the *THX* project to the studio, claiming that the film could be delivered for the quirky but unlikely sum of $777,777.77 (seven being Coppola's lucky number), but the company was not sold on the picture. Coppola managed to push it through only when he packaged it as part of his seven-picture deal with the company. Even then, the studio insisted that Coppola assign a line producer to the project, to assure Lucas's coming in on time and budget.

One didn't have to look long to see why Warner Bros.–Seven Arts was reluctant to endorse the film. *THX*, although quirky enough to enjoy a cult following in years to come, and fascinating in its commentary on futuristic technology and human relationships, was often cold and cynical. Lucas's subterranean world was a place where humans lost their identities and walked about in white uniforms and with shaven heads, their daily lives overseen by computers and computer-programmed robot guards. People were required to take mind-numbing drugs, which kept them in a docile, obedient state. At the heart of the story were THX-1138 (played by Robert Duvall) and LUH-3417 (Maggie McOmie), who defied the system by having sex and birthing a child. THX-1138 was captured and imprisoned, but after a bold prison break, he escaped to a surface world, where he would begin a new life.

To help Lucas launch the project, Coppola took a familiar approach—one that had been successful with his own films.

"He pushed Warners into giving us the go-ahead to make the movie," Lucas explained. "Francis's attitude was, 'We'll just start making it and they'll have to catch up with us.' So he put up some of his own money and got us going. We started casting and scouting locations and hiring an art director and doing all kinds of things before Warners knew what was going on. Finally, he just said, 'Look, you're either going to make this movie or not.'"

Even so, it looked as if *THX* might be indefinitely suspended in prepro-duction limbo, stalled by Warner Bros.–Seven Arts' delays in providing the agreed-upon funding. Coppola jumped to Lucas's defense, flying to Holly-wood and angrily confronting startled company officials. "What's going on here?" he demanded. "We're ready to shoot! Where's our go-ahead? Here's the script, here's the cast. . . . What kind of organization are you guys run-ning? Where's our money? You wanna be with us or don't you?" When, a few days later, the money still hadn't arrived, Coppola sent a pointed telegram: "PUT UP OR SHUT UP!" The studio put up—reluctantly.

Coppola appointed Lawrence Sturhahn to the position of line producer for the film—a decision that did not rest well with Lucas, who regarded Sturhahn as the kind of company bureaucrat that Zoetropers were trying to escape. In all likelihood, this was true enough, and Coppola intentionally installed Sturhahn, who had worked with him on *You're a Big Boy Now*, as a kind of oppositional force to Lucas—as someone to keep Lucas on his toes as well as help him. Lucas, who was receiving a piddling fifteen thousand dollars to write and direct *THX*, didn't need constant reminders about time and budget.

THX-1138 took only ten weeks and $800,000 to make—a tribute to Lucas's skills as a filmmaker. Cutting corners whenever possible, he worked on a pro-duction schedule that would have wilted Hollywood veterans. Much of the filming was done in the partially completed San Francisco BART subway tun-nels, or in the underground parking garage at the airport. Whenever he could, Lucas used existing light, and he rarely shot more than a couple of takes of any given scene. On some occasions, he shot—and used—the rehearsals. Cop-pola would stop by the set from time to time, and he would talk up Lucas to Warner Bros.–Seven Arts officials, trying to keep things copacetic between the young director and his increasingly anxious sponsors. As a mediator, Coppola turned out to be almost as gifted as he was as a pitchman. He would assure the studio that he was supervising Lucas, that everything was under control, and that the film would be delivered to the company's liking; with Lucas, he took an entirely different approach, telling him to make the movie that he wanted to make. In taking such an approach, Coppola was not playing a game with the studio or Lucas, at least by his thinking. He was utterly convinced that any of the film's shortcomings could be corrected during postproduction. Besides, it was Lucas's first feature film; people couldn't expect him to come up with a landmark film the first time around.

While Lucas worked on the postproduction of *THX-1138,* Coppola tried to guide American Zoetrope along. The studio's heady beginnings had lapsed into the rugged realities of day-to-day business—and business wasn't very good. There was never a lack of projects to pursue, or talented young minds to work on them; there was, however, a serious lack of money. *The Rain People* had not rewarded Coppola with profits to sink back into the company, and with no new pictures to place before the public, American Zoetrope had to rely on the rental of its facility and equipment for a good portion of its income. Equipment began to disappear. Suddenly, Coppola's paradise for young filmmakers had turned into a personal nightmare.

"I found that many young people who want to make films can be very selfish and one-sided about it," he lamented. "Suddenly here was this enormous playground and everybody wanted a piece of it. There was an incredible free-for-all."

As Coppola recalled, American Zoetrope was overrun by thousands of letters and unsolicited film submissions—all from putative filmmakers hoping to find a sponsor in the new studio. At one point, Coppola hired three women whose only job was to open these packages and letters and take calls from people inquiring about the facility. Coppola estimated that nearly forty thousand dollars' worth of equipment was lost or stolen during Zoetrope's first year in business, including company cars that were borrowed and wrecked in traffic accidents.

Coppola likened the experience to the Beatles' founding of Apple, which had faced similar problems in England, though on a much larger scale. Like the Beatles, Coppola had been too trusting of people who, quite often, were ripping him off.

George Lucas, for one, held Coppola accountable for some of Zoetrope's problems. Lucas's father, a conservative businessman with an office-supply store, had instilled in George a much more traditional view of how business was conducted, and Lucas was amazed by Coppola's willingness to let just about anybody handle Zoetrope's expensive equipment. ("Francis would have given a camera to a street cleaner who expressed an interest in the company," he noted.) He suspected that Coppola was burying some of Zoetrope's expenses in his *THX* budget, which was a common-enough practice in the big studios and wouldn't have been a major point of contention had Lucas himself not been called to task for some of the expenses that he charged to Zoetrope. On one occasion, Mona Skager challenged some of Lucas's telephone expenses, accusing him of charging eighteen hundred dollars' worth of noncompany calls to Zoetrope. Hurt and embarrassed, Lucas approached his father for a loan to pay back the money. Coppola hit the ceiling when he heard about it. "I never would have done that to a friend," he fumed to writer Peter Biskind. "Mona was way out of line. I always believed that that incident was one of the things that pissed George off and caused a break."*

(When questioned about it in 1999, both Lucas and Skager claimed to have forgotten about the incident long ago, both insisting that it was never as contentious as reported. Skager, however, defended her position. "I was plunking my own money into Zoetrope," she said, "and I felt justified in taking that position. We survived—that's the important thing.")

Coppola was undoubtedly giving himself the benefit of the doubt—or at least showing how selective memory can be, for if anything caused the first serious crack in his relationship with George Lucas, it was his handling of *THX-1138*. Lucas and Walter Murch had spent the winter of 1969–1970 in postproduction, trying to piece together a movie that was becoming an albatross to Warner Bros.–Seven Arts. The company was extremely unhappy with the film's dailies, which, from a technical standpoint, looked more like the work of a gifted amateur than the efforts of a polished professional, and as the months dragged on and a finished film was still not forthcoming, the company

---

*In their remarks to the author, both Coppola and Lucas protested the way their relationship— professional and personal—had been portrayed by the media over the years, both filmmakers insisting that their disagreements had been so blown out of proportion that the public record was terribly inaccurate. "George Lucas and I have always been good friends—and we're good friends to this day," Coppola stated. "George has been very helpful to me throughout the years, and I hope I have also been helpful to him. So often, reports of the past went out of their way to leave out the great help, affection, and friendship that we had—and have—for each other." Added Lucas: "The arguments we had weren't very serious. You could take the amount of time that Francis and I have actually been mad at each other and it would probably be less than a dozen times in the thirty years we've been together. We hardly ever fight, and considering we've been close friends for that long, I think it's a better-than-average record."

worried about Lucas's ability to pull it off. Coppola tried to reassure the studio that everything would work out, though he himself had not seen a rough cut of the movie.

He finally got the chance to watch a few reels of the completed *THX* in May 1970, when he dropped by Lucas's Mill Valley home, where the film had been edited. Coppola had scheduled an important meeting with Warner Bros.–Seven Arts executives for the next day, and he wanted to get a sense of the movie that they would be watching together. *THX*, however, confused him. "This is either going to be a masterpiece," he confided to Walter Murch, "or a masturbation."

In his heart, he probably knew the answer. People close to Lucas had offered less than jubilant reactions to the picture. The director's own wife, Marcia Lucas, hadn't liked *THX*, which, she said, had not involved her emotionally. Other friends found the film's plot too thin and confusing.

Coppola had no choice but to gather the reels of film and head south to Burbank. Who knew? Maybe the Warner Bros.–Seven Arts people would find it acceptable.

8.

COPPOLA'S MEETING WITH THE STUDIO bigwigs was supposed to have been special. Not only were they all going to be screening George Lucas's—and American Zoetrope's—first film; Coppola also intended to pitch seven new projects—in effect, the future of his studio—to the executives. Among the properties in development were Coppola's *The Conversation;* Lucas and John Milius's *Apocalypse Now;* Carroll Ballard's *Vesuvio*, a tale of life and love among northern California's early 1960s bohemians; *Atlantis Rising,* a science fiction rock opera, written by Scott Bartlett; *Santa Rita,* an account of the People's Park riots in Berkeley, to be directed by Steve Wax; and new work by Willard Huyck and Gloria Katz, who in a couple of years would help George Lucas rewrite his screenplay for *American Graffiti.* Coppola liked his odds, as well he should have: He was presenting project proposals by people destined to become mainstays in the next wave of talented young filmmakers.

Although Coppola would bitterly refer to the Warner Bros.–Seven Arts group as "the most unlikely group of executives," inexperienced and guilty of "a lot of stupid decisions," the group screening *THX-1138* was a fairly talented lot. After the Warner Bros.–Seven Arts merger, the new company had been purchased by Kinney National Service, a corporation that had started out in funeral parlors and parking lots, only to expand into the entertainment industry. Ted Ashley, the head of a major talent agency, had been hired to oversee operations, and he immediately sent most of the old executives packing, retaining only three of the company's top twenty-one officials in his new regime. John Calley, producer of *Catch-22,* was hired as head of production, and Frank Wells, an attorney and Rhodes scholar, took over business affairs. Dick Lederer, who had worked in marketing for the old Warner Bros., was appointed vice president of production. As part of its youth movement, the studio hired Barry Beckerman and Jeff Sanford, both in their early twenties, to work as story editors. As a collective, the executives were young, laid-back, and knowledgeable about films and film history; they were also savvy-enough businessmen to know that their jobs depended upon their making profitable decisions, and that these decisions often required their eschewing art films in favor of pictures that filled the seats in the larger theaters—movies like *Love Story,* the sappy Paramount flick that had become the hit of the year.

They hated *THX-1138* from front to back, and they were prepared to blame Coppola for the movie's failings. "What's going on?" one of them challenged Coppola at the end of the screening. "This is not the screenplay we said we were going to do. This isn't a commercial movie."

It got worse. The studio executives, no longer trusting Coppola or Lucas to restructure *THX* into a marketable picture, decided to take the film from Lucas and edit the movie themselves. Furthermore, they were angry enough about *THX* that they weren't inclined to entertain notions of making any of American Zoetrope's new projects. Crushed, Coppola returned to San Francisco to deliver the horrible news. Then he took off for Europe, where he hoped to regather his thoughts.

Fred Weintraub, a former music producer hired by Warner Bros.– Seven Arts as its vice president of creative services, volunteered to work with Lucas on *THX,* but Lucas despised Weintraub's suggestions. The task of editing *THX* eventually fell to Rudi Fehr, one of Warner Bros.' old in-house editors. Fehr took a light touch, cutting only four minutes from the film, but Lucas was still unhappy. As far as Lucas knew, no director and producer in Hollywood history had ever had their picture taken away from them in this fashion, and as far as he was concerned, the cuts were more of an added insult than an improvement over the original. He now hated the big studios more than ever.

"I was sort of hoping that Francis could do more to stop them," Lucas reflected, years later, "but ultimately he wasn't able to stop them from recutting it, either. It's been portrayed that I was angry about the fact that Francis couldn't stop them from recutting the movie, but that's not true. I was angry about Warner Brothers recutting the movie, and I was frustrated that Francis couldn't do anything about it, but I certainly didn't blame him for what Warner Brothers was doing."

Although they never liked any version of *THX*, studio officials promised to distribute the picture, as per their earlier agreement with Zoetrope. The film, however, had totally soured the studio on Zoetrope. If Coppola and Lucas had let them down once, there was no telling what lay ahead.

The end of the Warner Bros.–Seven Arts/American Zoetrope relationship came on Thursday, November 19, 1970—forever known by Zoetrope as "Black Thursday"—when Coppola appeared before Warner Bros.–Seven Arts executives in a last-ditch attempt to market his company's future projects. He had carefully prepared his proposal, placing seven screenplays into beautifully bound black binders, each embossed with the American Zoetrope logo, which were distributed to studio officials. Unfortunately, Coppola had grossly underestimated the company's position, and by the time the meeting had ended, the studio had not only rejected all of his ideas; it had also severed its agreement with Zoetrope and demanded repayment of its loan.*

To Coppola, the rejection was tantamount to the stock market crash of 1929. He was nearly half a million dollars in debt and had no work ahead. His studio was sinking before his eyes. *Patton,* released earlier in the year by Twentieth Century–Fox, had reinforced his reputation as a screenwriter when the movie turned out to be one of the season's biggest hits, but he could not get his own pet project, *The Conversation,* off the ground. Resourceful as ever, Coppola trimmed his staff, cut expenses, raised the rent for office space, and tried to adapt, turning American Zoetrope into a postproduction facility that also specialized in making television commercials and educational films. But

---

*Three decades after striking his Zoetrope deal with Warner Bros., Coppola still bristled at the way the studio interpreted the agreement. "Warner Brothers loaned me $300,000," he told the author, "and they financed about $300,000 against development of our projects, including *Apocalypse Now*—and this was not a loan. After the success of *The Godfather,* I paid them the $300,000 loan. However, when I was about to begin *Godfather II,* they made a claim to Paramount, saying that I owed them another $300,000, which was not true. Paramount just wanted to get rid of it—it was a nuisance—but I refused, saying that this was money they had invested in scripts that they ultimately turned down. When did you ever hear of a studio executive leaving a studio and having to pay them back for all the development costs? It was bogus, a way of helping alleviate their embarrassment over the fact that all these young guys that they had abandoned were becoming successful. My agent told me, 'Look, Paramount will pay the $300,000, so don't worry about it.' Of course they did, but they deducted it from my percentage. However, because of this reimbursal, American Zoetrope got back all the scripts rights, including those to *Apocalypse Now.*"

even so, things were very grim. As visiting reporter Gerald Nachman wryly observed, "Zoetrope was down to one mini-skirted secretary, and instant coffee instead of espresso."

No longer able to make their movies at Zoetrope, the young filmmakers began to look elsewhere. John Korty, unable to afford the higher rent on his office, left Zoetrope, as did Carroll Ballard, who looked into television and movies for children. George Lucas considered his options, as well. Coppola couldn't help but feel bitter: He had put up his own money to start a studio, but he had been abandoned as soon as he was no longer useful.

"Zoetrope was picked clean," he recalled. "Everyone had used it, no one had contributed, and there was a time when I literally was staving off the sheriff from putting the chain across the door."

Just when things seemed bleakest, Coppola received a call from Paramount. The studio wanted the author of *Patton* to direct one of its upcoming features, a low-budget adaptation of the current best-selling book, a gangster novel called *The Godfather*. Coppola read a portion of the book and hated it, and when Paramount called with its offer, he did what any broke and down-on-his-luck director would have done if offered a high-visibility, high-paying project: He turned it down.

Chapter Four

The Godfather

"It was the most miserable film I can think of to make. Nobody enjoyed one day of it."

—AL RUDDY, producer of *The Godfather*

"Coppola will never make another big picture. Everyone agrees he doesn't know what he's doing. He's overwhelmed by the job!"

—UNIDENTIFIED CREW MEMBER

"The Godfather *is a stunning confirmation of Coppola's talents: vividly seen, richly detailed, throbbing with incident and a profusion of strikingly drawn characters."*

—WILLIAM S. PECHTER, *Commentary*

1.

WHEN MARIO PUZO BEGAN writing *The Godfather* in 1966, the notion of creating a polished, enduring work of art was not one of his high priorities. He had published two earlier novels, *The Dark Arena* (1955) and *The Fortunate Pilgrim* (1965), both to generally favorable reviews, only to realize one of the publishing industry's longest-standing axioms: Good works are not necessarily rewarded with bankable (or even livable) wages. Puzo, a pragmatist with a taste for high living and gambling, was astute enough to concede that he could devote a lifetime to paying homage to high art, but if he ever expected to support himself and his family, he was obliged to write the kind of books that appealed to the people buying, not reviewing, his work. When he set out to write *The Godfather,* he was mired in debt, toiling as a writer and editor for several men's adventure magazines, yet somehow managing to hold his own in an ongoing battle against becoming cynical about his chosen profession.

"I had been a true believer in art," he explained in an essay, "The Making of the Godfather," published in his 1972 collection, *The Godfather Papers.* "I didn't believe in religion or love or women or men, I didn't believe in society or philosophy. But I believed in art for forty-five years. It gave me a comfort I found in no other place. But I knew I'd never be able to write another book if the next one wasn't a success. The psychological and economic pressure would be too much. I never doubted I could write a best-selling commercial novel whenever I chose to do so. My writing friends, my family, my children and my creditors all assured me now was the time to put up or shut up."

For all his bluster about his ability to write a best-seller on command, Puzo procrastinated on accomplishing the task. All told, the novel took him three years to complete, mainly because he made a point of working on anything *but* the book. By his own admission, he finished *The Godfather* only when mounting debts inspired him to honor his contract. While putting his words to paper, Puzo nurtured what he felt was an ambitious hope of earning $100,000 for his efforts; the book, of course, wound up amassing exponentially more, making Puzo a very surprised millionaire.

The book's appeal was undeniable. Peter Maas's *The Valachi Papers,* a nonfiction account about the Mafia published in 1968, had whetted the public's appetite for information about the secretive mobster society, and Puzo's book, although written entirely from research rather than from firsthand knowledge of or experience with the topic, brought readers even closer to the subject, affording them a curious fly-on-the-wall sensation as they listened to convincing tales of a Mafia don making decisions and directing his soldiers. Significantly, the Mafia chieftain and main character in the novel, Don Vito Corleone, bore little resemblance to the foulmouthed, bloodthirsty thugs of previous gangster books and movies. Even in a milieu that required iron-willed and occasionally forceful control over New York's gambling and assorted business interests, Corleone preferred negotiation to firepower. In Puzo's novel, there was plenty of the brand of sex and violence that helped propel books onto best-seller lists, but none of the mayhem came at the expense of ordinary people. As one critic observed, "The victims of the Corleone 'family' are hoods or corrupt cops—nobody you or I would actually want to know. . . . You never glimpse regular people in the book, let alone meet them, so there is no opportunity to sympathize with anyone but the old patriarch, as he makes the world safe for his beloved 'family.'"

Puzo would have been the last to dispute the reviewer's remarks; if anything, he had crafted his novel for just such an observation. "*The Godfather* was really, to me, a family novel more than a crime novel," he would insist years later, after the motion picture and its two sequels had become part of the American cultural idiom.

In *The Godfather,* Don Vito Corleone presides over two distinct families— his immediate one—which includes his wife, daughter, and three sons—and the largest, most powerful organized crime syndicate on the East Coast. The elder Corleone had emigrated from Sicily to the United States as a twelve-year-old boy and had grown up in the Little Italy section of Manhattan, where, at a very early age, he had learned the laws of the street and the laws of business, and how the former, if applied judiciously to the latter, could act as a great equalizing force in the constant struggle that immigrants faced in turn-of-the-century America. By acting as a benefactor to the powerless people in his neighborhood, young Corleone rose in stature, gaining influence and respect that he could parlay into a lucrative business during the Prohibition era, when he bootlegged liquor and provided a protection service for the small speakeasies run by the families and businesses around him. "By the end of the Prohibition period and the start of the Great Depression," writes Puzo in a lengthy flashback passage, "Vito Corleone had become the Godfather, the Don, Don Corleone."

Although barely educated, the Godfather built his empire by instinctively combining old-world and new-world values, yet by the time he has reached middle age, when the novel begins, he is finding it difficult to keep up with the times, at least in terms of what the other rival Mafia families are doing. Despite his criminal background, Corleone despises the prospects of investing his business interests in prostitution or drug trafficking; no matter what the financial rewards, these types of criminal activities are beneath him. The other Mafia families view this attitude as a sign of weakness and believe that Don Corleone is beginning to slip.

At the book's opening, there is very little tangible evidence of Don Corleone's losing stature, as he fulfills the Sicilian tradition of granting favors on the day of his daughter's wedding. He promises to help arrange for citizenship for a young Italian man about to be deported. He loans a friend the money needed for a down payment to start up a pizzeria. He agrees to avenge the beating of an undertaker's teenage daughter, who also happens to be his wife's goddaughter. All the Godfather asks in return for his favors is friendship and loyalty, along with a promise to provide a small service for him in the future, if and when he should ask.

These favors require very little on Don Corleone's part, for he has the money and influence to grant them without much effort. The real challenge comes along when Corleone's own godson, a down-on-his-luck singer/actor named Johnny Fontane, pays him a visit at the wedding reception. Fontane needs a break to turn around his sagging career—the kind of advantage he would gain by starring in an eagerly anticipated, high-profile war movie scheduled to be filmed in the near future. Unfortunately for Fontane, Jack Woltz, the film's producer and one of the most influential moguls in Hollywood, has taken a strong personal dislike to him and vowed that he will never appear in one of his films.

"The guy is a personal friend of J. Edgar Hoover," Fontane informs Don Corleone, the implications of his statement obvious. "You can't even raise your voice to him."

"He's a businessman," responds Don Corleone. "I'll make him an offer he can't refuse."

The statement, possibly the most memorable in the novel, coming as early on as it does, speaks volumes about the Mafia chieftain. He prefers to negotiate, with the implicit understanding that he will set the terms; he believes in the effectiveness of reason, and he will employ it in all matters of importance. When Woltz rejects Vito Corleone's request to give Fontane the movie role that he so badly needs, the Godfather pushes the negotiations to the next level. Woltz's prized possession, a legendary English thoroughbred racehorse, for which he paid a royal price and has put out to stud, becomes Don Corleone's bargaining chip: A few days after turning down Don Corleone, Woltz awakens, to find the horse's severed head at the foot of his bed. In a matter of hours, Fontane has landed his coveted role.

While establishing the Godfather's position of wealth and influence, Puzo also introduces the members of his immediate family and his tight circle of friends. His oldest son, Santino, known as Sonny, is intelligent, generous, and fearless, but his hotheaded disposition will prohibit him from ever taking over the reins of the family business. The second son, Frederico (Fredo), although dutiful to his father and family, lacks the intestinal fortitude to make and back tough decisions. Tom Hagen, Sonny's childhood friend, adopted by the Corleones after he is found wandering, sick and homeless, in the streets, is the Godfather's trusted consigliere—a lawyer holding "the most vital subordinate position in the family business." Clemenza and Tessio, two friends dating back to Vito Corleone's youth, are his most valued *caporegimes,* or lieutenants, destined to be awarded enviable slices of the business after Don Corleone retires.

Michael Corleone, the youngest and favorite son, a Yale graduate recently returned from a stint in the marines during World War II, is the most evident and qualified choice to succeed Vito Corleone as the head of the family—if, in fact, he can be persuaded to join the business. Although Michael possesses "all the quiet force and intelligence of his great father, [and] the born instinct to act in such a way that men had no recourse but to respect him," he has thus far shown no interest in his family's dealings. Instead, he has intentionally avoided involvement in his family, to the point of outright rebellion. His joining the service was an act of defiance against his father's wishes, and now, as if to test his father further, he has taken up with a non-Sicilian girlfriend, a Yankee schoolteacher named Kay Adams.

The story begins to unfold when a rival mobster named Virgil "the Turk" Sollozzo pays a formal visit to Don Corleone and tries to persuade him to help finance and offer protection to a new narcotics racket that he hopes to start up in New York. Corleone refuses, and three months later, Vito Corleone is gunned down in the street and his main enforcer is executed. Sollozzo reasons that, with Don Corleone out of the way, he will be able to talk Sonny, the next in command, into cooperating.

The plan backfires when Vito Corleone manages to survive. Furthermore, the assassination attempt sparks Michael's sense of family loyalty, and he volunteers to involve himself in a way that will permanently alter his life. To avenge the action against his father, Michael murders Sollozzo and his police-captain bodyguard, setting off a war among New York's Five Families and resulting in Michael being sent to Sicily, where he is to stay in hiding until the heat dies down.

Vito Corleone recovers slowly, his condition symbolic of the hit that his business interests have taken in recent months. With the police searching for the murderer of a fellow officer and cracking down on all mob activities in the process, the Corleone family finds itself battling on divided fronts, fighting with other families and trying to stave off the police. When Sonny is machine-gunned to death in classic gangland manner, a saddened and largely defeated Don Corleone calls a meeting with the heads of the other families and hammers out a truce.

Meanwhile, Michael, still in Italy, has settled into a peaceful life under the protection of a Sicilian don. He meets and marries the daughter of a businessman, but not before he reveals his reasons for being in the country. It is only a matter of time before news of Michael's whereabouts reaches the States, and a subsequent attempt on Michael's life fails when a car bomb intended for him explodes but kills Michael's wife instead. The attack, coupled with the events in the United States, set Michael's resolve. "Tell my father to get me home," he orders his Sicilian protector. "Tell my father I wish to be his son."

Michael is sincere in what he says, and as soon as he returns to the United States, he begins the process of learning and running the family's affairs. Michael, however, hopes eventually to convert the family's business interests into legitimate enterprises, and with this in mind, he looks into purchasing a hotel in Las Vegas, even as he plots revenge on those responsible for his brother's and wife's death, and the attempted murders of his father and himself.

Don Corleone, weak and infirm and formally retired as head of the family, counsels his son at every turn, knowing full well that Michael's plans will destroy the truce that he so carefully established a couple of years earlier. During that period, the Corleone family suffered horrible losses, both business and personal, but as Vito Corleone himself is presently quick to admit, his heart is no longer in the family's day-to-day operations. He realizes that the end is coming soon, and he dies while playing in the garden with his grandson, but only after he has taught Michael everything he needs to know to elevate the Corleone family back to its former prominence.

The book closes with an account of Michael's revenge on his enemies, including his brother-in-law, who had helped arrange Sonny's death, and Tessio, who, fearing the consequences of Michael's taking over for his father, had set up Michael for another assassination attempt at the hands of a rival gang. No one is spared. The bloody purge reinstates the Corleone family at the top of not only the New York crime syndicates but all the Mafia families in the United States. Still, as Mario Puzo makes clear at the end of his novel, such victories do not arrive without a price. In one of the book's most compelling scenes, Michael is attacked by his sister, who angrily accuses him of murdering her husband. Michael denies her charges, dismissing them as the ravings of a hysterical woman. When Kay Adams, now married to Michael and present at the confrontation, privately challenges her husband to tell the truth, he looks her directly in the eyes and repeats his lies. Michael, once a deliberate outsider in his family's business affairs, has thus rejected his immediate family in return for his leadership in the Corleone Mafia family. He has clearly traded his soul for mammon.

The public responded immediately to *The Godfather*, launching it to the top of best-seller lists across the nation and establishing it as one of the biggest publishing events in recent years. Critics, although generally favorable in their reviews, were hard-pressed to explain the book's success: At the close of one of the most turbulent decades in the country's history, when writers were laboring to contribute socially conscious works, *The Godfather,* like the Nixon administration itself, seemed to defy the odds—or, perhaps, it indicated a change in thinking, an indication that the public, weary of what it considered to be a freewheeling, overly permissive society, was willing to embrace a more rigid, almost Machiavellian, leadership in exchange for order in the house. Whatever the reasons, *The Godfather* was an unqualified triumph.

Despite its remarkable sixty-seven-week stay atop the *New York Times* bestseller list and its eventual status as the biggest-selling paperback of its time, *The Godfather* failed to impress the movie industry as anything other than a potential low-budget gangster flick. Paramount purchased the option for *The Godfather* for a paltry $12,500, with escalator clauses arranging to pay Puzo the sum of $50,000 if the novel was eventually made into a movie. The agreement, forged when Puzo was badly in need of cash but only one hundred pages into the novel that he had tentatively entitled *Mafia,* would prove to be one of the biggest bargains in motion picture annals. If Puzo could revel in the moment of having attained international best-seller status with a novel that was less than the best he had to offer—"I wrote below my gifts in that book," he eventually confessed—he could also spend the rest of his years wondering what he might have earned had he been able to afford to hold out for a better movie offer.

2.

FRANCIS FORD COPPOLA'S commitment to direct *The Godfather,* like Mario Puzo's decision to write the novel, was based almost entirely on financial need—an irony that did not escape the attention of all parties involved when it came time to tally the profits of the film's phenomenal run.

Not that Coppola was Paramount's first choice of directors—far from it. Gangster movies had become box-office poison, and studio executives took a cautious, if not skeptical, view of *The Godfather*'s chances of bucking the trend. Paramount's distribution department, in particular, objected to making the movie. "Sicilian mobster films don't play," they informed Robert Evans, the studio's head of production. *The Brotherhood,* a 1968 Paramount gangster picture starring Kirk Douglas and featuring an excellent cast, had received good reviews but had died at the box office.

Evans, still boasting of having obtained, in *The Godfather,* a blockbuster property for what amounted to little more than chump change, strongly disagreed. A savvy executive accredited with all but saving Paramount from oblivion by shepherding *Love Story* to the screen, Evans found himself in a mighty struggle to use *The Godfather* to add to his already-hefty reputation. "I felt like a kid picking up a stone in the street that turns out to be an emerald, but you can't sell it because it's the wrong color that year," he remarked.

To make matters more difficult, prospective directors were either already committed to other projects or wanted nothing to do with the picture. A list of some of the industry's finest directors, including Richard Brooks, Elia Kazan, and Arthur Penn, rejected directorial offers, as did Peter Yates, Fred Zinnemann, Richard Lester, and a host of others. Constantin Costa-Gavras liked the novel's rough treatment of American capitalism but feared that he was too much of an outsider to do it justice. Of those declining, the majority cited not wanting to be involved in a project that, in their eyes, glorified or gave any kind of sympathetic treatment to the Mafia.

The selection of Coppola ultimately boiled down to attrition and, to a very large extent, the young director's Italian heritage. After studying a number of contemporary gangster films, Evans concluded that the movies suffered from authenticity problems: Without exception, the films had been made by, and starred, people of Jewish, rather than Italian, descent. *The Godfather*, reasoned Evans, had to feature Sicilians in the key roles, starting with its director.

Nevertheless, he was horrified when Peter Bart, his right-hand man and Paramount's vice president of creative affairs, suggested Francis Ford Coppola as a candidate for the job. In his earlier films, Coppola had proven himself adept at delivering a movie on time and on budget. Evans was unconvinced. Coppola, he argued, had a terrible track record at the box office, not to mention the reputation of being a brilliant but eccentric director. Still, with the studio pressuring him to get the movie into production while the book was still at the pinnacle of its success, Evans had little choice. There were no other experienced Italian directors available.

Coppola, for all his money woes, followed the other directors in passing on the movie. In the wake of his success as a screenwriter for *Patton*, he was confident that he could earn a living by writing for the movies, and if he was going to direct another picture, he wanted it to be another personal film, along the lines of *The Rain People*—perhaps *The Conversation*, which he still dreamed of seeing into production. As far as Coppola was concerned, *The Godfather* was essentially a garden-variety potboiler in the Harold Robbins tradition—"a popular, sensational novel, pretty cheap stuff"—and he was offended by some of the novel's violence and explicit sexual content.

As the weeks passed, Coppola began to reconsider his stance. Zoetrope was withering on the vine, and he owed Warner Bros. $300,000. With no immediate directing or screenwriting offers on his desk, Coppola consulted his family and colleagues for their thoughts on his working on *The Godfather*. Carmine Coppola urged his son to take the job, reasoning that Francis could always use the money he earned to finance his more artistic endeavors. George Lucas was perhaps most direct in his assessment of the situation. "Take it," he advised Coppola. "We're broke."

Coppola heeded the advice. He met with Charles Bluhdorn, head of Gulf & Western, which owned Paramount, and the two talked through the night; by morning, an agreement had been reached. Coppola would draw a $150,000 salary for directing and cowriting the film, plus he would get 6 percent of the picture's net profits.

To celebrate, Coppola called Mona Skager and told her to pack her bags. "We're all going to Italy," he announced.

"I took four hundred dollars out of my checking account, and all of my credit cards, and Eleanor and the two boys and I jumped on a plane and met Francis in New York," Skager remembered. "Freddie Fields paid for the tickets, and we sailed off to Italy. That's when Francis broke down the book. He was up in the bar, and he ripped up the book and taped the pages on the windows of the bar. I'm not sure the captain liked it, but he kind of took over the bar. He had his little typewriter with him, and away he went."

Once he had agreed to direct the picture, Coppola immediately asserted his authority on it. Paramount executives, intent on holding the movie's budget to the $1–2 million range, had demanded that it be totally revamped, set in contemporary St. Louis or Kansas City, as opposed to 1940s New York. The company had commissioned Mario Puzo to adapt a screenplay from his novel, incorporating this significant change, and during the months that Paramount spent firming up the plans for the music and hiring a director, Puzo had worked on just such a script.

Coppola had other ideas. With pen in hand, he reread the novel, taking copious notes on what would work and not work in the film, softening his original harsh judgment on the value of the book. By cutting some of the less successful or less interesting passages from the novel, a powerful theme began to emerge. *The Godfather* contained not only all the elements of a solid, crowd-pleasing drama, it also possessed an allegorical undercurrent, with the crime boss and his family symbolizing the strengths and weaknesses of corporate America. In taking a more objective second look at the novel—his judgment aided, no doubt, by the fact that he was now signed on to direct the movie—Coppola concluded that his film could be both good *and* successful. His notes expanded, growing to include his own commentary on the book, a fifty-scene outline, queries that he wanted to pose to the author, and actual pages from the book, pasted onto binder paper and marked up with additional ideas and questions—altogether, a three-inch-thick volume of research that blended his director's sensibilities and screenwriting skills.

While collaborating with Puzo on the screenplay, Coppola insisted that they work separately, Puzo in his office on the Paramount lot in Los Angeles, Coppola at the Cafe Trieste in San Francisco. Oddly enough, the idea earned him the novelist's respect. "I suggested we work together," Puzo recalled. "Francis looked me right in the eye and said no. That's when I knew he was really a director."

As Puzo learned, a director has the ultimate creative control, and while the two were generally compatible, there were inevitable disagreements. The Puzo-written first draft had been set in the late sixties, complete with references to hippies, and many changes had to be made once Coppola had convinced Paramount that the movie would be better if set in the forties and fifties, as in the Puzo novel. Coppola cut most of the Johnny Fontane scenes from the book, reducing him to the status of a minor character. Puzo complained, with some justification, that Coppola had made the Mafia members *too* palatable, that Coppola was squeamish about dealing with the violence in the book. Coppola was willing to discuss any direction that the screenplay might take, but he remained firm on keeping it in accordance with his own vision for the movie, comparing his collaboration with Puzo to the way a conductor works with a composer's music.

"Usually in a film," he explained, "there is a person who conceives and designs it, like a composer writes music. A conductor is a great interpretive artist, but you wouldn't compare the conductor to the composer. But if the conductor had the power to change the music at will and then the music is very bad, it's not the writer's fault anymore."

So it was with the adaptation of the novel. "I wrote the *Godfather* script," said Coppola. "I did the adaptation. I credit Mario completely with creating the characters and the story. On the other hand, his book took in a lot more than what the film took in. I feel that I took the right parts. I also did a lot of things in that movie that people *thought* were in the book that weren't. The act of adaptation is when you can lie or when you can do something that wasn't in the original but is so much like the original that it should have been."

The memorable montage at the end of the movie, Puzo remarked years later, was one instance where Coppola's creative mind took the action in the book to a new level. "He knew what made a movie," said Puzo. "For instance, after I wrote the first draft of *The Godfather* script, I said to Francis, 'There's something missing from the ending. I don't quite know what.' He said, 'That's easy. We'll combine the executions with the christenings.' As soon as he said that, I knew we had the answer. In the book, those events are separate, but he saw them in cinematic form."

As Puzo recalled, their collaboration never grew hostile. "The great thing about Francis is he never criticized my work. If I sent him a draft and he didn't use some of it, I knew he didn't like it. He never criticized it or said, 'Gee, this is shit.' He just didn't use it."

Puzo was not alone in realizing that Coppola could be very strong-willed. Paramount brass might have suspected that they had misjudged their choice of directors when Coppola made it known that he was unhappy with the film's meager budget, or when he began to parry with studio executives over the casting of the film's major characters, particularly the roles of Vito and Michael Corleone. Producer Al Ruddy, a relative newcomer to the movie business, who had made a name for himself by producing the hit television sitcom *Hogan's Heroes,* wanted Robert Redford for the role of Michael Corleone, and thus he had instructed Mario Puzo to open the first draft of his screenplay with a love scene between Michael and his eventual wife, Kay Adams—the type of scene that would have appealed to Redford's large following. Puzo reluctantly complied, only to drop this dubious opening when Redford and Paramount failed to agree on the actor's salary for the role. Coppola and Puzo, along with Ruddy and casting director Fred Roos, favored hiring Marlon Brando for the part of the Mafia don, but their preference was vigorously opposed by Paramount president Stanley Jaffe, who refused even to consider him. As long as he was head of the studio, he informed Coppola, there was no way that Brando would work on the film.

3.

JAFFE'S OPPOSITION TO BRANDO had roots that dug deep, and which had been nurtured by a decade of the actor's difficult behavior and appearances in mediocre or money-losing ventures, beginning with the well-publicized turbulence on the sets of *Mutiny on the Bounty,* which had clocked in at $10 million over budget, and continuing through such disappointing pictures as *Candy, Burn!,* and *The Night of the Following Day.* Brando's magnificent acting talent, so overwhelming in *A Streetcar Named Desire*, *The Wild One*, and *On the Waterfront*, appeared to have sunk into a quagmire of disinterest and poor choice of roles. His box-office appeal had evaporated, and in an industry fueled by the sight of dollar bills piling up in the cash register, he was now considered a poor risk, regardless of his ability.

It was Brando, however, that Puzo wanted to play Vito Corleone, even though, at forty-five, the actor was actually much younger than the aging Mafia don at the end of the book.

"What happened," Puzo explained, "was I'd read an item in the newspaper saying Danny Thomas was going to buy Paramount Pictures just so he could play the role of *The Godfather*. I panicked. I knew a guy who knew Brando, and he gave me Brando's address. I wrote him a letter and asked if he would play the role if I could get it for him. He called me on the phone and said, 'No studio will hire me right now unless the director insists, so wait until you get a director.' I told the people at Paramount, and they were absolutely against it."

Nevertheless, when Puzo and Coppola met and began to discuss their ideas for the casting of *The Godfather*, Puzo proposed Brando as a good candidate. Coppola, who had recently been rejected by Brando after inquiring about the actor's interest in starring in the lead of *The Conversation*, originally believed Brando to be too young for the Corleone role, but after talking it over with Puzo, he added Brando's name to a short list that included Laurence Olivier and George C. Scott. Coppola made no secret of his belief that Don Corleone had to be played by one of the world's great actors, and he was intrigued by the challenge of directing Brando in the role.

Unfortunately, by the time Brando got around to reading the book and deciding that he was indeed interested in the part, Paramount brass had made its position known to Coppola and Puzo. Robert Evans joined Stanley Jaffe in opposing Brando. Evans and other Paramount officials had already anticipated and discussed what they felt would be inevitable protests to the movie from Italian-interest groups, and the notion of anointing Brando, a non-Italian, into the title role only exacerbated the problem. "If Brando plays the Don," renowned producer/director Dino De Laurentiis reportedly warned Charles Bluhdorn, "forget opening the film in Italy. They'll laugh him off the screen."

Without abandoning hope of changing influential minds, Coppola began testing others for the role. Paramount had initially announced that the movie would feature unknown Italian actors in the key parts, and of the scores of candidates taking screen tests for the role, the overwhelming majority fell into this category. Well-known actors were considered as well, including Richard Conte, Anthony Quinn, Lee J. Cobb, Raf Vallone, and Ernest

Borgnine. Burt Lancaster was said to be interested in the part. Frank Sinatra, who had publicly berated Mario Puzo at a dinner party for what he felt was an unfair portrait in the book, confided in Coppola that he would be willing to play Vito Corleone, provided he and Coppola could find a way to buy the rights to the movie from Paramount. Robert Evans entertained the idea of hiring Carlo Ponti, the internationally acclaimed film producer and husband of Sophia Loren, to play the lead. Everyone, it seemed, wanted to take a shot at such a high-visibility role, including, incredibly, Melvin Belli, the flamboyant defense attorney who had no acting credits on his résumé but who knew, beyond anyone's doubt, a thing or two about theatrics.

Coppola considered every suggestion, and continued his screen testing. Finally, after hearing from Brando, and after looking at an endless number of would-be dons, Coppola announced that it had to be Brando or nobody. Paramount seriously considered firing him, but Coppola held his ground. In a last-ditch effort to plead his case, Coppola asked for a special meeting with Paramount officials.

The gathering, attended by Jaffe, Evans, and a handful of corporate lawyers, turned out to be memorable. Jaffe held fast to his position that he would hear nothing about Brando's taking the role ("Furthermore," he insisted, "as president of the company, I will no longer allow you to discuss it."), but Evans, as unlikely an ally as Coppola could ever hope to find, persuaded the Paramount president to grant Coppola a few minutes to present his side of the story.

"Auguste Rodin molding clay with his hands did not have the agility of Francis's brain when it came to seduction," Evans later recalled. "Whether personal or professional, his persuasive powers made Elmer Gantry look like Don Knotts."

With very little to lose, Coppola launched into a passionate dissertation on the merits of Marlon Brando. The actor, argued Coppola, was not only one of the greatest performers in motion picture history, but, with the possible exception of Laurence Olivier, who was ailing and unavailable to appear in *The Godfather,* he was also the only man alive who could tackle this challenging role. Brando's involvement, Coppola continued, would only help the movie. Others would certainly line up for the opportunity to appear in a movie with him, and the actor himself would be a sort of patrician on the set, establishing a sense of family within the company. As Coppola described it, "I stood up as if I were a lawyer pleading for someone's life."

Upon completing his presentation, Coppola added a flourish that shocked the people seated in the room. Clutching his chest as if having a seizure, he collapsed to the floor.* The sight of Coppola writhing on the carpet, quite possibly suffering a heart attack as the direct result of his highly charged defense of his convictions, unnerved Jaffe to the point of caving in. Coppola could have Brando . . . but only on three strict, undebatable conditions. First, Brando would have to agree to work for a percentage of the film; he would receive no salary for his work. Second, he had to agree to allow Paramount to deduct overrun costs from his percentage if the overruns were the result of his unruly behavior. Last, Brando had to submit to a screen test—something he was loath to do, and something he had not done since he tried out for *Julius Caesar* in 1953.

Coppola correctly assumed that the screen test would be his biggest obstacle. Brando had money problems of his own, and since *The Godfather* whispered the promise of a huge payoff if it even approached the popular success of the novel, he had little objection to accepting Paramount's financial terms. The screen test was another matter. By his own admission, Coppola was still frightened of Brando and his reputation, and he could think of no reasonable way of broaching the subject with the actor. Fortunately for Coppola, Brando presented a solution when he admitted that he was not absolutely certain that he could play an aging Italian. "Why not get together and try it out?" he suggested to Coppola. "Wonderful," replied Coppola. "Let's videotape it." He said nothing about his immediate interest in using the tape as a screen test.

Coppola met Brando at the actor's home. Coppola brought along a borrowed video camera and camera operator, and the group went to work.

"I made this black-and-white videotape, and it was very impressive," Coppola recalled. "On the tape, you get to see Brando come out of his bedroom with a long, blond ponytail and in a Japanese-style kimono jacket. Then you see him roll his hair up in a bun and put shoe polish on it, talking the whole time, saying things like 'I want him to look like a bulldog.' Then you see him rolling up Kleenex, stuffing it in his mouth and starting to evolve his way of talking. He figured the guy had been shot in the throat. All this is happening right in front of you. He puts on a shirt and jacket, and bends the corner of the collar 'the way,' he says, 'those old Italian guys always have.' I had brought

---

*Coppola told the author that the seizure, a long-standing bit of *Godfather* lore, was actually intended to be "a joke." When Jaffe objected to the casting of Brando, Coppola went into his spiel. "I started talking as fast and furious as I could, trying to enumerate all the reasons I thought Brando was our only option. After this long tirade, I humorously fell down on the carpet and feigned exhaustion, as though *What else could I do?*"

little dishes of Italian cheese and salami and Toscano cigars, and he just wordlessly started working with these props. His phone even rang, and he picked it up, gesticulating and mouthing wordlessly into the phone."

The ploy worked. Upon returning to New York, Coppola visited the Gulf & Western building and asked Charles Bluhdorn if he could talk to him for a few minutes. Bluhdorn agreed, and Coppola set up a video recorder to show him the tape he'd shot of Brando.

"I turned on the set and you could see Brando coming out in his ponytail," said Coppola. "Bluhdorn recognized him and backed up, saying, 'No, absolutely not.' Then, as the transformation was taking place, he stepped closer. 'That's incredible,' he said. He was knocked out. I knew that if Bluhdorn bought the idea, the others would follow along—and they did. The others saw the tape later, but by then it was already a fait accompli."

4.

BRANDO PROVED TO BE ONLY ONE—albeit significant—battle in the casting wars for *The Godfather*. Buoyed by his success, Coppola forged ahead, trying to match actors with the critical roles of Sonny Corleone, Tom Hagen, Kay Adams, Fredo Corleone, Johnny Fontane, and, most crucial of all, Michael Corleone. Some of the decisions, such as the casting of Fredo, came easily; John Cazale, the brilliant stage actor, had the frail, sensitive looks required to play the middle Corleone brother, and he had little competition for the role. Other parts demanded extensive testing and discussion, prompting a flood of media speculation and rumor. Rudy Vallee lobbied for the role of Tom Hagen, but the septuagenarian singer was four decades too old to play the thirty-five-year-old lawyer; similarly, Rod Steiger was far too old to portray Michael Corleone, a role that Steiger coveted. Coppola, wanting a real-life singer to authenticate the Johnny Fontane character, considered Eddie Fisher, Frankie Avalon, Vic Damone, Bobby Vinton, Buddy Greco, and even Frank Sinatra, Jr. (who dropped out of the competition, reportedly at the prompting of his father), before settling on nightclub singer Al Martino. James Caan, who tested first for the role of Michael, was also considered for the parts of Tom Hagen and Sonny Corleone.

Assembling a cast for the movie might have been a challenging task for an extensively experienced and influential director given carte blanche to select his players, but for Francis Ford Coppola, who had been hired largely because studio executives hoped he could be more easily manipulated, the chore became almost blood sport. He nearly had been replaced for fighting over Brando; he found himself battling over other roles. In addition, ethnic-interest groups, such as the Italian-American Civil Rights League, issued not-so-veiled threats about trouble if *The Godfather* went into production, while others tried to pressure Coppola and Paramount into enlisting more Italian actors for the movie. Carried by unemployed Italian actors, picket signs crying out for ITALIANS FOR ITALIAN ROLES and MORE ADVANTAGES FOR ITALIAN ACTORS, popped up at the Paramount studio gate.

Coppola's most daunting debate—a battle that took months to resolve and actually jeopardized the film's shooting schedule—stemmed from the casting of the Michael Corleone part. Coppola strongly favored Al Pacino, a thirty-year-old stage actor who would soon be staking his claim in the movies with his critically acclaimed portrayal of a drug addict in *The Panic in Needle Park*. Pacino had the Sicilian appearance that Coppola was looking for, with expressive dark eyes that could be, in turns, mournful or flatly menacing—in short, just what Coppola wanted in a role that would find a quiet, reluctant family member evolving into the head of the crime family. Coppola had seen Pacino in a Broadway play, and from that moment on, he had him fixed in his mind as the right man to play Michael.

Paramount officials strenuously objected, and once again Coppola feared that his job was on the line. According to Paramount, Pacino had no marquee value whatsoever. He was too Italian-looking for the most Americanized character in the Corleone family; at five feet seven inches, he was too short. Pacino only hurt his case further when he tested poorly for the part, forgetting his lines and lamely trying to improvise through the scene. The lack of preparation frustrated Coppola, who branded Pacino a "self-destructive bastard," and while Pacino fared no better in two subsequent tests, Coppola continued to push against the odds. Pacino himself expressed doubts about his compatibility with the role. "When I read the book," he remembered, "I didn't think I was right for it, but Francis did."

Others would have agreed with Pacino. Fred Roos, who in years to come would become renowned for his casting skills, including some of his selections on *The Godfather,* confessed that he was nowhere near as excited about casting Pacino as Coppola was.

"I wish I could say I was," he admitted, "but I hadn't had the advantage that Francis had. He'd seen Al in a couple of plays in New York, but I hadn't. When I first saw him, I saw this sort of runty little guy—and not particularly good-looking. Al is good-looking, but he was the kind of New York actor who played against all that when he came around. He tried to be as scruffy as he could be. He was not what was thought of as a young leading man. I saw it as the auditioning and testing process went on, but I didn't see it instantly."

Neither did Mona Skager: "If you could have seen Al at that time, your eyes would have crossed when you tried to envision this person as the son of the Godfather. He was a little, diminutive thing, dressed kind of strangely. But Fred Roos and Francis thought he was a great actor, so that's history."

Paramount ordered Coppola to look at other candidates. Robert Evans suggested Ryan O'Neal, who had previously worked for him in *Love Story*, or Jack Nicholson; both actors had proven star power, as did Charles Bronson, Charles Bluhdorn's early nomination. There was talk of using Warren Beatty, but he turned down the role. James Caan, a Mario Puzo favorite for the role, scored as poorly on his screen test as Pacino. Others—Martin Sheen, David Carradine, Dean Stockwell, and Tony Lo Bianco—were considered but rejected. Robert De Niro, at the time an unknown actor, also failed to make the cut—a fortunate and ironic turn of events, given De Niro's prominence in the film's sequel.

Coppola grew more dispirited with each passing week. The tedious process of casting the film was pulling him away from other important pre-production activities, and the constant warring with Paramount had him convinced that it was only a matter of time before he was removed from the picture. Even the casting of his own sister in the role of Connie Corleone did not come without disagreement. Talia Shire tested well for the role, but Coppola felt she was wrong for the part.

"I thought Tally was too beautiful to be Connie Corleone," he explained. "The whole plot idea was that Connie was somewhat plain, and here came Carlo, a good-looking guy, marrying the don's homely daughter. Tally tested very well, but she was beautiful, so I wasn't enthusiastic about her playing the part."

Soon after seeing her screen test, Coppola traveled overseas to consult with Marlon Brando, who was in London finishing *The Nightcomers*. When he returned to the States, he learned that Robert Evans had loved Tally's test and felt she was fine for the role.

"I figured that I was probably not going to direct—that I was going to be ousted—so I thought that at least it would be good if my little sister got the part," Coppola said, refuting Evans's claim that he (Evans) was responsible for Shire's getting the role. "I cast her," Coppola insisted. "I wouldn't have stood between her and the role, and I was happy that she was in the film."

In giving her version of the story, Talia Shire—who would go on to earn Oscar nominations for her portrayal of Connie Corleone in the two *Godfather* sequels—judged the battle as being typical of her brother's struggle to make a film of artistic merit in the face of studio interference and politicking.

"When I asked him for an audition, all hell broke loose," Shire recalled. "It may have been that I caught him on a bad day, but he was in a no-man's spot with the movie. He could have been fired every two minutes. I think his being upset had far less to do with my request than with the fact that he had a fight with every single unique choice that he made. People were using people like chess pawns: 'We'll give you one of these for one of those. If she's your sister, that'll buy me three of these.' There was a whole political thing that had nothing to do with me, and I didn't know what was going on. It was a terribly difficult time for me because those around my brother—those who loved him personally—were aware that I was not somebody that he *needed* in this political situation, and they weren't always supportive. It was a shitty spot, but it was shitty for Francis, too."

By early 1971, *The Godfather* looked as if it might collapse under the weight of its director's ambitions, time constraints, indecision, politics, and corporate infighting. Coppola had managed to finagle more money for the film, hiking its budget to $5 million, but there were doubts as to whether he was capable of bringing in the movie under the revised figures. Paramount kept insisting that the film had to be ready for a Christmas 1971 release, yet casting and other problems made it highly unlikely that Coppola could begin filming on his projected March 1 starting date. A final shooting script had yet to be approved.

As anticipated, the Italian-American Civil Rights League, represented by Anthony Colombo, son of reputed Brooklyn crime boss Joseph Colombo, Sr., proved to be a major obstacle. A powerful organization, which had successfully lobbied against the FBI and Justice Department's use of the names La Cosa Nostra and Mafia in their statements about organized crime, the Italian-American Civil Rights League complained that *The Godfather* continued a hurtful trend of linking Italians with organized crime. This tendency, the league contended, was discriminatory and damaging to law-abiding citizens of Italian descent.

It was difficult to deny the validity of the argument, at least to some extent, but Paramount officials countered by taking the position that *The Godfather* was a presentation focusing on one small fictitious group of Italians, not an indictment of an entire ethnic group. Paramount's case did little to mollify the league, and the production company found itself struggling to secure key New York locations for the filming of *The Godfather*. In addition, the league petitioned state and national government officials, encouraging them to pressure Paramount into making the movie less ethnic in its handling of its subject matter. Frank Sinatra appeared at a huge rally for the league at Madison Square Garden, raising $600,000 for the cause.

There were darker, more ominous signals that someone or some group, if not the league, was prepared to resort to more persuasive methods of blocking production of the film. On two occasions, Charles Bluhdorn's Gulf & Western building received bomb threats and had to be evacuated. Al Ruddy's car was riddled with bullets, though no one was hurt. With time running out, some kind of settlement had to be reached.

Ruddy initiated the negotiations, meeting with Italian-American Civil Rights League representatives at the Sheraton Park Avenue Hotel and agreeing to strike the names La Cosa Nostra and Mafia from the script—an easy concession, given the fact that Coppola and Puzo had already avoided using those words in their script. Ruddy also agreed to search the league's membership for people who could be given small parts or roles as extras. Finally, as a gesture of goodwill, the producer promised to donate proceeds from the film's New York premiere to the league's hospital fund.

The pact set off a firestorm of criticism from the press and, to a quieter extent, within the offices at Paramount. In a blistering editorial, the *New York Times* accused Ruddy of hiding from the truth, calling his deal with the league a "hypocritical, craven act." While conceding that it was "despicable" to imply that any particular ethnic group was prone to criminal behavior, the *Times* went on to state that "the overwhelming majority of Italian-Americans have no need to buy self-respect or the esteem of their fellow Americans by pretending that the Mafia never existed." Industry trade journals such as *Variety* and *Show Business* gave the Ruddy deal front-page coverage, much of it disapproving in tone.

The negative publicity, when added to the already-intense media scrutiny surrounding the making of *The Godfather,* upset Paramount authorities, especially Stanley Jaffe and Robert Evans, who had been out of the country and not consulted prior to Ruddy's meeting with the league. The studio immediately rescinded the promise of a donation of premiere moneys to the league, and rumors circulated that Ruddy, along with associate producer Gray Frederickson, might be pulled from the picture.

"When I made my deal with the league, I had no idea how controversial it was going to become," Ruddy recalled, noting that Paramount had been especially upset when he called a press conference to announce the agreement. "I was called into Charlie Bluhdorn's office and fired. My position was very simple: I was there to produce a movie and I made this deal. Bluhdorn was beside himself. He called Francis in and said that they'd fired Al Ruddy because he was fuckin' demented, and Francis said, 'You better get him back, because he's the only guy who can keep this movie going.' I got another phone call and was told to come back to the Gulf & Western building, and Charlie told me, 'Well, you're back on the picture again, but if you talk to one person in the press, I will kill you myself with my bare hands.' So Francis saved my ass."

In hindsight, the agreement was a pragmatic solution to a sensitive problem, intended to buy time and resolve what appeared to be an impossible situation. Ruddy worked from a no-win position, caught between alienating a group that could shut down operations and enraging company officials who could fire him for making what they considered to be inappropriate concessions. As it was, the compromise might have led to the loss of one major company position. A short time after the deal was struck, Stanley Jaffe announced his resignation from Paramount, ostensibly to "resume his career as an independent supplier of films," although the unofficial word making the rounds in Paramount offices and on the *Godfather* set was that Jaffe departed because of his differences with company officials over their handling of the Ruddy agreement.

The debate, far from resolved, would continue long after the movie was completed and released, spawning reviews and critical articles that criticized *The Godfather* for glorifying the Mafia while denigrating an ethnic group in the process. Only the film's enormous critical and popular success would lay the argument to rest.

5.

DESPITE THE PROBLEMS, Coppola managed to hold on to his extremely tenuous authority over his picture. By the time he began rehearsals on March 16, he had broken through two barriers that had threatened his job: the shooting on location in Sicily and the hiring of Al Pacino to play Michael Corleone.

The Sicilian sequence, in which Michael hides in rural Italy after avenging his father's shooting by murdering a mobster and a crooked police captain, boiled down to a battle of wills between Coppola, who wanted to film on location for the sake of authenticity, and Robert Evans, who suggested that money could be saved by shooting the segment in upstate New York. Evans had grown tired of Coppola's disregard for budgetary concerns; some of his ideas bordered on the frivolous. Earlier in the year, Paramount had nixed Coppola's request to reconstruct the famous Camel cigarettes smoke-ring sign on Broadway, a task that would have set the company back five thousand dollars for just a few seconds' screen time. Evans tried to talk Coppola into eliminating the scenes in Italy, but Coppola refused to budge. The sequence, he said, was an essential interlude in the midst of some of the film's most violent scenes.

Tension grew between the two men over the weeks, Evans relenting only after Coppola scouted locations in Sicily and promised to film the scenes at a reasonable cost. As Coppola remembered, relations between him and Evans had become so strained that, upon returning from Europe, he found a note written by Mona Skager, his production coordinator. "Don't quit," the communiqué advised. "Make them fire you."

The antagonism between Coppola and Evans flared again as the two bickered over the casting of Pacino. As of March 1, the role had yet to be filled, and with cast and crew already scheduled to meet and rehearse, an immediate decision had to be made. Once again, Evans gave in to Coppola, only to learn, to his great disbelief, that Pacino was not even in a position to work on the film. Pacino, it turned out, was already under contract to MGM to star in the movie adaptation of Jimmy Breslin's best-selling gangster novel, *The Gang That Couldn't Shoot Straight,* scheduled to begin shooting in May. Disgusted by the entire affair, Evans shipped a copy of *The Godfather* script to director Elia Kazan, adding still more grist to the gossip mill. Hasty meetings were called among company attorneys, MGM and Paramount officials, and Pacino's agent, and, to everyone's great relief, MGM released Pacino from his *Gang That Couldn't Shoot Straight* obligations, on the condition that he make another picture for the company in the future.

At long last, Coppola was ready to bring *The Godfather* to life.

6.

ON WEDNESDAY, MARCH 17, the principle cast members of *The Godfather* gathered in a private room at the back of Patsy's, an Italian restaurant in Manhattan. The get-together, intended by Coppola to be part rehearsal and part informal dinner, was designed to show cast members what Italian family life was like. To create this effect, Talia Shire served the pasta while Marlon Brando, never stepping out of character, presided over the table.

"We were all new to each other," John Cazale reported. "We stood there, not knowing what to do. It was Brando who broke the ice. He just went over, opened a bottle of wine, and started the festivities. I think we all realized then that he was acting with us the way the Don would have acted with his own family."

It had been an eventful day—Brando's first day of rehearsal—and Coppola had been given a strong indication of what he might expect once the cameras started rolling in earnest. Coppola had chosen to rehearse the opening scene of the movie, wherein the Godfather meets an undertaker in his study on the day of his daughter's wedding. Chairs had been set up to approximate the placement of furniture in the room, and the four actors involved in the scene—Brando, James Caan, Robert Duvall, and Frank Puglia—lurched through the script, stopping often as Brando, true to reputation, insisted on lengthy discussions with the director about character, motivation, and action. During one such encounter, Brando and Coppola debated over when Don Corleone should begin to show his evil side, Coppola believing it should occur in the opening scene, Brando wanting to keep it hidden until later in the picture. With each interruption, Coppola tried to nudge Brando back into the rehearsal, with only marginal success.

The other actors sat around during these discussions, saying very little, no one wanting to offend Brando on his first day on the job. Finally, Robert Duvall, who knew Brando from their work on *The Chase,* began to make faces and mimic the actor behind his back. The others suppressed laughter until Duvall addressed the situation directly. "Keep talking, Marlon," he quipped, "none of us want to work, either." The room erupted in laughter.

Such levity was sorely needed, given the film's rocky preproduction history, the high expectations for a major hit, and the tendency for people to be initially nervous around Brando. Coppola admitted that he was "scared shitless" of Brando in the early days of filming, and acknowledged that cast members would go out of their ways to make an impression on him. Al Pacino, in awe of Brando since seeing him in *On the Waterfront* as a teenager, remembered his initial introduction to Brando with amusement.

"Diane Keaton was at that first meeting," he noted. "We went in and sat at a table and everybody was pretending that he was just another actor, even though we were all nervous. But Diane was open enough to admit how she felt. She sat at the table and Brando said hello to me and to Diane. And Diane said, 'Yeah, right, sure,' as if she couldn't believe it. She really did it. She said, 'I just cannot take that.'"

The company learned, soon enough, that Brando had a wicked sense of humor, which he would unleash at the most unexpected moments. One of his more notorious pranks occurred during the filming of a scene in which the Godfather, recovering from an assassination attempt, is brought home from the hospital in an ambulance and carried on a stretcher up a flight of stairs to his bedroom. The first take was scrapped when two extras, hired to play orderlies, struggled to transport Brando up the stairwell. Coppola immediately reassigned the parts to a couple of burly grips from the film crew. The new orderlies managed to heft Brando up the stairs, but only with great difficulty, and only after buckling under the weight and having to pause on the landing of the stairway. While cast and crew on the set howled with laughter, Brando pulled back the covers and rolled off the stretcher. Beneath the bedding were six fifty-pound sandbags, which had been loaded onto the stretcher while the two grips were being given their costumes. Brando, enjoying the practical joke as much as anyone on the set, admitted to having hatched the scheme. The prank, coming during a particularly tense time of the filming, loosened up Coppola and his crew and further endeared the actor to the others in the company.

Al Pacino, in contrast, was a quiet, brooding presence on the set, rarely joining the others in their antics, preferring to stay in character. From the moment of his first audition for the part of Michael Corleone, Pacino had felt like an outsider, barely tolerated by the higher-ups at Paramount and unwelcome on the set. By his account, only a handful of people—Coppola, Brando, Cazale, Keaton, and Al Ruddy included—offered the type of support that he needed.

"I never felt wanted," he maintained, long after he had established his film career with this role. "I always felt that I still had to win these people over. And I'm not the kind of person who wins people over. I never have been. . . . I would go there every day, and I would feel them all thinking, 'Who *is* this guy? *He's* playing Michael?'"

Pacino hated shooting out of sequence—as a stage actor, he was accustomed to allowing his character to grow and develop in a straightforward, linear fashion—and he wrestled with the role, acutely aware that he could be replaced if he did not measure up to expectations. He questioned whether it was worth the effort. "I just wanted to quit and go back to something else," he admitted. "I kept feeling as though this was not the medium for me."

Coppola believed otherwise, and he prodded Pacino into reaching for his best-possible performance. "I created you," he would tell Pacino. "You're my Frankenstein."

Coppola, knowing intimately how it felt to report to work each day with your job on the line, sympathized with the young actor. The part of Michael Corleone, he realized, was the most demanding in the film, involving a character shift from Ivy League student to cold-blooded Mafia leader. The role would have tested the finest, most experienced actor, but to a newcomer like Pacino, it could be excruciatingly difficult.

7.

FILMING PROGRESSED SLOWLY, greatly due to Coppola's deliberate, methodical work habits. The director made a practice of ordering numerous takes of individual scenes, many requiring lengthy setup times before they could be reshot. The scene in the Italian restaurant, in which Michael murders

Sollozzo and McCluskey—the mobster who set up the assassination attempt on the Godfather and the police captain acting as his bodyguard, respectively— seemed to take an eternity to film, even though the murder itself lasted only a few seconds on-screen. For each new take, Sterling Hayden and Al Lettieri, the actors portraying McCluskey and Sollozzo, required a new application of makeup; in addition, they had to be rewired so their blood and wounds would erupt in the gunfire. While these steps were being taken, crew members cleaned up the set from the previous take, removing all the artificial blood from the table, wall, and floor and resetting the scene, right down to the half-eaten dinners sitting on the table at the time of the murders. At an estimated cost of forty thousand dollars per average eight-hour workday, delays exacted their own high price, and as the filming fell behind schedule, crew members started to grumble among themselves, questioning Coppola's competence as a director.

Coppola, although far from oblivious of his running behind schedule, continued at his own pace. *The Godfather,* as he had determined long before the first day of shooting, March 23, was proving its potential to be much more than a typical gangster flick; excellence, however, took time and patience, and the kind of care that could send studio executives for ulcer treatments. When the movie was being planned, Coppola had asked for an eighty-day shooting schedule; Paramount had given him fifty-three. He was not surprised, then, when he found himself falling behind a day or two for every week of filming.

Nor could he be held accountable for some of the problems and delays that dogged the production. Unfavorable weather conditions undermined exterior shooting, starting on day one, when temperatures were too mild for the snow machine brought in for the Christmas holiday scene. On the fifth day of filming, Al Pacino suffered a badly sprained ligament in his ankle while jumping onto a car's running board, putting the actor on crutches and under doctor's orders to stay off his feet. Word arrived from overseas that the Sicilian sequence might have to be put off until after the country's elections.

Coppola was convinced that he was—again—only a step or two away from being replaced. Rumors of Elia Kazan's taking over the directorial duties were so persistent that Coppola actually began to dream of Kazan arriving on the set and relieving him of his post. Anxiety left him irritable and restless—so much so that, less than a month into the filming, he requested and received sleeping pills from the company physician.

To prepare for their roles, some cast members met or hung out with local mobsters. Marlon Brando met Joe Bufalino, who repeatedly referred to him as "Marlo" while being given a tour of the set representing the olive oil company. Al Pacino admitted to convening privately with a member of the Mafia, as did Robert Duvall, who noted that, while the gangsters would joke about being criminals, he detected "a viciousness underneath it with every one of them." James Caan spent so much time with Carmine "The Snake" Persico, and learned to imitate him so well, that New York plainclothes police actually suspected that he might be a mobster himself. Said Caan of the research that made his portrayal so realistic: "I noticed how they're always touching themselves. Thumbs in the belt. Touching the jaw. Adjusting the shirt. Gripping the crotch. Shirt open. Tie loose. Super dressers. Clean. Very, very neat."

For all his attention to authenticity and detail, Coppola preferred to stay away from the underworld figures when they made themselves available to him. The decision, Coppola later confessed, was the result of advice he had been given by Mario Puzo, who had warned him against becoming too friendly with the mob. According to Puzo, the Mafia was attracted to show-business glitz and would try to become involved if allowed to do so. Puzo suggested that Coppola refuse to deal with them on any level. "They respect that attitude," he told Coppola. "If you turn them off, they won't intrude into your life."

Such intrusions would have been difficult in any event, if for no other reason than Coppola was so ensconced in work that he had little time for his own family, let alone mob figures. Beside a demanding shooting schedule and nighttime rehearsals that kept him occupied for the better part of his waking hours, Coppola busied himself with constant script revisions, breaking one of his cardinal rules never to commence filming until a final shooting script was in place. His schedule was so overwhelming that he could view rushes only on weekends, and he spent a number of nights sleeping on James Caan's couch. On April 15, the night of the Oscar ceremonies in Los Angeles, he stayed in New York to work on the film and enlisted a proxy to claim his first Academy Award.

Nothing about the movie was predictable. A good day of shooting would more often than not be followed by a dreadful one. On one occasion, the film-processing lab underdeveloped a day's worth of film, forcing Coppola, his actors, and his crew to repeat their work. Nature refused to cooperate, fouling up exterior lighting and threatening the film's continuity. Coppola always seemed to be at odds with someone—if not a studio executive, then a member of his own crew.

Some of his battles with Gordon Willis, the extraordinarily gifted but temperamental cinematographer, became the stuff of legend. Willis, who had recently worked on *Klute* and *Little Murders,* and who would later garner critical acclaim for his contributions to many of Woody Allen's films, made little effort to disguise his contention that Coppola knew little if anything about the technical aspects of filmmaking. The two would clash whenever Willis felt that Coppola was infringing upon his area of expertise.

"You don't know how to do anything right!" he shouted at Coppola after the director had spent what Willis felt was an inordinate amount of time rehearsing a scene. At one point during the rehearsal, Coppola and Brando had an extended discussion about whether the Godfather's suspenders should be up or down during the scene. Disgusted by all the standing around, Willis left the set.

Coppola had heard Willis's outburst but refused to respond to it. He carried on with the rehearsal until he was satisfied that he was ready to shoot the scene. "Let's film it now," he called out, only to find Willis's assistants and main cameraman reluctant to take their boss's place.

Enraged, Coppola threw his hands in the air.

"Fuck this picture!" he bellowed. "I've directed five fucking movies without anyone telling me how to do it. I want to make the fucking shot now and we will, even if the fucking director of photography has to be thrown off the picture."

Efforts to calm Coppola were futile, and, unable to shoot the scene, the director stormed off the set and retreated to his office. A short time afterward, a loud, sharp report came from the direction of Coppola's second-floor office, followed by the sound of splintering wood.

"My God!" a stunned crew member gasped. "Maybe he's shot himself!"

During a hastily announced break, production manager Fred Caruso checked on Coppola and found him to be quite all right. An uneasy truce was established on the set, and Coppola returned to shoot the scene. Caruso pulled two company carpenters aside. "Please go upstairs and put a new door on Mr. Coppola's office," he instructed them.

In all likelihood, Coppola's disagreements with Willis were unavoidable. Both had different temperaments. Coppola, while never accused of being a beam of sunshine on the *Godfather* set, was by nature gregarious and energetic; Willis, at least by Coppola's assertion, was "a cranky, grumpy guy." Willis, a master craftsman, was all business and had very little use for any antics on the set, his disposition undoubtedly shaded by the challenges of his daily work. Coppola wanted a dated look to his film, the kind found in movies from the forties and fifties, and to achieve the effect, he asked his cinematographer to use antiquated equipment. Further, Coppola and Willis, along with production designer Dean

Tavoularis, agreed that dim interior lighting and dark-colored sets would establish the proper tone for the underworld environment depicted in the film. Such
technical details were occasionally difficult to achieve. Some of the scenes
demanded up to fifty camera settings, and Willis would grow impatient with
Coppola's tendency to think more like an artiste than a technician.

"At that point in his career, Francis didn't realize that you can't get art without craft," commented Willis. "You can't just arbitrarily block a scene and forget
the fact that you're making a movie. The blocking has to be basically comfortable for the actors and it has to function for the director, and then finally it has
to work for the camera. If the scene doesn't fit in that little hole that you're looking through, then it's all irrelevant. Unless a director can transpose his feelings
and interpretation into a visual structure, they're meaningless."

Coppola felt defensive around Willis, protective of his authority and of
the people he was directing. "He hates and misuses actors," he said of Willis.
"He wants them to hit marks. I said no. They're not mechanics, they're artists.
I was their protector. Gordy acted like a football player stuck with a bunch of
fag actors. I was in the middle."

Coppola, in fact, was always in the middle, directing a large crew and
company of actors while trying to appease Paramount officials, always knowing that, on a day-to-day basis, he was pleasing neither group. He overheard
the complaints on the set and knew that he was being second-guessed at every
turn. As if that wasn't enough, he had to deal with company officials. There
was never a shortage of Paramount representatives overseeing his activities
and offering advice. He resented the constant presence of Jack Ballard, Paramount's head of production in California, who had been dispatched to New
York to file daily reports to Robert Evans on the movie's planning, scheduling, and shooting. Aram Avakian, assigned to the position of supervising editor, regularly conferred with Coppola about script revisions and the quality
of the movie's rushes. First assistant director Steve Kesten was never lacking
an observation about how the filming could be more effectively accomplished. Coppola, on edge to begin with, suspected a conspiracy to undercut
him and have him yanked from the picture.

His concerns, as he was to learn later, were not without foundation. In his
autobiography, *The Kid Stays in the Picture*, Robert Evans recalled a telephone
call from Avakian and Ballard, along with Al Ruddy, in which the three accused
Coppola of making a film that was all but impossible to edit. "Shot by shot, it
looks great," Avakian told Evans. "Kubrick couldn't get better performances,
but it cuts together like a Chinese jigsaw puzzle. . . . The fucker doesn't know
what continuity means."

"Here you are, trying to make this movie, and your assistant director is bad-mouthing you and the film editor is going to the studio," a disgusted Dean Tavoularis remembered. "They're supposed to be coming to you—the director—and saying, 'I can't cut this together. I need a shot of this or that.' You don't call the studio and say, 'This stuff doesn't cut together.'"

"I had hired Aram Avakian because I really admired him," Coppola recalled. "He'd cut *You're a Big Boy Now,* and I was very pleased when he accepted the job on *The Godfather.* Aram suggested that I give a friend of his a break, and that's how Steve Kesten got the job. Aram had already directed a movie with Kesten producing. However, when the two were in place, they really started to conspire against me. Steve figured that if I was off the picture, Aram could direct and he could coproduce. Aram, whom I really loved and looked up to—even after the fact—felt that I was doing a terrible job and would probably get fired anyhow. But I nipped that in the bud."

Avakian and Kesten were removed from the picture, but Jack Ballard, to Coppola's dismay, remained. "I would have loved to have fired him," Coppola remembered, "but he was there, a thorn in my side throughout the entire production. He hated the film and had no regard whatsoever for my ability."

If Coppola found a measure of satisfaction in his survival, he hid it well. He was weary of the struggle. He had watched a number of people lose their jobs over the film; the president of Paramount had resigned. He had endless miles of film, and while he believed that he was in the process of making a memorable movie, he wondered if it was worth the effort.

"Do you still want to direct films?" he wearily asked one of his assistants after one long day of shooting. "Always remember three things. Have the definitive script ready before you shoot. There'll always be some changes, but they should be small ones. Second, work with people you trust and feel secure with. Remember good crew people you've worked with on other films and get them for your film. Third, make your actors feel very secure so they can do their job well."

Pausing for a moment, Coppola considered his advice.

"I've managed to do none of these things on this film," he concluded.

8.

COPPOLA'S WORDS, DELIVERED in a moment of self-doubt and exhaustion, while addressing several key problem areas associated with the production of *The Godfather,* overlooked the fact that, even in the vortex of the storm, some outstanding work was being accomplished. Something strong and powerful was being forged in the struggle—even if no one, including Paramount and Coppola himself, immediately recognized it.

For all the wizardry brought to the production by Gordon Willis, Dean Tavoularis, and others, it was the actors who kept Coppola's operatic approach to the film from becoming bombastic. Coppola admitted a distaste for violence, but his characters lived violent lives in a violent world, and *The Godfather* might have failed had the actors not shared Coppola's obsession with character over action.

Nowhere was this as evident as in Marlon Brando's interpretation of the film's title character. To watch Vito Corleone gently stroking a cat, selecting oranges at the marketplace, or playing with his grandson in the garden, one might have a difficult time imagining the same man killing or ordering executions of rival mobsters, bribing judges and union officials, strong-arming the opposition, and, in general, attaining a position of wealth and influence through a life of crime. The line most often associated with the movie—"I'm gonna make him an offer he can't refuse"—while suggesting the menacing force backing the Godfather's method of negotiation, only partially defines Puzo's (and Brando's) subtle characterization of the Mafia don. Earlier, in that very same scene, Vito Corleone mutters an ironic aside to Tom Hagen that might define him better: "We're not murderers, in spite of what this undertaker says." In the Godfather's world, violence was employed only when reason failed.

Brando, of course, had been given a lot to work with in the screen adaptation of Mario Puzo's well-conceived novel, but Brando himself brought a lot to the game. During his research and preparation for his role, he had listened to audiotapes of Frank Costello testifying before the Senate hearings on organized crime. Costello, Brando noted, did not have the gravelly, tough-guy voice so familiar in gangster films, nor did he speak in a loud, confrontational way while addressing the senators questioning him. When Coppola, listening to the tapes with Brando, remarked that "powerful people don't need to shout," Brando had to agree. His characterization of a Mafia don, he decided, would be modest and soft-spoken, more in keeping with the way he wanted to underplay the part.

"I thought it would be interesting to play a gangster, maybe for the first time in the movies, who wasn't like those bad guys Edward G. Robinson played, but who was a kind of hero, a man to be respected," Brando stated, adding that he wanted Don Corleone to be gentle and stand apart from mobsters like Al Capone, who had earned his reputation through violence. "I had a great deal of respect for Don Corleone," Brando continued. "I saw him as a man of substance, tradition, dignity, refinement, a man of unerring instinct who just happened to live in a violent world and who had to protect himself and his family in this environment."

The don would also be a vulnerable figure, physically weakening with age. He would still possess the insight and stubborn sense of purpose that had elevated him to the top, as well as an aura that commanded respect whether he was in the presence of family members or presiding over a summit meeting of the Five Families, but it would be clear to those around him (and to those watching the film), that his advancing years were demanding that he entrust more of the family business to his sons.

To create this physical image, Brando relied heavily on the skills of makeup artist Dick Smith, who had worked so effectively with Dustin Hoffman on *Little Big Man,* and Philip Rhodes, a longtime friend and personal makeup artist. Smith devised a plastic triangular mouthpiece that pushed out Brando's cheeks and lips, similar to the way the Kleenex had worked when Brando had done his screen test for Coppola. By stretching the skin on Brando's face, painting on latex rubber, and then allowing the skin to relax again, Smith and Rhodes were able to create a fine network of wrinkles that added years to the actor's face. Ten-pound weights were placed in each of Brando's shoes, forcing him to walk in a tired shuffle. Padding was added to his waistline. Finally, to make Don Corleone appear as if he was losing his hearing, Brando wore flesh-colored earplugs that muffled the sound around him and made him strain to hear what the other actors were saying.

Other personal touches brought color and depth to the film. When we first see Vito Corleone at the beginning of the film, we encounter a powerful figure, flanked by his oldest son and his attorney, granting favors on his daughter's wedding day. For a portion of the scene, he fondles a cat while going about his business. One might have complimented Puzo or Coppola on what appeared to be a nicely placed metaphor in their script, but in reality, the cat's presence was an accident. It had wandered onto the set while Coppola was setting up the shot, and Brando had improvised it into his performance.

Improvisation also added texture to Brando's final scene in the film, which finds him playing in the garden with his grandson moments before he is struck down by a fatal stroke. Philip Rhodes had once spoken to Brando of how his father liked to cut an orange rind into the shape of monster fangs, which he would slip into his mouth while playing with his grandchildren—a game that Brando himself adopted while playing with his own children. For his death scene in *The Godfather,* Brando fashioned a set of orange-peel fangs and bared them at his grandson, adding a memorable final touch to his role. The once-mighty head of New York's most powerful crime syndicate had been reduced to a weakened old man, now wonderfully human, his bite ineffective and comical. Brando's unexpected improvisation had a bonus effect: The little boy playing the grandson was genuinely surprised when Brando turned on him with his artificial fangs, and his frightened reaction added credibility to the scene.

According to Coppola, the scene almost didn't make it into the film.

"Evans and Ballard and all felt Brando's death was unnecessary, that you could cut right to the funeral," he recalled. "I loved the scene in the book, with the old man and his grandchild, so I fought to do it. Finally, we were allotted thirty minutes to shoot it before lunch. We had this child and Brando, and I set up two cameras to rush it. When we tried the first take, the kid was just too fidgety and wouldn't do it. There were only ten minutes left, and I knew if I didn't get it before lunch, I'd get no chance later. Then Brando said, 'Look, the kid is uncomfortable. Let me try something.' I didn't know what he was going to do, but Brando loves children and I figured he was up to something. He sprung the orange-peel trick on all of us, with two cameras running. The little boy was scared and played the scene as it appeared in the movie. I yelled *cut!*, they yelled *lunch!*, and we almost lost having it at all."

Coppola was pleasantly surprised by how easy it was to direct Brando, given the actor's reputation. Indeed, Brando habitually held up filming on Monday mornings after returning late from his weekends in Los Angeles, and, to Coppola's chagrin, he had a difficult time memorizing—and even, on occasion, refused to learn—his lines, forcing the crew to place hidden cue cards all over the sets, but, as a general rule, Coppola found him to be engaging and professional. Even the actor/director conferences, while disruptive, almost always added depth or insight to a character or scene.

"Everyone advised me to assert myself with him and say, 'Now, Marlon, I'm the director, you just act,'" Coppola remembered. "That would have been suicidal. I could understand how he got his reputation because his ideas were so bizarre, so apparently crazy. Yet without exception, every one of his crazy ideas I used turned out to be a terrific moment."

James Caan, who witnessed the dynamics between the director and actor, agreed that Coppola's approach to Brando sealed their professional relationship. "I think Marlon and Francis got along so well because Francis didn't try to control him," Caan observed. "I think everybody tried to control Brando. He just wanted to be talked to, not controlled."

Not all of these moments were easily reached. At one point, later in the filming, Brando disagreed with Coppola over a scene involving the don's counseling of his son outside the family home. The scene was designed to be a revealing look at the relationship between the Godfather and Michael Corleone, but Brando despised it and refused to leave his dressing room the morning it was scheduled to be filmed. In an effort to pacify Brando and salvage a day's work, Coppola offered to film the scene in a long shot, the camera following Brando and Pacino as they walked around the garden; the actual dialogue, Coppola said, would be dubbed in later, after that portion of the script had been rewritten. Brando consented to Coppola's solution and the scene was filmed. Later that evening, legendary script doctor Robert Towne was flown in from the West Coast to make the necessary dialogue revisions.

Although this was precisely the type of behavior that had earned Brando his reputation as being difficult, the actor had his reasons for holding out for a better scene. This was a critical moment in the film, in which the baton was being passed from father to son; in addition, it was revealing the father's love for his youngest son, as well as his regrets for getting Michael involved in the family activities. Throughout the film, Brando's Vito Corleone had shown a rough-hewn, old-world wisdom, the kind gained through experience rather than from a textbook, yet for this scene Brando wanted the don to rise intellectually to the occasion. "Just once," he told Coppola and Towne, "I would like to see this man *not* inarticulate. I would like to see him express himself well."

The scene, rewritten as per Brando's suggestions, worked well in the film. It also acted as an effective bridge to the movie's sequel, in which Vito Corleone's youth and Michael Corleone's early years as head of the Corleone family are explored in depth.

9.

BRANDO WOULD RECEIVE the most attention of any cast member for his role in *The Godfather,* yet his supporting cast, to the actor or actress, was invaluable in elevating his performance and making the film one of the most time-honored movies in American motion picture history.

Al Pacino, whose $35,000 salary was, arguably, the bargain of the decade, contributed a performance that would earn him an Academy Award nomination. However, unlike Brando, Duvall, and Caan, who established a camaraderie that found them frequently wisecracking and pulling off practical jokes, Pacino never loosened up enough to relieve some of the pressures involved in making the movie; instead, he hung around with Diane Keaton, his screen wife, or kept to himself. "I stayed a little bit out of it," he suggested, "because I felt Michael was a private person. And I kept that with me all the time. Michael was always a little outside. He was the youngest, so he really had to observe, to look, and he was prepared when he finally took over because he'd learned a lot of things just by observing."

For Pacino, observation was one of the keys in his preparation for his roles. He would watch people in cafés and restaurants, in stores or on the street, learning how they walked and talked and gestured, determining how they related to what was going on around them. "I used to walk from 92nd Street and Broadway right to the Village and back again, bopping along the street, thinking of parts," he said. "I worked out a lot of my role in *The Godfather* that way."

Paramount's initial reservations about Pacino's suitability for his role dissolved in time as Pacino, like Brando, turned in the type of understated performance that allowed moviegoers the chance to see and understand the many layers of Michael Corleone—a character portrayal that did not go unnoticed when the movie was released. *New Yorker* critic Pauline Kael, praising Pacino's acting as being "marvelous, big without ostentation," zeroed in on his subtle character transformation in the film. "Like Brando, Pacino is simple," she wrote in her review of *The Godfather.* "You don't catch him acting, yet he manages to change from a small, fresh-faced, darkly handsome college boy into an underworld lord, becoming more intense, smaller and more isolated at every step."

Pacino never found his work easy. He fretted about being replaced and, at least in the early stages, was genuinely surprised when he was not. Such worries only intensified the anxiety he felt over developing and playing his part. "Once I got the role," he said, "I was waking up at four or five in the morning and going into my kitchen to brood over [it]." Coppola found his moodiness troublesome and had to coax performance after performance out of the actor. "I don't want to do this anymore," Pacino complained after one emotionally brutal take. Coppola assured him that he had nailed down the scene precisely as it was intended to be.

Robert Duvall, for one, sympathized with Pacino. He was all too aware of Pacino's history in the casting of the role, and he defended Pacino when he was questioned about Pacino's growing reputation for being difficult. "*Time* magazine—trying to get something started, I guess—asked me what did I think of Al Pacino, was he difficult," Duvall recalled. "I said, 'I dunno.' I realized later I should have said that if he *was* difficult, which he wasn't with me, he had good reason to be. What they put him through to get that part!"

Duvall, whose portrayal of Tom Hagen would also merit high critical acclaim and an Oscar nomination, was bothered by the tension that he witnessed during the making of *The Godfather,* much of it arising, in his opinion, from the high expectations for the film and the vast sums of money being sunk into the venture. "This film should have been made with an all-unknown New York cast, low budget, and no big studio pressure," he suggested.

To alleviate some of the tension, Duvall, along with Brando and Caan, engaged in schoolboy high jinks that, under other circumstances, might not have been tolerated. They began early on in the filming, during one of the lengthy work stoppages, when Coppola and Brando were discussing and rehearsing a scene. Duvall and Caan, passing their downtime in the studio lobby, joked with a number of Teamster drivers on hand about the practice of "mooning" someone—the dropping of one's pants and baring of one's naked backside to a surprised victim. The best moons, they agreed, were those accomplished at the most unexpected times and in the most inappropriate places. Thus inspired, Caan and Duvall sneaked to the soundstage where Coppola and Brando were convening. The two actors hid behind some scenery until what they deemed to be the perfect moment arrived, and then, whooping and jumping out, they dropped their pants and exposed their buttocks to Coppola and Brando. At first, the joke looked like a dud. Coppola was only slightly amused, and Brando frowned in disapproval.

Brando's initial response had been misleading, for he was soon a major participant in what was turning out to be a mooning competition, and the game of one-upmanship reached preposterous proportions. One time, Duvall and Caan scaled the studio rafters and mooned Brando from above while he was working on a scene. One could never be certain about where or when the next prank would be pulled. "My best moon," Caan boasted, "was on Second Avenue. Bob Duvall and I were in one car and Brando was in another, so we drove up beside him and I pulled down my pants and stuck my ass out of the window. Brando fell down in the car with laughter."

All agreed, however, that Brando pulled off the ultimate stunt. It occurred on May 26, the forty-fourth day of filming, when Coppola assembled the principal cast and eight busloads of extras for the filming of the outdoor wedding reception, which occurs at the beginning of the movie. The logistics involved in setting up and shooting the sequence were staggering. A helicopter flew overhead, taking aerial shots of the enormous party, while four cameras were positioned around the garden area, complementing the footage taken by the main camera. Thirty vintage cars were moved into the long driveway leading to the estate, while nearby, in a college gymnasium, the 350 extras being used as reception guests were outfitted in period clothing. Coppola wanted a cinema verité look to this part of the picture, and he encouraged the extras to behave as they would at an actual wedding, their improvised dialogue to be picked up by a soundman weaving through the party with a portable tape recorder.

Predictably, the shooting of this segment was a mixed success, with Coppola stopping the action every so often and shouting instructions to the assembled multitude. Then it was back to the action, complete with Carmine Coppola conducting a six-piece Italian combo on a small stage, couples dancing, women leading children through a maze of people, and men drinking wine and cavorting at tables.

At one point, the script called for a group photo of the Corleone family and wedding party to be taken in the garden, and it was here that Marlon Brando decided to stage his coup de grâce. With hundreds of people looking on, he made his entrance to the area where the family portrait was to be taken, and despite protests from James Caan, who knew Brando's intentions and tried to discourage him, Brando wheeled around, dropped his tuxedo trousers, and mooned the entire ensemble. Robert Duvall, not to be outdone, did likewise. The film crew doubled over in laughter and most of the extras roared their approval. Some of the women looked away in disgust, while others complained about the stunt being pulled with children present. Caan, embarrassed by the display, kept his distance from the two actors.

Caan and Duvall had to concede that Brando had won the contest, and on Brando's last day of filming, at a going-away party for the famed actor, they presented him with a silver belt buckle engraved with the words *MIGHTY MOON KING*.

10.

FOR SOMEONE INITIALLY reluctant to become involved with the movie at all, Coppola turned *The Godfather* into a family experience, employing family members for various duties in the film. Beside composing incidental music used in the movie, Carmine Coppola appeared in two of its scenes, first as a restaurant patron in the Sollozzo/McCluskey shooting scene, and later, in an entirely different role, as a piano player in the mattress scene, which found Corleone family mobsters in hiding during the gang wars immediately following the shooting. Italia Coppola did double duty as well, appearing with her husband in the restaurant scene and playing a switchboard operator at Vito Corleone's Genco Olive Oil office. To Coppola's delight, Talia Shire was admirable in her role, turning in a portrayal impressive enough to earn her the same part in the movie's two sequels. Coppola also worked his own immediate family into the picture, assigning his wife and two sons parts as extras in the crucial baptism scene. The baby in the scene was none other than Coppola's three-week-old daughter Sofia.

The May 12 birth of Coppola's third and last child had been a joyous occasion sandwiched in an especially trying work period. As soon as he heard that Eleanor was in labor, Coppola had made a mad dash for the equipment needed to photograph the birth, and from there he was off to his Manhattan apartment, where he picked up his wife and accompanied her to the hospital.

"Francis had a big video camera," Ellie remembered, "and he was shooting it in the delivery room. We had two boys and were more or less expecting another. When Sofia was born and the doctor said, 'It's a girl,' Francis forgot he was shooting and the camera taped several minutes of the floor, table legs, shoes, and cords, with his excited voice on the track."

If Coppola, like Mario Puzo, was seeking a strong sense of family in *The Godfather,* the filming in Sicily deepened the feeling, bringing him in touch with his ancestry. The area around Taormina, where the sequence was shot, had become a tourist trap over the past century, but Coppola found that he could easily work in the tiny rural towns in the vicinity, where people still lived modest lives not unlike those of Coppola's ancestors. Al Pacino, in Italy for the first time, was also deeply moved by seeing the land of his forebears.

When filming was completed in July, Coppola began the arduous postproduction work of piecing together the final product. He had shot enough material to assemble a movie exceeding three hours in length, but Paramount opposed anything much longer than two. The company's reasoning was purely pragmatic: The film was still scheduled for release during the Christmas holiday season, when moviegoers traditionally flocked en masse to theaters, and a lengthy movie meant fewer showings per theater per day, which translated into substantial losses in potential gate receipts.

Coppola, weary of his battles with Paramount, struggled to comply with the company's demands for a shorter film, viewing and cutting and restructuring until he had a rough cut running just over two hours. Company officials, Robert Evans in particular, were underwhelmed by the results. Evans had seen the film's rushes, which he had deemed to be excellent, and he was gravely disappointed by the way Coppola had put together his movie. In typical fashion, he did not mince words when offering his opinion.

"You shot a good film," he told Coppola. "Where the fuck is it—in the kitchen with your spaghetti? It sure ain't on the screen. Where's the family, the heart, the feeling—left in the kitchen too?" Evans then stunned his now-defensive director by challenging him to make the picture longer. "You shot a saga and turned in a trailer," he goaded Coppola. "Now give me a movie."*

Coppola was by no means alone in his surprised reaction to Evans's suggestion that he lengthen the movie. Evans's colleagues at Paramount, including Charles Bluhdorn, balked at Coppola's doing anything that might jeopardize the film's Christmas release date. Any delays, they argued, would affect not only the picture's potential earnings; they could also damage the film's reputation. Exhibitors had a habit of interpreting premiere postponements or delays as evidence of weakness in a film, and *The Godfather* did not need such speculation added to its already-spotty history.

Even Coppola's choice of music—a time-honored feature of *The Godfather*—was contested by Evans.

"He wanted Henry Mancini and I wanted Nino Rota," Coppola recalled. "When I came back with the recorded music, Evans hated it and demanded that it be taken out. He liked the period source music we had put in it, and he wanted it back. I refused. I told him he didn't have the right to order me to take it out, but he could fire me, hire another director, and order him to take the music out. I knew that, this close to opening, they'd never do this. There was a stalemate that went on for almost two weeks, with Walter Murch and me going to Evans's house every day and just sitting there, waiting for his decision.

"Finally, I suggested a way out. I told Evans that if he'd let us screen the film for a small audience of just regular people and they reacted negatively,

---

*Coppola resented Evans's claims in his book, *The Kid Stays in the Picture,* that he (Evans) was largely responsible for the film's final cut. "After the film was shot," Coppola told the author in 1999, "I had the right to edit it in San Francisco, but Evans told me that he would yank it down to L.A. if the cut ran longer than two hours and fifteen minutes. When the cut was done, it was over two hours and forty-five minutes, and we were so terrified that they were going to yank it, as warned, that we lifted as much as we could, getting it down to two hours and twenty minutes. We showed it to them, and Evans said that we had cut out all the texture, the good stuff. Therefore, he said, he was taking the film down to L.A. In L.A., we put back the stuff that we had taken out to conform to his dictum, and he then said—and has been saying ever since—how much better it is." In an interview with the author, James Caan echoed Coppola's sentiments, as well as those of many people who felt that Paramount officials were guilty of selective memory: "I love the fact that all these guys wanted to take credit. Evans told me he had cut the picture. This guy couldn't cut his toenail. Francis had to fight. When it was over, they told Francis his picture was a piece of shit, but when they read the reviews, they wanted credit: 'Yeah, I did this, I did that.' They're all full of shit."

we'd take the Rota music out. 'Who will decide if their reaction is negative?' he asked, and I said, 'You could.' He agreed and we got ready to do this. To this point, the film had never been shown to a small preview audience, and I think Evans was afraid to do so, lest it get a bad reaction. But we had this little screening for about thirty or forty people at a theater in the studio, and when it was over, the audience was glowing. We realized, for the first time, that an audience liked the film, and we were so pleased that we even forgot about the music for a second. Finally, we asked, 'What did you think about the music?' and they said that it was great, that they loved it. So even Evans saw that it worked. However, he insisted that we keep one piece of source music in—during the scene where Hagen's plane is landing in Hollywood— but the Rota music, which was almost out, was in."

11.

COPPOLA WORKED RELENTLESSLY on the postproduction of *The Godfather*, yet, as both he and Paramount had suspected, there was no way he could complete the movie in time for the 1971 holiday season. Instead, the film premiered on March 11, 1972, opening in five Loews theaters in New York City for exclusive showings before national release one week later. Any apprehension that Paramount might have experienced pertaining to the public's acceptance of the film was quickly resolved: One had only to look at the long lines ever present outside the theaters to conclude that *The Godfather* was going to be a runaway success. In its first week in New York alone, the movie grossed an unprecedented $465,148 in sold-out performances run virtually around the clock.

From the very beginning, it was clear to industry observers that *The Godfather* had achieved event status. Demand for limited seating led to the employment of creative capitalism. Ticket prices, normally in the three-dollar range, were raised fifty cents to a dollar per ticket; scalpers hawked tickets for twenty to thirty dollars each, and they had no trouble finding takers. In Los Angeles, UCLA students charged five dollars to stand in line for people with better ways to fill their time. Theatergoers engaged in a variety of tricks, including bribing security guards and feigning illness, all in desperate attempts to be admitted into theaters or to the front of lines. Each week saw new records being established in venues across the country, and with such figures came the speculation that *The Godfather* might eventually break all-time box-office earnings for a movie.

For Coppola, the film's enormous popular success softened some of the sting he felt from the mixed reviews he was receiving for his movie. He had known, from the moment he agreed to work on the picture, that it would be controversial in some circles, from those politically correct reviewers who lambasted him for glorifying the actions of criminals to watchdog groups condemning the film's violence. For every positive notice, such as the *New York Times'* enthusiastic pronouncement that *The Godfather* was "one of the most brutal and moving chronicles of American life ever designed within the limits of popular entertainment," there appeared to be offsetting commentary condemning the picture, such as historian Arthur Schlesinger, Jr.'s review, published in *Vogue,* stating that "in the reverent hands of Francis Ford Coppola, [*The Godfather*] has swelled into an overblown, pretentious, slow, and ultimately tedious three-hour quasi-epic."

Most prevalent, perhaps, was the opinion offered by critics who tried to have it both ways, frowning on the film's subject matter while praising Coppola's artistry, all the while suggesting that a viewer was likely to enjoy the movie much more than he or she ought to. *The Godfather,* offered a critic for *Commonweal,* was "class trash," a movie "unashamed of its own gauche appeal."

"[It] is as immoral and violent as any other movie one might object to," the same reviewer wrote. "But people are not objecting to this one because it is a well-made narrative film, free of obscurantist tricks and false artistic pride. . . . It is evil, but we cannot help ourselves: we admire it."

Time, along with the film's and Coppola's continued success, would prompt reevaluations of the movie's artistic merits and position in motion picture history. Coppola himself would eventually confess to having underestimated *The Godfather*'s appeal. As Coppola recalled, he, Al Ruddy, and Robert Evans were talking about the film's chances to exceed the fifty-million-dollar mark in gross receipts—a figure previously reached by only *Gone with the Wind* and *The Sound of Music.* Coppola, who was tired of being picked up with other crew members in a station wagon whenever he was summoned to a meeting with the Paramount bigwigs, offered an interesting proposal.

"If it does seventy-five million," he said, "would you buy me a Mercedes limo, since I always ride in a crummy, dirty station wagon."

Ruddy had no problem with the idea. "If this film does seventy-five million," he answered, "we'll be glad to buy you that damn limo."

The Godfather surpassed *Gone with the Wind* in gross receipts in its sixteenth week. Accompanied by George Lucas, Coppola went out and purchased a top-of-the-line 1972 Mercedes-Benz 600. He sent the bill to Paramount.

Chapter Five

Renaissance Man

"The Conversation was very ambitious, and I hung in not because it was going right, but because I couldn't accept within myself the judgment that I couldn't succeed in doing it."

—FRANCIS FORD COPPOLA

"When Francis Ford Coppola insisted that he made The Godfather *for the freedom big money would bring him to work on his own personal projects, many people jeered at what they took to be the guilty old Hollywood bull, the promise so often made, so often not delivered. Well, Coppola has delivered and the cynics stand mute."*

—DAVID DENBY

1.

THE GODFATHER REWARDED Francis Ford Coppola in ways that he could only have dreamed of a few years earlier. He was now respected, wealthy, and in constant demand; his name was internationally known.

Such success was quite agreeable to Coppola's substantial ego, and in the months following the release of *The Godfather,* he basked in his newfound fame, granting interviews and expounding upon every imaginable topic until he had grown weary of the sound of his own voice. With interviewers, he would make every attempt to avoid coming across as being cocky or conceited, and he tried to be generous when assessing the talents of those with whom he had worked, but he was clearly enjoying his position. He had aspired to be rich and famous—and to show his parents, in the finest of Italian traditions, that he could amount to something—and now that he had attained those goals, his sense of self-satisfaction blossomed.

Of particular pleasure to Coppola was the fact that he had accomplished the difficult task of becoming enormously popular while being seriously regarded as an artist. Magazines such as *Time, Newsweek,* and *Life* ran large feature spreads on *The Godfather,* adding momentum to the film's already-enviable word-of-mouth boost, while such respected trade journals as *Sight and Sound* and *Film Quarterly* treated Coppola as the great new arrival on the motion picture scene. Coppola's old film school colleagues and rivals could only stand back in wonder as they watched the first of their numbers rise to prominence.

Nor was Coppola shy about displaying the fruits of his success. Not long after signing on to write and direct *The Godfather,* he had purchased a twenty-eight-room mansion in the Pacific Heights section of San Francisco. Built at the turn of the century, the home boasted the kind of luxury usually reserved for the film industry "haves," including a gorgeous view of the Golden Gate Bridge, spacious living quarters, and a basement ballroom (which Coppola converted into a screening room); after purchasing the place, the Coppolas put in the obligatory swimming pool. It was, in every respect, the mansion on the hill, proof positive that Coppola had arrived.

Not surprisingly, Coppola tried to apply his new stature as leverage to further not only his own career but those of others, as well. George Lucas, looking to find a way to launch his latest movie project, *American Graffiti,* approached Coppola and asked him to add his name to the film's production credits. The endorsement, arriving on the heels of *The Godfather,* would help Lucas, still smarting from the commercial failure of *THX-1138,* with the financing of his new picture. Coppola was willing to comply, though he was peeved that Lucas had approached other potential producers before coming to him.

There was no end to the workload. Paramount was pressing for a sequel to *The Godfather,* and Coppola, after some discussion, agreed to write and direct the picture, tentatively scheduled to begin shooting in the spring of 1973. In the meantime, he devoted his prodigious energy to such other concerns as directing Noel Coward's *Private Lives* for the American Conservatory

Theater in San Francisco; writing a screenplay adaptation for *The Great Gatsby;* directing the Gottfried von Einem opera, *The Visit of the Old Lady,* for the San Francisco Opera; and realizing, at long last, his hope of ushering *The Conversation* into production. Although he would grumble about how the work was keeping him from relaxing and having fun, Coppola also admitted that the whirlwind of activity was the realization of what he described as his "youthful desire to do everything."

"I'm open to almost anything," he said, weary but happy. "That's the fun I'm having, now that I don't have to work for money anymore."

2.

To outsiders, Coppola's activities might have appeared to be an energetic, perhaps even ill-advised series of adventures—a willy-nilly dash on the small, slippery surface of momentary fame—but in actuality, Coppola, for the most part, was only marrying his enormous appetite for the arts to his ambitions and successes of the past. His work on *The Great Gatsby* continued a screenwriting career that had begun over half a decade earlier, reaching its apex with *Patton.* His involvement in the Coward play was not unprecedented—he had directed plays and musicals at Hofstra—and his love of opera could be traced back to his father and grandfather. If pursuing such projects seemed self-indulgent, Coppola was not inclined to offer defensive explanations. He could *afford* self-indulgence.

His involvement with *American Graffiti* turned out to be unexpectedly lucrative, eventually earning him nearly $3 million when the movie became a smash hit and Coppola tallied his share of the film's profits. His initial involvement, however, was far more an act of "friendship, love, and belief in George," as Coppola recalled, than a calculated investment in a potentially hot commercial property.

His friendship with Lucas was evolving with the development of their respective careers. The two had remained close personal friends, seeing each other socially and gathering their families together on holidays, but the two had gone in different professional directions. From the beginning of their friendship, they had been an unlikely pair, Coppola a boisterous and whirling dervish of activity, driven by relentless ambitions and an ego tempered by insecurities and self-doubt, while Lucas, shy and sedate by nature, worked quietly and purposefully, uninterested in the spotlight, the antithesis of Hollywood bluster. In becoming the first of his number to score a huge commercial and critical success, Coppola had assumed a place at the head of the class; at the ripe old age of thirty-three, he was a sage, a mentor, a don in the New Hollywood. Lucas had no problem congratulating Coppola on his success, but it would cause him some irritation in the future, when it was insinu-ated, by ignorant or insensitive members of the press, that he might have never succeeded without Coppola's intervention on his behalf. Still, there was no denying that Coppola was at the apex of a team of industry newcom-ers poised to change the direction of modern filmmaking.

"Francis has charisma beyond logic," Lucas commented years later, openly admitting that his life, to some extent, was "a kind of reaction against Francis's life." But, at the same time, he also stated that his professional rela-tionship with Coppola had been largely beneficial. "I can see what kind of man the great Caesars of history were," said Lucas. "That's one reason I toler-ate as much as I do from Francis. I'm fascinated by how he works and why people follow him so blindly."

What the two had in common was their unstinting creative vision, which they refused to compromise, even in showdowns with corporate officials. Both were pragmatic inasmuch as they recognized the need to balance art with commerce, and both would make unhappy concessions in lesser dis-putes, yet neither would sacrifice vision for the sake of the dollar—a creative temperament that did little to endear them to company presidents, executive producers, and other officials, who tended to view each new movie, especially of the sort proposed by Coppola and Lucas, as guarded risks.

American Graffiti was a case in point. The project, thought some potential producers, had all the earmarks of a box-office flop. It was set in the past, in 1950s Modesto, California, where Lucas had spent his formative years, and it was so deeply personal that industry higher-ups feared it might lack the uni-versal appeal necessary to attract large audiences. Would teenagers, always the bedrock of box-office receipts, embrace a movie that was, in essence, about their parents as teenagers? Industry officials were skeptical. In addition, casting the film's major parts would, by nature, involve using a number of unknown actors and actresses, which brought into play the usual debate about marquee appeal. Finally, Lucas intended to use songs from the period as the backbone of his movie—an expensive and risky proposition at the very least.

"After the Warner Brothers' 'Black Thursday,' Zoetrope pretty much dis-solved," Lucas recalled. "Francis had to go off and make enough money to pay back Warner Brothers, so he went off and made *The Godfather.* I had to do something with my life. I was trying to get *Apocalypse Now** off the ground,

*At the time, *Apocalypse Now*—one of the films that would become synonymous with Cop-pola's name—was a project under development by George Lucas and screenwriter/director John Milius. A complete history of *Apocalypse Now* will be provided in Chapter 7.

but nobody wanted to do it, so I put that on the shelf and started working on another project that I had—*American Graffiti*. When I took *American Graffiti* around to all the studios, nobody wanted to do it. I finally talked United Artists into giving me money to develop a screenplay. I did a couple of drafts and took it to United Artists. They hated it. I took the screenplay all around town and nobody wanted to do it."

After being rejected by a number of studios, Lucas found one company—Universal—willing to take him on, provided he would agree to work under a strict and tiny budget, and the studio found a big name to act as producer for the film—hence, Francis Ford Coppola. By terms of the agreement, Coppola was not only expected to supervise all the details of the film's production, he was also required to assume financial responsibility for any of the music permissions fees exceeding ninety thousand dollars, a sizable commitment given Lucas's intention of having classic late 1950s and early 1960s music playing during every moment of the film.

Coppola liked the idea and prospects of Lucas's project, and for a while he even attempted to find financing for it himself. He had no intention of meddling in his friend's movie, acting like the kind of corporate goombahs he despised, but when he failed to secure the backing needed to finance the production on his own, he had no alternative but to agree to do it Universal's way. In the months ahead, he would visit the *American Graffiti* set from time to time, but he generally tried to stay out of George Lucas's way.

He had more pressing matters on his mind—the Noel Coward play, for one. Coppola relished the thought of helping to boost the artistic community in the Bay Area, and the production of *Private Lives* was a good place to start. Unfortunately, he scarcely had time to humor his expanding ambitions. He was accustomed to working under tight schedules and crushing deadlines, but the demands on his time were presently such that, barring his accomplishing the feat of bilocation, he would find it impossible to give every project the time it deserved.

Such was the case with *Private Lives,* which sounded like a great project when Coppola agreed to direct it, but which ultimately demanded too much work in too little time. Coppola might have been able to crank out play productions successfully under tremendous time constraints while he was a student director at Hofstra; putting together a polished production as an adult, not to mention a critically acclaimed film director, was something else entirely. When he signed on as the American Conservatory Theater's guest director, Coppola had less than a month to prepare the Noel Coward comedy for its February 22 opening.

To the surprise of even Coppola himself, he pulled it off. The play might not have been the crowning jewel in his career up to that point, but given the logistics of progressing from planning and rehearsals to the final product, he did amazingly well. While critics offered their applause, Coppola seemed relieved. "I was very, very lucky it turned out all right," he told a reporter from *The Saturday Review,* noting that the dress rehearsal had been a disaster. The work had been more than he anticipated and, as he mentioned two decades later, it did not necessarily represent the best use of his time.

"It is as much work to do a play for ACT," he observed, "as it is to make a $15 million movie."

3.

FOR ALL THE DIVERSITY IN HIS professional life, Francis Ford Coppola continued to think of himself primarily as a screenwriter who happened to direct movies. The writer, he would tell interviewers, was the ultimate creator, and in Coppola's perfect world, he would create the story and then go on to see it into production. After nearly a decade in the business, he had accomplished this only twice, with *Dementia 13,* which was not the sort of film that he could boast about, and with *The Rain People,* which he loved, but which had been seen by so few people that he could hardly hang his hat on it. His other pictures— *You're a Big Boy Now, Finian's Rainbow,* and *The Godfather*—had been the products of others' imaginations, with Coppola eventually steering them to the screen. Although he could find satisfaction in his overall body of work, as well as in the fact that he had stayed busy within the film industry since his film school days, Coppola still coveted the life of the auteur. *The Conversation,* along with the sequel to *The Godfather,* promised to guide him further down that path.

But first he had to work on a screen adaptation of *The Great Gatsby,* the F. Scott Fitzgerald masterpiece, which had never been satisfactorily captured on the big screen. For the filmmaker, the novel presented serious challenges. The novel's story is told from the viewpoint of a narrator—a difficult perspective for a motion picture, whose point of view tends to be omniscient. In addition, one of the devices used by Fitzgerald to great success was his use of texture, which worked brilliantly on the printed page but proved to be problematic for screen adaptation.

Coppola was familiar with the difficulties that the novel posed to the screenwriter, and, if anything, they made the project all the more attractive to him. Truman Capote had attempted and failed to come up with a suitable script for producer Robert Evans, who hoped to feature his then wife, Ali MacGraw, in the female lead. Coppola, who took on the project as a favor to

Evans, was full of ideas on how to apply creative spin to an adaptation that remained faithful to the book, and he worked on the screenplay for an intense five-week period, running from the completion of his involvement in *Private Lives* until the end of March. Ironically, he was working on the script during the opening of *The Godfather.*

The experience was less than ideal. Since he was acting only in the capacity of screenwriter, he was ultimately the liege of director Jack Clayton, who had thoughts of his own on how to adapt the novel to the screen. To Coppola's disappointment, many of his ideas were rejected, ignored, or altered in the final product. For instance, rather than attempting to use a series of flashbacks to relate the history shared by Gatsby and Daisy Buchanan, Coppola decided to write a scene in which the two, their affair in tatters, try to understand what has gone wrong, the nature of their relationship to be revealed through dialogue. Clayton, however, deemed the lengthy exposition to be too dull, and he decided to cut it into five scenes, to be spread throughout the final third of the film—a decision that, Coppola complained, threw off the delicate construction of his narrative.

"In the novel, there are no scenes, really, between Daisy and Gatsby, so I did a lot of research and found similar characters and situations in Fitzgerald's short stories," Coppola explained. "I crafted a long scene—about nine pages—in which they spend a night together. I thought it would be interesting to feel the tension of their thinking about each other and behaving in reaction to each other, and then give this long, developed scene. Jack used little pieces of the scene rather than play it out the way I planned it."

Nor was he pleased with the way Clayton reacted to some of the more subtle points in his screenplay. In his opening, Coppola had the camera passing over select Gatsby possessions—his car, his clothing, his photographs of Daisy, a book from his childhood—all significant at one point or another in the film. Once again, Clayton maintained that this passage, like the dialogue between Gatsby and Daisy, was too slow. This threw off Coppola's intended ending for the film, a full-circle swing from the opening, in which Jay Gatsby's father, while going through his dead son's possessions, looked at many of the same objects shown at the opening of the film. "Look," Coppola had the father saying, "this is a book he had when he was a kid. Even then he was going to make something out of himself." The film would then close with the father seeing the picture of Daisy and asking, "Who's this girl?" This scene, too, was replaced in the final cut of the movie.

Coppola tried to take a diplomatic stance with the press when the film was eventually released, after a lengthy delay, to disastrous reviews in 1974, the same year he was receiving the highest accolades for *The Godfather, Part II* and *The Conversation.* He was put off by the final version of the film, which was so far removed from his original screenplay that he was reminded of his days at Seven Arts, particularly the disaster of *Is Paris Burning?* In interviews, he kept the harshest of his opinions to himself, avoiding the kind of criticism that would hurt the film's chances at the box office or offend its director.

Still, he was not about to accept any great burden of blame for the picture's shortcomings. "It's not my place to say how I would have done the film," he declared. "But I still say that if you have a cast and a good script, you've got eighty percent of the film. In *Gatsby,* I disagreed with the casting and I didn't think the script ever got to see the light of day in the form I think it should have."

Fortunately for Coppola, the *Gatsby* script was never as attached to his name as his earlier screenplay for *Patton,* and he was in the position to shrug off his work on the film as a matter of his doing Paramount and Robert Evans a favor while he earned a paycheck in uncertain times. "They were in trouble over a script," he said, "and I was very unsure about what would happen with *The Godfather.* I had no money, so I accepted the job of doing a rush script, knowing full well that, as things go, the director usually only wants to get into shooting, wherein he'll make the film the best he can. A final script is just to get the money flowing, and less to really follow."

Although he had no way of knowing it at the time, he would never again write a script for a film he did not direct.

4.

COPPOLA HAD NEVER BEEN IN better position to be self-righteous. He was Hollywood's boy wonder; he had pitched uncertain battles over *The Godfather* and spirited away victoriously with what promised to become the highest-grossing movie to date. The money and power were affording him the opportunity to reestablish his reputation as a motion picture mogul, even in the wake of the Zoetrope failure. In August 1972, he and two other hot, bankable directors—Peter Bogdanovich (*The Last Picture Show*) and William Friedkin (*The French Connection*)—had teamed up with Paramount to form the Directors Company, a business venture requiring each of the three filmmakers to produce and direct three new projects and act as executive producers for at least one other film over the forthcoming six-year period. In exchange, Paramount agreed to finance and distribute a minimum of twelve films, to the tune of a $31.5 million investment. All profits from the partnership would be divided fifty-fifty, with Paramount taking half and the directors dividing the other half among them.

Coppola was brutally frank when explaining why he, a maverick filmmaker hoping to break away from Hollywood, would suddenly reverse field and consummate a deal with one of the industry's biggest production companies.

"Part of my desire to get involved with them," he said, "is revenge. Part of me really wants to take control and own a piece of that film business, for lots of vindictive, Mafia-like reasons—because I'm so mad at Warner Brothers. And I know that I can't do it alone. Billy Friedkin, Peter Bogdanovich and I are old friends, and we've all had a super-success this year. What if we get together? We could really take over the business. In a company like that, for six years' work, you could make $20 million, and then spend the rest of your life making little movies that don't have to make money."

The first project he intended to release under the Directors Company banner, *The Conversation,* represented a return to the kind of personal filmmaking that he had temporarily abandoned while making *The Godfather.* It was the kind of film that he needed to make if he intended to avoid being branded as a gangster-movie director—a realistic possibility, given his plans to work on *The Godfather, Part II* in the near future.

In retrospect, *The Conversation,* with its stern yet almost resigned commentary on modern electronic surveillance, seems to be remarkably prophetic, not only with regard to some of the events associated with the Watergate break-in and its aftermath but also to the electronic revolution two decades later, in which issues concerning privacy have become a growing concern to people all over the world. It could be easily argued that Coppola's sixth film represents one of those rare occurrences where a movie gains added meaning and importance over time.

However, as Coppola would go to pains to explain, *The Conversation* was far less interested in making a political statement than in exploring the concept of moral responsibility. The latter, of course, could be a highly charged political issue, especially coming, as it did, when a cynical Nixon administration was using any means possible to denigrate the idealism of the 1960s, but as a screenwriter and director, Coppola was far more concerned with his art.

"I'm not interested in 'messages,'" he volunteered at the time. "As in *The Godfather* I want to get inside a very specialized individual, discover what motivated him. And I feel the only way to show his character in the action is to show something horrifying, a nightmare, the nightmare we live in, in which any personal privacy can be invaded with too much ease."

The Conversation sprang from several sources, not the least of which was the filmmaker's lifelong interest in gadgets. In his early teens, Coppola had learned how to tap the telephones in his home; he also devised a plan wherein, by planting microphones in the radiators throughout the house, he could listen in on conversations, ostensibly to learn what he was getting for Christmas. "I wasn't much of a hotshot," he recalled of his exploits, "but there was a tremendous sense of power in putting microphones around to hear other people. There was a sense of being important and superior because I could tap a phone and no one knew."

Years later, in 1966, during a casual conversation about eavesdropping and wiretapping with director Irvin Kershner, Coppola learned of the existence of microphones so powerful and selective that they were capable of isolating voices in a crowd. These microphones, Kershner told Coppola, came equipped with gun sights that the person recording the conversation would aim at the mouth of the speaker. The recording would come out fine, as long as no one blocked the line of vision.

Coppola was intrigued.

"I thought what an odd device and motif for a film," he remarked afterward, when recalling his talk with Kershner. "The image of two people walking through a crowd with their conversation being interrupted every time someone steps in front of the gunsight. From just a little curiosity like that, I began to very informally put together a couple of thoughts."

When he began writing *The Conversation*, Coppola was reading *Steppenwolf*, a contemporary classic about a loner who lived by himself in an apartment and kept to himself. Coppola liked the book so much that he named his bugging technician Harry, after the main character in the Herman Hesse novel, and assigned him many of the same traits.

As the character evolved over the coming years, he became very familiar to his creator. He was the type of guy, Coppola would explain, who was probably an oddball in high school, the type of person who would probably be the president of his school's radio club. "I was one of those guys," Coppola openly admitted. "I was president of the radio club."

However, Coppola realized, as he was mapping out his screenplay, that his film's main character was too dull and passive to be of much interest to a moviegoing public that, as a general rule, liked plenty of action in its pictures. To bring people to the theater, Coppola needed a strong storyline, perhaps within the framework of a thriller, in which to place his central character. At the same time, Coppola was searching for a new challenge—a fresh way to tell the story and, by extension, construct his movie.

"There's no real difference between *The Godfather*, *The Exorcist*, or *American Graffiti*," he maintained. "They are done the same way: actors are instructed to 'play a role' on an invisible stage in front of cameras, the film is shot in shattered fragments and their performance doesn't jell until the editing is done. These routines haven't changed in decades, and I'm bored by them.

"The Conversation," he continued, "is an attempt to go beyond this. It was written long before Watergate, as a psychological horror film. My plan was to start a movie with a couple having a conversation in a public square, and show that they were being recorded. But then, instead of going with them, I decided to go with the man who recorded it and examine him."

In constructing his "psychological horror film," Coppola drew from two earlier models: the films of Alfred Hitchcock and Michelangelo Antonioni's *Blow-Up*. Perhaps the greatest director in the history of suspense films, Hitchcock was a master of making the mundane seem menacing; his pacing was exquisite, particularly in the ways in which he layered events to slowly (and almost painfully) build and maintain suspense. Coppola, however, was not impressed with the way Hitchcock used his actors. In the younger filmmaker's opinion, all but a few of Hitchcock's films were poorly acted, and if he was going to make *The Conversation* work as intended, he needed to entice nothing but the finest in performances from his actors. Despite these misgivings, Coppola screened Hitchcock's films while he was preparing *The Conversation*, making notes on what he felt worked and did not work in the filmmaker's movies.

The Antonioni movie was an even greater source of inspiration. In *Blow-Up*, the main character, a photographer, is horrified to discover that he might have captured more than intended in an innocent photograph taken in a park; upon enlarging—or blowing up—the photo, he sees the image of a body in the background. In *The Conversation*, Harry Caul's recordings take on a different meaning when he enhances—or blows up—the sound, revealing a disturbing remark buried in the midst of otherwise-innocuous conversation.

Coppola spent six years, off and on, researching and developing the script. He read articles and catalogs on surveillance devices; he attended bugging conventions, which, at the time, were still open and legal. Through Irvin Kershner, he met Bernard Spindel, a real-life bugging expert who, over the course of his career, had worked with Jimmy Hoffa in the Teamster leader's efforts to thwart Justice Department surveillance. Each experience contributed texture to a screenplay that would become the finest personal film in Coppola's career.

Production designer Dean Tavoularis also consulted a bugging expert when he was building props and stocking the sets with surveillance equipment. The expert, said Tavoularis, had been instrumental in the way Harry Caul's surveillance van was designed.

"He put me in touch with these Department of Justice guys who, in fact, had built a van like this. Only it was a laundry truck—in Berlin," Tavoularis explained. "They told me how they'd covered the surface with carpeting, so you wouldn't make a noise if you dropped a lens. You put heavy springs on the van, so it wouldn't wobble when you moved from one side of the van to the other. You had bottles to urinate in. All those kinds of details."

5.

FROM THE STANDPOINT OF STORY alone, *The Conversation* contains enough intrigue, surprising revelations, high incident, quirky characters, and suspense to work effectively as a thriller.

For all of his reputation of being the best surveillance man on the West Coast, Harry Caul is a man of little distinction or identity. He lives in a generic apartment in San Francisco, guards his privacy as if someone out there would really go to the bother of invading it, wears nondescript clothing (except for a plastic raincoat, which he wears everywhere, rain or shine), and goes out with a woman who knows nothing about him, including his age, what he does for a living, or even his telephone number. Harry's only source of contentment, it would seem, is playing saxophone along with the jazz records in his collection.

At the opening of *The Conversation*, Harry is walking about San Francisco's Union Square, supervising the recording of a young couple's lunchtime conversation. Under the usual circumstances, hiding in a crowd is the best way to avoid being bugged or overheard, but Caul possesses the finest surveillance equipment available. He has stationed people everywhere—two in buildings overlooking the square, aiming riflelike microphones at the couple, one on foot in the square, following the couple with a microphone planted in a wrapped package—and he is all but assured of getting a decent recording.

At first, it appears as if Harry has gone to a lot of trouble to record what looks to be no more than an illicit but harmless encounter between a married woman (Ann) and her lover (Mark), theirs the kind of small talk that one would expect to hear from two people just happy to be in each other's company. Harry is not interested in the nature of their talk; to him, the recording is just another job for which he is being very well paid. When his assistant, Stanley, stationed in a camouflaged van set up as a sound station, complains that the job is boring, Harry shrugs him off. "I don't care what they're talking about," he tells Stanley. "All I want is a nice, fat recording."

It is Harry's birthday, and when he returns home after work, he is disturbed to find a card and bottle of wine from his landlady. The gift, left inside his apartment door, angers Harry: Not only does the landlady know that it is his birthday; she also knows how old he is—facts, Harry surmises, that she could have obtained only by reading his mail. He is further disarmed by the knowledge that she has keys to the apartment, and that she had to enter his private domain to disengage his alarm system.

His day only gets worse when he goes out to visit his girlfriend, Amy, who is waiting for him in bed at her apartment. He has been hoping to spend a quiet evening with her, but he grows perturbed and leaves when she asks what he considers to be too many questions about his private life. In reality, her queries are the type that someone might ask on a first or second date, but Harry, already unnerved by the earlier events at his apartment, is not in the mood for any more questions or playful musings. Before departing, he drops rent money on the kitchen table, even though Amy mentions that she is tired of waiting for him to come around and might be moving on.

The mystery begins the next day, when Harry pays a visit to an enormous office complex to deliver the tapes of the conversation he'd made the day before to his employer, a man known only as "the Director." Harry is greeted by Martin Stett, the Director's assistant, who, in the absence of his boss, is to accept the tapes and pay Harry fifteen thousand dollars. Harry insists that he will deliver the tapes to the Director only. On his way out, he catches a fleeting glimpse of Mark in a hallway, and then of Ann on the elevator.

Back in his warehouse lab, a deeply troubled Harry Caul takes a closer listen to the contents of his tapes. By using high-tech equipment, he is able to piece together the entire conversation, including one scrap of dialogue previously buried in the sound of a band playing in the square. "He'd kill us if he got the chance," Mark says. The comment worries Harry. What will happen when he delivers the tapes to his employer? Will the Director, who is paying a high price to learn of his wife's affair, actually murder someone? Harry has reason for such concern: A previous bugging job on the East Coast had led to the murder of a couple and their child.

To clear his conscience, Harry visits a Catholic church, where he goes to confession and admits to committing such sins as petty thievery and impure thoughts. At the end of his confession, he blurts out a few words about being involved in work that might hurt others, but even as he seeks absolution for his minor infractions, he refuses to accept any blame for whatever might happen as the result of his work.

Later that evening, Harry attends a wiretappers' convention, where he is shocked by the news that Stanley, his assistant, with whom he had quarreled earlier in the day, has now accepted a job with a rival named Bernard Moran, a sleazeball paladin who sells his equipment with all the panache of a carnival barker. Moran patronizes Harry, coming on like an old friend and admirer and slipping a company pen into Harry's pocket with a flourish, but Harry's mind is elsewhere. He tries to call Amy, only to discover that her phone has been disconnected. Worse yet, he sees Martin Stett lurking about the convention floor. The two confront each other later in the men's room, where Stett demands that Harry turn over the tapes the following Sunday, but Harry remains noncommittal.

The convention closes for the night, and Harry invites Moran, Stanley, and a small group of others to his lab for a spur-of-the-moment party. Moran, drunk and abrasive, airs some of the painful incidents of Harry's past, as if to challenge his colleague's reputation in front of the group attending the party. Harry plays along for a while, but he eventually seeks solace in the company of one of Moran's assistants, a woman named Meredith, who has been flirting with him throughout the evening. Hoping to talk to her in private, he takes her to another area of the warehouse, only to discover later that their conversation has been recorded by a microphone hidden in the pen that Moran had slipped into his pocket earlier that evening. Infuriated, Harry orders everyone but Meredith to leave.

After making love to Meredith, Harry falls into a fitful sleep. He has two nightmares, the first involving his seeing Ann at the entrance of the park, the second placing him at a hotel where a murder is about to occur. In his nightmare about Ann, Harry tries to assuage his guilt over recording the private conversation by telling her secrets of his past. He fails to connect with her—a failure that is all the more troubling in the subsequent nightmare when Ann is murdered because Harry cannot offer her an ample warning.

When Harry awakens, he finds Meredith already gone. So, too, are the tapes. Defeated, he returns to his apartment, where he is contacted by Stett, who somehow has obtained his unlisted telephone number. Stett informs Harry that he has the tapes and that Harry will be paid for them if he drops by the Director's office. At the office, Harry witnesses the Director listening to the taped conversation, and, fearing for the safety of the young woman, Harry asks, first the Director and then Martin Stett, what is going to happen to her. "We'll see," Stett replies.

From what he has heard on the tape, Harry knows that the couple have planned a rendezvous at a hotel later that day; the Director, of course, is aware of the same. Harry rushes to the hotel and takes the room adjacent to the one that Mark and Ann have already reserved. He drills a hole in the wall between the two rooms and plants a bugging device. A short time later, Harry hears what he has feared most: The Director arrives, confronts the couple, and a fight breaks out. Harry walks out onto the hotel balcony just in time to see a bloody hand smearing the frosted glass on the window to the next room. Horrified, he retreats to his own room, turns on the television, and jumps into bed, curling into a fetal position, his hands covering his ears and shielding him from any further sounds of violence. He falls asleep in this position.

When he awakens, all is silent next door. He steps into the corridor and, after receiving no answer when he knocks on the door, picks the lock to the room. The place is empty and in perfect order, as if no one had ever been there. Harry gives the room a thorough inspection but finds no blood or even a hint of a struggle. In the bathroom, he checks the shower stall and then, almost as an afterthought, he flushes the toilet. The clear water suddenly turns crimson as bloody towels work their way back into the toilet bowl.

Rage and guilt lead him back to the office complex, but security personnel refuse to admit him. He tussles briefly with them, but he has no fight left in him. Outside the building, he sees Ann, the Director's wife, sitting in the back of a limousine. In a flash, he realizes that he had been mistaken all along, that he had misjudged what he had heard on the tapes. Instead of "He'd *kill* us if he got the chance," Mark had actually said, "*He'd* kill *us* if he got the chance." By misinterpreting the voices on the tape, Harry had failed to recognize that he was playing an unwitting but very serious role in setting up the Director's murder.

His nightmare, however, is far from over. When he returns home, he receives a call from Martin Stett, who cautions Harry that he is being watched. As proof, he plays back a recording of Harry playing his saxophone. Harry scours his apartment for a bugging device, moving methodically from room to room and becoming more frantic when he fails to find anything. Finally, in frustration, he peels off wallpaper and tears out the floorboards in the apartment, his search still yielding nothing. The master surveillance expert has been beaten at his own game. As the story closes, he is seated in the rubble, playing his saxophone, his life a shambles.

6.

COPPOLA WORKED ON *THE CONVERSATION* script throughout much of the spring and summer of 1972. He had a commitment to direct *The Visit of the Old Lady* opera in the fall, but once he had honored that obligation, he had a few months before he was scheduled to begin work on the *Godfather* sequel—time he hoped to fill by filming *The Conversation*. In the meantime,

he continued what was now a yearlong juggling act, working on the preproduction for *The Conversation,* keeping tabs on *American Graffiti,* and preparing
The Visit of the Old Lady for the stage.

His work on the opera tested him even further than his earlier work on
the Noel Coward play. By his own admission, Coppola was no authority on
opera, and the one he had agreed to direct, a contemporary work of questionable box-office appeal, could have easily flopped and cast doubts on his judgment, all at a time when he might have been shoring his reputation by
working on another film. The failure of *Finian's Rainbow,* only four years
removed, was still fresh in his mind.

Nevertheless, he plowed ahead, mainly because, as he would later confess,
he underestimated the task at hand. When he had told San Francisco Opera
general director Kurt Herbert Adler that he would direct *The Visit of the Old
Lady,* Coppola had not heard so much as one note of the opera's music, which
was not especially memorable. As one who earned his living in a visual
medium, Coppola reasoned that he might compensate for some of the opera's
shortcomings by making the presentation visually interesting, but as he
quickly determined, directing an opera was much more involved than he had
anticipated. With only limited funds at his disposal, he had to abandon some
of his plans for elaborate sets. Rehearsal time was hard to come by, and Coppola, accustomed to allowing his actors and actresses their own input into the
shaping of a production, suddenly found himself in a situation where he had
to provide more direction within a fairly rigid framework, one with which he
was only vaguely familiar. Then there was the issue of time itself: Although he
had signed on to do the opera in March, by the time he was able to free himself from other obligations to work on it, Coppola was again under the gun,
attempting to put together a major production in a three-week period. The
same opera, when it had premiered at the Vienna State Opera a year earlier,
had required more than two months of preparation.

Coppola, who likened the frenetic preparation of the opera to "running
in front of a locomotive," struggled with his on-the-job training, which
showed him the wide gulf between directing a motion picture and directing
an opera.

"At the first run-through on the Opera House stage," he recalled, "I realized that nearly all the intimate detail I had been working on simply got lost.
I had given the chorus members individual bits to do, for instance, like in the
wedding scene in *The Godfather.* But at the run-through, from that distance,
they all merged into a mob. Things get lost in opera, and music slows time
down. It's simply not a natural art form, so you have to bring in stylization."

The Visit of the Old Lady elicited mixed response when it opened on October 25, 1972, with reviewers treating Coppola's involvement more as an interesting oddity than as a serious career move. For his part, Coppola remained undaunted by the criticism, hinting that he might tackle something even more ambitious in the future—something involving, perhaps, a multimedia presentation—provided he could clear away more time to stage it. If nothing else, he walked away from the experience with a newly acquired respect and knowledge of the inner workings of opera.

"I'll never work on this kind of crazy schedule again," he stated. "Opera people work harder than anybody else I've ever seen."

7.

FILMING OF *THE CONVERSATION* commenced, as planned, on November 26, 1972, with a budget set at $1.6 million. In assembling a cast and crew for his movie, Coppola stayed with the familiar, employing a company consisting largely of people from *The Godfather* and *American Graffiti.*

Harrison Ford and Cindy Williams, both relative unknowns prior to their appearances in *American Graffiti,* were cast in the important roles of Martin Stett and Ann. Robert Duvall, marking his third (although, in this case, uncredited) appearance in a Coppola-directed film, played the Director, while John Cazale followed up his impressive work in *Godfather* with the meaty role of Stanley, Harry Caul's business associate. Teri Garr, a comedic actress who had previously appeared in several Elvis Presley movies, won the part of Harry's girlfriend, Amy, and Frederic Forrest, another newcomer, who would turn up in a number of Coppola's future projects, played Mark.

Gene Hackman, in what proved to be a casting coup for Coppola, signed on to play the movie's leading role. Hackman, busy establishing himself as one of the industry's hardest-working actors, had won Golden Globe and Academy Award statuettes for his portrayal of Popeye Doyle in 1971's *The French Connection,* and subsequent appearances in *The Poseidon Adventure* and the critically acclaimed *Scarecrow* (the latter with Al Pacino) had elevated his marquee appeal. While this could have been seen as beneficial for the future marketing of *The Conversation,* Coppola was more immediately concerned that Hackman's history of playing intense, macho roles might make him seem miscast in the more subdued, internalized part of Harry Caul. To be effective, Hackman had to let his emotions simmer, rather than boil, throughout the picture; he had to bear the weight of both anger and resignation simultaneously, both tempered by his belief that he was simply a professional going about his job.

The casting of Hackman was both ironic and fortuitous. Coppola had originally intended the Harry Caul role for Marlon Brando, but the actor had turned him down when offered the part in 1969, deeply disappointing the director who, less than two years later, would play a pivotal role in reviving Brando's career. Immediately after appearing in *The Godfather*, Brando set to work on *Last Tango in Paris*, in which he portrayed a man obsessed with his own anonymity and privacy.

Hackman, on the other hand, had agreed to star in the picture before his stock in Hollywood had risen to its present level. Hackman had seen and admired *The Rain People*, and, later, *The Godfather*, and he had agreed to play Harry Caul, if and when he and Coppola could align their busy schedules. Whether he would have accepted this part if it had been offered to him for the first time a few years later is anyone's guess, but there is no doubting that in landing Hackman, Coppola had lucked out again, securing the services of a top-notch actor at bargain-basement prices. Hackman's portrayal of Harry Caul, which would eventually earn him a Golden Globe nomination for Best Actor, was brilliant, his character as subtle and slowly revelatory as the story line itself.

In its own way, *The Conversation* posed as many problems to Coppola as *The Godfather* had. There were no battles over casting decisions, nor were his abilities as a director called into question by studio bosses, but to get the movie made, Coppola had to overcome a variety of creative and technical difficulties. For one, he had not completed a screenplay to his satisfaction, and when cameras rolled and Coppola found himself up against a serious time crunch, he still had not worked out a suitable ending to his thriller. The characters were fully realized and the film's main events locked into place, but he was at a loss as to where to go with them.

Coppola, however, was nothing if not an artist of substantial faith. He had gone into *The Rain People* with only a few characters and pivotal events in place, and he had trusted that his actors, along with the circumstances surrounding the filming itself, would provide him with clues as to how to flesh out his movie; so it would be with *The Conversation*, another character-driven film.

"I tried to obtain emotions from Gene Hackman that would have been passed over if the picture had been done in the usual manner of thrillers," Coppola remarked, noting that William Friedkin had eliminated introspective scenes from *The French Connection* for the sake of keeping the film's pacing fast. "We worked the other way," explained Coppola, "letting Hackman's character determine the pacing of his scenes."

Hackman, for one, was not entirely comfortable with this method of working. His character was relentlessly depressing, and without a clear indication of how, exactly, some of the story's main questions were going to be answered, Hackman was essentially on his own. "It's a depressing and difficult part to play," he observed at the time, "because it's so low key. The minute you start having any fun with it, you know you're out of character."

Coppola and Hackman had done an admirable job in transforming the young actor into his character. When he had arrived in San Francisco for the shooting, Hackman had been fit and trim, well tanned—the physical opposite of the frumpy, pale, repressed middle-aged man he was to portray. A hairstylist supplied Hackman with his new balding appearance, while the costume designer outfitted him with a wardrobe that was ill-fitting and just out of style. To add to the aging effect, Hackman grew a mustache and wore a pair of glasses that looked as if they might have been passed down to him by his father. Coppola wanted Hackman to look like a "nudnik" and he succeeded.

To save money, Coppola shot entirely on location, using no soundstages except a Zoetrope warehouse that was converted into Harry Caul's warehouse office. Dean Tavoularis's selection of locations was deliberately designed to give the city a universal appearance, with only a few locations easily identifiable as being in San Francisco. The roller-coaster streets, Victorian houses, wondrous visions of the Bay and the Golden Gate Bridge—all were overlooked, prompting one journalist to observe that "San Francisco, for once in its life, is presented as it must seem to conventioneers."

The locations might have been right on hand, but the script requirements for Harry Caul's apartment had Tavoularis scrambling to find a suitable location.

"We had to find an apartment that was across the street from a building that was being torn down," Tavoularis explained, noting that you had to be able to see the building from Harry Caul's window. "We found such an apartment, and we coordinated the demolition of the building so that when you're in Gene Hackman's apartment and looking through the window, you could see it coming down across the street."

These locations might have saved Coppola money, but they caused him all kinds of headaches during the shooting, creating numerous technical difficulties in lighting, sound, and continuity. The film's celebrated opening sequence—a slow, overhead zoom of San Francisco's Union Square, where Caul and his associates are recording the central conversation used in the movie—was a work of technical wizardry, involving four camera crews, six cameras, and a battery of sound technicians recording with radio mikes. No one, including the crew, seemed to know precisely what was going on. In an effort to make the scene as realistic as possible, Coppola had ordered his cameramen to locate the actors mingling in a mass of extras and real-life passersby, focus on them, and follow them as they moved about the square. It was a slow, tedious process, repeated day after day, threatening to throw the schedule and budget out of whack and, on at least one occasion, leading to comical results when a camera crew, unaware that the filming had ceased, shot Hackman giving an interview to a reporter. On another occasion, several soundmen were briefly apprehended by police, who saw the rifle-sight microphones and mistakenly feared that they were snipers out to murder the director. In the finished film, a number of the people seen on the square were actually technicians working on the street.

"We did it very much the way Harry was supposed to be doing it in the story," Coppola offered. "It was total chaos. Half our crew was in all those shots. And you can see them! But there were a lot of cameras. It was really John Cassavetes time: cameras photographing cameras."

Coppola could remark—perhaps even laugh—about it in hindsight, but at the time, the shooting caused the kind of tension he could have done without. Cinematographer Haskell Wexler and production designer Dean Tavoularis were at odds over some of the scheduled locations for the film, and Coppola soon found himself in the middle of the tussle, trying to maintain peace without offending either man's artistic sensibilities. Coppola admired Wexler's work, which he had witnessed firsthand during the filming of *American Graffiti,* and which he had applauded in *Medium Cool,* Wexler's award-winning film about the 1968 Democratic National Convention in Chicago—the latter a powerful commentary on the relationship between an event and the person witnessing it, making Wexler a natural choice for *The Conversation.* Still, Wexler had no sooner filmed the opening of the movie than it became apparent that something had to be done. Since he sided with his production designer on the location issue, Coppola decided that Wexler had to go. He would be replaced by Bill Butler.

"The relationship was just not working out in a way I was comfortable with," Coppola explained. "He didn't like certain locations, said they were impossible to light, impossible to shoot. One was the Director's office. Remember the strange office where Bobby Duvall is? Haskell vetoed that, and we were shooting it somewhere else; it was tense, and I was having to make the movie differently than I wanted to."

The firing of Wexler was messy. Unable to tell him directly that he was being replaced, Coppola called a ten-day recess in the shooting, during which he sent word to Wexler that he was no longer part of the production. Wexler was justifiably upset by this turn of events, especially when, a short time later, he read Coppola's published comments about the firing—comments that did not exactly jibe with the reasons Coppola had given him for the termination.

However, as time would show, Coppola accomplished some of his finest work under adverse conditions, and *The Conversation* was no exception. For all of his problems, Coppola was on the way to creating one of his more memorable films.

8.

ON SUNDAY, JANUARY 28, 1973, Coppola attended a special premiere showing of *American Graffiti* at San Francisco's Northport Theater. George Lucas had accomplished a remarkable feat in bringing the picture in on time and budget and, most important, to his satisfaction; he was eager to see how it would play in front of a live audience. Since he had yet to show it to Universal executives, the San Francisco presentation of the director's cut would be providing a response to a movie unadulterated by the customary studio demands for prescreening changes.

The audience and studio responses could not have been more different. The audience loved the picture from the beginning, and when the theater lights went on after the screening, people stood and applauded. The reaction, however, was of no encouragement to Universal's Ned Tanen, the production executive most responsible for convincing the studio to take on the project. The film, thought Tanen, was in no way ready to release for national distribution, and furthermore, by previewing the movie, Lucas had set his movie up for serious criticism. Confronting Coppola and Lucas in the theater, Tanen made his feelings known. "You boys let me down," he said. "I went to bat for you and you let me down."

As Lucas looked on in stunned disbelief, Coppola launched an attack that has become legendary in Hollywood film circles.

"You should get down on your knees and thank George for saving your job," he roared, his indignation undoubtedly fueled by recent memories of all his problems with Paramount over *The Godfather.* "This kid has killed himself to make the movie for you, and he brought it in on time and on schedule. The least you can do is thank him for doing that!"

The outburst drew the attention of dozens of people still inside the theater. Coppola continued his tirade, berating Tanen's judgment and insensitivity and backing his old protégé in a passionate defense rarely seen beyond closed studio doors.

"This movie's going to be a hit!" he shouted. "This audience loved this movie! I saw it with my own eyes!" Then, in a grandstand gesture that would have people talking for years to come, Coppola fumbled around for an imaginary checkbook. If the company didn't like Lucas's picture, he said, he would be happy to take it off their hands right then and there.

The outburst capped what in recent weeks had amounted to an emotional roller coaster. Coppola was feeling the strain of his work on *The Conversation,* still nearly a month from completion of principal photography, meaning not only that he was running over schedule and budget but also that he would have virtually no time to oversee the film's critical postproduction work before he had to turn his attention to *Godfather II.* He had yet to write a screenplay for the new picture, which only caused him additional anxiety, given the high expectations for the sequel.

The Godfather continued to pay dividends, financial and, as expected, in the honors accumulating during the awards season. The film picked up five Golden Globe awards (for picture, direction, actor, screenplay, and score) in what Coppola and Paramount hoped would be a prelude to a big night at the Academy Awards. A short time later, Coppola was honored with the Directors Guild of America award for Most Outstanding Direction Achievement of 1972–arguably his most prestigious award to date and, for Coppola, another indication that he might be spending plenty of time onstage when the Oscars were being awarded. As far as he or anyone else could see, the *Godfather* juggernaut was rolling on.

9.

AFTER THE BLOWUP AT THE *AMERICAN GRAFFITI* screening in San Francisco, Coppola had interceded on George Lucas's behalf with Universal officials. Using his powers of persuasion, Coppola argued that the Lucas film, in its present state, was a work of considerable achievement, in need of only a small cut here or there. The company wanted more, but Coppola eventually won the day. When all was said and done, *American Graffiti* remained essentially the same, with only about four and a half minutes of Lucas's original cut excised from the film.

Unfortunately, Coppola did not possess such insight into his own work, which was still giving him grief. The day-to-day operations on *The Conversation* might not have been as tempestuous as they had been during the making of *The Godfather,* but Coppola had his hands full, with everything from his continuing script problems to his customary complaints about dealing with the local unions. On one occasion, in February, he became involved in a squabble with a local television reporter and cameraman when they showed up on the set to investigate citizen complaints about a smoke generator being used in a scene Coppola was shooting in the park. "Stop taking pictures," he told the cameraman. "You're going to make me look bad." When the cameraman ignored the order, a minor scuffle broke out, with the television people being pushed around and the camera damaged. It was hardly the kind of publicity that Coppola needed.

"We were shooting a so-called foggy day," Coppola explained years later, "so of course there was not any fog. We had these fog machines running, trying to get the effect we needed. Some neighbors complained about the noise, and the fact that the fog machine was leaving some oily residue on some of the cars. A local TV crew arrived and started shooting while we were shooting; they were getting close-ups of the machine. I could tell that all the shots they were getting were done to make us look bad, so I stood behind one of the guys and quietly tried to flip the drive band off the pulley of the magazine with a pencil, which would have messed up the film that he shot. He saw what I was doing and turned the camera and came at me. I told him not to photograph me, but he continued to do so. He said I pushed him down, but I don't think I did. He sued me and collected some money—unfairly, I thought."

The Academy Awards ceremony turned out to be a mixed blessing, with *The Godfather* represented in awards given to Marlon Brando (Best Actor), Coppola and Mario Puzo (Best Screenplay), and to the movie itself (Best Picture). Under normal circumstances, such recognition would have thrilled any filmmaker or studio, but Coppola and Paramount were disappointed that the movie did not fare better. After all, it had been *the* motion picture event of the preceding year, and when the Oscar nominations had been announced in late January, *The Godfather* had led the field with eleven nominations. As it was, Bob Fosse's *Cabaret,* second in nominations with ten, wound up the big winner, receiving eight Academy Awards: those for actress, supporting actor, cinematography, editing, art direction, sound, original score, and, to Coppola's chagrin, director. It was only the second time that the Directors Guild winner was not also given the Academy Award.

There was additional fallout from Oscar night—apart from whatever disappointment the *Godfather* company might have felt from not winning more recognition for its achievement—when Marlon Brando declined to accept his Academy Award for Best Actor. Such refusal was not unprecedented—just two years earlier, George C. Scott had turned down the same award for his performance in *Patton*—but Brando had taken a more confrontational approach in rejecting his Oscar, sending a representative, a young woman going by the name of Sacheen Littlefeather, to read a statement when his award was announced. In his statement, Brando, an advocate for Native American rights, lambasted the entertainment industry for its treatment of the country's native peoples. "You may be asking what the hell does this have to do with the Academy Awards and why am I coming into your home," Brando wrote, anticipating the reaction of the program's millions of worldwide television viewers. "I believe that the motion picture community and television community have been as responsible as any for degrading the image of the American Indian."

Littlefeather never got the opportunity to read the speech. Word of Brando's plans leaked out prior to the presentation of the award, and Littlefeather was summoned backstage and warned by the program's producer that she would be cut off if she attempted to read the speech. Rather than defy the producer, Littlefeather spoke off-the-cuff. Mentioning that Brando had prepared a long speech, she said that she could not deliver it "because of time" but that she would gladly provide it to the press afterward. She then paraphrased the heart of Brando's speech, declining the award because of the way American Indians had been treated in Hollywood, and closed by stating that Brando would have delivered the speech himself but felt he "could do more good at Wounded Knee" (where a small band of Indians were currently engaging government agents in a tense standoff). As promised, Littlefeather delivered copies of the Brando text after she left the podium.

Brando's remarks cast serious doubts upon Coppola's plans for *Godfather II*. Much was written and said in the aftermath of the controversial speech. Frank Yablans and other Paramount brass had been infuriated by Brando's statement, and Yablans in particular made no attempt to hide his disgust with the actor. Brando, in turn, made it clear that the studio would have to pay him an exorbitant amount of money—reportedly half a million dollars plus 10 percent of the film's gross—if it had any hope of signing him for so much as a brief appearance in *The Godfather* sequel. Coppola, who had originally had every intention of casting Brando in at least some flashback scenes in the new movie, was now caught in the crossfire, undecided as to whether he could write Brando into his screenplay at all.

Chapter Six

The Death of Michael Corleone

"When you start you want to make the greatest film in the world, but when you get into it, you just want to get it done, let it be passable and not be embarrassing."

—FRANCIS FORD COPPOLA

1.

BY THE SPRING OF 1973, FRANCIS Ford Coppola found himself in the throes of two major film projects, uncertain about what to do with either, knowing only that time was running out. Had he had any less stamina or dedication to his projects, he might have crumbled under the demands for his attention. *The Conversation,* in postproduction, required a lot of editing work; *The Godfather, Part II,* in preproduction, needed a screenplay and Coppola's final approval on the locations selected for the upcoming shoot. Coppola scrambled as well as he could, working on *The Conversation* in San Francisco during the week, checking out locations in Las Vegas and Lake Tahoe, around Italy, and elsewhere on weekends, and plugging away at his screenplay whenever he caught a moment in between. In his exhausted state, he must have wondered if he was being punished for all his ambition.

His hopes of somehow finding another level of meaning to *The Conversation* during the shooting of the movie had failed him, and now, with principal photography completed, he was surrounded by film but, to his growing consternation, possibly no movie—or, at least, a story that added up. In the past, he had been successful in bringing together his plotlines by rearranging scenes and through skillful editing, but the going was slow on this latest venture. His psychological thriller was missing something, yet he was at a loss when he tried to pinpoint what it needed. Nor did it help that his attention was so severely divided among his various projects, depriving him of the chance to focus on the task for any great length of time.

With *Godfather II* looming in the near future, Coppola delegated much of the decision making on *The Conversation* to Walter Murch, the gifted sound technician who had worked with him on *The Rain People* and *The Godfather,* and who had done the sound montages for *American Graffiti.* Coppola's reliance on Murch was logical, inasmuch as the sound in *The Conversation* was vitally important to the plot itself. In essence, Coppola was asking Murch to discover the film that he, the director, thought he had made.

The oppressive workload did not prevent Coppola from investigating other ways to invest his money and talents. Over the months, his widespread interests—as well as money—had gone in so many directions that a team of agents and accountants would have had their hands full just keeping track of them. Coppola's property purchases included an estate in Mill Valley, complete with film-editing facilities, and San Francisco's landmark Sentinel Building, an eight-story structure built in 1905 (and the miraculous survivor of the great earthquake and fire a year later), which he used to house Zoetrope's offices. In addition, he purchased *City* magazine, which he also installed in the Sentinel Building, and the Little Fox Theater, a three-hundred-seater that Coppola hoped to use for an informal acting school, where he could encourage and mold new talent while he developed potential film projects. Coppola and others would write their material, which would then be performed by his repertory company.

"I want to write a scene, change it, rewrite it, try it for an audience with my class," he explained. "If it works, it works. I essentially want to do my stuff in a modest way, perhaps some eccentric films without worry whether they will be profitable or not."

The plan, noble in intent, reflected conflicting sides of the man now being referred to in print as "the Sultan of San Francisco" and a "baby tycoon." One could not question Coppola's sincerity in pursuing what he felt were modest projects, his intentions of acting as a local patron of the arts in San Francisco, or his hopes of using his status and money to help clean up San Francisco's run-down North Beach area, but it was also clear that Coppola reveled in his ballooning status as a major player in the movie business, rich beyond belief (at least for a film director) yet revered as an uncompromising artist of substantial importance. In his many interviews with the press in years to come, Coppola would speak frequently about wanting to take on small projects—or even of retiring altogether from the business—yet, as much as anyone around him, he understood the core of his ambitions. It was all but impossible for a man of his stature, ambition, ego, personality, and talent to hold things to a modest level, no matter how much effort he devoted to proving otherwise.

Nowhere was this as evident as in his connection to *City* (or, *City of San Francisco*, in its extended title). He had initially become involved as a patron of the magazine, pumping money into the periodical when it looked as if it would go under without help from outside funding. Coppola, who liked the idea behind the magazine but disliked the quality of the publication itself, sunk thousands of dollars into *City*, praying that it would somehow stabilize and improve. When it didn't, Coppola met with the magazine's publisher and set up a deal, wherein he would invest fifteen thousand into the magazine on the condition that he would take over the publication if it did not show a profit within a year's time.

The year passed and, ignoring advisers cautioning him that he was bound to lose a lot of money on the magazine, Coppola assumed ownership. Predictably, he could not simply hire an editor and take a position on the sidelines, where he could watch others do what they were being paid to do. In the months ahead, despite a full slate of activities demanding his attention elsewhere, Coppola would become more and more heavily involved in the magazine, dropping a small fortune into its sagging prospects, taking an active role in editorial decisions, and, in general, finding his energy leeched by a project he would have done well to avoid.

2.

THE GODFATHER, PART II HAD been in the works for a long time. The original had yet to hit the screens in 1972 when rumors of a sequel began to make the rounds. Paramount officially confirmed the reports and quietly went about the task of assembling the team to guide the follow-up to what the studio hoped would be its golden goose. Mario Puzo was again recruited to write a first draft of the screenplay, and Robert Evans hoped that he would be able to attract the rest of the brain trust behind *The Godfather* to work on the new picture.

It wasn't easy. Producer Al Ruddy, for one, wanted no part of *Godfather II*. The original film, with its ongoing battles with the Italian-American Civil Rights League–and the subsequent controversy over his deal with the league–had nearly cost him his sanity, and he had been around the business long enough to know that he could make a good living as a producer without going through the trials he had endured with *The Godfather*.

"I told them I had no interest in ever getting involved with *The Godfather* again," Ruddy noted. "I'd had it up to my nose with the project, between the mysterious phone calls at one o'clock in the morning–to take some meetings–to all the bullshit with the FBI and all the other nonsense. I finally thought I'd gotten through the film unscathed, and I just didn't want to see it anymore. I'd had it."

Nor was Coppola an easy mark. He, too, was burned out from his *Godfather* experiences and, as he put it, he "never wanted to see another gang or explosion again." As far as he was concerned *The Conversation* beckoned him as his next film.

"The idea of a sequel seemed horrible to me," he reflected in an interview released after the opening of *Godfather II*. "It seemed like a tacky spin-off, and I used to joke that the only way I'd do it was if they'd let me film *Abbott and Costello Meet the Godfather*."

Coppola remained adamant in his rejection of Paramount's offers, turning down the studio time and time again–on six occasions, according to one published report. But Charles Bluhdorn, one of Coppola's strongest allies during the shooting of *The Godfather*, stubbornly insisted that Coppola be involved in the sequel.

"Bluhdorn was very persistent," Coppola recalled. "Finally, I said I would produce it, pick a director, and help with the production, which is where things lay for a long time. Then I went to them and said that I had the perfect young director for it–Marty Scorsese–at which point Bob Evans had one of his tantrums and said he hated the idea. This put the whole thing into a new gear."

In trying to persuade Coppola to change his mind, Bluhdorn tried to appeal to Coppola's sense of artistry, proposing that he would be making history if he succeeded in presenting a sequel that was better than the original. One idea that did appeal to Coppola was the notion that he would be making not so much a sequel as a companion piece to the earlier film, in which he could explore Vito Corleone's rise to power while simultaneously depicting Michael's continuing fall from grace. From his earliest involvement with *The*

Godfather, Coppola had been ultrasensitive to criticism that he was glorifying the Mafia; *Godfather II* would give him the chance to put that ugly accusation to rest.

Each offer from Paramount was sweeter than the preceding one. Coppola could have complete artistic control of his film, including its casting; he could name his own fee for writing and directing the picture. He could even, as he insisted, kill off Michael Corleone, thus jeopardizing the chances of any other *Godfather* sequels that might be lurking in the shadows somewhere up the road.

Peter Bart, so instrumental in Coppola's hiring in the first *Godfather,* met with Coppola and asked him outright what it would take to get him signed.

"*You* were the star of *The Godfather,*" he told Coppola, not even attempting to disguise the ego stroking. "What does a star get?"

"A million dollars."

"If I can get you a million to write and direct," Bart went on, "will you do it?"

Coppola said that he would, as long as Paramount met two other conditions. First and foremost, Coppola wanted Robert Evans completely out of the picture.

"I said that I wanted Evans to have zero to do with it," he stated in 1999. "He was not to read it, not to have any say in it whatsoever, and not to be involved when it was being edited." Coppola vigorously disputed Evans's published claims of having been involved in the film: "Evans had zero involvement in *Godfather II*—not in the writing phase, the preproduction phase, the shooting phase, or the editing phase. A little research could easily confirm this."

Coppola also wanted to call the new picture *The Godfather, Part II*—a title that was not immediately embraced by Paramount. According to the studio, people would find the title confusing, and believe that the new movie was the second half of the original *Godfather.* Besides, they told Coppola, no one had ever entitled a film in this fashion.

"What about *Ivan the Terrible, Part II*?" Coppola argued.

"Oh, but that's a Russian film," Paramount countered. "We mean an American film."

When Bart called Charles Bluhdorn to relay the finer points of his conversation with Coppola, Bluhdorn was ecstatic. "Close the deal!" he cried. "Where are the papers! Do it, do it!"

The million-dollar offer, however, turned out to be only a display of Coppola's readiness to negotiate seriously. By the time he had agreed to terms with

Paramount and the press was alerted to the fact that he was on board as the producer, writer, and director of *Godfather II*, Coppola's tough stance had been rewarded handsomely with a contract calling for him to earn $250,000 for cowriting the screenplay, $200,000 for directing the movie, and an additional $50,000 for producing it. The big money, however, rested in the film's potential, in Coppola's whopping 13 percent of the film's adjusted gross earnings. Almost as important, from Coppola's perspective, was the agreement that he would be working without the kind of studio interference that had driven him to the brink while he was shooting *The Godfather*. He would be virtually autonomous in the sequel, making all the important artistic decisions.

On July 31, 1972, Paramount officially announced that it would be making *The Godfather, Part II*, ending months of rumor and speculation about the sequel. The movie was scheduled to premiere on March 27, 1974—almost exactly two years after the opening of the original—and with Coppola once again writing and directing, the picture promised to deliver the same quality as *The Godfather*.

"It will not be an exploitation picture," Paramount insisted in its announcement to the press. "The new film will have the same look, the same integrity of the original. Coppola believes the new story will be even better than the first one."

3.

PARAMOUNT HAD ACTUALLY SIGNED Mario Puzo to write a script for *Godfather II* in August 1971, more than six months before the premiere of *The Godfather*. Coppola had just completed shooting the *Godfather* scenes in Sicily, and despite the fabled difficulties with the first movie, and the fact that Paramount could only speculate about how the picture was going to go over with the public, the studio felt confident enough in its prospects at least to explore the possibilities of a sequel. Buoyed by a significant raise in his writing fee, which included a percentage of the movie's take, Puzo began working on a screenplay tentatively entitled *The Death of Michael Corleone*.

Coppola quite naturally had his own ideas about the story line for *Godfather II*, and once he had agreed to work on the script, he and Puzo collaborated in the same fashion as they had on *The Godfather*, each working separately. From the beginning, Coppola had been enticed by the prospects of telling two stories in the movie, the first showing Vito Corleone as a young man on his way up, establishing what would become the most powerful crime family on the East Coast; the other depicting his son Michael at virtually the same age, presiding over the same family, now in tatters and losing its influence. Coppola still viewed the story as being quintessentially American—no different, he insisted in interviews, from the stories of such families as the Kennedys or the Rothschilds, each founded by powerful, influential patricians, each experiencing both subtle and dramatic changes as one generation succeeded its predecessor. Americans had always been attracted to stories of wealth and power, and in continuing the *Godfather* stories, Coppola would be fleshing out what was turning into a morality play of epic proportion.

"From the very beginning, when people started to write plays, they always wrote about the head man, the king," he explained. "And in some way, through that kind of drama, people are able to better understand themselves or learn some way of looking at themselves. Maybe, in the attempt to grapple with our own sense of powerlessness or insignificance, these dramas make us feel we amount to more than we really do. But it was always the king. People have a fascination for power, and some an appetite for it."

For Coppola, it was crucial that the sequel show Michael, for all his wealth and apparent worldly success, as a loser in life. He would "kill" Michael, but not in the literal sense. Instead, Michael would lose his wife and children, be betrayed by friends and family, and wind up utterly alone, a victim of his own character flaws. Unlike his father, who had earned his slice of the American dream, Michael would lose what had been given to him, including a standard he could not follow, the dream eroded into a stark, haunting memory.

Mario Puzo also favored exposing Michael's moral bankruptcy, but he differed with Coppola on one critical point. In Puzo's opinion, Coppola was being too didactic in driving home the moral of his story. If Puzo had had his way, he would have taken a darker, more subtle approach, in which evil wasn't necessarily punished by Michael's losing as much as he does in the film. Instead, he would gain the world but lose his soul.

"I would have showed Michael at the height of his power, everybody around him," said Puzo. "Everybody loves him, his wife comes back, his children come back. Everything is great with him. He's the only one who knows what's happening to him." Although he conceded that it was hard to second-guess Coppola's approach, since it had worked so well with audiences, he nevertheless maintained that the final version was "too much on the nose, too blatant."

Significantly, *The Godfather, Part II* opens in Sicily. Rather than offer an affirmation of the American dream, as at the start of *The Godfather*, when Bonasera utters the famous opening line, "I believe in America," *Godfather II* begins with a funeral procession for young Vito's father, who has been murdered for slighting a local don. The don, fearing a vendetta when Vito and his older brother grow up, orders the two boys killed, as well. After seeing her older son murdered, Vito's mother takes her remaining son to the don and pleads for his life. When the don refuses to reconsider, Vito's mother holds a knife to his throat while Vito escapes. She is shot dead for trying to protect him.

Local villagers hide the young boy until he can be sent to America. At Ellis Island, Vito's surname is changed from Andolini to Corleone, the name of the Italian village from which he has come. Doctors determine that Vito has smallpox, and he is quarantined at Ellis Island, left alone in a room with a view of the Statue of Liberty.

At this point, the story jumps forward to 1958, to Lake Tahoe, Nevada, where Michael Corleone and his family are now living. Michael's son, Anthony, has just received his First Communion, and in a scene designed to echo the wedding scene at the opening of *The Godfather,* a huge party is taking place on the Corleone estate. However, unlike the wedding scene, in which the Godfather is shown respect while granting favors to friends and acquaintances, the Communion party scene reflects the mob family in a downslide. A Nevada senator, after publicly accepting a large donation from Michael Corleone, privately berates him and tries to shake him down for a kickback in exchange for a liquor license for one of the Corleone family's casinos. Angered by the senator's insults, Michael refuses to give him a cent.

Frankie "Five Angels" Pentangeli, one of the family's *caporegimes,* meets with Michael and Tom Hagen and reports on the family's activities in New York. The times are not good. Pentangeli suggests that the family take action against the Rosato brothers, a rival faction cutting into the Corleone family's profits, but Michael nixes the idea, telling Pentangeli that he has plans that require peace between the Corleones and the Rosatos.

Later that evening, gunfire erupts on the Corleone compound and the windows to Michael's bedroom are shot out, Michael and Kay narrowly escaping assassination. Michael immediately suspects that the murder plot was instigated from within his own organization, and he hastily prepares to leave Lake Tahoe for Miami. In his absence, Tom Hagen will be running operations. In one of the film's few truly touching scenes, Michael visits his son's bedroom to kiss him good-bye, and Anthony asks if he can help his father.

In another flashback, we see Vito, now a young adult with a family, living in the Little Italy section of Manhattan. Vito has been in the United States for over a decade, but he is still ignorant of the ways of the New World—a fact that is brought home when he and a friend attend a small local opera production and Vito's friend accidentally insults Don Fanucci, the most powerful and feared figure in Little Italy. Although he has witnessed firsthand the consequences of angering the local don in Sicily, Vito initially finds it difficult to accept that the same kind of business is taking place in the United States.

He quickly learns otherwise. He has a job at a small grocery store, and one day Fanucci walks in with a nephew in need of employment. The store owner, the father of Vito's best friend (and future business partner) has no choice but to fire Vito and replace him with the don's relative. Vito surprises his boss by taking the news in stride, even though he is now without a means of supporting his family.

A short time later, he is sitting at home, eating dinner with his family, when he hears a rap on the window. It is Clemenza, a young neighborhood tough, who asks Vito to hide a package for him—guns wrapped in a towel. Vito does so without questioning Clemenza. When he comes back to reclaim the gun, a grateful Clemenza offers to give Vito a rug as a gift, but he needs Vito to help him carry it back to Vito's apartment. Vito accompanies Clemenza to an unfamiliar apartment, only to learn that his "gift" has to be stolen. The theft is briefly interrupted by someone knocking at the door, and for a few tense moments, Vito hides and watches Clemenza stand near the door, out of sight but with his gun drawn, until the visitor leaves. Vito's life of crime has officially begun.

The action again jumps forward to 1958, to the film's longest segment involving either Michael or Vito. Michael has taken a train to Miami, where he meets with Hyman Roth, the powerful chieftain of the Jewish mob. Both Michael and Roth feign affection for each other, but their apparent friendship is actually a relationship forged out of respect (if not fear) of each other's power, and the need to do business together. In many respects, Roth is similar to Michael's late father, who never let the personal interfere with business.

Roth is very dangerous, and Michael knows it, even as he prepares to join forces with Roth in a lucrative deal that will all but have them taking over the gambling establishments in Cuba. Michael correctly suspects that Roth's organization was responsible for the attempt on his life, but he has no way of knowing—or suspecting—that the insider who set him up was none other than his older brother Fredo, who has been secretly dealing with the Roth organization with the intention of strengthening the Corleone's interests in Las Vegas. After years of toiling in Michael's shadow, and having little say in any of the Corleone family's business dealings, Fredo is looking for a way to contribute, and thus, in a small way, make a name for himself. Unfortunately, in his association with the Roth organization, he unwittingly jeopardized Michael's life.

However, as we saw in the last half of *The Godfather,* and as we see in its sequel, Michael has grown accustomed to living in the midst of treachery; it's all part of the game, of doing successful business. In New York, the Rosato brothers, working under Roth, stage an attempted assassination on Pentangeli, which they try to hang on Michael Corleone. Meanwhile, the Corleone family exacts its revenge on Senator Geary by drugging him and placing a murdered prostitute in his room. By blackmailing the senator, the Corleone family no longer has to worry about the senator's using his political clout against them.

In Cuba, Michael attempts to close his deal with Roth and the corrupt Cuban government, but his journey is tainted when, at a New Year's party, he learns of Fredo's duplicity and when, a short time later, his ordered assassination of Roth is thwarted. He returns to Lake Tahoe, only to learn that Kay has miscarried what would have been his second son.

In a contrasting flashback, we see young Vito Corleone's moment of truth. Vito has been engaged in small-time criminal activities with Clemenza and Tessio, another friend, much to the displeasure of Don Fanucci, who demands an exorbitant cut of the take. Vito explains that he doesn't have the money, but Fanucci makes it clear that he had better come up with it. Vito meets with Clemenza and Tessio and discusses an alternative plan, in which they will give him some—but not all—of the money that he is demanding. Clemenza and Tessio balk at Vito's suggestion, but Vito holds his ground. Fanucci, he insists, is a reasonable man, and Vito intends to make him an offer he can't refuse.

Vito meets with Fanucci in the back of a restaurant. He had brought only a portion of the money he owes Fanucci, which elicits a mixed response from the don. On the one hand, he is unhappy that Vito has defied him; on the other hand, he is impressed by Vito's courage—so much so that he tells Vito that he probably can find a place for him in his organization.

Both leave the restaurant, Fanucci walking down the streets of Little Italy, now flooded with throngs of people celebrating a religious festival, Vito following him by jumping from rooftop to rooftop of the buildings overhead. Vito arrives at Fanucci's apartment building before the don, and after disconnecting the lights in the hall, he hides in the hallway and waits for him. When Fanucci shows up at his apartment, Vito murders him with a gun wrapped in a towel. With Fanucci out of the way, and Clemenza and Tessio loyal to him, Vito is poised to become the new don of Little Italy.

At this point, the contrasts between Vito and Michael couldn't be sharper, and the crosscutting of their stories picks up at a faster pace. While Vito's star continues to rise in his portion of the dual plotlines, Michael struggles mightily to maintain his position. A Senate committee investigating organized crime has its sights set on the Corleone family, with Willi Cicci, once a loyal member of the family, testifying against Michael and his organization. To make matters worse, Michael has lost his immediate family: He is estranged from Connie, who defied him by marrying a gigolo interested only in the family fortune, and from Fredo, who betrayed him; he is barely on speaking terms with Kay, who has given up hope of Michael ever honoring his promise of going legitimate.

Vito, conversely, has become a sort of benign dictator of Little Italy—a figure of power and authority who looks after the best interests of the people in the neighborhood, particularly immigrants being squashed by other authoritarian forces. In a scene both humorous and poignant, Vito intercedes on the behalf of a woman who has been evicted from her apartment by a greedy landlord looking to earn more money by renting the apartment to another tenant. Vito offers to pay the difference in rent himself, but the landlord, unaware of Vito's standing in the community, sneers at his offer. Later, after learning about Vito from others, he approaches the new don, offering the apartment to the woman at a reduced rate.

The Senate hearings drive the final wedge between Michael and Kay, who watches Michael lie under oath about the nature of his business. Michael's testimony had been anticipated by the Senate investigators, who promise to bring forth a star witness who will corroborate everything that Cicci told the committee earlier. The witness, to Michael's surprise, is Frankie Pentangeli, who, contrary to the information given to Michael, was not murdered by the Rosato brothers, but who is instead living under the government's witness protection program.

Michael has a trump card of his own. When Frankie enters the Senate chambers to testify, he looks out in the audience and sees his brother, flown in from Sicily, seated with Michael and Tom Hagen. The implications are obvious, and Pentangeli suddenly has nothing to say to the committee. Kay, disgusted by Michael's behavior, confronts him. The two quarrel, and Kay reveals that she did not have a miscarriage, as she had previously reported to Michael. Unable to bear the prospects of having more of Michael's children, she had the baby aborted.

(This particular plot twist, remembered Talia Shire, was one of her major contributions to the movie. According to Shire, the original script called for Kay to bear Michael a son, only to leave with him when she left her husband. To Shire, this didn't ring true. "We were all up in Lake Tahoe, and Francis was writing the scene. And I said, 'You know, Francis, Kay would never have the baby and run off with him. She would terminate the pregnancy—which is a very brutal thing to do—and say, "I cannot carry your line."' And Francis said,

'You know, you're right!' What Francis did was give me a huge gift for that suggestion: one of the movie's most beautiful speeches, which comes later in the movie, when I walk across the room and kneel at Michael's feet and say, 'You know, we've never gotten along. . . .' That scene gave me hope for an Oscar nomination.")

In the final extended flashback scene, Vito returns to Sicily to avenge the murders of his family members. By this time, the Sicilian don is old and feeble, barely able to move, let alone threaten anyone. Nor does he remember who Vito is. This is of no concern to Vito, who plunges a knife into the old man's abdomen and eviscerates him. He has put his past to rest.

The death of Mama Corleone gives Michael the chance to settle some of the issues of his own past when Connie approaches him, seeking a reconciliation, and then begs him to forgive Fredo. Michael approaches Fredo at the funeral home, and the two embrace, the family seemingly together again.

Except, of course, for Kay, who has left Michael and the children. Kay visits the children regularly, but it is clear that Michael has turned them—particularly Anthony—against her. On one of her visits, she stays too long, trying to solicit a good-bye kiss from her son, and she is confronted by a stony, silent Michael, who coldly closes the door in her face, symbolically shutting her out of his and their children's lives.

The closing, like the montage ending of *The Godfather*, shows Michael ridding himself of his enemies. Hyman Roth is gunned down in the Miami airport as he returns from Cuba to live out his final days in the States. After talking to Tom Hagen and being reassured that his family will be taken care of, Frankie Pentangeli commits suicide. Most shocking of all, Michael has Fredo shot while he is fishing on the lake.

(According to Mario Puzo, he and Coppola disagreed about Michael's having Fredo murdered. "When he first said that he wanted to kill Fredo," Puzo recalled, "I said, 'You cannot do that. He would never kill his brother.' But Francis was adamant. So I said, 'Well, you can't kill him until their mother is dead.' And Francis listened. We both gave way, and we both came up with the solution.")

The story concludes with a brief flashback of the Corleone family—Sonny, Fredo, Michael, and Tom Hagen—assembled for their father's birthday in 1941. In a scene that effectively ties the two films together, Michael announces that he has ignored his father's wishes and has joined the marines. Sonny, true to form, is outraged. Fredo congratulates Michael. Tom expresses disappointment, mentioning that Vito Corleone has great hopes for his youngest son. The group leaves to greet their father in another room, leaving

Michael alone, as he is in the film's final frames, when he is seen sitting alone after the murder of his brother, his expression as hollow as his life has become.

4.

COPPOLA'S INTERCUTTING OF STORIES proved to be very controversial when *The Godfather, Part II* was released in December 1974. Viewers and critics alike found the film's dual plots difficult to follow, especially in some of the more complex sequences, such as the bogus attempt on Pentangeli's life. Reviewers complained, with some justification, that some of the movie's scenes were implausible and that other scenes were left unresolved, as if crucial details had been sacrificed in the film's editing. After seeing an early version of the picture, George Lucas urged Coppola to simplify his film. "Francis," he told his friend, "you have two movies. Throw one away. It doesn't work."

Coppola, of course, disagreed. When he first set out to write the script for *Godfather II,* he claimed, to anyone who would listen, that he had no intention of following the traditional Hollywood pattern for a sequel. He realized that because of the success of *The Godfather,* he had a built-in audience for the follow-up, but one of his stiffest challenges was to design something equal to or better than the original. Two years earlier, he had been limited by the necessity of staying reasonably faithful to the source material, a novel that had all but become part of the popular culture. There was very little unused material that he could work into the new picture, and he had ideas for the small portion of the novel—the flashback scenes in Little Italy—that he planned on using. *Godfather II,* he decided, could be developed into a personal film in which he could address his own ancestry.

Thus, the scenes in Little Italy became his favorites, and, in writing the screenplay (and eventually filming the movie), he labored to bring the early-twentieth-century Italian immigrant experience alive, historically accurate and compelling. In addition, he was able to add personal touches that gave the story heightened meaning for his own family. Young Vito's being quarantined on Ellis Island reflected on Coppola's aunt Caroline, who had been similarly isolated, or on Coppola himself, and his lonely battle with polio. When Vito and his friend attend the opera, the musical production being performed is *Senza Mama,* a popular tale about immigrants in America, written by Francesco Pennino, Coppola's maternal grandfather.

Although Coppola insisted that the formal screen title to the movie be *Mario Puzo's The Godfather, Part II,* the authorship would belong more to Coppola than to the novelist. In the end, Puzo's main contributions included the stories of young Vito Corleone taken from the book, along with the Senate investigation scenes. He was still the creator of the major characters, of course, but in the sequel, Coppola assumed greater authority in guiding their actions.

"I don't know whether it's an original screenplay or an adaptation," Coppola responded when asked about how he and Puzo had written the script. "Obviously, the overall architecture and the body of the script is mine, but then again, the overall concept of the family and the characters is his. So, because of all that, I feel justified in crediting the script to both of us."

Coppola struggled with the screenplay for months, puzzling over characterization and pacing, trying to find a way to make it compatible with *The Godfather* yet, at the same time, a separate work of art. A master of rewrite, Coppola found his own skills continuously tested, especially when, shortly before the filming commenced, Al Pacino told him he didn't like the way his part had been written. Coppola, already hopelessly overworked, rewrote all of the Michael Corleone scenes in just three days.

As Coppola would admit, writing a script in this fashion was a less than optimum experience. "I got myself in a real bind," he reported. "When a novelist takes on an ambitious theme, he works on it for two years. I had to write the script for *Godfather II* in three months, and then go right into preproduction. I was making a $13-million movie as if it were a Roger Corman picture."

5.

IN THE MONTHS LEADING UP to the shooting of *Godfather II*, Coppola managed to re-sign most of the principal cast and crew members from *The Godfather* to work on the sequel. To Coppola's disappointment, Marlon Brando was out, unable to reach agreement with Paramount on how he would be compensated for his return in *Godfather II*. Coppola, counting on having Brando for a pivotal scene at the end of the movie, devised an innovative way to make the scene work without the star.

"Originally, Brando was going to be in the last scene," Coppola explained. "My idea had been to have the movie straddle the two time periods—modern and old—and end in the same period as the first movie. In fact, it was to end with a scene between Vito and Michael, about Michael's decision to join the marines. We spent a lot of money getting the actors for that—Jimmy Caan, for example. But the night before we were going to shoot the ending, Marlon pulled one of his stunts and said he wouldn't show. Or perhaps it's true that Paramount antagonized him. Whatever.

"I was in a real mess. I had spent all this money getting the other cast members for it, and now Marlon wasn't going to show. Late that night, in bed, the answer came to me: have the scene be a surprise birthday party for Vito, and have everyone else run out of the room, leaving Michael alone. I typed it on my little Olivetti in my bed. That's how we shot it the next day, and that's how it is in the movie."

Richard Castellano, Clemenza in *The Godfather,* was out, as well. Castellano not only wanted a substantial salary increase for reprising his role in the new picture but also demanded that Paramount hire his girlfriend to rewrite his dialogue. Conversely, James Caan and Abe Vigoda, whose Sonny Corleone and Sal Tessio characters had been rubbed out in *The Godfather,* agreed to appear in a brief flashback scene at the end of the sequel.

Others returning from the first part included Robert Duvall (Tom Hagen), John Cazale (Fredo), Diane Keaton (Kay), Talia Shire (Connie), and, in greatly expanded roles, Tom Rosqui (Rocco Lampone) and Richard Bright (Al Neri). Coppola had been impressed with the way Cazale and Keaton had handled their rather limited roles in *The Godfather,* and, in putting together the screenplay for the sequel, he searched for ways to deepen their characters and involve them more in the film's plot.

Once again, it took some effort to cast Al Pacino as Michael Corleone, but this time around, there were no disputes over Pacino's qualifications for the part. After appearing in *The Godfather,* Pacino had gone immediately to work on *Scarecrow* and *Serpico,* his portrayal of the title role in the latter eventually earning him another Oscar nomination. Now one of the most sought-after leading men in Hollywood, Pacino hesitated before accepting his old role in *Godfather II.* There was little to be gained, he felt, by repeating himself, and he was insulted by Paramount's initial $100,000 offer.

It soon became apparent that Pacino would not be enticed into the role merely by waving more money at him. After rejecting a number of offers, each proposal increasing the actor's salary until the number stood at $450,000, Pacino met with Paramount officials in the company's New York office.

"There was a bottle of J&B on the table," Pacino recalled of the meeting. "We began drinking, talking, laughing, and the producer opened his drawer and he pulled out a tin box. I was sitting on the other side and he pushed it over in my direction. He said, 'What if I were to tell you that there was $1,000,000 in cash there?' I said, 'It doesn't mean anything—it's an abstraction.' It was the damnedest thing: I ended up kind of apologizing for not taking the million."

It took Francis Ford Coppola to change the actor's mind. Pacino had seen an early Mario Puzo draft of the screenplay, which, while intriguing him, was not enough to make him reverse his stance. However, when Coppola offered him one of his patented sales pitches, talking up the screenplay and his plans for *Godfather II,* Pacino could refuse no longer.

"He was so wigged out by the prospect of doing it, he would inspire anybody," Pacino remembered. "The hairs on my head stood up. You can feel that sometimes with a director. I usually say, if you feel that with a director, go with him."

The money wasn't bad, either. In the end, Pacino signed on for $600,000 and 10 percent of the movie's adjusted gross income—quite a jump from the flat $35,000 he had received for the first picture.

With the exception of some opposition by Frank Yablans, the decision to cast Robert De Niro as the young Vito Corleone was both easy and ironic. Coppola had been greatly impressed with De Niro when the actor auditioned for the role of Sonny Corleone in *The Godfather*—"I thought he was very magnetic and had a lot of style"—and he had noticed what he felt was a vague resemblance between De Niro and Marlon Brando, especially in the way they both smiled, which led him to believe that De Niro would work out well in the sequel. Like Pacino, De Niro had registered some very impressive work since his *Godfather* tryout, most recently as a street hood in Martin Scorsese's *Mean Streets.*

"When Marty showed me a very early cut and I watched Bobby, I just decided that it would be him," said Coppola. "Bobby was not as well-known then as he became two months later when *Mean Streets* and *Bang the Drum Slowly* came out. So very early I just made the decision, unilaterally, that he was right and that he could do it."

Bold, if not ingenious, casting paid off elsewhere, as well. Michael Gazzo, an actor and producer/director perhaps best known for his 1955 play, *A Hatful of Rain,* was hired to play Frankie Pentangeli, a character created by Coppola when Richard Castellano was written out of the picture; Italian actor Gastone Moschin, whom Coppola had admired in Bertolucci's *The Conformist,* was awarded the meaty role of Don Fanucci. Former teen idol Troy Donahue was offered the part of Merle Johnson, Connie Corleone's third husband.

Coppola's biggest casting surprise, however, was in his hiring of Lee Strasberg, the seventy-three-year-old director of New York's renowned Actors Studio, to play Jewish gangster Hyman Roth. Both Al Pacino and Robert De Niro had studied at the Actors Studio, and Pacino had suggested that Coppola cast Strasberg in the role. Strasberg had never appeared in a motion picture, and it had been decades since he had acted onstage, yet his reputation as the world's foremost acting teacher frightened Coppola in much the same way that Marlon Brando had intimidated him a couple of years earlier. How could he, Francis Ford Coppola, give direction to a man who had trained some of the greatest actors in the business? Would Strasberg respond by spouting acting theory at him?

Before offering Strasberg the part, Coppola got together with him socially. The meeting, arranged by Sally Kirkland, went well, with Coppola and Strasberg talking about classical music, Toscanini, and Coppola's father's days with the NBC Orchestra. Several days later, Paramount called and formally offered Strasberg ten thousand dollars for his appearance in the movie. Strasberg, put off by the offer, immediately rejected the studio, holding out until Paramount raised its offer to $58,000. A year later, Strasberg was still shaking his head over the initial offer. "Ten thousand dollars," he scoffed. "That was silly."

Strasberg would eventually receive an Academy Award nomination for Best Supporting Actor—as would Robert De Niro and Michael Gazzo—proving, if nothing else, that Coppola's casting instincts were as sharp as they had been when he battled Paramount executives over his selections for *The Godfather.*

6.

AS IMPORTANT AS THEY WERE, the casting decisions for *Godfather II* were only part of the selection process. Early in the game, while he was still roughing out the plot for his new screenplay, Coppola decided that he wanted to create a story so connected to the characters and events in *The Godfather* that he could eventually edit the two movies into a single six-hour epic. While this would be challenging enough to accomplish just in terms of the screenwriting, it also required a strong continuity from a technical standpoint. Ideally, this meant bringing back as many of the original crew as possible.

Production designer Dean Tavoularis, so instrumental in creating the moody atmosphere in the first movie, would be returning, as would makeup artist Dick Smith and special-effects men A. D. Flowers and Joe Lombardi. Nino Rota, composer of the haunting *Godfather* theme song, would be handling the music, with Carmine Coppola assuming a greater role in both conducting and composing.

Coppola debated asking Gordon Willis to return as the director of photography. Although he admired Willis's technical skills and readily attributed much of *The Godfather*'s success to his camerawork, Coppola winced at the thought of reprising the kind of heated exchanges that had marked his and Willis's working relationship in the first movie. With this in mind, Coppola contacted Vittorio Storaro, the Italian cinematographer who had recently earned kudos for his work on *Last Tango in Paris,* but Storaro, believing that the sequel could not possibly measure up to the lofty standards of its predecessor, declined Coppola's invitation. Coppola called Willis and hoped for the best.

Principal photography began on October 1, 1973, with a budget set at $11 million, which would balloon to $13 million by the time Coppola had finished his picture. The first scenes, shot in Lake Tahoe, set a tone for all that would follow: While the work was top-notch in every imaginable way, the going was slow and tedious, fraught with complications and, to some extent, a feeling of impatience. The First Communion and party scenes gobbled up two weeks of shooting, the slow pace placing Coppola behind schedule almost as soon as he had left the gate.

Michael Corleone's Lake Tahoe residence, as designed by Dean Tavoularis, could not have been more different from Vito Corleone's compound in the first movie. The elder Corleone had gathered his family around him, preserving at least a semblance of a home; Michael's place was a fortress, surrounded by walls and shielded by a lake, his isolated family virtually captive in their own house. The actual estate used for the compound, built in 1934 by Henry Kaiser, also served as living quarters for the cast and crew, while Coppola and his family stayed in a stone bungalow near the lake.

The fall shooting schedule proved to be problematic. The decreasing daylight hours created lighting problems and cut into the available shooting time for the daytime exterior scenes. Chilly temperatures, compounded by winds whistling in from over the lake, wreaked havoc on the filming of the Communion party scenes which, according to the script, were supposed to be taking place outdoors during the summertime. Crew members bundled the cast in heavy coats whenever the cameras were not rolling; extras wore long underwear beneath their summer clothing. The director himself donned a wool stocking cap and stowed an old-fashioned hand warmer in his coat pocket. Temperatures were even more brutal after sundown, when Coppola shot the nighttime exterior scenes.

The weeks of isolation wore on people's nerves, including those of Eleanor Coppola, who grew depressed by the gray, almost Spartan conditions, so different from the cosmopolitan environment she normally enjoyed in San Francisco. Al Pacino, temperamental to begin with, and no longer the rather wide-eyed young actor he had been during the filming of *The Godfather,* took exception to Coppola's slow working pace, especially when he compared it to the faster pace of other directors with whom he had worked. "Why the hell does it take so long to shoot a scene?" he wondered, shortly after the company relocated to Las Vegas after six weeks in Lake Tahoe. "Lumet shot *Serpico* in eighteen days!" The complaint, eventually spawning an altercation between the actor and his director, didn't spur Coppola to move any faster.

The Las Vegas shoot, lasting several days and finding Coppola and company working between 4:00 A.M. and noon, when business around the city and at the Tropicana Hotel were at a crawl, provided a welcome improvement from the harshness of Lake Tahoe, even if very little of the footage found its way into the final cut.* With the holiday season and year's end rapidly approaching, Coppola moved the production to soundstages in Hollywood, where most of the film's interior shots were filmed.

Despite the hectic daily pace and the fact that he had fallen behind his shooting schedule, Coppola felt much more relaxed than he had felt during any period during the filming of *The Godfather.* This time around, he was in charge, getting along as well as could be expected with his acting and production companies, slowly but surely assembling his movie and determining its course without interference from corporate officials. In the grueling, uncertain process of filmmaking, Coppola was as close to being satisfied with his work in progress as he could be.

7.

HIS FORTUNES CHANGED DRAMATICALLY in late February of 1974, when Al Pacino came down with pneumonia and was incapacitated for the better part of a month.

On January 2, Coppola had brought the production to Santo Domingo, which was to serve as the shooting location for all of the movie's scenes taking place in Cuba and Miami. Unfortunately, the Caribbean weather refused to cooperate, and rather than work in the sunny, tropical environment that he was hoping for, Coppola had to contend with nonstop rain. An exhausted Al Pacino, who had enjoyed very little downtime since his work in the first *Godfather* picture, fell victim to the combination of heavy workload and inclement weather. Doctors ordered him to take several weeks off.

While Pacino recuperated, Coppola turned his movie's dual plots to his advantage by filming the Little Italy scenes in New York. To re-create the streets of Little Italy as they appeared around the time of World War I, Dean Tavoularis and his crew had cordoned off a section of East Sixth Street in

---

*In fact, none of the Las Vegas footage was used in *Godfather II,* and only fragments in the restored *The Godfather Epic.*

lower Manhattan, between Avenues A and B, which was then given a complete makeover, from construction of authentic-looking storefronts and outdoor markets to the dirt in the street. This was the most personal portion of the film for Coppola, and he spared no expense and overlooked no detail in making Little Italy appear as if viewers were stepping into a time capsule transporting them back to a time when immigrants were still struggling to gain a foothold in the new country, when old-world and new-world customs met almost cataclysmically, creating a new chemistry in America's melting pot.

Robert De Niro had gone to great lengths to prepare himself for his role. In the months prior to his appearance before cameras, De Niro had traveled to Sicily to live among and observe the local people so that he could familiarize himself with as much of their culture and history as time permitted; in the United States, he worked with a tutor on learning his Sicilian lines, listening to them on a tape recorder and repeating them endlessly until he was confident that he could speak them convincingly.

"You just have to put in the time," De Niro explained when asked about his crash course in Sicilian. "I wanted to have those lines down so securely that I wouldn't have to think about it. I probably understand more than I speak, but it's a hard language."

Coppola, for one, was impressed by De Niro's ability and professionalism.

"His assignment is incredibly difficult when you consider he's being asked to play one of the most famous actors in the world in a character that he received tremendous credit for," Coppola said in an interview at the time. Furthermore, Coppola continued, De Niro was expected to develop the character in an unfamiliar language. "Learning and working in a foreign language could be a tremendous liability for an actor," Coppola remarked, "but Bobby is such a unified, concentrated guy that he did it."

De Niro, wise enough to realize that he could only harm his portrayal of young Vito Corleone by closely imitating Brando's performance as the elder Vito, watched the original *Godfather* numerous times and decided to take a subtle approach in his interpretation of the part. While he could not deny or ignore the work that had come before him, he could use Brando's portrayal as a guideline and go from there.

"It's like being a scientist or technician," De Niro observed. "Audiences already know Vito Corleone. I watch him and I say, 'That's an interesting gesture. When could he have started to do that?' It's my job as an actor to find things I can make connections with. I must find things and figure out how I can use them, in what scenes can I use them to suggest what the older man will be like."

Coppola's faith in casting De Niro in the role was rewarded by a tour de force performance that ultimately earned the actor an Academy Award. While comparisons of Brando and De Niro were inevitable in the reviews of *Godfather II*, as well as in the minds of moviegoers, De Niro pulled off the role in such a way that there was little disputing that he *was* Vito Corleone in his youth, and viewers were all too willing to suspend any skepticism arising from the actors' physical differences in favor of their absorption in the performances themselves.

8.

ALL TOLD, *THE GODFATHER, PART II* took nearly nine months to shoot, from its opening sequences filmed in October 1973 to its wrap in June 1974. The ambitious project exacted its toll on everyone connected to the picture, from director on down, presenting physical and psychological challenges that, on more than one occasion, found Coppola wondering aloud if he might be better off retiring from the movie business and taking on a less stressful career. Life had been much easier when he was an unknown working on smaller projects, as either a screenwriter or director; he was presently a kind of Godfather himself, overseeing a big-budget movie and the activities of a large company, knowing that he alone would be held accountable if the new movie failed to live up to expectations. The ambitious side of him, of course, desired the attention, responsibility, and respect, but at the same time, he regretted the way that filmmaking took away from his family life. He could have done without the constant pressure that left him drained and irritable, and the self-doubts that edged him into worrying about whether he was creating something of lasting value.

As with *The Godfather*, Coppola trusted his ambition and artistic vision wherever they took him, regardless of the work involved, or the knowledge that it was likely that some excellent footage would wind up being cut from the movie. This proved to be true enough, as a number of the Little Italy scenes—of Italian immigrants working on the construction of the subway system; Enrico Caruso turning up in the neighborhood and singing "Over There" to encourage young men to enlist in the service; and young Vito's courtship of his wife, to name three such scenes—were never filmed, to Coppola's disappointment. Other scenes required extensive preparatory work for relatively short screen time. The Festa of San Rocco scene, in which Vito stalks Fanucci through the streets of Little Italy, involved what was at the time the largest call for extras ever registered by the Screen Actors Guild in New York. The sequences set at Ellis Island, filmed in Trieste over the Easter weekend of 1974, boasted of similarly complicated logistics—all for about two minutes of actual screen time.

Producer Gray Frederickson recalled another sequence in which Coppola took extraordinary measures to gain the exact effect that he was after.

"In the train station sequence, in which Robert De Niro revisits Sicily with his family, there's a scene where the train pulls into the station and they get off and go into town," Frederickson said, "and then there's a scene where he gets on the train and goes away. We found that station in a little town about an hour's drive from our hotel. Every morning, we'd load up everybody and drive over to this little town, and every morning it would be cloudy when we arrived. And we'd never get a shot. Gordon Willis would be standing around, looking up at the sky for hours and hours, and every once in a while he'd say, 'I think we're going to get a break here. It looks like the clouds are moving. Everybody hustle—run, run, run.' They'd get everything ready to go, and then the clouds wouldn't break. This went on for about ten days. They wouldn't shoot the scene without the sun because Sicily was supposed to be hot and sunny, in contrast to the gloomy scenes in New York. Everybody was going crazy. We finally wrapped and went home. We later found out that this town was at the base of Mt. Etna, and when the heat came out of the volcano, it hit the cold air in the sky and created clouds that always hung over this little town. No one had known that when we scouted locations. We eventually went back and got the scene at a better time of the year."

Throughout the late winter and spring, while he labored to keep his now overbudget and behind-schedule movie in control, Coppola received a number of mixed signals about how his work was being received by the press, the film industry, critics, and the general public—all contributing, no doubt, to his volatile mood swings. *American Graffiti,* already a blockbuster hit, earning Coppola an unexpected windfall for his investment as the movie's executive producer, captured a Golden Globe as 1973's Best Motion Picture—Musical/Comedy, leading Coppola to proclaim that the award, "in a way, [is] the best one I have." Coppola's moment of glory was brought into sharper focus a short time later when the film, nominated for five Academy Awards (including Best Picture), failed to take home a single statuette on April 2. But that was not all. Just a week before this, Coppola had cringed as *The Great Gatsby* premiered to largely hostile reviews, tying Coppola's name to still another Hollywood failure in adapting a classic novel for the big screen.

The mixed reaction to the release of *The Conversation* was perhaps the most perplexing of Coppola's concerns that spring. Walter Murch had done a magnificent job on the movie, not only in his sound editing but also in tying together some of the film's flimsier plot threads. "Walter Murch," Coppola told fellow director Brian De Palma, "collaborated with me on the film as much as possible. . . . He was cutting and a lot of the editorial decisions were his. He also constructed the tracks and mixed it alone in our little Zoetrope studio."

At best, the initial audience response to *The Conversation* was lukewarm. Box-office receipts were barely passable, and critics seemed confused as to how to react to a character as unlikable as Harry Caul, or to a plot that came off as paranoid, even when stacked up against the newspaper headlines issued during the Watergate era. Reviewers wrote respectfully of Coppola's mastery in writing and directing his film, but some took exception to the way that he distanced himself from his subject. "Like the conversation that Harry Caul eavesdrops on, this film seems to record life at a great distance and by purely mechanical means," offered Colin L. Westerbeck, Jr., in a review typical of the complaint. "However impressed we may be with Coppola's control over his material, we don't come away from the film feeling that he has even Harry Caul's pathetic capacity to let his passions interfere with his work."

Writing for *Esquire*, John Simon, always a tough critic, deemed the film's plot to be contrived and improbable, given Harry Caul's reputation in his business. "There is something profoundly irritating," Simon declared, "about a movie that presents its hero as a celebrated mastermind, and then proceeds to have him fall for a row of transparent stratagems."

In a review that spent most of its space praising the movie, especially its sound and cinematography, only to judge the film "a disappointment" that "lost me somewhere along the line," John M. Dower of the *Washington Post* best represented the ambivalence that some reviewers felt about *The Conversation*.

Coppola reacted angrily to the criticism—with some justification. Critics, he complained, wanted him to make art films like *The Conversation,* but then they turned on him and judged the work as if it was just another commercially driven movie. When he tried to do something in an unconventional manner, such as his development of Harry Caul's character, critics attacked him for not taking a conventional approach. The same critics who complained about the shoot-'em-up action of *The Godfather* were now grumbling that *The Conversation* moved too slowly and was too understated. Coppola conceded that the film was gloomy, but he denied being negative by nature.

A veteran of the passionate debates over the merits of his films, Coppola could take solace in the positive reviews, some of which ranked among the most enthusiastic reviews that he would ever receive. Jay Cocks of *Time* called *The Conversation* "a film of enormous enterprise and tension," while Paul D.

Zimmerman of *Newsweek* lauded the film as being "brilliantly original in its basic style and mood, and prophetically American in its vision of a monitored society." Penelope Gilliatt of *The New Yorker* was impressed by Coppola the auteur: "This is a screenplay of the first quality, written with the eerie foresight of a real writer. It is very simply directed. Nothing gets in the way of the intended double meanings of the script."

In the *New York Times*, Stephen Farber offered a glowing review, in which he echoed Gilliatt's observations about Coppola's skills as a director and screenwriter, concluding that although *The Conversation* was "one of the darkest and most disturbing films ever made in this country," . . . "it deserved a place in the pantheon of great art.

"*The Conversation* may not give *The Godfather* much competition in *Variety*'s list of top grossers," Farber allowed, "but it is Coppola's best movie, a landmark film of the seventies and a stunning piece of original American fiction. Literary critics who still look down on American movies should be required to see this film. I doubt that any American novel published this year will have the imagination and immediacy, the sheer dramatic power of *The Conversation*. Coppola has caught what it *feels* like to be living through this period of disillusionment and full-scale social disintegration."

Reviewers had noted that *The Conversation* had the feeling of a foreign film, so it should not have come as much of a surprise to Coppola when, at the end of May, his movie received a better reception overseas than in the United States, particularly at the Cannes Film Festival, where it received the prestigious Golden Palm for Best Film. The victory, however, was far from being totally satisfying. By the time *The Conversation* had claimed the top prize in the international film competition, it had all but slipped from sight in the United States—a box-office flop that forced Coppola to reconsider the types of films he was making and the kind of audiences he hoped to attract.

9.

COPPOLA SPENT MOST OF THE SPRING of 1974 overseas, first in Trieste, where he filmed the Ellis Island scenes for *Godfather II,* and then in Sicily, where he shot the sequences involving Vito as a young boy attending his father's funeral and, later, as an adult, avenging his father's murder.

In Trieste, Coppola embarked on a highly ambitious scene, even by his own standards. Il Grande Mercato Ittico all'Ingrosso, the city's enormous fish market, bore an uncanny structural likeness to the Ellis Island Immigration Arrival Center, and by the time Dean Tavoularis and his crew had finished their extensive reconstruction of the location, one could have sworn that

Coppola had shot the scenes at the American landmark itself. The call for extras, like the earlier call for the festival scene in Little Italy, was prodigious, with over eight hundred locals, all outfitted in turn-of-the-century costumes, milling about the set and playing the roles of immigrants awaiting the processing that would grant them entrance into the United States. In addition, Coppola enlisted the help of U.S. Marines Corps and U.S. Navy personnel, stationed on troop and ammunition-transport ships nearby, to stand in as American customs officials, medical personnel, and police stationed at Ellis Island.

By the time he had completed the principal photography for his new movie, Coppola had enough material for a five- or six-hour film, yet he was still uncertain about where *Godfather II* was going. Paramount remained uneasy about the story's ending, and there were plot elements that had to be worked out in postproduction. The answers would arrive in the months ahead. For the time being, Coppola could rest assured that he had the raw materials for a movie that rivaled his earlier masterwork.

Chapter Seven

Skirmishes Before the War

"I'm at a Y in the road. One path is to become a manager and an executive who brings about great changes. On the other, there's a very private notion to put my energy into developing as a writer and an artist. In the next five years, I want to break through creatively by my own standards. I don't think any film I have made even comes close to what I have in my heart."

—FRANCIS FORD COPPOLA

1.

THROUGHOUT HIS CAREER, Francis Ford Coppola has engaged in a remarkable range of activities apart from making major theatrical motion pictures. Oftentimes, his interest in such endeavors as directing an opera, making a high-tech video, or overseeing the operations of a vineyard have appeared to be in conflict with his work as a filmmaker, as if he cannot hold his concentration on writing or filming or postproduction—or, worse yet, as if he is searching for activities that might give him an excuse to avoid the *real* work. Much of the activity, of course, has arisen from financial necessity—Coppola has needed to earn huge sums of money, not only to pay debts, seed future film projects, and support a staff of employees but also to sustain his own expensive tastes and lifestyle—and much of it can be attributed to Coppola's need to satisfy his expansive ambitions.

Still, some of Coppola's activities are hard to understand. His increased involvement in *City* magazine, which commanded a fair amount of his attention during the summer of 1974, is one such example.

Upon completing the principal photography for *Godfather II* in mid-June, Coppola returned to the United States with an imposing workload ahead of him. Paramount still intended to release the movie on December 12, in time to capitalize on the increased number of moviegoers during the holiday season, but to have his film ready to meet this date, Coppola needed to pare down hundreds of hours of footage into a picture that, first and foremost, stood on its own, and, second, fit neatly into his plans for eventually combining both *Godfather* movies into a single epic film. Under the usual circumstances, the kind of postproduction work and time frame that Coppola faced might have frozen a director; the pressure was even greater for *Godfather II,* given the high expectations for the follow-up to the film industry's most successful movie.

Coppola recognized his professional stakes in *Godfather II*—in interviews, he expressed worry that he might lose artistic control over future films if the picture failed to live up to its advance billing—yet even as he and his postproduction staff worked feverishly on piecing the film together, working double time to beat a looming deadline, Coppola decided to take a more active role in the workings of *City* magazine.

One could easily understand Coppola's concern. He had already invested a substantial amount of money in a publication that he, by his own admission, did not particularly care for, yet as the months rolled on, it became apparent to media observers and the staff of the magazine that, for all his genius in other endeavors, Coppola knew virtually nothing about how to successfully publish a service magazine like *City.*

2.

THIS IS NOT TO STATE OR IMPLY that Coppola spent the great bulk of his waking hours on the magazine, especially in comparison to the amount of time that he would devote to the publication six months up the road. As expected, most of his attention was devoted to postproduction on *Godfather II,* with each passing workday reminding him that his race against the clock could influence the quality of his film. The movie's dual plots, Coppola realized, did not fit together as hoped, and though the original idea of presenting stories of Vito Corleone on the rise and Michael Corleone in decline appealed to his artistic sensibilities, Coppola knew enough about film audiences to conclude that he would lose them if he didn't construct an almost seamless story.

Public expectations for *Godfather II* were elevated even more in mid-November when, less than a month from the film's premiere date, NBC broadcast *The Godfather* for the first time on television. NBC had paid an eye-opening $10 million for the privilege of airing the film over a two-day period during sweeps month, and as an extra added attraction, Coppola was persuaded to appear as the on-screen host. By the time the numbers were tallied, *The Godfather* had drawn 90 million viewers, making it the fourth-largest audience draw for movies shown on television.

With the deadline for *Godfather II* closing in, the press reported every little development in the postproduction process. On the positive side, Coppola had trimmed the movie to a manageable running time of three hours and twenty minutes, down from its original rough-cut time of four hours and forty-five minutes. Portions of the plot had been changed or cut entirely, and Coppola felt he could still lop nearly ten minutes from the picture. On the negative side, there was talk that the film moved too slowly—an especially troubling criticism in the wake of the nagging, persistent rumor that the movie's plot, with all its cutting back and forth in time, was difficult to follow.

"The pressure is on, but no one seems nervous," reported Jon Carroll in the November 13 issue of *New York* magazine. "The progress of *Godfather II* has done nothing to refute another Coppola legend—his rough cuts look terrible. There are embarrassed silences after screenings. Old friends mutter darkly and avoid his eye. But it has happened before. It happened with the original *Godfather.*"

Coppola needed the feedback from a live audience, and on November 27, he flew to San Diego with Ellie, a group of friends, editors, coworkers, Paramount officials, and actor John Cazale for a sneak preview of his film. The showing drew a mixed response, with the full-house audience reacting favorably to much of the movie, but with Coppola coming away unhappy with the overall results. Throughout the screening, he muttered notes into a tiny tape recorder, and at a postpreview gathering at a nearby restaurant, he and his party agreed that there was still a great deal of work to be done. The film's final hour, they felt, was cold and confusing, and there was far too much intercutting of scenes. Some of the scenes needed to be combined, others compressed. The intermission that Coppola wanted was out of the question. Still, despite the results of the screening and the daunting task of pulling the movie together in the less than three weeks remaining before the New York premiere, Coppola kept at least an outward appearance of staying calm. "Would you believe this?" he quipped during the restaurant meeting. "It's just like college, doing a play: Johnny Cazale acts in it, Ellie does the sets, and Bob [Evans] . . . Bob is the rich kid whose father will print up the programs."

Over the ensuing weeks, Coppola and his editing crew worked feverishly to fine-tune the production.

"We were working day and night to get the mix finished," editor Barry Malkin explained. "I remember sleeping on the floor of the studio, just getting catnaps. We were almost on a 24-hour schedule. As I recall, we came back from the preview, put everyone's notes together, and made a large number of cuts in the film–eighty-some cuts, but nothing of tremendous import. It was mostly a lot of tightening up."

The Godfather, Part II appeared, on schedule, at the same five New York theaters that had originally introduced *The Godfather.* The movie, once released nationally, dominated the holiday season's box-office receipts, topping the *Variety* charts by Christmas, but it became evident early on that the film was not bound for the same level of success enjoyed by its predecessor.

Reviews of the movie underscored what Coppola and Paramount officials might have suspected: *Godfather II* was the kind of movie that took some time to sink in. The original *Godfather* had hit audiences on an immediate, visceral level, but the sequel, much more understated in its approach to its subject, had a way of occupying one's thoughts long after the running of the end credits; the more one thought about it, the better the movie played. Critical response seemed to reflect this, as well. Early reviews of the film, written for newspapers and weekly magazines with tight deadlines, tended to be rougher on Coppola and his picture than the notices written for publications with greater lead times.

In a review posted the day after the film's premiere, *New York Times* critic Vincent Canby ripped into *Godfather II* with one of the nastiest reviews the picture would ever receive. "It's a Frankenstein's monster stitched together from leftover parts," Canby stated. "It talks. It moves in fits and starts but has no mind of its own. Occasionally, it repeats a point made in *The Godfather* . . . but the insights are fairly lame at this point." Canby, who would never be accused of being a fan of Coppola's films, was especially harsh in his assessment of what he felt were recycled ideas from the first movie. *"The Godfather, Part II,"* he wrote, "is not very far along before one realizes that it hasn't anything more to say. Everything of any interest was thoroughly covered in the original film, but like many people who have nothing to say, *Part II* won't shut up."

Calling *Godfather II* "ambitious, imposing but essentially superfluous," a *Washington Post* critic joined the *New York Times* in complaining about the similarities between the two movies. "The new film, exquisite and impressive as it often looks, fails to provide a fresh narrative, a fresh concept or fresh revelations. It simply continues what we know at the devastating, unforgettable fadeout of *The Godfather:* that Michael Corleone, powerfully impersonated once more by Al Pacino, had become a moral monster in the process of shouldering the burden of responsibilities of his criminal heritage."

Although much more favorable in their overall assessments of the movie, both *Time* and *Newsweek* found *Godfather II* too flawed for unqualified endorsements. Michael Corleone, offered the *Time* reviewer, was never convincingly human, and Coppola's efforts at making him a tragically flawed character within the context of a gangster picture was "a tall and slightly pretentious order."

The *Time* reviewer continued: "Yet despite this overreach, a rather messy structure, and great length, *The Godfather, Part II* is a worthy successor to its predecessor. Francis Coppola has made a richly detailed, intelligent film that uses overorganized crime as a metaphor to comment on the coldness and corruption of an overorganized modern world."

The reviews improved over time, especially when the monthly magazines begin to weigh in with their appraisals. While a few continued to harp on the film's length and sense of repetition ("This is not a sequel, it's just more . . . a vastly bloated mediocrity"), most were more charitable in their conclusions about the film's value.

If Vincent Canby's early review had pounded away at the movie, Pauline Kael of *The New Yorker* at least balanced the scale. "Coppola is the inheritor of the traditions of the novel, the theatre, and—especially—opera and movies," she declared. "The sensibility at work in the film is that of a major artist. We're not used to it: how many screen artists get the chance to work in the epic form, and who has been able to seize the power to compose a modern American epic? And who else, when he got the chance and the power, would have proceeded with the absolute conviction that he'd make the film the way it should be made? In movies, that's the inner voice of the authentic hero."

Audience response wound up being as wildly mixed as the critics'. After a hot start at the box office, the movie's receipts dwindled substantially, and while *Godfather II* was by no means a failure at the gate, it disappointed studio officials, who hoped to see it match or approach the revenue generated by its predecessor.

3.

THE 1974 RELEASE OF TWO MAJOR pictures reaffirmed Coppola's position as perhaps the best and the brightest that Hollywood had to offer. Equally adept at making small personal films and huge commercial blockbusters, he was as close to being an auteur as could be found in American film. In a system as complex as that of the motion picture industry, in which large production companies, financial backers and lending institutions, artists and filmmakers, and distribution companies are inextricably connected through the making of a huge variety of movies, Francis Ford Coppola enjoyed as much leverage as the system would allow. His control over his productions, hard earned over a decade of experience, defied the norm; his influence on the business was enormous.

Nevertheless, Coppola was not entirely satisfied. In his mind, he was still tethered too tightly to the old Hollywood system, and he yearned for a way to create a working system more favorable to the way he wanted to make movies. American Zoetrope, his utopian dream of restructuring the system in northern California, had been a failure, and by late 1974, the Directors Company had fallen apart as well, a victim of the never-ending battle between commerce and art. On paper, the Directors Company had looked fail-safe to all parties involved. The risks seemed minimal and the potential rewards boundless. The three directors involved—Coppola, William Friedkin, and Peter Bogdanovich—had been given a wide berth to create the kind of films they wanted, in exchange for their allegiance to Paramount. All three had displayed a knowledge of the business aspects of filmmaking uncommon to directors their age; all three had directed huge critical and financial successes. Paramount's hopes were high at that time. If any of the directors came through with a picture that even approached the success of *The Godfather,* Paramount's initial investment in the company would be covered—and then some. If all three made blockbusters, people would be rolling in wealth.

Artistic vision, however, became a major obstacle. At the time of the formation of the Directors Company, Gulf & Western CEO Charles Bluhdorn was confident that Coppola, Friedkin, and Bogdanovich had graduated from making arty, film-school movies to the more grown-up world of big commercial pictures, and he encouraged the formation of the company. Paramount president Frank Yablans was not so certain, and he expressed his reservations—strongly—to Bluhdorn and the others. Coppola, he complained, had used his remarkable salesmanship skills to sell Bluhdorn a bill of goods, and he was certain that the Directors Company was headed toward failure, to be sunk by the egos of its participants. Despite these feelings, Yablans went along with the idea—at least in public. "They've gone through their growth period, indulging their esoteric tastes," he said of the three directors during an August 20, 1972, luncheon announcing the formation of the Directors

Company. "Coppola isn't interested in filming a pomegranate growing in the desert. They're all very commercial now."

Or so he hoped. In the months following the formation of the Directors Company, Yablans and Paramount became increasingly concerned about the return on their investment. The obvious blockbuster in the making was *Godfather II,* which Yablans coveted, but the terms of the arrangement between Coppola and Paramount with regard to this film precluded the founding of the Directors Company. When Yablans tried to shuffle *Godfather II* to the new company, he was blocked from doing so by other Paramount officials.

Then, to Yablans's horror, Coppola delivered *The Conversation,* a movie that Yablans and others at Paramount correctly predicted would not stand a chance at the box office. Coppola would complain that *The Conversation* was shortchanged in its promotion and distribution, but in a year finding such movies as *The Towering Inferno, Chinatown, Murder on the Orient Express,* and *Godfather II* jockeying for box-office receipts, Paramount was more inclined to get behind *The Great Gatsby,* another one of its pictures. With Robert Redford headlining, *Gatsby* had a better chance of making a dent in the marketplace than *The Conversation.* If Yablans and Paramount were sending Coppola a message, it was a simple one: Don't waste our time with art-house films; bring us a *big* picture.

Coppola, quite rightly, balked at the notion, as did the other two members of the Directors Company. This, however, was only part of the problem. Neither Friedkin nor Bogdanovich cared much for *The Conversation—*"I thought it was like watching paint dry or listening to hair grow," Friedkin told writer Peter Biskind—but at least Coppola had made a film. Friedkin seemed to be in no hurry to chip in with his contribution.

Bogdanovich was another story. His first picture for the Directors Company, *Paper Moon,* a wonderful period piece starring Ryan O'Neal and his young daughter, Tatum, was a critical and box-office success, earning Coppola and Friedkin $300,000 each for their share of the collective's profits. Yablans, sensing a ripe opportunity to create discord among the three directors and possibly break apart a company that he despised more and more with each passing day, filled Bogdanovich's ears with talk of how he was being taken advantage of. "When are these guys going to make a movie?" he asked Bogdanovich. "They have your money, what's going on here?" Bogdanovich listened.

The dissension among the ranks grew stronger when Bogdanovich announced that his next picture for the Directors Company would be *Daisy*

Miller, a film adaptation of the Henry James novel. In fact, the picture was a thinly veiled attempt to find a star vehicle for Cybill Shepherd, Bogdanovich's lady of the moment, whom he had cast in *The Last Picture Show.* Friedkin tried to talk Bogdanovich out of making the movie, arguing that Shepherd had no acting ability, but Bogdanovich went ahead with the project—with disastrous results. The movie, almost universally hated by the critics, fell on its face with a resounding thud, and Friedkin, not wanting to be associated with a group that produced such flops as *Daisy Miller* and *The Conversation,* opted out of the company.

Coppola, in his "us against them" mind-set, chose to blame the downfall of the Directors Company on Paramount, which, in his view, had not allowed the three directors the kind of artistic freedom it had originally promised.

"There was disagreement between us and Paramount," he commented later, "the nutshell being that we wanted to be a truly independent company. The three of us got along well, and even to this day we never had an argument, although Bogdanovich and Friedkin were always feuding to some extent. But I think the reason we ultimately liquidated it was because Paramount never really wanted there to be a company with the autonomy that we wanted."

For Coppola, the demise of the Directors Company amounted to only a minor, temporary setback. In short order, he formed his own new company, Coppola Cinema 7, and then bought into Cinema 5, a New York–based exhibitor-distribution chain highly respected for its distribution of foreign films.

Coppola's involvement with Cinema 5 was both political and pragmatic. When he purchased 10 percent of the company's stock in August 1974, paying $180,000 for 72,000 shares, Coppola had cut a sweetheart deal that, like his Directors Company agreement with Paramount, appeared to offer great profit potential at virtually no risk. At the time, Cinema 5 was embroiled in serious internal conflict, with Donald Rugoff, the company's president and one of its principal owners, fighting off a takeover by William Foreman, another Cinema 5 investor, who also owned Cinerama, a domestic distribution chain. With an antitrust suit in the works, Rugoff needed allies on the board of directors. In exchange for Coppola's support—as well as that of Fred Roos, who also bought stock in the company—Rugoff guaranteed the loan to Coppola for his purchase of the company stocks, then went one step further by promising to buy back Coppola's stock if he ever wanted out of the deal. By October, Coppola and Roos were seated on Cinema 5's board of directors.

When discussing Cinema 5 with the press, Coppola assumed his now-familiar position of the embattled filmmaker searching for a way to circumvent an oppressive system. If all went well, Coppola would be able to make art-house films and distribute them through Cinema 5, putting him in the position of circumventing some of the usual kinds of agreements that filmmakers had to arrange—deals that often found them losing control or even ownership of their movies in exchange for the front money needed to make a film.

"Ultimately, my objective in getting involved with Cinema 5 was to have some sort of hold on distribution and exhibition," said Coppola, "because, as you know, it owns theaters, the best theaters in New York, for opening this kind of film." Coppola could see the possibility of a future merger or buyout involving the two companies. "Coppola Cinema 7 would take over Cinema 5, or vice-versa," he proposed, "and it will be an interesting new arrangement."

Coppola had several projects that he hoped might fit into his agreement with Cinema 5. The first, his long-planned biography of maverick automobile manufacturer Preston Tucker, would be written, produced, and directed by Coppola and would feature Marlon Brando in the title role; Coppola had announced his intentions of pursuing this project in June, while he was still in Sicily working on *Godfather II* and well before his purchase of Cinema 5 stock. The second film would find Coppola acting as an executive producer of a movie directed by Carroll Ballard—an adaptation of Walter Farley's *The Black Stallion*. Coppola had been high on the project for some time, and he was hopeful that the movie might spawn a number of sequels and maybe even a television series. With this in mind, he had purchased the rights to all of Farley's *Black Stallion* books and had commissioned Walter Murch to work with Ballard on a screenplay for the first installment.

According to Ballard, the project was almost torpedoed before the script had been written.

"I really didn't like the book that much," he admitted. "I thought it was kind of a *Leave It to Beaver* story. But it was something. Francis decided that it would be really great if Walter Murch and I would work together on this, and he set a date for Walter and me to meet with him in his San Francisco office. I flew up there, and Walter and I talked a little bit before we went in to see Francis. Walter wasn't too hot about it, either: He thought it was kind of a namby-pamby story. When we went in and started talking to Francis, we were both really straight with him. We said, 'You know, this is the sort of movie that's been done before. The story about the shipwreck and the kid on the island is kind of unique, but when he gets back home, it's like a million movies, with the horse winning the big race and everything.' Francis just sat there and listened to us. Finally, he got really furious: 'What the hell are we talking about? What are we doing? What a waste of time! You guys don't want to make a movie? To hell with you! Get out of here! I don't want to talk to you!' Walter and I kind of looked at each other and said, 'Wait a minute, Francis. There are possibilities here.' We tried to keep the thing going."

The third project on Coppola's list was, by Coppola's description, "a macabre comedy, set in the midst of the Vietnam War."

The project's working title was *Apocalypse Now*.

4·

APOCALYPSE NOW'S ORIGINS could be traced back half a dozen years, to 1968, when John Milius, then a bright young screenwriter and putative filmmaker from Southern Cal's film school, and classmate George Lucas began to talk about making a movie about the Vietnam War. Milius had heard a number of wild, disturbing stories about the war from soldiers returning from Southeast Asia, and one particular image—that of soldiers surfing in the aftermath of a bloody firefight—brought home the insanity of the war to him. Milius, who in years to come would write the scripts for *Jeremiah Johnson* and *The Life and Times of Judge Roy Bean,* and who would direct such movies as *Dillinger* and *The Wind and the Lion,* was not interested in writing a dark anti-war comedy along the lines of a *Catch-22*. A gung ho militarist, Milius was incensed that the United States didn't seem committed enough to the war to try to win it.

"George Lucas and I were great connoisseurs of the Vietnam War," he recalled. "Of course, we hadn't lost it then so it was a little easier to be interested. As a matter of fact, I wanted to go to Vietnam but I had asthma, couldn't get in anything. I was the only person I knew who wanted to go in the Army. George and I would talk about the battles all the time and what a great movie it would make. I had the title to call it *Apocalypse Now,* because all these hippies at the time had these buttons that said 'Nirvana Now,' and I loved the idea of a guy having a button with a mushroom cloud on it that said 'Apocalypse Now,' you know, let's bring it on, full nuke. Ever hear that Randy Newman song 'Let's Drop the Big One Now'? That's the spirit that it started in right there."

Further plans for making the movie came together during the early days of American Zoetrope, when Milius and Lucas were part of the original group that Coppola assembled in San Francisco. In its early permutation, *Apocalypse Now* was to be directed by George Lucas, who wanted to shoot it in 16 mm, giving it a cinema verité appearance. The fictional material would be shot with real soldiers and recruits, and this would be mixed with actual news footage, adding authenticity while holding down expenses to somewhere in the range of $1.5 to $2 million for the entire film.

Unfortunately, Zoetrope was not in the position to finance the film at any price, and the project was shelved until the summer of 1974, when Coppola resurrected it and proposed that it be filmed in time for release during the American Bicentennial in 1976. Coppola had gained ownership of the project in a strange, roundabout way. When Warner Bros.–Seven Arts cut its original deal with Zoetrope, it had obtained the rights to *Apocalypse Now.* After the demise of American Zoetrope, when Coppola repaid his loan to Warner Bros.–Seven Arts, the ownership of the film's rights was transferred to Coppola, rather than to Milius or Lucas.

Lucas, however, had initiated his own efforts to get the production off the ground. He had worked out his own development deal with Columbia Pictures shortly after the completion of *American Graffiti,* and he had even sent Gary Kurtz—a friend and colleague who at one time had agreed to produce *Apocalypse Now*—to scout locations in the Philippines.

"I sort of had a deal with Columbia to do it," Lucas pointed out, "but we really couldn't reach an agreement with Francis over the participation with Columbia. There was a big disagreement about it. Columbia wouldn't give us enough points, and Francis didn't want to do it with them, so we ended up not doing it at Columbia."

When Coppola approached Lucas about directing *Apocalypse Now* in 1974, Lucas was tied up in the making of his new motion picture, a space fantasy called *Star Wars.* Lucas still wanted to make *Apocalypse Now,* but he was too deep into his own picture to even consider the new project. He asked Coppola to wait until he had finished working on *Star Wars.* Coppola insisted that he wanted the movie released in time for the Bicentennial, when it would have maximum impact on a country wrapped up in patriotic sentiment. After some discussion, Lucas surrendered to Coppola's persistence. "If you want to make it," he told Coppola, "go make it."

After Lucas rejected his offer, Coppola offered the job of directing the picture to John Milius, who consented to writing the screenplay but refused to direct the film. It was just as well: Coppola and Milius held very different opinions on the Vietnam War, and Coppola readily admitted that their differences might have presented a problem had Milius directed the film.

Never especially political to begin with, Coppola was not interested in filming a commentary on Vietnam. Instead, he wanted to make a deeper, yet more general, statement. As he told *Playboy* interviewer William Murray, he wanted to say something "about war and the human soul."

"But it's dangerous," he noted, adding his typical sense of drama to his pronouncements, "because I'll be venturing into an area that is so laden with so many implications that if I select some aspects and ignore others, I may be doing something irresponsible. So I'll be thinking hard about it."

5.

WITH THE RELEASE OF *THE CONVERSATION* and *Godfather II,* Coppola's relationship with the press and film critics underwent another change. In the past, his ego and gregarious nature had always made him a fascinating interview—eminently quotable and always good for a colorful anecdote, even if he did come off, in some cases, as being a little too full of himself for his own good. The press, for the most part, recognized Coppola's creative gifts and was eager to inquire about how he used them, just as Coppola understood the necessity for publicity whenever he was issuing a new film.

The mixed reaction to *The Conversation* and *Godfather II* soured Coppola on the press, even though eventually, after the dust had settled and the critical appraisals had been filed, the majority of reviews and critical articles wound up favoring both films. It was difficult enough, Coppola lamented, to deal with studios and corporate officials, actors and actresses, batteries of production workers, distributors and exhibitors—all in an effort to create a single motion picture; the last thing he needed was a lot of negative criticism and commentary from people who had never negotiated contracts with studios, hit a mark in front of a camera, or worked out travel arrangements for an entire production company. *The Conversation* and *Godfather II* had taken a lot out of him, and he seethed whenever he read what he deemed to be unjustified or mean-spirited remarks.

At times, his anger approached the absurd, as on the occasion when he told an interviewer that critics practiced a lot of blackmail and extortion on the filmmaker, forcing him "to participate in certain things that accrue to the critics' advantage under the implicit threat of a bad review." When pressed to be more specific, Coppola declined, stating that not all critics behaved this way. "But suffice it to say," he cautioned, "that if this sort of extortion continues, it may blow up in the biggest scandal the field of criticism has known. It's corrupt right down to the bottom."

Apart from unfavorable reviews, Coppola's hostility was difficult to understand. As he himself admitted, he was generally treated well by critics and the press. He was continually fielding a barrage of interview requests, and his words and likeness graced the pages of the most prestigious newspapers and magazines in the country. He was presently regarded as perhaps the most talented filmmaker in the United States.

This much was evident when he reaped the rewards for all the work he had put into *The Conversation* and *Godfather II.* He scored first with *The Conversation,* when he was given the Best Director award and his movie was cited as English-Language Picture of 1974 by the Committee on Exceptional Films of the National Board of Review. For Coppola, the awards signaled not only the beginning of many walks to the awards podium but also the satisfying conclusion that his small personal film, which he had spent years wanting to direct, might receive the kind of recognition expected for *Godfather II.*

As it turned out, the two films wound up competing with each other in both the Golden Globes and Academy Awards—and in a very big way. *Godfather II* was nominated for six Golden Globe awards—Best Motion Picture—Drama, Best Director, Best Actor (Al Pacino), Best Screenplay, Most Promising Newcomer (Lee Strasberg), and Best Original Score—while *The Conversation* was nominated for four—Best Motion Picture—Drama, Best Director, Best Actor (Gene Hackman), and Best Screenplay—putting the two movies in direct competition in four categories. It was more of the same when the Oscar nominations were announced, with *The Conversation* and *Godfather II* going head-to-head in the Best Picture entry. All told, *The Conversation* received three Oscar nominations, while *Godfather II* garnered eleven, tying it in overall nominations with *Chinatown,* another of 1974's highly regarded movies.

It had been a remarkable year, finding a number of directors issuing some of their finest films. Besides Coppola's work on two critically acclaimed movies, Roman Polanski had released *Chinatown;* Bob Fosse had contributed *Lenny,* his powerful biography of comedian Lenny Bruce, adapted from the Broadway play and starring Dustin Hoffman in the title role; John Cassavetes had directed his wife, Gena Rowlands, in *A Woman Under the Influence,* one of the high points in his remarkable career; and French director François Truffaut had made *Day for Night.* As an indication of the level of excellence in 1974: Martin Scorsese (*Alice Doesn't Live Here Anymore*), Sidney Lumet (*Murder on the Orient Express*), Mel Brooks (*Young Frankenstein*), and Paul Mazursky (*Harry and Tonto*) were *not* cited with Academy Award nominations for direction, even though any one of these movies might have been nominated—and maybe even won—in another year.

Coppola coveted the Best Director Oscar, which he had lost two years earlier to Fosse for *Cabaret,* but indications were strong that this was going to be his year when, in March, he took home his second Directors Guild Award, winning for *Godfather II.* Once again, he found himself competing against himself—the only time in DGA history that a director had been nominated for two pictures in one year—and while he knew all too well from past experience that one could win a DGA and still lose the Oscar, tradition, if not sentiment, was on his side.

Godfather II blew out the competition on April 8, when it won six Academy Awards in what insiders had projected to be a tight competition between *Godfather II* and *Chinatown*. (The latter received only one Oscar, for Robert Towne's original screenplay.) Robert De Niro edged out two of his *Godfather II* colleagues—Lee Strasberg and Michael Gazzo—in the Best Supporting Actor category, while Dean Tavoularis took home a well-deserved award for art direction. The evening, however, belonged to the Coppola family, with Carmine Coppola sharing an Oscar with Nino Rota for the Best Musical Score, and Francis taking the stage three times to accept statuettes for Best Picture, Best Screenplay, and Best Director.

For Carmine Coppola, winning the Oscar was long overdue recognition, and he was grateful that his youngest son had given him the opportunity he'd been seeking in a career that spanned more than three decades. "If it wasn't for Francis Coppola," he said, "I wouldn't be here tonight. However, if it wasn't for me, *he* wouldn't be here." The packed house at the Dorothy Chandler Pavilion ate it up.

Italia Coppola, however, was not amused. Talia Shire had been nominated for an Oscar for Best Supporting Actress but had lost to Ingrid Bergman (*Murder on the Orient Express*), and Mrs. Coppola felt that her husband and son might have been more sensitive when giving their acceptance speeches.

"Francis is jumping up in the air saying, 'This was the best night in our lives,'" she recalled. "Well, Tallie lost that night, and she said, 'I'm a girl, so you forgot about me.' Then Carmine gave his speech about how if it wasn't for him Francis wouldn't be here. I said to him afterward, 'Gee, Carmine, you did a great job. I hope the labor pains weren't too bad.'"

According to Talia Shire, Italia Coppola was looking for a little recognition herself. "When Francis was giving his acceptance speech, my mother wanted him to say, '... and to my mother, Italia Pennino Coppola.' She wanted some of her old friends, who hadn't seen her in all these years, to know what happened to her."

6.

LIKE IT OR NOT, COPPOLA WAS now king of the gangster flicks, and there was never a shortage of requests for him to direct this type of movie. In recent months, Dino De Laurentiis, the biggest independent producer in the business, had approached Coppola with the proposition that he direct the film adaptation of Peter Maas's *King of the Gypsies*. De Laurentiis, easily Coppola's equal as a pitchman, insisted that, despite their obvious similarities, *King of the Gypsies* and *The Godfather* were two entirely different pictures.

"They're only alike in one respect—box office potential," De Laurentiis told Coppola. "No one but Francis Coppola could make *The Godfather* more than just another gangster picture."

When Coppola showed no apparent interest in the project, De Laurentiis played his final card.

"Look, Francis," he urged, "the only way to do business is to screw the major studios."

"Dino," Coppola replied, "*you* should be the Godfather."

Nor could Coppola rest with any assurances that, with the release of *Godfather II*, he was finished with the Corleone family. The new film had been out for only a brief period when Coppola started hearing rumors that Paramount was interested in a third installment. Coppola adamantly refused to consider another sequel.

He had other projects to hold his interest. Borrowing against his *Godfather II* profits, he purchased KMPX-FM, one of San Francisco's premier underground rock stations during the sixties. Although the move might not have been the best investment that Coppola could have made at the time, it was consistent with his recent interests in purchasing media and entertainment properties. The station, Coppola explained, could be used as another venue to explore story ideas. He could air a radio adaptation of, say, *Apocalypse Now* and see how it was received.

"Filmmakers need ways to try out ideas short of starting a film," he said. "Too often, the fate of a film is sealed before the first photography begins. In radio especially, you can get the sense of context and what the whole thing means; it's a wonderful springboard to discuss content and character. Also, it's a good test of audience reaction: if it's a total bore on radio, it will be a total bore on film."

Coppola was so encouraged by the idea that he suggested that every major Hollywood studio follow his lead. Theater and radio workshops, such as those that he wanted to develop with the Little Fox Theater and KMPX-FM, could be the foundation of developing new talent and movie properties. "A guy who could knock me out with a radio drama could also write me a movie," he stated. "I think I've introduced more new talent than all the majors together, and that's a disgraceful comment. It is also suicidal for them. I'm not attacking them; they've been wonderful to me. But it's their future, as well as mine."

With *Godfather II* out of the way and *Apocalypse Now* still being worked into a usable screenplay, Coppola had more time to oversee some of his investments. *City* magazine, though doing better than before in attracting advertisers and new subscribers, was still losing money, and throughout the early part of 1975, Coppola kept a close watch on what the magazine was publishing. He could not have been more dissatisfied with the direction his publication was taking. Although the magazine aspired to be a service magazine—"It's full of news you can use week after week; it tells you inside stories and it lets you know where to go to have fun and where to get a great meal," crooned an ad soliciting subscriptions—Coppola could find little in the publication that related to him or, for that matter, to the kind of upscale readers and advertisers needed to keep the magazine afloat. Coppola began to report to the magazine offices every day. *City* editors and writers hated having him around, kibitzing with them about editorial content and questioning their decisions, and by the end of April, Coppola recognized the tension at the office.

Feeling that he needed to take drastic measures to protect his investment and turn the magazine around, Coppola fired the entire staff on May 1. *City,* he informed the staff in a memo, would temporarily suspend publication until a new staff could be hired.

In the months to come, Coppola would try anything to get *City* back on its feet. He hired new editors in chief, engaged in an expensive ad campaign pushing new subscriptions, changed the format of the publication, and eventually turned the magazine over to his wife. Nothing worked. *City* continued to lose large sums of money, just as some of Coppola's advisers had predicted when he bought the publication, and in February 1976, he finally pulled the plug, announcing that there wasn't enough local talent to keep the magazine running.

In retrospect, Coppola, who would publish another magazine two decades later, viewed his involvement with *City* as "a learning experience."

"I think that *City* was an exciting, innovative magazine," he said when asked about the publication in early 1999. "What I didn't know anything about was how to access a potential market for a type of magazine first, to see if there's a readership to support it. I also learned that putting out a big, beautiful weekly magazine is really a tough task."

7.

USING THE EARNINGS FROM his *Godfather* films, Coppola purchased a seventeen-hundred-acre estate, complete with a majestic Victorian house, breathtaking gardens, olive groves, and vineyards—all set in the fertile countryside in California's Napa Valley. The estate had been established in 1879 by

Gustave Niebaum, a former Finnish sea captain and furrier who, after years of travel, had invested his wealth in land that he hoped to use to create a vineyard similar to the ones he had seen in Italy. The estate's illustrious history was not lost on Coppola, even if, while house hunting, he was actually seeking a modest bungalow set on two or three acres of land. The availability of the Niebaum estate had been an unexpected bonanza.

"We were looking for a little summer house with a couple of acres of grapes, where Francis could make home wine and our kids could run around in the country sun," Eleanor Coppola remembered. "One day, our real estate broker said, 'Let's take a look at the Niebaum estate, just for fun. It's not what you're looking for, but it will only be on the market once in a lifetime.' So we just drove by without an appointment or anything. It was stunningly beautiful! It looked like a movie set. We couldn't imagine being able to actually own it, but it was just at the time that money started coming in from *The Godfather.* We made an offer at an auction but we didn't get it. It was purchased by a consortium of land developers. We continued to look for a property in the Napa Valley, but everything was disappointing. Several years later, the area was zoned Agricultural Preserve, and we heard that the owners of the Niebaum estate couldn't proceed with their plans and wanted to sell. Francis aggressively pursued and bought the property."

By late spring of 1975, Hollywood's rumor mill was buzzing over *Apocalypse Now.* Vietnam was still relatively taboo as a topic for a major motion picture—*The Green Berets,* a piece of propaganda starring John Wayne, released at the height of the tension over the war in Southeast Asia, had proven how poorly the controversial subject could be handled—and Coppola's tackling it, in what he promised to be the bloodiest movie he'd ever made, seemed par for the course for the maverick director. Some of the rumors swirling around *Apocalypse Now* were tasty. Marlon Brando and Steve McQueen were said to be at the top of the list for the film's male leads. Freddie Fields, Dino De Laurentiis, and, most surprisingly, Bob Hope, were connected at one point or another with the picture—rumors that Coppola immediately squelched. There was even talk that the film's provocative title would be changed to *Heart of Darkness,* no doubt in an effort to give the picture a more serious literary dressing, as well as to pay homage to the Joseph Conrad novella that inspired it.

Coppola refused to provide the press with much information about his plans. Nothing could be done, especially in terms of casting, until the finished script had been delivered. He did confirm that John Milius was rewriting his original screenplay and that the movie would be totally self-financed under his Coppola Cinema 7 banner.

To this day, the origins of the plot for *Apocalypse Now* remain rather mysterious, largely because of conflicting statements issued by those involved in its development. Coppola always maintained that the core of the screenplay was John Milius's work, and that his (Coppola's) main contribution was bringing the plot closer to *Heart of Darkness*. Milius acknowledged that the original idea was his, and that it was enhanced by his discussions with George Lucas, but his feelings about how the story turned out—and who was responsible for it—fluctuated with his mercurial moods. In one interview, he would be pleased with the film ("That one movie justifies my career. I feel I really did something worthwhile by writing it. Even though I share credit [with Coppola] and I didn't direct it, it's a real piece of me"), while in another, he would speak disparagingly about Coppola's work on the screenplay ("Basically, he wanted to ruin it, liberalize it, and turn it into *Hair*"), as if to distance himself from a script that he disapproved of.

Then there was Carroll Ballard, who staked his own claim to originating a film adaptation of *Heart of Darkness*, although not anything like the movie *Apocalypse Now* became.

"At the time when I was working on *Finian's Rainbow*," said Ballard, who shot the picture's title sequence, "Joe Landon, the producer, asked me if there was any project that I was interested in doing. My fantasy was to make *Heart of Darkness*. I felt it was a great subject for a movie if you could get the gears in your head to run right. I proposed that we try to get the rights to it, but it all came to naught. Nobody was really interested in making that film. Many years later, I discovered that Francis and George had sort of taken that idea and run with it."

At first, the fact that someone else was making a film based loosely on *Heart of Darkness* did not sit well with Ballard, especially since the people making the picture were friends. "At one time, I was very bitter about it," he confessed, "because nobody said anything to me about it. If somebody had said something, it probably would have been different. The fact is, I tried to go down the straight line with it and failed, and they took another approach to it. But I'm not bitter anymore."

"I have no idea why Carroll would feel that it disturbed his chance to make the original," Coppola countered, when asked about Ballard's wanting to make a film adaptation of *Heart of Darkness*. "Years had lapsed and he could have done it. But to my knowledge, neither he nor I optioned the Conrad material or registered the title.

"There's no question that *Apocalypse Now* was John Milius's idea, with George egging him along. George was going to direct it. Carroll really had nothing to do with it, but he was around, talking about wanting to do *Heart of*

Darkness. So John and George just naturally started to borrow the river journey from that, though they didn't think of it as a version of *Heart of Darkness.* They were listening to Carroll's enthusiasm about *Heart of Darkness* and it influenced them."

Both Coppola and Milius agreed that their differing political views were responsible for their disagreements over the tone, if not the actual incidents, in *Apocalypse Now.*

"The original script was profoundly interesting, and made a really interesting and unusual statement about the war, that was not political in a very short or myopic sense, but in a big sense was really political," said Coppola. "It [had] a lot of offensive paramilitary stuff that [was] irrelevant and shouldn't be stressed—Milius's whole mythology of hunting people down and so on, which I am not particularly in. Yet aside from that there was an incredible film in *Apocalypse.*"

"To make an anti-war movie as Francis is trying to do," scoffed Milius at the time, "is about as foolish as trying to make an anti-rain movie. It's gonna rain. It was not an anti-war movie when it started out; it was apolitical. It deals with the nature of war in man altogether, and man's inherent bestiality. It went right into war. It said, 'Here you're going to see it all: you're going to see the exhilaration of it all, you're going to see the horror of it all; you're going right into the war with no holds barred.'"

Joseph Conrad's allegorical novella had always been a kind of Everest to filmmakers—Orson Welles had been obsessed with making a movie out of it, only to give up on the project—and superimposing the Vietnam War on the Conrad story complicated the task exponentially. Milius wrote his first draft of *Apocalypse Now* with *Heart of Darkness* very much in his mind—he even kept the name Kurtz for his demented Special Forces character, but he changed the Marlowe character's name to Willard—although he structured his story on the accounts he had heard from Vietnam vets. Milius had stories about the surfing; a friend had told him the horrific tale about the Vietcong hacking off the arms of the children that had been immunized for smallpox. His script told the story of a young GI sent up the river to murder a Special Forces officer who had gone AWOL and established his own mad kingdom in the heart of the Cambodian jungle. The farther Willard traveled up the river, the farther he moved from civilization. When Willard finally met Kurtz, he not only was unable to kill him; he wound up fighting beside him, defending Kurtz's compound against American helicopters attacking it.

Milius rewrote his script in the late spring of 1975, and Coppola then took over and revised the rewrite, installing even more shading from *Heart of*

Darkness in the Milius story. Of all the Coppola changes, two were especially significant. In the original draft, Kurtz, badly wounded and literally rotting from within, was seen at the opening of the film; Coppola, however, preferred to keep Kurtz offscreen until near the end of the film, allowing Kurtz's mythological presence to build in Willard's mind as he journeys up the river. In the second major change, Coppola adjusted Kurtz's psychological makeup. Milius's version of Kurtz was of an ordinary man driven over the edge when he discovered his power over his Montagnard minions. ("Do you know what it is to be a white man who can summon fire from the sky?" Kurtz challenges Willard in the Milius script. "You can live and die for these things—not silly ideals that are always betrayed.") Coppola's Kurtz was just as insane, but he was also a brilliant man capable of recognizing his own madness and seeing his death as a solution. The differences in these two characters reflected the differences between Milius and Coppola, between Milius's belief that war was natural to the human condition and Coppola's abhorrence of war and his belief that intellect could stop it. It was Coppola who insisted that Kurtz's last words be "the horror, the horror," just like the last words of Kurtz in *Heart of Darkness.*

"All the great scenes and lines are Milius's," Coppola generously allowed years later, when asked which screenwriter made which contribution to the script. Milius, he said, was responsible for the memorable "Ride of the Valkyries" helicopter attack scene, as well as for the Kilgore character and dialogue. "My contributions were to make it more like *Heart of Darkness.* I made the [Dennis] Hopper character out of the Russian in the book. I came up with the opening with Willard in Saigon, and the weird ending. The overall spaciness of the style came from me."

Milius disapproved of Coppola's rewrite of his script. Milius was not interested in delivering messages—especially if they were liberal ones—and he took Coppola to task for the way the director had altered his original vision.

"He sees himself as a great humanitarian, an enlightened soul who will tell you such wonderful things as he does at the end of *Godfather II*—that crime doesn't pay," a disgusted Milius said sarcastically. "We may come up with some great statement at the end of *Apocalypse,* to the effect that war is hell."

8.

IT'S DOUBTFUL THAT COPPOLA would have characterized himself as a great humanitarian. He did, however, see himself as a filmmaker facing a very difficult task. To obtain the kind of financing necessary for *Apocalypse Now,* he would have to convince foreign distributors that overseas audiences, still carrying a bitter taste about U.S. involvement in Vietnam, might be willing to watch his movie. In addition, Coppola hoped to gain the approval and assistance of the U.S. Army and the Department of Defense when making *Apocalypse Now*—a touchy situation regardless of how he approached his film. Finally, he was going to have to worry about American film distributors and exhibitors and their concerns that American audiences might not be ready or willing to watch a graphic depiction of the madness of war. *Apocalypse Now* promised to be Coppola's most controversial film to date, and its very nature demanded the best of Coppola's skills in balancing his artistic vision with the more pragmatic aspects of marketing his product.

In May 1975, while John Milius was still rewriting his screenplay, Coppola and Fred Roos flew to Washington, D.C., for a meeting at the Pentagon. Coppola dropped off Milius's early draft of the script, explaining that it was still being rewritten and that he personally would oversee the work on the film's ending. He was approaching the Pentagon, he said, because he hoped the Department of Defense would help him with some of the research for his film, as well as supply him with stock footage for "study purposes."

The Pentagon's Public Affairs Office forwarded the script to the U.S. Army's Office of Information. Coppola intended to make his film with or without the cooperation of the army or the Department of Defense, the Pentagon informed the army, so it might be best if the army cooperated with the filmmaker—provide him with facts and try to keep a "proper perspective" on the unpopular war.

It didn't take long for the army to render its decision on the script, which it judged to be unacceptable. The army particularly objected to the script's dark humor, and to some of the scenes that found soldiers surfing during combat, scalping the enemy, and smoking marijuana. "*Apocalypse Now* contains simply a series of some of the worst things, real or imagined, that happened or could have happened during the Vietnam War," the army responded, contending (in what must have amused both Milius and Coppola) that these objectionable episodes placed the army and war "in an unrealistic and unacceptable bad light."

In its critique of the screenplay, the army insisted that the entire basis of the script was unrealistic and would never have taken place. An officer like Kurtz would have deserted only if he had lost his mind, and even under these circumstances, the army would never order his murder; instead, it would have brought him home for medical treatment. Feeling that "to assist in any way in the production would imply agreement with either the fact or the philosophy of the film," the U.S. Army's Chief of Information refused to help

Coppola. "[If he] wants to make a bundle with this type of garbage, so be it. But he will do so without the slightest assistance from the Army."

Neither the Department of Defense nor Coppola was happy with the army's decision. For the better part of a decade, the Defense Department had been practicing as much damage control as possible, all in an effort to maintain an acceptable image during the turmoil of the Vietnam War, as well as to maintain the volume of recruits needed to keep the defense system solid. The department realized that it could not expect the kind of whitewash seen in *The Green Berets*, but it hoped that, by cooperating with filmmakers, the final product wouldn't be totally negative. With this in mind, the Public Affairs Office at the Pentagon tried to act as an intermediary between Coppola and the army, suggesting that Coppola visit Fort Bragg in North Carolina, where a simulated Vietnamese village had been constructed for training purposes. Coppola could do some of his research there, meet with army officials, and, afterward, fly to Washington, D.C., where all parties could get together and discuss script changes.

Coppola was hearing none of it. At that moment, he had no way of knowing where he was going to shoot his movie, or if he would actually require military assistance during the filming. It would have been nice to have had the army's cooperation, but not at the cost of its rewriting his film.

Chapter Eight

"The Most Important Movie
I Will Ever Make"

*"You aren't going to see this picture—This picture is going
to happen to you."*

—ORSON WELLES, in the prologue
to his unreleased movie *Heart of Darkness*

1.

ONE DAY IN THE LATE FALL of 1975, Francis Ford Coppola
snatched up his five Academy Award statuettes, marched them to the
window of his Pacific Heights estate, and flung them into the courtyard,
smashing four of them to pieces. As far as he was concerned, all of his
past success meant nothing if he couldn't get his next picture off the
ground—and it was beginning to look that way.

Casting *Apocalypse Now* had been a miserable experience. According to the terms of his agreement with foreign distributors, Coppola was
obligated to sign big-name stars for the movie's leading roles—a task that
Coppola had assumed he could accomplish with little trouble—but as
the months passed, it was beginning to look as if nobody wanted to
have anything to do with the movie. In May, *Variety* had reported Steve
McQueen and Marlon Brando as prime candidates for starring roles; a

few months later, in early September, it was going to be McQueen and Gene Hackman. By the end of November, nobody had been signed, though certainly not for any lack of effort on Coppola's part.

Virtually every major star had been approached and, to Coppola's mounting concern, the actors had other things to do, weren't interested, or wanted too much money to appear in the picture. Steve McQueen liked the script but was not interested in playing Willard, which would demand a lengthy absence from the country and would have disrupted his family life; when Coppola subsequently offered him the role of Kurtz, which would have called for McQueen's being on location for only three weeks, the actor agreed to take the part, but for the same $3 million he had been offered to play Willard. James Caan, wanting $2 million rather than the $1.25 million Coppola offered to play Willard, declined, citing his wife's pregnancy and her reluctance to have her baby in the Philippines, where the film was to be shot. Jack Nicholson was not interested in either part, and Robert Redford had promised his family that he would take a break from lengthy location shooting. Marlon Brando's attorney informed Coppola that his client refused to discuss any role in the film.

Frustrated by his inability to secure a single major star, and angered by what he felt were excessive salary demands, Coppola considered casting unknowns in his film. If need be, he would find other financing for the movie. He called a casting agent and asked him to arrange a casting call in New York.

While there, Coppola met with Al Pacino. They had discussed the part of Willard over the previous weeks, and while Pacino liked the role and the script, he did not want to spend four or more months in the jungle, especially after the health problems he had endured while shooting *Godfather II* in the Dominican Republic. In New York, Coppola and Pacino discussed the idea of Pacino's playing Kurtz, but Pacino disliked the part as written. Coppola promised to rewrite it to Pacino's satisfaction if the actor would only make a commitment to the movie, but Pacino refused to sign on without first seeing a finished script.

The New York trip only added to Coppola's feelings of helplessness. He was scheduled to begin production within a couple of months, sets were being built half a world away, and he had yet to sign the two leads for his movie.

Shortly after Coppola had boiled over and tossed his Oscars out the window, Marlon Brando's lawyer called again. It was time to talk.

2.

FINDING LOCATIONS FOR *Apocalypse Now* had been difficult, although not nearly as trying as assembling the movie's cast. At first, Coppola hoped to shoot the picture in Australia. Fred Roos and Dean Tavoularis had flown there for the Australian premiere of *Godfather II* and had scouted locations during their visit. Queensland, they reported to Coppola, had a tropical climate and environment suitable as a stand-in for Vietnam. However, when Coppola subsequently flew to Australia to check out the situation for himself, he found the government unwilling to meet some of his needs. He wanted to use B-52 bombers in the movie, but he learned that they had never been sold overseas. When he asked for four hundred helicopters and ten thousand troops, the government replied that its army was "not a film-extra agency." The unions, unimpressed by Coppola's stature as a filmmaker, or by his promises to employ as many Australian technicians as possible, were equally unresponsive.

Coppola fared better when he approached President Ferdinand Marcos of the Philippines. Marcos, intimately familiar with the value of an American buck, was more than willing to grant Coppola permission to shoot *Apocalypse Now* in his country. He would supply all the American-built helicopters operated by the Philippine Air Force, provide all the needed security, and cooperate in every other way possible. All Coppola had to do was pay the necessary fees. It didn't hurt, either, that Fred Roos had previously made a couple of low-budget films in the country and had contacts who could help pave the way, or that the Philippines could offer cheap labor—a bonus not to be underestimated, given Coppola's testy relations with labor unions in the past. An agreement was reached, and Coppola dispatched Dean Tavoularis to the Philippines to begin construction on the sets.

Back in the States, Coppola continued to work on casting his film, rewriting its script, and structuring the picture's financing. Coppola intended to hold the budget to somewhere between $12 and $14 million, but with only $7 million locked in from foreign distributors, he had a ways to go. He had already sunk a million dollars of his own money into preproduction, and he now understood that he was not going to be able to realize his original plan of independently financing the film. The trick was to find additional backing without relinquishing ownership in the film. He struck such a deal with United Artists, which agreed to advance Coppola $7.5 million in exchange for the film's distribution rights in the United States.

On March 1, 1976, Coppola flew to the Philippines with Ellie, their three children, a baby-sitter, a housekeeper, Francis's nephew Marc, and a projectionist. The household was to stay in a ritzy section of Manila, in a large house elaborately furnished in beautiful rattan and velvet. A huge dining room table would serve as a conference table, and the heat would be somewhat assuaged by ceiling fans and a swimming pool. After traveling through the country to reach the house, passing over endless miles of rice paddies and sugarcane fields and seeing people living in nipa huts in tiny villages, Ellie, for one, was feeling the early effects of culture shock. "My reality feels like a foreign movie," she wrote in her diary. "Part of me is waiting for the reels to change and get back to a familiar scene in San Francisco or Napa."

Her husband's reality was probably closer to a nightmare than a foreign film. From the onset of the scheduled five-month shoot, the Philippines presented a full slate of problems, from contending with the cultural differences on a day-to-day basis to trying to make a movie under strange and occasionally dangerous working conditions that included oppressive heat, constant dampness, guerrilla warfare being waged nearby, poisonous snakes, and an assortment of insects not usually seen by city slickers. In such an environment, the production company welcomed any forms of creature comforts. Cinematographer Vittorio Storaro and his Italian crew kept a supply of imported olive oil, canned tomatoes, and pasta for gourmet meals; Coppola installed a small espresso pot on the set.

Casting for the movie had not been completed until after Coppola's arrival in Manila, and though it was not the all-star group that investors demanded, the cast was impressive. Marlon Brando had finally been persuaded to play Kurtz—at a cost of $3.5 million for one month's work. Robert Duvall, now a Coppola regular, had taken the crucial role of Lt. Col. Bill Kilgore, the gung ho militarist surf freak, whose real-life counterpart had been the inspiration for the original John Milius screenplay. Frederic Forrest and Harrison Ford, both of whom had appeared in *The Conversation,* had taken roles in *Apocalypse Now,* Ford in a cameo appearance, Forrest portraying "Chef" Hicks, one of the main characters on Willard's boat. Dennis Hopper, best known for his role in *Easy Rider,* had signed on to play an unnamed American photojournalist living in the Kurtz compound.

Filling the Willard role had been difficult to the bitter end. After being rejected by McQueen, Caan, Nicholson, and Pacino, and learning that he couldn't even find a suitable unknown in New York or Los Angeles, Coppola had approached Martin Sheen, a talented character actor who seemed right for the part, and who would come at a price that Coppola could afford. Sheen wanted the role, but he was committed to another project, *The Cassandra Crossing,* currently being filmed in Italy, and was unavailable when Coppola needed him for shooting in the Philippines. Coppola eventually signed Harvey Keitel, a Martin Scorsese regular, who had appeared in *Mean Streets* and *Taxi Driver.*

Casting *Apocalypse Now* had driven Coppola to the edge, and he publicly aired his gripes in a series of articles published in *Variety* and other newspapers, in which he fumed about the high fees commanded by major stars of the day. Coppola proposed that the film industry return to the old studio system of yesteryear—statements that amused Hollywood observers, who noted that Coppola had never been shy about taking his share of the cut.

Nevertheless, Coppola hatched a new plan, made public in a full-page ad published in *Variety* in March, in which he stated that he hoped to sign actors to seven-year contracts binding them to his Cinema 7 company. Unlike the old studio agreements, in which actors were essentially treated as slaves, forced to work on pictures they would have preferred to avoid, and loaned to other studios in arrangements profitable to the studios but not to the actors themselves, the Coppola contract would encourage actors to work on outside projects, and they would be given a generous percentage of the profits for such work. The contracted actors would be paid for fifty weeks of work (as opposed to the forty weeks' pay in the old Hollywood system), and they would be encouraged to develop their careers further by writing and directing their own projects.

"The reason for the term contracts," Coppola explained, "is that there are few companies willing to give newcomers big starring roles that can turn a career around overnight. If we can make a continued success of the practice and show the studios the dollar value of doing it, it won't be too long before the studios are copying us copying them."

Immediate reaction to Coppola's announcement was mixed. Director Robert Altman declared himself to be morally opposed to the optioning of actors' services ("It's not a baseball team," he scoffed), while Martin Scorsese went along with Coppola to a certain extent, saying, "I think it's the right concept to break down the $3,000,000 syndrome."

Others were suspicious of the plan. Noting that Coppola had signed three young *Apocalypse Now* cast members (Laurence Fishburne, Albert Hall, and Sam Bottoms) to such contracts and was presently negotiating with Harvey Keitel, *Variety* speculated that Coppola's new contracts system might have been the direct result of his failure to sign Al Pacino and James Caan for his latest feature. "Coppola felt abandoned by people whose careers he felt he had significantly advanced," *Variety* mentioned.

Frederic Forrest, another actor signing the contract, looked back on it all with mixed feelings.

"There was no choice, really, if you wanted to do the part," he contended. "I didn't want to do any big contract, so I called Jack Nicholson for advice. I'd just worked with Jack on *The Missouri Breaks*. When I told him that they wanted me to sign a seven-year contract, Jack said, 'Don't sign it, Snake. Seven fuckin' years is too long. We don't sign with anybody for that.' But I wanted to do the movie, so I signed."

Over the long haul, Forrest noted, the contracts didn't amount to much—not in the way business is traditionally conducted in the motion picture industry.

"It all depended," Forrest said. "If the movie was a big hit, the contract was valid. If it wasn't a hit, the contract didn't mean anything. And that's really what happened on *Apocalypse Now*. They finally said the contract wasn't valid anymore, that it was dissolved. It was crazy."

Whatever Coppola's intentions, his announcement, issued on the eve of his start-up of *Apocalypse Now*, was a characteristically bold move, an innovative response to a system that was, at least in Coppola's view, making it more and more difficult to realize artistic vision.

3.

ON MARCH 20, NEARLY THREE weeks after Coppola's arrival in Manila, *Apocalypse Now* lurched into motion, its opening day's shooting set on a salt farm near a river. In the first scene filmed, Harvey Keitel, as Willard, was being taken by helicopter to the patrol boat that he would direct up the river. It was not an especially difficult scene to set up and shoot, but if Coppola needed an omen for how things would work for him in the future, he might have seen it on that first day, when a mix-up found Keitel and several others abandoned on a raft on the river. When he realized that no one was coming to pick them up, Keitel repeatedly tried to contact someone with his walkie-talkie. "Hello, this is Harvey Keitel," he called again and again. When no one answered, he grew edgy. "You wouldn't do this to Marlon Brando," he complained.

Brando wasn't even around. The superstar wanted to spend the summer with his family on his island near Tahiti, and by terms of his agreement with Coppola, he was not due on the set until September. Keitel, for one, was not pleased by the arrangement. There had been talk of shutting down the production during the summer and reconvening when Brando was ready to shoot his scenes, but Keitel had already sought and gained Coppola's permission to appear in another movie that fall. Brando's special treatment grated on Keitel, who hated the jungle to begin with and who loathed the prospects of having to return for several weeks to finish the film.

Coppola had far more serious problems to consider. A small cluster of southern islands, largely inhabited by Muslims, was seeking a break from the Philippines, and rebel soldiers were battling Ferdinand Marcos and his government in a series of skirmishes that had a direct bearing on the filming of

Apocalypse Now. The production company would no sooner set up for a difficult battle sequence than the helicopters on loan from the Philippine Air Force would be needed to fight the insurgents, frustrating Coppola and forcing him to rearrange his shooting schedule. The huge arsenal of props and special-effects equipment, which included an army's worth of M16s and enough explosives to set off half the jungle, had to be guarded by security specialists, lest they be taken by the rebels. Coppola himself was assigned a full-time bodyguard, lest *he* be kidnapped and held for ransom.

Early on, Coppola filmed on the sets that Dean Tavoularis had constructed near Baler, a small town on the northeastern coast of Luzon, about a six-hour drive from Manila. To the production company, the location must have seemed like the farthest outpost from civilization as they knew it. Afflicted by abject poverty and boasting of virtually nothing modern, the town and surrounding area might have been a reasonable stand-in for Vietnam, but it was hardly suited to supporting the needs of a motion picture company. Coppola began hearing complaints almost as soon as he began filming.

After only a few weeks on location, Coppola was at a loss as to where his movie was going. Not that this was out of the ordinary—he habitually had doubts about his movies while filming them, and even afterward, when he was in postproduction—but this was more difficult than usual. For Coppola, much of filmmaking involved a process of self-discovery, in which he addressed the important themes and concerns of his own life, but in the past, he had known what those themes were. With *Apocalypse Now,* his main character was discovering himself throughout his long trip up the river, through a series of revelatory episodes that Coppola had yet to finalize in his script. All Coppola knew for certain was that he wanted to address as many aspects of war and human nature as possible, and he literally drew up a checklist to make certain that they were integrated into his movie.

On April 16, just over a week after celebrating his thirty-seventh birthday with an elaborate party that included three hundred guests, a cookout featuring hundreds of pounds of hot dogs and hamburgers shipped in from San Francisco, and a six-by-eight-foot cake with the legend HAPPY BIRTHDAY, FRANCIS, APOCALYPSE NOW, and less than a month after the beginning of the filming, Coppola reached one of the most important decisions that he would make during the shooting of his picture: Harvey Keitel had to be replaced. He arrived at the decision after watching the first week's rushes with producers Fred Roos and Gray Frederickson, with Coppola concluding that Keitel wasn't right for the part. Still, his decision to fire Keitel came as a shock. "Jesus, Francis," Frederickson said, "how do you have the guts to do it?"

It was not a move that Coppola took lightly. "Firing my lead actor—that was bad," he said later, when recalling all the turmoil during the making of *Apocalyse Now*. "It's a terrible thing to do. Sure, it jeopardizes the production, but it can also ruin an actor's career, to be fired like that. It was a very, very hard decision."

Still, Coppola felt it was the correct decision. Keitel, he believed, had been miscast from the beginning.

"I had searched hard for someone to be in the film," he explained. "I had hoped for McQueen for the part. After I realized that that wasn't going to happen, I settled on Martin Sheen, but he wasn't available. Fred Roos pushed hard for Keitel, whom I admired as an actor, but I didn't feel he was right for the role, which was really very much that of an observer—a man gazing out into the jungle, thinking. Keitel is a very active actor, always attracting attention to himself, and I didn't think he'd be the kind of passive man—a face, if you like—gazing out into the jungle.

"When we got [to the Philippines], I could see that he was very uncomfortable about conditions in the jungle, and I thought, Not only do I think he's wrong casting, but what's it going to be like for six months in these difficult conditions in the jungle, for a city guy who's afraid of it? I just decided to make this tough decision. Harvey's always been gracious about it, and I'm very grateful to him for that. He's proven himself over and over, so I'd say that this was just one of the difficult things that happen. But I feel I made the right decision for the picture."

Producer Gray Frederickson, who had the unpleasant task of delivering the bad news to Keitel, remembered Keitel as being almost relieved by his dismissal. "I think Harvey realized, as well as Francis, that it wasn't his kind of role. He's a New York street guy, and this was a different role for him; he didn't quite feel right with it. It was a mutual thing."

As for Keitel's becoming a part of Coppola's new plan to sign actors to long-term contracts: Although Keitel had reached a verbal agreement to work under contract before the filming commenced on *Apocalypse Now*, both he and Coppola agreed to void the agreement.

The day after deciding to replace Keitel, Coppola rose early, shaved off his beard so he could move around unrecognized, and caught a flight to Los Angeles. The news about Keitel was bound to travel quickly, and Coppola hoped to recast the part before the rumor mill swung into overdrive. With any luck, he could check into Los Angeles without attracting attention from the press. He had lost thirty-five pounds during his month in the Philippines, and that, along with his freshly shaved face, might do the trick. He had already contacted Martin Sheen's agent and asked him to instruct his client to meet him in the airport's VIP lounge.

For Sheen, it was the beginning of a strange journey.

"I left Rome on Good Friday," said Sheen, recalling that after the long flight from Italy and a check through customs, he had about fifteen minutes with Coppola before the director's flight back to the Philippines. Coppola gave Sheen a copy of the script and briefed him on the situation, adding that Sheen was one of several candidates for the role. Sheen didn't have to read the script to know that he wanted the part. "The next day," he continued, "I got a call from Coppola's associate saying that Francis wanted me."

Sheen wrapped his work on *The Cassandra Crossing* the following Monday. The next day, he said good-bye to his wife and four children and flew to Manila.

4.

COPPOLA HAD NOT ABANDONED HOPE of enlisting the Defense Department's help in making *Apocalypse Now*. He could have used the military's technical assistance in what was easily his most complex film to date, and, in light of the problems he was experiencing with the Marcos government, he could have used the U.S. government's jets and helicopters. Coppola's arrangement with the Philippine Air Force was barely functional. Not only was he being charged an outrageous price for the use of helicopters that might or might not be available, depending on how the war was going, he also found that he had to deal with significant problems when the helicopters *were* available. Coppola could never count on seeing the same pilots from day to day, which meant he could rehearse an elaborate battle scene one day, only to find that he had to run through the same routine all over again the next day, when another set of pilots arrived on the set. In addition, Coppola needed equipment that the Philippine military could not supply, such as a large Chinook helicopter necessary to carry and drop Willard's patrol boat in the river. On April 20, Coppola contacted Secretary of Defense Donald Rumsfeld, explaining his various needs and submitting another script.

The Defense Department remained uncooperative, though officials stated that they would be willing to change their position if Coppola made revisions in some of the areas they found objectionable. The department still took great offense at the idea that it would contract the murder of one of its officers, and in reply to Coppola's request for assistance, officials suggested that Coppola could have Willard "investigating and bringing those guilty of wrongful action back for a courts-martial or medical/psychiatric treatment"—a far cry from the script's call for Willard to "terminate with extreme prejudice." Coppola, trying to reach a compromise, offered to change the script so that a civilian, rather than someone from the army, sends Willard on his mission. "I will present the situation in such a way," Coppola proposed, "that it will be obvious that there is no alternative but to terminate Kurtz if he does not comply."

Coppola's new counterproposal was received no better than his earlier suggestions, leading him to wonder if the Defense Department was practicing its own brand of censorship. The department had willingly rented equipment to the production of *The Green Berets,* and people making pictures about World War II never ran into this kind of problem.

The Defense Department's rejection, added to the other difficulties he was experiencing, left Coppola in a foul mood, utterly convinced that his film was going to be a failure. He confided as much to Ellie, who was taping their conversations, without his knowledge, and filming a documentary about the making of *Apocalypse Now,* with her husband's blessing, for Paramount's publicity department.

"When we were in the Philippines for several weeks," Ellie remembered, "United Artists told Francis that they wanted to send a documentary team over to get some material. At the time, it was customary to run five-minute pieces on television to promote films. Francis was already having difficulties and didn't really want a team coming out and snooping around, plus all the systems of getting people out to the locations were overtaxed and he just thought that having more people to look after would be too much. He told UA that he would do it 'in house.' He looked around and everyone but me had a job. He said, 'So, Ellie, you do this.' I had never made a movie or been to film school, though I had made some very short art films and he knew I had a good eye.

"The equipment arrived on the porch of our house in Manila, and I sat down and read the instructions, taught myself how to load magazines, and so on. I was using a small 16-mm newsreel camera, but it was still fairly heavy for me. I made every mistake there was to make. The tripod blew over while I was trying to shoot too close to the helicopters, and I left the lens cap on for a big shot on the main set. I thought that if I shot everything in sight, surely I would get five minutes of usable film. I wasn't getting paid—just getting raw stock. At home, Francis would start talking about all his problems, and I would just stick the tape recorder on the table and turn it on. He didn't care. He was too overwhelmed with what he was saying. By the end, I had sixty hours of film and about forty hours of sound tape."

Her footage, eventually used in the documentary *Hearts of Darkness: A Filmmaker's Apocalypse,* showed Francis to be in a terrible state of anxiety, typing feverishly at a script that refused to come together and complaining that the movie was headed toward oblivion. "The film is a $20 million disaster," he moaned. "Why won't anyone believe it?"

He meant it. During the filming of *The Godfather,* beset as he was by the interference and doubts of studio officials, daily concerns on the set, and the constant fear of being replaced as the film's director, Coppola could work with the knowledge that his stakes in the picture were relatively low. He had had none of his own money invested in the movie, and even had he failed as a director, critics would have been willing to write off the failure as the workings of a young director in over his head. The enormous success of *The Godfather,* coupled with the artistic success of *The Conversation* and *Godfather II,* pinned Coppola to his own expanding reputation as a filmmaker. With *Apocalypse Now,* he was in over his head; plus, he had his own money staked on its success. If he brought the movie in way over budget—or, worse yet, failed to deliver the movie at all—he was in a position to lose heavily.

Almost lost amid Coppola's dark predictions was the fact that, for all his trouble, he was getting some mind-boggling footage. Scenes took forever to set up, and they were often sabotaged by bad luck, as when special-effects explosions went haywire, but for all the hassles, uncertainty, and mayhem facing him, Coppola was slowly (and at great expense) assembling a film that would take people into the center of conflict. In early May, Robert Duvall, playing Kilgore (originally named Kharnage in the Milius script), wowed the company with his intense portrayal. The battle scenes were riveting ("With my helicopters, the boats and the high morale of the well-trained extras we had, there were three or four countries in the world we could have taken easily," proclaimed Dick White, a Vietnam vet and helicopter pilot, who oversaw the aerial battle sequences), and the special effects, when working according to design, were spectacular, prompting special-effects coordinator Joe Lombardi to remark, "I hate to say it, but this whole movie is special effects. You got three stars, but the action's gonna keep the audience on the edge of their seats."

Producer Gray Frederickson was impressed by the footage being shot, but he had more than a few anxious moments during the filming.

"I was a wreck for about two weeks, with all these explosions and helicopters and everybody running around," he remembered. "There would be all of this smoke going up in the air, and two or three helicopters coming from different directions would be flying into these smoke clouds. I would just sit there, crossing my fingers: 'Don't let them hit each other up in those clouds. I hope they can see.' They could see, obviously, but it was horrifying when you were looking from down below. Then they'd have these explosions that would blow these fishnets way up into the sky. I'd think, 'My God, if a helicopter rotor caught one of those fishnets, that would be the end of everybody in the cast inside that helicopter.' It's lucky we didn't get anybody hurt."

There was some truth to Joe Lombardi's statement about the special effects: Apart from the action, there was very little substance to the film. Some of this was understandable, since movies, traditionally shot out of sequence, often seem confusing and out of sync until they are edited. This might not have been the case with *Apocalypse Now* had Coppola exuded more confidence on the sets. As it was, he impressed his crew as being lost at times, struggling with his own production—which, in fact, he was. He still had no ending for his movie, and he was dissatisfied with the way he had written the parts for Willard and Kurtz.

"I had gotten totally sucked into the problems of setting up the big scenes," Coppola confessed. "But in movies, people are not interested in just seeing helicopters fly by, or seeing explosions. They want a story and character interaction. I finally realized that the script wasn't really engaging, that it didn't weave the characters and themes together to some high point which then resolved itself. I had left a flank totally open—I should have been working more as a writer."

5·

AT FIRST, WHEN HURRICANE OLGA blew in from the South China Sea on May 19, it was little more than another disruption—a typhoon bringing heavy rains for days on end, causing local flooding that washed out roads and crept into houses, including the Coppolas', which, after a couple of days, had six inches of water on the floors. The Coppolas initially found the storm a rather exciting change of pace from the sweltering heat and humidity and tensions of moviemaking, and the family tried to make the best of it, the boys playing cards and Sofia chasing frogs in the flooded backyard, Francis and Ellie entertaining a group of stranded crew members. Francis cooked pasta, played *La Bohème* at top volume until the electricity went out, and marveled at the way his guests looked by candlelight. For a short time, the wars of recent weeks had ceased.

However, as the days passed and the rains never let up, the typhoon became a huge obstacle in a film already riddled with as many hurdles as it could handle. Transportation became difficult, if not impossible; water rose to the point where there was a foot-deep lake in the Coppolas' backyard. The constant wetness made everything smelly and moldy. The production, $2 million over budget and six weeks behind schedule, became further bogged down by the rains and typhoon damage. Through it all, Coppola persisted, as if engaged in a gigantic war of wills with nature itself.

On May 21, the production moved to the coastal town of Iba, where Coppola intended to spend the next six weeks filming, among other things, the scene in which the GIs are entertained by a visiting troupe of Playboy Bunnies. The intensifying storm ripped through the area, destroying sets and blowing away a tent housing the costumes for eight hundred extras. Still determined, Coppola shot during breaks in the storm, and even during the storm itself, although he was beginning to believe, with each lost day of production, that he ought to shut down operations until the bad weather passed. He saw destruction everywhere he looked. The patrol boat had been pushed forty feet onto the bank, the speedboat blown onto the helicopter pad; the entire medevac set was destroyed. Supplies and props were washed away by the rising river, and a generator had been rendered useless by water damage. Coppola, his wife observed, was looking run-down, "on some brittle edge."

"I remember sheets of corrugated steel coming off the roofs and flying through the air," said Dean Tavoularis. "The howling winds and bamboo trees bent way over. This yellow light. It was strange. When it was over, the set had been blown away."

In early June, Coppola finally surrendered. The storm, now officially upgraded to hurricane status, offered no sign of weakening, and the sets needed to be rebuilt. Coppola and Ellie were feeling poorly—victims of dehydration, salt deprivation, and malnutrition—and both had been ordered to spend several days in the hospital, where they would be tested and given intravenous feedings and medication. Ellie's weight had plummeted to eighty-nine pounds, her lowest weight since she was fourteen, and Francis had lost the burly appearance that had become his calling card in the movie world.

According to Coppola's new plan, *Apocalypse Now* would shut down for six weeks. During that time, new sets would be constructed near Pagsanjan, a quiet agricultural community north of Manila. With any luck at all, he would be able to regroup and save his picture.

6.

COPPOLA SPENT MOST OF JUNE and July in California, dividing his time between his home in Rutherford and his place in San Francisco, trying desperately to bring the different elements of his screenplay into a cohesive story.

Fishing for ideas about how to improve the Kurtz character, he read through a biography of Genghis Khan, one of John Milius's heroes. ("Attila was a slob," Milius told an interviewer, "but Genghis Kahn was a great man.") While reading, Coppola took vocal notes on his tape recorder.

The pressure was on. While filming *Apocalypse Now,* Coppola had tried to maintain a secrecy about its details, with only marginal success. Hollywood will always be one of America's hardest-working gossip mills, and Coppola had heard an assortment of rumors connected to his picture. The film was supposedly out of control; *Coppola* was out of control. He was running out of money. . . . As usual, there was a grain of truth to most of the rumors.

Shortly after returning to the States, Coppola screened the rough footage that he'd shot in the Philippines for a group of friends, only to go into a funk when their response was less than enthusiastic. He was well aware of his reputation for indecision on the sets—which reminded him of an incident that had occurred during the shooting of *The Godfather:* He had been in a stall in the men's room when two crew members sauntered in and began grumbling about what a lousy movie *The Godfather* was turning out to be and what a horrible director Coppola was; Coppola had lifted his feet so the men wouldn't recognize his shoes.

As for the money, Coppola needed no reminders that he was in trouble. By the time he had shut down operations in the Philippines, he was $7 million into the budget—and all for what would take up about fifteen minutes of the finished film's time. The hurricane, along with the unanticipated high costs of working with the government, had put him in a deep financial hole, with no hope of completing the picture at its assigned budget. In an effort to put himself back on budget, Coppola flew to Los Angeles and met with lawyers and officials of United Artists. The parties struck up an agreement in which UA would loan Coppola the $3 million in current overruns, but only on the condition that *Apocalypse Now* earn $40 million in rentals. If it didn't, Coppola would be personally responsible for paying back the loan. It was a gamble, but a calculated one. All Coppola had to do was complete the movie on his original budget and hope that its reputation carried it at the box office.

While rewriting his screenplay, Coppola solicited the opinions of a number of his trusted friends, including Fred Roos and former classmate Dennis Jakob, who had worked as a crew member on *The Rain People.* Jakob, whom one observer described as "a brilliant eccentric who quotes Nietzsche and lives with a trunkful of original screenplays in a men-only hotel," worked with Coppola on stitching the elements of mythology in *Heart of Darkness* with the Vietnam experience. Within a few months, Jakob would play a vital role in helping Coppola find his movie's ending.

The script struggles left Coppola depressed and doubting his ability. Perhaps he wasn't quite the screenwriter he thought he was. To Susan Braudy, an admirer profiling him for *The Atlantic Monthly*, he confessed his greatest fear of the moment. "I got problems," he admitted. "I'm too good at adapting other people's scripts. Better than writing my own. I don't want to be known as an adapter of other people's work."

Ellie saw his script problems from a different perspective. Her husband could still write with the best of them, but he had spent so much time on *Apocalypse Now*, researching, reading, writing, filming, and talking about it for the better part of a year, that he was too close to the material. Maybe it would be helpful, she suggested, were he simply to dictate what he knew about his movie into his tape recorder. Willing to try almost anything, Coppola gave it a shot.

7.

THE COPPOLAS HEADED BACK to the Philippines in late July, stopping briefly in Hong Kong before continuing on to their new digs in Pagsanjan. To the locals, accustomed to earning an average of a dollar or two a day, the arrival of a high-spending film-production company meant an incredible financial windfall, and for the next nine months, the standard of living increased dramatically, especially for those who rented their houses to people in the company for previously unimaginable amounts. Laborers working on the set construction enjoyed three times their normal salaries. Concerned about the effect the money was having on the townspeople, Pagsanjan's high school principal took to driving from bar to bar, trying to convince the suddenly flush Filipinos to refrain from blowing their paychecks on women and liquor. "Our people have lost their sense of values," he complained.

After watching his film's rushes and hearing one of his friends observe that the acting seemed tentative, Coppola decided to try to push Martin Sheen to another level of performance, beginning with the first day's shooting, in a scene that depicted Willard alone in his room at a Saigon hotel. Coppola had recently dreamed that he had met with Sheen and a Green Beret at the hotel and that the Green Beret had told him that he had the Willard character wrong. In real life, a soldier like Willard would be more vain—the kind of guy who would stand in front of a mirror and admire himself. For the first day's filming, Coppola had concocted just such a scene.

August 3, the day of the shoot, was Sheen's thirty-sixth birthday. By his own admission, he drank and smoked too much, and he wasn't in good physical condition. He hadn't been in the Philippines a month when he fainted in the street from the heat and humidity; he received four stitches for a cut he sustained from a special-effects explosion. He was emotionally fragile, as well. Earlier in the shoot, before the hurricane, he had brooded about the poverty he'd seen in the streets outside his hotel in Manila, where pigs ran around freely, chased by children without teeth. During the hiatus, he started having second thoughts about returning to the Philippines, and he had demanded more money; he and Coppola fought over it, and they had what Sheen later described as "a very heavy falling out," but Coppola won the day. When Sheen returned to the shoot, he was still worried about what lay ahead. "I don't know if I'm going to live through this," he confided to a friend. "Those fuckers are crazy; all those helicopters are really blowing things up."

Coppola was aware of Sheen's emotional state, and he believed that if he pushed him in the right direction, forcing some of his inner turmoil to surface on-camera, he might be able to draw out the Willard in Sheen. To that point, Willard had been an observer, as he would remain for much of the picture. However, Coppola felt that viewers needed to know how someone like Willard could actually be capable of accepting and carrying out his mission; they needed to see Willard as a man who kept himself under tight control.

Prior to shooting the scene, Martin Sheen drank so heavily that, by his own later admission, he was barely able to stand when the time came for him to do the scene. Believing that Sheen was in a state where his innermost feelings might be explored, Coppola began to prod his actor.

"He would tell Martin, 'You're evil; I want all the evil, the violence, the hatred in you to come out,'" recalled a crew member. "You tell that to a guilt-ridden Irish Catholic and he hasn't a chance. . . . It was devastating."

When cameras rolled, Sheen was highly charged emotionally, barely in control. As instructed, he walked to the hotel room's full-length mirror, admired his seminaked body, and, in a moment of improvisation, lashed out at his image with a vicious karate chop, shattering the mirror and cutting his hand. Coppola offered to halt the shooting, but Sheen insisted on continuing. With his own blood running freely and the cameras capturing every moment of his private agony now bursting to the surface, Sheen turned in an astonishing performance, his rage and despair so real that Eleanor Coppola feared that Sheen might actually attack her husband or the cameramen. By the time the scene had ended, Sheen was collapsed in a heap on the floor, naked, his body smeared with his own blood. He wept uncontrollably, tried to persuade the people in the room to sing "Amazing Grace" with him, and begged them to pray with him. The incident left Coppola and the camera crew visibly shaken.

Coppola defended his tactics afterward, claiming that they were needed to obtain the performance necessary for the picture.

"Marty's character was coming across as too bland," he explained. "I tried to break through it. I always look for other levels, hidden levels in the actor's personality and in the personality of the character he plays. I conceived this all night drunk; we'd see another side of the guy."

Although both Coppola and Sheen were pleased by the outcome of the scene, not everyone agreed with Coppola's method of direction.

"Francis did a dangerous and terrible thing," said one witness to the shooting. "He assumed the role of a psychiatrist and did a kind of brainwashing on a man who was much too sensitive. He put Martin in a place and didn't bring him back."

A place, dark and imposing, not unlike Vietnam, where basic instincts warred with all things civil, reducing a man to his lowest price, easily purchased by awaiting madness.

8.

WHILE REWRITING HIS SCRIPT, Francis Coppola had decided to give a surreal shading to parts of his movie, as if, in presenting the phantasmagorical elements of warfare, viewers might better understand the way reality blended with the unreal—or, more importantly, the way the characters of Willard and Kurtz could be separated by only the thinnest, filmy line. In his original perception of the story, John Milius had seen the jungle as a character unto itself, as important as the war; the jungle was alive and primitive, bringing a man in touch with the animal within. While Coppola integrated some of this into his film—particularly in the scene in which Willard and Chef encounter a tiger in the jungle, and in the scenes at the Kurtz compound—he used the river, more than the jungle, as the major touchstone. As a literary device, water has always had a multitude of applications and meanings—baptism, danger and death, life, timelessness and perpetual motion, to name a few—and Coppola, as much as any of his peers, was adept at working with literary devices in his films. In *Apocalypse Now*, the river became a place of severe realities and horrible nightmares.

Immediately after shooting the hotel-room scene with Martin Sheen, Coppola moved to one of the most important sequences in his picture, in which Willard's boat reaches the Do Long Bridge, set as far away from civilization as seems possible. It was, in the words of one frightened but exhilarated soldier, "the asshole of the world," where warfare was constantly staged with no winners or losers—only casualties. Every night, the enemy destroyed the bridge, and the following day the American soldiers rebuilt it. There wasn't a commanding officer to be found; there was no discipline or moral order.

The scene, shot over the course of thirteen nights, setting the film even further over budget and behind schedule, was a Coppola masterpiece, exquisitely set up and shot, a perfect metaphor. Strings of light, reminiscent of Christmas tree bulbs—or, in Coppola's case, the lights suspended over Little Italy during the religious-festival scene in *Godfather II*—gave the bridge a strange definition in the midst of battle, where flares lit the night and colored sulfuric smoke rose and enveloped the river in a hellish fog. In this surreal place, the war seemed both life-threatening and dazzlingly beautiful. The soldiers never seemed younger. (In fact, Coppola used his twelve-year-old son, Gio, as an extra in the scene.) Over three decades earlier, during World War II, the Japanese had blown up this very same bridge; it had been left as it was, a series of concrete footings jutting out of the riverbed, until Dean Tavoularis and his crew rebuilt it.

Filming this sequence was painfully slow, weighed down by difficult lighting and camera settings, changing weather conditions that fouled up continuity, Coppola's occasional script revisions, and tedious rehearsals. Tempers shortened as people made their way through a quagmire of mud and muck. One day passed into the next, the only certainty being that each day was costing between thirty and fifty thousand dollars on an already-ruptured budget.

Coppola recognized that he was barely holding his production in check, but he had little choice but to let the movie, now with a life of its own, move toward its own destiny. "The way we made it," he would say, "was very much like the way the Americans were in Vietnam. We were in the jungle, there were too many of us, we had access to too much money, too much equipment; and little by little we went insane. I think you can see it in the film. As it goes up the river, you can see the photography going a little crazy and the director and the actors going a little crazy. After a while, I realized I was a little frightened, because I was getting deeper in debt and no longer recognized the kind of movie I was making."

"He went over the edge," associate producer Mona Skager remarked. "His mental state was a big part of the movie. When you watch the film, you can see how it gets a little crazier as it goes along. Well, that was the state of mind. The whole thing was crazy."

The next scene, the French plantation sequence, was a complete contrast in tone from the Do Long Bridge segment. Early in the film's planning stage,

Coppola had determined that he wanted to make a statement about war in general, as opposed to commentary exclusive to Vietnam. Part of his decision was pragmatic—he still hoped to obtain the army's assistance in making *Apocalypse Now*—and part of his decision was artistic: Rather then delve into the politics of Vietnam, he aimed to get audiences to experience the war, as if they had been dropped into the center of the conflict and had to survive the movie itself.

The French plantation scene was a subtle exception. In this scene, Willard and his army escort encounter a small group of wealthy descendants of the original French colonists in Indochina. Through fragments of conversation, we would be given a brief history lesson—or at least a sense of history—of a time before United States involvement in Vietnam, the segment ending on a violent, symbolic note when a French woman is raped and her husband murdered by GIs.

The art department had gone to great lengths in designing the interior of the plantation's main house, dressing it with authentic antiques, patterned rugs, paintings and framed photographs, vases and fans, mirrors, books, and animal heads. Under the usual circumstances, Coppola, a stickler for detail, might have admired his set designers' efforts. However, with the budget rocketing out of control, he groused about a set so exquisitely designed that he could not possibly fit everything into his movie. As it was, he couldn't step backward to look through his viewfinder without bumping into something.

"We were aware that we were going over budget, and I asked everyone to make their best efforts to spend less money," Coppola remembered. "For example, I didn't cast some of the European actors we were considering for [the scene]. A French actor had agreed to do it, but it was for decent money and I decided to cast lesser actors who'd work for a more modest budget. But then, when I got to the set, I saw that the art and decorating departments had not stinted one little bit; they'd spent a fortune on the set and furnishings. I was very annoyed and angry at the set, which was basically beautiful, but I would have rather had a cheaper set and the actors I originally was going to have."

To make matters worse, he couldn't get his actors in sync. The French actors, including Aurore Clément and Christian Marquand, were accustomed to working very methodically, speaking their dialogue in a series of short takes that were subsequently pieced together during the editing process. The American actors preferred to play out an entire scene, lest some of the emotion be lost in repeated takes. As the awkward, unusable takes piled up, Coppola wondered if part of the problem might be attributed to the fact that the French were speaking their lines in a foreign language, or if he should blame himself for casting a number of people who were not professional actors.

In retrospect, the scene became the ultimate symbol of Coppola's problems and frustration during the filming of *Apocalypse Now*. Shot over a period of five days, at a cost of hundreds of thousands of dollars, the French plantation scene was intended to be an important segment in the early part of the movie. Instead, it wound up on the cutting room floor, never seen by the public except in fragments in the *Hearts of Darkness* documentary.

9.

MARLON BRANDO ARRIVED, on schedule, on August 31. The superlative actor had been on a career upswing since his appearance in *The Godfather*, and Coppola had traded on his name and reputation while financing *Apocalypse Now*.

Brando had come at a high price. Instead of charging the $3.5 million he had originally demanded to appear in the movie, Brando, at Coppola's urging and as an act of friendship, agreed to amend his contract and make the movie for three million dollars against 11.5 percent of the picture's adjusted gross profits. The new agreement had been reached during the filming hiatus, when Coppola was vulnerable, trying to cut costs and drum up additional money to finance his picture, gambling that it would still come in at a reasonable price and score big at the box office. To Coppola, Brando would be worth every penny of his salary if he turned in another brilliant performance, showed the kind of leadership he'd displayed during the shooting of *The Godfather*, and helped the director find the ending to his film.

Instead, Brando turned up terribly overweight and totally unprepared for his role.

Coppola had been aware of Brando's weight problem—the actor had ballooned to over 250 pounds, with one report estimating 285 pounds—and earlier in the year, he had asked Brando to take some of it off. Coppola had originally envisioned Kurtz to be an imposing figure, a brilliant warrior gone mad, capable of turning a tribe of natives subservient by his powerful presence; the Brando he was looking at now hardly filled the bill.

In addition, Brando had given very little thought to his role. Coppola had provided him with a copy of *Heart of Darkness*, along with T. S. Eliot's epic poem *The Waste Land*, to prepare him for his role, and Brando had assured Coppola that he had read the material. It soon became apparent that Brando hadn't looked at the Conrad novella, and after some preliminary discussion about the Kurtz character, Brando admitted his deception. "I lied," he told Coppola. "I never read it."

This was not good news. From his experiences on *The Godfather*, Coppola knew that Brando liked to work out the details of his character and performance through lengthy discussions with his director, and with Brando signed on for only five weeks, there was precious little time to spare. Other directors might have found this situation intolerable, but, as a huge fan of Brando's work, Coppola was revitalized by his discussions with Brando, and by the actor's extraordinary improvisations. Brando, he proclaimed, was the finest actor he had ever worked with.

Brando had a different view of what was taking place. Coppola's script, he felt, was a horrible mess, with Kurtz being little more than a stereotypical character showing very little resemblance to the Conrad character. Brando suggested that Kurtz be even more ominous and mysterious than the part Coppola had written for him, and he even offered to rewrite the script to improve the character. All this was immensely helpful, but as Brando later confessed, he had another motive when he engaged Coppola in their endless hours of conversation. "I was good at bullshitting Francis and persuading him to think my way," he declared, "and he bought it, but what I'd really wanted from the beginning was to find a way to make my part smaller so that I wouldn't have to work as hard."

Through their discussions, the two reached a compromise on Kurtz's character. Whereas Coppola envisioned Kurtz to be a wild Gauguin-like character now living alone in his excess and madness, Brando took a more benign approach to Kurtz. As Brando perceived him, Kurtz had indeed gone mad, but he had been driven to it by the war. Brando proposed playing Kurtz as a kind of David Berrigan; he would wear black Vietnamese pajamas and fill Willard's ears with talk about America's guilt in the war. The sentiment might have approximated some of Coppola's personal feelings about the war, but after his conversations with John Milius and their arguments about politics and war in Southeast Asia, Coppola was not about to turn Kurtz into a demented peace activist. "Hey, Marlon," he told Brando, "I may not know everything about this movie, but one thing I know it's not about *our guilt.*"

Brando's weight also played a significant role in the discussions about Kurtz. Brando, embarrassed by his obesity, wanted to find ways to disguise his size. ("He wasn't what everyone expected to see because he had gained so much weight," Gray Frederickson recalled. "We had drawings of what we thought he was going to look like, in these boots and fatigues, looking the way you remembered him to look. We had to shoot it differently.") The loose-fitting black pajamas were a start. In addition, if his character dwelled in a world of darkness—adding, by Brando's rationalization, to his air of mystery—the sets would be lit only sparingly, further camouflaging Brando's excessive weight. Coppola, on the other hand, suggested that they use Brando's size to further define Kurtz's excesses. Overindulgence could be viewed as an indicator of how far Kurtz had slipped.

The two finally agreed to make Kurtz a gigantic, hulking presence, adding to the myth that Willard had developed in his own mind as he traveled upriver to assassinate him. To achieve this effect, Coppola hired Pete Cooper, a six-foot-five-inch Vietnam veteran working on the film as a military adviser, to stand in for Brando during the long shots. Brando requested and received five-inch lifts for his shoes, but it wound up being a disaster. On his first day of filming, he twisted his ankle and was unable to work.

10.

THE MAKING OF *APOCALYPSE NOW* was beginning to take a huge toll, not only on Coppola, who suffered from both nightmares and sleepless nights throughout the filming, but on just about everyone associated with the production. Some of the cast and crew used drugs, particularly marijuana, to ease the tension, while others retreated to local bars, where they got drunk and occasionally fought and tossed around furniture. For Pete Cooper, the production brought him back to his own experiences in Vietnam; for months, he screamed in his sleep.

Dean Tavoularis, growing more depressed and alienated with each passing month in the jungle, immersed himself in the macabre task of designing the Kurtz compound, spreading blood and skulls everywhere, and piling up garbage and arranging bones that he obtained from a restaurant until rats started to gather on the set and crew members complained about the stench. "I was living in the house of death I was making," he recalled. "It became such a low level in my life that somehow putting blood on staircases and rolling heads down steps seemed natural to me."

Alex Tavoularis worked with his brother on the *Apocalypse Now* sets, and he, too, was having second thoughts about the horrors of the Kurtz compound.

"For the Kurtz compound, which was supposed to be the ultimate madness—Joseph Conrad's vision of the depths of human depravity," he recalled, "Dean wanted us to create these piles of human skulls. Of course, many were plastic skulls from Hollywood, but we created these heaps, and there were rats crawling around everywhere. When Martin Sheen came to the set, he was astounded. He had his two young sons—Emilio and Charlie—with him, and he was very concerned. To that point, he had not been involved in this kind of madness, and he asked Francis to dismantle these piles of squalor. In our hearts we knew he was right, but we were on a road, hell-bent on creating this world of madness. But Martin Sheen shook us up a little bit."

The Kurtz compound, modeled after the Cambodian ruins of Angkor Wat, was a work of art, constructed by nearly seven hundred laborers. To build the temple, local workers carried handmade adobe blocks, weighing three hundred pounds apiece, on bamboo poles to the construction site, where they were lifted into place on bamboo hoists. To a craftsman like Dean Tavoularis, accustomed to building elaborate sets with state-of-the-art equipment and tools, the construction work was very primitive, not that far removed from the way the ancient temples themselves had been built, but he had learned early on that in this part of the world, human labor was cheaper than machinery.

"The original idea," Tavoularis explained, "was that the compound was going to be blown up, and if you're going to do that, you have to build in a different way than if you're not going to blow it up. You can't just put up a wall or scaffolding and attach the stone or skin. I remember looking at this *National Geographic* with a centerfold of the building of Angkor Wat. They had used sleds and carabao and bamboo poles, and had created a miniature crane to lift the blocks off these barges or sleds. We were building the same way."

Instead of employing local extras to populate the Kurtz compound, Coppola asked Eva Gardos, a production assistant, to travel to Luzon, a northern province, to recruit members of a local tribe, the Ifugaos, to live on the set and appear in the film in exchange for food, medical supplies, betel nuts, a small salary, and animals for sacrificial purposes. The primitive mountain tribe, reportedly cannibalistic as recently as World War II, offered the kind of verisimilitude Coppola wanted for Kurtz's Montagnard guard.

During the weekend of their arrival in Pagsanjan, the Ifugaos held a feast that lasted the better part of two days. Wearing loincloths and ceremonial blankets, the tribal elders assembled in the priests' house and, for nearly fifteen hours, sang and chanted a long tribal legend about a couple and their life together. Eleanor Coppola, who had asked permission to observe and film the ceremony, found herself absorbed by the hypnotic chanting, which at one point found the elders chanting, "Coppola, Coppola, Coppola" in honor of their host. Outside, a group of Ifugaos danced around a pole.

The chanting continued through the night and into the next morning, until around ten o'clock, when the tribesmen assembled outside and began the ritualistic slaughter, first of a chicken, whose bile was read for omens and signs, and then of five pigs, butchered in order of size and boiled in a large cauldron. Ellie, who had risen early to observe more of the ritual, was taken by how natural the ritual seemed. When the tribal mayor informed her that they were going to sacrifice a carabao, she rushed to get her husband, who was working on the script in his room. They arrived in time to see two priests praying by the huge animal. Suddenly, four men rushed up to the carabao and hacked it with bolo knives, killing it with four blows to the back of its neck and butchering it within minutes. Francis and Ellie were honored with a gift of the carabao's heart. Afterward, at the request of the Ifugaos, Coppola posed with two of the priests for a photograph.

That same evening, Marlon Brando threw a party at a resort hotel for the Ifugaos and the entire *Apocalypse Now* cast and crew. Four hundred people attended festivities that included entertainment by local dancers, acrobats, and a magician and concluded with a fireworks display engineered by the company's special-effects department. Although there would be many tough months ahead of them, several crew members pointed to the weekend's ceremonies as a turning point for the company. The Ifugaos, supposedly the most primitive people on the set, offered a sense of calm amid the craziness of modern moviemaking.

11.

FRANCIS FORD COPPOLA NEVER INTENDED *Apocalypse Now* to be a magnum opus or cornerstone to his career as a filmmaker, and he certainly never dreamed that it would give him the grief that it did. He had simply aspired to make a good action picture about Vietnam before moving on to the film that really mattered to him—his biopic of automaker Preston Tucker.

But here he was, deep in the Philippine jungle, questioning his own sanity and ability to pull off the picture, battling with his own crew, and worrying about what people were saying about him back home. *Apocalypse Now* had become his personal Vietnam and, whispered many of the people around him, including his wife, he had become Kurtz. He could not write a good scene for Brando; much of what he filmed was either improvisation or the result of lengthy conversations with his actor.

"There'd be long discussions with Brando," Coppola recalled, "and I would take these ideas and go back and write them up as dialogue or sequences. We'd record the longer speeches on a tape recorder, which Marlon would use to refresh himself. He would go off whenever he wanted to, but there was always a written script."

According to Frederic Forrest, this was not always the case. There were times, Forrest insisted, when a scene was shot with only skeletal dialogue or, in some cases, when it was totally improvised.

"That whole scene where we shoot up the sampan was improvised," he remembered, referring to the tense, memorable scene in which Willard and his crew come upon a small boat filled with a Vietnamese family, only to murder everyone on board after a terrible misunderstanding. "It flowed like music," said Forrest. "Francis set it up so the improv really flowed. Before we started, he gave each of us something to do. For instance, I was to search the sampan. And it was an incredible, powerful scene! When we had finished, it was absolutely quiet. Vittorio Storaro was just stunned. He said it was the best scene that he'd ever seen. But none of it was written down."

Besides dealing with Brando, Coppola had to contend with Dennis Hopper, who seemed to be in his own little universe. Hopper brought an odd, hyperkinetic energy to the picture that Coppola wanted to include, but he had a maddening inability to learn his lines. Coppola had made significant changes in the script to accommodate Hopper, adding prominence to his role, but he and Hopper never seemed to be on the same page. If that wasn't enough, Hopper disgusted a number of the crew by wearing the same clothes, day in and day out, throughout his time on the movie, until he had become so ripe that people hated to go anywhere near him.

Coppola was at a crossroads: He had mortgaged everything he had, literally and figuratively, on a picture he was no longer certain he could deliver. One evening, he climbed on a lighting scaffold and lay on the platform in the rain, unable and unwilling to go on. Hundreds of crew members were waiting for him on the set, but he had nothing to shoot. Brando refused to go to the set until Coppola had given him material he deemed acceptable, but Coppola had no idea what that might be. Instead, he lay on the platform in the rain, totally miserable. Finally, Vittorio Storaro suggested that he might be able to capture a certain effect through the use of smoke and strange lighting—something that might appease Brando—and Coppola agreed to return to the set. Brando eventually joined them, and the evening was saved.

Desperate for any kind of creative input, Coppola sent for Dennis Jakob, who had worked so well with him on the script earlier in the year. Jakob arrived on September 22, carrying an armload of books and a suitcase filled with fruits, vegetables, spices, and roses from Napa. He was shocked by Coppola's condition. "By the time I got there, he had run out of emotional gas," Jakob recalled, adding that he felt that the director was in over his head with *Apocalypse Now.* "The typhoon killed him," he continued. "He was taking dope and his mind was like jelly."

Jakob conferred with Coppola and Brando, going over the script and arguing that Kurtz had to die at the end of the movie—an ending Coppola had considered but had yet to adopt. Jakob explained that, as far as he could see, *Heart of Darkness* had been a retelling of the myth of "The Fisher King." Coppola was aware of the story from his student days, but he had not considered it while writing *Apocalypse Now*. Jakob gave the director a copy of Sir James Frazer's *The Golden Bough,* which discussed the myth, and a copy of *From Ritual and Romance,* which had directly influenced T. S. Eliot when he was writing *The Waste Land.*

Suddenly, it all started to come together for Coppola—the war, *Heart of Darkness,* "The Fisher King," and even the Ifugaos' sacrifice of the carabao, which seemed to bear an eerie parallel to Willard's sacrifice of Kurtz. Coppola had always understood Willard and Kurtz to be conflicting sides of the same person, but he didn't know how he was going to resolve this conflict once Willard had made his journey and confronted Kurtz. Now, with the additional influence from *The Golden Bough,* the theme and resolution of the movie became clear: The search was for the truth, but in order to accept the truth, one had to accept both good and evil, life and death, as part of the same *whole.* When all was said and done, *Apocalypse Now* was a movie about choices and the paths that are taken to discover the truth.

Brando, too, was taken by Dennis Jakob's ideas, and in one of his final appearances before the camera, he performed two lengthy, astonishing improvisations intended to be inserted into the movie just before his assassination. During the improvisations, Brando proved why he is regarded as one of the greatest actors in film history. He ran the gamut of emotions, digging inside himself and his character until he reached an amazing fusion. When he had finished, he was totally drained.

"Francis," he said, "I've gone as far as I can go. If you need more, you can get another actor."

12.

BRANDO CONCLUDED HIS WORK on October 8, and from that point until December, when the company shut down for the holidays, Coppola devoted almost all of his time to polishing the scenes at the Kurtz compound. In a sense, Brando's performance had formed the outer wall of the film's final third; it was now up to Coppola to build his ending around the structure Brando had given him.

Coppola might not have known how his film would be received when it was eventually released, but he knew one thing for certain: It was going to be beautiful to look at. Vittorio Storaro was making *Apocalypse Now* a much better film than it might have been under another cinematographer's supervision. Storaro had taken numerous photographs throughout the filming, and Coppola was amazed by the images. "God! I'd go to see that movie, wouldn't you?" he exclaimed one evening after looking over the latest batch of Storaro's photos.

At first, Storaro had been reluctant to work on *Apocalypse Now*. He and Coppola had met previously on a couple of occasions and had gotten along splendidly, and Storaro openly admired Coppola's work, but he did not want to infringe on Coppola's working relationship with Gordon Willis. He agreed to join the *Apocalypse Now* team only when Coppola assured him that Willis was unavailable to work on the film, and when Coppola promised to give him the artistic freedom needed to put his own signature on the picture.

"The original idea," said Storaro, "was to depict the impact of one culture which had been superimposed over another culture. I was trying to show the conflict between natural energy and artificial energy. For example, the dark, shadowy jungle where natural energy reigns, in contrast to the American military base where big powerful generators and huge, probing lights provided the energy." As Storaro saw it, Vietnam was "a conflict between technology and nature as well as between different cultures. I tried to use the lights and camera to suggest this."

Ironically, nature thwarted some of Storaro's technology while he and his crew worked on the film. The rainy season was particularly difficult, especially at night, when the rains created a mud mire that hindered dolly shots and kept the crew scampering to protect equipment. Then, on the nights when it didn't rain, Storaro and his men had to create artificial rain so the night-to-night shootings would match. "I don't believe anyone anticipated that it would be that long and difficult," Storaro said of the shoot.

Least of all the film's director. Throughout the fall, Coppola's moods continued to fluctuate wildly from intolerable anger, when filming was going badly, to an almost irrational ebullience when the going was good and he was convinced that he had all the answers. The tiniest negative remark during the screening of the rushes could send him into a blind rage; on other occasions, he would shrug off the latest bit of adversity with barely a notice.

"I have a lot of mixed feelings about Francis," said Martin Sheen. "I am very fond of him personally. The thing I love about him most is that he never, like a good general, asked you to do anything he wouldn't do. He was right there with us, lived there in the shit and mud up to his ass, suffered the same diseases, ate the same food. I don't think he realizes how tough he is to work for. God, is he tough. But I will sail with that son of a bitch anytime."

Working with Coppola was challenging enough; living with him could be a trial. Throughout the fall, Eleanor Coppola dealt with her husband's moods as well as she could, enduring the tirades and trying to keep his upswings in perspective. Still, she was relieved when Francis announced that he had to get away for a few days, spend some time on his own, and sort out what was troubling him. Like everyone else, Ellie felt the strain of all the months in the Philippines, and of staying supportive of her husband and being a good mother to her daughter. She missed her sons, who had returned to San Francisco earlier in the fall to attend school.

The holiday season found Coppola in fine form, upbeat and convinced that he finally had his film under control. Before returning to the States, he had come up with the idea of making a montage of Willard's killing Kurtz and the Ifugaos' sacrificing the carabao, drawing a direct parallel between the two. He had spent a couple of nights filming the Ifugaos' reenactment of the ceremony that he and Ellie had witnessed shortly after the tribe's arrival in Pansanjan, and he came away with excellent footage. Finally, after months of agonizing indecision, the ending of his movie was locked into place.

He was further thrilled when he assembled five hours of rough footage and screened it with Dean Tavoularis and Dennis Jakob. It was amazing, he told Ellie, to think that he had improvised so much of the ending and had managed to pull it off; it wasn't just a good movie—it had the markings of a masterpiece. All he had to do was trim away the material that didn't belong and he would have his picture.

Ellie viewed some of the footage a few days later and agreed that it was amazing, perhaps even the work of a visionary filmmaker. She was troubled, however, by Francis's manic state, terrified that he could no longer differentiate between the visionary and the insane. In addition, she was feeling personally unfulfilled as an artist. When in the Philippines, she had been busy with her documentary; now back in California and removed from that work, she was beginning to feel lost in Francis's shadow. Her needs were always secondary to those of her famous filmmaker husband.

The gulf between the two widened even more after Coppola returned without his wife to the Philippines to shoot the final scenes for *Apocalypse Now*. Francis, Ellie believed, was losing his perspective. He was now living in a luxurious cottage in Hidden Valley, a resort located inside an extinct volcano; his telexes home contained orders for stereo equipment, gourmet wines and frozen steaks, and other luxurious items. He wrote of extending his stay and shooting new scenes. Although she feared for what was happening to her husband, Ellie maintained her silence, afraid to speak her mind lest she be accused of disloyalty.

Finally, she decided that she had to say something. In a toughly worded telex sent toward the end of February, she accused him of becoming a Kurtz, revered by hundreds of people at his beck and call, living in luxury in Hidden Valley. He had gone out to the Philippines to expose Vietnam, but somehow, in the process, he was creating his own Vietnam. He was, said Ellie, "an ass-hole," and she was saying as much because she loved him and there was no one else around who would tell him what she was saying. Then, as if to prove her point, Ellie sent copies of the letter to Dean Tavoularis, Vittorio Storaro, and others on the production staff.

Coppola responded angrily. Here he was, doing the best work of his life, and rather than support him, Ellie was accusing him of self-indulgence. And if this betrayal wasn't bad enough, she had transmitted her message over a wire service that could have been picked up by just about anyone around. The least she could have done, he felt, was send him a letter and give him the opportu-nity to explain his actions.

Given his situation, Coppola's wrath was ironic. He was indeed accom-plishing some of the best work of his life, but he was doing so at the cost of his own psychological well-being. Ellie had been on the mark when she accused him of self-indulgence—"All those things did contribute to the state of mind that was a little like Kurtz," Coppola later admitted, although he contested the notion that his behavior was meglamanical—but there was one part of his life that he had kept hidden from her: For months, he had been involved in a serious affair with a young screenwriter working as an executive assistant on *Apocalypse Now.*

As Coppola would later admit, the tryst had started innocently enough, as a kind of mentor-student relationship, but it soon blossomed into some-thing deeper, continuing even after Coppola returned to the States during the movie's hiatus, when he would meet with her during his overnight stays in San Francisco. Later, when he was back in the Philippines and left the com-pany to go off on his own, supposedly to straighten out his inner turmoil, he spent a good portion of his time with this new lover. Not that such liaisons would have been unusual during the shoot: The rumor mill was rife with gos-sip about the different affairs taking place in the Philippines, and Coppola's name was not omitted from all the talk.

"The particular person at the time of *Apocalypse,*" he told interviewer David Breskin in 1991, "always made me feel like a million dollars in terms of 'I was talented, and I could do it.'" Such encouragement, said Coppola, was badly needed at the time, and he didn't feel he was getting the same reassur-ance from Ellie.

His deception, however, tormented him. He fancied himself to be a good husband and father, a traditional family man and provider; he had grown comfortable with Ellie, and even when times were rough, as they were now, he could not realistically see himself leaving her. Nevertheless, he had great affection for the younger woman, and he was deeply troubled over how to resolve his dilemma.

Coppola kept the affair a secret throughout the filming of *Apocalypse Now*, and if Ellie had any suspicions of her own, she kept them to herself. The tension between them continued, especially after Ellie rejoined Francis in the Philippines in early March. By that time, however, Francis had another problem to confront—one that threatened the completion of the movie and, by extension, his very future.

13.

APOCALYPSE NOW HAD WEIGHED heavily on Martin Sheen from the beginning. The Willard role had been difficult enough, especially for a liberal-leaning individual like Sheen, who considered himself patriotic but who, like so many, questioned the country's leadership during the war in Southeast Asia. Acting in Coppola's war-nightmare had drained him physically and emotionally. The constant heat and rain, the squalor and poverty in the streets, the mosquitoes that seemed to be eating him alive, the tension on the set, his horrible eating habits and excessive smoking—all made the movie an endurance test, the greatest ordeal of Sheen's acting career.

On the evening of March 5, while sitting alone in his cabin room and reading, Sheen felt sharp pains in his chest. His wife, Janet, was in Manila for the weekend, but rather than speak with anyone else about his pain, Sheen, thinking that he'd better quit smoking, lay back and listened to the wind howling outside his window. "I kept waking up, feeling like there was a hot poker on my chest," he recalled.

The pain increased throughout the night, and the following morning, Sheen decided to seek help. He lay on the floor, pulled on his clothes and boots, and crawled outside, inching his way to the road. In time, a public bus pulled over and loaded him on board. From his window in the bus, Sheen spotted the film company's wardrobe van, which took him to the production office.

"Dean Tavoularis," Sheen remembered, "stuck his head in the van, looked at me and started to cry. A doctor came in and he looked real worried. I just said, 'Get me a priest.' And he came and gave me the last rites."

"I was at the production compound that morning," said Tavoularis, "and there was a very agitated Filipino waving his arms and saying something I didn't understand. He led me to a wardrobe truck full of army shoes, and in the back, lying on all these shoes, was Martin Sheen. He was pale and sweaty. I held his hand and said, 'What happened?' Finally, another Filipino said they had been bringing in these shoes when they found Marty on the side of the road. He'd apparently had a heart attack. I felt the main thing to do was to get a helicopter."

Sheen was eventually transported to Manila, where doctors determined that he had suffered a serious heart attack. In addition, he was having a nervous breakdown.

"I completely fell apart," said Sheen. "My spirit was exposed. I cried and cried. I turned gray—my eyes, my beard—all gray. I was in intensive care. Janet slept on the floor beside me. She called a therapist in New York and I talked to her every day and these two ladies pulled me through. I knew I would never come back until I accepted full and total responsibility for what had happened to me. No one put a gun to my head and forced me to be there. I had a big ego and wanted to be in a Coppola film."

Twenty years after *Apocalypse Now* appeared on screens around the world, Sheen still found it exceedingly difficult to talk about his time in the Philippines. He recalled wonderful experiences with Frederic Forrest, Albert Hall, Laurence Fishburne, and Sam Bottoms—which led to lasting friendships—but the overall experience was so overwhelming and powerfully emotional that Sheen hated to dredge them up.

"I'll just say that it was a deeply personal, long, and painful journey," he remarked. "There was a lot of darkness and a lot of despair—and a lot of humanity, too—but if you'd told me, 'This is what you're in for,' I would have passed in a minute. When they were rolling me down that corridor in the hospital, some four or five hours after I'd had a heart attack, my wife appeared alongside me, running with the gurney, and she leaned down and whispered in my ear, 'It's only a movie, babe.' And that saved my life. She saved my life. *It's only a movie.*"

Coppola feared for both his actor and his film. After talking to Janet Sheen and hearing that Martin's condition was stable, and that in all likelihood he would recover and eventually be able to finish the picture, Coppola let his business instincts take over. In a sense, the experience was similar to what he'd faced when he replaced Harvey Keitel: Word about Sheen would spread, and once it did, Coppola's picture would be in jeopardy. United Artists had been pushing him for months to wrap up production, and now there was a good chance that the company's higher-ups would demand that he remove Sheen from the picture. He would have to act quickly and decisively.

His options weren't good. If he pushed to keep Sheen on the picture, he would appear to be placing his movie's completion above the welfare of one of his actors; if he dropped Sheen from the production—or if Sheen decided to leave—he would have to scrap almost everything he had filmed, all but guaranteeing him a devastating financial loss. The best immediate course of action, Coppola decided, was to downplay Sheen's condition to the press and film around Sheen while he recovered. In the days immediately following Sheen's heart attack, the official line was that he had collapsed while jogging in the hundred-degree heat. The explanation spawned other rumors, including one that had Sheen actually dead and Coppola keeping it a secret. Soon enough, everyone knew the truth. United Artists dispatched a representative to the Philippines, the press continued to dog Coppola for the real story, and Coppola had to address an avalanche of questions.

Years later, when recalling these tense times, Coppola still bristled in response to queries about how he had reacted to Sheen's heart attack. "I sort of panicked that rumors would start flying, and of course they did, and I knew that that alone could finish me off," he explained. "In a crisis like that I'm usually calm, but when everyone started yapping away I remember becoming outraged, and I think that was misunderstood by a lot of people, the press in particular."

The misunderstanding, said Coppola, lingered for a long time, and it was exacerbated over a decade later, in 1991, when *Hearts of Darkness*, the documentary about the making of *Apocalypse Now*, was finally made public. In the documentary, an agitated Francis Ford Coppola can be seen raving on about Sheen, claiming that the actor wouldn't be dead until he declared him such.

The scene, Coppola insisted, was seriously misleading.

"The idea was not to tell anyone that it was more serious than it was," he said of his position with the press in the days following Sheen's collapse. "Then I heard that people and crew members were calling home and saying that he had died. So I was furious, which was that whole bit about me saying, 'He's not dead unless I *say* he's dead.' I'd say that again. But if you view that out of context, then it seems I don't care about him."

To his credit, Coppola managed to keep his production running while he juggled his various personal and professional crises. He used doubles, including Sheen's brother, Joe, to stand in for the recovering actor; he orchestrated the destruction of the Kurtz compound in a series of impressive special-effects explosions, prompting some of the crew to remark that it was the most incredible spectacle one could see outside of an actual war. For Coppola, the work was vital, if for no other reason than to maintain his company's morale.

His own morale, however, had hit rock bottom. His earlier confidence in the film had again been replaced by despair, triggered by Sheen's heart attack and his own marital difficulties. He and Ellie were fighting all the time, and they were thinking about divorce. Ellie, for her part, was convinced that her husband had been suffering through a slow but continuous nervous breakdown for the better part of a year. The filming had been going on for an unbelievable two hundred days, and here they were, still thousands of miles from the comfort of their home in California, risking everything important to them for a movie that still required more work than either of them wanted to consider.

14.

MARTIN SHEEN RETURNED TO WORK on April 19–less than two months after his near-fatal heart attack. On that same day, Coppola announced that he intended to wrap up the filming on May 15, even if he hadn't finished the movie. If necessary, he would cut incomplete scenes from the picture.

Sheen's presence did little to elevate Coppola's spirits. He felt as if he was under siege–by the film, his disintegrating marriage, the press and rumor mill, and his escalating debt. *Apocalypse Now* had attained legendary status, both for the length of the shoot and its enormous cost–on April 11, a short item in *New York* magazine quipped that the film was "in the running for this year's *Lucky Lady* award as the Hollywood film farther over budget than any other"–and Coppola worried about how he was going to come up with the money needed for postproduction. As it was, the picture was already $15 million over its original $12 million budget.

Giving what the *Los Angeles Times* interpreted as "a fascinating view of an artistic temperament struggling to bring order to the unwieldy business structure that has grown up around it," Coppola dictated a lengthy memo to be distributed to all of his associates and employees. The memo, eventually passed along to *Esquire* by a disgruntled Zoetrope employee and published by the magazine, to Coppola's great embarrassment, depicted the embattled director as caught up in his frustration and paranoia, trying to pull in the reins on his own company.

In the opening of the memo, Coppola conceded that he had been inconsistent in his recent business operations and that he might have confused some of his employees by his behavior. The memo, then, was his way of detailing the future relationship between him and his company.

In the future, Coppola advised his employees, he would be trying to limit his work to his own creative endeavors, rather than continuing the scattershot approach of the past. He was no longer interested in servicing other filmmakers through facility and equipment rentals, nor was he interested in sponsoring other filmmakers' pictures. "To this end," he explained, "I have decided to reduce all the various companies and enterprises, wherever financially and legally prudent to do so, to one company. This company will be known as AMERICAN ZOETROPE and, purely and simply, it is *me and my work.*"

The rambling memo covered a range of topics, including Coppola's recent decision to drop the "Ford" from his name ("Never trust a man who has three names") and his pique at those employees who couldn't correctly pronounce his name ("If you aren't sure how to pronounce it, inquire"); his displeasure with company gossip and politics ("I would like to hereby sever the so-called 'grapevine'"); his new guidelines for memos, letters, and other communications; his policies for office expenses and waste, and attitudes toward money in general ("I am cavalier with money because I have to be, in order not to be terrified every time I make an artistic decision. Don't confuse that technique with the idea that I am infinitely wealthy"); and his feelings about establishing a more professional atmosphere in the office, as opposed to the big-happy-family environment of the past. Coppola tried to maintain an air of cordiality in the memo, but more often than not, he came across as a stern schoolmaster scolding his disruptive or ignorant students. On occasion, he sounded almost frantic to reaffirm his position as company boss, as if anyone had ever doubted it.

Although the memo addressed general issues of importance to any business operation, many of Coppola's statements were reactions to problems, large and small, that had plagued him during the shooting of *Apocalypse Now.* As a result of a misunderstanding, he had been sent eleven hundred dollars' worth of French crystal; lack of communication had resulted in his receiving three cameras just alike. Such problems, though, shrank in comparison to what Coppola strongly hinted was a lack of respect from the people working for him. His personal life, including the rumors of his affairs, were nobody's business but his own; his private property, including his homes and automobiles, were not intended for use by his employees. Most important, *he* was the one making the final decisions, not his wife or business associates. Coppola admitted that he was embarrassed to say these things in print, and that he himself was largely to blame for misunderstandings of the past; he implored his employees not to look upon the memo as a negative communication. Still, he could not have been more clear in asserting his position: "Your reward for your work is your salary and your benefits. The more successful I am, the faster they will go up. There really are no fringe benefits working with me, other than what you might learn, and how you might advance yourself, on the basis of your experience with me." And: "Anyone who feels doubtful or confused or negative about whether or not I know what I am doing really should not be working for me—that goes without saying. The others are welcome and hopefully will find that working for me in the future will be far more rewarding than it has been in the colorful, but somewhat chaotic, past."

In discussing *Apocalypse Now,* Coppola remained upbeat, stating that it had the potential to be a great film. He was troubled by all the rumors swirling around the production, and he asked his employees to be discreet when discussing him and the film with the press. ("APOCALYPSE NOW has generated a kind of mystery—and you will be amazed at how an idle remark will turn up in the press. At this point, we would like to control what the public and the press know about the film, until we are ready to spring it on them. Please help me in this.") The same could be said about his personal life: In the past, he had been a very public figure, the subject of books and newspaper and magazine articles. He now wished to become more private, and he hoped his employees would honor that request.

The press, of course, sneered at these remarks when the memo surfaced in *Esquire.* Coppola, of all people, was a master of media manipulation; he had made an art form of seducing the press with well-timed remarks, piquing its interests with strategically planned news blackouts, and buttering it up with luxurious, high-visibility media events and parties; he complained only when the press responded negatively to one of his movies, or when it presented stories outside the party line. Coppola was by no means unique in this regard, but he had few equals in the motion picture industry when it came to working the press to his advantage.

In retrospect, while it might be argued that Coppola could have better timed or worded his remarks, and that he was unquestionably betrayed by having the memo delivered to a magazine for publication, he was nevertheless justified in trying to state his priorities formally. He was acutely aware that he had been ruthlessly ripped off during his stay in the Philippines, by thieves who literally stole money and equipment, and by moneygrubbing individuals who took advantage of their position and power to gouge him for their services. The high costs of *Apocalypse Now* placed Coppola in a precarious financial position, and it was only natural that he would move to strengthen his day-to-day operations at Zoetrope. In the future, he would dismiss his communiqué as an embarrassment, "a memo from a desperate guy trying to hold on to his company from 6,000 miles away," even if his concerns were legitimate.

Coppola might have received a more receptive, sympathetic audience if he had shown any indication of cutting back on his own lavish lifestyle. Life in the Philippines was a far cry from what Coppola and his family enjoyed in the States, but they were living as well as could be expected, staying in a resort hotel and sacrificing very little in terms of food and drink. For Ellie's forty-first birthday, Coppola flew in his parents from California, took over a restaurant, where a surprise party was held, and hired a small orchestra to play "Tango Eleanora," a tango that his father had composed for the occasion. It was a touching gesture offered in the wake of Coppola's recent marital discord, yet it probably seemed a bit extravagant to those hearing all the tales of the director's financial woes.

15.

COPPOLA COMPLETED PRINCIPAL photography for *Apocalypse Now* in mid-May. The film had taken 238 days to shoot, at a cost of about $27 million, leaving the cast and crew totally blown out from the ordeal and prompting Coppola to remark that he had never seen so many people happy to be unemployed.

His work, he knew, was only beginning. He had over a million feet of raw footage to cut and shape into a compelling story that people would line up to see. Postproduction had given him all kinds of grief in the past, and he had no reason to suspect that the upcoming work on *Apocalypse Now* would be any different.

Still, he never would have guessed that another two years would pass before his movie hit the big screen.

Chapter Nine

Apocalypse When?

"Even if Coppola isn't haunted by the specter of financial fiascos like Cleopatra, *there's no assured future for* Apocalypse. *It's a complex, demanding, highly intelligent piece of work, coming into a marketplace that does not always embrace those qualities."*

—DALE POLLOCK

"Apocalypse Now is finally here. It is incredible. It is breathtaking and awe-inspiring. Sensitive, moving and inspired, it is beautiful, acute, brooding, magnificent, spectacular, and stupendous, but also wise, witty, a monument to human dignity, and eternal testament to man's inhumanity to man. I look forward to seeing it someday."

—RUSSELL BAKER

1.

A LOT HAD HAPPENED IN the film industry since Francis Ford Coppola began work on *Apocalypse Now.* There were new players at the top of the roster of powerful, influential filmmakers. A new blockbuster mindset had taken over the industry. Audience tastes had shifted, ever so slightly, but significantly nevertheless. All were inextricably connected, and all would have a profound effect on Coppola's career.

Most significant, perhaps, was a blockbuster mentality that had invaded the motion picture industry like a virus, influencing the type and number of movies released each year. Ironically, the fixation on the blockbuster could be largely traced back to *The Godfather,* as well as to *Jaws, Star Wars,* and *Close Encounters of the Third Kind,* all released within a five-year period. All grossed staggering sums of money, making their directors rich and powerful, and all contributed immensely in lifting their respective studios out of the kind of doldrums that had affected the film industry for nearly three decades, since the advent of television.

In 1946, the theatrical film business boasted a $1.69 billion gross, but with the arrival of the television in American homes, the figure declined in each succeeding year, bottoming out in 1962, when domestic box-office grosses were only half of the 1946 figure. The numbers increased slowly throughout the sixties, but studios continued to lose money and production decreased. The huge success of both *The French Connection* and *Love Story* earned their studios (Twentieth Century–Fox and Paramount, respectively) enough money to stay afloat, and it helped to generate a revived interest in the movies, but as of the early seventies, the 1946 mark had yet to be equaled.

During this period, the major studios underwent important changes. MGM ceased making movies altogether, while Warner Bros., Paramount, Universal, and United Artists were absorbed by large corporations, which, on the one hand, might have saved them from extinction, but which, on the other hand, altered the business practices of the studios. Making movies became a business, as opposed to an industry—and neither had much to do with art.

"Film used to be an industry: its aim was to make films first, money second," wrote James Monaco, who drew the industry-business distinction in his book *American Film Now.* "Today, film is clearly a business." In analyzing the evolution from industry to business, Monaco drew a conclusion that would strike the white-hot center of the successes and failures of Francis Ford Coppola's career: "Film in America has always been better understood as industry rather than as art. . . . Let the Old World worry about art and auteurs, aesthetics, levels of meaning, and deeper significance. Meanwhile, we make entertainment products. And a great deal of money."

Coppola knew art and, after *The Godfather,* he knew money. But, as it turned out, he was merely breaking ground. In 1972, the year that *The Godfather* took in $43 million and was well on its way to becoming the biggest box-office attraction to that point in time, the top-ten grossing films tallied a total of $123 million; a mere five years later, the year of *Star Wars* and *Close Encounters,* the top ten films grossed $424 million. The industry as a whole had recovered, but fewer movies were being made, and the fewer movies being made were earning more money.

This was both good news and bad news for Coppola. Companies were willing to invest more in the production and marketing of a movie, with the hopes that it would be the next blockbuster, yet with the rising expectations came a broader definition for disappointment or failure. It was no longer acceptable for a picture to earn a modest profit; companies were looking for the *big* money. "Everybody in the business is trying to put out another *Star Wars* or *Jaws*," noted Max Youngstein, one of UA's founders. "They're looking for the kill."

These expectations had a direct bearing on the type of movies being made—or at least the ones receiving the green light for large budgets. For all that had been written or said about the ballooning expenses of *Apocalypse Now*, the film was by no means unique—or at the top—among the big-budget movies being produced. *Moonraker*, the latest James Bond picture; *Star Trek*, the first of many movies spun off the popular television series; and *Flash Gordon*, a Dino De Laurentiis science fiction extravaganza, could claim equal or larger budgets. A remake of *King Kong*, a film version of the Broadway musical *The Wiz*, and Steven Spielberg's *1941* were nearly as costly. *Heaven's Gate*, Michael Cimino's first picture since *The Deer Hunter*, was running a tab that was threatening to go out of control.

With only a few exceptions, the high-buck pictures were light entertainment, designed to appeal to the broadest audience base possible, and were, in general, aimed at the lucrative summer or holiday seasons. Also at play, in some cases, was the possibility of merchandising tie-ins, which George Lucas had worked to perfection with *Star Wars*, when the picture took in over $500 million in merchandising—more than its $467 million in box-office receipts.

Apocalypse Now ran firmly against the grain. Obviously, there were going to be no action figures or fast-food restaurant tie-ins with the Coppola movie, and Coppola was not even certain that he wanted the picture to be shown on television. All of this might have been fine had Coppola not placed himself in the position where he would have to release a blockbuster just to break even, and with all the problems he'd embraced during the filming of *Apocalypse Now*, and all the work ahead of him, he had every reason to feel the heat when he finally wrapped production on his latest motion picture.

2.

AFTER PACKING UP AND LEAVING the Philippines, Coppola took a roundabout way home, first accompanying Vittorio Storaro and his crew to Rome, then stopping off at the Cannes Film Festival in France, sight-seeing in

Paris, attending the bull fights in Madrid, and stopping briefly in London before heading to New York. If the whirlwind tour had been designed as a means of relaxing after tempestuous months of work on *Apocalypse Now*, it was a miserable failure: Coppola was in a foul mood when he finally arrived in San Francisco in mid-June 1977.

On his trip home, he had flown on a private jet, where he spent much of his time watching footage of *Apocalypse Now*. It showed flashes of great promise, but Coppola worried about how the picture would fare in postproduction. It still needed inserts and pickup shots, which he intended to shoot in California, and it still lacked the feeling of a total story. The early and middle portions seemed to work, but Coppola was not yet sold on the ending.

Apocalypse Now had become the film that refused to go away. For reminders, Coppola needed only to look out the windows of his Napa Valley home: A helicopter was parked in his driveway, and Willard's patrol boat sat beneath an oak tree by the road. In the meadow nearby, military tents were being set up, along with a partial set of the Kurtz compound. Costumes and props occupied parts of the barn and the cook's quarters.

Coppola had devoted a lot of energy over the past month in restructuring his finances for the final push to finish the film. In May, he sold his 72,000 shares of common stock in Cinema 5 back to Donald Rugoff for the same $2.50 per share he had spent when investing in the company in 1974. A few weeks later, in early June, he cut a new deal with United Artists, using all of his personal assets, including his houses and real estate holdings, as collateral in a $10 million loan for film-completion money. As it now stood, *Apocalypse Now* would have to be a huge box-office success for Coppola to realize any profit for all his work. If the movie bombed, he would go down in flames with it.

To protect its investment further, United Artists took out a $15 million life-insurance policy on Coppola, leading the director to remark that he was now worth more dead than alive. For all his talk about being cavalier with his money, or of his willingness to put himself on the line for his art, Coppola was genuinely frightened by his latest gamble. He had upped the ante considerably, but he still had grave doubts about whether his footage would fit together in the end. After spending a couple of days going over it with sound editor Walter Murch, a dispirited Coppola announced that there was only a 20 percent chance that he could pull off the movie.

Oddly, the financial risk affected Ellie far less than she might have expected. She, like her husband, enjoyed the possessions and lifestyle that accompanied great wealth, and she hated to watch Francis agonize over *Apocalypse Now*, knowing, as she did, that he was risking his reputation as well as his money on the film. Nevertheless, as she noted in her diary, a part of her almost wanted him to fail. With wealth and fame came numerous complications that Ellie, as a wife and mother, would have preferred to avoid. Shy by nature, she wasn't thrilled by all the large parties and gatherings that they hosted or attended, where she was expected to play the role of the famous filmmaker's spouse. She hated even more the lack of privacy that she had around her own home, which always seemed to be overrun by her husband's associates. A part of her yearned for the old days, when Francis was young and unknown and laboring for footing in the film industry, when the simpler life had been, in some respects, a happier one.

"I came from a family that felt that material possessions were not the biggest deal in life, that other values were more important and lasting," she noted. "I grew up in a small house, which was a way of life familiar to me. When Francis put up what we had to finance *Apocalypse Now,* we were living in a huge, twenty-two-room house and we had lots of responsibilities, so it would have been simpler for me if we went back to living on a smaller scale. It wouldn't have been that hard on me. At the bottom line, I always felt that Francis was very talented and intelligent, and if he lost one fortune, he had the potential to create another."

Coppola spent the summer working on *Apocalypse Now* and overseeing preproduction on *The Black Stallion,* scheduled to go before the camera in Canada. He had been enthusiastic about making the picture a Zoetrope release since 1974, when he purchased the film rights to the book with some of his *Godfather* earnings, but he and the film's director, Carroll Ballard, had been at odds over the script. Ballard originally wanted to alter the story, changing the gender of the main character from a boy to a girl in order to exploit the almost mythical relationship between young girls and their horses, but Coppola had vetoed the move. In addition, the two differed over what Ballard perceived to be the preachiness of the Walter Farley book; again, Coppola won the dispute. Coppola kept a watchful eye on the development of a suitable screenplay, rejecting script after script and assigning new screenwriters to work with Ballard until, at last, he found one who met with his approval.

Or so it seemed. In midsummer, only days before principal photography was to begin on *The Black Stallion,* Coppola flew to Toronto for yet another script consultation with Ballard. Since the film's future earnings were presently tied into Coppola's recent deal with United Artists, Coppola insisted that the screenplay meet his every specification. His meddling nearly drove Ballard to distraction, but, to Ballard's great relief, Coppola didn't yank the picture from production.

"We were in a terrible mess," Ballard allowed. "We still weren't very happy with the script, and we were struggling to get the script together. I was having some big problems with the Canadians. I was having terrible problems communicating. Prior to that time, I had been kind of a one-man band: I would shoot a movie and I would edit it—I would do practically everything. With *The Black Stallion*, I was in my first experience of having to communicate so much information to other people, who would have to carry out really vital tasks on their own. And I was failing on all accounts. Everything seemed to be going wrong.

"Francis had bought himself a jet plane and was flying around with his friends, and he just flew into town a few days before we were scheduled to start shooting. I understand that, at that time, he was thinking of pulling the plug on the whole thing. But we started shooting, and a couple of days in, Francis saw the dailies and liked them and decided to hang in there. So we kept going, and shot through the summer of 1977."

3.

COPPOLA'S INDECISION OVER *Apocalypse Now* and *The Black Stallion* mirrored his indecisiveness in another important area of his life: Not only had he not broken off his affair with the young screenwriter, begun over a year earlier in the Philippines, but the relationship had intensified since Coppola's return to the States, to the point where Coppola was now deeply in love and pondering how he was going to handle this extremely difficult situation.

Finally, in late September, he broke down and told Ellie about the affair. Weeping as he spoke, Coppola tried to explain how he could love two women—his wife and his mistress—and how he did not want to abandon either. Each, he said, represented a different side of him.

Ellie, as disturbed by her own blindness to her husband's lies as she was in hearing the truth, pitched a vase of flowers at him. "I listened to the person I love, in complete anguish and pain," she wrote of the confrontation in her diary. "Suddenly I could see the conflict for him was not about peace and violence. The conflict for him would be about romantic ideals and practical reality. A man who loves romance, loves illusion. He's a filmmaker, in the very business of creating illusion. And he loves his wife, he loves his children and fifteen years of that reality. I could see it so clearly."

Years later, Coppola still puzzled over the dilemma of loving two women at the same time. "I have wept over the impossible question of dual loyalties," he said. "You feel loyal to your wife and your family, but you feel loyal to another person who you have singled out for mutual confidence. That's probably the most destructive thing I've ever been through."

Despite Coppola's tearful confession and promises to discontinue his affair, there were no easy or immediate solutions to the problem. Within days of his talk with Ellie, Coppola had returned to his mistress. Ellie learned of this and other transgressions that followed, and she struggled with her own responses to her husband's infidelity. One day, she would rationalize his actions, going so far as to accuse herself of straying from their marriage by pursuing her interests in est, meditation, and other aspects of the "nonphysical world"; other days, she would be furious with him for his deception, hurt by his lies and her inability in the past to see the truth in the notes and small gifts that she found in his pockets. She was humiliated by the realization that everyone else seemed to know the story, and that she and her husband had been favorite topics in the hated gossip mill. Their lives, she felt, bore an astonishing resemblance to the film director and his wife in Fellini's *8 1/2*, a movie that she and Francis screened in the midst of their falling-out; even their conversations and fantasies were similar.

Ellie stayed with Coppola throughout the ordeal for any number of reasons, the most important being that she still loved him. Most of his problems, she hoped, were the result of his difficulties with *Apocalypse Now* and the intense pressure it was putting on him. There was no question that he was different from the man he'd been before he started the movie. Perhaps his problems were chemical. He had recently been diagnosed as manic-depressive and given a prescription for lithium, which they both hoped would help stabilize his fluctuating moods.

In trying to sort through his conflicting emotions, Coppola kept coming back to one central issue: He loved his wife and family. He could analyze his situation from every angle and rationalize his actions in a million different ways, but he knew, at the core, when he truthfully addressed the important matters in his life, that he was traditional in his beliefs.

"I didn't want to lose my family," he admitted years later, when discussing this difficult period in his life. "I didn't want to lose my children. A lot of men can do that. But I was just not the kind of person who could go and wipe out my family like that and do a second family or something. I'm just not that kind of person."

The marriage endured, despite the trials. In 1999, Coppola still bristled when reminded of the letter that his wife sent him while he was filming in the Philippines, though he could now take a more reflective, analytical approach in explaining how his marriage had survived some of its toughest tests.

"That was a low point for us," he said of the *Apocalypse* period. "I still feel that Ellie was out of line and bending to advisers when she wrote that letter censoring me while I was shooting. But our family meant a lot to us, and the marriage survived, step by step. It's been better than ever these last fifteen years. She has learned to believe in me more, and in the 'experts' less. She has seen more of my crazy dreams bear fruit, and maybe that helped. As for me, I've learned to give her more privacy and the space to create, and I've supported her work. I think the most important thing in marriage is to give one another the right to express oneself and the privacy to do it. Being married should never be a limitation—it ought to be an advantage."

4.

BY THE END OF 1977, *Apocalypse Now* had attained the unenviable reputation of being a film in serious trouble. Earlier in the year, before Coppola imposed his total press blackout on the project, newspapers and magazines had issued progress reports that included relatively optimistic remarks from Coppola and others working on the film; as time went on, the reports became more and more vague, fueled mostly by speculation, or by sources asking to remain anonymous.

To industry observers, the signs were anything but encouraging, beginning with the continual postponement of the film's release date. Originally slated to premiere on April 7, 1977—Coppola's thirty-eighth birthday—the film's release date had been pushed back on several occasions, first to December 1977, then to Coppola's thirty-ninth birthday, and, a short time later, to October 1978. Postponements were never favorably greeted by distributors, who feared a subsequent loss of exhibitor interest or confidence, but the *Apocalypse Now* story, with its history of hurricanes and heart attacks and replaced actors, was by now so familiar to the public that the postponements might have been understandable—perhaps even adding an air of mystique to the film—if anyone in the Coppola camp had given reason for optimism. Instead, the press was greeted with silence—or, worse yet, rumors that were neither confirmed nor denied.

Coppola, in fact, had very little to say. He had pored over his film's footage so many times that he could no longer watch it with any sense of objectivity. His other films—*The Conversation,* at the top of the list—had given him trouble in postproduction, but they had been easy in comparison to this. All he needed for a reminder was the history of the two *Godfather* pictures. Prior to his experiences with *Apocalypse Now,* making *The Godfather* had been, hands down, the most miserable experience of his life. He'd had more say in the creation of its sequel, but he'd struggled with the script and postproduction on that one, and he hadn't known until the very end if his film was going to make any sense. You would never have known any of this when looking at the two movies now: They are highly polished, were enormously successful at the box office, and had picked up a ton of awards.

Coppola finally realized a goal for the two films when they were combined and reworked into *Mario Puzo's The Godfather: The Complete Novel for Television*, which aired on NBC in mid-November. The carefully prepared new version, running just over seven hours and featuring an hour of footage that had been excised from the theatrical versions, ran in strict chronological order, eliminating some of the confusion that had arisen from the flashback scenes in *Godfather II*. Since Coppola had been preoccupied with the filming of *Apocalypse Now* when it came time to prepare the production for television, the yeoman task of reassembling the footage into a single, smooth-running story had fallen on Barry Malkin, Coppola's editor on *The Rain People*. Coppola made extensive notes on how he wanted the movie to go, gave his instructions to Malkin, and trusted that he would come through.

"I had worked on *Apocalypse Now* in the Philippines," Malkin remembered, "and I learned, about that time, that this was a project in the offing. It was mentioned that when we got finished shooting the film and got back to San Francisco, we would put this thing together when we could find the time. Well, some months into *Apocalypse Now*, my personal life got a little troubled and I left the film. I knew what the reality of *Apocalypse* was going to be—how much longer it was going to take than we all thought when we began to film. I felt guilty about having left the film, and I felt it was kind of incumbent upon me to offer my services on the *Godfather* television project. And Francis jumped at that."

Malkin had worked on *Godfather II* recently enough that he didn't need to reacquaint himself with it, but he only knew the original *Godfather* as a viewer, and thus had to familiarize himself with the picture before he began the splicing of the two films together. In addition, Malkin had to format the massive picture for television, complete with openings for commercial breaks, as well as create the promotional teases used by the network to generate interest in each night's showing. It was a lot of work—the kind of work that Malkin was not accustomed to doing—but in time, Malkin had enough finished that he felt confident about flying back to the Philippines and showing the work to Coppola.

"As it turned out," he said, "there was so much chaos going on around *Apocalypse* that we never really screened it. We started to look at it, but we stopped. I went back to New York and got into the more detailed finishing of it. I hired a sound crew, and we used the music from the two movies as a kind of library for the music needed for the new scenes. I ran around the country and looped the actors, to change the dialogue that wasn't suitable for television. Then I went to L.A. for a number of weeks, to oversee the videotaping, which, I guess, was of a more primitive nature than it is today. It was a pretty long project, but when it was all over, Francis was still in the Philippines."

Shortly after the first of the year, Coppola arrived at another important decision: Rather than seek a unifying style in *Apocalypse Now,* he would make each of the movie's scenes stylistically self-contained, separate unto itself, so that Willard (and moviegoers) would be experiencing something new on each leg of the journey upriver. The decision, of course, was largely practical, born out of Coppola's frustrating problems with continuity, but it was also a sound decision from an artistic standpoint: Each scene would become a kind of tone poem—part of the story's evolution, to be sure, but also compelling on its own terms.

Coppola now had the first two-thirds of the film all but locked into place, but there were still too many holes in the story to allow the movie to run smoothly. He had debated using a voice-over narration for some time—a practice frowned upon by the critical establishment, which found it pedestrian—and in January 1978, he decided to give it a try. He sent for Michael Herr, author of *Dispatches,* perhaps the finest in the canon of nonfiction books about Vietnam. Herr watched the footage and listened to Coppola's detailed plans, and over the course of the next year, he produced the internal monologue that provided viewers with a psychological profile of Capt. Benjamin Willard. The laconic, almost trippy voice-over etched out Willard's role as an observer while contrasting strongly with the on-screen violence and mayhem.

5.

IN THE YEARS FOLLOWING THE release of *Apocalypse Now,* reviews, essays, and journalistic reports would depict Francis Ford Coppola's creation of the film as an exercise in madness, with the director out of control, barely holding the film together and losing all sight of budgetary concerns. The reports, though largely true, made Coppola cringe and added to his increasing hostility toward the press. What his critics damned as an ego running amok (and, indeed, there was plenty of that) was too often a misinterpretation of Coppola's need, grown desperate over time, to make something monumental out of a project that had begun on a much more modest scale. "I've got to do this picture," he confided to John Milius. "I consider it the most important picture I will ever make. If I die making it, you'll take over. If you die, George Lucas will take over."

Postproduction on *Apocalypse Now* mirrored the bedlam of filming it, from the manic-depressive atmosphere in the editing rooms to some of the crazy antics that arose from it. In the early editing stage, one assistant editor became so obsessed with the movie that he would sneak into the Zoetrope editing room after hours and rework the footage; when Coppola told him to stop, he retaliated by stealing several reels of work print, burning the footage, and sending the ashes to Coppola every day for a week. On another occasion, Fred Rexer, the Vietnam vet who was a friend of John Milius and a strong influence on the early script for *Apocalypse Now*, arrived at the studio and began telling war stories, including an especially gruesome tale about how he would execute Vietcong officers by pushing his thumbs through their eye sockets and pulling their skulls apart. He later frightened Martin Sheen and Coppola, at work on the voice-over narration in the basement studio, by handing Sheen a loaded revolver. "You could shoot anyone in this room," he told the startled actor. "You have the power of life and death in your hands."

Never had the costs of postproduction become as high for Coppola, not just because of the enormous length of time devoted to putting the film together but also because, in attempting to place an audience in the midst of a war, he needed the kind of state-of-the-art technology that came with a high price tag, such as the four-screen editing equipment that allowed him to layer his film. For sound, he proposed something equally innovative.

"When I started the film, he said he wanted three things," Walter Murch remembered. "First, he wanted it to be quintaphonic, he wanted the sound to fill the room, to seem to come from all sections of the room." This, said Murch, had never been done in a dramatic film. Ken Russell had used quinta-phonic sound in *Tommy*, his movie adaptation of the rock opera by the Who, but the sound in that film had been mostly music and had rarely used sound effects. For the helicopter strike on the village in *Apocalypse Now*, movie audiences would be hearing the sound of the helicopters, Wagner's "Ride of the Valkyries" blaring from speakers in the helicopters, explosions and gunfire, and people screaming—all coming from different speakers located through-out the theater. The trick, Murch explained, was to arrange the sound so people wouldn't be overwhelmed by a wall of noise, and to accomplish this, he tried to see that only two dominant sounds were playing at any given moment. In addition, Murch had to determine when, for dramatic purposes, it was best to have sound coming from a single point and when it should expand to include parts or all of the theater.

"Second," Murch said of Coppola's instructions, "he wanted it to be authentic, by which he meant the weaponry had to sound like it really sounded in Vietnam. He had very much in mind the veterans who had been in battle in the war who would be looking at the film. He wanted them to feel that the film was an accurate portrayal of what they went through just simply on the level of the hardware—the helicopter and the boats and the gunfire and all of those things."

Murch, a perfectionist himself, could appreciate Coppola's devotion to detail. During the making of *The Godfather,* Murch had gone to the trouble of recording the sounds of vintage automobiles, just so the movie would sound authentic. Still, Coppola's requirements for the weapons' sounds was a pretty tall order, since, during the filming of *Apocalypse Now,* not all of the weapons had been recorded specifically for the sound track, and since soliciting the army's help was long out of the question. Murch somehow managed to come up with the needed weaponry, and for three days he and his crew retreated to the hills outside of San Francisco, where they fired off the weapons and recorded their sounds.

"The final thing he wanted," Murch continued, "was the film soundtrack to partake of the psychedelic haze in which the war had been fought, not only in terms of the music for the soundtrack—The Doors and what kids listened to on the radio—but in general, kind of far-out juxtaposition of imagery and sound; for the soundtrack not to be just a literal imitation of what you saw on the screen but at times to depart from it."

Murch, who would eventually receive an Academy Award nomination for his sound editing on *Apocalypse Now,* even came up with a new title for his job.

"We were moving into uncharted waters," he said. "I thought I was doing a job similar to that of a production designer, so I called what I did sound design."

6.

THE EXTENDED TIME AND COSTS of postproduction on *Apocalypse Now* had not escaped the attention of United Artists, whose investment in the film was in a strange sort of limbo. Company officials had heard the disturbing rumors that the picture was an unreleasable mess, but they were without a clear course of action. If they shut down the picture, they would be guaranteed an enormous financial loss (one report estimated it at $30 million) and the unsavory prospects of how—or if—they should collect on Coppola's collateral. If they continued to stand behind Coppola, they faced the prospects of having him approach them for even more completion money.

The company's position was complicated by its own recent history. United Artists, founded in 1919 by Mary Pickford, Charles Chaplin, Douglas Fairbanks, and D. W. Griffith as a means of distributing independently produced movies, had been purchased in 1967 by insurance giant Transamerica, which for the better part of a decade had allowed UA officials to run their affairs without much corporate involvement. This had changed recently, however, with the San Francisco–based Transamerica growing more and more concerned about the bottom line earned by UA movies. The corporate concern was not unjustified. In 1970 alone, UA had lost or written off about $85 million, and while the company's fortunes had taken a turn for the better in the following years, peaking in 1974 and 1975, when UA led the movie industry in theatrical rentals, Transamerica insisted on taking a more active role in the business practices not just of UA but of all its subsidiaries. Angered UA executives insisted that Transamerica was violating its promise to give UA autonomy in its business decisions—charges that Transamerica contested. UA's chairman, Arthur Krim, once the co-owner of the company and still regarded as one of the great minds in the movie business, finally tired of what he believed was too much interference from Transamerica and resigned from the company, taking with him other high-placed UA officials. The new UA regime subsequently found itself caught in the middle, trying to appease the moviemakers, upon whom they depended for survival, while trying to earn the kind of profits that Transamerica demanded.

Apocalypse Now, with its shaky reputation and potential for financial disaster, was about the last kind of property that UA wanted to address with Transamerica executives and investors. True, Francis Ford Coppola had one of the best reputations around, as well as two moneymakers in his *Godfather* movies, but in the motion picture business, memories and reputations have a way of fading with dwindling profits. Coppola, of course, was sensitive to this, and as a businessman, he made a point of schmoozing with the right people—in this case, with Jim Harvey, the chairman of United Artists and executive vice president of Transamerica. The two got along famously, but Coppola knew better than to overlook Harvey's position and what it meant to his film. As both a gag and a gesture of friendship, Coppola bought a telescope mounted on a tripod, which he installed in Harvey's twenty-fifth-floor Transamerica office and aimed at his own Sentinel Building office. The telescope had a small metal plaque that read: "To Jim Harvey from Francis Coppola, so you can keep an eye on me."

Realizing that he had to show the company some kind of product, Coppola set up screenings of his work in progress, first for United Artists executives, and then, on April 25, for a selected audience at San Francisco's Northpoint Theater. The film, Coppola warned, was nowhere near completion, and he begged area critics and writers not to crash the public screenings and write about what they'd seen. The press complied, happy just to see the recently reclusive director in public again. "Francis Ford Coppola finally comes out of hiding," crowed one Los Angeles newspaper.

The response to the two screenings disappointed the director. The UA officials offered nothing to boost Coppola's confidence, and the Northpoint audience, although more enthusiastic, liked all the wrong parts of the film. Before the screening at the Northpoint, Coppola distributed flyers soliciting a written response from the audience. When reading over the questionnaires afterward, Coppola was disheartened to notice that people were most favorable in their comments about the "Ride of the Valkyries" battle sequence—a memorable scene but not, by Coppola's estimation, one of the high points of the movie.

"The film reaches its highest level during the fucking helicopter battle," he wrote in his notes. "My nerves are shot—my heart is broken—My imagination is dead. I have no self-reliance—But like a child just want someone to rescue me. . . ."

7.

BUT THERE WAS NO ONE TO RESCUE him—or even point him in the proper direction. Throughout the summer and fall of 1978, while he toiled on a film that threatened to bankrupt him, Coppola watched his contemporaries bask in the spotlight that he had enjoyed only a few years earlier. George Lucas, who had declined the director's job on *Apocalypse Now* in favor of working on *Star Wars*, had seen his space opera blast off the charts throughout the summer of 1977, filling theaters week after week until it unseated Steven Spielberg's *Jaws* as the top-grossing film of all time. Spielberg, whose film had taken the box-office title from *The Godfather* a few years earlier, had issued *Close Encounters of the Third Kind* at the end of 1977, and it was still showing considerable profits well into 1978. Lucas and Spielberg had been supportive during Coppola's struggles with *Apocalypse Now,* offering suggestions and encouragement when they got together with Coppola, both sympathetic about the pressures placed on a director once he had a huge blockbuster on his résumé.

Coppola could afford to feel happy for the success of his two friends, who had released movies that he would never have dreamed of writing or directing himself, but he might have felt a little differently, perhaps even threatened, when Michael Cimino, another contemporary, came out with *The Deer Hunter* at the end of 1978. Prior to his work on the film, Cimino had been a successful screenwriter, but he had directed only one notable movie,

Thunderbolt and Lightfoot, an action picture starring Clint Eastwood. In *The Deer Hunter,* Cimino had not only beaten Coppola to the theaters with a Vietnam War movie, he had also scored heavily with the critics, who seemed ready to anoint Cimino as the next major film director.

Whatever his private feelings about the movie, Coppola tried to be gracious to Cimino when he flew to New York for the premiere of *The Deer Hunter,* but Cimino, already comfortable in his newfound celebrity, was slow to reciprocate. Instead, he seemed more interested in promoting his movie by offering disparaging comparisons and remarks about *Apocalypse Now.* His film, he told a *New York Times* reporter, had been shot in Thailand, "which is more like Vietnam than the Philippines, where Francis shot *Apocalypse Now.*" The nastiness, however, did not stop there. On several other occasions in the interview, Cimino—who had never served in Vietnam, and who could only claim to have learned about the war in the same manner as Coppola—took cheap shots at Coppola, implying that he, Cimino, was more qualified to make an authoritative film on the war than Coppola. "Vietnam," he scoffed, "is not the only war in the history of the world where there have been terrible atrocities. There have been and there probably will be far worse. Vietnam was not the apocalypse."

Coppola wisely elected not to address Cimino's comments in public immediately, but he had his own final word later, when he was baited into discussing *The Deer Hunter* at the 1979 Cannes Film Festival. "When I saw *The Deer Hunter,*" he said, "I thought that it was a film that dealt with serious subject matter, that it had good performances, and that it attempted to do something serious; but I thought it was politically naive. But it was an attempt, and I felt that was something. *The Deer Hunter* is a different kind of film from my film, which is in a different world."

All hype and bickering aside, *The Deer Hunter* raised the stakes in the Hollywood pictures about Vietnam. After a lengthy hands-off approach to making films about Vietnam, Hollywood had seen a smattering of movies about the war and its effects on soldiers, including 1977's *Heroes,* starring Henry Winkler and Sally Field, essentially a love story involving a Vietnam vet and a woman he meets after the war, when he's on the road and trying to sort out his life; and, a year later, *Coming Home,* a more ambitious effort, which is about a disabled Vietnam vet (Jon Voight) who returns to the United States, falls in love with a married woman (Jane Fonda), and ultimately confronts viewers with challenges about U.S. involvement and guilt in the war. Loosely based on the experiences of Ron Kovic, whose own 1976 memoir, *Born on the Fourth of July,* would be made into a successful film, *Coming Home* was by far the most critically acclaimed movie dealing with this unpopular subject.

Neither of these pictures, nor any of the others made during this period, were overwhelming successes at the box office, and none, arguably, brought viewers into the heart of the Vietnam experience. In *The Deer Hunter,* Michael Cimino came very close, due largely to the performances of a superlative cast (Robert De Niro, Christopher Walken, Meryl Streep) and Cimino's decision to take viewers to Vietnam and back. The film also set an important precedent elsewhere. "Not until *The Deer Hunter* appeared," wrote Lawrence Suid in a lengthy study of Hollywood and Vietnam in *Film Comment,* "did the war itself become a financially viable subject for filmmakers."

In addressing the effects that *The Deer Hunter* might have on Coppola's film, *Apocalypse Now* coproducer Fred Roos took an optimistic tone. "We were not banking on being the first out," he said. "*The Deer Hunter* . . . seems to be a big success. We look at this as being good for us. All these years, the industry has thought the audiences did not want to deal with the Vietnam War. *The Deer Hunter* is the first tangible proof that this may not be true."

Coppola was keenly aware of *The Deer Hunter*'s reputation as being *the* Vietnam War movie—and coming at a time when his unfinished picture was being jeered at as "Apocalypse When?" and "Apocalypse Never" by an increasingly skeptical press. One can only imagine what ran through his mind when, as the presenter of the Academy Award for Best Director at the April 1979 awards ceremony, he opened the envelope and announced Michael Cimino as the winner. It was time to get his own movie in front of the public.

8.

HE DID JUST THAT IN MAY, when, ignoring the pleas of United Artists executives, he took *Apocalypse Now* to the Cannes Film Festival and entered it into the competition as a work in progress. In a career that seemed to have been built on equal parts enormous talent and creativity, dedication to craft, and outright moxie, Coppola was taking one of his biggest chances.

The weeks leading up to the festival had been both encouraging and infuriating—and as busy as ever. On April 7, Coppola celebrated his fortieth birthday with a gigantic party at his Napa Valley vineyard, complete with a six-foot cake hoisted on a stretcher and over a thousand guests. A few weeks later, he was in Washington, D.C., attending a black-tie barbecue at the White House with President Jimmy Carter, Japanese prime minister Masayoshi Ohira, actor Peter Falk, and singer Bobby Short. Through Gerald Rafshoon, an old friend currently working as one of Carter's media advisers, Coppola was able to arrange a private White House screening of *Apocalypse Now,* attended by the

George Lucas and Francis Ford Coppola, shown here on the set of *THX 1138*, which Lucas directed and Coppola produced, met on the set of *Finian's Rainbow*. The two became close, lifelong friends.

TOP: Roger Corman, king of the B movies, provided numerous aspiring filmmakers and actors an entrée into the business. BOTTOM: After working on several Corman films, Coppola was given his first film to direct—a low-budget psychological thriller titled *Dementia 13*. Corman produced.

TOP: *You're a Big Boy Now*, featuring Elizabeth Hartman and Peter Kastner, owed much to the films of Richard Lester. Coppola submitted the film at UCLA as his master's thesis. BOTTOM: On the set of *Finian's Rainbow* with Fred Astaire. Always a lover of musicals, Coppola relished the thought of directing *Finian's Rainbow,* partly because he wanted to work with Astaire, and partly because he wanted to show his father that he could make the picture. The experience, however, proved to be a disappointment, and the movie was a box office flop.

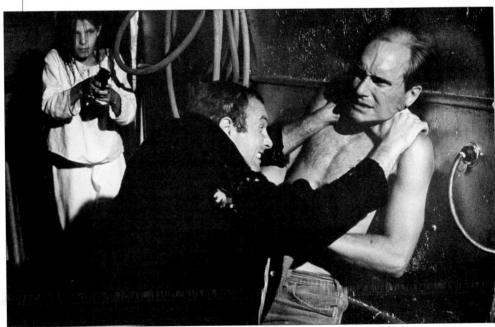

TOP: Coppola tailored his screenplay for *The Rain People* as a vehicle for Shirley Knight. The two clashed during the making of the picture, which was shot entirely on location as Coppola and a small road crew made their way across the country, starting in New York and winding up in Nebraska. BOTTOM: James Caan and Robert Duvall were virtual unknowns in the movie business when Coppola cast them in *The Rain People*. Caan would appear in three future Coppola films, Duvall in four.

The Godfather would always be remembered for its powerful cast, which included Al Pacino, Marlon Brando, James Caan, and John Cazale. Coppola's casting struggles with Paramount became legendary in the industry and, in the cases of Pacino and Brando, nearly resulted in his removal from the picture. Despite his reputation for being "difficult," Marlon Brando worked well with Coppola in *The Godfather*. Brando won the Best Actor Oscar for his portrayal of Don Vito Corleone.

ABOVE: Gene Hackman and Coppola confer on the set of *The Conversation*. The picture, generally regarded as one of Coppola's finest, won the Palm d'Or at the 1974 Cannes Film Festival. BELOW: Carmine Coppola always dreamed of composing music for the movies, and his work on *The Godfather, Part II* earned him an Academy Award. His son didn't do badly, either, taking home Oscars for Best Picture, Best Screenplay Adaptation, and Best Director.

In *The Godfather, Part II,* John Cazale and Al Pacino reprised their roles as Fredo and Michael Corleone. The film remains one of the most successful sequels in motion picture history.

Robert De Niro had originally tested for a role in *The Godfather,* but Coppola decided not to use him in the picture—a move that proved to be most fortuitous. De Niro won great acclaim and an Oscar for his portrayal of young Vito Corleone in *The Godfather, Part II.*

Apocalypse Now was the most physically and psychologically challenging film of Coppola's career, taking the director to the outermost boundaries of his creative powers, and nearly costing him his marriage and fortune in the process. Coppola worked tirelessly with Marlon Brando on the actor's pivotal role as Colonel Kurtz, the two developing the part and dialogue as Coppola struggled to find the inner meaning—and ending—to his film.

TOP: Coppola gambled the future of *Apocalypse Now* by taking the film as a work in progress to the Cannes Film Festival. His meetings with the international press were both easygoing and contentious. In the end, he was awarded his second Palm d'Or. BOTTOM: Robert Duvall *(left)*, with Albert Hall and Martin Sheen in a scene from *Apocalypse Now.*

Coppola meets with the press on the gigantic Las Vegas set of *One from the Heart* *(bottom)*, while his crew shoots a miniature of Las Vegas set *(top)*. The ambitious picture, which introduced Coppola's visionary method of "electronic cinema," was a terrible failure, eventually driving Coppola to bankruptcy.

TOP: Coppola hoped his adaptation of S. E. Hinton's *The Outsiders* would be a "*Godfather* for kids." Like *The Godfather*, *The Outsiders* featured a solid cast of actors unheralded at the time, including C. Thomas Howell *(left)*, Ralph Macchio *(back to camera)*, and Matt Dillon. BOTTOM: Working with Kathleen Turner and nephew Nicolas Cage: Coppola might have viewed *Peggy Sue Got Married* as a kind of cinematic confection—beneath, perhaps, his talents as a director—but the picture was a hit with moviegoers and earned Turner an Oscar nomination for Best Actress.

TOP: Studio executives hoped that Coppola's involvement in another mob film would produce the same kind of financial rewards as the earlier *Godfather* pictures, but nothing about *The Cotton Club* came easily, including Coppola's work with Richard Gere. BOTTOM: On location for *Kagemusha*, Coppola and George Lucas meet with the great Japanese director, Akira Kurosawa.

TOP: Gordon Willis *(left)* served as director of photography on all three *Godfather* pictures. His relationship with Coppola was testy at times, but there was no doubting the quality of the results of their collaboration. BOTTOM: In *The Godfather, Part III*, Al Pacino *(left)* portrayed an aging Michael Corleone, seeking redemption and turning over the family leadership to Vincent Mancini (Andy Garcia), the illegitimate son of his brother Sonny. Coppola envisioned the movie as Shakespearean in scope, but it also contained strong personal underpinnings.

Sofia Coppola had worked with her father in a number of his pictures, as an actress, cowriter, and costume designer. Coppola's decision to use his daughter in *The Godfather, Part III* was one of the most controversial casting choices of his career.

In *Bram Stoker's Dracula,* featuring Gary Oldman and Winona Ryder, Coppola tried to present a film that was faithful to the time-honored novel. The movie's enormous success enabled him to escape a decade's worth of financial worries.

TOP: With Robin Williams and Jennifer Lopez on the set of *Jack*. BOTTOM: Claire Danes and Matt Damon were two of Hollywood's rising stars when Coppola directed them in *John Grisham's The Rainmaker*.

TOP: Attending the 1975 Golden Globe Awards ceremonies with his wife, Eleanor, and sons, Gio and Roman. Throughout the ups and downs of his career, Coppola turned to his family for balance in his life. BOTTOM: Like father, like son: Gio Coppola hoped to follow in his father's footsteps and was well along the way to a career as a successful filmmaker when a tragic boating accident claimed his life at age twenty-two.

President and fifty guests, who gave the picture a "very, very mixed" reaction. Although he offered no public statement about the movie, Carter was reportedly moved by the film, applauding at its conclusion; others, including CIA director Stansfield Turner, sat in silence. The audience reaction cards—now standard fare at Coppola's *Apocalypse Now* previews—were equally mixed.

The film's White House screening was merely a prelude to a much larger event—a public showing on Friday, May 11, 1979, at Mann's Bruin Theater in Westwood. Thus far, Coppola had avoided previewing *Apocalypse Now* anywhere near the nerve center of the motion picture industry, so the Bruin Theater screening, held a short distance from the UCLA campus, took on *event* proportions to people who had heard all the rumors but had not yet seen so much as a trailer for the film. Ticket seekers turned out in droves, gathering at the box office at 9:30 A.M.—eight and a half hours before the scheduled opening of the box office—and growing in number until 2,500 people had amassed in what one report called "the Cinematic equivalent of a gas line," all clamoring for entrance to the evening's 8:00 P.M. showing. Everyone in the city seemed to be calling connections to obtain the sought-after tickets. High-profile names requested tickets—one report had John Travolta asking for two, Dustin Hoffman for four, and Gene Hackman for five—while United Artists executives, exhibitors, writers, and other film industry workers, including people from rival studios, jockeyed for admission. Seeing the enormous turnout, Coppola expanded the evening to three showings, the final one to be screened during the wee hours of the morning. No one seemed to mind.

Coppola was very visible throughout the evening, chatting with people waiting in the long lines, talking with selected members of the media, discussing the film with people after the showings, and even throwing a tantrum when he saw a large section of the theater roped off for dignitaries, leaving the poorer seats to people who had spent hours in line. The questionnaire, sealed and distributed to attendees as they entered the theater, invited the audience "to help me finish the film," leading one observer to remark that he was "disturbed by the clear evidence that Coppola had not discovered an inevitable shape for the picture, that he was searching desperately to find something that worked."

The film, presented in a magnificent 70-mm version, ran without beginning or end credits—a move that Coppola was contemplating for all of the 70-mm prints to be shown in art houses. For those showings, people would be handed programs with the credits printed inside, while regular beginning and end credits would be displayed on-screen in the standard 35-mm prints running in the great majority of theaters nationwide. The picture also ran without quintaphonic sound, which Coppola and Walter Murch were still trying to work into an acceptable final version.

If Coppola had been confused about audience response prior to the evening, the three screenings could only have deepened his concern. At one showing, the audience sat in stunned silence at the end of the film, with only a handful of people applauding; at another screening, the theater erupted in applause when the screen went black. Was the silence a display of disapproval, or could it be interpreted as a reaction to the profundity of the movie? Were people confused by what they had seen? Coppola had no way of knowing, and the questionnaires offered little to clarify his uncertainty. The response was generally favorable yet, as one viewer noted, "It's like watching your mother being killed and asking you what you think of it."

The screening, judged a risk by industry insiders, backfired on Coppola in one important sense: The press, up to this time respectful of Coppola's pleas for a moratorium on reviews, was going to be silent no more. Rona Barrett was the first to break ranks when, on the May 14 edition of ABC's *Good Morning America,* she summarized the film's plot, commented on the actors' performances, and ultimately dismissed the movie as "a disappointing failure." The same day, Gene Siskel published a lengthy review of the event and movie in the *Chicago Tribune,* in which he declared the opening two hours of the film to be "mostly stunning" while writing off the final twenty minutes as a muddy mess.

"Apocalypse Now, in the version I saw, is not easy to comprehend," wrote Siskel. "It does not have the broadly drawn, good-and-evil characters of *Coming Home* and *The Deer Hunter.* It's a much more subtle film, which appeared to hold the audience's attention until the ending, when many people seemed confused." Siskel, who had interviewed Coppola after the second screening, was not buying the director's explanation that his film was not ambiguous. "The film is about moral ambiguity," Coppola had stated, drawing a distinction between overall ambiguity in the plot and in the characters themselves. "That's quite a difference," Coppola insisted. "What the film says is that we are all straddled between good and evil, that we make each decision as we go along and we always will, that there is no such thing as absolute good and evil—there never is and never will be."

Other reports followed, including an account of the evening and a review in *Variety*'s weekly edition (the trade publication had avoided a review in its earlier daily edition, deferring to Coppola until after the Barrett television review), a brief piece in *Newsweek,* and extensive coverage in *New York* magazine. The *New York* article, written by critic David Denby, attacked Coppola for presenting an uncompleted movie, but he praised the film itself: *"Apoca-lypse Now,"* he wrote, "feels like one of those awesome pieces by the Rolling Stones or the Grateful Dead that seem to go on forever in a spreading luxuri-ousness of panic and dread, leaving a residue of anxiety in your stomach while making you high at the same time."

Coppola exploded when he saw the write-ups. Not only had he been betrayed by the press but reporters seemed to be deliberately distorting the big issue about the film's ending, as well. He had heard all the rumors about the different endings to *Apocalypse Now*—he had even shown different end-ings at the various previews—but he had made a special point of announcing that the ending shown at the Bruin Theater was going to be the final ending of the finished film. "The version you just saw," he told *Variety* writer Dale Pollock after the first Westwood preview, "is my version. That's it. There are no other versions, just things people would like to see me do. But this is my version, my ending and my film."

With the August release date for *Apocalypse Now* closing in, Coppola might have been excused for his concern that no more confusing details about the picture be spread around, but his anger over the published reviews was hard to comprehend. After all, *he* had been the one to make a major event out of the screening, charging $7.50 per ticket (an exorbitant sum at the time, almost double the usual price, even if the proceeds were going to the Pacific Film Archive) and taking out full-page newspaper ads announcing the preview. He must have known that the press would write about the merits of the movie—either that or he was being uncharacteristically naïve. After all, he was working in an industry where, all too often, one's word was more of a sound than a promise, and a promise bore all the value of cab fare from Malibu to Westwood. *Apocalypse Now* had become one of the most highly anticipated and written-about movies in motion picture history, yet Coppola expected the media to sit on its collective hands when actually given the chance to see it? Not likely.

Coppola was feeling every bit the embattled warrior when, a few days after the preview, he boarded Kirk Krekorian's private jet, along with his wife, their children, and an entourage of forty, and flew with the movie mogul to France for the Cannes Film Festival. Here, too, he found himself at the center of con-troversy. No work in progress had ever been entered in the Cannes competi-tion. United Artists executives were none too pleased about his competing against such other American entries as *Manhattan, Norma Rae, Days of Heaven, The China Syndrome,* and *Hair,* or with the notable films from all around the world. Although one UA official tried to put a decent spin on the controversy, insisting that "UA is in perfect harmony with Coppola" in his decision to screen *Apocalypse Now* at Cannes, another savaged Coppola's tactics as "momentary insanity born of arrogance." An executive from competing Warner Bros. chimed in that the move "might easily be called the dumbest idea in filmmaking history." Coppola and his movie, these people believed, stood to lose greatly if the film was ignored or poorly received; negative reaction at Cannes could finish off a film with an already-dubious reputation.

Coppola, ready to gamble and prepared for whatever wars lay ahead, waved off the criticism, labeling his Cannes screening an "out-of-town try-out," similar to the way plays were tested outside of New York prior to their presentation on Broadway. Besides, *he* was the one taking the risks, not his critics or distributors.

"Ten people at United Artists had nervous breakdowns when we took the film to Cannes," he later remarked. "But the fact that I held the note at the bank—that it was my neck—meant that UA couldn't stop me. Other directors who keep their $10 million in their bank accounts don't have the right to make their distributors face catastrophe."

Nor was he especially concerned about his film's winning the festival's Golden Palm award.

"I'm not afraid to lose," he countered when it was suggested that he might have been better off if he hadn't entered *Apocalypse Now* in the competition. "I'm not interested in the prize."

9.

ONE COULD NOT HELP BUT ADMIRE Coppola's swagger. He might have been speaking truthfully when saying that he was unafraid of losing the prize at Cannes, but he didn't need advisers, the press, or industry hotshots to remind him that he had much more on the line than an award. Through it all, Coppola exuded a confident air, receiving guests and reporters aboard the *Amazone*—a chartered yacht that he occupied, to the tune of four thousand dollars a day—and holding forth on any topic that struck his fancy. The interview requests were staggering. Coppola was easily the center of the film festival's attention, a status underscored when Coppola was offered the entire Palais des Festivals for a mass press conference—an honor bestowed upon a director on only one other occasion during the seventies, when Ingmar Bergman spoke about his classic *Cries and Whispers*.

After all the hype leading up to the 10:00 A.M. press screening of *Apocalypse Now* on Saturday, May 19, the showing itself was almost anticlimactic. Coppola arrived at the Palais in an edgy mood, only to be greeted by a theater that was less than filled. (One account speculated that people, facing the prospects of an overwhelming crowd, simply stayed away.) As in virtually all of the previous screenings in the United States, response to the film was polite but mixed, with critics voicing the now-familiar complaint that the ending was confusing, as well as film executives worrying about the picture's commercial appeal.

The press conference afterward, attended by over a thousand reporters, proved to be more eventful than the screening itself. Coppola chose to use the occasion to vent years of frustration and rage over his struggles with making and completing the picture, as well as comment on the American press, the state of film criticism, and his plans for the future—all in a virtuoso performance in which Coppola, in turns, played the role of stern lecturer, wounded victim, arrogant artiste, and media manipulator. Years later, he would express regret for allowing his anger to get the better of him, but on that rainy afternoon in 1979, he was finally going to have his say.

"My film," he said, "is not a movie. It's not about Vietnam—it *is* Vietnam. It's what it was really like. It was crazy. . . ."

From there, he aimed his sights on the group he considered to be his greatest tormentors.

"American journalism," he charged, "is the most decadent, most unethical, most lying profession you can encounter. I learned it on this picture. There wasn't a truthful thing written about it in four years—about the film, about the budget, about what we were doing about the film. Journalists would promise that they would come to see an unfinished work, but wouldn't write about it, and then they *would* write about it. So I said, 'If there are no rules, if there are no ethics, then let me show the film right in Hollywood, right in Cannes so that everyone can see it and get off my back.'"

Coppola's attack was relentless. His movie, he said, had been beset by so many problems that he and his crew had slowly gone insane and the movie wound up making itself. Here he was, creating "the world's first thirty million dollar surrealistic movie"—about one of the most controversial conflicts in American history, to boot—and he had to contend with people second-guessing his budget or criticizing the violence in the film. He had made the movie with his own money; he had taken the risks. "Why is it a crime that I, the first one to make a film about Vietnam, a film about morality, am so criticized when you can spend that much on a film about a big gorilla, or on a fantasy, or about some jerk who flies around in the sky?" he asked, referring to the large budgets allotted to *King Kong*, *The Wiz*, and *Superman*. He was equally dismissive of the criticism of the excessive violence in *Apocalypse Now*. "Despite *The Godfather* and *Apocalypse Now*, I dislike violence. What you see here is a fraction of what occurred in Vietnam." Sneering at those offended by the sacrifice of the water buffalo at the end of *Apocalypse*, Coppola compared the reaction to one he received for the horse's head scene in *The Godfather*. "Americans," he said, "are again more outraged by the killing of animals than of people."

The press loved it: As always, Coppola made great copy, even when he was in the process of killing the messenger. Steven Bach, UA's head of East Coast and European production at the time, attended the press conference, and while certain that Coppola's tirade was only adding to the ulcers of UA executives in attendance, Bach was impressed by the passion and authority coming from the "big, bearded bear wearing a panama hat."

"Coppola is not just a great self-promoter; he is a genuinely articulate and infectious speaker," he recounted. "Lionel Trilling once observed the gulf between 'sincerity,' which many film people have and communicate handily, and 'authenticity,' which is something of a different order. Coppola communicates authenticity in good times and in times of disaster, and he is familiar with both. This was one of the good times."

That evening, Coppola presented another screening of his film, this one for exhibitors, and it was very well received. By all accounts, Coppola's strategy of taking the offensive, by showing his movie at Cannes and in his remarks at the press conference, had worked. The press, perhaps feeling sympathetic because of its past transgressions, flooded the papers with favorable stories, thus establishing *Apocalypse Now* as a favorite to win the festival's grand prize. Doing so, however, would involve beating considerable odds. The competition was especially stiff, and there were no Americans on the panel of judges. In the previous thirty-one years of Cannes festivals, only seven American films had taken the top prize.

The awards, announced on May 24, honored Americans in every major category. Jack Lemmon, the veteran character actor known mostly for his comedic roles, took Best Actor honors for his portrayal of a nuclear power plant technician in *The China Syndrome*, and Sally Field won the Best Actress award for her role as a union organizer in *Norma Rae;* Terrence Malick was cited as Best Director for *Days of Heaven.*

The Golden Palm for Best Film wound up being controversial. Unable to reach the unanimous vote required to honor a single picture, the Cannes panel split the award between *Apocalypse Now* and German director Volker Schlöndorff's *The Tin Drum*, a film adaptation of Gunther Grass's novel about the rise and fall of Nazism as seen through the eyes of a young boy. Coppola was now the only director in history to have won the Palm d'Or more than once—a status that did not sit well with purists, who noted that, by tradition, a winning director at Cannes refrained from entering the competition again, and who booed the selection when Coppola's name was announced, one dissenter commenting disparagingly that the jury should have awarded Coppola a "prize in progress."

The nit-picking, of course, meant nothing to Coppola, who celebrated the award as an indication of the artistic merits of his troubled film, and as vindication for his standing firm against his naysayers. He had rolled his dice and come up a winner.

That evening, Coppola, with his family and entourage, repaired to a small Italian restaurant far from the glitz of Cannes. The party began at a rather subdued level, but "when the celebratory mood finally struck, it did so literally," one witness remembered.

"A Chianti bottle flew from one corner of the little restaurant to another, crashing against a wall. Someone let out a whoop of release, a signal that the frustrations and uncertainties of four years' work were over. Another bottle followed the first, then another, then the glasses. The restaurant floor was a sea of wine and shards of glass, a red sea one expected for a moment Francis might try to part. He didn't; he joined in the celebration as glass followed glass."

10.

BOLSTERED BY HIS VICTORY at Cannes, Coppola returned to San Francisco for the final round with his movie. Winning the Golden Palm had given him a tremendous emotional lift, but the award also meant that he was more obligated than ever to honor the movie's August release date and place the film in front of the public while he and UA could capitalize on whatever benefits the award might bring. Cannes winners rarely fared well at the U.S. box office, as Coppola knew all too well from his own experiences with *The Conversation*. But in the case of *Apocalypse Now*, where skeptics wondered if the film was ever going to get off the ground, let alone be a movie of great merit, the Golden Palm offered added credibility.

The award also boosted Coppola's confidence, not only in his ability to complete his film but in his own business instincts. It hadn't been that long since his infamous memo announcing the downscaling of his studio, but in the aftermath of Cannes, he reconsidered his position. Hollywood General Studios was up for sale, and Coppola considered purchasing it and resurrecting some of his old Zoetrope dreams. Throughout the summer, the movie trade publications, along with area newspapers and magazines, tracked Coppola's activities, as well as various rumors, which had him thinking about purchasing United

Artists or MGM, unlikely as that seemed, or establishing an alternative school for children, in which students would study computer and video technology. Later in the summer, he talked to Orion Pictures about setting up a nonexclusive distribution deal for six pictures. Here was the Coppola of old, back in operation. He had hocked everything he owned for a movie yet to be released, yet he was looking into expensive new projects and purchases. "He's in a manic frame of mind," an unnamed source told a reporter from *New West*, "and I think he's trying to say *Apocalypse* is small change compared to what he's about to get into." Not surprisingly, the Coppola camp remained tight-lipped about his plans.

Coppola, who resented having the details of his life and business practices "spread out like a sheet of butter," took an unwelcome hit when, a few weeks before the release of *Apocalypse Now,* his wife published *Notes,* her diary on the making of the movie. The diary, originally intended as notes for a documentary, started out as a collection of observations about the process of filmmaking, but as the months dragged on and the Coppolas' marriage began to show the strain brought on by the difficulties with the film and Francis's philandering, the notes took on a much more personal dimension. Or, as one reviewer noted, "the book [became] a highly personal report on the difficulties of being Mrs. Francis Coppola."

Coppola, quite naturally, was unhappy about the prospects of having some of the more delicate aspects of his personal life aired in public, yet, after hearing Ellie read passages from the diary to him, he felt it might be educational to those interested in the difficulties of making a film on location. This was true enough, though Coppola undoubtedly realized that the accounts of his infidelity would become one of the book's selling points. Although he was in a position in which he could have vetoed the book's publication, realistically he was in no position to do much but watch the book go into circulation, then suffer through any resulting embarrassment, and live with the old axiom that any publicity is good publicity—a point that one book critic underscored when he noted that "[*Notes*] made me want to see his movie."

Notes, like the *Hearts of Darkness* documentary, would become a valuable companion piece to *Apocalypse Now,* for precisely the reasons that Coppola predicted when he first heard selections read aloud to him. Moviegoers rarely had the opportunity to see how a film was actually made—shot out of sequence, full of blunders and false starts, and weighed down by logistical hassles. *Notes* supplied an insider's view of the creation of a controversial masterpiece and of its equally troubled, and very human, director. Coppola might have been angered or hurt by some of the book's details, but it ultimately stood as a testament to a marriage strong enough to endure its most difficult times, and of a man, so often characterized by the press as irresponsible and arrogant, battling at all costs to realize his vision, reaching for (and finding) courage under circumstances that would have driven others to surrender.

11.

WHILE COPPOLA, WALTER MURCH, Richard Marks, and the editing team worked to assemble *Apocalypse Now* into its finished form, Coppola and United Artists planned and debated the best way to promote the film. Nothing could be taken for granted. Coppola's name, the turbulent history of the film, and the public's apparent anticipation of its release, and the victory at Cannes—all might be useful in putting together a marketing strategy for the movie, but none guaranteed success at the box office. The summer movies, which included *Rocky II, Alien, Moonraker,* and *The Amityville Horror,* brought in respectable gate receipts, but overall theater attendance declined 6 to 10 percent from the previous summer, with some studios, such as Columbia and Universal, taking terrible broadsides. Sequels to *The Poseidon Adventure (Beyond the Poseidon Adventure), Airport (The Concorde–Airport '79),* and *Butch Cassidy and the Sundance Kid (Butch and Sundance: The Early Days),* featuring different casts and obviously attempting to cash in on the phenomenal success of their predecessors, were dismal failures, as was B.W. L. Norton's *More American Graffiti,* which brought back most of the original cast and was trading on the success of the original, along with Lucas's *Star Wars* reputation. Even the tone of the summer's releases seemed to work against *Apocalypse Now.* "Winners and losers alike, this summer's movies were almost unanimously light entertainment," wrote Aljean Harmetz in a long analytical piece for the *New York Times,* while Gene Siskel, in the *Chicago Tribune,* questioned the appeal of a film like *Apocalypse Now.* "The guess here," offered Siskel, "is that the general public is not interested in another Vietnam film."

Coppola disagreed. *Apocalypse Now,* he felt, should be marketed like a major theatrical event, complete with ten-dollar ticket prices for reserved seating and handsome programs to be passed out at each screening. He had recently sponsored a showing of Hans-Jurgen Syberberg's seven-hour German epic, *Our Hitler,* in San Francisco, where two thousand people had shelled out ten dollars each to view the controversial film. The success of the *Our Hitler* screening, along with the clamor for tickets to the earlier Los Angeles previews of *Apocalypse Now,* had convinced Coppola that he could follow a similar path with the national release of his new picture. Classy films, he insisted, could be marketed as cultural events.

Others were not so certain. Joseph Farrell and his National Research Group had been enlisted to help launch *Apocalypse Now*, and in his discussions with Coppola and UA, Farrell contended that Coppola risked losing his mass audience by making his film a high-ticket event, and with a record $9 million committed to advertising and promoting *Apocalypse Now*, UA tended to agree. It was simply too risky. A compromise was reached: After its premiere in New York City, *Apocalypse Now* would run as a major, reserved-seat event, without titles and in its 70-mm grandeur, in New York, Los Angeles, and Toronto for twelve weeks prior to national release. Marketing of the film would be subdued, focusing on Marlon Brando, with no mention of the Golden Palm or favorable review blurbs in the ads.

Although not entirely satisfied with the strategy, Coppola had grown accustomed to the art/commerce compromise. In recent weeks, he had made a few in the film itself, abandoning his planned intermission and, despite his earlier proclamations that his Cannes ending was final, changing the ending to something less depressing and uncertain.

"There are those who want something pleasant, something warm to end the film with," he'd said while reveling in Cannes, after showing an ending that placed Willard, after killing Kurtz, on the steps of the temple, undecided about which direction he should take. UA executives and foreign distributors had pleaded with Coppola to change the ending to something more acceptable to audiences, perhaps along the line of Willard's calling in an air strike to destroy Kurtz's village, but Coppola had resisted. "I've got that ending, too," he admitted in Cannes. "But that's a lie. Maybe during the next month I will decide to end the film with a lie anyway, but I don't think so. Vietnam and America have had all the lies they need already."

Coppola's remarks bore a remarkable similarity to a line spoken by Kurtz at the end of the picture, when the demented colonel, inviting Willard to fulfill his mission by murdering him, implored his assassin to meet with his son afterward in the States and tell him of everything he had witnessed in Vietnam. He must tell the whole truth, Kurtz insisted, "because there is nothing I detest more than the stench of lies."

The ending that Coppola assigned to *Apocalypse Now* wound up being a compromise, the product of the unhappiest of artistic marriages, yet somehow it seemed to be as true as the ambiguity of the war itself.

12.

AT THE OPENING OF *Apocalypse Now*, we see helicopters moving languidly across the screen, their blades moving in slow motion, accompanied by the opening bars of the Doors' phantasmagorical song "The End." As the lush green tree line silently bursts into bright orange, decimated by a napalm strike, we understand that the movie we are about to see, like the Vietnam War itself, will be hellish reality superimposed on a bad acid trip. We are being transported to a place where you can be killed in battle, or you can die in the darkest regions of your mind, where all that you believe and hold sacred will be mocked by the grinning death's-head of civilization stripped to the primordial.

In a Saigon hotel room, Capt. Benjamin Willard awaits his assignment. He, too, seems to be moving in slow motion, imprisoned by hotel walls, drinking and smoking away his boredom, going physically and mentally soft. His past includes a failed marriage, a couple of tours of duty in Vietnam, and unspecified operations for the CIA, for which he performed unspeakable tasks, including murder. He is a man on edge, not entirely at peace with who he is, as we see when he drunkenly lashes out with a lightning-quick karate chop and shatters a mirror, cutting his hand and prompting an agonized scream.

He is eventually summoned to a general's headquarters and given his assignment: He and a small crew are to take a patrol boat up the river to a point just inside Cambodia, where he will encounter Col. Walter E. Kurtz, once one of the finest officers in U.S. military history, now living as a renegade in the jungle and ruling over a Montagnard tribe of warriors. Willard's job is to terminate Kurtz and his command "with extreme prejudice."

Willard's crew represents a cross section of the kind of grunt soldiers assigned to duty in Vietnam. "Chef" Hicks (played by Frederic Forrest) is a kid from Louisiana, an aspiring *saucier* who just wants to get out of Vietnam in one piece and return to the kitchens of New Orleans. Lance Johnson (Sam Bottoms) is a world-class surfer, obviously not bright or ambitious enough to attend the California college that would have given him the 2-S deferment necessary to avoid the draft. "Clean" (Laurence Fishburne) is a seventeen-year-old who, like many blacks during Vietnam, wound up serving in the war because there was no alternative. Chief Phillips (Albert Hall), the patrol boat's pilot, quietly yet authoritatively controls the crew.

Willard needs someone to airlift his patrol boat from the ocean to the river, and he finds assistance in Lt. Col. Bill Kilgore, a character who would have felt at home in such black war comedies as *Catch-22* or *M*A*S*H*. Kilgore is a man who understands war as adventure and, in a sense, adds to his identity (and legend) as he moves from battle to battle, swaggering with confidence with each new risk taken, regaling his troops with fireside stories of conquest, shrugging off danger as a mere annoyance. Incredibly cool under fire, he seems unconcerned when shells explode only a few feet from where he's walking, or when a lighted flare clouds his helicopter during an air strike.

Kilgore is also a surfing fanatic, and he's delighted to meet Lance Johnson, whom he hopes to see in action. As a rule, the waves in Vietnam are not conducive to good surfing, but Kilgore learns of one spot, currently occupied and heavily guarded by the enemy, where surfing is possible. It's here, he informs Willard, that he will drop the patrol boat.

At dawn the following morning, Kilgore leads an air strike on the occupied coastal village. As helicopters blaze over the ocean and gather in battle formation, Kilgore orders his pilot to play Wagner's "Ride of the Valkyries" at top volume over speakers installed in his helicopter. The music, he tells Willard, frightens the enemy. The helicopters swoop over the village, cutting down everything in sight, sustaining losses from return fire and, in one case, from a grenade tossed inside a landed helicopter by a young woman from the village. Once on land, Kilgore walks amid the carnage as the battle continues, tossing playing cards from a custom-made deck onto the corpses of the enemy as a grim message to the Vietcong. A horrified Willard can only watch. After a while, when it becomes clear that he will not secure the beach without outside help, Kilgore calls for a napalm strike. The jungle erupts in flames, leading Kilgore to utter the most often-repeated lines from *Apocalypse Now:* "I love the smell of napalm in the morning. It smells like . . . victory." He orders several of his men either to fight or surf, and before long, young soldiers are shooting the curls while shells drop and explode in the water around them.

Willard and his crew begin their journey up the river. Chef talks Willard into stopping the boat so he can go into the jungle for some mangoes, violating a survival code that commands soldiers never to leave the safety of their transport. In the jungle, Chef chirps on aimlessly about his life in the States as he and Willard make their way through the greenery, climbing over huge prehistoric-looking tree roots and observing plants taller than humans. Willard hears a noise and, gun at the ready, searches for the source of the sound. A tiger suddenly leaps out of the jungle growth and Willard and Chef, frightened out of their wits, open fire on the tiger, the jungle, and anything else that might be lurking there.

The group visits a black-market supply depot, where a USO show featuring a group of Playboy Bunnies is scheduled to perform for the troops. The show, the ultimate fantasy in the macho world of death and destruction, ironically representing the last look at civilization that Willard and his crew will see, weirdly reflects the bedlam of Altamont, in which festive music and entertainment were shattered by hair-trigger adrenaline: Frustrated, sex-deprived soldiers rush the suggestively dancing Bunnies, who wind up running for their safety, their exit by helicopter framed by huge phallic missile silos rising out of the bleachers.

The farther the patrol boat ventures upriver, the stranger and more hostile the environment becomes: broken, mangled bodies litter the trees and river; a burned-out helicopter rests in a tree, perched awkwardly like a giant insect shot down in midflight. The enemy is everywhere—but never seen. Lance, showing signs of losing his mind, paints his face in green camouflage, while Willard, totally obsessed with Kurtz—his own hidden enemy—pores over the dossier given him at the general's headquarters.

The group encounters a sampan, and though Willard would prefer to let the boat proceed unmolested, Chief Phillips insists on following protocol by pulling alongside and inspecting it. A family of terrorized Vietnamese stands by as Hicks, angered at drawing inspection duty, ransacks their vegetable cargo. In the middle of this tense scene, a woman dashes toward a covered basket, and in an instant, Willard's nervous crew opens fire on everyone aboard, killing all but the woman, who is mortally wounded but still alive. Phillips wants to take her somewhere nearby for help, but Willard ends the discussion by shooting her in the head. Hicks, traumatized by the events, looks into the basket that the woman had been approaching, and he finds not the expected cache of arms, but a little puppy. The shocked group takes the dog aboard and continues up the river.

(It was at this point that Coppola wanted to have his intermission. At the beginning of the movie's second act, the screen was to remain black, with only Willard's voice filling the theater. In the videotape version of the movie, the screen fades to black at the end of the sampan scene, remaining silent and black for fifteen seconds before action resumes.)

The group reaches the Do Long Bridge on the Cambodian border, a sort of no-man's-land technically occupied by the Americans and South Vietnamese but constantly under siege by the NVA, who blast away at the bridge and taunt the troops in the night. There are no winners or losers here—no leaders or troop morale—only sheer survival. Willard picks up further instructions and a pouch of mail before fleeing the nightmare. All that's left ahead, he notes, is Kurtz.

Now deep in enemy territory, Willard and his crew find themselves under attack, first by Vietcong troops concealed along the riverbank, then by Kurtz's warriors, who are armed with arrows and spears. At this point, the story has shifted toward the surreal, with Coppola using colored smoke from flares and thick fog to shroud the patrol boat in a haze. The battle sequences, however, produce very real and sobering results: Clean is cut down in the battle with the Vietcong and, a short time later, Chief Phillips is struck and killed by an enemy spear. The only ones left to accompany Willard on the remainder of his journey are Chef Hicks, completely traumatized by recent events, and Lance, who has lost his mind.

Willard finally reaches the Kurtz compound, where his boat is greeted by the former Green Beret's Montagnard servants, along with a whacked-out American photojournalist, who babbles incessantly about Kurtz's greatness. With its random display of severed heads and rotting corpses, the compound could have been the work of Vlad the Impaler, who mounted heads and bodies on spears to spook the enemy, but Willard suspects, when he finally meets Colonel Kurtz, that there is no method to Kurtz's madness. He is taken prisoner by Kurtz's guard, but not before ordering Chef to stay on board the patrol boat and call in an air strike if he doesn't return within a specified time.

Kurtz, riddled with malaria, comes across as part Buddha, part Jim Jones, and though he seems resigned to Willard's mission, he is initially scornful of Willard and his superiors. Lurking in the cavelike darkness of his temple, Kurtz appears only in brief moments of light, his huge bald head and massive frame concealed in shadow. "You're an errand boy," he says mockingly to Willard, "sent by grocery clerks to collect a bill."

Imprisoned in a bamboo cage, Willard endures the elements and the photojournalist's ravings until Kurtz appears, face painted in camouflage, and silently tosses Chef Hicks's severed head into his lap. Willard is set free, but he is too weak to fulfill his mission; instead, he stays in the temple, recovering slowly, while Kurtz rambles on, reading aloud (from *Heart of Darkness* and *The Waste Land,* among others) and speaking haltingly about his life and philosophy. While a member of the Special Forces, he tells Willard, he witnessed an event that changed him forever. The Americans had come into a village and inoculated the children for smallpox and other diseases; as soon as they left, the Vietcong arrived and hacked off the arms of the children, proving to Kurtz that moral judgment was of no use in war, when horror was a deadly but effective enemy that one had to learn to embrace. "If I had ten divisions of these men," Kurtz concludes, "our troubles here would be over very quickly."

Kurtz, however, recognizes the inevitable, and he makes no attempt to hold Willard prisoner or keep him at the compound. Willard, in turn, is still undecided about what he will do. He despises Kurtz and what his life has come to, but there is also something attractive, in a terribly horrible way, about Kurtz, just as there is something horribly appealing about war itself. Back at the patrol boat, Willard ignores a radio communication, apparently (though not explicitly) to confirm Hicks's earlier call about the air strike.

Willard reaches his decision the evening the tribespeople are performing a ritualistic slaughter of a water buffalo. Slipping unnoticed into the temple, his face painted in the camouflage that has come to symbolize the madness of war and the mask one needs to survive it, Willard murders Kurtz at precisely the same moment that the water buffalo is being sacrificed, his machete strikes echoing the machete strokes used on the animal outside the temple. Kurtz, bloody and dying, mutters as his final words those from *Heart of Darkness:* "The horror . . . the horror."

His mission accomplished, Willard lingers inside the temple, where he riffles through one of Kurtz's autobiographical manuscripts before heading outside. The tribespeople, seeing Willard's bloody machete and sensing what has occurred inside the temple, kneel down in unison to their new leader. Willard pauses momentarily, as if considering the idea of replacing Kurtz, but he rejects the notion and drops the machete on the temple steps. Willard finds Lance and together they return to the patrol boat. The film's final moments juxtapose Willard's face and a death's-head, with Kurtz's final words playing in the voice-over. Whatever Willard decides to do, whatever lessons he has learned, will never change the fact that war is an ancient horror, as inescapable as passing time itself.

The final fade to black did not put an end to the controversy over the *Apocalypse Now* ending. In the 35-mm print for theatrical release, Coppola shows the Kurtz compound being destroyed by an air strike while the end credits run, whereas in the 70-mm format, the screen goes black and there are no end credits. When the film was released, Coppola asserted that there was a practical explanation for the two endings. In theaters showing the 70-mm version, viewers were given a program with the credits, which was not feasible for the more widely distributed 35-mm version.

"We had to put titles in," Coppola explained, "and we had a choice of putting it on black at the end or over some footage, and I had tons of this gorgeous infrared stuff so I put it under the titles." This footage, Coppola continued, was not intended to change the film's ending, because, according to the director, "it's so clearly the credits."*

---

* Coppola apparently rethought his position on this, because in the videotape version of *Apocalypse Now,* the movie fades to black and the end credits run white on black, with no further footage.

13.

APOCALYPSE NOW PREMIERED, to great media fanfare, on August 15, 1979, in New York City's Ziegfeld theater, and in the weeks following, crowds packed the Ziegfeld, Hollywood's Cinerama Dome, and Toronto's University Theater, making Coppola's limited-run gamble an unqualified success. In New York alone, the picture, bolstered by a higher-than-average five-dollar ticket price, took in $311,000 during its first week—an astonishing figure for a single theater. Attendance figures were so impressive that United Artists announced, before the picture had even been released nationwide, that it anticipated a full recoupment of its investment.

Critics were almost unanimous in their appraisals of the film, lauding the first two-thirds of it and condemning the final third. All seemed to agree that the movie's reach exceeded its grasp, especially when Coppola tried to tie his movie into *Heart of Darkness*. There were a few total pans ("emotionally obtuse and intellectually empty") and a few complete endorsements ("a stunning and unforgettable film"); the reviews were generally mixed, although respectful.

"For two-thirds of the way," offered historian Arthur Schlesinger, Jr., for *The Saturday Review,* "*Apocalypse Now* is really an extraordinary movie. Like the Vietnam War itself, it gets out of control at the end." Vincent Canby's *New York Times* review similarly dismissed the final portion of the film, which Canby felt ineffective and anticlimactic. "I assume that Mr. Coppola's intention was to create in the finale a sense of Capt. Willard's disconnection from reality," wrote Canby, "but what we get is a disconnection from the rest of the film. When we arrive at the heart of darkness, we find not the embodiment of evil, of civilization junked, but an eccentric actor who has been given lines that are unthinkable but not, unfortunately, unspeakable."

Canby's remarks represented a consensus, not only in the opinion of the film's ending but in the mixed feelings that critics had toward the film in general. Canby, who thought enough of the picture to publish two separate reviews in a four-day period, was enthusiastic about the earlier episodes in the film: "In dozens of scenes, Francis Coppola's *Apocalypse Now* lives up to its grand title, disclosing not only the various faces of war but also the contradictions between excitement and boredom, terror and pity, brutality and beauty. Its epiphanies would do credit to Federico Fellini, who is indirectly quoted at one point."

Critics lined up to take potshots at Brando's role and performance—"a literature-lacquered version of the arch-villain in *Superman* or the James Bond scripts," griped Stanley Kauffmann in *The New Republic*—with a number of reviews singling out Brando's meandering improvisation in the temple as a major reason for the confusion in the film's ending. "Obese and photographed in shadows, Brando's character comes on like some kind of burlesque clown," wrote Gene Siskel in the *Chicago Tribune*. "What he has to say is mostly inaudible, and what is audible doesn't make any sense. That's a powerful letdown when you've been traveling upriver for two hours to meet the guy."

Conversely, Robert Duvall received the highest praise, even by those who found other parts of the film unsatisfying.

"The movie peaks early, both pictorially and metaphorically, when Willard and the crew of a patrol boat assigned to ferry him up the river encounter Col. Kilgore, a cheerfully brutal, gung ho air cavalry officer, played by Robert Duvall," wrote the *Washington Post*'s Gary Arnold, who gave *Apocalypse Now* one of its most scathing reviews. The air strike scene, Arnold maintained, was "a visual rouser and sums up whatever points the filmmaker has to make about wanton American violence in Vietnam."

David Denby of *New York* magazine agreed. "Kilgore is a vaunting, strutting caricature of military prowess, yet when we watch him in action, riding in with him as the copters pulverize a village, we may experience for the first time the insane electric fantasy of power that draws some men into war. . . . Dramatizing how war can be a crazy, beautiful turn-on yet totally alienating and self-destructive at the same time is Coppola's greatest achievement."

While critics checked in on the artistic merits of Coppola's film, Vietnam vets offered their own opinions on the picture's credibility in a glut of articles and companion pieces published shortly after *Apocalypse Now*'s premiere. As one might expect, some veterans took great exception to what they believed was a Hollywood trend of portraying the average soldier (and returning vet) as "baleful, explosive, spiritually exhausted, tormented, with brains like whipped cream."

"Whether the war was moral or immoral, that's not the point," said Robert Santos, an infantry platoon leader during his tour of duty. "The films should not show us as being unstable." Most of the people he served with, Santos maintained, were emotionally traumatized by having to kill, but Hollywood seemed hell-bent on depicting them as trigger-happy lunatics. "Filmmakers don't know enough about the war and seem not to want to find out the truth. They're motivated by ego and money—will the story sell, will people pay to see it?"

Al Santoli, an infantry sergeant in Vietnam, judged *Apocalypse Now* to be "a cartoon. It's a kind of cocaine fantasy. It's an infatuation with explosions and blood. The characters are all sterile. There's no sense of human interaction."

The problem, said vets and writers analyzing the Vietnam War movies, rested largely in the way Hollywood catered to the public's perception of war. Movies about World War II–the "good war," as it was often called–tended to portray war as a necessary evil, and its warriors as heroic; no one wanted to take any responsibility for the unpopular war in Southeast Asia, so filmmakers served up soldiers who reflected the public's sense of guilt, anxiety, anger, and shame. God forbid an enlisted man believe in his country's cause and want to serve, or complete his tour of duty and return home relatively stable.

The *Apocalypse Now* criticism cut Coppola to the quick. Here he was, trying to make a movie that disdained the usual war-picture formula–something that dared to surprise its viewers by giving them something different from what they'd come to expect–and he was being attacked for his efforts. He was heartened by the film's success at the box office, but, as he conceded to interviewer Greil Marcus, the public's response to the movie, like the critics', was largely divided. "Half the people thought it was a masterpiece," he declared, "and half the people thought it was a piece of shit."

The early responses to the movie, it should be noted, were probably as visceral as intellectual. It was impossible to stay neutral on the topic of Vietnam, and in 1979, the war was still so fresh in American minds that critics and the public were bringing a lot of emotional baggage to their viewing of the film. In time, *Apocalypse Now* would be regarded as one of the finest movies ever made on the war and, without question, one of Coppola's greatest achievements, but for the time being, in the immediate aftermath of making the film, Coppola was exhausted and more than a touch embittered.

"Sometimes I think, why don't I just make my wine, do some dumbbell movie every two years, and take trips to Europe with my wife and kids," he mused. "I've had it in terms of going to incredible extremes, half-blowing my personal life just to make a movie. I'm always going to bed in a cold sweat– will that star do the picture, how am I going to film the scene, will they like it. I know that feeling translates into your insides; I know I'm losing years of my life."

Chapter Ten

The Shape of Things to Come

"The new technology is as important to modern man as the discovery of fire was to early man. We are going to turn in the distant future into a race of people who possess extraordinary communication with one another—and the language of communication will be art."

—FRANCIS FORD COPPOLA

"Pretending that advanced technology will revolutionize movie art is a bit like claiming that the invention of the electric typewriter resulted in better writers."

—PETER RAINER

1.

DURING THE SUMMER OF 1979, while preparing *Apocalypse Now* for release and, in the words of one Hollywood observer, "moguling it up" by looking into a possible studio purchase, Francis Ford Coppola began to develop a new vision for what he wanted for his career, his Zoetrope enterprise, and, on a much grander scale, the structure of moviemaking as a whole. *Apocalypse Now* had sapped his interest in shooting on location—"In the mud of *Apocalypse,* I realized I wanted to make films in a studio again"—and, as always, the pressure of putting together another movie caught him pondering how films could be better produced and distributed. Nearly a decade had passed since "Black Thursday" and the end of Coppola's first run at American Zoetrope, and over the ensuing years, Coppola had hung on to the dream, hoping to see Zoetrope rise from the ashes and become the bold, successful studio that he had once imagined.

The core of his dream had changed very little over the years. He still wanted to lead a company of writers, actors, and production specialists, all working in a contemporary version of the studio system, where he could take the best of tradition and infuse it with bright new business and creative practices. An electronics revolution was at hand, and Coppola wanted to integrate it into a new, more efficient way of filmmaking. In April, during the Academy Award ceremony, he had spoken confidently of his vision. "I can see a communications revolution," he said, "that's about movies and art and music and digital electronics and satellites but above all, human talent—and it's going to make the masters of the cinema, from whom we've inherited the business, believe things that they would have thought impossible."

A perennial enthusiast when it came to gadgetry, Coppola had been awed by the possibilities presented by the constant advancements in technology, from the employment of high-tech equipment in the creation and editing of pictures to the use of satellites for the electronic distribution of finished movies. Pictures still had to focus on good stories and performances, but after that, everything else was up for grabs. In Coppola's opinion, the best way to start was to buy an old studio lot, completely overhaul it and install state-of-the-art equipment, and set up shop.

The Hollywood General Studios offered an ideal place to begin. The ten-and-a-half-acre lot housed nine soundstages, thirty-four editing suites, projection rooms, a special-effects lab, offices and bungalows, plus a history that could be traced back to the era of silent films. Built by John Jasper in 1919, the Jasper Hollywood Studio, as it was then known, was the envy of the motion picture business, and the only facility in Hollywood capable of twenty-four-hour production. Harold Lloyd had shot *Grandma's Boy* on the lot in 1922 and, five years later, Howard Hughes had used the facility to film *Hell's Angels*, the first picture he directed. Michael Powell had made *The Thief of Baghdad* (Coppola's "all-time favorite movie"), and Henry Hathaway had directed Mae West in *Go West Young Man* at the studio. Mary Pickford had lived in one of the lot's bungalows, and in the 1930s, when the studio changed its name to General Service Studios, Bing Crosby and Gary Cooper had resided there. The facility fell out of favor over time, as more and more directors chose to shoot their films on location or rent other facilities, but the renamed Hollywood General enjoyed success when Lucille Ball and Desi Arnaz used the lot exclusively to film their *I Love Lucy* television series. By May 1979, when Coppola was making serious overtures about buying the studio, Hollywood General, though still renting space to major and independent film producers, had fallen into disrepair and was, according to word circulating around Hollywood, available for the right price.

There was never a shortage of projects to pursue. According to his new agreement with Orion Pictures, finalized shortly before the opening of *Apocalypse Now,* Coppola would personally supervise the production of six new movies, which Orion would cofinance and distribute. Coppola already had *Hammett*—a detective story involving the real-life mystery writer—in development, and he had a slew of other projects in various stages of development, including a sequel to *The Black Stallion,* which he wanted Bob Dalva to direct; a picture called *The Escape Artist,* slated for Caleb Deschanel; and *The Secret Garden,* intended for Carroll Ballard. Coppola was uncertain about which picture he himself would pursue, though he was warming up to *One from the Heart,* a love story that he had rejected earlier in the year, when MGM offered him a record $2 million, plus a percentage of the film's gross receipts, to direct it. Coppola had also hinted, off and on over the past year, about making his next picture a screen adaptation of Goethe's *Elective Affinities.* In any event, after years of working on *Apocalypse Now,* he felt no pressing urge to rush into a new film.

The Orion deal fit neatly into Coppola's plans. With a studio lot and a decent distribution deal, he was ready to push Zoetrope to the next level.

2.

ONE CAN'T HELP BUT WONDER what Coppola felt privately about the state of contemporary motion pictures and the way they were being created. In his public statements, he enjoyed playing the part of the high roller who had bet the farm and won, but with *Apocalypse Now* and, a short time later, *The Black Stallion* holding their own at the box office, it was an easy position to take. Reaching that point was another matter.

The Black Stallion, plagued by script problems and bad weather on location, had taken what seemed like forever to complete, giving United Artists fits even as the company worried about the prospects for *Apocalypse Now.* UA hated the movie and considered shelving it, but Coppola, who liked it, convinced UA officials that they had nothing to lose by entering the picture in the New York Film Festival. The film was given a slow national release, but once it was out and had accumulated decent (though mixed) reviews and the all-important word-of-mouth recommendation, *The Black Stallion* maintained a strong position at the box office, eventually becoming one of the most successful debut features ever made. To Coppola, the *Black Stallion* story must have borne an element of déjà vu.

The history of *Hammett* followed a similar pattern of prolonged frustration. When Fred Roos read former detective Joe Gores's novel in 1975 and optioned it as a potential film, Coppola, too, had been intrigued. The novel, a mixture of fiction and nonfiction, combined the details of Dashiell Hammett's real-life story as a developing writer with a fictitious mystery in which he becomes involved. Both Roos and Coppola were enthusiastic about the prospects of blurring the line between fact and fiction in a movie, and Coppola was eager to cast Frederic Forrest, now signed as a regular Zoetrope player, in the lead. Nicholas Roeg, the British director of *Performance, Don't Look Now,* and *The Man Who Fell to Earth,* was hired to develop and eventually direct the picture, and Gores was given the assignment of adapting his book for the screen.

The wheels started to come off the project early. For openers, Lillian Hellman, Hammett's longtime lover and executor of his estate, was reluctant to sign the necessary releases and throw her support behind the film. The early scripts were a bust. Then, just when it seemed as if the project was gaining momentum, United Artists, having agreed to give $8 million in financing in exchange for the domestic distribution rights to the film, nixed Frederic Forrest as the lead, arguing that he lacked the star power needed to justify the company's investment. Roeg grew weary of the search for a replacement for Forrest and left. For a while, Robert De Niro seemed interested in playing the lead, but he was hard to nail down to a definite commitment. Similarly, director François Truffaut looked at the script and praised it, but ultimately he passed on directing the movie. Subsequent searches for an actor and director moved at a crawl, and by the end of 1977, when Coppola was wrapped up in his own battles with *Apocalypse Now, Hammett* looked like a lost cause.

The film's fate improved the following spring, when Roos saw and was greatly impressed by Wim Wenders's *The American Friend.* Both Roos and Coppola agreed that the German director was just the person they wanted for *Hammett,* a stylish period piece set in 1920s San Francisco. Wenders, who proposed shooting the film in black and white as a homage to the 1940s film noir, regretted that Montgomery Clift was not around to play a role so perfectly suited for him, but he was pleased by Coppola's and Roos's new choice for the lead—playwright and actor Sam Shepard.

The script problems continued. After a number of unsuccessful rewrites, Joe Gores departed in September 1978 and was replaced by USC alumnus Tom Pope, a young screenwriter who joined forces with Wenders on a new draft of the script. Their efforts, although an improvement over the earlier attempts, still failed to pass muster for Coppola, who felt the plot was too complicated for most film audiences. When the two delivered a subsequent draft, this one integrating portions of Hammett's *The Red Harvest* into the movie's plot, Coppola was frustrated to learn that the novel's rights were unavailable. When the two delivered still another draft, an increasingly impatient Coppola decided to test it on a radio audience, to disastrous results. He hired Gene Hackman to read the lead, and Frederic Forrest and Ronee Blakley (Wender's wife at the time) to read the other roles. The radio play showed just how far the screenwriters had yet to go: The dialogue was good, but no one could follow the action. Pope left the project and another young writer, Dennis O'Flaherty, an Oxford Ph.D. in Russian literature, was brought aboard to rework the script with Wenders. Four years after Roos had originally read the novel, when *Apocalypse Now* and *The Black Stallion* were finally hitting the screens after years of lengthy delays and problems, *Hammett* had yet to see a single frame of film.

The delays on *The Black Stallion* and *Hammett* were often linked to Coppola, with critics charging that he interfered too much with the development of the projects. Others, however, contended that Coppola, as a gifted and experienced screenwriter, was enhancing the projects with his guidance, and that, as the head of Zoetrope, he had every right to insist on the very highest quality before affixing his company's name to the pictures' credits. Some observers weren't interested in drawing a distinction. "Whether he's controlling you for good or bad, he's still controlling you," remarked a former employee. "I don't know many writers who are willing to work in that kind of manipulative environment." "He's a true visionary," noted another. "But no director with any clout will work over there. Who'd put up with the interference?"

Carroll Ballard, who had spent some nerve-racking times in the trenches with Coppola during the *Black Stallion* saga, was unhappy about some of Coppola's interference, as well as with the low payment he received for directing the film, but he was also grateful that Coppola had given him the work. "Sure, I can gripe," he stated. "But without Francis, I would have had no chance to make a picture in Hollywood."

3.

COPPOLA RANG IN THE NEW DECADE, along with his hopes for his new version of Zoetrope, by planting a small palm tree on the Hollywood General lot. Although the courts had yet to issue a final decision on the sale of Hollywood General, Coppola felt confident that all would work out in his favor. While he waited, he continued to fill out his roster of talent. He, of course, would be acting as the company's chairman of the board, though he preferred to be referred to as the company's "artistic director"—a title that seemed less formal. Robert Spiotta, a Hofstra classmate presently working as an oil executive, was named president and chief executive officer, and Lucy Fisher, a former production vice president at Twentieth Century–Fox, was appointed Zoetrope's vice president and head of production—the first woman to hold the position in Hollywood history. Both Spiotta and Fisher would be stationed in the company's San Francisco offices, which Coppola intended to keep as his main base of operations.

The department chairs and other staff positions were equally impressive. Dean Tavoularis would be running the art and design department; other positions included casting (Jennifer Shull), special effects (Raymond Fielding), and sound (Walter Murch). Dennis O'Flaherty, Dennis Klein, and Bill Bowers signed on as staff writers, while Teri Garr and Raul Julia joined Frederic Forrest, Laurence Fishburne, and Albert Hall as part of Coppola's acting company. Coppola optimistically figured that, all told, he would eventually be employing as many as fifteen hundred people in his company, all working toward putting out six to eight quality pictures per year.

"I believe the most natural forum for films to be made in," said Coppola, "is the repertory system, in which the talent is held together as a team, where actors, producers, directors, and writers are encouraged to work and socialize together, and out of all the fraternization can achieve the same sort of craft that you find in a theater company or a ballet company."

Coppola was brimming with enthusiasm. His revamped Zoetrope Studios, he reasoned, would finally place him in the position of complete artistic control of his films, from the earliest preproduction meetings through the completion of a picture. Ideas for a movie would be generated internally, from creative minds that he employed, and the production would be carried out by a loyal cast and crew. Having soundstages meant he would never again have to slosh around in the muck or worry about climate and natural lighting, as he had during the filming of *Apocalypse Now*. Most important of all, he would be able to make the kind of motion pictures that he chose to make, rather than the kind of movie dictated by exhibitors and market researchers.

"We must never allow the cinema to become driven into little categories," he warned, "that after a while we can only make certain kinds of films because some sort of market research tells us that it's the only kind that people will go to. We used to make the greatest cars in the world, and then market research got hold of cars, and I even see a certain trend in motion pictures slowly moving towards this idea that you can only make this kind of film or that kind of film, and only that."

Coppola, however, was not merely content with establishing Zoetrope as a small production company operating independent of Hollywood; he aspired to set the pace for a future in which pictures would be made and distributed in a more cost-effective manner. The key, he insisted, was in electronics.

"My idea," he said later, "was to go back to the old system—have an art department, special effects department—except try to be more economical." The basic technology, he pointed out, had not changed much since the 1920s; film- and sound-editing techniques were essentially the same. "We began to think, what if the studio could be arranged to be made totally into an electronic studio that approached movie-making as a combination of live theater, live television, and 24-track recording as used in making a record?"

Hollywood, quite expectedly, reacted with skepticism to Coppola's visions for the future. Here was Coppola, always the showman, popping off again about how he was going to reinvent the wheel—and this coming from a man who could barely scrape together the money needed to purchase a run-down, outdated studio lot. As far as Hollywood was concerned, Coppola could go off on his little adventure and experiment to his heart's content. Hollywood, like the American government, had gone along basically unchanged, governed by the same rules, because the old way worked. Coppola was running around, comparing himself in public statements to Darryl Zanuck, but if memory served, American Zoetrope, Coppola's first attempt at revolutionizing the industry, had produced mixed results.

Coppola hated the cynicism, especially when it originated, as it did, from people enslaved by the dollar. All anyone around him, particularly the media, talked about was how much a movie cost and how much it grossed at the box office. The ledger on *Apocalypse Now* had been public knowledge almost from the beginning, and despite all the caustic predictions and naysaying, the movie was still heading toward the break-even point. Even with his ideas for a new, electronic cinema, all people wanted to know was, "How much is it going to cost?"

It would cost Coppola plenty, but for reasons he might not have anticipated in 1980. His ideas, in fact, *were* nothing short of visionary, even if, in his customary way, he charged about without having all the details and possibilities considered and worked out.

For the moment, he had a studio to run, and since *Apocalypse Now* was not providing the kind of immediate profits needed to support the studio, he had to come up with another project.

4.

COPPOLA'S FIRST EXPERIMENT with electronic cinema—a thirty-minute live broadcast of presidential candidate Edmund G. Brown, Jr.'s campaign rally in Wisconsin—was an embarrassing disaster, foreshadowing problems the director would experience on his next film. Entitled "The Shape of Things to Come," the broadcast was so horrible that the media rechristened it "Apocalypse 1980."

Coppola's association with the California governor and presidential hopeful began on March 7, when Brown appointed Coppola to a position on the California Arts Council, ending a controversy dating back to the previous July, when Brown had offered the same position to Jane Fonda, only to see his recommendation rejected by a state senate that refused to confirm the appointment because of the actress's political activities during the Vietnam War. The two-year position, which Coppola announced that he was "very pleased to accept," involved the dispensing of grant money to artists and artistic groups, and it would require very little of the filmmaker's time.

In many respects, Brown and Coppola were a good match. Brown's father had also been governor of California, defeating Richard Nixon in a bitterly contested race in 1962, but the younger Brown was more of a political maverick, a self-styled political visionary definitely outside of the national mainstream. His futuristic ideas found very few sympathetic ears at a time when Americans were seething over the hostage crisis in Iran, and his vote tallies in the presidential primaries gave little indication that he had much chance of defeating the incumbent, President Jimmy Carter, for the Democratic party's nomination. In Coppola's eyes, Brown must have seemed like the Preston Tucker of the political scene.

Brown realized that he had neither the votes nor the money to continue much longer in the race, and he decided to make a final stand in the April 1 primary in Wisconsin. Coppola threw his support behind Brown, and the director and his brother, August, created four television ads for the Wisconsin campaign. Then Coppola had a major brainstorm: Why not take a full film crew to Wisconsin and present Brown's Madison campaign rally as a full-blown event on live television? "Instead of spending the little campaign money that he had for a commercial here, a commercial there," Coppola proposed, "why not blow it all on one live media event? In other words, take everything we had and somehow try to attract a big commotion."

Unfortunately, despite his good intentions, Coppola had no experience working on either live television or political campaigns, and when he and his crew blew into Madison "like a little Zoetrope SWAT team," as Coppola described it, he'd had only two weeks to prepare for the event. Not that he arrived unarmed for battle: To put together the show, Coppola intended to deploy a helicopter and two video-control trucks, seven cameras, five search-lights, eight carbon-arc spotlights, an enormous high-resolution television screen, twenty-five walkie-talkies, three camera lifts, and thirty steel drums (in which he intended to light fires for effect, as well as a means to warm the crowd); rock promoter Bill Graham agreed to emcee the event, and Dean Tavoularis and Caleb Deschanel were on hand to assist Francis and August Coppola with the program's staging. Coppola had even ordered three thou-sand cups of chicken and vegetable soup to pass out to people in attendance. When asked about what Coppola was up to, one Brown staffer pleaded igno-rance. "I have no idea what he's going to do," he told a reporter. "All I know is that Coppola intends this thing to be one of the collector's items in his career."

Nor did the local residents know how to react to the beehive of activity swarming around the capitol building. The helicopter frightened residents of a nearby nursing home, who were awakened by the noise and, looking out their windows, became worried that the capitol had been invaded. Another local, looking up in the night sky and seeing the helicopter moving about the building tops, exclaimed, "Holy shit! Francis is going to napalm us!" One could only imagine what went through the mind of John Anderson, another presidential candidate campaigning in Madison, as he looked out his hotel window and saw Coppola's crew taking over the town. Even Governor Brown, by one reporter's account, seemed overwhelmed by the preparations. His staff worried about what all this was going to cost.

Coppola made the most of his time in Madison, stumping for Brown and promoting his electronic cinema in press interviews, as well as turning up at high school assemblies and college classes, and even at a PTA meet-ing. While he spread the word, his technicians and video consultants wres-tled with his elaborate plans for the program. As Coppola envisioned it, Brown would appear on a bare stage, much the way George C. Scott had appeared at the opening of *Patton,* and when he spoke, a montage of corre-sponding images would be projected onto a twelve-by-twenty-foot screen behind him. Coppola and his staff agreed that, with such ambitious plans, there was very little margin for error. Since the rally was being broadcast on live TV, the decisions and equipment had to be flawless. "If something goes wrong," Coppola allowed, "I'll have to show it."

The event was a disaster from start to finish. Brown's wireless microphone failed as soon as he began his prepared speech, and even after the problem was solved, the helicopter drowned out the sound coming from the public-address system. The chroma-key montage process failed as well, resulting in some of the most outrageous juxtapositions imaginable. At one point, as Brown spoke about the country's deteriorating cities, a farm scene played on the screen behind him; when he spoke about reindustrializing the United States, the audience was treated to footage of astronauts floating weightlessly in space. Coppola scrapped the montage before Brown had completed his speech, but the damage had already been done. The grand finale, which was to have the candidate reciting the "Pledge of Allegiance" while his image and an image of the American flag played on the screen, wound up a blurry mess, rather than the emotional climax that Coppola had intended, leading one of Brown's aides to remark that the governor looked like Claude Rains in *The Invisible Man.*

"It was as spectacular a failure as any of his awesome filmic successes," the *Los Angeles Times* reported of Coppola and his show. "Everything that could possibly go wrong, did."

Whatever his private feelings about the debacle, Brown defended Coppola at a postrally press conference. "The fact is you wouldn't all be here [without the Coppola production]," he said. "There's a real barrier, so I had to take extraordinary steps. You are under a negative spell that I am attempting to exorcise."

Coppola admitted that the program had been a failure, but he hoped that it had at least generated the kind of badly needed publicity the Brown campaign needed. Some time later, when recalling the botched attempt, Coppola could find humor in his failure.

"It looked as if we were coming from the moon," he said. "The chroma-key didn't work, so instead of the images being behind Jerry Brown, they were in his face. And it was altogether one of the funniest things you've ever seen in your life. It looked as if it were a transmission from some clandestine place on Mars."

He wasn't willing, however, to accept total responsibility for the fiasco. "It was typically overambitious," he admitted, "and depended on some degree of technical competence, which was just not available to us from the rentals and teams that came from the local [television] station. The video trucks that we rented and the typical broadcast cameramen weren't up to what we were asking to do. The intercom in the switching truck went out before we started, and we had zero communication with the cameramen out there. Instead of pointing their cameras at what was going on, they walked around with cameras pointed toward the ground, so all we had in the truck were these images of feet and the ground, and we had no way to communicate with them. Primarily, it was the intercom failure that did us in."

"The Shape of Things to Come": The title of the broadcast, the press noted, was deliciously ironic. Four days after the rally, after pulling a tepid 12 percent of the vote in the Wisconsin primary, Brown withdrew from the race. The title had ironic implications for Coppola as well, as he would learn when he tried to apply his electronic cinema to his next motion picture.

5.

BY MID-APRIL 1980, COPPOLA had decided to make *One from the Heart* his next movie—and the first that he would be producing by electronic cinema for his Zoetrope studio. The sale of the studio had been finalized on March 25, with Coppola agreeing to pay $6.7 million for the property, a sum that he would be able to afford only by working on another film. *One from the Heart*—a simple love story about a couple who break up on the eve of their fifth anniversary, only to reunite after engaging in overnight flings with other partners—might have struck Coppola followers as a lightweight follow-up to *Apocalypse Now,* but Coppola refuted the notion. Love and sex, he declared, were large, universal subjects, and they were certainly more personal to the average moviegoer than war.

"The movies I make for the next ten years," he predicted, "will focus on one major theme: love, the male-female situation, sex. I want to examine it like a novelist. . . . I feel I can finally deal with the subject matter. I was thrown by it before, and I think that's why I've had too few women in my films. But now. . . .Well, maybe I've slowed down enough to get a handle on the subject."

Hammett, which had gone before cameras on February 4, was still distracting him to no end. Frederic Forrest, whose marquee value had risen substantially with his performance in *The Rose,* had won the title role, as Coppola originally intended, and he was joined by a cast that included Brian Keith, Sylvia Miles, and Ronee Blakley. Coppola had yet to see a screenplay that met his approval—the tally of completed screenplays was presently standing at twelve—and for several weekends at the beginning of the shoot, he himself had tried to doctor the script. When his attention was required at the new studio, he hired Dennis Jakob to work on the script, but Jakob could not come up with anything suitable, either. Discouraged, Coppola shut down the production at the end of its tenth week of shooting, figuring that it might be best to assemble the rough footage and see what could be done to salvage a picture that Wim Wenders claimed was already 90 percent completed. Rather than hold the decision to shut down against Coppola, Wenders was relieved by it. "I was so exhausted by the end of the tenth week," he recalled, " I wasn't at my best any more."

In recalling the trials of the making of *Hammett*, Coppola saw the picture as a problem almost from the start.

"We had a script, a director, and a budget," he said. "When we were getting around to casting, Wim inquired whether it would be okay to consider Ronee Blakley–whom he was in the midst of a romance with–for the leading lady. Fred Roos and I felt she was wrong for the part, and we politely told him so. He then cast Marilu Henner. Then he married Ronee. They started to shoot in San Francisco, and the stuff looked excellent. However, Wim later came to tell us that he wanted to cast Ronee as another character, which he–they–had invented for the film. She was supposed to play an old woman, and it was going to be a one-day scene. We said okay. However, after they shot the scene, Wim wanted to add another one for her. Word was coming back from the set that they were writing together, and that Ronee was very aggressive on the set, making herself the focus of the scene. My son Gio came back and said that they were arguing on the scene, and that Ronee was starting to almost direct, belittling Wim in front of all the crew. I asked Fred [Roos] and the others to hang around and watch, and they confirmed that not only was this happening, but that new pages were coming in, focusing on this 'one-day' character, totally changing the approved script. When I asked Wim about it, he said that this was the way he always worked–hand in hand with the woman he was with–and that he felt it would be great. We were rapidly getting into a 'no-man's-land' with the script: We weren't shooting what we had, and step by step Ronee's character was becoming the lead of the film. Since I couldn't dissuade Wim from this path, and seeing that we were using up the resources we had on the script with Ronee in the lead, and not sure where it was leading, I stopped production."

Dean Tavoularis, working as production designer on the film, remembered it similarly: "It all started so great and promising, but then it went to this weird kind of scene. You'd go to the set and everybody would be standing around, and you'd hear a typewriter in the corner. Everybody's standing around, drinking coffee at ten or eleven in the morning, and somebody's in this dark corner, working on the script. You don't go to the stage and then write the movie."

Frederic Forrest, for one, appreciated the job that Blakley was doing on the film.

"I didn't think that she was taking over the film," he insisted. "She and Wim were married, but I'll tell you one damn thing: Her performance was more interesting than anything in the film that they made later. She was perfect for that part. It was like the Mary Astor part, a quirky sort of thing, as if he was writing *The Maltese Falcon,* not some nebulous shit that they did later. In the first version of the film, Wim Wenders and I were trying to put in all of Hammett's attitudes. We read all of his books, and did everything we could to get all that in there. I was caught in the middle: Francis was my boss—I loved him and he got me the job—but Wim Wenders was my director, and I respected him and loved the way he was working."

While Wenders tinkered with his rough cut of *Hammett,* Coppola tried to hammer out the details for his work on *One from the Heart.* Armyan Bernstein had set his original screenplay in Chicago, but Coppola favored placing the story in Las Vegas, for reasons both pragmatic and symbolic. With *Hammett* on the shelf indefinitely, the Las Vegas sets could be constructed on the Zoetrope lot, sparing Coppola the headaches of shooting on location. Besides, Coppola wanted his movie's version of Las Vegas to be the Las Vegas of people's dreams—bright, promising, and magical—rather than the garish Las Vegas of real life, and he could construct such a dream city in his own studio. "The real Las Vegas is like Burbank," he maintained. "We're going to tell this simple story in a fantasy way, so we'll make our own fantasy of Las Vegas, which for me is a metaphor for America itself."

"I wanted to take a fable-like story and treat it almost the way Disney would approach a story in his animated films," he said on another occasion. "Treat it with very expressive sets and lighting and music that heighten the story. If we had made the movie in Las Vegas, it would have been just another relationship movie set on a real location with people jumping in and out of cabs, talking about their love affairs. I wanted to do something people hadn't seen before."

But first he had to find a way to finance his film, which was proving to be difficult. The industry's focus on blockbusters had spawned some colossal failures, headed by Michael Cimino's *Heaven's Gate,* which had started out as a modestly budgeted action Western, only to evolve into a fiasco of nightmare proportions when the picture's expenses skyrocketed out of control and Cimino delivered an unreleasable five-and-a-half-hour movie. The film was eventually chopped down to a manageable two and a half hours, but by then the advance publicity on the picture had all but sunk it before its release.

The failure of *Heaven's Gate* hurt Coppola on a number of fronts. In the wake of that film's demise, along with the well-publicized problems with *Apocalypse Now,* there was great discussion about the death of the auteur in Hollywood. Bright, talented, yet largely self-absorbed directors, the rising stars in the industry less than a decade ago, needed to be reeled in and controlled by the studios backing the pictures. After all, when all was calculated, there was a price tag on ego and artistic vision. There was also a price tag on perception. If the public *perceived* a picture to be a failure before its release, the movie could be doomed before it had the chance to establish itself with critics or viewers. *Apocalypse Now* suffered (and, to some degree, would always suffer) from a perception problem: Despite the fact that it would eventually earn a respectable amount of money, *Apocalypse Now* would always be perceived as a grand failure—the victim of a director out of control and a box office that failed to respond to the movie. This was not the kind of reputation that one wanted to overcome during the best of times, but in the aftermath of *Heaven's Gate*, Coppola found himself taking a defensive posture.

"Of course, not everyone acknowledged it was made largely with my own money," he told Jeffrey Wells of *Film Journal*. "The general prediction was that *Apocalypse Now* wasn't any good and that it would fail, that I would lose all of my money and my house, and that I was a fool to have done it." This kind of perception, Coppola complained, was terribly damaging not only to an individual film or filmmaker but to the industry as a whole. "They've never really said that *Apocalypse* was a success, and that it made this much money. In other words, if they predicted it would fail and it succeeds, they never acknowledge it. But the next time you do a picture, they say it's going to fail. If you look back at all the press clippings, you'll see this is exactly what happened. . . . Of course, sooner or later, I *will* fail, and at that point the press, no doubt, will say, 'We told you all along.' It's a pity because the real loss is that you'll put these kind of people . . . the Michael Ciminos and all the rest, whatever their flaws, out of business, and we won't see these kind of films anymore, and we'll all be looking at television."

If all this weren't enough, Coppola had to contend with his own reputation and track record. His talents as a director or screenwriter were well established, and his reputation had served him well throughout the seventies. Still, there was no denying that Coppola's most recent films, though beautiful works of art, had been disappointing at the gate. Financial backers might have been willing to overlook this and support Coppola as a prestige artist—as has always been the case with directors like Woody Allen—if Coppola and Zoetrope hadn't stubbed their toes on *The Black Stallion*, *Apocalypse Now*, and, most recently, *Hammett*. To some potential backers, such films, however admirable as works of art, weren't worth the headaches.

In this sense, Coppola's timing on *One from the Heart* could not have been worse, and all the talk of the new studio and a radical new way of filmmaking only hurt him further. Just when Hollywood was talking about taking back the night, so to speak, here came one of its biggest renegades, looking for financing from traditional sources while he spoke endlessly about how he was going to change the system. It was like investing one's life's savings on a brilliant but mad inventor.

Finally, Coppola was not interested in the standard movie deal, which, in essence, would find him working as a studio's employee, collecting a director's fee and perhaps a percentage of the take, while the studio owned the movie itself. Coppola had his own studio and he wanted ownership of his films, as well as final say about how they were made. MGM, which owned the rights to *One from the Heart*, was intent on striking a deal with Coppola, but not entirely on the director's terms. Some kind of compromise had to be reached.

6.

FOR ALL THE TROUBLES HE WAS having with *Hammett*, Coppola truly wanted the film to work out, but by midsummer 1980, the picture had become a burden that diverted his attention from other projects, including his own. Wim Wenders had edited a fine cut of his footage and had made a detailed storyboard for a newly proposed ending, but Coppola rejected this new version, claiming that the story still wasn't right. To correct the problem, he ignored Wenders's pleas that he be allowed to work out the plot on the set. He hired yet another writer—best-selling mystery author Ross Thomas—to build a beginning and ending around the existing Wenders footage. No new filming on the project would be permitted until early 1981. Wenders, reaching the limits of his patience with what was starting to look like an endless project, decided to use the hiatus to make another film in Europe.

With the exception of its problems with *Hammett*, Zoetrope was operating smoothly. Caleb Deschanel's *The Escape Artist*, starring Griffin O'Neal and Raul Julia, was moving along on schedule, and a number of other projects, including *Tucker*, were under development. As a distributor, Zoetrope had picked up several prestigious films, including *Napoleon*, the 1927 Abel Gance silent classic, for which Carmine Coppola was currently writing a musical score; *Sauve Qui Peut (La Vie)*, Jean-Luc Godard's first major production in eight years; Hans-Jurgen Syberberg's *Our Hitler*, which had enjoyed a sold-out run at Avery Fisher Hall in New York City; and *Kagemusha*, Akira Kurosawa's latest film.

Coppola was especially pleased by his association with the Kurosawa film. The Japanese director had been a hero of Coppola's for as long as he could remember, and he considered it an honor to serve, along with George Lucas, as executive producer of the first Japanese picture ever released worldwide by a major American studio.

The film, cowinner of the 1980 Golden Palm at Cannes, almost didn't get made at all. Kurosawa was revered throughout the world as the greatest director in Japanese cinema history—two of his films, *Rashomon* (1950) and *Dersu Uzala* (1975), had won Oscars for Best Foreign Film—yet, at seventy, Kurosawa was considered too old to direct, a slight that George Lucas quipped "was like telling Michelangelo, 'All right, you're 70 and we're not letting you paint anymore.'" *Kagemusha* had originally been approved for production by Toho, Kurosawa's Tokyo studio, but the financing for the director's twenty-seventh film had fallen through when Toho executives deemed its budget to be too rich for their taste.

"I contacted Kurosawa and asked him if it was true that they didn't have enough money to do it, and he said yes," Lucas recalled. "I said, 'How much do they need in order to finish the movie?' It was about two or three million, or something like that. So I turned around and went to Laddie [Alan Ladd, Jr.] at Fox, and I told him that I wanted him to buy the international rights to the film and pay them the difference between what they had and what they needed to finish the movie—about two or three million. This was right after I did *Star Wars.* Fox had done very well for themselves with *Star Wars,* and Laddie was in a great mood at that time, so they said yes, they would do the movie. I then went to Francis and said, 'You're a friend of Kurosawa's. Would you like to be the cointernational producer on this picture with me?'"

Coppola jumped at the opportunity. In addition, Zoetrope agreed to be *Kagemusha*'s American distributor.

Coppola's connection to Japanese theater and cinema went far beyond his appreciation of Kurosawa's talents. Over the years, Coppola had studied Japanese theater—especially Kabuki, the traditional Japanese form of drama, which brought him back to his youthful days when, incapacitated by polio, he had staged his puppet shows. For Coppola, there was something magical about the way the Japanese worked outside the traditional methods of telling a story. "In Japanese drama," he explained, "scenery, story, actors, and dance are all components. To them, the illusion part is better at getting to the mysteries of life than the naturalistic."

Significantly, Coppola looked at his first script for *One from the Heart* shortly after the completion of *Apocalypse Now,* while he was in Japan, reading Goethe and trying to figure a way to adapt *Elective Affinities* in a way that addressed Eastern and Western cultures. In Goethe's novel, a husband and wife take in a young girl, and the man subsequently falls in love with the young girl, while his wife has a relationship with another man. Coppola had a grand plan for *Elective Affinities*—which he was in no financial position to execute—in which he would make four films over a ten-year period, each film set in a different time in history, in America and Japan, the four long episodes telling the story of the married couple, the other man, and the girl. *One from the Heart,* with its somewhat similar story line, was an appealing alternative. Coppola even got the idea for setting the movie in Las Vegas when he was walking in the Ginza section of Tokyo and observing the similarities between the two cities.

At first, Coppola conceived *One from the Heart* as "a little musical Valentine," as he told a BBC interviewer in a 1985 television special presented in England. A musical would give him the chance to use song, dance, fantastic effects and lighting, as well as unconventional settings and props—more like those used onstage than in the movies—to create the romantic illusions that he wanted for his film. In time, however, he amended this to an even bolder and more innovative idea: The movie's musical sound track could be a series of songs corresponding with the action on-screen, sung by people other than the film's actors. It would become a kind of musical within a movie, contributing further to the ethereal qualities of the picture.

The more it was developed, the more ambitious *One from the Heart* became, with a budget rising accordingly. Fortunately, Zoetrope employed some of the finest creative minds in the business, and Coppola called on them to help him with his project. Veteran actor and dancer Gene Kelly, who had starred in such classic musicals as *An American in Paris* and *Singin' in the Rain,* joined Zoetrope to offer his expertise on *One from the Heart,* as well as on such projected musicals as *Tucker* and *Sex and Violence,* the latter intended as a vehicle for Cindy Williams. Kelly loved the Zoetrope facilities and Coppola's plans for *One from the Heart* and electronic cinema, and he optimistically pronounced that he and Coppola were "like a couple of school kids" eager to begin the projects. Although he would not be listed in the film's credits as its choreographer, Kelly worked closely with Kenny Ortega on choreographing the dance numbers for the picture.

By now, Dean Tavoularis had become one of Coppola's most trusted associates, and Tavoularis was again assigned the task of production design, which, for *One from the Heart,* amounted to nothing less than reconstructing Las Vegas on the Zoetrope soundstages—a job that proved to be both awe-inspiring on-screen and very costly to the film's budget.

"The idea was not to go to Las Vegas," said Tavoularis, "but to do everything on the stage. Naturally, it took on a certain look. We had a list of scenes—a home, a car driving on an open street, a guy parking and getting out in front of his house. I said, 'To try to scrunch a whole street into a soundstage, we can't make it that realistic; it's going to be theatrical.' So the theatricality became the design."

Coppola needed an especially gifted cinematographer to create the difficult illusion of an animated film shot in live action, and he hoped to bring back Vittorio Storaro to lead the camera crew, only to find himself fighting another round with the unions, who wanted the job to go to an American. In a tense meeting with union officials, Coppola threatened to shoot the movie in Italy if that's what it would take for him to have Storaro as his cinematographer. He then punctuated his statements by picking up a chair and smashing several of his office windows while horrified union officials watched in stunned silence. They relented, but only on the condition that Coppola list a local cinematographer before Storaro in the film's credits.

For *One from the Heart,* Coppola wanted to use color to establish mood, much the way he and Storaro had used light for effect in *Apocalypse Now.* Storaro, who had recently brought home an Oscar for his work on *Apocalypse Now,* and who would be nominated for another for his brilliant work with color in *Dick Tracy,* was the perfect candidate for the job.

"In *One from the Heart,*" Storaro remembered, "I went to the physiology of color, in the sense that I wanted to show the kind of reaction the body could have in the presence of one color instead of another. Part of human development, through the centuries, has been the way we respond physically to color." People, Storaro pointed out, reacted differently to bright colors than to dark colors; they were more active in light. People were sluggish if placed in rooms in which the walls were painted black, and they would be distracted or excitable in rooms painted red.

Las Vegas would be an interesting study, bathed almost entirely in artificial light, especially inside the casinos, where artificial light and color is employed to work on people's subconscious, to encourage them to stay in the casinos and gamble. In Las Vegas, casino windows are tinted to block out the sunlight, creating an illusion of time stopped. There is no day or night—only *now.*

"For characters in a story that takes place in Las Vegas," Storaro said, "I wanted to use the physiology of color to create an atmosphere. *One from the Heart* was about the feelings of people in such a place, where the environment works to ease restraint."

Coppola had a number of familiar faces, along with several newcomers, to play the major roles in his film. Frederic Forrest, currently free due to the shutdown of *Hammett,* and Teri Garr, who had worked for Coppola in *The Conversation,* were cast in the lead roles of Hank and Frannie, a couple on the verge of splitting up on the eve of the anniversary of their meeting. Raul Julia, who had recently completed his work on Zoetrope's *The Escape Artist,* and Nastassia Kinski, a relative newcomer who had won critical raves for her work in *Tess,* were assigned the parts of Ray and Leila, Frannie and Hank's partners during their brief flings away from each other. Lainie Kazan, one of Coppola's Hofstra classmates, and Harry Dean Stanton, who had made a very brief appearance in *Godfather II,* took the roles of Maggie and Moe, Frannie and Hank's closest friends. Allen Garfield (billed as Allen Gorwitz), the sleazy Bernie Moran in *The Conversation,* rounded out the cast of principal characters by portraying Ray's unnamed boss.

The cast and crew in place, Coppola threw a huge barbecue at his Napa Valley estate, inviting around 350 members of the cast, production team, and Zoetrope staff. Coppola's enthusiasm rubbed off on his guests, who talked optimistically about the upcoming shoot.

Coppola was thrilled. He seemed to be poised at the threshold of his dream of running his own studio, making the kind of film that he wanted to make, and leading a revolution in a new, electronic cinema.

"Something incredibly good," he told his family and friends, "is about to happen."

7.

WHEN *ONE FROM THE HEART* was released in 1982, critics almost unanimously agreed that the film was a technical wonder, full of the kind of romantic, whimsical beauty that Coppola had intended for his picture. However, these same critics, almost to the writer, also agreed that the film fell flat in its story, as if Coppola, while working his technological wizardry, could not be bothered with the heart and soul behind what he was filming. Or, as Andrew Sarris wrote in the *Village Voice:* "With all this technological huffing and puffing, Coppola has thrown out the baby and photographed the bath water."

Indeed, as a story, *One from the Heart* is a sweet confection, as familiar as cotton candy and, unfortunately, just about as filling and nutritious. At another time, coming from another director, it might have qualified as a charming, satisfying made-for-television movie, but, coming from Francis Ford Coppola, with his background of making large, operatic big-screen productions, the film is a disappointment, its characters and action far too commonplace to be coming from someone of Coppola's prodigious capabilities.

One from the Heart's protagonists, Hank and Frannie, are unmarried lovers who have fallen into a dull day-to-day routine. Hank is co-owner of a junkyard called Reality Wrecking, while Frannie works for a travel agency. Their relationship has grown so stale that a night out usually means a trip to a restaurant; lovemaking has become less frequent. The two fit together more out of the comfort of familiarity than from any spark of passion. Both have let themselves go—Hank complaining that Frannie doesn't shave her legs, she noticing that he's developing a spare tire around his waist—but neither says anything about it until they quarrel on the eve of their fifth anniversary together.

Their fight goes a long way toward defining the root of their differences. For an anniversary gift, Hank has invested the couple's savings in the deed to their home; Frannie, on the other hand, has purchased airline tickets for Bora Bora. When neither displays what the other feels is sufficient appreciation for the gifts, an argument breaks out, escalating quickly to the point where both hurl insults that they will later regret. The two reconcile briefly and make love, but they resume their fighting, which ends with Frannie leaving to spend the night with a coworker named Maggie. Hank, in turn, goes to confront his business partner, Moe, who, according to Frannie, kissed her during a New Year's Eve party. Hank and Moe go at it over the incident, but they come to terms and Hank stays overnight at Moe's.

The next day finds Frannie and Hank back at their respective jobs, the issues between them still unresolved. While working on a window display, Frannie meets a passerby named Ray, who chats with her and appears to be the kind of exciting man that Hank is not. Ray impresses Frannie by telling her that he has been to Bora Bora, and that he is a singer and pianist at a local club. The flirtation bothers Frannie, who still has feelings for Hank but who nevertheless agrees to meet Ray at the club where he works.

Meanwhile, Hank is sorting through his own feelings. After a heart-to-heart talk with Moe, during which he spoke of his dissatisfaction with the business, Hank goes on a lonely walk down the Strip, his glum spirits contrasted by crowds and endless neon. During this walk, Hank encounters a young high-wire acrobat named Leila who, for reasons Hank can't quite understand, seems attracted to him. The two flirt for a while, and Leila suggests that she and Hank get together later in the evening.

Hank and Frannie are reunited back at their house, where they both prepare for their individual rendezvous. Hank, who has had flings of his own in the past, is more surprised than angry to learn that Frannie intends to meet with Ray, but since he has plans of his own, he makes no effort to straighten out their differences or win Frannie back. Both are clearly intrigued and excited, after years in an exclusive relationship, to know that they are appealing to someone else.

At the club, Frannie learns that Ray is a waiter, not the performer he claimed to be. Rather than do his job, Ray sits at a table with Frannie, until his irate boss approaches the table and berates him in front of her. The two men argue vehemently and, in a fit of pique, Ray quits his job. He may not be employed, but at least he is now totally free to use Hank's ticket and accompany Frannie on a romantic vacation in Bora Bora. Ray and Frannie take a walk through the packed streets of Las Vegas, where they break out in a spontaneous dance in the midst of a mob of people, Frannie overwhelmed by the excitement of the moment. It's almost too good to be true.

Hank's evening with the exotic German acrobat has a similar dreamlike quality. He, too, has had the opportunity to see his new partner at work—performing in a giant champagne glass—but he is more interested in having a quiet interlude away from the glitter of Las Vegas. He drives Leila to the junkyard, where, he tells her, he likes to go when he's in the mood to be alone and think. At the junkyard, Leila performs her old circus high-wire act, which, she assures Hank, she has no intention of ever repeating.

The next morning, both Hank and Frannie awaken with feelings of guilt. For Hank, the regrets mean very little—Leila disappears quickly. Frannie, however, still intends on flying to Bora Bora with Ray, if for no other reason than to satisfy a dream that she probably will never realize with Hank. Her plans are interrupted when Hank, who has been searching frantically for her, breaks into the motel room and carries her off over his shoulder. During an ensuing conversation, Frannie reveals that she's leaving Hank and Las Vegas for good; her new lover, she claims, sings to her rather than shouting at her. For the moment, Hank can think of nothing to say or do to stop her.

Hank comes up with an idea at the last moment and races to the airport. Frannie and Ray are getting ready to board their plane. Desperate, Hanks sings "You Are My Sunshine" to Frannie, but it appears that his gesture has come too late: Frannie and Ray board the plane, and, totally defeated, Hank returns to his house, where he mopes around and, in despair, begins to burn some of Frannie's belongings. The story concludes with the vintage Hollywood ending, with a car pulling up outside the house and Frannie returning to Hank—the two not walking into the sunset, perhaps, but standing in a house that suddenly seems much brighter than it had just a few moments earlier.

8.

COPPOLA BELIEVED THAT his electronic cinema would save him a bundle of time, making it possible for him to shoot a modest production such as *One from the Heart* in a mere six to eight weeks. The key to the method was what he termed a *previsualization technique*, which basically involved combining modern technology with a radical restructuring of the preproduction and production steps of filmmaking, all in an effort to cut back drastically on repetition and time-consuming (and, therefore, costly) work in postproduction. Inspired by Coppola's nightmarish editing experiences on *The Conversation, Godfather II,* and *Apocalypse Now,* previsualization seemed like a well-conceived solution to myriad problems.

The first step of the process involved committing the screenplay to computer disk. Each scene was written as an individual paragraph, giving Coppola a better opportunity to rearrange, cut, or rewrite scenes than he had conceived when hammering out scripts on a typewriter or, worse yet, trying to firm up a story during the editing process. A conventional storyboard was then pieced together, complete with rough sketches of the movie's scenes. The storyboard was put on Betamax videotape, along with a sound track of the actors and actresses reading their lines, which added an entirely new dimension to the screenplay. Coppola now had an idea of which scenes worked and which ones did not, which ran too long, and which needed to be eliminated entirely. During rehearsals, Polaroid photographs were taken of the actors and actresses, replacing the original artist sketches on the storyboard.

For the next step in the process, Coppola took the cast to Las Vegas, where they spent two days videotaping the script in the film's real-life setting. Coppola now had an idea of how he wanted things to look on the Zoetrope soundstages. After returning from Las Vegas, Coppola videotaped his film one more time—in what he called "technical rehearsals"—on the Zoetrope soundstages. This run-through was of special interest to Dean Tavoularis, who could use the videotapes as guidelines for the completing of set construction.

In a sense, Coppola had made his movie four times before he had actually shot a single frame of film, and while this involved a lot of work in preproduction, he was in better shape than ever to know exactly where his story was going. This, he told reporters, would save him a lot of time, translating into substantial savings in virtually every aspect of filmmaking, including the amount of money he would be paying to lending institutions, which traditionally charged 20 percent interest.

There were, however, some costly hitches in the plan, most notably in the costs of the previsualization and in Coppola's decision to forgo location shooting in favor of the soundstage. For the most part, previsualization cost money that Coppola might not have normally written into a film's budget, and, as it turned out, what he was saving in postproduction, he was spending in preproduction—which still could have worked out had he actually saved the time he anticipated.

What really hurt was the money spent on set construction. Dean Tavoularis believed that "God [was] in the details," and the production designer went all out in building sets that took up all nine of Zoetrope's soundstages and included a scale model of the city of Las Vegas, a nightclub and casino, a department store, Hank and Frannie's house, a section of a jet airplane, a motel, and a junkyard—each constructed in the finest detail.

As impressive as all this was, it was beginning to add a lot of heft to Coppola's $15 million movie, hoisting the budget to $23.1 million, much to the growing concern of MGM, which had a considerable stake in the picture. In cutting his deal with MGM, Coppola had managed to purchase the *One from the Heart* property and keep complete artistic control over his film, as well as agree to a $3 million director's fee (the largest to date in the industry), in exchange for 20 percent of the film's adjusted gross receipts and the U.S. and Canadian distribution rights to the film. Zoetrope would be responsible for all production costs, though MGM guaranteed it would provide an unspecified amount of completion money. Armed with his MGM agreement, Coppola was able to secure a loan for production costs from Chase Manhattan Bank. The loan, however, was not enough to cover the film's escalating budget.

Once again, Coppola found the creative process being stifled by the realities of big business. He was approximately $8 million shy of what he needed to make *One from the Heart*, plus he still had to find a way to maintain his Zoetrope payroll. His *One from the Heart* problems were temporarily resolved when a group of German investors agreed to supply him with the needed funds. A subsequent sale of the television rights to *Apocalypse Now* provided an additional $2.5 million, which helped Coppola stay afloat a little longer.

Although Coppola had long ago achieved the reputation of working best when under extreme pressure, his tightrope act never ceased to amaze his friends, colleagues, and employees. Even as he struggled to meet his payroll, Coppola continued to conduct rehearsals for *One from the Heart*, oversee work on *The Escape Artist*, which was nearing completion, and wheel and deal on what he hoped might be future Zoetrope projects. One rumor had Coppola talking to Joseph Papp, director of the New York Shakespeare Festival, about the possibility of making a film out of Gilbert and Sullivan's operetta *The Pirates of Penzance*, or of Coppola's joining forces with Papp in the production of a Broadway play. There was also talk of Coppola's making a film adaptation of Gay Talese's *Thy Neighbor's Wife*, a best-selling novel about marital infidelity, but Coppola was finding it difficult to obtain the film rights from United Artists, which had optioned the property.

Coppola's position was growing desperate. After nearly a year in existence, Zoetrope had yet to place a single new film of its own in theaters, and without new product, it was nearly impossible to generate any substantial income, other than from money earned from occasional distribution deals or the sale of ancillary rights to earlier films. Zoetrope could not even pick up badly needed funds by renting its soundstages to other productions—not with the *One from the Heart* sets taking up all the space. As Coppola himself admitted, he was trading on his reputation and talent, which might have been enough to keep him going on a personal level, but it was far from what he required to stabilize a studio that by the end of 1980 seemed to be in danger of sinking unless Coppola could pull off a miracle.

9.

ONE OF COPPOLA'S PET PRESTIGE projects, the presentation of Abel Gance's *Napoleon*, reached fruition on January 23, 1981, when the epic film began a highly anticipated three-day run at New York's Radio City Music Hall, capping a long, colorful history for a classic film that had seemed on the verge of extinction for the longest time.

For serious film students, Gance and his 1927 epic represented not only a great bygone era but also a virtuoso creative mind that stretched or broke every rule and, in the process, set up signposts for the continuing development of filmmaking in the future. In *Napoleon*'s grand finale, Gance had presented a sensational triptych of on-screen images, accomplished by using three synchronized projectors—a process that, several decades later, would evolve into Cinerama. The French filmmaker also pioneered such techniques as superimposition, rapid intercutting for montage, and split-screen projection; he was believed to have been the first to use the camera dolly and the handheld camera.

In its original release print, *Napoleon* had run nearly three and a half hours—a whopping running time for a silent film—and was accompanied by a musical score written by Arthur Honegger. This version, however, was altered and edited over the years, including an hour-and-a-half version shown in the United States in the late 1920s, and an updated version, using a musical sound track and spoken narration, that was released in 1934. By the 1950s, the film had been cut and reassembled so many times that no one, other than Gance himself, could say for certain what had gone into the original. Entire reels of the film had been lost, dispersed, or put in storage.

Fortunately, a young British film buff named Kevin Brownlow purchased two reels of the film and, overwhelmed by what he saw, decided to try to piece together the entire original. He succeeded nearly two decades later, and on October 22, 1972, a sound version of the film was shown as part of the San Francisco Film Festival's Homage to Abel Gance. A few weeks later, the silent version was screened, accompanied by a fragment of its original score, at the Avenue Theater in San Francisco. Coppola and Tom Luddy, the director of the Pacific Film Archive at the University of California at Berkeley Art Museum (and, by 1980, the head of special projects at Zoetrope), were in attendance at the Avenue Theater screening.

Coppola and Luddy felt that the film was too good to wind up stashed in archives, available only to critics, film historians and students, or filmmakers. *Napoleon*, Coppola told Luddy, ought to be seen in its full splendor, accompanied by an orchestra—perhaps in a venue such as Radio City Music Hall. Around the time of his purchase of Hollywood General, Coppola put his plan into motion. He asked his father to compose a new score for the film, and looked into securing the distribution rights. The latter did not come cheaply: In exchange for the distribution rights, Coppola had to pay $400,000 and 50 percent of the film's gross.

Not everyone was happy with the arrangement. The British Film Institute, so helpful during Brownlow's restoration of the picture, took exception to Coppola's involvement in the project. The BFI, along with Thames Television, planned on screening the film, along with its own specially commissioned score, at the London Film Festival in November 1980, and the Coppola production, scheduled to be presented in New York only a couple of months later, threatened to rub some of the shine off the BFI event. In addition, Coppola's assigning the score to his own father smacked of the kind of nepotism that could possibly cheapen the overall production. Coppola was too busy with his own projects to be too concerned about such complaints. The London screening came and went, and in late January of 1981, it was Coppola's turn.

The Radio City Music Hall premiere proved, once again, that Coppola possessed as much savvy as anyone when it came to staging a movie as an event. Every seat for each of the eight performances—the top ticket price going at twenty-five dollars—was sold, and though such expenses as renting the six-thousand-seat theater, advertising the event, and paying the orchestra and theater employees took a huge bite out of the gate receipts, the presentation was an unqualified success, furthering Coppola's reputation as a patron of the arts. Gene Kelly acted as the emcee at the premiere, Carmine Coppola conducted the sixty-piece American Symphony Orchestra, and Francis hosted a post-premiere party at Sardi's. Immediately following the first screening, a Zoetrope employee called Abel Gance in Paris so the ninety-one-year-old director could listen to the sound of the enormous ovation that his film was receiving.

For Coppola, the triumph was a badly needed reprieve from the ever-tightening grip of money problems. He could not say with any certainty where his studio would be in a year or two—or even in a month or two—but for a few memorable moments, he and Zoetrope could take a bow for their role in presenting a gem from the past.

Chapter Eleven

Fatal Gamble

"It's like I'm at a poker table with five guys. And they're all betting two or three thousand dollars a hand, and I've got about eighty-seven cents in front of me. So I'm always having to take off my shirt and bet my pants. Because I want to be in the game. I want to play."

—Francis Ford Coppola

"Francis calls me the seventy-year-old kid, which means that I play it very, very safe. I'm very much a build-a-concrete-foundation-and-build-a-house-of-bricks-and-don't-go-higher-than-you-know-can-support person, and Francis is the opposite. Francis is build-this-sandcastle-up-here-and-tell-everybody-what-it-is-and-somehow-or-other-through-the-whole-concept-of-creating-dreams-they'll-come-true."

—George Lucas

1.

It was probably inevitable that Coppola would be forced to place his own property on the line to save *One from the Heart* and his studio, which is precisely what he did in February 1981, when it became evident that he would have to resort to this measure if he ever intended to make his movie.

The previous couple of months had been brutal. The German investors, originally poised to sink $8 million into the production, had backed out at the last minute, leaving Coppola at square one, with no prospective investors on the horizon. MGM balked at lending Coppola more money, as did Chase Manhattan, which was already heavily into the production. With *One from the Heart*'s February 2 starting date on the horizon, Coppola had to find a way to keep things rolling, even if on a week-to-week basis.

Although his studio was in dire straits, Coppola himself was anything but poor. Over the years, he had sunk huge portions of his earnings into real estate, which boosted his personal worth to an estimated $55 million and made him one of the wealthiest men in the movie business. Nevertheless, Coppola's decision to invest his money in this manner left him with crippling cash-flow problems. He'd put his property in hock for *Apocalypse Now*, and now he would have to do it again—only this time, he was going to do it piecemeal, with the hope that somehow, at some point in the very near future, someone would provide him with the backing he needed. Using his real estate as collateral, Coppola took out a million-dollar personal loan from Security Pacific Bank, a process he would repeat each week until he had accumulated the $8 million needed to make the movie.

Still, this influx of money did not address the issue of meeting the Zoetrope payroll, and at the beginning of February, Coppola began a painful series of staff layoffs, beginning with the company's story department and followed soon by the entire San Francisco staff. Other staffers agreed to take 50 percent pay cuts and, in perhaps the most surprising development yet—and one that moved Coppola to tears—union workers employed for *One from the Heart* volunteered to work for two weeks on a deferred-payment basis.

Coppola's plight attracted plenty of press attention, which, under different circumstances, might have angered or embarrassed the embattled filmmaker. In this case, however, the reports served to magnify Coppola's image as a heroic artist willing to gamble everything for his work. Before long, the Zoetrope offices were opening envelopes stuffed with checks from well-wishing private donors—offerings that, a Zoetrope spokesperson made clear to the press, were to be returned. Money arrived from other, higher-placed sources, as well. Paramount Pictures purchased the rights to *Interface*, a Zoetrope property with no immediate future, for $500,000, and Barry Diller, chairman of Paramount, and Michael Eisner, the company's president, offered Coppola an additional half-million-dollar interest-free loan. Television mogul Norman Lear extended another half a million in an unsecured loan.

The reason for such generosity and goodwill was not difficult to pinpoint: Whatever his flaws as a person or businessman, Coppola was a genuinely decent, generous man who, over his up-and-down career, had given more than he had received—through his enduring films, his patronage of others' projects, his restoration and distribution of films that other studios wouldn't touch, and his vigilant research into methods and technologies that benefited the overall motion picture industry. There was that faction in Hollywood that would have been delighted to see Coppola fall on his face, yet he also had a strong base of support, from some of the most influential names in the business to Zoetrope executives (who had secretly taken 15 percent pay cuts in December) and staffers (who donned I BELIEVE IN FRANCIS C. buttons), all rooting for Coppola to overcome the odds.

Calling his loan to Coppola "a supportive act," Barry Diller summed up the feelings of many Coppola backers. "Francis is, by any definition, the best in the business," said Diller. "His monumental risk-taking, his pushing everything to the wall, is the essence of what any creative enterprise is about. When you go to Zoetrope, you can feel the passion there about making movies."

"The mood here is one of hope," reflected a Zoetrope staffer. "We're all behind him. We all support him. People with all their hearts want it to go."

"A practical man would have said, 'Let's get out of this thing,' but Francis was determined to see it through," observed Alex Tavoularis, who was working on the film's sets and witnessed the daily turmoil caused by money problems. "Francis is like many great men, who were always teetering on the threshold between the rational world and madness. That's how great artists achieve."

Throughout the ordeal, Coppola stayed true to character, alternately playing the role of martyr for his art and issuing bombastic statements that must have caused some observers to wonder if he had taken leave of his senses. He remained adamant about maintaining control over his studio, even when associates advised him to declare bankruptcy to protect his personal interests. On at least two occasions, he turned down people who wanted to buy his studio. In the face of tremendous financial loss, he defiantly maintained that he intended to take his film and studio to the limit. "I'm trying to hold something together," he told reporters, conceding that unless things changed dramatically, "the studio could be dismantled piece by piece."

Unwavering in his faith in electronic cinema, Coppola chided the nonbelievers in the industry for failing to share his vision, accusing them of being "so worried about advertising and directors [that] they don't care that much about theoretical things."

While discussing the bigger studios, Coppola could not help but let some of his bitterness show. There were a number of studios, he said, that resented the fact that he and Zoetrope were trying something new—especially his insistence on owning his movies.

"The majors don't like the fact that we make movies and keep the negatives," he said. "If you own a grocery store, why would you want another grocery store to compete with you? Especially since the motion picture industry, as it exists now, is the new Detroit, a group of lackluster companies. How many times do I have to be laughed at? They laughed at me for *Apocalypse.* They laughed at me when I decided to present Abel Gance's *Napoleon* at the Radio City Music Hall. They're laughing because, for *One from the Heart,* I'm building Las Vegas at Zoetrope instead of going to Las Vegas. . . . By now people should realize that what I do is different."

2.

IN THE MIDST OF GREAT UNCERTAINTY, *One from the Heart* went before cameras on February 2, as scheduled. No one, from Coppola on down, could predict if the film would be finished, or even if the company would be working the following week. "It's very hard to work," Coppola noted, understating his case, "when every day there is a crisis."

It was also very challenging to work under Coppola's new method of filmmaking.

To implement his electronic cinema, Coppola established a nerve center inside a customized silver Airstream trailer—officially dubbed "Image Control" but nicknamed "Silverfish"—in which he had installed a bank of Betamax recorders and monitors, a complex communications system, editing equipment, and such creature comforts as a bed, kitchenette, espresso machine, and Jacuzzi. The mobile headquarters, designed to permit Coppola to use his electronic cinema on both Zoetrope soundstages and location shoots, allowed him, through a series of video cameras directly connected to Vittorio Storaro's cameras, to direct and immediately play back scenes on his video monitors, eliminating the customary wait for the rushes of the day's work. Theoretically, Coppola could shoot, edit, revise, and fine-tune a movie during the production stage.

There was a downside to all this, most notably in the communications between the director and his actors. While stationed in Silverfish, Coppola issued his communications to the set via loudspeaker, leading a visiting reporter from *Life* magazine to remark that Coppola had a heard-but-not-seen, Wizard-of-Oz quality to him, and that "the amplified power of his voice made him seem omnipotent but not necessarily infallible"—an ironic comment, given Coppola's well-deserved reputation as an actor's director.

Coppola later admitted that this technique was less than perfect—especially during the making of *One from the Heart*—but he defended his decision to test his electronic-cinema method of filmmaking on the picture.

"The idea of my working in there was greatly exaggerated," he contended. "Certainly I experimented with it a little on *One from the Heart,* because the whole concept was to make it a live-TV-style production, and that's how it's done, with the director editing or switching from the control booth. I also knew that music was done this way—with the producer in a booth, where he could really hear what was being done. I always liked to experiment, and I experimented with this. The truth is, I would only go into the 'Fish' to see certain shots that were involved in elaborate moves, or when it was otherwise the best place to see what was going on. I never directed a whole film from it. It was new on *One from the Heart,* and I wanted to learn."

The movie's cast and crew found that dealing with Coppola's disembodied voice required a considerable adjustment to their usual way of working with a director; Big Brother, it seemed, was watching their every move and controlling them by remote control. While Nastassia Kinski tactfully stated that Coppola's method took "some getting used to," Teri Garr struck closer to the heart of the matter in her assessment. "It's okay," she said, "but we can't talk. Just listen and be seen and take direction. We're little puppets." Frederic Forrest, a staunch Coppola ally, admitted that he felt that there were times when electronic cinema seemed too impersonal and tied into style over substance. "The way it was shot," he observed, "meant that sometimes you were more accommodating the character than living the character. You had to stand in a certain way because of the lighting. When you're doing it, as an actor, you're thinking in conventional terms, and for a while you think Francis is more interested in the scenery. But in the end you see what he's doing."

The problem with Coppola's electronic cinema, offered Forrest, was that actors could be made to feel as if they were working "in the lab"; *One from the Heart*'s story, he said, was so thin that, in an effort to dress it up and make it visually pleasing, Coppola and his crew risked making the movie look as if it was about "technique—what they could do, how they could show the pictures."

"I think what happens now," he speculated in a 1999 interview, "is people have sometimes emulated Francis so much that they miss the point: A movie has to have a *soul.* Francis always has a soul involved in his story, but a lot of people just let their knowledge of technical stuff take over. The films have no basis or substance. They're about filmmaking."

Forrest's observations largely reflected the criticism that Coppola would receive for his movie. "In interviews," wrote *New Yorker* critic Pauline Kael,

"Coppola has talked about directing from inside a trailer while watching the set on video equipment. This movie feels like something directed from a trailer. It's cold and mechanical; it's at a remove from its own action." "This one," offered Judith Crist in the *Saturday Review*, "is from the video control board. The heart is missing."

Just how Coppola—who knew nothing if not how to place believable characters in a compelling story—missed this is anyone's guess. Perhaps, as a number of reviewers suggested, he was too absorbed in his movie's style and in his technological toys to recognize the shortcomings in his characters. Or it could be that his financial woes and the need to place a movie in theaters clouded his judgment. Or maybe it was clouded from the onset, inasmuch as the story itself offered too little, in terms of characters and dramatic event, to carry a feature-length motion picture. Or perhaps there was a grain of truth to Coppola's assertion that a number of influential forces, most notably the media, were actually hoping he would fail, if for no other reason than to justify their own pessimistic predictions, and thus neglected to notice or mention that there were charming elements to his characters and story.

Most likely it was a combination of all of the above, although, in the end, it mattered very little. *One from the Heart* was destined to be a beautiful, yet stillborn, baby.

Coppola himself could only wonder what had gone wrong.

"My idea for *One from the Heart*," he said, "was to make it essential as 'live cinema' in much the way that John Frankenheimer had made his fantastical live TV dramas. The idea was to build the sets in a continuous manner, so the actors could perform the entire story walking directly from one set to the other, with a number of film cameras (that had video viewfinders attached) following. Special little elevators would have been provided so as the actors, for example, went up the stairs, the camera would be able to rise and get that. The idea would be to film the movie in ten-minute blocks, already edited and monitored by the director in a control station—Silverfish—much the way recordings or TV is done. It was to have the beauty and magic of cinema, but the life of theater.

"Of course, typically, it backfired. After going to all the trouble of designing the entire film beforehand—much as it is done today in animated films—and of introducing such things as 'video assist' and 'previsualization'—now known as Animatics, several things got out of control while I kept trying to evolve the script and songs. Vittorio, late in the game, decided that we could shoot with one camera as efficiently as doing it in ten-minute blocks with multiple cameras. Obviously, photographers prefer the control of light that this gives. Dean decided that he needed to use all nine stages—and he wanted to take more at the nearby Goldwyn lot—so true connectivity became impossible. I ended up spending a fortune to prepare for a 'live cinema' production that could be shot in two weeks and ended up shooting it conventionally, which took a normal schedule. It was the worst of both worlds, and it broke me."

3.

NOW THAT HIS PICTURE WAS finally in production, Coppola had to deal with additional headaches, including the realization that after only a few weeks of shooting, the film was already behind schedule. Coppola wanted to make a picture with fewer cuts and seams than normally exist in a movie or television program, and to accomplish this, he wrote lengthy scenes, some extending as long as ten minutes each. Under the usual circumstances, fewer scenes would have translated into less overall set-up time, but Coppola, ever the perfectionist, negated this advantage by shooting multiple takes of each scene and by taking the time to edit and assemble his film as he went along. In no time, what was designed to be a quick shoot was starting to look like an average shoot—which was not encouraging news for a nearly bankrupt studio looking for ways to trim expenses.

By the end of its first month before the camera, *One from the Heart* was in such danger of its production being suspended that Coppola was holding weekly wrap parties for the cast and crew. The personal loans had gone only so far, and on any given Friday, Coppola could not assure his company that they would be working together by the end of the following week. MGM, citing large budget overruns, backed out of the picture, claiming that Coppola had broken his contract. Creditors were hanging around to such an extent that, according to one Zoetrope department head, Coppola was using Silverfish as a refuge as well as a workstation. Something had to give—and soon.

At this point, Coppola might have been wise to surrender. He did not have the money to complete his picture or pay his studio employees; millions of dollars of his own property had either been sold or mortgaged, and he had no one to distribute his film if he managed to find a way to finish it. Nevertheless, Coppola plowed ahead. When he first started shooting, he had reasoned that after a couple of weeks, he would have enough of the movie in the can to attract more money. As for MGM, he would just have to find another distributor.

Temporary salvation arrived in the form of two new deals, arranged several weeks apart: the first from Jack Singer, a wealthy Canadian investor eager to enter the film business; the second from Paramount Pictures, which agreed to distribute the picture.

According to reports published at the time, the sixty-two-year-old Singer was worth around half a billion dollars, his fortune stemming from real estate, oil, and building developments. He had met Coppola earlier in the year, when he had approached him for an autograph, and after reading about the director's financial problems, he decided to become involved with the picture. "I think that people like this should have a chance to go on," Singer said of Coppola, noting that he had "a gut feeling" about the filmmaker.

In his interviews with the press, Singer insisted that his association with Coppola was purely business, and not as a hobbyist wanting to dabble in the movies. "My interest," he stated, "is to enable him to finish the picture, and hopefully we will continue our association. I'm really interested in becoming involved in the motion picture industry. I'm interested in doing it and doing it properly." His involvement in *One from the Heart* offered him a good entrée into the business. "At least with Francis Coppola," he said, "we're starting at the top."

There was no question that, as a businessman, Singer knew how to cut a deal. When he initially approached Coppola, Singer was willing and ready to purchase 50 percent of Zoetrope and back Coppola. When Coppola nixed selling even a portion of his studio, Singer offered to lend Coppola $1 million—desperately needed to meet payroll—and an additional $7 million up the road. In return, Coppola promised an unspecified percentage of *One from the Heart*'s grosses until the loan, plus interest, was paid, as well as one-third of the film's net profits thereafter. In addition, Singer, who quickly established Jack Singer Productions on the Zoetrope lot, would have the right to look at and invest in future Zoetrope projects. It was a hard—and risky—bargain, underscored by the fact that Coppola cemented the deal by putting his studio up for collateral. If *One from the Heart* failed, Jack Singer would have his own studio at a bargain-basement price.

On paper, the new deal that Coppola consummated with Paramount was better than his previous arrangement with MGM. Coppola was still responsible for financing *One from the Heart,* but Paramount would guarantee to release six hundred prints of the movie and sink $4 million into the film's advertising, as well as help Coppola, if necessary, with completion funds, in exchange for a distribution fee. A new release date was set for February 10, 1982, giving Coppola additional time to finish his film.

"What Paramount has done," announced Zoetrope president Robert Spiotta, "is take over the completion obligation of MGM and the distribution obligation of United Artists. MGM still shares in a percentage of the gross revenues, but we own the property now. We bought it from MGM."

The jubilation over both deals would sour in months to come, but for the moment, Coppola had again dodged another bullet.

4.

DESPITE ALL OF COPPOLA'S statements to the contrary, electronic cinema was not turning out to be any kind of big money saver. *One from the Heart* was no *Apocalypse Now*, to be sure, but it was no bargain either, especially for the kind of love story that might have been shot by another director, with less ambitious intentions, for about half of what Coppola was spending. With *One from the Heart*, Coppola was not up to his neck in mud; he was up to his eyeballs in the costly video equipment, technicians, and sets needed to pull off his film's Disneyesque look. If his method seemed frayed around the edges while he clumsily attempted to direct a film and piece it together within the confines of Silverfish, his electronic cinema seriously began to unravel after the completion of principal photography, when Coppola shot the movie's title sequence, an utterly brilliant bit of filmmaking, which, while being perhaps the most captivating opening sequence in recent history, wound up costing Coppola in more ways than one.

Shortly after he had finished shooting *One from the Heart*, Coppola decided, against the advice of Rudi Fehr, one of the film's editors, to hold an advance screening of the rough cut in Seattle. The response to such a preview, Coppola figured, would give him an indication of what an audience wanted. He could then use the responses to help determine how the film could be edited, how much (if any) additional shooting would be required, and where the story was weak and needed shoring. However, to his great dismay, the preview was attended by critics, who took one look at the unfinished film and declared it to be a holy disaster.

"Disheartened" by the reviews, Coppola lashed out at his critics, much the way he had, several years earlier, when reviews of the unfinished *Apocalypse Now* had appeared in print. "It really has got me depressed," he admitted. "I mean, to think I can't even finish my picture without it getting reviewed already! The point is, isn't there some kind of understanding that you review pictures when they come out, when they're finished?"

With journalist Gay Talese he was even more blunt, assailing the press as being dishonest and unethical—"a bullshit racket," as he put it. "Let me say just one thing," he fumed. "I have never read anything about myself that has been totally accurate. Now if *that's* the case, what about all the other stuff I'm reading? The press is going to get its ass kicked. The press is out of control. The press is a millstone around this country's neck. It does not tell the truth. It does not push for change."

The Seattle preview turned out to be only minor turbulence compared to an exhibitors' screening held in San Francisco a few months later, on August 16. The Seattle showing had convinced Coppola that more shooting was necessary, and for the next month and a half, he labored to get the kind of material needed to make the movie run more smoothly. This, along with the shooting of extra special effects and the film's title sequence, expanded the costs of the film to over $25 million, but rather than approach Paramount for the completion money he felt the studio was going to provide, Coppola took out another loan and sold off more property, including his San Francisco mansion. Paramount, Coppola reasoned, would reimburse him his completion costs when the film was finished.

He could not have been more mistaken. Instead, without consulting Coppola, Paramount held a blind-bidding screening of the rough cut for Bay Area exhibitors, with the worst possible results. The exhibitors hated the film and, to make matters worse, a few talked about it for the record with Judy Stone, film critic for the *San Francisco Chronicle*. Stone's article, "Coppola Has 'Heart' Trouble," appearing in the August 21 edition of the paper, profiled a film in serious trouble, and included some of the most damning of the exhibitors' remarks. "It's like the emperor's new clothes all over again," said a disgruntled viewer. "People were twitching—they were so uncomfortable." Another grumbled, "It was one of the worst movies I've ever seen." And someone else commented, "I almost think the film is unreleasable. How can these talented Big People be so wrong?"

Coppola, in New York at the time of the screening, seethed when he saw the article, which was subsequently quoted at length in *Variety*. Paramount, he said, had betrayed him by showing the print to exhibitors not covered by blind-bidding laws, and the media, as always, had cut his legs out from beneath him by writing negative articles about an unfinished film. The whole affair, he raged, was similar to a novelist discovering that his work in progress had been shown to the manager of a chain bookstore, only to have the manager call a book critic with negative remarks, which were then printed in a newspaper.

Labeling his battles with such reviews a "no-win war," Coppola complained bitterly, as he had after the Seattle screening, of the effects the San Francisco showing might have on his film. "They showed a duped color print of *One From the Heart* in a tiny room to twenty exhibitors and out came a great big feature story in the San Francisco paper, which was basically a review of the picture," he said. "So, you know, now . . . for the next three months, I'm going to be working on a picture that's already been judged."

Coppola's worries, however, extended beyond how the public might perceive his picture. Paramount executives, discouraged by the exhibitors' reactions, were looking for ways to dump the film, and when Coppola approached them for his completion money, he was rejected outright. Paramount argued that he had violated his contract by extending the film's shooting schedule, and that he should have consulted with them about the added expenses before he went ahead with the additional shooting. Faced with the now-familiar do-or-die proposition of coming up with his own financing, Coppola approached Chase Manhattan Bank for one final loan, placing the rest of everything he owned, including his Napa Valley estate, on the line as collateral.

5·

WHILE *ONE FROM THE HEART* simmered in a gumbo of mounting debt, Zoetrope resurrected *Hammett* and placed it back into production with a whole new script and several new cast members. Ronee Blakley, recently divorced from director Wim Wenders, had been written out of the updated script, as had been Sylvia Miles; Peter Boyle replaced Brian Keith as Hammett's friend from his Pinkerton days. Wenders, rumored to have been fired at the time of the shelving of *Hammett,* was back at the helm, fresh from the critical success of his most recent film, *The State of Things,* the story of a European director making a movie for a quirky, financially strapped American mogul not unlike Coppola himself. In announcing the new shooting schedule for *Hammett,* Coppola expressed the same kind of confidence he had exuded before the filming of *One from the Heart:* "It will only take about a month to do the additional filming, and it'll take another five months to get the film ready for final release."

This time around, his predictions proved accurate. Working on "a nonexistent budget," Wenders ripped through the production, shooting ninety pages of script in just twenty-three days. The new Ross Thomas screenplay stressed the pace of Hammett's writing over the slow, more esoteric aspects of his life.

"Orion had been pressuring me to put on another director and return to the original script," Coppola remembered. "We had only a small percentage of the money left—about a million and a half. I contacted Wim and said I wouldn't replace him, and asked him if he could go back to more of the original script, now that he'd broken up with Ronee. We then started up a second time, with a new set that had pieces of all the necessary scenes that we needed. Wim shot very efficiently, and we shot what is effectively 80 percent of the film during this time, using the exteriors and a few scenes from the other shoot."

Coppola, who had earlier claimed that the biggest problem with *Hammett* was Wenders's wandering away from the script, made certain that things stayed on track, supervising the shooting from Silverfish and offering advice whenever he felt it appropriate. Within a month, an entirely new film had been completed.

Coppola had other projects on his mind, including Zoetrope's first fling into television—producing an NBC movie called *Sweat Shop*, a fictional account of the abuse of Mexican aliens, based on a sixteen-part undercover story written by Merle Linda Walin for the *Los Angeles Herald-Examiner*. Coppola still toyed with the idea of making *Elective Affinities*, but with the financial turmoil connected to Zoetrope and *One from the Heart*, it was improbable that he would find financing for such an ambitious project—unless, of course, *One from the Heart* turned out to be the blockbuster he hoped it would be. Instead, Coppola focused on a smaller, more commercial endeavor—a movie adaptation of S. E. Hinton's best-selling young adult novel, *The Outsiders*, a story about a teenage gang war. This, he decided, would be his next picture.

But first he had to find a way to launch *One from the Heart*, which was still suspended between completion and release and had become the subject of increasing ill will between Coppola and Paramount. Coppola, still angry about Paramount's exhibitors' screening and its refusal to provide completion money, was considering the possibility of finding another company to distribute his film—a scenario that would have pleased Paramount immensely, since it had lost faith in the movie and would have been delighted to cut it loose. Unfortunately, Coppola had been absolutely on the mark in his statements about the damage the negative publicity had done to his film. A year or two earlier, any company in the business would have been pleased to distribute a new film by the director of the *Godfather* pictures and *Apocalypse Now;* the reports about *One from the Heart* had given potential distributors second thoughts.

In his boldest move since his screening of *Apocalypse Now* at Cannes, Coppola decided to take his new film directly to the public, without sponsorship or approval from Paramount. He had successfully placed *Our Hitler* and *Napoleon* in front of audiences as film events, and if he could do the same for his own movie, and receive favorable response from critics and the public, he might be able to salt away a distribution deal outside of Paramount. The action, Coppola knew, would be certain to infuriate Paramount, but he was feeling no sense of allegiance to the company.

"As soon as things started going bad with Parmount," he told *Time* magazine's Richard Corliss, "I decided to open the film. It's like being rejected by your lover: it gives you an excuse to call someone else. Every day I heard that somebody else didn't like it. So I thought, let's have a perfect screening—a big screen, good projection. . . . Let six thousand people see it, not six exhibitors."

To some, Coppola's decision might have seemed desperate or serendipitous, but Coppola insisted that he had been wanting to present such a preview for months but had only recently set the plan in motion—a decision surprising even his own studio executives. "I knew that if I were going to pull this off, I'd have to do it fast," he said. "If I'd delayed a week, someone would have talked me out of it."

The arrangements were indeed very sudden. Zoetrope contacted Radio City Music Hall and set up arrangements for two January 15 screenings—at 7:30 and 10:00 P.M.—with tickets set at ten dollars for reserved mezzanine seats and five dollars for general admission. Paramount knew nothing of Coppola's plans until alerted by a full-page advertisement for the event running in the January 10 issue of the *New York Times.*

Paramount, still planning to release the film (albeit reluctantly) on February 10, reacted predictably to Coppola's showmanship, issuing stiff-lipped "No comment" replies to inquiries about the preview while weighing its options. Coppola's move set an industry precedent—no one had ever done an end run around distribution and privately staged a premiere—and Paramount was none too pleased about being shown up by a man it had bailed out less than a year earlier. From a business perspective, the screening presented a problem, since Paramount had yet to receive final bids from a number of potential exhibitors.

Coppola openly acknowledged that he was taking a potentially fatal risk in showing the picture in this manner, and he was as dramatic as always when addressing his gamble with the press.

"If the picture isn't strong," he stated, eight days prior to the screening, "this will totally annihilate it."

6.

THE TWO SCREENINGS, AIDED by a blitz of media coverage and the movie's already colorful history, sold out quickly. On the morning of the shows, people hoping to secure general admission seats lined up at ticket windows in the cold twenty-degree air; moved by the spectacle, Coppola ordered split pea and sausage soup to be delivered, free of charge, to those waiting in line.

Last-minute preparations were hectic. The master print, complete with final changes, had arrived from Rome the day before the screenings, and Coppola had worked around the clock on the sound mix, completing the task at six o'clock the morning of the preview. That afternoon, Coppola bustled around the hall, checking lights and going over every tiny detail for the evening's festivities. The event, he said, reminded him of his days of directing plays at Hofstra, when the anticipation before the opening curtain was almost electric. Just before the lights dimmed in Radio City Music Hall for the first screening, Coppola gathered family and well-wishers in a circle around him, and the group, clasping hands, chanted "Pa-wa-ba!" three times.

"It dates from my days at Hofstra," Coppola told a visiting reporter, "when we put on plays. It exorcises evil spirits and invokes the good spirits. I still do the 'pa-wa-ba' before we do the first shot of all my movies."

But, as Coppola learned, nothing was going to drive the demons away on that night—not the chants, not his constant pacing at the back of the hall throughout the screening, not the lingering hopes of taking on and defeating the system. When the movie ended, Coppola retreated to a backstage rehearsal studio for a press conference. The first question set the tone for the rest of the session: "How do you feel, now that everyone dislikes the picture?"

Coppola tried to hold his patience. Most people, he answered, appeared to have enjoyed the picture. Most people responded to the film, very few had walked out, and when the movie ended, people applauded throughout the titles. "That's what I saw," he said. "If someone saw it a different way, maybe that's so."*

The questions came at him in a wave, addressing every angle of the film's storied past and Coppola's uncertain future. Coppola might have manipulated the media in the past, but on this occasion, he was clearly a target, if not of a totally hostile press, then at least of a skeptical one. Coppola defended

---

*Coppola never retreated from his stance that his movie had been a hit with the Radio City audiences. "The film played really well," he told the author in 1999. "The audience was responsive and seemed totally charmed—more than I had hoped for. When it was over, there was a very enthusiastic hand, and I felt in my heart that I had made it. As I walked through the applauding crowd, Norman Mailer ran up to me and said something like, 'Wonderful, I so enjoyed it. Brilliant!' The applause kept going and I called out to the crowd, saying something banal like 'There's no business like show business.' Then Joseph Papp rushed up to me and said, 'Brilliant. I loved it. Totally original. Congratulations.' My heart was beating and I felt totally redeemed. Then I went to where the press was waiting, and the first question was 'How do you feel, now that you know that no one likes your picture?'—which took me by surprise. I realized later that the press had already formulated its opinion, even before we had the preview."

his film, but at times he sounded weary, as if the long haul of making the picture and battling for money had taken away some of his snarl and bravado.

He did use the occasion, however, to announce publicly that he had terminated his distribution arrangement with Paramount, though he also stated that he had not yet ruled out the possibility of working something out. "Whether that happens or not," he said, "depends on the reaction of people to the film, so I don't really know what's going to happen."

After the second showing, Coppola went to the Tower Suite of the Time-Life Building, where he and 647 guests dined on shellfish, pasta, cabbage soup, cold cuts, and desserts, and people toasted the movie while an orchestra provided the entertainment. Norman Mailer, Andy Warhol, Liza Minnelli, Robert De Niro, Martin Scorsese, Robert Duvall, and Joseph Papp were among those congratulating Coppola on his film, and he held out hope that the reviews would favor his picture.

Coppola had taken some beatings from the critics in the past, but nothing could have prepared him for the salvos fired on *One from the Heart* in reviews that were smug, sarcastic, mean-spirited, and downright sadistic, as if critics were using the occasion to puncture the bombast and arrogance of Coppola's past by hurling darts at his precarious future. Rex Reed, who never saw a movie that he couldn't suffocate with his exaggerated self-importance, dismissed *One from the Heart* as "hogwash" in the *New York Daily News,* while across town, in the *Village Voice,* Andrew Sarris, a sharp critic of Coppola's previous films, berated the film for paying more attention to style than to substance. "Whatever made Coppola think," wrote Sarris, "that contemporary audiences were nostalgic more for the sets in the background of the old movies than for the sweet sentiments in the foreground?" Comparing *One from the Heart* to "one of those brand-new, ultra-modern, multimillion-dollar arts centers with nothing going on inside," the *New York Times*'s Vincent Canby took Coppola to task on his methods of making the film: "The one thing Electronic Cinema doesn't yet do, obviously, is write a screenplay that can be directed, acted and edited into a coherent piece of popular entertainment." David Denby of *New York* magazine, although not nearly as nasty as some of the other Gotham writers ("I certainly didn't hate *One From the Heart,* but I was disappointed"), ultimately panned the movie as "more bizarre and pointless than anything else," saying it was "all visual candy—tricks, transformations, partings, interweavings." *New Yorker* critic Pauline Kael, who had championed Coppola's *Godfather* movies as modern classics, trounced *One from the Heart* in a pitiless review. "Eventually," she wrote, "the audience realizes that there is nothing—literally nothing—happening except pretty images gliding into each other, and you can hear people saying to each other, 'It's a pastry chef's movie' and 'I didn't know Coppola had become such a ding-a-ling.'"

The reviews outside of New York were generally less caustic, but negative nonetheless. Both *Time* and *Newsweek* singled out Dean Tavoularis and Vittorio Storaro for their respective work in production design and cinematography, but both concluded that there was not enough story in *One from the Heart* to carry the dazzling effects. *Variety,* while conceding that "the film does have a shot at audience embrace," described the picture as "a curiously surface affair that, for all its glitter, tends to evaporate almost as quickly as it unfolds."

In the midst of all the negative notices, Coppola could find solace in two unqualified raves—one from Sheila Benson of the *Los Angeles Times,* and the other from James M. Wall of *The Christian Century*—both finding the story charming, the movie visually exciting, and Coppola successful in his innovative filmmaking. "It's so easy to love *One From the Heart,*" wrote Benson. "You just let yourself relax and float away with it. A work of constant astonishment, Francis Coppola's new film is so daring it takes your breath while staggering you visually." Wells, too, praised *One from the Heart* for its daring, calling it "innovative and imaginative—a breakthrough in film style."

Of all the critics, Richard Corliss might have come closest to the white-hot center of the problems facing anyone attempting to review the movie.

"The hope and the hype surrounding Francis Coppola's latest exercise in free-fall parachuting should not obscure one fact: *One From the Heart* is also a movie," wrote Corliss. "But with the fate of Zoetrope Studios riding on this crapshoot, it may be difficult for audiences and critics to pay attention to what is on the screen."

7·

DESPITE THE GLUT OF BAD REVIEWS, Coppola steadfastly maintained that if audiences were given the chance, they would fall in love with his new film. In counterpunching with his critics, Coppola allowed that people, by nature, are attracted to the spectacle of someone taking great risk, much the way they are attracted to a street fight, but he confessed that he was hurt by the fact that he wasn't taken seriously as a professional.

"They call me reckless, on a business level," he said, "but I've had Zoetrope for twelve years. We've never made a flop. We've never lost large amounts of money. Exhibitors and theater owners have made money on pictures I either directed or produced, or on talent that I discovered or gave their first start to, and yet they resent even putting me in a position where I don't have to go to one of them with my hat in my hand and have them tell me what movies I can or cannot make."

Why Coppola risked so much on what should have been a modest bit of entertainment would baffle critics and movie buffs for years to come, but August Coppola, who knew his brother as well as anyone (except, perhaps, Eleanor Coppola), and who knew his brother's films well enough to lecture about them in the United States and abroad, had a compelling theory for why Francis pursued *One from the Heart* the way he did.

"There are Francis Ford Coppola films, and there are Francis Coppola films," August observed, "but there's only one *Francie* film, and that's *One from the Heart*. Francie is the name that we used when he was young. When he had done everything that he wanted to do, he made a Francie movie. He wanted to do the things that delighted him as a child. As a child, he was delighted by a musical, and in *One from the Heart*, you can see every element of all the films that we had seen as children."

In August Coppola's opinion, *One from the Heart* represented a progression from his brother's earlier films, both in terms of art and technology.

"The last great location film was *Apocalypse Now*," August proposed, "so after you've shot that, where do you go? He thought of going back to the studio, with the sense that he could electronically extend the frontiers of reality. Just as *The Thief of Bagdad* was a fantasy, so he wanted to make a fantasy out of the visual imagery itself, using electronic means. He hoped to push the frontier of what was ultimately the end of location shooting in *Apocalypse Now*. If you go from the flare scene in *Apocalypse Now* to the electronic scenes in *One from the Heart*, you have a direct correlation with his figuring he was going to go back to the studio, into a new, more exact reality. Unfortunately, at that time, society had become less and less fantastic."

In the weeks following the disastrous reviews, Coppola attempted to find a distributor willing to take on his movie—on his terms. Three days after the Radio City screenings, Paramount publicly announced that it would not be distributing the film, saying that it had reached the decision the day before the previews—and, therefore, a day before Coppola told the press that he had terminated his arrangement with the studio—but had delayed making the decision public "so that it would not interfere with the previews of *One from the Heart*." Undaunted, Coppola scheduled a preview similar to the Radio City showings in Los Angeles and continued to shop his picture to perspective distributors.

He found very few takers, and he couldn't come to terms with those companies that were interested. Some of the offers, Zoetrope president Robert

Spiotta told the trade papers, were "respectable and generous," but the bidding distributors wanted too much in return. Warner Bros., an early front-runner, wanted the distribution rights to *One from the Heart* in perpetuity, and Universal, another serious bidder, wanted ancillary rights that Coppola refused to relinquish. In addition, Coppola was requiring, as part of a special handling provision in any agreement, that premiere screenings of the film be shown on screens at least twenty-five feet wide.

Unable to reach an agreement with distributors, Zoetrope took yet another bold step, announcing that it would release the film itself, not to a nationwide audience (which, in any event, it was in no position to do), but to twenty-five theaters in eight cities—New York, Chicago, Los Angeles, Las Vegas, Denver, San Francisco, Seattle, and Toronto. The picture would premiere on February 11 and be marketed as an event.

Realistically speaking, Coppola was reaching the endgame portion of his chess match with the major studios, and, like a chess player unwilling to concede defeat, he was praying for what amounted to a draw. He didn't have the money to make release prints for extensive national release, nor did he have time to assemble trailers to advertise the film. He was dodging bad press from every direction; both Chase Manhattan Bank and Jack Singer were demanding payments on their loans. Limited release could at least generate revenue and further interest in the film.

On January 29, Coppola closed a deal with Columbia Pictures for distribution of *One from the Heart* in the United States and Canada. Columbia had approached Zoetrope earlier but had offered no up-front money and wanted *The Outsiders* as part of the deal. In the new deal, Columbia still offered no money, but it agreed to distribute the film at a lower fee. *The Outsiders* was not part of the pact, although Columbia speculated that it would be able to work with Coppola in the future.

The agreement illustrated how far Coppola's stock had fallen. It wouldn't have been that long ago when Coppola might have felt insulted by Columbia's offer, and undoubtedly he would have held out for a better deal. As it was, Columbia was offering the best available deal that allowed him to maintain ownership of his movie, which, at this point, was his only hope for salvation. If the film took off at the box office, he would need as much money as he could earn if he ever hoped to pay back his creditors. Although insiders could not have helped but see the deal for what it was, Coppola and Robert Spiotta tried to give the impression that Zoetrope still held on to some bargaining power. According to Spiotta, during the initial negotiations with Columbia, the studio had indicated "less than the required enthusiasm" for the picture, but after giving the movie a second look, the company had given a more encouraging response. The deal afforded the opportunity for *One from the Heart* to open on schedule.

"The deal does not involve a great deal of up-front money. None, in fact," Spiotta reported. "We've decided to gamble on the back end—to go with a lower distribution fee and retain control of all rights, rather then take the Universal deal, which provided six million dollars up front but meant losing control of all rights."

Columbia immediately went to work on an advertising campaign. The original ad, focusing on the film's romanticism, had depicted Frederic Forrest and Teri Garr coming together in a kiss, with a legend reading "Francis Coppola Takes a Very Special Look at Love"; for a tag line, the ad agency debated between "A New Kind of Old-Fashioned Romance" and "A New Kind of Valentine." Columbia, to Zoetrope's displeasure, wanted something snappier and less traditional, as well as something that traded on Coppola's past. In the new ad, Raul Julia would be pictured lying on top of Teri Garr, with the line "Francis Ford Coppola, the Man Who Brought You 'The Godfather' and 'Apocalypse Now,' Takes a Light Look at Love in a Spectacular Way" running over the picture and "Sometimes You Have to Break Apart to Come Together" running beneath.

While Columbia prepared to advertise the film and get it placed in theaters by its scheduled opening date, Coppola hit the road in a torrid promotional blitz, appearing on *The Merv Griffin Show* in Los Angeles, heading to Las Vegas the next day for a press conference at Caesar's Palace, and, later the same day, flying to Chicago for an interview with Gene Siskel. Then it was on to Toronto for a press conference and a handful of one-on-one interviews with journalists before heading to New York City. Somehow, in the face of endless inquiries about his financial misfortunes, Coppola managed to keep his composure, if not his humor. In New York, he sandwiched casting calls for *The Outsiders* around appearances on *Good Morning America* and *Late Night with David Letterman*. He then flew off to Washington, D.C., where he sat for more interviews and, in the evening, appeared at a black-tie opening of *Napoleon* at the Kennedy Center.

The interviews, like most interviews scheduled during promotional tours, varied from fluffy chatter to grueling interrogation. Coppola must have cringed when he learned that he would be following Australian pop singer Olivia Newton-John, who sang "Let's Get Physical," and humorist Erma Bombeck, who offered a television column on "The Cost of Wives," on *Good Morning America,* just as he must have blanched when Gene Siskel asked why he didn't "act more like his co-equal as the greatest of American filmmakers, Martin Scorsese, who manages to release his extraordinary movies with a manner of dignity and without going nuts in public." ("Why does one weigh two hundred and forty pounds and the other weigh something like ninety-six pounds?" Coppola responded. "Obviously, it has to do with a difference in personality.")

At times, he could be hypersensitive and testy, especially when discussing his bad reviews. In an interview with the *Los Angeles Times,* published on the eve of *One from the Heart*'s opening in the city, Coppola lashed out bitterly against the critics, allowing his paranoia to surface when he hinted that Pauline Kael might have written him off because he didn't follow the example of other directors and take her to lunch or show her private screenings of his latest film. "Everybody knows Pauline has been struggling to maintain her level among the critics," he griped, even though he would have been thrilled had she written a glowing review of *One from the Heart.* "Rex Reed once said I didn't know how to thank them for making me," he continued. "Those two and Andrew Sarris are the boring old guard. The New York film critics in particular are like those who run the Golden Globes. All these little people you wouldn't care about if they didn't have their little thing going."

Coppola's words might have sounded like an embarrassing case of sour grapes—which, to a large extent, they were—but there was more at play in Coppola's attack than the press realized at the time. Two days after Kael's review appeared in *The New Yorker,* Jack Singer hit Zoetrope with a ninety-day foreclosure notice, and while no one, Coppola included, would have been foolish enough to blame a critic or review for the demise of a studio, Coppola was most certainly relying on reviews to help launch his film and, by extension, save his studio. Zoetrope and *One from the Heart* were literally facing a terrible demise unless Coppola found a way to elevate the movie's stature in the eyes of the skeptical public.

8.

THERE WOULD BE NO STAYS of execution, no last-minute reprieves.

A gala premiere of *One from the Heart,* attended by Coppola, Columbia executives, principal cast members, and other celebrities, was held on February 10 at Plitt's Century Plaza Theater in Los Angeles, followed by the film's official opening the next evening in forty-one theaters in the selected eight cities. Attendance was encouraging in four cities—New York, Los Angeles, San Francisco, and Toronto, all great supporters of Coppola's films in the past—but after a couple of weeks, the gate receipts in even these cities were dwindling. With only a few exceptions, the reviews were dreary.

Columbia, hoping to find a way to mount a successful promotional campaign for the film, conducted exit polls at theaters showing *One from the Heart*, with discouraging results. Only half of the people seeing the film claimed to like it, and a disarming number of people weren't even aware that the picture had been directed by Coppola. Zoetrope hired Patrick Caddell and Cambridge Survey Research, the company that had worked on the polls for Jimmy Carter during his successful 1976 presidential run, to do further market research. The firm targeted four cities and, after interviewing 451 moviegoers, drew essentially the same conclusions. Half the people seeing the movie admitted to liking it, and those who didn't said the film wasn't what they had expected. The negative publicity had had a mixed effect on the people polled, some saying they were aware of the movie because they had read reviews and articles about Coppola's problems but had attended the movie in any event, while others responded that they had avoided the film because of the bad reviews. Most surprising was the finding that men, by a large margin, preferred the movie over women, and that women disliked its surreal element. Cambridge Survey Research concluded its report by recommending that Columbia and Zoetrope draw up a marketing strategy stressing Coppola's direction of the film and accentuating the idea that it was the kind of innovative adventure that he alone could do, complete with fantastic music, lighting, photography, and scenery.

While Columbia restructured its distribution strategy, the movie continued to sink. After twenty days in theaters, *One from the Heart* had grossed an appalling $804,518, leading Columbia to trim the number of theaters to eight venues in eight cities. Coppola, committed to beginning production on *The Outsiders* on March 1, left for Tulsa, Oklahoma.

The attendance for *One from the Heart* had become so dismal that, by April 1, only one theater in the country—the Guild in New York—was showing the picture, and on that day, a reporter counted forty-three people at the last showing. The next day, Coppola pulled the plug on the picture.

Zoetrope and Columbia officials tried to remain optimistic—at least in public—about the movie's future, announcing that it would reopen in several target cities in the United States later in the year. By then, with any luck, a better marketing strategy would be mounted, the sound track album would be released, and there would be some distance between its rerelease and all the negative publicity.

In fact, Columbia was disposed to shelve its involvement in the movie indefinitely, if not permanently, especially when, within weeks of closing down *One from the Heart*, Columbia Pictures was purchased by Coca-Cola. In light of the $5.9 billion grossed by the soft-drink magnate in 1982, and the $700 million grossed by the motion picture company during that same period, the money that Columbia had invested in distributing and promoting *One from the Heart* looked like loose change.

For Coppola, it was an entirely different matter. He had gambled and lost on one of the biggest flops in motion picture history. He had *Hammett* completed, and *The Escape Artist* was scheduled for release over the Memorial Day weekend. He had also purchased *Too Far to Go,* a made-for-TV movie based on several John Updike short stories, which Zoetrope intended to revamp and release in theaters. These properties, however, were not enough to save his studio.

Resigned to the inevitable, Coppola formally announced on April 15 that he was placing the Zoetrope studio up for sale. The dream, at least in its latest permutation, was over.

Chapter Twelve

Paladin in Oklahoma

"Francis was so far ahead of his time. He was really sinking his teeth into the next, deeper phase of 'art film for teenagers.' An art film for teenagers? Even we thought he was crazy, and we were making it. But Francis has always been that kind of visionary."

—Diane Lane

1.

As soon as he realized that there was no immediate hope for *One from the Heart* or Zoetrope, Francis Ford Coppola began to contemplate his options seriously. He was tempted to leave the business entirely and put behind him all the hard hours, haggles with the money men, and wars with the press, but this, of course, would have been an unsatisfactory conclusion to a career that, for all its ups and down, had provided him with a life that others could only have dreamed of. He had taken a substantial beating over the last half decade, but he had struck out only with one film. For all the abuse he'd been taking, he was still regarded as one of the most important and influential filmmakers of his time. So getting out of the business was not a realistic option.

What, then, was left?

Coppola concluded he was best off by making another film as quickly as possible, in time for a 1982 release. From his meetings with his attorneys and Zoetrope officials, he realized that he had only a small window of opportunity—no more than several months—in which he could work before all the legal red tape ensnaring Zoetrope was resolved and he would again be burdened with the crushing financial responsibilities of his past. If he could complete a film during that time, he would at least have a product capable of earning him some money and, with luck, a chance to edge his way out of trouble. This time around, he had no alternative but to play the Hollywood game: Find a project with decent commercial potential; approach studio executives with hat in hand; work as a director for hire; and complete the picture on time and on budget.

In this respect, *The Outsiders* was an ideal project. The S. E. Hinton novel had been a runaway best-seller—one of the biggest young adult books ever— and a film adaptation of it could plug into one of the film industry's ready-made audiences. In addition, since there were no major adult roles in the story, Coppola could save on the film's budget by hiring a relatively unknown (and, therefore, relatively inexpensive) young cast. The prospects were exciting. Coppola loved kids—more, he claimed, than he cared for adults—and working on *The Outsiders* promised to be an enjoyable experience, not unlike Coppola's old days as a camp counselor. Filming on location in Tulsa also tossed in the added bonus of being geographically removed from Hollywood and the attendant nonstop ringing of the telephone, with all its reminders of his recent financial crises and the failure of a movie he dearly loved.

"Rather than go through six months of being whipped for having committed this sin of making a film that I wanted to make, I escaped with a lot of young people to Tulsa and didn't have to deal with the sophisticates," Coppola would recall after finishing *The Outsiders*. "It turned into a way for me to soothe my heartache over the terrible rejection."

2.

COPPOLA'S INVOLVEMENT WITH *The Outsiders* (and, by extension, *Rumble Fish*) had a storybook quality to it, beginning a decade earlier, in 1972, when a newly hired librarian's aide at the Lone Star School in Fresno, California, read the book and recommended it to her thirteen-year-old son. The librarian, Jo Ellen Misakian, was simply searching for a way to encourage seventh and eighth graders at the school, particularly the boys, to read. *The Out-*

siders, a straightforward tale narrated in language that refused to compromise or talk down to its readers, was a hit.

The reasons for the book's success required very little analysis. Susie Hinton (who used her initials, for Susan Eloise, rather than risk having her critics use her gender as reason to challenge her book's authenticity) wrote *The Outsiders* when she was sixteen years old, and she saw it published, to great fanfare, two years later, in 1967. Over the next fifteen years, *The Outsiders* sold around 7 million copies and became a staple in classrooms across the country. Hinton, who characterized herself as being something of an outsider, attributed her success to the fact that she liked teenage kids, especially the ones a bit rough around the edges, and found the teen years, "where ideals are clashing against the walls of compromise," one of the most interesting times in life.

"So many adults are hostile toward teenagers," she observed. "Adults like little kids because they're cute and controllable, but there's something about teenagers that absolutely sets them off. I don't know if it's because they don't want to remember how miserable they were as teenagers, or because they don't want to realize how much they've compromised since they had those ideals."

Over the years, several motion picture producers had approached Hinton about making a movie of *The Outsiders,* but the author rejected their offers, mainly because she wasn't convinced that the book needed to be adapted for the big screen. Nor did she respond when Jo Ellen Misakian sent her a letter with her own proposal that the book be turned into a movie.

Fortunately, Misakian was not the kind of person to be easily discouraged. She had approached a number of people who she hoped would assist her in finding someone with a friendly ear—and the right connections—but she had always come up empty. Then, after reading a favorable review of *The Black Stallion* in *Newsweek,* she and her students decided that Coppola was the man for the project and that they should approach him directly. In a letter dated March 21, 1980, Misakian told Coppola that, in her opinion, the Lone Star School's student body of 324 probably represented America's youth, and that everyone who had seen the book, regardless of background, felt strongly about his directing a movie version of *The Outsiders.* The letter was signed by thirty students and sent, along with a copy of the novel, not to Coppola's San Francisco office but to Paramount's offices. The mistake turned out to be a lucky break.

"We get tons of that kind of mail," Fred Roos, a coproducer of the film, recalled. "It was lucky for the kids that we were in New York when it was sent over [by Paramount]. Francis doesn't get much mail in New York, so he read the letter."

Impressed by what he'd read, and believing that the students might indeed have a good notion about what would make a good movie, Coppola turned the material over to Roos. "Check it out," he told Roos, "if you want to."

Roos had no interest in the book, which, he felt, looked like the product of a vanity press, complete with what he regarded as a tacky cover. For weeks, he carried the book around without so much as giving it a glance. Then one day while on a plane trip, he decided to read a few pages and see what he thought. "I ended up reading it cover to cover," he remembered, "and I agreed with the kids. I thought it was a movie." He enthusiastically recommended the project to Coppola.

Later that summer, Roos traveled to Tulsa to meet with Hinton. He learned, as had producers before him, that she wasn't dying to see her book translated into a movie. Nor was she impressed when Roos told her that the filmmaker interested in making the picture was the director of *The Godfather* and *Apocalypse Now.* She did, however, like *The Black Stallion,* and she felt that the people responsible for this movie might be the kind of people who could do justice to her book for young adults. She asked for five thousand dollars for the option on the book—a steal, by Hollywood standards—but at the time, Zoetrope was in such terrible financial shape that it couldn't afford even that paltry sum for a project that might not reach fruition. Hinton wound up settling for five hundred dollars, a percentage of the picture's earnings, and a small part in the movie.

Coppola assigned the screenplay duties to Kathleen Knutsen Rowell, a young scriptwriter, but he was dissatisfied with her adaptation, which, in his view, lost some of the book's charm. The story had to remain as gritty as the original, but the characters still had to hold the fine line between youthful innocence and darker adolescent behavior. Coppola opted to write the screenplay himself, turning the Hinton story into what he described as "a *Godfather* for children," but the *One from the Heart* and Zoetrope distractions made the going tough, forcing him to put the project away for a while. When he finally returned to it, he worked closely with the source material, producing fourteen drafts, until he had written a script he could live with. By then, he was so buried in problems that work on *The Outsiders* was starting to look like a pleasant diversion.

The casting decisions, once again, illustrated Coppola's uncanny knack for placing unknowns in precisely the right roles. Teen heartthrob Matt Dillon, who had established himself in 1980's *My Bodyguard,* and who had just completed the filming on *Tex,* an adaptation of another Hinton novel, was cast in the role of Dallas Winston, and C. Thomas Howell, who had had a small part in *E.T.*, was given the part of Ponyboy Curtis. Ralph Macchio, who would go on to star in the *Karate Kid* movies, but who at the time had appeared mostly in television roles, won the role of Johnny Cade, Ponyboy's friend. Filling out the youthful cast were Emilio Estevez, Tom Cruise, Patrick Swayze, Rob Lowe, and Diane Lane—all destined to attain star status in the future, but all relatively inexperienced when auditioning for their roles.

Cruise recalled how grateful he was to work with a director of Coppola's stature. "I had been offered some leading roles," he said, "but I didn't feel that I could carry a film. I hadn't learned enough and I felt that I would be eaten alive. So when they started auditioning for *The Outsiders*, I remember pulling Francis aside and saying, 'I'll do anything it takes; I'll play any role in this.' And he was nice enough to hire me."

For two of the small adult roles in the film, Coppola gave Susie Hinton a part as a nurse, and he offered the part of Buck Merrill, a barroom bouncer, to musician Tom Waits, who had recently nabbed an Oscar nomination for his score for *One from the Heart*.

In what was becoming a tradition, Coppola found work for his own family in the production. Carmine Coppola, absent from *One from the Heart*, except for a cameo appearance, was back as the composer for his son's film score. Son Gio, who had written him a formal letter asking permission to drop out of high school in order to become his apprentice, was appointed associate producer, while younger son Roman worked as a production assistant. Twelve-year-old Sofia made her acting debut (appearing under the pseudonym "Domino") as a young panhandler at a Dairy Queen drive-in restaurant.

For his production crew, Coppola stuck with familiar faces, with Dean Tavoularis returning as production designer, and Robert Swarthe, responsible for some of the dazzling visual effects in *One from the Heart*, working in the same capacity on *The Outsiders*. Cinematographer Vittorio Storaro was gone, but Coppola was more than content with his replacement, Stephen Burum, a former UCLA classmate who had proven himself on *Apocalypse Now* and *The Black Stallion*, for which he had worked as director of second-unit photography, and on *The Escape Artist*, for which he had been the director of photography. All were familiar with Coppola's electronic cinema, which the director intended to use, with some modifications, on *The Outsiders*.

By the beginning of March 1983, Coppola had assembled his cast and crew in Tulsa; Silverfish, with all its gadgetry, awaited another shot at electronic filmmaking. It was time to begin.

3.

THERE WAS, HOWEVER, ONE major drawback: Coppola had yet to secure financing for his picture. While waiting for a deal to be hashed out, he went into an extended period of rehearsals, videotaped in the gym of a local school, which gave him the opportunity to watch his young actors develop their roles.

"We had workshops with all the actors in which we'd ad-lib and play around," Tom Cruise recalled. "And I remember feeling very good, building up my own instincts on acting. And understanding more of each level, learning more about film acting and what I wanted to do."

Coppola wanted his cast to delve into their roles as deeply as possible, to live the parts of the upscale Socs (pronounced *soh-chez*) and their wrong-side-of-the-tracks counterparts, the Greasers, and to help them achieve this, he arranged to have the actors treated in ways that corresponded with their roles in the movie. The cast members playing Greasers were treated poorly, assigned the worst rooms in their hotel and given tiny expense allowances, while those playing Socs were treated like royalty, given the best rooms in the hotel and larger allowances. Coppola even encouraged the Greaser actors to disrupt business at a local restaurant, and Matt Dillon to do some petty shoplifting at a drugstore—with the assurance, of course, that he would bail them out should they get into trouble.

Filming began on March 29, with a (for Coppola, relatively small) budget set at just under $10 million. By then, Coppola had negotiated a distribution arrangement with Warner Bros., production financing from Chemical Bank, and a completion guarantee from National Film Finance Corporation in England. The terms of the agreements were strict—Coppola would not be permitted to veer from the budget without prior approval—but after the *One from the Heart* experience, the director was happy to be back at work and not having to back the project with his own money and property. Hyping his new picture as a "*Gone With the Wind* for 14-year-old girls," to be shot in operatic, *Godfather* style, Coppola sounded hopeful on the eve of the shoot. "It's not a little picture," he cautioned the press. "It's a heartbreaking story, with nobility." Then he added, as if remembering the past criticisms about his pictures' being too negative, that "it's sort of uplifting at the end."

This time around, Coppola issued no lofty pronouncements about his electronic cinema or changing the industry, even though his previsualization process worked beautifully on *The Outsiders*. The rehearsals in the gym had been videotaped as designed, against blue backgrounds, and the performances were then superimposed on stills of the locations to be used in the movie. By the time cameras rolled in earnest, Coppola had his production mapped out.

The movie's plot was the least complicated of any Coppola screenplay to date, with shadings from *Rebel Without a Cause, West Side Story,* and even *The Godfather* making their way into the finished film. Ponyboy Curtis (the novel's narrator) lives in Tucson with his two older brothers, Darrel and Sodapop. Their parents are dead, victims of an automobile accident, and the three are simply trying to hold their meager family together, Darrel working as a roofer and Sodapop at a gas station. Though sensitive and reasonably bright, Ponyboy has fallen in with a local gang called the Greasers, and he has been in enough scrapes with the system that only luck seems to be separating him from residence in a reform school.

As the story opens, Ponyboy is walking through town with two fellow Greasers. Dallas, an older member, was recently released from prison and is presently living in a room above a tavern. Johnny, a likable Sal Mineo look-alike, would give anything to live in a peaceful place far removed from the domestic violence of his household and the gang violence that he has to contend with on the street. The three wind up at the local drive-in, where they run into two girls who have just fought with their drunken boyfriends, who happen to be members of the rival gang, the Socs. Dallas tries to impress them with his crude bravado but turns them off instead. Ponyboy, however, makes a connection with Cherry, a redheaded cheerleader who, despite her higher social standing, seems willing to accept Ponyboy and Johnny as peers. While walking the two girls home, Ponyboy and Johnny are confronted by a carload of Socs, including the girls' boyfriends, and a fight is avoided only when Cherry and her friend reluctantly agree to leave with the Socs.

Ponyboy and Johnny repair to a local park, build a small fire, and talk long into the night. Earlier in the evening, Johnny had witnessed his parents fighting, and now he plans to spend the night in the park. Ponyboy eventually returns home, but after a quarrel with his eldest brother, which quickly becomes physical, he rejoins Johnny in the park and announces that they both should run away. As they talk, the drunken Socs drive into the park and a fight breaks out. Three of the Socs gang up on Ponyboy and hold his head underwater in the fountain until he nearly drowns.

After an indeterminate amount of time, Ponyboy regains consciousness, only to see Johnny, armed with a bloody switchblade, sitting across from him. The leader of the Socs lies facedown on the ground nearby. Johnny explains that he murdered the boy because he feared that the three Socs were going to kill Ponyboy. Frightened and uncertain about what to do, the two look up Dallas for advice. He gives them dry clothing, fifty dollars, and a gun, and instructs them to take shelter in an old abandoned country church miles away from Tulsa. He will join them, he promises, when things settle down in town. Ponyboy and Johnny jump a freight train and, a few hours later, stumble into their hideout.

Over the next several days, the bored and lonely boys amuse themselves by smoking cigarettes, talking, playing cards, and reading a paperback copy of *Gone With the Wind*, which Johnny picked up during an excursion into a nearby town. They cut each other's hair so they won't be easily recognized, and Ponyboy dyes his hair blond. Dallas arrives with news from home. Cherry has vowed to testify at a trial that the Socs were drunk at the time of the fight and that Ponyboy and Johnny had only acted in self-defense. In addition, Dallas has brought a letter from Sodapop, in which he begs Ponyboy to come home. Dallas, however, is skeptical about the odds of a fair trial, if his friends should decide to turn themselves in; he knows the system too well. He offers to drive Ponyboy and Johnny to a drive-in restaurant, where they make further plans and grab a bite to eat.

Upon returning to the church after lunch, they see the building in flames, with a school bus parked nearby. A kindergarten field trip has taken a tragic turn. Johnny instinctively bolts into the burning building, followed by a somewhat reluctant Ponyboy. The two rescue the children, but the church's roof collapses before Johnny can escape. Dallas pulls him out of the building, but Johnny has been badly burned and has a broken back. Dallas and Ponyboy have also been hurt, but their injuries are not life-threatening.

Ponyboy is reunited with Sodapop and Darrel at the hospital, and the three brothers return to their home. An all-out rumble between the Greasers and the Socs, to be staged without weapons, has been called for the park. Dallas, seeking revenge for all that's happened to Johnny, leaves the hospital and joins the Greasers, and in the middle of a driving rainstorm, the Greasers thoroughly trounce the Socs and chase them from the park. For Ponyboy and Dallas, any satisfaction in the victory is totally rubbed away when they return to the hospital to deliver the news to Johnny. Johnny is near death, and as he lies dying, he advises Ponyboy to "stay golden"—a direct reference to a Robert Frost poem that Ponyboy has committed to memory.

Johnny's death drives Dallas to despair. When the good guys are punished, there is no hope, no reason to live. He holds up a drugstore with an empty revolver, and while fleeing the police, he is gunned down in the park, near the scene of his earlier triumph against the Socs. In an epilogue to the movie, Ponyboy mulls over everything that has happened in recent days. He finds a letter from Johnny, hidden in his copy of *Gone With the Wind*, in which Johnny informs him that he has no regrets; the lives that he saved, he tells Ponyboy, are more valuable than his own. Deeply moved, Ponyboy opens a composition notebook and begins to write his account of the story.

Critics sneered when *The Outsiders* premiered in March 1983, thumbing their noses at the story that Coppola praised as "sweet and youthful, [with] something in its little, simple theme that was of value," their appraisals saturated in the kind of cynicism and regret that had inspired S. E. Hinton to write her novel. "Who would have expected a teary, teen soap opera from the maker of *The Godfather* and *Apocalypse Now?*" wrote *Newsweek*'s David Ansen, who accurately predicted that the movie would be a hit with adolescent viewers, but who also complained that "the disappointment is that Coppola didn't make a movie for the rest of us to love." To Vincent Canby of the *New York Times*, *The Outsiders* was "spectacularly out of touch, a laughably earnest attempt to impose heroic attitudes on some nice, small characters purloined from a 'young adult' novel by S. E. Hinton."

The generally negative critical response to the film failed to take into account (or refused to acknowledge) one crucial point: Coppola had not made the picture for adults, any more than Hinton had written her novel for grown-ups. It might be argued that the gang activities in the story, supposedly set in 1966 (although the movie never specifies as much), seem tame in comparison to urban gang warfare nearly two decades later—just as the choreographed rumbles of *West Side Story* seem hopelessly dated today—but the central theme of *The Outsiders*—the aching need to belong—was, and is, a universal feeling among teenagers everywhere.

4.

THE OUTSIDERS SHOOTING proceeded smoothly, with Coppola and his teenage cast forming a kind of mutual admiration society. The hours were long, but no one seemed to mind. There were some minor problems, such as trying to direct the kindergarten class during the fire sequence, or choreographing the rumble scene (in which Tom Cruise broke a thumb, Emilio Estevez suffered a cut lip, and Thomas Howell received a shiner during rehearsals), but as a rule, Coppola hadn't had this much fun working on a film in a decade. Matt Dillon referred to him as "Father Film," and Emilio Estevez, who had once taken a role as an extra in *Apocalypse Now*, and who had watched his father, Martin Sheen, survive the ordeal, was happy to report Coppola's "getting his credibility back as a director who can deliver on schedule."

Ironically, Coppola's biggest hassle arose not from the filming itself, but over the picture's scriptwriting credit. Coppola had written the film's shooting script, but when he approached the Writers Guild of America, West, with the request that he be given writing credit for the screenplay, he found his case going to arbitration—the customary procedure whenever a production executive requests screenwriting credit. The arbitration board ruled against him, deciding that Kathleen Knutsen Rowell, author of the first two drafts of the screenplay, written before Coppola was formally listed as the film's director, should receive sole writing credit. Coppola was furious.

"The woman simply did not write the script for the film I made," he insisted in 1999, a decade and a half after the dispute. "However, in the Writers Guild rules, they weigh very heavily for the first person to do an adaptation— for the screenwriter who first adapts a book and uses the characters by their names and uses the basic plot, even if it isn't a particularly effective or even do-able script. You are credited for being the one who had those characters and plot, even though they are from the book. By the same token, the Guild weighs very heavily against a producer or director who claims credits—and rightfully so, due to years of abuse by directors who gave ideas but really didn't sit down and write.

"So, those two facts considered, the Guild ruled against me getting any credit, even though I sat down and wrote the script that I used; it gave her *all* the credit, even though her script wasn't, in fact, even on the set. This happens often, as it did later with *Tucker,* when they gave a credit to a writer who had nothing to do with the script that I used."

As hoped, Coppola enjoyed a temporary reprieve from his many worries. Jack Singer had agreed to delay any further action on his foreclosure notice, and Chase Manhattan Bank agreed to hold off on legal action against Coppola and Zoetrope, as well. A few parties had expressed interest in buying the studio, and rather than go through the courts, Coppola's creditors took a wait-and-see approach, hoping that he would be able to repay the loans with money gained through the studio's sale.

One thing was certain: No significant money would be forthcoming from Zoetrope's other releases. *Too Far to Go,* a negative pickup, opened at a New York art house, only to disappear after six weeks when Zoetrope failed to find a national distributor for the picture. *The Escape Artist,* delayed on numerous occasions, finally premiered in May, but, after taking a whipping from the reviewers and seeing only marginal box-office receipts, it was pulled from circulation. *Hammett* appeared a few weeks later at the Cannes Film Festival, but it, too, was panned mercilessly and shelved before national distribution.

The demise of *The Escape Artist* and *Hammett* affected Coppola in more ways than just lost revenue. While working on *The Outsiders,* he read *Rumble Fish,* another S. E. Hinton novel for young adults, and he decided to steal a page from his old Roger Corman days: As long as he had a cast and crew at his disposal, he would shoot *Rumble Fish* immediately upon completion of the principal photography on *The Outsiders.* As Coppola saw it, he could work on the postproduction of *The Outsiders* during those hours when he wasn't shooting *Rumble Fish.*

Warner Bros. saw it another way. The company had been the distributor for both *Hammett* and *The Escape Artist,* and in the wake of its disappointment over the failure of these two movies, it was not inclined to pick up another Coppola film, especially one that, in a sense, would be riding on the coattails of *The Outsiders.* Warner Bros. executives had previewed and hated an early cut of *The Outsiders,* and they were now concerned about its commercial appeal. If it went nowhere after its release, it was almost certain that *Rumble Fish* would follow suit. After some discussion, Warner Bros. decided to pass on the new picture.

Coppola responded by plunging even deeper into the project, working late into his evenings with Susie Hinton on a screenplay, rounding up a cast, and roughing out a production schedule. *Rumble Fish,* he decided, would be entirely different from *The Outsiders*—an "antidote to the saccharinity in *Outsiders,*" as he would later claim. Whereas *The Outsiders* had been a strictly commercial venture, shot in lush colors and backed by what he called a "schmaltzy classical" score, *Rumble Fish* would be a return to art, shot in black and white and backed by a modern, percussion-dominated score. He had always boasted of never making similar films, with the possible exception of the two *Godfather* pictures, and he was excited by the prospects of making back-to-back, yet contrasting movies out of two Hinton novels. "I really started to use *Rumble Fish* as my carrot for what I promised myself when I finished *The Outsiders,*" he recalled.

Assembling a cast and crew for the new film required only minor effort. Virtually the entire production crew from *The Outsiders* would be staying on, as would Matt Dillon and Diane Lane, who would be playing Rusty-James, the movie's protagonist, and his girlfriend, Patty; Tom Waits, Susie Hinton, William Smith, and Glenn Withrow, along with Gio and Sofia Coppola, would again have minor roles. Coppola's nephew, Nicolas Cage, signed to play Rusty-James's competitive friend Smokey and Dennis Hopper won the part of Rusty-James's alcoholic father.

The pivotal role of the Motorcycle Boy, Rusty-James's rebellious but burned-out older brother, went to Mickey Rourke, a volatile, enormously talented young actor who had previously appeared in such films as *Heaven's Gate, Body Heat,* and, most recently, in *Diner*. Rourke had auditioned for a role in *The Outsiders* but had been deemed a little too old and not quite right for a featured part in the picture. Fred Roos, however, had been very impressed with the young actor, and when Coppola began casting *Rumble Fish*, Roos highly recommended him for the part of the Motorcycle Boy.

The decision to shoot the film in Tulsa, although obviously practical, was based largely on an effect that Coppola wanted for his film. The hot summer months were just settling in, and Coppola felt that he could use the weather to his advantage.

"Francis wanted that for his film: the dampness, the stifling humidity," Fred Roos explained. "It is a tortured, moody film, full of moisture, steam, and smoke. It had to be shot in a steam bath and that was the result. From the beginning, we renamed the company 'Hot Weather Film Productions.'"

The energy and passion behind *Rumble Fish*, not readily apparent to observers, who thought it was just another teen gang flick—or even to Coppola's crew, who initially refused to believe that he was going to do the picture—could be attributed to the collective enthusiasm of its creator, star, and director. Although *Rumble Fish* was the least successful of her young adult novels, Susie Hinton had a special fondness for her third book, which could be traced back to 1967, when she was putting the finishing touches on *The Outsiders*. She had been paging through a magazine when she came across a photograph of a young man on a motorcycle. She clipped the photo out and used it as inspiration for a short story. Unable to get the photo out of her mind, she eventually featured the Motorcycle Boy, as she called him, in a book of his own.

Matt Dillon had met Hinton on the set of *Tex*, where he pleased her greatly by confiding that *Rumble Fish* was his favorite of her books. The novel, Dillon insisted, had to be made into a movie, and when that happened, he wanted to star in it. Hinton was doubtful. No one seemed to understand the book, she told Dillon, and it might be some time before they could find someone willing and able to adapt it for the big screen. Both rejoiced when Coppola read *Rumble Fish* during the shooting of *The Outsiders* and agreed that it would make a great film.

The book had special meaning for Coppola, who easily understood the mentality of a teenage boy trying to live up to his older brother's reputation. There were more than a few parallels between Coppola and his older brother, Augie, and Rusty-James and the Motorcycle Boy, which meant that Coppola could make *Rumble Fish* into more of a personal film than others might have suspected—so much so that Coppola wound up dedicating the movie to his brother.

Rehearsals began as soon as Coppola had his cast locked in, and in no time he had produced a rough videotaped version of the movie. By now, Coppola had most of the bugs worked out of his electronic cinema, which in a movie as stylized as *Rumble Fish* was of special importance, allowing Coppola, Dean Tavoularis, and Stephen Burum the chance to work out complex production details prior to the filming. As with *The Outsiders*, Coppola had to wait to start the actual shooting until he had hatched a distribution deal, which was reached at the end of June, when Universal Pictures agreed to act as the domestic distributor on both *Rumble Fish* and the new theatrical release of *Napoleon*.

5.

THE SIAMESE FIGHTING FISH—the "rumble fish" of the movie's title—is an apt symbol for the youths in the S. E. Hinton novel. The female of the species is generally nonaggressive and capable of coexisting with most kinds of fish, but for the males, it is an entirely different story. As a rule, aquarium owners must keep the brilliantly colored males separate, lest they attack one another and fight to the death—an instinct so engrained that the male will attack its own reflection. In their native Thailand, these fish are often raised for sport: Two males are placed in a small tank and gamblers wager on the results of the inevitable confrontation.

At one time, the Motorcycle Boy was the ultimate rumble fish—winner of countless fights in his younger days, gang leader extraordinaire, legend in his hometown. Significantly, we learn of his existence before we see him: Graffiti proclaiming THE MOTORCYCLE BOY REIGNS can be found spray-painted on walls throughout the city. For his younger brother, Rusty-James, the legend is both a curse and a vocation; he idolizes his absent brother—the Motorcycle Boy had left for California some time ago—but he also realizes that he can never live up to his reputation.

Like so many teenagers in S. E. Hinton novels, Rusty-James finds a greater sense of family when he is with his friends than when he is at home. The Motorcycle Boy is gone, his mother had left the family years ago and is presently living with a television producer in Hollywood, and his father, a lawyer, fell apart after his wife abandoned the family, and he currently lives in an alcoholic stupor, staggering home every evening to collapse on his bed. The only stable influence in Rusty-James's life is his girlfriend, Patty, who comes from a traditional family, attends a school with a uniform dress code, and, like most female characters in stories of this nature, somehow manages to see the poet in the brute.

All live in a city that is never identified but which, like the town in Peter Bogdanovich's *The Last Picture Show*, seems to be slowly dying from the cancer of ennui. Clouds rush by in Coppola's sped-up photography, but life in the city is languid and repetitious. Kids move from one place to another, more because they have to be *somewhere* than out of any sense of purpose, and it is clear from the onset that part of the Motorcycle Boy's legend stems from the fact that he may be the only person ever to have escaped the town. Teenage boys fight, not with the conviction of youth gangs risking skin and blood over turf, as in the old days, but because something internal drives them to it.

So it is at the beginning of the story, when Rusty-James is challenged to a fight by Biff Wilcox, another tough kid in town, who has taken exception to remarks Rusty-James has made about a girlfriend. Rusty-James accepts the challenge with a shrug. He will fight Wilcox, but he feels so little emotion or conviction behind it that he falls asleep at his girlfriend's house and almost misses the fight.

The two meet at the agreed-upon location, each backed by a small group of friends. Rusty-James, believing the fight will be carried out with fists, is surprised when Wilcox, hopped up on drugs, pulls out a knife and claims he's going to cut him to pieces. Rusty-James, however, is a superior fighter, and he is about to finish off Wilcox when the Motorcycle Boy suddenly and unexpectedly turns up. Wilcox, using the temporary distraction to his advantage, slashes Rusty-James, opening a deadly cut in his side. In retaliation, the Motorcycle Boy sends his riderless bike charging at his younger brother's attacker.

The Motorcycle Boy takes the wounded Rusty-James home and patches him up, allowing us the opportunity to see the interaction between the two brothers, as well as learn more about the Motorcycle Boy. The two brothers, it turns out, are quite different. The Motorcycle Boy is actually very intelligent, and one suspects that with different guidance, he might have amounted to something. He has the charisma of a leader, but at this point, he is comfortable being off on his own. Even his legend bothers him: "It's a bit of a burden to be Robin Hood, Jesse James, and the Pied Piper," he tells Rusty-James later on in the story. "I'd just as soon stay a neighborhood novelty, if it's all the same to you. It's not that I couldn't handle a larger scale, I just plain don't want to."

Rusty-James, on the other hand, is not intellectually gifted, and as a result of his being abandoned by his mother and older brother, he can't bear the thought of being alone. He instinctively understands that he will probably amount to very little other than what he might earn through his reputation—and so much of that reputation, he realizes, is tied to the Motorcycle Boy.

The trip west has exacted a terrible toll from the Motorcycle Boy, even if Rusty-James doesn't immediately notice it. The Motorcycle Boy had hoped to escape from his hometown and find a better life in Los Angeles, but he had been disappointed in California. The return home represents a life sentence to an existence with little hope. He is as trapped as the beautiful Siamese fighting fish he has seen confined in small bowls at the pet store.*

Over the next few days, Rusty-James begins to lose the few anchors that he has in his life. He is expelled from school and, after attending a wild party, he is dumped by his girlfriend, Patty, who winds up dating Smokey Bennett, Rusty-James's friend—and rival for leadership.

Things are going no better for the Motorcycle Boy. The town is a dead end, and he is now existing day to day, rather than living with any measure of ambition. He is hounded by his past, symbolized by a policeman determined to find a reason to arrest him, and his future offers no promise. Finally, in an act of utter desperation, he breaks into the pet store and steals the "rumble fish," intending to set them free in the river. He is gunned down by the police before he accomplishes his mission, leaving Rusty-James to sort out what it all means. He, too, will head west, but with the lessons he's learned, he might find something worthwhile.

6.

RUMBLE FISH WENT INTO PRODUCTION on July 12 and was as different from *The Outsiders* as one could have imagined. Its language, much of it improvised, was rough, more in keeping with the real speech patterns of teenagers; its atmosphere buzzed with flashing violence. There would be no shots of bunny rabbits watching the main characters, as in *The Outsiders,* or of juvenile pranks at the drive-in movies. The teenagers in *The Outsiders* were just learning how to smoke, just learning where their hormones were taking them; in *Rumble Fish,* the cigarette dangling from the corner of Mickey Rourke's mouth, copped from a photo of French existentialist writer Albert Camus, suggested experience, as did the orgy scene, or even Matt Dillon's scenes with Diane Lane. In *Rumble Fish,* the kids were steaming and ready to blow, just

---

*Although *Rumble Fish* was shot in black and white, Coppola, in one of his more interesting moves, decided to show the fighting fish in color—an apt symbol of the colorful youth trapped in drab surroundings.

like the pipes in the city. *The Outsiders* was rated PG-13, *Rumble Fish* R all the way.

Critics unfairly accused Coppola of pretentiousness when *Rumble Fish* was released in October 1983, proving, if nothing else, that the fine line separating the ambitious and the pretentious is often interpretative, and often determined by those with myopic vision. Indeed, there were occasions in the movie, such as Coppola's use of a large handless clock, when the symbolism seemed forced or hyperbolic, or when the dialogue jumped track, but given Coppola's ambitions and execution in the project, *Rumble Fish* deserved better than it received.

Coppola's attention to detail, a trademark in all of his films, as well as a forte of Dean Tavoularis, was again evident in *Rumble Fish,* as was his awareness of—and willingness to pay homage to—his predecessors. The fight scene in *Rumble Fish,* choreographed by Michael Smuin and stuntman Buddy Joe Hooker, and staged near the tracks of an elevated train, mirrored the rumble in *West Side Story,* which was staged beneath a highway. Smuin, codirector of the San Francisco Ballet, had choreographed fight scenes in *Romeo and Juliet* and *Medea,* which Coppola had seen and appreciated, and he was looking for a similar grace in *Rumble Fish*'s big fight scene. Smuin obliged with an intricately planned sequence, complete with bursting pipes, flapping pigeons, swinging lights, and, as the grand finale, a riderless motorcycle running down the rival gang leader. Film writer Peter Cowie, author of biographies of both Coppola and Orson Welles, noted the technical similarities between *Rumble Fish* and such Wellesian classics as *Citizen Kane* and *The Magnificent Ambersons,* stating that "the fight scene between Wilcox and Rusty-James might well have been shot by Welles himself. . . . Like the old master, Coppola captures the *visual* properties of heat."

The similarities were far from coincidental. Coppola wanted his film to look like some of his favorite classics—particularly the German Expressionist films of a half century earlier—and he, Steve Burum, and Dean Tavoularis, along with other members of the cast and crew, watched a number of films, including Robert Wiene's *The Cabinet of Dr. Caligari,* F. W. Murnau's *Sunrise,* Anatole Litvak's *Decision Before Dawn,* and Welles's *Macbeth,* for ideas and inspiration. Coppola had quipped that he wanted *Rumble Fish* to look like an art film for young people, and the camera work in the film suggested his European influences.

The movie's avant-garde score was another matter. Rather than mix a couple of rock songs into a classical score, as he had done in *The Outsiders,* Coppola was looking for something heavily rhythmic, a combination of the primitive and the modern—something suggestive of passing time. He initially worked on the score himself, using bass and assorted percussion, but he eventually turned the job over to Stewart Copeland, the drummer and percussionist for the Police. Copeland hit the streets of Tulsa, recording the sounds of blaring horns and sirens, traffic, and machinery, which he integrated into his basic rhythm track. Few sound tracks had been anything like it.

Coppola finished shooting *Rumble Fish* in mid-October, concluding a half-year interlude from the bedlam he'd been facing from as far back as the beginning of the filming of *Apocalypse Now*. None of his old problems had gone away, but at least he'd had the opportunity to work on not one but two pleasant projects, leaving most of the studio headaches in the hands of Robert Spiotta while he put in some extremely long yet ultimately rewarding hours on what he hoped would be some good, profitable work.

7.

WARNER BROS. DIDN'T LIKE Coppola's edited version of *The Outsiders* any more than the rough cut that he had showed them earlier in the year. Coppola wanted to present an operatic film for young people; Warner Bros. wanted a polished, highly commercial teen flick that ran no more than an hour and a half, which meant that Coppola would have to shave off nearly one-fourth of the movie he hoped to release. In addition, as further indication of their lack of faith in the project, the company decided to postpone the picture's release date, October 1982, to the late winter or early spring of 1983, which, on the upside, gave Coppola plenty of time to edit it to their approval. On the other hand, *The Outsiders* would be missing out on the lucrative holiday season and would turn up in theaters at a time when movie attendance was traditionally at its lowest ebb.

Coppola was in a bad position. Warner Bros. undoubtedly reasoned that *The Outsiders* was too weak to compete with bigger, higher-profile films scheduled to premiere at the end of the year, but with the movie being delayed for another six months, Coppola was losing money he greatly needed. In addition, the postponement threw off the release date of *Rumble Fish*, probably until the following summer or fall. With creditors pounding on the door and threatening foreclosure on their loans, Coppola needed to offer something more than promises.

The sale of the Zoetrope studio was going nowhere. Earlier in the year, a couple of bids for the studio had been submitted, one matching Coppola's $20 million asking price, but Jack Singer, who had already served Coppola with foreclosure papers and therefore had the right to approve the sale, nixed the bids on the grounds that there was not enough up-front money being offered. A second round of bidding, in mid-July, also failed to produce a buyer. Two other lien holders, James Nasser and Glen Speidel (the lien holder on Hollywood General prior to Coppola's purchase of the studio and the former president of Hollywood General, respectively), served foreclosure notices, but they, like Singer, had been persuaded to hold off, in the hope that everyone might be paid off once Zoetrope was sold.

In essence, the studio had become a house of cards, held together by red tape, the goodwill that Coppola was able to generate from creditors, juggled payments, and time; that the studio was still functioning, however meagerly, in the fall of 1982 was testament to Coppola's (and Robert Spiotta's) business acumen and powers of persuasion. In October, a fourth foreclosure action, filed by Security Pacific Bank, followed Zoetrope's defaulting on its mortgage payments. A public auction seemed inevitable until, like the others, Security Pacific agreed to put off proceedings for three months. Coppola now had until January 14, 1983, to come up with $7 million or watch his studio sold to the highest bidder.

By this point, Coppola's financial distress had been so highly publicized that he had become legendary simply for surviving as long as he had. In the November 8 issue of *The New Yorker,* Lillian Ross published "Some Figures on a Fantasy," a fascinating and extremely lengthy piece that presented, in gory detail, Coppola's struggles with *One from the Heart* and his Zoetrope studio. The article, a primer for those unfamiliar with the business machinations of Hollywood, offered mind-numbing figures and statistics, from the actual number of videocassettes used in the making of *One from the Heart* (1,231), to the cost of the party thrown at the Time-Life Building after the movie's Radio City Music Hall screening ($19, 410), to the finest points of Coppola's distribution deals.

Aside from being embarrassing to a man who must have wondered if—or when—his tax returns were going to become part of the public record, the accounts of Coppola's money problems added to the filmmaker's image as a Hollywood maverick. He might not have been the kind of businessman that contemporaries such as George Lucas and Steven Spielberg were proving to be, and he might have produced a flop for his latest movie (but then again, so had Lucas with *More American Graffiti* and Spielberg with *1941*), but he seemed unbowed from the battle. "It's so silly in life not to pursue the highest possible thing you can imagine," he told Ross, "even if you run the risk of losing it all, because if you don't pursue it you've lost it anyway. You can't be an artist and be safe."

What Coppola wanted to avoid during these turbulent times was to leave the impression that he had grown desperate. He had his pride; he was head of a studio and a major filmmaker. The talk of budgets and money problems had worn him down, but he still had enough tooth to bite back. Hollywood, he said, was full of phonies interested more in the bottom line than in making good, creative pictures, but he was going to do it his way—including the decisions about the future of Zoetrope. "Although I wanted to keep the studio," he reflected shortly after the studio went on the block, "I'd rather sell it than go through bankruptcy and legal proceedings."

Nor did he want people to think that he was so hard-pressed that he would take on any project, as long as the money was good, or that Zoetrope was merely a paper studio. Quite the contrary: Coppola was as committed as ever to presenting important, overlooked films. Upon Tom Luddy's recommendation, Zoetrope picked up the world distribution rights for Godfrey Reggio's iconoclastic *Koyaanisqatsi,* with its haunting score by composer Philip Glass. The studio also sponsored Phillip Borsos's first film, *The Grey Fox,* a Canadian picture about an aging train robber—a highly regarded and awarded film that no major American studio would touch. Despite his own precarious financial situation, Coppola refused an on-screen credit for his role in the picture (other than the "Zoetrope Studios Presents" banner) or any share of the film's profits.

The project that Coppola liked enough to consider directing himself was a big-budget film adaptation of *The Pope of Greenwich Village,* a best-selling novel about two low-level gangsters. Intended as a vehicle for Al Pacino and Mickey Rourke, *The Pope of Greenwich Village* offered Coppola the opportunity to work with two actors he admired and had previously directed, along with the potential to make a highly commercial picture with some artistic spin. "I had some good ideas on it," he recalled. "I had Vittorio Storaro and the idea of making a kind of George Orwell, down-and-out movie in New York. I got excited about that."

Pacino, however, was locked into prior commitments, and as time dragged on, Coppola lost his enthusiasm for the project—which was just as well, because, although he had no way of knowing it, there would be another gangster movie waiting for him a few months up the road.

8.

COPPOLA DEVOTED THE FIRST couple of months of 1983 to working on a new screenplay for an ambitious project he was calling *Megalopolis,* producing four hundred pages of notes and script fragments in a two-month period. He would remember this time spent at his Napa Valley estate as a hopeful, creative period, even though, by all indications, he was barely hanging on to his studio.

To no one's surprise, he had been unable to repay the money owed to Security Pacific Bank, which promptly announced a foreclosure auction set for February 11—ironically, a year to the day after *One from the Heart* went into limited release. Coppola's biggest fear, it appeared, was about to come true. He was spared the worst, however, when the auction was subsequently postponed on two occasions, and when the bank decided to grant Coppola several extensions, during which he was to sell the studio.

Such a sale, Robert Spiotta announced, was imminent, although it was difficult to determine how much of this was fact, how much was wishful thinking, or if some of it was simply bluffing. The rumor mill was rife with speculation about potential buyers, or of the possible declaration of Chapter 11 bankruptcy by Zoetrope. Frustrated by the lack of a sale and Security Pacific's extensions, James Nasser threatened to take legal action himself. "It's got to be settled," he said impatiently. "It can't go on any longer."

In all likelihood, Coppola felt the same way. He had sold and mortgaged property, rented facilities, laid off employees, wheeled and dealed, and watched as his dream of the future had been reduced to all but an empty lot; the stays of execution must have been torturous.

The Outsiders, at long last, was ready for release. Warner Bros. still disliked Coppola's cut, but a sneak preview indicated that it was a hit among teenagers—a response that stayed consistent long after the movie's release. As a rule, critics despised the picture, but young audiences went to see it in flocks, making it one of Coppola's most profitable movies to date. The film's success would always have a mixed effect on Coppola. He was not one to look askance at the box-office figures—although, sadly, the money was coming in too little and too late to bail out Zoetrope—but as an artist, he was less than thrilled with the way the film had turned out. Some of his critics' complaints, he'd have to admit, were justified, but reviewers had not seen the film before it had been whittled down to its present state.

Coppola also resented what he perceived as a double standard in the way his movie was judged. "People expect me to demonstrate more of my own style," he grumbled. "Many directors make movies in the same style as *The Outsiders*. The actors are good; the story was the story and that's it. Yet when I do a film like that, people now expect it to have some loaded trap door. People expect me to be nutty, weird, or at least a little unusual or strange."

About the time *The Outsiders* was making its way into theaters across the United States, Coppola heard from Robert Evans, the former head of production at Paramount, now working as an independent producer. Evans had seen gangster lightning strike twice with the two *Godfather* pictures, and he was presently teamed up with Mario Puzo on a new mob picture, this one set in Harlem during Prohibition and the Harlem Renaissance. A lot of money had been invested in the picture's development and cameras were scheduled to roll within a few months.

Evans was in a panic. He and Puzo had yet to produce an acceptable shooting script, and investors were getting nervous. On a day-to-day basis, Evans had little use for Francis Ford Coppola, whom he regarded as a gifted but self-indulgent artiste committed to making the kind of movies that didn't stand a snowball's chance in hell of making big-time Hollywood money. Nor was Evans fond of Coppola personally. He was, however, an astute and pragmatic businessman who, like Vito Corleone, knew the difference between business and personal, and with his movie in trouble, he knew better than to stumble on his pride. Coppola might have been a lot of things, but he knew how to write a script.

Evans picked up the phone and called.

Chapter Thirteen

Tap Dancing Through Minefields

"I specialize in being the ringmaster of a circus that's reinventing itself."

—FRANCIS FORD COPPOLA

1.

ROBERT EVANS BECAME INVOLVED with *The Cotton Club* in late 1980, when he paid $350,000 for the motion picture rights to James Haskins's book about the storied Harlem nightclub. The book, a pictorial history of the club, might not have given Evans much of a plot for his movie, but he liked the concept: a glamorous nightclub set in Roaring Twenties Harlem, frequented by a glitzy whites-only crowd, which was entertained by some of the greatest black performers of the era. Duke Ellington and Cab Calloway had fronted the house band, and such performers as Ella Fitzgerald, Bessie Smith, Lena Horne, Josephine Baker, Bill "Bojangles" Robinson, Fats Waller, and Ethel Waters were regular entertainers; the tall, leggy, scantily clad coffee-and-cream-skinned dancers, the Cotton Club Girls, were the talk of the town. Mobsters, celebrities, members of high society, and political bosses were equally at home in the establishment. Evans saw great potential in the setting. He could present a *"Godfather* with music"—or, as he put it less delicately on another occasion, a movie with "gangsters, music [and] pussy—how could I lose?"

Evans needed a hit. After his unparalleled stint as head of production at Paramount, during which he had overseen production on a string of hits that included *Love Story, The Odd Couple, The Godfather,* and *Rosemary's Baby,* Evans had been awarded his own "Robert Evans Presents" banner at the studio. He struck gold with his first major production, Roman Polanski's *Chinatown,* but the films that followed, most notably *Black Sunday* and *Players,* had been nowhere near as successful with either the critics or at the box office. Evans was still a major player in Hollywood, but on the industry's "What have you done for me lately?" ladder of success, he had slipped a few rungs. A highly publicized drug bust and conviction had knocked him back a few more rungs. By his own estimation, his new gangster picture was going to redeem him.

"I've been involved with 200 pictures," he stated when announcing his plans for *The Cotton Club,* "and I've gotten to a time in my life when I'd rather spend four years on a movie that is a happening or an event than do four movies in a year. I'd rather be remembered than rich."

Evans knew nothing if not how to pitch a film concept, and for *The Cotton Club,* he came up with a poster and slogan before a single word of the screenplay had been written: "Its violence startled the nation; its music startled the world." A few years earlier, the slogan, along with Evans's impassioned sales pitch, might have caught the attention of a number of studios, but in this case, Evans met nothing but resistance. At the time, movies about African-Americans fared poorly among mainstream audiences, and the most recent black musical, *The Wiz,* had been box-office poison, despite its prior success as a Broadway musical and its stellar cast. Nor did it help that Evans had yet to receive any kind of firm commitment from a major star to appear in *The Cotton Club,* or that he didn't have a script to show around.

Eventually, Evans abandoned his attempts to sell his movie idea to the big studios and decided instead to finance the picture himself through private investors. Through Melissa Prophet, an actress friend who had appeared in *Players,* Evans met Adnan Khashoggi, an Arab arms trader who, a few years later, would gain notoriety as a result of his involvement in the Iran-Contra fiasco. Rather than finance the entire cost of the production, as Evans had hoped that he would, Khashoggi offered $2 million in seed money—more than enough to hire a scriptwriter and develop the project into something more than an idea. Evans offered Mario Puzo a million dollars to write a screenplay, hoping that he might do for *The Cotton Club* what he had done for the two *Godfather* pictures.

The Puzo connection had a mixed effect on the movie. Although Puzo struggled with the script and ultimately failed to present anything workable, the best-selling author's involvement in the movie raised the interests of several previously uninterested studios—a fortuitous turn of events, since Khashoggi dropped out of the project as soon as he saw Puzo's script. Employing the rumor mill to his advantage, Evans continued to firm up his project by trying to nail down bankable actors to appear in the movie. Al Pacino, Evans's first choice for the lead, wasn't interested, but Sylvester Stallone liked the project. After some negotiations, the *Rocky* and *Rambo* star agreed to play the film's lead for a $2 million salary. Robert Altman, who had directed *Popeye* for Evans, expressed interest in directing *The Cotton Club*. And Richard Pryor seemed willing to take the lead black role in the film.

Unfortunately, Evans's luck deteriorated quickly. Stallone, a hot commodity with the release of *Rocky III,* doubled his acting fee and was scratched from the picture. Pryor, advised that the film was headed for failure, escaped by similarly raising his acting fee to $4 million. Altman, tired of waiting for the plans to materialize, decided to direct another picture. Evans was able to find foreign distributors for *The Cotton Club,* but no studio in the United States would touch it.

He caught a huge break in October 1982, when he met with Ed and Fred Doumani, two wealthy brothers who owned, among other things, the Tropicana Hotel and the El Morocco Casino in Las Vegas. The Doumanis liked the project, which Evans pitched as a can't-miss proposition. Evans said he would be making his directorial debut on the movie, tentatively budgeted at between $18 and $20 million—a rather hefty price tag at the time, but by no means out of line for the kind of classy picture that Evans intended to make. The Doumanis, impressed with Evans's presentation, hooked up with Victor Sayyah, a Denver insurance tycoon who was a partner with the brothers in an oil interest, and in January 1983, the three agreed to back the production of *The Cotton Club.* Encouraged, Evans moved the picture into gear, setting a July start date and working on a rewrite of the Puzo script.

To Evans, the signs looked good. After losing Richard Pryor, Evans had signed Broadway dancer Gregory Hines as his replacement. Hines had seen a copy of the *Cotton Club* script in his agent's office, and over the ensuing weeks, he had actively campaigned for the role, deluging Evans's office with phone calls and, in one memorable encounter, leaping onto Evans's desk and improvising a tap dance. Evans, still holding out hope that he might talk Pryor into joining the picture, eventually caved in and hired Hines.

About the same time, Evans signed Richard Gere, fresh from his performance in *An Officer and a Gentleman,* for the movie's lead. Gere's involvement,
however, was problematic from the beginning. He agreed to appear in the picture on the condition that he have script approval, which assured the blos-
soming, image-conscious actor that he would be playing a sympathetic
character (rather than a gangster) in the movie, and that the role be written in
such a way that allowed him to play the cornet in the movie. Gere's first condition was relatively easy to accommodate, but the second created serious
problems, since white people never performed at the Cotton Club. In addition, Gere, who signed to do *The Cotton Club* for a $1.5 million fee, plus 10 per-
cent of the film's adjusted gross, was committed to appear in the title role of
King David at the end of the year, and to ensure a strict shooting schedule, he
demanded a fee of $125,000 for every week that the film ran over schedule. It
was a hard-nosed bargain, but one that Evans was happy to oblige.

With Gere on board, Evans was able to secure a $10 million distribution
agreement with Orion Pictures, which meant that he had enough money, at
least on paper, to make his picture. Evans began to assemble his production
team and, in a virtually unprecedented move, he negotiated with the New York
unions in an effort to convince them to alter their customary working and overtime arrangements, thus cutting back on some of the movie's expenses.

Everything appeared to be moving along, except for one major hitch: A
shooting script had yet to be approved. The Doumani brothers hated Evans's
revision of the original Puzo script and threatened to withdraw their money;
Gere, likewise, was making noises about pulling out unless the script was
given a considerable overhaul.

In an act of desperation that he would live to regret, Evans called an old
nemesis—a man he would bitterly refer to as "Prince Machiavelli."

"I have a sick child," he pleaded with Coppola. "I need a doctor."

2.

THE COPPOLA-EVANS COLLABORATION was as unlikely a union as one
could imagine. Neither cared for the other, personally or professionally,
although each conceded the other's considerable talents. Evans had decided to
stay away from studio financing for *The Cotton Club* because he wanted total control over his movie—a position that Coppola understood all too well—but in
approaching Coppola for help, Evans must have heard the sound of warning signals. Coppola, after all, had the well-earned reputation of taking over anything
in which he became involved. When he contacted Coppola, all Evans was looking for was a script doctor; he wound up getting much more.

Despite his negative feelings toward Evans, Coppola felt sorry for the man's predicament, and he volunteered to look over the *Cotton Club* script, free of charge, as a personal favor. After reading the screenplay, Coppola delivered a verdict that Evans already took for granted: The script, in its present form, was useless. Evans could talk all he wanted of putting together a movie with lots of guns, gangsters, sex, and jazz, but what he had in his present screenplay was joyless, unfilmable glop.

Coppola suggested that Evans, along with Richard Gere, Gregory Hines, and producer Dyson Lovell join him at his Napa Valley home for a brainstorming session. He then impressed them with his own vision for the film. It could be the story of the rise and fall of the Cotton Club, filtered through the perspectives of two minor characters—"Rosencrantz and Guildenstern, Harlem style," as he described it. The group was excited by the idea, and Evans offered Coppola a quarter of a million dollars to rewrite the script. Coppola accepted.

For Coppola, the move represented yet another step backward. *The Cotton Club*, even with its gangsters, was hardly the type of property that he would have chosen to work on had he not been so badly pressed for money. He loved opera, not jazz, and he knew virtually nothing about black culture, the Harlem Renaissance, or the political dynamics that governed the Cotton Club during its heyday in the twenties. The screenplay fee itself, while nothing to scoff at, was less than Coppola had commanded in the past.

Still, Coppola needed the work. It seemed that he could not call the office or look at a newspaper without being confronted with more bad news about the status of his studio. By the late spring of 1983, there had been so many foreclosure notices, threats of public auctions, and last-minute reprieves and reschedulings that *Variety* was characterizing the ongoing drama as boring, "something of an industry yawn"; by June 1, Security Pacific Bank alone had scheduled and rescheduled eleven auctions of the Zoetrope studio. There seemed to be no ending to the saga. "Just how much muddier the waters can get is anyone's guess," *Variety* offered, "but on top of all the other debts heaped up on the studio, the studio is also two and a half years delinquent in its county real estate taxes to the tune of $67,511.89."

Coppola threw himself into the *Cotton Club* script, flying to New York and researching the Harlem Renaissance and the Cotton Club. Before long, he had fallen in love with the excitement of the era. Evans, Coppola discovered, had been on the money when he saw the great potential for a film about the period; he and Puzo simply hadn't taken the right approach in working it into a screenplay. There were really two distinct stories to be told—divided, like the Cotton Club itself, along racial lines—but if they were properly integrated into a single script, much the way the stories of the two Corleones had been combined in *Godfather II*, *The Cotton Club* could be an amazing tale of a forgotten time, when some of the greatest cultural activity in America was taking place in a small section of upper Manhattan. The film could be both entertaining and educational.

Evans recoiled in horror when Coppola submitted his screenplay on April 5. Evans still wanted a slick, commercial dance and shoot-'em-up flick, and Coppola delivered a script that, as far as Evans was concerned, read like a PBS documentary, rich with details about the Harlem Renaissance but lacking the kind of story that Evans felt the movie needed. Worse yet, in bringing the Harlem Renaissance story to the forefront, Coppola had greatly shrunk Richard Gere's part, which was certain to meet both Gere's and the investors' disapproval. What had happened, Evans wondered, to the Rosencrantz and Guildenstern approach that Coppola had described at the Napa meeting? Disheartened, Evans asked Coppola to rewrite his script, which Coppola agreed to do—for an additional quarter of a million dollars.

At this point, Evans was caught in a bind, staring at nothing but problems. Preproduction on *The Cotton Club* was running at full speed in New York, with costly, extravagant sets being constructed and overall work on the film, at $140,000 per week, chewing up Evans's budget. The Doumanis, whose refusal to pay for Coppola's rewrite had forced Evans to pay the fee out of his own pocket, were willing to work with the Puzo-Evans script, if need be, while Orion, which had been touting the Puzo-Evans-Coppola *Godfather* team reunion, insisted on the Coppola script. Gere was pushing Evans to hire Coppola as the film's director. Meanwhile, Coppola slipped away to New Mexico to attend the Spirit of Zoetrope, a three-day film festival held in his honor in Santa Fe.

Evans continued to dance—for more time and money—with the worst possible results. The Doumanis had been demanding a look at Coppola's rewrite of the Puzo script, and on the weekend of the Academy Awards ceremony, Evans flew to Las Vegas to present the screenplay in person. Knowing that there was little chance that the brothers would approve the Coppola script, Evans composed a fake cover letter, supposedly written and initialed by Coppola, in which Coppola referred to the script as a "blueprint" for the screenplay that he intended to write. "Background makes foreground," the letter read, "now let's get to the foreground." As Evans feared, the Doumanis were not buying: They took one look at the script and promptly cut off all further funding of the movie.

A frazzled Robert Evans began searching for financing to keep his film's preproduction afloat, but he found no takers. He still hoped to avoid conventional studio financing, and private investors weren't interested. Finally, he heard from a woman calling herself Elaine Jacobs, who offered to connect Evans with Roy Radin, a variety-show promoter interested in becoming involved in Hollywood. Radin and Evans met in New York, and after an extended weekend of negotiations, the two formed a holding company in Puerto Rico, to the tune of $35 million (to be financed, supposedly, by the Puerto Rican government), which would back *The Cotton Club* and four future Robert Evans productions.

The pact, for Evans, amounted to a bargain with the devil, and it indicated just how desperate the producer had become. According to the two-page agreement, signed by Evans and Radin on April 26, 1983, the relationship between the partners was mutually exclusive, and neither could pursue a project without written permission from the other. Each owned 45 percent of the company, with the final 10 percent going to the Puerto Rican banker who set up the union with the government. In retrospect, the arrangement was hardly the kind of deal favorable to an independent producer hoping to maintain ownership of his films.*

In fact, Evans was having second thoughts about the partnership almost as soon as he had signed the papers. Radin continually badgered him about not talking to anyone without his permission, and Evans, who took great pride in his maverick reputation in Hollywood, resented Radin's position.

The partnership was short-lived. Soon after the agreement was drafted, Elaine Jacobs began demanding a cut of Radin's take as compensation for her part in introducing Evans to Radin. Evans backed Jacobs in the dispute, but Radin refused to part with the money, offering instead a flat fee of fifty thousand dollars. A few days later, back in Los Angeles, Radin and Jacobs decided to meet and see if some kind of deal could be worked out. Radin was last seen leaving his hotel and climbing into Jacobs's limousine, supposedly heading to a restaurant for dinner. Radin apparently feared for his safety, for he had arranged to have Demond Wilson, costar of the old television show *Sanford and Son,* follow the limousine. Wilson, armed in the event that anything went wrong, lost the limo in traffic. It was the last time anyone saw Radin alive. His decomposed remains were located a month later in a canyon north of Los Angeles. He had been shot in the head.

---

*Coppola maintains that he knew nothing about any of these arrangements.

3.

AFTER RETURNING TO CALIFORNIA from Santa Fe, Coppola resumed his work on a new rewrite of the *Cotton Club* script. Evans had hired an African-American actress named Marilyn Matthews, who had appeared in *Players,* to serve as an adviser and script consultant, but after working with her for a day or two, Coppola realized that she was there to carry the Evans banner. While Coppola campaigned for artistic integrity and historical accuracy, Matthews argued for employment. Blacks, she maintained, struggled to find any kind of work in Hollywood, and *The Cotton Club* presented a golden opportunity for a lot of people. Seeing his role as strictly work for hire, Coppola capitulated and rewrote the script that Evans wanted: more Gere and gangsters, less Harlem Renaissance.

The problems swirling around *The Cotton Club* blunted Evans's enthusiasm about making his directorial debut on the picture, and he offered Coppola the job when he, Richard Gere, Gregory Hines, and Dyson Lovell reconvened at the Napa estate to read and amend the new script. To Evans's surprise, Coppola turned him down. Coppola knew too much of the film's troubled past, as well as of Evans's history of interfering with his directors, to take on a project that was likely to make him unhappy. He told Evans that he would gladly assist him during the shoot, but he would not direct the movie.

"I always thought it was for him to direct," Coppola remembered. "Then he said that it was too big for him to direct, and that I had to. I refused many times, always offering to help him—to spend the first few weeks backing him up on the set. I didn't realize that he needed me to get the money, and he never said that. He was never honest with me."

Evans's troubles compounded, first with the disappearance of Roy Radin and then, a few weeks later, with the discovery of his remains. Suddenly Evans found himself at the police station, being questioned as a possible suspect in a crime that, to everyone's discomfort, would be known as "the *Cotton Club* murder." If there was one thing the picture did not need at this point, it was more bad publicity. Evans contacted attorney Robert Shapiro (who would later gain international notice as part of the O. J. Simpson defense team), and over the ensuing weeks, Evans's attention was understandably removed from the day-to-day operations of his motion picture.

He now needed Coppola more than ever, and, after giving the idea added consideration, Coppola agreed to direct *The Cotton Club* for $2.5 million, a cut of the gross, and the condition that he have complete creative control of the film. Evans agreed. He secretly believed that he could control Coppola—and he assured the Doumani brothers of as much when they worried about Coppola's reputation for being difficult to manage. By Evans's reasoning, Coppola, in his present financial position, would be so grateful for work on a good picture that he would be more malleable than usual. Coppola, quite naturally, saw it differently. "I told Evans that as a writer I would do it any way my director instructed me to," he remembered, "but if I became the director, I would need to have total control and the final cut."

Coppola wasted no time in establishing his authority in such vital decisions as the hiring of a production crew and casting his players. The issue of production crew was particularly sticky, since Evans, when planning to direct the picture himself, had hired his own crew, many with pay-or-play provisions in their contracts, meaning they would be paid their salaries whether they worked on the film or not. Nevertheless, Coppola, like all directors with clout, insisted on working with his own handpicked crew, and the bloodbath was on, beginning with Jerry Wexler, the movie's musical director (and legendary producer at Atlantic Records), who accepted an $87,500 buyout of his contract. Other Evans loyalists followed.

Two key positions—production designer and cinematographer—were more problematic. Coppola would have preferred Dean Tavoularis as production designer on *The Cotton Club,* but Tavoularis was already committed to another project. Richard Sylbert, a *Chinatown* veteran hired by Evans for *The Cotton Club,* was retained. Cinematographer John Alonzo, also of *Chinatown* fame and, more recently, the director of photography on *Black Sunday,* was a different story. After paying Alonzo $160,000 to leave the picture, Coppola cast around for a cinematographer more likely to achieve the stylish look that he wanted for *The Cotton Club.* Gordon Willis rejected the offer, and Evans talked Coppola out of hiring *Rumble Fish* lensman Steve Burum, who impressed Evans as being too artsy for the kind of commercial film the Doumani brothers wanted. After going over a list of candidates Coppola and Evans eventually agreed on Stephen Goldblatt, a British cinematographer best known for his work on *The Hunger.*

Evans was unhappy. Not only were Coppola's moves a kind of personal affront to the decisions he had made earlier; they also loosened his grip on the picture. In some cases, the positions represented rewards for past work on Evans productions, and Evans had been thrilled to work with these people again. Still, by terms of his agreement with Coppola, he had no alternative but to allow Coppola his choices.

The tension between Coppola and Evans finally erupted during a dispute over casting. Coppola wanted Fred Gwynne, whom he had seen in a standout performance in a stage production of *A Streetcar Named Desire,* to play the role of Frenchy, the sad-eyed mobster friend of Cotton Club owner Owney Madden. Evans, who could only picture Gwynne as Herman Munster, the Frankenstein-like character in the television sitcom *The Munsters,* hated the choice and demanded that Coppola find somebody else. Coppola, undoubtedly remembering his battles with Evans over the casting of *The Godfather,* flatly refused. He reminded Evans of his promise of complete artistic control, which included casting decisions; if Evans refused to honor the agreement, Coppola warned, he was going to pack up and head back to the West Coast. Gwynne stayed with the picture. Totally fed up with a director and film that seemed to be slipping from his authority on a daily basis, Evans concluded that it might be best if he stayed away from the *Cotton Club* set and Coppola entirely.

Other casting decisions were arrived at with far less difficulty. Richard Gere and Gregory Hines stayed on as Dixie Dwyer and Sandman Williams, the movie's leads, and Maurice Hines, Gregory's real-life brother, was signed to play his tap-dancing brother in the film. Bob Hoskins, the British character actor who had appeared in *The Long Good Friday,* was assigned the role of Owney Madden. Diane Lane, who had impressed Coppola with her work in *The Outsiders* and *Rumble Fish,* took the part of Vera Cicero, Dutch Schultz's (and Dixie Dwyer's) young lover, and Lonette McKee earned the role of Lila Rose Oliver, Gregory Hines's love interest. Coppola's nephew, Nicolas Cage, was given the part of Vince Dwyer, Richard Gere's younger brother.

As spring edged into summer with still no indication of a final shooting script, the film's start date was postponed until August, which might have bought Coppola more time to prepare but which, in turn, added hundreds of thousands of dollars to a budget long out of control. Evans had hoped to make *The Cotton Club* for about $20 million; the movie was more than three-quarters of the way there before the first day of shooting. Ironically, Coppola would inherit much of the blame for the picture's burgeoning expenses when, in fact, the film was a runaway train before he jumped aboard.

In mid-July, Coppola contacted novelist William Kennedy and asked him to help with the film's dialogue. Kennedy, the Pulitzer Prize–winning author of *Ironweed,* had come to Coppola's attention when Mickey Rourke sent the director a copy of *Legs,* Kennedy's novel about gangster Legs Diamond. Kennedy's sparse, spring-loaded dialogue seemed more authentic to Coppola than the words he had been assigning to his characters, and with the rescheduled start date only a month away, something had to be done to spruce up the script.

Over the following weeks, Kennedy, a novice to the business but a big fan of the movies, including Coppola's *Godfather* films and *Apocalypse Now*, received a crash course on screenwriting, Coppola-style. As a novelist, he was accustomed to working at his own pace, polishing and revising each passage until it had been pared down to its essence. After years of working under tight deadlines as a journalist, he found the method very satisfying—and effective. But after a few brainstorming sessions with Coppola in his Kaufman-Astoria Studios office, Kennedy discovered that Coppola not only wanted everything written at a rapid pace; he wanted economy of phrasing, as well.

"Concision is the operative word with Coppola, who will intercut even a shot scene with another one to accommodate the pace," Kennedy noted. "I thought I was already a concise writer, but after Astoria I created a screenwriting axiom: what you wrote yesterday, cut in half today."

Or, as Kennedy learned, much of what was written yesterday could be completely chopped from the script or moved to another part of the movie, necessitating more rewriting. The pace was frantic, the hours long. On one occasion, the two worked thirty-four sleepless hours; on another, they came up with five different scripts during a marathon forty-eight-hour session. Kennedy estimated that he and Coppola produced between thirty and forty scripts. Exhausted as he may have been, Kennedy wasn't complaining: He was eating and drinking well, hobnobbing with some of Hollywood's elite, and, in general, having the time of his life.

By now, Coppola had all but abandoned the Mario Puzo screenplay, and the efforts that he and Kennedy were producing differed significantly from the rewrite he had shown to Robert Evans, Richard Gere, and the company at the Napa meeting. Many of the changes were creative decisions, but some were inspired by budget. If money could be saved by shifting a scene from one location to another, Coppola did not hesitate to do so. The changes were quite unsettling to Richard Sylbert, who saw six of his seven shooting locations, along with ten of the sets he had designed, cut from the script. Worse yet, with time running out, Coppola could not give definitive directions about what he wanted. "Francis just flails around, hoping he'll pull it out of the air," Sylbert complained to a reporter. "He desperately wants to be Kurosawa, Fellini, Bergman. He resents being in the commercial, narrative Hollywood movie business."

Robert Evans, still camped out in his Manhattan town house and avoiding the set, sent along his comments on the screenplay, which, he told

Coppola, was "on the way to being not good—but great." Coppola, however, did not trust Evans's judgment or intentions, nor did William Kennedy, who was irked by Evans's blatant refusal to acknowledge his contributions to the script. ("I was the Invisible Writer," Kennedy lamented in "The Cotton Club Stomp," his entertaining account of his work on the movie.) For his part, Coppola continued to treat Evans as persona non grata, occasionally throwing his messages away without looking at them.

Evans, in fact, was in the process of making one final attempt to wrestle the film away from Coppola. Approaching Victor Sayyah, the Doumanis' partner in the film's financing, Evans criticized Coppola's screenplay, complaining that it wasn't the same as the previously approved script, and furthermore, with new drafts arriving every couple of days, there was no telling where Coppola was heading. It was time, Evans suggested, to issue an ultimatum to Coppola: Either turn in a final screenplay that everyone liked or shut down the production.*

"Let's go out there and take it over," Evans said, "and if Francis wants to walk, then forget the whole thing."

The two discussed their options throughout the night, but by the following morning, they had decided to drop the matter.

The Coppola-Evans feud, however, was only heating up.

4.

FILMING OF THE COTTON CLUB began on August 22, 1983, the production still plagued by problems, still lacking a final shooting script . . . and missing the headliner. When Coppola gathered his cast and crew at Prospect Hall in Brooklyn for the first day of shooting, Richard Gere was nowhere to be found.

Nor was he on the set the next day. Or the next. Throughout the first week of filming, Gere was a painfully noticeable absence, causing no end of concern to the people trying to film around him.

Gere's grievance regarding The Cotton Club was twofold, beginning with his frustration over the ever-evolving script. In rehearsals, Coppola had encouraged his actors to improvise their dialogue, which did not sit well with Gere, who, beside having a script-approval provision in his contract, took a more traditional approach in preparing for his role. Improvisation was not part of the

---

*According to Coppola, the major obstacle to completing the script was money. "They kept asking me to figure out ways to rewrite, to lower the budget," he told the author. "We always had a script, but they always wanted it cheaper. We kept trying."

deal. In addition, he was extremely dissatisfied with all the production delays, which, by August 22, had pushed the movie more than two months behind schedule. If he was going to appear in a film that was going to run over schedule, cause him a lot of grief on the set, and, in all likelihood, fare poorly at the box office, Gere wanted his contracted restructured—immediately.

During the first weekend of shooting, Gere, Evans, and their attorneys met to hash out a new agreement. Rather than receive $1.5 million and 10 percent of the adjusted gross, as per the original arrangement, Gere was paid a flat $3 million for appearing in the film, alleviating any of his concerns about box-office figures *and* establishing his salary as comparable to the highest-paid actors working at the time. In addition, Evans sweetened the kitty for Gere's compensation if the shooting went beyond October 29. Now, if Coppola insisted on making the movie by the seat of his pants, without a firm script and shooting schedule, Gere was in the position to score a handsome sum for working beyond the end of October. Happy again—or at least mollified—Gere returned to the fold.

Gere wasn't the only problem that Evans and the movie's investors had to face during the first week of shooting. On August 24, the film's title was challenged when a variety-show promoter named Bud Diamond filed a restraining order against Evans, Mario Puzo, the Doumanis' holding company, and others, claiming he owned the rights to the title, which he had been using for his programs for eight years. After checking into Diamond's story and determining that the promoter did indeed hold a patent on the title, the Doumanis settled out of court.

If all the chaos bothered Coppola, he showed no sign of it, at least not early on. If anything, he seemed to thrive on it. Perhaps, as in some of his other movies, he harbored the hope that something good would rise out of all the chaos and confusion—a memorable nugget shining amid the uncertainty clouding his script. He would have had reason for such faith. On the first day of shooting, Gregory Hines had improvised a dance that found its way into the finished film. Later in the shoot, Fred Gwynne improvised a scene with Bob Hoskins—in which Frenchy smashes Owney's treasured watch, only to replace it with a more valuable platinum one—that became one of the picture's more memorable moments.

Coppola might have been comfortable in allowing the events in the movie to develop at their own pace, but for those acting and investing in the film, it was an entirely different story. Richard Gere loathed what seemed to be such a reckless and unprofessional way of making a film, and Bob Hoskins complained that he had gained twenty pounds from inactivity. "You sort of sit around and eat and drink and philosophize," he said, "and suddenly you've forgotten what you do for a living."

Diane Lane made a similar observation. "My main experience on *The Cotton Club*," she remarked, "was lying down like I was in a tomb. I'd come in every day at 4:30 and they would start: They would tweeze my eyebrows and work on my hair. They would make me perfect. I was wearing clothes that Jean Harlow had worn in some of her films—archived costumes that came from Paramount. When they were finished, I'd lay down and cross my hands over my chest like Nosferatu when he went to bed at dawn, and I'd stay in my dressing room. Then, at four o'clock in the afternoon, they'd come and knock on my door and say, 'Miss Lane, it's okay to go. We're not going to use you today.' And this went on for months. We never knew when we were going to shoot."

Not everyone was content to sit and wait. Nicolas Cage, angered by the delays, took out his frustrations on his trailer, trashing it in a widely reported fit of rage. "I was very frustrated on *The Cotton Club*," he recalled. "I was slated for three weeks of work. I was there for six months, in costume, in makeup, on the set, in case Francis got an idea that would involve my character. Meanwhile, I'm getting offers for starring roles in other movies and I can't do them. So my behavior—all the acting out—came from frustration. I was young."

The investors were similarly displeased. With the film tallying enormous expenses, Ed and Fred Doumani, along with Victor Sayyah, tried to find ways to supervise the spending. For a while, Sayyah hung around the set and at Evans's town house, reading through the script revisions, watching Coppola at work, and growing increasingly frustrated with the whole affair. He finally boiled over after a heated argument with Melissa Prophet, now listed as an associate producer, and slammed the actress into a plate-glass window. He returned to Denver shortly thereafter.

Ed Doumani was next, flying in from Las Vegas for a personal look at the production. Although he would have been the first to admit that he knew very little about the motion picture business, he knew plenty about business in general, and what he saw in New York sickened him. Overspending was rampant, and everyone connected with the picture seemed to be living in an extravagant manner, something that Doumani could not understand. The Las Vegas businessman was accustomed to flying coach and taking cabs, and while in New York he stayed at Evans's town house, but such frugality escaped the people in the production, who flew first-class, stayed in the finest New York hotels, and were driven by limousine to the set. The shoot, costing roughly three hundred dollars per minute, was equally perplexing. Coppola was shooting seven to nine takes of each scene, spending what seemed to Doumani to be an inordinate amount of time and money in setting up and reshooting a scene that appeared to be quite suitable the first or second time around. "I tried very hard to stay calm," Doumani recalled.

Convinced that he needed a watchdog to protect his interests, Doumani contacted Sylvio Talbet, a Lebanese B movie producer, whom he installed as a coproducer and paid $200,000 to hang around the set and prod Coppola into moving more quickly and less expensively. Talbet, however, had little effect on the production. Coppola continued to work at his own pace, and the meter continued to run.

5.

UNBEKNOWNST TO COPPOLA, the Doumanis were running low on money. At its original $18 to $20 million budget, *The Cotton Club* was manageable, but after his trip to New York, Ed Doumani could see that there was no chance that the film was going to come in anywhere near those early projected figures. If he and his fellow investors couldn't come up with more money, the production was going to have to be shut down.

Coppola might not have known the gory details of the Doumanis' financial plight, but he was painfully aware of one thing: He was not receiving checks for his work on the picture. After a month on the shoot, he had yet to receive a cent of his director's fee—a situation that did not sit well with a man overwhelmed by his own financial woes, working endless hours on a film beset by problems, and trying to find ways to accommodate investors who insisted that he trim 20 percent of the picture's budget. Every day he seemed to hear more and more bad news from California, where the Zoetrope problems continued and creditors were making noises about taking his property; things were so tight that American Express canceled his credit card.

Meanwhile, the Doumani brothers went from bank to bank, hunting for a solution to their cash crunch. Lending institutions in Las Vegas, to Ed Doumani's dismay, suggested that he and Fred approach New York banks that traditionally financed motion pictures. New York banks wondered why they didn't approach the Las Vegas bankers they knew. A desperate Ed Doumani had to ask his son for a loan from his trust fund.

After five weeks of filming, Coppola moved the production to the Kaufman-Astoria Studios, where his production designer had constructed a replica of the Cotton Club interior. The New York studio, located in Queens, had a resonance of its own, which Coppola, as a student of film, was bound to appreciate. At one time, the Astoria had been a hotbed for the production of silent movies, and with the advent of talkies, the studio had been the site for films starring W. C. Fields, the Marx Brothers, Gary Cooper, and Claudette Colbert; Rudolph Valentino had lunched with his mother in the Astoria's cafeteria. The army had commandeered the studio during World War II, churning out armed forces radio broadcasts from the studio and housing soldiers in barracks built on the back lot. Like Coppola's own Hollywood General, the Astoria had fallen into disrepair, although in recent years, filmmakers had utilized the studio for interior scenes in such movies as *Fort Apache, the Bronx, The World According to Garp,* and *Arthur.* Recently, however, real estate developer George S. Kaufman, funded by government grants and loans, and private investors, who included Johnny Carson, Neil Simon, and Alan King, had undertaken a massive renovation program designed to turn the old studio into a modern state-of-the-art facility. *The Cotton Club* had been one of its first new customers.

On the studio's soundstages, Richard Sylbert had taken extraordinary measures to reproduce the club right down to the finest details, including the menus, wooden drink stirrers, and tiny frying pan ashtrays, his efforts soliciting raves from some of the older Cotton Club vets visiting the set. For Coppola, the dance routines to be shot here were extremely important—the only remnants of his original hopes of presenting some of the culture of the Harlem Renaissance in his film. In all, forty-eight dance numbers were to be worked into the movie, to be presented, for the most part, as fragments. A casting call held the previous August for dancers and extras had resulted in a turnout of 4,600 hopefuls. There would be little difficulty populating the screen version of the club. Coppola, however, was unhappy with Dyson Lovell's choreography. He had asked Lovell to design routines that were faithful to the period; instead, Lovell had come up with routines that impressed Coppola as being more like "an Ice Capades salute to Duke Ellington."

On September 25—known afterward as "Black Sunday" by the *Cotton Club* crew—Coppola fired Lovell and seventeen production technicians, many of whom had been hired by Robert Evans before Coppola's involvement in the movie, and who, Coppola felt, were too critical of his directing. Coppola replaced Lovell with Michael Smuin, who had choreographed the fight sequence in *Rumble Fish;* he was immediately put to work on redesigning the dance routines. In addition, Coppola hired jazz clarinetist Bob Wilber to oversee the picture's music—a wise choice but for one logistical problem: Wilber was currently playing a gig Tuesdays through Saturdays in Bern, Switzerland, and was unavailable indefinitely. On a couple of occasions, Coppola solved the problem, albeit expensively, by flying Wilber in on Sunday and sending him back, via the Concorde, on Tuesday, giving the jazzman two days a week to supervise the music on the picture.

By the end of September, Coppola's nerves were shot, the victim of one too many money worries. He tried to maintain his composure on the set, but, as reporter Michael Daly recounted in "The Making of *The Cotton Club*," his lengthy and exhaustively detailed *New York* magazine article on the movie, Coppola could be volatile away from the set. On one occasion, after taking a call from an attorney, Coppola smashed his hand onto his desktop, sending him to the hospital for X rays. Another time, he exploded and kicked a hole in his office door. Even for someone like Coppola, so experienced in working under the most trying of conditions, the pressure was intolerable.

Coppola rightfully resented not being paid for his work, and he finally lost his patience after a Saturday meeting with the Doumani brothers in early October. The Doumanis had finally run out of money and were unable to meet the weekly payroll. Just as vexing, as far as Coppola was concerned, were the brothers' latest efforts to cut costs and bring the budget under control. At the meeting, Ed Doumani informed Coppola that his share of the movie's profits was being reduced, and that he would be penalized if *The Cotton Club* came in over its schedule. Coppola, who had been working without a contract, went through the ceiling. Two days later, when it became evident that neither the Doumanis nor Robert Evans had any intention of backing off the terms set at the meeting, Coppola caught the Concorde for London, leaving the entire *Cotton Club* company to speculate on the future of the picture.

"I made a bargain with myself that I would be tolerant and helpful," Coppola explained at the time, "but now that we're beyond the halfway mark, my position is getting weaker and weaker." When asked how long he anticipated staying away from the picture, Coppola refused to speculate.

From a negotiating standpoint, Coppola had the upper hand in the dispute. As he pointedly reminded Evans and the Doumanis, they needed him more than he needed them. Industry insiders were presently projecting a $40 million price tag on the completed *Cotton Club,* and if Coppola left the picture, there was no telling how high the final numbers would rise. Coppola himself was not particularly worried. He needed money—lots of it—but he could always find work elsewhere. Ed Doumani backed down on Tuesday, agreeing to begin paying Coppola's salary, and to buy back some of Coppola's profit percentage. Coppola agreed to return to the set.

The next morning, Coppola was back at the Kaufman-Astoria studios, only to learn that the paychecks still hadn't been distributed and, as a consequence, the unions had shut down the production. Upon hearing the news, Coppola jumped up on one of the soundstages and, in one of his typical grand gestures, vowed to pay the cast and crew out of his own pocket if need be. Exactly how he intended to do so, given his financial situation, is unknown, but he was relieved of his promise when the checks arrived by armored car a short time later that day.

Rather than immediately return to work, Coppola decided to halt filming until the following Monday. Instead, he tried to boost spirits by throwing a huge party for the four hundred members of the company, capped by a showing of the assembled rough footage. Robert Evans, who had been barred from the daily screenings of the rushes and was therefore seeing the footage for the first time, watched with mixed emotions. Some of the scenes, he had to admit, were as powerful and beautifully rendered as Coppola's work in *The Godfather;* other scenes reminded him of Coppola's work in *Rumble Fish.* Evans held his breath. "I didn't know which way Francis was going to go," he told Michael Daly. "I was only hoping he wouldn't esoteric it up."

That weekend, *Rumble Fish* premiered at the New York Film Festival, touching off a new wave of controversy, first among the festival's five-member selection committee, which had haggled over whether to include the film in the festival, and then among critics, who disagreed vehemently about the film's merits.

If Coppola needed further evidence of the difference between the esoteric and the commercial, all he needed to do was compare the box-office performances of *The Outsiders* and *Rumble Fish.* Shot strictly as a commercial venture, *The Outsiders* enjoyed brief number-one status on the *Variety* box-office charts and eventually became a very profitable picture. *Rumble Fish,* with its black-and-white photography, darker theme, and R rating, barely made it out of the gate, performing so poorly that it was pulled from circulation after a brief, ignominious run.

6.

By mid-October, no one questioned whether Richard Gere would be collecting his overtime pay. *The Cotton Club* was so far behind schedule that Coppola was hoping to have the principal photography completed by Christmas. Insiders delighted in tallying up estimates for the film's final costs, most agreeing that the picture would have to be an enormous blockbuster on the scale of *The Godfather* to avoid losing money. Robert Evans's picture-book project had ballooned into a nightmare lasting over four years to date, and the clock was still ticking. Rumors coming from the set, including stories of extensive marijuana and cocaine use, festered like open sores. Evans and Coppola were barely on speaking terms.

According to Diane Lane, Coppola's relationship with Richard Gere was essentially a matter of an unsteady truce. "I didn't know what the hell was going on," she said, "but there was an unspoken awkwardness between them. When I worked with them, there was this tension—they were tolerating each other—and that was an uncomfortable position for everybody because the unspoken things are the things that scream out loud. I couldn't understand why it felt like Francis was Atlas, holding up the world while everybody was just beating him up, and I felt very protective of Richard, who's a private, vulnerable, spiritual man, and who's easily misunderstood. I felt like I should run between both camps and try to cheer them up. There was so much negativity going around."

Ironically, as a number of critics pointed out, the story behind the making of *The Cotton Club* proved to be more fetching than the plot of the movie itself. For all its problems, *The Cotton Club* was a relatively modest enterprise, featuring a plot that belies the extensive, maddening work done on the screenplay.

The action opens in 1928, with Michael "Dixie" Dwyer playing cornet in a small nightclub in Harlem. Dutch Schultz, a tough, violent bootlegger, is in attendance, as are a group of his henchmen and an aspiring young singer and nighclub owner named Vera Cicero. Both Dwyer and Schultz have their eyes on Vera, but she seems to be more taken with the musician than the gangster. Toward the end of the evening, gunmen from a rival gang burst into the club and open fire on the Schultz table. Dwyer pushes Schultz to the floor, saving his life. The grateful gangster promises Dixie that he will reward him for his efforts. After the club closes, Dixie takes a very drunken Vera home, but he resists her advances.

In parallel expository scenes, we see Dixie Dwyer and Sandman Williams, an aspiring black tap dancer, in their homes. In the absence of their fathers, both have assumed positions of authority, and both have brothers who resent it. Vince Dwyer, Dixie's younger brother, is a recently married street punk hoping to rise in the Harlem numbers racket, and he uses Dixie's newfound favor with Dutch Schultz to land a job with the mobster. Clay Williams, Sandman's brother, is also a tap dancer, and though the two work together as a team, it's obvious that Sandman is the more gifted of the two.

The Williams brothers have an audition at the Cotton Club, the finest of the Harlem nightclubs, and while they are there, Sandman meets and instantly falls in love with Lila Rose Oliver, one of the light-skinned dancers employed by the establishment. Lila Rose, with show business dreams of her own, is flattered by Sandman's attention, but she repels his initial advances.

As it turns out, Dutch Schultz's way of repaying Dixie is to make him little more than an indentured servant. Dwyer is expected to escort Vera Cicero, now Schultz's mistress, whenever Schultz's wife is around, or perform odd jobs that include such degrading tasks as fetching Dutch's laundry. Dixie dislikes the job from the onset, but Dutch makes it clear that Dixie will not be voluntarily leaving his employ.

The Harlem bootlegging scene has become volatile in recent days, capped by the attempt on Dutch Schultz's life. Owney Madden, the Cotton Club owner—a gangster himself and arguably the most influential figure in Harlem—arranges a meeting between Schultz and his biggest rival, Irish mobster Joe Flynn, to try to score a truce. It's not meant to be. During the meeting, Schultz and Flynn quarrel violently, and Schultz stabs Flynn to death as Madden, Dixie, and Vera look on.

For Dixie, who only wants to play his cornet in the area nightclubs, life suddenly seems to be spiraling out of control. He is working for a murderous thug and, despite his sometimes testy relationship with Vera, he has fallen in love with his boss's mistress. However, Dixie is blessed with a chance for escape when, one evening at the Cotton Club, actress Gloria Swanson, one of the club's celebrity customers, spots him and declares that he has the looks of a movie star. Owney Madden, aware of Dixie's feelings for Vera and fearing for his safety, arranges for Dixie's screen test.

Meanwhile, things are going poorly for Sandman Williams. He and his brother have a falling-out after the Cotton Club gives Sandman some solo work. Lila Rose, tired of the abuse heaped upon the black performers in the club, decides to look elsewhere for work. Sandman asks her to marry him, but she turns him down.

Time passes. The stock market crashes. Dutch Schultz, now at the height of his powers, wages a war on the Harlem numbers gangs. Vera, as promised, has been given a nightclub by the mobster, which she subsequently turns into one of the most popular clubs in town. Dixie makes a movie called *Mob Boss,* modeling his character after Schultz. Sandman becomes one of the top acts at the Cotton Club.

Vinnie Dwyer, however, is unhappy. He wants a bigger percentage of the numbers racket, but he is rebuffed when he confronts Dutch Schultz and demands a better cut of the action. Rather than submit to Schultz, Vinnie strikes out on his own, setting off additional gang warfare, climaxing in a bloody street scene, in which five children are caught in the gunfire and killed by a carload of Vinnie's thugs. Knowing that he is a marked man, and needing money to leave town, Vinnie kidnaps Frenchy, Owney Madden's right-hand man, and demands fifty thousand dollars in ransom. Vinnie insists that the money be delivered by Dixie, who is in town for a visit. Dixie takes the ransom money to Vinnie, realizing that this is probably the last time he will see his brother alive.

In a contrasting scene, we see the reconciliation between the Williams brothers, when Sandman visits a club to watch his brother's act. Clay and Sandman perform an impromptu tap dance duet to "Crazy Rhythm," sealing their reunion. (Dixie and Vera are similarly brought back together, when Dixie visits her club and they perform "Am I Blue?" together, Vera singing while Dixie plays cornet.) Sandman has also been reunited with Lila Rose, although their relationship seems as uncertain as ever. Lila is singing at Vera Cicero's nightclub, passing herself off as white, and Sandman is angry that she would work in a place where blacks are not welcome.

Vinnie, as feared, is cut down by Dutch Schultz's men, but the victory will be short-lived. These are times of change, symbolized by Cab Calloway's taking over Duke Ellington's position as leader of the Cotton Club's orchestra. To the underworld, Dutch Schultz is dangerous and out of control, and Lucky Luciano, now a Cotton Club regular, is eager to assume his status as head of the underworld.

Dixie Dwyer, eager to return to California, is trying to figure a way to get Vera to leave with him, especially in the wake of an ugly confrontation at the Cotton Club, where Dutch Schultz's wife catches Vera and her husband together. Dixie defends Vera against both an enraged Schultz and his wife. He punches Schultz in the face, and the gangster vows revenge.

The story reaches its conclusion in another classic piece of Coppola montage. While Sandman tap-dances, providing a rhythm for the action on-screen, Dutch Schultz and his men are gunned down by Luciano's men in a tiny restaurant; Vera and Dixie discuss their relationship and reluctantly agree that they should split up; Owney Madden is arrested and sent off to prison; and Sandman and Lila Rose marry. Then, in an epilogue staged at Grand Central Station, the Cotton Club dancers perform while Dutch Schultz's casket is being wheeled through the station, Sandman and Lila depart for their honeymoon, and, in a surprise development, Dixie finds Vera waiting for him on the train platform. She will be leaving with him after all.

7.

ED AND FRED DOUMANI were justifiably bitter over having to hire babysitters to watch over their investment. Victor Sayyah had been unable to figure out the motion picture business, and Sylvio Talbet, who supposedly knew something about making movies, had been unable to control Coppola. The brunt of the Doumanis' anger, however, was directed at Robert Evans, the original producer-director of the picture, who, the Doumanis felt, should have worked more vigilantly to see that their money was being well spent.

"He abnegated that responsibility," Fred Doumani said. "Most of the fighting should never have happened. But Bob Evans went to New York, worked out of his townhouse, visited the set for about one hour and never went back again."

The Doumani brothers were receiving the worst-possible kind of education about the film industry. The agreement with Orion did not include completion money, and there was great uncertainty about the Doumanis' ability to come up with the cash needed for postproduction, and there was still no guarantee that Coppola would be finished by the holidays. What they needed, the Doumanis reasoned, was someone with real muscle—somebody who could frighten Coppola, if necessary, into completing his picture sometime in the near future.

Joey Cusumano, hired by the Doumanis to fill those shoes, had a history that, if not coming from *The Cotton Club,* sounded as if it had been scripted for *The Godfather.* A friend of Anthony Spilotro, reputedly the head of the Mafia in Las Vegas, Cusumano had been the target of a decade's worth of bugging and wiretapping, and while he would eventually be convicted of labor racketeering, at the time of his association with *The Cotton Club,* he was simply the kind of shady figure that the FBI liked to tail. Unfortunately for the Doumanis, Coppola had dealt with people like Cusumano in the past, and he was adept at playing games involving ego and power.

Every day, Cusumano would arrive on the set, where he stood quietly and watched the action, occasionally posing questions to production workers but never challenging Coppola, and taking mental notes on how films were made. Instead of finding fault with Coppola's method, Cusumano grew to respect the director—and vice versa. One morning, upon arriving on the set, Cusumano found a chair labeled "Joey" placed next to Coppola's. ("I'm glad you're sticking around," Coppola told him.) It was a brilliant move. Before long, Cusumano was schmoozing with Coppola, watching the videotaped rushes in Silverfish, dining on Coppola's spaghetti, and—most important to Coppola—assuring his bosses in Las Vegas that all was well on the set, that Coppola needed to make his movie without worries about its budget.

Such sentiments, however, were not shared by the people backing the picture. The Doumanis were again running perilously low on cash, to such an extent that it looked as if they might not be able to meet the company's payroll even if Coppola completed the film by Christmas. The Doumanis impressed upon Cusumano the importance of finishing the movie on time, and he, in turn, passed the point on to Coppola. As a reminder, Cusumano printed T-shirts with DECEMBER 23, 1983 emblazoned on the backs for members of the crew. With Coppola, he was much less subtle. "You see this Silver Fish?" he said. "If we go past the twenty-third, this is going in the ocean with the rest of the fish."

Robert Evans had reached the limits of his own patience with the project. For months, he had watched his authority over the picture gradually stripped away to nothing, even though he was expected to help find more money to keep it running; he had not received a penny in salary for his efforts, and his percentage in the film's profits was looking like so much ink on paper. His personal credit was in serious jeopardy. As recently as mid-October, Evans had been issuing blustery proclamations about his position in the production—"I am the producer. I hired Mr. Coppola. He did not hire me"—but now, faced with the prospects of having to mortgage his Beverly Hills mansion and possessions to keep the picture afloat, he erupted angrily at the injustice of it all. Not surprisingly, Coppola was the focus of his discontent. Coppola's script problems, Evans told the *Washington Post,* had made it impossible for investors to negotiate completion money for the film.

Infuriated by the article, Coppola fired off a vitriolic telegram to Evans's town house, accusing Evans of double-crossing him. Evans, Coppola vowed, would see none of *The Cotton Club* until it was an answer print. "If you want a PR war or any kind of war," Coppola warned, "no one is better at it than me."

The next day, Evans responded in kind, telling Coppola that he couldn't understand what prompted his outburst "when all I do is praise your extraordinary talents as a filmmaker." Evans went on to accuse Coppola of being unconcerned and dishonest, and he concluded his message with a warning of his own: "Do not mistake my kindness for weakness." The macho posturing between the two became so ridiculous that, according to one account, they actually considered fighting a duel, not with guns but with fists.

In all likelihood, Evans could see the harsh reality of his predicament. He almost certainly knew the significant details of Coppola's travails during the making of *One from the Heart,* and Evans was presently in much the same position with *The Cotton Club.* He had gone to extraordinary measures to hold on to the property, but he could see it sliding away, even as he slipped beneath the surface of an ocean of money problems.

He lost his final hold on the movie a short time later, when he made a last-ditch effort to come up with the funds to finish the production. After

Orion steadfastly refused to release any money until the film was in the can, Evans approached Barry Diller of Paramount to see if his old company would bail out the movie. The problem was, no studio—Paramount included—could become involved as long as Orion held the distribution rights—unless Evans declared bankruptcy, voiding his contract with Orion, and started over. The legal proceedings alone would have put an end to *The Cotton Club*.

Orion, although upset by Evans's dealings, eventually agreed to provide $15 million for completion financing, on one important condition: Robert Evans was to relinquish the rest of his control over *The Cotton Club*, including his interests in production, distribution, and advertising. He could still hold on to his 32 percent of the film's profits, but in every other respect, he was out of the picture. Evans reluctantly agreed.

"It was like giving up your kid," a dejected Evans admitted, "but I had no choice. I gave up everything."

The acrimony, however, was far from over, as Evans, Coppola, the Doumanis, and others would discover in the months ahead, when legal battles over *The Cotton Club* bound the reluctant participants together until all would regret ever having heard of the movie.

For the time being, Coppola rushed to meet the production's December 23 deadline. Script revisions were no longer part of the equation; whatever they shot would have to be pieced together into a coherent story during the editing process. Throughout December, Coppola worked at breakneck pace, pushing cast and crew through marathon shooting sessions, including a sequence at Grand Central Station that lasted from 6:00 one Friday evening until 1:30 the following afternoon. In one three-day stretch, Coppola accomplished an incredible forty setups before moving his crew to Harlem for a week of location shooting. After months of deliberate structuring of his picture, Coppola was shooting a huge portion of it in a three-week period. December 23 arrived, and Coppola, not quite finished, forged ahead, working through the day and night, stopping at 6:00 A.M. on Christmas Eve. Somehow, to everyone's amazement, the bulk of the principal photography had been completed. All that remained was a couple of weeks' worth of close-ups and special-effects shooting. Rather than have the traditional wrap party, the exhausted production company members broke up and went their separate ways for the holidays.

8.

THE FINAL TAB ON THE *Cotton Club* production stood at a hefty $47 million, and even so, stopping at that figure required some fancy footwork. When shooting resumed after the holiday season, there was only $1.5 million left from the Orion money, and Coppola found himself cutting corners to finish the film. Props were cut back or eliminated and bargains were struck on location rentals.

It was a difficult period for Coppola. On February 19, 1984, a dream came to an end with a public auction of the Zoetrope Studios property. Through a series of agreements with his creditors, Coppola had been able to avoid personal bankruptcy, but his studio had not been as fortunate. Jack Singer filed a Chapter 11 involuntary bankruptcy petition against Zoetrope, cutting off further talk of selling the studio and forcing its sale at a public auction. Robert Spiotta, who had worked tirelessly in trying to generate a sale of the studio, resigned as Zoetrope's president, and all that seemed to remain was the determination of the studio's future owner.

The minimum bid on the property was set at $12.2 million—roughly $4.5 million less than its appraised value—but even so, there was little interest in the studio. Jack Singer's $12.3 million bid wound up being the highest offer, and the Hollywood lot, to the wealthy businessman's delight, became Singer Studios. "The studio is a historic site," he noted, sounding a lot like its previous owner. "We're going to do our best to make it a beautiful, viable studio." On March 10, to raise money to pay his loan, Singer held a public auction of Zoetrope's props, costumes, and memorabilia. While the sale of the property was painful to Coppola, he managed to retain Silverfish and a lot of technical equipment, as well as his personal property in northern California. He had also worked out an agreement whereby he would be able to retain and use the Zoetrope title in the future, even though the actual studio had ceased to exist.

Coppola completed the filming of *The Cotton Club* on March 31, and after a brief vacation in England, he began the task of trying to edit nearly half a million feet of film into a two-hour movie. The Doumanis, sorely in need of Orion's distribution money to make payments on short-term loans, pressured Coppola about finishing the postproduction in a hurry—a tall order, since Coppola was still trying to make sense of his movie's plot. He had shot much more film than he could ever squeeze into the movie, so sacrifices had to be made. Dance numbers fell by the wayside, as did scenes that fleshed out the film's main characters. William Kennedy, on hand to help firm up the movie's plot during the editing process, hated to see some of the cuts, but he admitted that he was in no position to second-guess the director.

"There was more in almost every direction you can imagine," he said, "including Dutch Schultz' mother, an old Jewish woman who goes shopping and has dinner with Schultz and Vera; Gregory's relationship with the black numbers barons; Diane's relationship, in more detail, to Dutch; Gere's family;

the Williams family; Winnie and Bumpy—all these were developed in a lot of directions. Great musical numbers were cut out."

Despite all the heavy-duty editing, the first cut ran about fifteen minutes too long, resulting in a pace that, to Kennedy, seemed to drag. Coppola, along with editors Barry Malkin and Robert Lovett, trimmed an added seventeen minutes from the movie, but the new version, shown to Orion officials in New York, seemed to be full of holes. It moved too quickly and, in Orion's opinion, needed more love scenes and less tap dancing. Unfazed, Coppola returned to the editing room.

"After that two-hour screening that didn't work," Kennedy remembered, "we put back about eleven minutes, and that made all the difference. And that week he had very good reactions. Now that wasn't, by any means, the final version. He kept changing and adding and going back, even after the print was in processing. He's a man who just doesn't give up until he gets exactly what he thinks works."

9.

COPPOLA WOULD NEED ALL the determination and stamina that he could muster, for even as he grappled with the postproduction on *The Cotton Club*, a series of nasty and complicated battles over the movie was being staged in the courtroom, delaying the film's release for nearly six months. At times, there appeared to be so many players involved in the different scenes of the drama that it was virtually impossible to follow the action with any true understanding of what was going on. However, one could cynically state that the entire messy affair was pure Hollywood, complete with warring egos, shameless moneygrubbing, melodramatic posturing, and just enough sleaze to keep the Hollywood rumor mills and trade papers buzzing for months.

Robert Evans had not faded into the background after the Orion bailout. If anything, he was as angry and frustrated as ever. Being cut out of the picture after years of involvement had frosted Evans beyond belief. As far as he was concerned, he had been publicly humiliated by Coppola, the picture's investors, and Orion; his professional reputation, cultivated over years in the business, had been sullied. In filing suit against the Doumanis, Coppola, and Orion Pictures, Evans hoped to be awarded at least some say in how *The Cotton Club* would be advertised and distributed.

A second lawsuit, filed by Victor Sayyah against Evans, the Doumanis, Orion, and the *Cotton Club* production company, was actually little more than a transparent attempt to recoup his investment money. The Doumanis, Sayyah posed, had been less than truthful when they approached him about becoming a partner in the film. For his $5 million, he was supposed to have been investing in a $20 million picture; instead, the costs had risen to the neighborhood of $50 million, which, he claimed, constituted a breach of contract.

Other suits followed, including an action taken by restaurateur John Rockwell, who wanted a $2.1 million finder's fee for introducing Robert Evans to the Doumanis. A suit filed by Susan Mechsner, who had supposedly been promised a starring role in the film, plus 2 percent of the movie's net, allegedly as a reward for her role in helping Evans deal with the Doumanis, sought damages for the mental distress that Mechsner felt when she saw the film and learned that she had been cut from all but one scene. Sylvio Talbet, the Doumanis' watchdog on the *Cotton Club* set, felt he had been slighted by the Doumanis and the production company, and he sued for a coproducer credit and $6 million in damages.

Of the many cases, the Evans-Doumanis clash appeared to be the most serious. Although each action had to be addressed, clogging up the courtrooms and filling lawyers' pockets for their participation in what amounted to little more than nuisance suits, the other suits were relatively easy to settle. Evans, on the other hand, in opening up such issues of power and prestige, was charging into sacred territory. Regardless of what people thought of him personally—and he had long lines of both supporters and enemies—it was undeniable that Evans was a major figure in the business, and that he had been muscled out of a picture that he had developed and pursued on his own long before the other principal figures had jumped on board. Questions needed to be answered. Perhaps most importantly this: Had Evans been pushed off his own picture as a result of a power play or conspiracy, or had he been removed as a result of his own actions, judged by the others to be detrimental to the picture?

In court, all the familiar complaints and accusations were trotted out before a judge so amazed by what he was hearing that he compared the various statements to Kurosawa's classic movie *Rashomon,* in which one event is seen and interpreted differently by a handful of witnesses. Evans was attacked personally and professionally, depicted as a man who lived the good life during the filming, never visiting the set and, in general, jeopardizing the production from the beginning, when he failed to show the investors a finished script or detailed budget. During his testimony, Coppola presented a balanced account, conceding that Evans had contributed significantly to the film's development but arguing that he had also been largely responsible for the chaos that plagued the picture. Any further involvement, Coppola insisted, would only hurt the picture by driving up its budget and delaying its release.

"It fills me with horror," Coppola stated, "to think that it could go back to the way it was. My only goal is to get out of the job and get on with my life."

It was Evans, however, who delivered the greatest performance. Breaking down in tears on the witness stand, he impressed the judge with his impassioned plea for a say in a project he had labored for so long to bring to the screen. Money, Evans told the court, was not an issue, even though he had sunk everything he had into the picture; what he wanted was at least a hand in how *The Cotton Club* was marketed.

The decision of the U.S. district court judge, Irving Hill, although technically a victory for Evans, was a mixed bag. On June 18, Hill granted Evans a preliminary injunction over his adversaries, tossing *The Cotton Club* into limbo until later hearings resolved the dispute. In addition, Evans regained marketing and distribution control of the film. He was not, however, given any say in the movie's postproduction, which meant that Coppola and his team would be free to complete the picture without any interference from Evans. Nevertheless, Evans was thrilled. "I gave the triumvirate a second asshole," Evans crowed in his 1994 autobiography, comparing his court battle to the confrontation between David and Goliath. "The kid stayed in the picture."

But not for long. In August, using his court victory as a bargaining chip, Evans met with the Doumanis and struck a settlement, whereby he would forsake all of his interests in the picture in exchange for a cash settlement and the forgiving of a $1.6 million note the Doumanis held on Evans's home. He would also be used by the Doumanis as an adviser, and would receive screen credit in *The Cotton Club*. Evans was ecstatic, the Doumanis were ecstatic, and the Hollywood trades reported the agreement the way they might have reported a reconciliation between longtime lovers. The Doumanis hinted of future projects, and Evans gushed about their newfound relationship. "Through hardship," he told *Variety*, "we have come close now. In essence, I'm working for the Doumanis; it's like working for a studio."

Evans could not have expected more. The court case had restored some of his bruised reputation, and the settlement had restored some of his cash. By Hollywood standards, it was a sweetheart bargain.

10.

COPPOLA, OF COURSE, had better things to do with his time than to while away his hours in a courtroom. Not only did he have a film to edit; he also had to start thinking about future projects. He had to keep working just to honor the terms of his payment agreements on his monstrous personal debt. He hated being in that position, which took away some of his options on the kind of films he would be directing, but it was better than the alternative deal. Better to work as a hired gun than to lose the Sentinel Building in San Francisco, the Napa Valley estate, or other prized possessions.

As he liked to boast to the press, Coppola never lacked projects to pursue. *The Outsiders* was being developed as a television series, the action to begin where the movie left off. After years in the planning, *Mishima*, the film biography of Japanese writer Yukio Mishima, to be directed by screenwriter and UCLA alumnus Paul Schrader, was finally coming to pass. Coppola had originally wanted to make the film a Zoetrope production, but in the wake of the *One from the Heart* disaster, he could not afford to finance it. Ironically, George Lucas rescued the picture, convincing Warner Bros. to sink $5 million into the production. Coppola, whose name would appear with Lucas's above the film's title, was pleased.

He was uncertain which full-length feature he would be directing next, but he was intrigued by a smaller television project that came his way. Actress Shelley Duvall, a veteran of a number of Robert Altman films, including a starring role opposite Robin Williams in *Popeye,* hosted a Showtime cable television series called *Faerie Tale Theater,* in which classic fairy tales were overhauled and given creative modern treatment, and for nearly two years, she had been trying to land Coppola as a director for one of the program's installments. Coppola had always been too involved in directing his big-screen pictures and running his studio to find time to work on the show. Coppola's daughter, Sofia, was approached about appearing in one of the segments, and Coppola had accompanied her when she taped the show in September. Duvall had made her first pitch at that time: The series would be taping its twenty-eighth and final installment shortly after Thanksgiving, so if Coppola intended to direct an episode, he'd have to do it then. Coppola jumped on board.

In a way, it was an ideal opportunity. He wanted to test some of his new video technology on television, and he viewed his contribution, a fifty-minute retelling of Washington Irving's "Rip Van Wrinkle," as a good vehicle. He was also eager to attempt something very different visually from the usual children's fare, and to achieve this new look, he hired Eiko Ishioka, the Japanese costume and production designer who had worked on *Mishima.* By Coppola's standards, the program's $650,000 budget and six-day shooting schedule was minuscule, but he was excited by the prospects.

"The bigger the budget, the less freedom you have and the less money you have actually available," he said, adding that such movies as *The Rain People, The Conversation,* and *Rumble Fish* were "much freer, more extravagantly artistic" than his big-budget movies. "I think I'm better suited to a medium where the budgets are smaller and yet the imagination is bigger."

By early October, Coppola was satisfied enough with the editing of *The Cotton Club* to preview the picture before audiences in San Diego, Boston, and Seattle. As usual, he used the occasions to gauge public reaction to the film; this response would then influence future cuts and edits of the picture. *The Cotton Club*, Coppola realized, had suffered as much negative prerelease publicity as *One from the Heart*, and he was anxious to see how real moviegoers, as opposed to studio executives and distributors, would respond to the movie. To his delight, people seemed to enjoy it.

He received one detailed, unanticipated response. Robert Evans had attended the San Diego preview as a paying customer and had been deeply disappointed by what he'd seen. In Evans's opinion, Coppola had edited *The Cotton Club* the same way he had edited *The Godfather;* he had left some of his best work on the cutting room floor. Great dance numbers had been butchered or cut entirely; the film's texture—always a Coppola long suit—was missing. Evans rounded up Ed and Fred Doumani and explained his feelings, saying that there was still a chance to save the film if Coppola was willing to listen to some of his suggestions. For the next fourteen hours, Evans composed a thirty-one-page epistle, complete with detailed suggestions on how to improve the film, from opening credits to ending. In his cover letter, Evans tried to strike a conciliatory chord, praising the director's brilliance and imploring that they put their past differences behind them for the good of the film.

Ed Doumani decided to deliver the letter personally to Coppola, and as soon as Evans had completed his opus, Doumani lit off for the Napa estate, racing along the highway as if he had a deadline to meet. He had hoped to speak to Coppola directly, but the meeting never occurred. At the filmmaker's home, Doumani was met by Barrie Osborne, who was working closely with Coppola on the *Cotton Club* editing. Osborne promised to pass along the letter. Whatever Coppola thought of Evans's letter, he did not see fit to respond.

What he thought of Evans's suggestions, however, was crystal-clear: When *The Cotton Club* was released, not one of Evans's suggestions had found its way into the finished film.

11.

THE COTTON CLUB PREMIERED on December 2, 1984, in William Kennedy's hometown of Albany, New York, at a gala charity event that included a costume ball after the screening of the movie. On December 10, the film opened in New York.

Coppola, at work on *Rip Van Winkle* in Los Angeles, attended neither event, nor was he feeling particularly gracious or charitable when questioned about the reasons for his absence. "I didn't want to show up at the premiere for one reason," he said. "I didn't want to be involved with those people. They have been my most horrible enemies. What's that word? Calumny. That's the word for it. Evans is a liar, you see. I almost think he would love this picture to be a gigantic flop."

Evans, also a no-show at the two premieres, was perhaps a bit more generous in his response to similar inqueries about his absence, but not by much. "*The Cotton Club* is a dazzling movie," he allowed, "but it's Francis's movie, not mine. The picture I wanted is on the cutting room floor."

The rancor between the two never abated, even when they gave interviews to promote the picture. Evans, now cozy with Ed and Fred Doumani, accused Coppola of running up the movie's budget. "Coppola came in with his contingent, his perks, and his per diems," Evans groused. "He had profiteered from the film and raped the Doumanis."

"Had they not hired me," Coppola responded, "the film wouldn't have been made. I got a call and took over the picture, and now they're blaming me for what happened in the last five years."

The verbal jousting, a fitting postscript to the film's beleaguered history, probably heightened the curiosity level for a movie that, under other circumstances, might have come and gone with only marginal interest. The picture itself, like *The Outsiders,* seemed nothing like a Coppola movie, and for all the effort, money, and emotion that he had sunk into the film, Robert Evans might have had good reason to feel cheated by the final product. It certainly was no *Godfather* with music, as he had originally hoped; at best, it was simply a cut above the ordinary.

The critics noted as much in their reviews of the film. Most reviewers appeared to be relieved that Coppola had abandoned the young adult market of *The Outsiders* and *Rumble Fish,* but few were ready to mark *The Cotton Club* as Coppola's comeback production. Nor were they willing to dismiss the movie's colorful history and judge the film strictly on its own merits. Two influential critics compared *The Cotton Club* to *Cleopatra,* the Richard Burton–Elizabeth Taylor epic that, like the Coppola film, had cost a small fortune and entertained gossip mongers at least as much as it entertained moviegoers.

"It is the sorry fate of some big-budget movies to be remembered as the indifferent sequels to their own prerelease publicity," wrote Richard Corliss in *Time.* "Mention *Cleopatra* and the memory swirls, not with images from the film but with tabloids screaming the latest indiscretion of Liz and Dick. Mention *The Cotton Club* 20 years from now, and the graybeards will have forgotten whether it was a good film or a bad one." *The Cotton Club*, Corliss concluded, was "not a bad film, just a bland one; not inept, just inert."

Vincent Canby, writing for the *New York Times*, echoed these sentiments almost to the letter: "Just as *Cleopatra* was somewhat better than its harshest critics said, and considerably worse than its supporters thought, *The Cotton Club* is not a complete disaster, but it's not a whole lot of fun. It just runs on and on at considerable length, doing obligatory things, being philosophically fancy but demonstrating no special character, style, or excitement."

Another focus of attention dealt with Coppola's own past. He had set a standard for the gangster picture with his two *Godfather* epics, and *The Cotton Club* seemed to have fallen short of that standard. "In *The Cotton Club*," noted Stanley Kauffmann in *The New Republic*, "[Coppola] has made a picture with much of the manner and matter of the very gangster films he once tried to supersede."

Pauline Kael, no fan of Coppola's electronic cinema, combined her disdain of his technique with her scorn for his abandoning the style she had praised in her earlier reviews of his two *Godfather* films. "If a whiz-kid director from the three-minute-rock-video field tried his hand at a Jazz Age gangster musical, the results might be *The Cotton Club*," she sneered. "Francis Coppola, who co-wrote and directed it, seems to have skimmed the top off every twenties-thirties picture he has seen, added seltzer, stirred it up with a swizzle-stick, and called it a movie." Kael's *New Yorker* review, by far the nastiest notice that Coppola would receive for *The Cotton Club*, attacked Coppola on every front, including the way he handled the Harlem Renaissance. "A great time in the history of black people has been screwed over," she charged. Coppola, who had tried so hard to fit more of the Harlem Renaissance into the film, only to be thwarted by the picture's backers, must have winced at the remark.

The movie, however, found plenty of fans among the critics. Jack Kroll, of *Newsweek*, after noting the film's tumultuous history, praised *The Cotton Club* as "one of the few original films of the year, a movie of driving pace and swirling style whose major fault is that it should be longer than its 2 hours and 8 minutes."

Richard T. Jameson, one of Coppola's most vocal critics in the past, off-set Pauline Kael's harsh comments in a bubbling review that must have pleased Coppola as much as it surprised him. "I love it!" Jameson wrote in *Film Comment*. "I think the movie's terrific. Nothing I've seen all year has given me a better, busier, more abundantly good time. It's a three-ring circus of a movie, a juggling act with so many balls in the air that it becomes its own bright constellation."

Given his history of mixed reviews, Coppola might have anticipated the notices assigned to his latest picture, but he never would have predicted the way *The Cotton Club* was treated by its distributor after its release. Although it struggled to compete with *Beverly Hills Cop*, the season's blockbuster, *The Cotton Club* managed to post respectable box-office numbers, charting fifth on the *Variety* list in its opening weekend, then rising to the number-two position the following week. Despite some of the negative or lukewarm reviews, the movie looked as if it would hold its own.

Much of the credit for the interest in the picture could be attributed to Orion, which aggressively promoted the movie in an all-out marketing blitz that included glossy three-page ads placed in such magazines as *Newsweek, Rolling Stone,* and *People* and a series of thirty-second television ads that played up Coppola and Richard Gere and the way *The Cotton Club* was a movie similar to *The Godfather.* However, with the appearance of the initial negative reviews, along with first weekend attendance figures suggesting that *The Cotton Club* might not be the blockbuster it needed to be in order to recover the movie's costs, Orion stockholders panicked and began selling off their stock, and Orion executives had to scramble to practice some kind of damage control. The numbers, they assured their stockholders, were nothing to be upset about. With only $15 million tied up in the film, Orion was all but assured of recovering its investment.

While this seemed to ease stockholders' minds, Orion officials themselves were unconvinced that they had a hit on their hands, and shortly after the first of the year, with the film less than a month in circulation, Orion appeared to be all but giving up on the picture. *The Cotton Club,* the studio announced, was going to be retooled and presented later as a four-hour television miniseries.

Attendance at *The Cotton Club* showings fell off dramatically, and while Orion could not be blamed with any certainty for the drop at the box office—it might have been that the people who wanted to see the film had gone during its first week or two—the announcement could not have helped: Why would people pay to see *The Cotton Club* now when, presumably, they could see a longer and better version on television, free of charge, sometime in the near future?

And what of Coppola's participation in the new television version of the film? At the time of the announcement, he had completed *Rip Van Winkle* and was vacationing with his family in Europe. In just a few weeks, he would be starting work on his next film, a time-travel fantasy entitled *Peggy Sue Got Married,* another work-for-hire adventure. Coppola hoped this new film would help him to whittle down his debt and to forget the hardships of the past year or so. It was unlikely that he would be returning to *The Cotton Club.*

Chapter Fourteen

Warm Nostalgia, Unbearable Grief

"I'm like that character in Yojimbo. *He's beaten, he's lost everything, so he lies low and gathers his strength until he's able to be a warrior again."*

—FRANCIS FORD COPPOLA

1.

FRANCIS FORD COPPOLA'S agreement to direct *Peggy Sue Got Married,* coming on the heels of his forgettable experience with *The Cotton Club,* must have seemed ill-advised to movie industry observers. *Peggy Sue* was even less likely a Coppola project than *The Cotton Club* and, more significantly, it came prepackaged with its own history of problems.

Originally designed as a vehicle for Debra Winger, who had reached marquee status as Richard Gere's costar in *An Officer and a Gentleman, Peggy Sue Got Married* was little more than a romantic comedy with a twist. Jonathan Demme, destined to direct such pictures as *The Silence of the Lambs* and *Philadelphia,* but at the time a relative unknown, was hired to direct *Peggy Sue,* but Winger wanted Penny Marshall instead. Marshall, who would also receive accolades in the future for such pictures as *Big* and *A League of Their Own,* had yet to direct a feature-length picture, but Winger was adamant about her preference. Demme left the picture, citing creative differences as his official explanation for leaving, and Marshall was installed as the new director. She, too, had her artistic differences—this time with producer Paul Gurian and screenwriters Jerry Leichtling and Arlene Sarner—and she, too, was out. Disgusted, Winger threatened to leave the picture unless an appropriate director was found—someone, she suggested, like Francis Ford Coppola.

Ray Stark, the renowned Hollywood producer and head of Rastar, the production company backing *Peggy Sue,* knew Coppola from nearly two decades earlier, when, as an employee of Seven Arts, Coppola had worked on the screenplay for Stark's *Reflections in a Golden Eye.* He was also aware of Coppola's well-publicized financial woes, which increased the odds of his hiring the director. At the time—fall 1984—Coppola was preoccupied with *The Cotton Club,* but with *Peggy Sue* not scheduled to go into production until March 1985, there was plenty of time to work out a deal.

For Coppola, the offer came at a critical time. He had been shopping around a couple of project ideas, including a screen adaptation of William Kennedy's *Legs,* but the studios weren't interested. Looming in the near future were two large payments—$1.7 million on his Sentinel Building in San Francisco, which was scheduled for a trustee sale on December 27 if Coppola failed to deliver the payment, and his annual $1 million loan and interest payment due on March 20—so he had to find work quickly. *Peggy Sue* became that work.

"*Peggy Sue,* I must say, was not the kind of film I normally would want to do," he admitted later. "The nature of my debts is that I have to make gigantic payments in March, millions of dollars. And so when the time starts getting closer to the payment and I'm looking around seeing what I should do, the project that was ready to go that wanted me was *Peggy Sue.*"

Even then, it took some persuasion from Fred Roos to convince Coppola to sign on to direct the film. Coppola felt that the script, while decent enough, was more suitable for a television movie than for the big screen. Roos, on the contrary, believed the picture had the potential to become a big hit.

Ironically, much of the project's charm centered on the comic potential in traveling to one's past, confronting one's teenage mistakes, and learning from what had been missed the first time around—an intriguing concept for a film comedy at that point in time. What Coppola and the others did not know, even as they prepared to put *Peggy Sue Got Married* into production, was that Steven Spielberg was developing a similar project—*Back to the Future.*

2.

UNHAPPY AS HE WAS ABOUT becoming a director for hire, Coppola was not about to work on a movie without putting his own personal touch on it, and as soon as he agreed to direct *Peggy Sue Got Married,* he began to shape the screenplay into something more to his liking. Coppola disliked the way the screenwriters jumped back and forth in time in their script, and in putting his own stamp on the story, he tried to push the humor and fantasy into the background in favor of emphasizing the bittersweet elements of the plot.

"My model," he explained, "was the last act in Thornton Wilder's *Our Town,* when the daughter goes back and sees her mother and her youth. I was looking for more of that kind of small-town charm and emotion than for jokes or effects."

His confidence, no doubt, had been nudged by the recent success of *Rip Van Winkle,* which he had not only delivered on time and on budget but in which he had also shown how he could add distinctive flourishes to a rather inflexible plot. The Washington Irving story, known and revered by millions, offered very little room to move, but with Eiko Ishioka, lighting director George Riesenberger, and his own electronic cinema, he was able to give the short film a dreamy quality that added depth and texture to the story. In the background of many of the scenes, he used a wonderfully surrealistic mountain, comprised of five people crowding under a canvas, which changed shape and color to reflect the characters' moods, adding what Coppola called a "magical, mystical element" to the presentation.

"I don't want to be limited to reality anymore," he told reporter Stephen Farber. "I'm more interested in impressionistic films that require fantastic images to be invented. In *Rip Van Winkle,* we're working with a surreal vision of America in Revolutionary times."

Coppola reportedly ran into resistance when his method of electronic cinema clashed with some of the program's established visual formats, but these problems were minor and easily resolved. "I guess the secret is to be honest with him," noted Shelley Duvall. "Keep him informed of what's going on, and don't surprise him in the end."

With *Peggy Sue Got Married,* the surprise came in the beginning: Coppola had no sooner immersed himself in the film's preproduction than Debra Winger was sidelined with a back ailment that doctors said would keep her out of action for an extended period—maybe for as long as six months. Winger dropped out of the production, and the search was on for a bankable new headliner—someone who could pull off the look of both a forty-three-year-old mother of two, and her earlier, seventeen-year-old former self.

Kathleen Turner was an excellent alternative. One of Hollywood's rising young stars, Turner, over the course of just a handful of movies, had distinguished herself as being remarkably versatile. In *Body Heat* and *Crimes of Passion,* she had shown an ability to play a sultry yet vulnerable character trapped in a web of her own making, and she had displayed a flair for comedy in *The Man with Two Brains. Romancing the Stone,* a lighthearted adventure movie, won her a Golden Globe and established her reputation as one of the most bankable female leads in the business. At the time of Coppola's call, she had just completed John Huston's *Prizzi's Honor,* and according to the Hollywood buzz, she had turned in another performance worthy of Oscar consideration.

Turner and Coppola met and went over the script. Turner thought that it was excellent, and she relished the thought of working with Coppola, who delighted her with his singing and his sense of family. Yes, she told Coppola, she would play Peggy Sue.

"I really wanted to work with Francis," she remembered. "I was intrigued by the thought that this was a great filmmaker who had never really had a leading lady. His films had basically dealt with men. In fact, he said to me, 'I don't really know how to treat a leading actress. You'll have to tell me.' I said, 'Well, you have a glass of wine ready for her at the end of every day.'"

There was, however, one major snag. Turner was scheduled to go before cameras in *Jewel of the Nile,* the sequel to the extraordinarily successful *Romancing the Stone.* She felt the *Jewel of the Nile* script was "an exploitation adventure movie" lacking the sense of fun of the original. In addition, she was having money squabbles with Twentieth Century–Fox. Turner hoped to find a way to resolve these differences before working on the movie, but the studio wanted to capitalize on *Romancing the Stone*'s success. "My agent tried to find out if they could postpone *Jewel* while we addressed the problems, so I could do [*Peggy Sue*]," she remembered, "at which point everything got mucked up." Under the threat of a $25 million lawsuit from Fox, Turner returned to the picture and the Coppola project was put on hold.

3.

NOT THAT COPPOLA SUDDENLY found himself without anything to do. Quite the contrary: While Kathleen Turner was away in Morocco, shooting *Jewel of the Nile,* Coppola busied himself with a number of projects, including further preproduction on *Peggy Sue.*

Coppola hated being in debt, not just because it forced him into a kind of Hollywood servitude but also because, as a proud man, he disliked the effect that all the publicity about his money problems had on his reputation. In interviews, he tried to downplay his reputation as a free spender, repeating ideas he had been issuing, off and on, for the better part of a decade. *The Cotton Club*, he insisted, had never had a formal budget drawn up, and it had been out of control when he took over as the picture's director. He was even more bitter about the persistent tongue wagging over *Apocalypse Now* and *One from the Heart*, which, he pointed out, he had financed with his own money, at his own risk. He was not reckless with other people's money, and he resented being portrayed as such. As for his personal debt, estimated at nearly $50 million at the end of *One from the Heart*, Coppola was working his way toward solvency, defying advisers who suggested that his life would be less stressful and complicated if he declared bankruptcy and started over. This, said Coppola, was not the way he was raised to behave.

New projects abounded, even as Coppola waited to start the filming of *Peggy Sue*. Victor Kaufman, the head of Tri-Star Pictures, approached Coppola with an invitation to direct Ron Bass's screen adaptation of *Gardens of Stone*, Nicholas Proffitt's 1983 novel about the army's Old Guard. As Coppola saw it, the story was sympathetic to the military while being antiwar in tone, and it could not have been more different from the way he depicted the army in *Apocalypse Now*. Always fascinated by rituals, and seeing an opportunity to earn another large chunk of money to apply to his debt, Coppola agreed to take on the project as his next picture.

A more immediate project, *Captain Eo*, arrived by way of an old friend. In September 1984, Frank Wells, president and chief operating officer of Walt Disney Productions, and Michael Eisner, the company's chairman, had been touring Walt Disney World in Lake Buena Vista, Florida, when the two began tossing around ideas for a new visual attraction similar to the three-dimensional travelogues presented in a process known as Circle-Vision 360. "What's the most exciting thing we can do with this process?" Eisner wondered.

It was not an idle question. In recent years, amusement parks had been pushing the limits with their rides and live attractions. In the very near future, people visiting the Universal Studios theme park would be confronted by a thirty-foot King Kong that moved realistically on an elaborate set that assaulted the senses. A Six Flags theme park offered a Sensorium that combined 3-D visuals with corresponding smells. In the works was a spaceship ride that promised to give customers the sensation of being hurled through an asteroid field in space. The proliferation of these and other attractions was largely attributed to the popularity of George Lucas and Steven Spielberg, whose movies, with their spectacular special effects, had redefined excitement in family entertainment. As one industry insider observed, "It's more exciting to see the mine-car chase in *Indiana Jones* than to go on the Matterhorn."

It was natural, then, that Disney would contact Lucas about designing a new 3-D film for its two theme parks in the United States. A big-budget spectacular, *Captain Eo* would be underwritten by Disney, and by Eastman Kodak, which wanted to test a new 70-mm 3-D process its scientists had developed. What Disney wanted was a short film (about ten to fifteen minutes) as visually stimulating as some of the action scenes in Lucas's *Star Wars*, complete with music and dazzling special effects. Michael Jackson, pop music's hottest act, was signed to act and dance in the production, as well as to write and sing its songs.

Lucas invited Coppola to direct the production, and Coppola, in turn, brought in Vittorio Storaro and Walter Murch to shoot and edit the film. Jeffrey Hornaday, the choreographer for *Flashdance* and, a short time later, *A Chorus Line,* served in a similar capacity in *Captain Eo.* John Napier, known for his staging of Broadway musicals, was hired as production designer. With a budget set at nearly $20 million, *Captain Eo* became, minute for minute, the most expensive movie ever made.

The final product was a combination of rock video and *Stars Wars* special effects, with Michael Jackson, as Captain Eo, singing and dancing his way through two numbers while taking on the forces of She-Devil Supreme, a planet's evil empress, played by Anjelica Huston, soon to win an Oscar for her role in *Prizzi's Honor.* Disney's Lance Johnson created a supporting cast of space creatures that looked like mutants from *Fantasia* or *Return of the Jedi,* including a green elephant who used his trunk as an oboe, a red monkey with butterfly wings, and assorted fuzzy aliens. The short film might not have been classic cinema but, as a critic for *Time* noted, it was entertaining. "What can be exhilarating and depressing about Walt Disney World," reported the reviewer, "is true of *Captain Eo:* it is a triumph of the artificial, of high-tech wizardry and second-hand emotions. All of which makes *Eo* just fine as a total three-dimensional experience, but only the fourth-best film at Epcot."

In terms of Coppola's career, the professional reunion with George Lucas was more important than the film itself. During his break from *Peggy Sue Got Married,* Coppola had blown the dust off his plans to make a biographical feature about Preston Tucker, and one evening around the time of the filming of *Captain Eo,* he decided to approach Lucas and see if he would become involved in the project.

As Coppola later admitted, it was a humbling experience. After all, he had been one of Lucas's early mentors, back in the days when Lucas was a skinny kid hanging around the *Finian's Rainbow* sets and, a short time later, when Lucas accompanied him on *The Rain People* shoot. Their history and relationship had been established. Even in the fledgling days of Zoetrope, when Lucas was developing his own projects and working with Coppola as a fellow filmmaker, it had been Coppola who had used his influence to help launch *THX-1138* and, more importantly, *American Graffiti*.

The success of *American Graffiti*–and the subsequent Coppola-Lucas disputes over the film–represented a fork in the road, and the two filmmakers, so different in personalities and goals, had gone their separate ways. If Coppola had been secretly scornful of Lucas's making *Star Wars* while he was sweating out the jungle in *Apocalypse Now,* he could not deny the bottom line: *Star Wars* had become the most popular movie of its time, making Lucas as wealthy as he could have ever hoped to be, affording him the opportunity to establish his own filmmaking facility; he and Steven Spielberg were now among the most powerful men in the film industry, and their influence was reshaping the way business was practiced in Hollywood. Lucas had warned Coppola of the follies of trying to take on the old system by setting up a studio in Hollywood, but Coppola had refused to listen. As a result, the Hollywood trades could fill their pages with accounts of Coppola's sinking fortunes while reporting Lucas's latest triumph.

Lucas, never as boisterous about his life and work as Coppola, would never have consciously held his position over Coppola, but Coppola nevertheless felt awkward in asking him to produce *Tucker*–an action painfully similar to a time when the young George Lucas had asked Coppola to attach his name to *American Graffiti*. "It took a lot of courage on my part," Coppola confessed when discussing his approaching Lucas about *Tucker.* "I wanted to do something with George, but I didn't know if he wanted to do something with me."

Lucas, of course, already knew of Coppola's affinity for Preston Tucker, and of Coppola's long-standing dream of making a movie about the automaker's life, and he immediately approved the project. Seeing Coppola pursue a film idea that he really cared about, Lucas reasoned, was much better than watching him grind out a series of movies strictly for the money.

"Francis had been wanting to do *Tucker* ever since I'd known him," Lucas remembered. "He would always show me industrial films of Tucker, and I knew he'd been working on *Tucker* forever and ever. So, during this period after *One from the Heart,* when he was having a lot of financial problems and doing some things for hire, I asked him, 'Why don't you do a movie that you really care about, that you really want to do? Why don't we do *Tucker* together?'"

So it was set: Coppola would shoot *Peggy Sue Got Married* in the fall, follow it up with *Gardens of Stone* the following spring, and, to cap off one of the most productive periods in his career, make a movie that, in a way, had been a part of his consciousness since his boyhood, when his father invested in an ill-fated company with great heart and vision but not the clout needed to survive in the established system.

4·

COPPOLA HEARD INDIRECTLY from another old friend—in an unsettling way—when the Steven Spielberg–produced *Back to the Future* was released just as Coppola was preparing to go before cameras with his own time-travel story. Directed by Robert Zemeckis and starring Michael J. Fox, *Back to the Future*, with its familiar theme, presented a potential threat to the way audiences might respond to *Peggy Sue*, especially when *Back to the Future* took off to become the season's biggest hit. There were bound to be comparisons between the two films when *Peggy Sue* was eventually released, and if Coppola did not come up with something special in his picture, he risked looking as if he was merely cashing in on the earlier movie's popularity. Not wishing to be influenced in any way, Coppola refused to see the Zemeckis film.

He had reason to be at least reasonably optimistic about *Peggy Sue*'s chances. The script was in good shape, and he had some of the old familiar faces, absent during the filming of *The Cotton Club*, back in his stable. Dean Tavoularis would be designing the sets and re-creating Santa Rosa, California, 1960, in Petaluma, California. Theadora Van Runkle, the costume designer for *Godfather II*, was back in the fold, in the same capacity in *Peggy Sue*, as were editor Barry Malkin, assistant director Doug Claybourne, art director Alex Tavoularis, and John Barry, who had worked with Bob Wilber on the music for *The Cotton Club*.

Cinematographer Jordan Cronenweth, known for his work on *Altered States* and *Blade Runner,* was a significant newcomer. Cronenweth, who would earn an Academy Award nomination for his work on *Peggy Sue*, and who called working with Coppola "the highlight of my career," was amazed by the amount of freedom given to him by his director. "Francis is [a] very visually oriented director," he said, explaining that, for *Peggy Sue*, Coppola wanted to use saturated colors to heighten the reality in what was, in essence, a dream picture. Many of the decisions, Cronenweth noted, were left to the cinematographer.

"He delegates more than any other director I've worked with," said Cronenweth. "He's a hands-off director."

In selecting a cast for his film, Coppola found a whole new list of young actors and actresses destined to distinguish themselves in years to come. Helen Hunt, later to star in television's hit sitcom *Mad About You* and an eventual Oscar winner for her leading role in *As Good as It Gets,* was cast in the role of Beth Bodell, Peggy Sue's teenage daughter, and Jim Carrey, one of the industry's biggest comic headliners in the 1990s, was given the role of Walter Getz, the high school's class clown; Joan Allen, a Best Supporting Actress nominee in 1995 for her work in *Nixon,* and Lisa Jane Persky, who played Dutch Schultz's wife in *The Cotton Club,* were signed to play Peggy Sue's classmates. Barry Miller, a standout in his portrayal of Yippie leader and antiwar activist Jerry Rubin in the 1987 television drama *Conspiracy: The Trial of the Chicago 8,* won the role of Richard Norvik, the nerdy science whiz headed for great success as an adult.

In retrospect, the selection of Nicolas Cage to play "Crazy Charlie" Bodell, the most important casting decision apart from the title role, might have seemed obvious, if not nepotistic, but it was anything but that. Judge Reinhold, who had earned his reputation as a rising young comic actor in *Fast Times at Ridgemont High* and, later, in *Beverly Hills Cop,* and *Saturday Night Live* regular Martin Short were considered leading candidates for the role, but producer Paul Gurian had his heart set on Cage, whom he had seen and appreciated in *Valley Girl.* Cage, however, was not interested in the role, and he turned Coppola down on four occasions before finally relenting. He was accustomed to seeing relatives working on his uncle's movies—he himself had worked on *Rumble Fish* and *The Cotton Club*—but he was sensitive to grumbles about nepotism, which had been one of his main reasons for changing his last name from Coppola to Cage.

"I started acting when I was seventeen, and my fellow actors didn't accept me. They said I was there because of Francis Coppola," Cage recalled. "I felt I had to work twice as hard as the next guy to prove myself. I felt the burden of being his nephew. . . .What really helped me was when I was able to disassociate myself from him. At first I was working as Nicolas Coppola. When I changed my name, everything changed."

Cage's blood relation to the film's director wasn't the only reason for his hesitating to take the male lead in *Peggy Sue;* he had professional reasons, as well. He was not especially impressed with the story, and he had less than pleasant memories about working on *The Cotton Club.* Coppola persisted, and

Cage finally signed on when he was convinced that the film was going to be a kind of modern *Our Town*.

Determined to bring the film in on time and on budget, Coppola set up a grueling shooting schedule, averaging, according to Kathleen Turner, eighteen hours per day. For Turner, who appeared in every scene of the movie, the schedule, coming so soon after her work on *Jewel of the Nile*, was exhausting.

"They were back to back," she said of the two movies, "and we had to get into Santa Rosa and do all the shooting in the school before the school opened. So we had a really tight schedule on the shooting end of *Peggy Sue*. I think I had ten days off between *Jewel of the Nile* and *Peggy Sue*, which taught me to never do back-to-back films again. It was a tough go, because Francis had a stop date, and we were desperately intent on coming in on schedule, which meant twenty-hour days. Poor Maureen O'Sullivan. On her first shooting day, she worked eighteen hours, but, God bless her, she was a trouper. What we did was unbelievable."

Turner found working for Coppola a rewarding experience—once the ground rules were laid down. "We made a deal," she remembered. "He asked me one day if I would mind if he went and directed from his trailer, and I said, 'No, I'll go act in mine.'" The two discussed their feelings about Coppola's electronic cinema, and Coppola agreed to direct from the set. "After that," said Turner, "we were fine."

Turner might have taken issue with some of Coppola's methods, but she came away from the film with great respect for her director. "His special talent," she told Gene Siskel on the eve of the film's premiere, "is that he's an intensely caring man. He gave me so much attention that I was both flattered and made to feel secure, secure enough to try a more risky approach when I was afraid the audience might think I was silly."

5.

INDEED, THE ROLE COULD have been viewed as Turner's most challenging to date, in the sense that she had secured her reputation by taking sophisticated adult roles in which she projected such a smoldering sensuality that critics were calling her "the Lauren Bacall of her generation." In *Peggy Sue*, she was not only required to pass herself off as a high school senior but she was also expected to confront her past with all the knowledge she had gained as an adult. She was physically more mature than a seventeen-year-old girl, yet she had to be convincing to both her fictional classmates and the people watching her in theaters. Further, Turner had history itself working against her. Although there are a number of historical references sprinkled through-out the picture, neither the screenwriters nor Coppola were interested in making a commentary on the political and social upheaval that took place between Peggy Sue's graduation and the reunion a quarter-century later. Still, Kathleen Turner had to work her (and the moviegoing audiences') awareness of history into her performance with very subtle nuances, closing what other-wise might have been a credibility gap.

"The fact that I didn't grow up in the States kind of worked for me," said Turner, who was raised in England, "because when Peggy Sue was rediscover-ing all those customs and phrases and all the stuff that came from television, I was sort of discovering them as well; I didn't have any history of this of my own. So, in a funny kind of way, it worked rather well."

As the film opens, Peggy Sue is standing in front of a mirror, squeezing herself into her old prom dress and fretting about her high school's twenty-fifth reunion. Her marriage to Charlie Bodell, her high school sweetheart, has fallen apart, fractured by Charlie's philandering ways. Separated but not yet officially divorced, Peggy Sue is raising a son and daughter on her own, and her bitterness surfaces anytime she sees her husband noisily hawking appli-ances on his "Crazy Charlie" television commercials. On top of everything else, he has become an embarrassment.

At the reunion, Peggy Sue discovers her former classmates have changed very little over the years—they're just older versions of their teenage selves. The one exception is Richard Norvik, the class brain, once the butt of count-less high school pranks but now very wealthy and respected, who is presently self-confident enough to be forgiving of his youthful tormentors. When meeting Peggy Sue at the reunion, Norvik comments that she was the only one who treated him decently during their high school years—a revelation that should surprise no one watching the film.

Richard and Peggy Sue are crowned king and queen of the reunion—a homage to present and past—and they take the stage for their coronations and acceptance speeches. Just as Peggy Sue is about to give her speech, she grows faint and passes out.

When she awakens, she has been transported, much like Dorothy in *The Wizard of Oz,* to another place and time. She is lying on a table, whoozy from just having contributed to her high school's blood drive. It is 1960 again, and everyone but Peggy Sue is the person he or she had been at that time. It takes some time, but Peggy Sue eventually realizes what has happened, and she makes clumsy attempts to adjust to her former self, her thoughts and actions tempered by her knowledge of things to come. She goes back to living at home with her parents and younger sister, attending classes, and living the life of a high school senior.

Her relationship with Charlie Bodell is the heart of the story; the movie becomes a process of discovery: How could Peggy Sue have fallen in love with someone who, by all appearances, seems so terribly shallow—and someone who will betray her so hurtfully twenty-five years up the road? Will Peggy Sue, knowing what's in store for her, reject him and spare herself an unhappy future? Charlie pales considerably when pitted against Richard Norvik's intelligence or, even more appealing to Peggy Sue, the fierce artistic intellectualism of Michael Fitzsimmons, the class beatnik and putative writer who rejects Hemingway in favor of Kerouac, and who affects an attitude that suggests that somewhere, at some later date, he might be overwhelmed by great sadness.

But Peggy Sue knows in her heart why she married Charlie, and nothing—not her fondness for Richard or her one-night stand with Michael—will prevent her from rediscovering it again. For all his fast-car, arrogant-teenager bluster, Charlie is doomed to be wounded by his own secret desires: By impregnating Peggy Sue on her eighteenth birthday and marrying her shortly thereafter, he can only watch helplessly as his dream of becoming a musician is replaced by the "stardom" of his obnoxious, whacked-out television persona. All he has left to hang on to is a loser's arrogance.

Peggy Sue, like Dorothy, cannot return to reality until she learns her important lessons. Unlike Dorothy, Peggy Sue will not necessarily return to a happier existence, although, in a coda to the story, Charlie visits her in the hospital in present time and hints that he will mend his ways. Only the future will tell.

6.

COPPOLA COMPLETED PRINCIPAL photography on *Peggy Sue Got Married,* on schedule and under budget, near the end of October, giving him plenty of time to fiddle with the film in postproduction before the picture's scheduled May 1986 release date. Compared to the insanity of *The Cotton Club,* the shoot had been a breeze, and for anyone skeptical of Coppola's ability to work in a swift, professional manner, the film's eight-week shoot proved, as Coppola had always claimed, that he could be responsible with other people's money. Rastar and its parent company, Tri-Star, were so impressed that they took out full-page ads in the trade papers, congratulating and thanking the production company for bringing the movie in on time.

Company officials might have been delighted by the results of Coppola's latest job, but they worried, nevertheless, about the timing of his movie. *Back to the Future* had exceeded all expectations at the box office, and there was concern that *Peggy Sue Got Married*, due to open less than a year after *Back to the Future*, might be overlooked by moviegoers. Kathleen Turner was expected to fare well during the upcoming awards season (and she did, winning a Golden Globe for her performance in *Prizzi's Honor*), but there was even question about whether her star status would attract the youthful market supporting the pivotal summer season.

Coppola provided a solution to the dilemma during *Peggy Sue*'s postproduction, when he decided that he would like to reshoot the movie's ending. Unlike some of his earlier films, Coppola had little trouble stitching together the story during the editing process; the script had supplied him with a complete, coherent story. However, Coppola felt that the filmed ending came up short. The cast looked tired and the scene lacked the emotional power that Coppola wanted for the conclusion of his film. Tri-Star agreed with Coppola's assessment, and the studio offered him additional money to reshoot the scene in Washington, D.C. The movie's release would simply be postponed until the fall of 1986.

The decision proved to be a sound one. In reworking the scene, Coppola decided to adjust the ending so it would echo the beginning. At the opening of the film, Peggy Sue is seen standing in front of a mirror, preparing to visit her past via her class reunion; in the revamped ending, she is again in front of the mirror, back from her dream visit to the past and ready to confront an unstable future. The added detail, along with fresh performances, made all the difference.

It's fortunate that the *Peggy Sue* experience had gone as easily as it did for Coppola, for he had no sooner finished reshooting the revised ending in March than he had to begin preproduction on *Gardens of Stone*, slated to go before cameras in May. To make the movie, Coppola needed the army's cooperation, which meant that he had to convince the Defense Department that he, the director of *Apocalypse Now*, had entirely different designs for his portrayal of the military in his new film. For Coppola, this was a fairly simple task: Since he was working as a director for hire on *Gardens of Stone* and wasn't the author of the book or screenplay, he could afford to be less rigid in his discussions with the army about the film. The movie, he said, was not designed to make great statements about war; in comparison to *Apocalypse Now*, it was a "small story" focusing more on the army as a large family, and showing how the elders in that family tried to give the younger members the benefit of their experiences, only to lose some of them tragically in battle.

"Obviously, there is a message there," Coppola explained, "that we are sworn to protect our children and we keep putting them in situations that make that impossible, that you want to save your kids but you end up burying them, all dressed up in ritual. But I didn't associate *Gardens of Stone* with *Apocalypse Now*."

Coppola backpedaled significantly when the earlier film was brought into conversation, taking pains to ward off the inevitable comparisons. *Gardens of Stone*, he offered, showed men as "very emotional and capable of love," unlike the way they were usually portrayed in war movies. "I don't know," he said, "maybe it might give a new look at the Army and make men a more beautiful kind of people instead of always making them so violent." *Apocalypse Now*, he pointed out, was entirely something else.

"I find the movies really so different," he insisted. "The hook is only that they relate to Vietnam. So many of the circumstances of *Apocalypse*—insane guys surfing in the middle of battle—to me were too extraordinary. Although elements of that were true, it was very clear that it was a dream . . . sort of an opera about this phenomenon that takes men to the point where they actually began to bend their sense of morality. To me, it was never very much about Vietnam."

Whatever his feelings about *Apocalypse Now, Gardens of Stone,* the army, or warfare in general, Coppola was able to sell the army on his intentions for *Gardens of Stone*. To seal the deal, he agreed to give the army approval of the movie's script—a concession he had refused to relinquish in *Apocalypse Now*. According to Coppola, the army asked him to tone down the foul language in the script, but other than that, and a few adjustments here and there for the sake of authenticity, the army left him alone. "From the Army's standpoint, the film's depiction of the military is beyond reproach," announced Lt. Col. John Meyers, who acted as a liaison between the Pentagon and the film company.

The army provided Coppola with everything he needed, from technical advice, to equipment, to personnel. Coppola would be allowed to shoot on location at Fort Myer and Fort Belvoir, as well as in Arlington National Cemetery; he would have army uniforms, weapons, and helicopters at his disposal. The army also volunteered a large number of its personnel to work in the movie, including 600 soldiers to appear as extras throughout the film and 450, including the army's marching band, to appear in a scene of a troop review. As the *New York Times* reported, Coppola was given "enough men and

material to invade a small country"—a complete reversal from the tense relations between the filmmaker and the Defense Department during the making
of *Apocalypse Now.*

In assembling his production team for *Gardens of Stone,* Coppola brought
back the core of his crew from *Peggy Sue,* including cinematographer Jordan
Cronenweth. Coppola's son Gio was given the important task of supervising
the electronic cinema, while Carmine Coppola, absent from his son's movies
since *The Outsiders,* was again assigned the job of composing the picture's
music.

In casting the movie, Coppola combined a number of familiar faces with
a handful of significant newcomers. James Caan, back in the business after a
five-year hiatus, during which he brought his substance-abuse problems
under control, took the male lead, while Anjelica Huston, who had recently
worked with Coppola on *Captain Eo,* won the female lead. Other Coppola
regulars with parts in *Gardens of Stone* included Sam Bottoms and Larry Fishburne—both veterans of the director's earlier war movie—and Lonette McKee,
who had appeared in *The Cotton Club.*

James Earl Jones, one of the country's finest character actors, headed the
list of first-timers, playing Sgt. Maj. Goody Nelson, the witty, intelligent, and
occasionally stern father figure to the honor guard trainees. D. B. Sweeney, in
his first major role, played a cadet hell-bent on leaving the honor guard and
serving his country in Vietnam. Mary Stuart Masterson played his young
wife.

Coppola led his company through the customary two weeks of rehearsals, encouraging his actors to improvise and develop their characters. By
now, he had the videotaped rehearsal routine down to a fine art, with few of
the problems that had undermined his electronic cinema in the early days,
particularly during the preparation for *One from the Heart.* His relaxed method
of directing the rehearsals rubbed off on the actors, who, rather than finding
the process confusing, as had been the case in the early days, now praised the
director for the license he gave them as artists. James Earl Jones compared the
experience to having an affair, when everything seems fresh and exciting.

"I've always searched for the best way to rehearse movies, and have tried
every permutation under the sun," Coppola explained in a 1999 interview,
"starting way back with *You're a Big Boy Now,* for which I wrote a special
'rehearsal script,' which was performed almost as a play and videotaped. No
actor has really balked at this opportunity, but some didn't like it as much as
others. Anthony Hopkins [who would appear in *Bram Stoker's Dracula*] didn't
like to rehearse, but most of them did."

7.

COPPOLA WAS ONLY PARTIALLY correct when he called *Gardens of Stone* a small story in comparison to *Apocalypse Now*. Indeed, the latter had grand, operatic battle scenes, high-voltage emotional impact, larger-than-life characters, and a message that seemed to embody much of the confusion, frustration, anger, and despair suffered by the country during the Vietnam War, but in *Gardens of Stone*, which might also be viewed as a companion piece to *Apocalypse Now*, Coppola was making important statements rarely addressed in war movies, especially on the topic of how we bury our dead warriors and go on to heal. Vietnam movies such as *Coming Home, The Deer Hunter,* and *Born on the Fourth of July* address the issue of war's aftermath, but in all three pictures, the focus is on the wounded—the physically and/or emotionally damaged—the victims of battle. In *Gardens of Stone,* Coppola was adding another dimension to the canon of war movies.

The story itself, as Coppola indicated, was straightforward and simple. The film opens with a military funeral at Arlington, complete with the ceremonial twenty-one-gun salute, the folding of the flag, and its presentation to the soldier's widow. We hear the dead soldier's voice, reading his last letter home—not to his wife, but to his sergeant, the father figure of his other family. It is 1969, and Vietnam is still sending too many young men to the cemeteries—or gardens of stone.

The story flashes back to a year earlier and the arrival of Jackie Willow (D. B. Sweeney) at Fort Myer. He is the young man whose voice we heard moments earlier. To his displeasure, Willow has been assigned to the Old Guard, a group of NCOs that, among other duties, serves the President and buries Vietnam casualties. Willow, a gung ho volunteer who would much rather be fighting in Vietnam, immediately makes it known that he would like to transfer out of the unit as soon as possible.

Early on, he is befriended by Sgt. Clell Hazard (James Caan), a veteran of the Korean War and two tours of duty in Vietnam. The army is the only family Hazard has: He has been married and divorced, and he never sees his son, who is about the same age as the young men under his command. Hazard, too, wants out of the Old Guard. He is a soldier to the marrow, but he is intelligent and sensitive enough to see war for what it is. Vietnam, he sneers, is not being fought properly, and he is reminded of this with each fresh body brought in for burial. He reasons that if he could transfer somewhere else, he might be able to train young men to be better soldiers—and, hence, survivors.

Hazard fought with Willow's father in Korea, and he has agreed to look after the young soldier while he is in the Old Guard.

Hazard's closest friend in the service is Sgt. Maj. Goody Nelson (James Earl Jones), an imposing bear of a man who, like Hazard, has spent a lifetime in the armed forces. He runs a tight ship, as we see during a routine barracks inspection, but he also cares deeply for the young men in the Old Guard. Unlike Hazard, who believes that one man can make a difference in the war effort, Nelson asserts that he and Hazard are little more than middle management.

Hazard meets Samantha Davis (Anjelica Huston), a reporter for the *Washington Post* and a neighbor in his apartment building. Sam, who opposes the Vietnam War on the grounds that it is genocide, sees the decency and humanity in Hazard and Nelson, and while she refuses to back away from her antiwar stance, she is attracted to Hazard and begins seeing him regularly.

Once the main characters have been introduced, *Gardens of Stone* becomes a character study. As one might expect, Jackie Willow becomes an ideal member of the Old Guard, never letting up on his intentions to fight in Vietnam, even when Hazard tries to discourage him. He is promoted to the rank of sergeant and shows signs of leadership. He is also reunited with Rachel Feld, his old girlfriend and the daughter of a crusty old colonel, and after a whirlwind courtship, the two are engaged and married. Although she hates the idea, Rachel is resigned to the idea that her husband will be fighting in Vietnam. Since we already know that Willow is going to be killed by the end of the picture, there is an edge of sadness and resignation to nearly everything he does.

These are the same feelings that bother Clell Hazard. Although he has no way of knowing how Jackie Willow's life will turn out, he fears for all young men like him, and he looks out for Rachel when Jackie finally leaves for Vietnam. He, Samantha, and Goody Nelson become Rachel's family, only to suffer a family's grief when, only days before he is to return to the States, Jackie is killed.

8.

OVER A DECADE AFTER MAKING *Gardens of Stone,* Francis Ford Coppola would claim to remember very little about the shooting of the movie. His mind, he said, had been elsewhere—and for good reason.

On Monday, May 26, with production shut down to celebrate Memorial Day, Gio Coppola, his girlfriend, Jacqueline de la Fontaine, and Griffin

O'Neal, son of actor Ryan O'Neal, rented a fourteen-foot McKee speedboat for an outing on the South River near Annapolis. The young Coppola and O'Neal had become friends during the making of *The Escape Artist,* in which O'Neal had a starring role, and O'Neal had a small part in *Gardens of Stone.* O'Neal had a troubled past, including a year of drug rehabilitation in Hawaii. Only a few days earlier, on May 23, he'd had a brush with the law when he was stopped, at 1:30 A.M., for racing a Lotus Esprit through the streets of Rosslyn, Virginia; he was charged with reckless driving, driving without a license, and carrying a concealed weapon—a six-inch switchblade, which, O'Neal told police, did not belong to him. The *Gardens of Stone* production company had bailed him out of his latest scrape.

On May 26, after a lunch that included several glasses of wine, O'Neal and Coppola, along with de la Fontaine, took the speedboat out on the river, with O'Neal at the wheel. De la Fontaine (nearly three months pregnant with Coppola's child, though his family was unaware of it at the time) was frightened by what she felt was reckless boating on O'Neal's part, and after a short time on the river, she was dropped onshore. O'Neal and Coppola then headed back out on the water.

Around 5:15, while moving at what was later deemed to be excessive but "[not] terribly excessive speed," O'Neal tried to steer the boat between two other craft on the lake. What he did not see, until it was too late, was that one of the boats was disabled and being towed by the other. The towline struck Gio and knocked him off his feet, his head hitting the back of the boat with tremendous force. He was taken by ambulance to Anne Arundel County General Hospital, where he was pronounced dead on arrival, his death attributed to massive head injuries.

O'Neal, who suffered only minor injuries and refused treatment at the scene, panicked when asked about the accident, telling police that Gio had been driving the boat when they struck the towline. "I didn't want to have to tell his mother," O'Neal would later say of his lie, "didn't want to have to carry that burden, which I will have to do for the rest of my life."

The truth would be revealed within days, when witnesses came forward and told police that they had seen a blond man (O'Neal), not a dark-haired man (Coppola), at the wheel at the time of the accident, but as far as the Coppola family was concerned, placing blame was the furthest thing from their minds. At twenty-two, Gian-Carlo Coppola, son and brother, was dead.

For Francis Coppola, the loss went far beyond a parent's ultimate nightmare of losing a child; he had lost a colleague and one of his closest friends. At sixteen, Gio had written his father a note seeking permission to leave school and work as his apprentice, and from that moment until the time of his death, Gio had been his father's right-hand man, serving as an associate producer on *The Outsiders* and *Rumble Fish,* directing the montage footage in *The Cotton Club,* and acting as second-unit director on *Captain Eo.* He had recently agreed to intern on Steven Spielberg's upcoming *Amazing Stories,* and he was also to work as second-unit director on Penny Marshall's *Jumpin' Jack Flash.* He was, in every way, on the road to becoming a filmmaker in his own right, and he was loved and respected by his friends and peers. Penny Marshall's daughter, Tracy Reiner, one of Gio's closest friends, described him as "a very, very old soul" who had taught her more about life and love than anyone she had known. "There's no elaborate story to Gio," she told William Plummer of *People* magazine two months after her friend's death. "He loved art, he painted and wrote and wanted to make films, and he could fix just about anything. He was a very formal, classic gentleman."

"I think there is something unique about the relationship of a father to his first child," Eleanor Coppola proposed. "It just seemed like such a miracle to have a child. Francis took Gio everywhere, even as a baby in a basket. Later on, Gio seemed to have a temperament of great patience for a kid. We used to say he was an 'old soul.' He could sit quietly on the set for hours. Roman and other children would make noise and wiggle around and have to be taken away during a take, but unlike most kids Gio seemed to have some reserve of patience. It turned out he was a bit dyslexic, and he finally got so frustrated at school that we let him out and he took the G.E.D. to graduate from high school. He went to work for Francis at age sixteen, and they were together daily; they went through production, thick and thin, and grew very close. There isn't much time in Francis's life to maintain men friends, and Gio became his best friend. Most kids that age would have been away at college, but Gio was at Francis's side, and his accidental death was the most profound blow imaginable. Gio had a healing, observant, 'old soul' personality—more like mine—that was a soothing complement to Francis's tumultuous Italian personality."

"The best memories I have of working on Coppola's films are about being around him and Gio," Frederic Forrest reflected, more than two decades later. "They had such love, and that carried over to everybody else. You felt privileged to be around that kind of love. Gio was the sweetest young man that I ever knew. I had watched him grow up, because I'd done *The Conversation* and *Apocalypse Now,* and then, later, I did *One from the Heart* and *Hammett.* He'd come in and say, 'Is there anything you need? Anything I should tell my dad? Anything you need for your trailer?' He was just the sweetest kid."

In years to come, a number of Francis Ford Coppola's associates would point to the tragedy as a major turning point not only in Coppola's life, which would have been expected, but in the way he pursued his career. In a sense, they speculated, the youthful fire had been extinguished. In the past, Coppola had used courage and bluster to take on bigger foes, particularly the Hollywood system, but Gio's death had taken the fight out of him. A family man first and foremost, Coppola had once remarked that his greatest fear was losing a loved one, and now, with Gio gone, he had to face the prospects of what that momentous occasion meant to his life and art.

"I realized that no matter what happened, I had *lost,*" he stated several years later. "No matter what happened, it would always be incomplete. The next day, I could have all my fondest dreams come true: someone could give me Paramount Pictures to organize the way I would do it, and develop talent and technology, and have my dream of dream of dreams, and even if I did get it, I lost already. There's no way I could ever have a complete experience, because there will always be that part of me missing."

In the immediate aftermath of Gio's death, Coppola tried to work through his grief. A memorial service had been arranged for Wednesday, May 28, but on the day between the accident and the service, as well as in the following weeks, Coppola insisted on carrying on with the film, partly because, as he told others, Gio would have wanted it that way, and largely because it was his own way of confronting his loss.

"I was in a dream—or a nightmare," Coppola recalled. "I didn't know what to do. I just didn't want to go somewhere where all I'd do is think of him, over and over, day and night. I dreaded the nights, and specifically the morning most of all, because what had happened would always hit me anew in the morning. It went on like that for over seven years, until I could wake up and that wouldn't be the first thought that hit me. I thought having the film to work on would give me something to do. I thought he'd want me to go on, since he had been there to work with me. It was horrible."

"Francis chose to go on with the movie because he felt it would be best for his psyche," production executive Gary Lucchesi concurred. "I remember him saying the last place he'd want to be after Gio's death was home. To see Gio's room, to confront him there . . . he wanted time."

What he did not want, in the days following Gio's death, was any kind of reprisal against Griffin O'Neal. The young actor asked to be released from the picture, and rumors flew that Coppola had thrown him off the set, or that cast members had pushed for his removal. Fred Roos claimed that that was not the case. Coppola, said Roos, was searching for ways to help O'Neal. As far as Coppola was concerned, there was nothing he could do for his son, and there was no need to destroy another life to gain reparations in what had amounted to a terrible accident. What was important was to go on.

9.

"I'VE OFTEN FOUND THAT the movies I make reflect a great deal of what's happening in my life," Coppola reflected in a 1988 interview with film critic Gene Siskel, "and, in turn, that influences the movies as I make them. We feed off each other."

So it was with *Gardens of Stone*. What had begun, in Coppola's words, as "a film about a man who loved his son" wound up becoming a movie with much deeper personal meaning than its director ever could have imagined.

In his fragile state, Coppola was a natural candidate for some kind of physical or emotional breakdown, and it was probably no surprise to the cast or crew when he collapsed on the set shortly after the resumption of the filming.

"He fainted," Eleanor Coppola remembered, "and he was taken to the hospital for tests. It was very scary for a few hours, until we learned that it was nothing serious. He just needed a rest and was ordered to take some time off. He stayed home for four or five days, and then proceeded to finish the film."

James Caan, for one, feared for Coppola's health, and while he understood his director's reasons for trying to work through his numbing period of grief, he strongly urged production officials to shut down the movie for the time being.

"Francis was so vulnerable," Caan remarked. "To this day, I've never met a man who enjoyed his family and children more than Francis. This was devastating. I kept begging these studio heads to put him in the hospital. 'He's gonna go down,' I told them. 'No,' they said, 'he wants to work.' *Of course he wants to work!* He doesn't want to go home and sit in some dark room and think about it. I told everybody, 'You have to trick him. You gotta tell him the helicopter broke down, or that the camera broke down. He has to lay down.' Finally, he just collapsed, and was he scared. He didn't want to go to the hospital because he was afraid of being alone. In the ambulance, I told him, 'We gotta stop. You're watching but you're not seeing anything.' Poor Francis. To this day, I can't imagine myself in that situation."

For Caan, Gio's death and the subsequent filming of *Gardens of Stone* had a sobering effect. By his own admission, Caan had watched substance abuse rob him of some of his priorities and perspective; he had been a problem even during the making of *Gardens of Stone*. Gio's death helped him reestablish priorities.

"It's the saddest thing," he said. "What the fuck are we doing, putting all this importance on a movie? What does it mean? Some of these actors think they're curing cancer with a movie. *It's a movie!* It's good for a week and then it's gone."

Throughout the summer, Coppola tried to harness his emotions in a setting that could be intolerably sad. Coworkers, as well as Coppola himself, had to overcome a somber set, occasionally punctuated by Coppola's sudden breaking down in tears. "Things were very hard on *Gardens of Stone*," Anjelica Huston remembered, "and it's a miracle he got through it."

Ironically, when *Gardens of Stone* was released in May 1987, one of the main complaints registered by critics focused on what they felt was a distance that Coppola had kept between himself and his subject, as if the director was disconnected from, or deliberately avoiding, a deeper exploration of the subject he was filming. "The most important missing ingredient is Mr. Coppola," remarked Vincent Canby in the *New York Times.* "*Gardens of Stone* is, finally, so commonplace that one longs for even the inappropriate grandeur of *Rumble Fish* and *The Outsiders.*" *Newsweek*'s David Ansen also noted a detachment that affected the way viewers could identify with the story: "One is left feeling like a stranger who's wandered into a wake of strangers: you respect their grief but are unable to share it." Dave Kehr, writing for the *Chicago Tribune,* was more sympathetic. "It's impossible to watch *Gardens of Stone* without remembering the tragedy that intervened in Coppola's own life," he wrote, adding that "the film is so distant, perhaps, because it is so close."

Coppola would have been the last to dispute the claims that he seemed removed from the film. In the months following Gio's death, he found it very difficult to address the tragedy in public, and the press, for once, maintained a respectful distance, even when, on July 28, a grand jury in Annapolis indicted Griffin O'Neal on six counts of criminal behavior, including manslaughter, in the death of Gian-Carlo Coppola. If convicted, O'Neal faced a possible five-year sentence.

Coppola completed the movie's principal photography in early August and immediately departed with his family for a vacation in Paris. The months ahead promised to be eventful, with work still to be done on *Peggy Sue Got Married* before its fall premiere, as well as postproduction work on *Gardens of Stone.* In addition, Coppola had been invited to participate in the ribbon-cutting ceremonies of the *Captain Eo* premiere at the newly constructed Magic Eye Theater at Disneyland on September 19. For the time being, he needed to be alone with his family.

Chapter Fifteen

Con Man, Reflected

"I like [Tucker] because he feels human, the lovable American con man, the used-car salesman with his heart in the right place. In a way he was a charlatan. . . . Some people say I identify with him because he was a con man who was talented. Do you think I am a con man?"

—FRANCIS FORD COPPOLA

1.

PEGGY SUE GOT MARRIED premiered on October 5, 1986, on the closing night of the New York Film Festival. The film had enjoyed a number of successful previews, and advance word predicted a hit for Coppola, despite the movie's similarity to *Back to the Future*. "Coppola is back on target again," wrote critic Ron Rosenbaum in a glowing review, "in touch with something human and real and frustrating and complex. He's left behind the artificial fantasies of such turkeys as *One from the Heart* and gives us, in *Peggy Sue*, one from the soul."

The generally favorable response to the movie must have been perplexing to Coppola. Although he engaged in the obligatory promotional interviews and said all the right things about how and why he had made the picture, he felt no special connection to *Peggy Sue*. It hadn't been his own idea or script—as with *The Cotton Club*, he had been hired after the project was already in the works—but here were the critics, so willing to slash apart his more serious and ambitious efforts in the past, now falling all over themselves in praising what, by comparison, was glorified fluff. In giving the movie their thumbs-up approval, Gene Siskel and Roger Ebert proclaimed the film to be "a classic," while Rex Reed, rarely in Coppola's corner in the past, called *Peggy Sue* "Francis Coppola's best film since *The Godfather*." Others were equally enthusiastic. "Who would expect a time-travel movie to tell us so much about marriage, compromise, and coming to terms with the past?" wondered David Ansen of *Newsweek*. "This is the movie that could have been called *One From the Heart*."

The notices, as one would expect, were far from unanimous. Pauline Kael continued her string of Coppola-bashing reviews ("I came away with the feeling that Coppola took on a piece of crap thinking he could do something with it, and when he discovered he couldn't it turned into sad crap"), and *New York Times'* critic Vincent Canby, although not as rough on Coppola as in his previous reviews, felt that the director had sold himself short in his latest effort. "Mr. Coppola is a risk-taker who thinks big," offered Canby. "It's not easy to recognize him when he pursues the ordinary for such inconsequential results."

Most critics agreed that Kathleen Turner excelled in her role, but they were divided on how effectively Nicolas Cage pulled off his performance as Peggy Sue's boyfriend/husband. "He is Coppola's nephew," wrote Stanley Kauffmann disdainfully in *The New Republic*. "Nothing else explains why this thin-voiced inadequacy was given the role. Errant charm is needed, and all we get is a goof." Richard Corliss of *Time* had much less of a problem with Cage, although he, too, had his reservations. "With his dinky voice and false teeth, professing ardor in a gold lamé jacket or smacking the dumbness out of his forehead, Charlie can endear or exasperate. Cage's brave turn teeters toward caricature, then tiptoes back toward sympathy."

The commentary on the actor's voice was not unexpected. Going into the filming, Cage had known that the high, reedy tone that he had assigned to his character's voice would be controversial. Kathleen Turner, apparently unhappy with the sound of his voice, had approached him during rehearsals and warned him that he was taking a risk. "You know," she told him, "film is a permanent record. Be careful what you do." Cage, however, wanted to attempt something different with his voice, which he fashioned after a sound he heard while channel-surfing on his television—the voice of Pokey from the *Gumby* cartoon. "It stuck with me," Cage remembered. "That's the way my brain works. My character was an adult who goes back to high school, when guys' voices haven't necessarily changed yet. Also, Francis was doing a story about a woman who goes back in time via her dream. He painted the trees pink and the sidewalk salmon. Why can't actors bend things a little bit, too?"

Peggy Sue Got Married was neither a classic nor an artistic failure. What it was was a hit: During its first three weeks in theaters, *Peggy Sue* took in nearly $22 million, pushing it up the *Variety* charts and establishing the film as Coppola's biggest box-office draw of the decade. With his percentage of the gross from *Peggy Sue,* his earnings from *The Outsiders,* his director's fees for his various projects, and other business profits, Coppola was reaching a point where he could finally see an end to his mountainous debts.

2.

TUCKER HAD BEEN ON COPPOLA'S back burner for so long, and it had undergone so many changes in his mind that it seemed impossible to believe that it was finally going to be made. Coppola had spoken whimsically of the film over the years, building it up in interviews and occasionally tinkering with its development, but the lack of time and money, along with the availability of other film projects, had kept him from actually pursuing the picture in earnest. Now, in late 1986, with the assistance of George Lucas, he was only a few months from realizing his dream.

Although Coppola would downplay the strong autobiographical elements in the film, the Preston Tucker story struck closer to home than any of his previous projects. Apart from the way that Tucker had actually touched upon Coppola's life—when his father had taken him to see the Tucker automobile at an auto show in 1948 and had invested (and lost) in the automaker's company—Tucker had come to symbolize the kind of visionary dreamer, family man, and risk-taking businessman that others associated with Coppola. A characterization of Tucker, published in *People,* might have been describing Coppola himself: "Tucker, in short, was a shameless showboat who spared no expense to maintain the illusion of lush success. He rented the most sumptuous suites, made routine business calls in private planes and threw monster parties. He hired top people and paid top salaries—above all to himself. Even his enemies admit that he was an inspirational leader and a messianic salesman. But even his friends admit that he was a disastrous manager." *Collier's* magazine, in a 1949 profile published after Tucker had declared bankruptcy, called the entrepreneur "a bewildering combination of P. T. Barnum, Huck Finn, Jimmy Walker and Baron Munchausen, with a talent for telling stories that people believed and a genius for spending money."

Coppola certainly would have disputed some of the comparisons between Tucker and himself, but he could see how people found similarities, which, in fact, had attracted him to the story. "People thought Tucker was a con man," he told *New York Times'* critic Janet Maslin in 1988, "and maybe in some ways he was, but he was also legit. That's a duality that interests me because I've been accused of being a con man in the last five years. People tell me, 'You've been successful because you're a good talker, and you wheel and deal.'"

Preston Thomas Tucker was struck down by cancer in 1956, at the age of fifty-three, ending a life as devoted to the automobile industry as Coppola's had been to the movies. The son of a Michigan peppermint farmer, Tucker had been very young, only six, when a Buick accidentally ran over his foot, but rather than be terrified by the experience, he was utterly enthralled by the sight of the red horseless carriage. From that point on, he lived and breathed the automobile, learning to drive when he was only eleven and, at sixteen, taking a job as a used-car salesman. He went on to sell Studebakers, Chryslers, Pierce-Arrows, and Packards. As much an innovator by nature as he was a salesman, Tucker began to think about designing his own cars. He met race car designer Harry A. Miller, and they, along with Eddie Offutt, designed ten cars for the 1935 Indianapolis 500, their sponsor being none other than auto magnate Henry Ford. According to legend, Ford had been impressed by Tucker's gumption when he demanded that Tucker put out a cigarette—"Nobody smokes around me," said Ford—only to be rebuffed by the brash young man. "Tell that to your flunkies," Tucker supposedly shot back. "Don't tell me."

By all accounts, the episode was vintage Tucker. Tall, muscular, and good-looking, with a flair for fashionable clothing and high living, Tucker oozed self-confidence, even when he was feeling his way around in the dark. His Indy cars were a flop—none so much as finished the 1935 race—but that did little to discourage him. By the onset of World War II, Tucker was heading production at the Ypsilanti Machine and Tool Company in Michigan, filling orders for the War Department. He designed a combat vehicle that could move up to 150 miles per hour, which the army rejected as being impractical, but he scored with the air force when he designed a gun turret that was used on bombers. During the war years, Tucker also gave some thought to a bold new type of automobile—stylish, safe, innovative, reasonably priced, and, above all, capable of high performance. Since, due to the war effort, no new cars had been manufactured since 1941, Tucker reasoned that the public might be ready to embrace his innovative automobile.

In 1946, he formally started his own company, announcing that he would be producing "the Car of Tomorrow, Today," to be built in Chicago, in an enormous factory used for building bomber engines during the war. The car would be the first to have such safety features as disk brakes, seat belts, a pop-out windshield constructed of shatterproof glass, and padded dashboards. It would be capable of seating six people comfortably, and it would come equipped with a rear-mounted six-cylinder engine that could push a cruising speed of one hundred miles per hour while, at the same time, using very little gasoline. The car's design changed slightly from the time it was initially announced to the public to the time the first cars hit the street, but the Tucker remained true to its creator's vision. Car collectors and aficionados would always remember it for its third headlight, positioned between the standard headlights and rotating with the steering wheel, offering drivers added illumination in the turns.

Unfortunately for Tucker, it took capital to fulfill such ambitions—more than he was capable of raising through the sale of stock and dealer franchises—and he and his team of engineers were hard-pressed to place even a prototype vehicle in front of the public. Tucker, ever the salesman, had done his homework: Interest and demand for the car were much greater than his small company could ever hope to satisfy. The first Tucker was ceremoniously unveiled in June 1947, but industry insiders correctly predicted that, for all his good intentions, Preston Tucker would not be able to produce enough cars in a given time period to make his business profitable.

Nevertheless, the big three—Ford, General Motors, and Chrysler—took a strong interest in Tucker. The new car might not have given them any worries in terms of direct competition, but if any of Tucker's innovations caught on, the other companies might be forced to redesign their own vehicles, at considerable expense. Although never totally substantiated, rumors circulated that the big three and Michigan senator Homer Ferguson pressured the Securities and Exchange Commission into investigating Tucker for fraud and other violations of SEC regulations, and in 1949, Tucker and seven of his associates were indicted on thirty-one counts of mail fraud, conspiracy, and other violations.

Tucker was eventually acquitted of all charges, but his company was finished, having produced only fifty-one automobiles during its brief existence. Ironically, many of his ideas wound up being adopted by the other automotive manufacturers, but it was of little consolation to Tucker, who tried to work on other projects in the years following his acquittal, but never with any success.

When he first heard the Preston Tucker story, Francis Ford Coppola saw it in allegorical shadings, as the dark side of the American dream. When, as a student at UCLA, he initially thought of it in terms of a movie, he envisioned the film as "a *Citizen Kane* kind of stark scandal in the corporate world." Like the famous Orson Welles character, Tucker would fall victim to cold reality, to forces larger and darker than his dream. Or, as Coppola succinctly summarized: "Preston Tucker dies and his car dies with him."

By the time Coppola formally approached Tucker's family and purchased the rights to the automaker's story, his plans for the movie had evolved into an entirely different kind of picture. The newer version was set to be a musical, "a dark kind of piece," as Coppola recalled, "a sort of Brechtian musical in which Tucker would be the main story, but it would also involve Edison and Henry Ford and Firestone and Carnegie." At that time, Coppola was riding the crest of his success. He was the renowned director of the two *Godfather* films, a Golden Palm winner at Cannes for *The Conversation,* and he had yet to endure all of the horrors visited upon him by *Apocalypse Now.* The film world embraced his moxie and ambition, and if he wanted to make a musical about an obscure American industrialist . . . well, who was to argue? After all, he had pulled off *The Godfather* as a symbol for corporate America.

Never one to think in small terms, Coppola later hired Leonard Bernstein to write the music and Adolph Green and Betty Comden the lyrics for *Tucker.* All visited Coppola in California, and drove around the scenic Napa Valley countryside in his Tucker, conferring on his ideas for the film. Bernstein, for one, wanted the picture completely mapped out. "This isn't *Apocalypse Now,*" he told Coppola, "where we just go improvising around. How do you want to do this?" Nothing was resolved. The plans become more complex, and before Coppola could go any further in pursuing them, he was engulfed in his Zoetrope and *One from the Heart* problems and ultimately forced to drop his plans in favor of work-for-hire pictures. As he later confessed, he was too embarrassed to call Bernstein, Green, and Comden, and tell them that he had abandoned the project.

Part of the problem, Coppola would admit, stemmed from his own perception of Preston Tucker. Coppola perceived him as a heroic figure and model for the way he fashioned his own career. Others dismissed him as a failure. At one point, Coppola approached Frank Capra with an invitation to produce the film, but after listening to the young director's plans, Capra turned him down. "I don't think we can make that," Capra said of the film, "because, in the end, Tucker doesn't get his dream. Are you saying that in America you can't make your dream come true?" Coppola disagreed with Capra's interpretation of success: Whereas Capra felt that Tucker was a failure in the larger scheme of things, Coppola believed that by just building a few cars, Tucker had achieved his dream.

Coppola might have abandoned all of his hopes of making the film had it not been for his son Gio. Every year on the Fourth of July, a festive holiday parade was held in Calistoga, a small wine-producing town not far from Coppola's Napa Valley estate. Gio, a car buff, had wanted to see his father make *Tucker* for some time, and he decided that it would be fun to enter one of his father's Tuckers in the 1985 parade. Gio talked Roman and Sofia into helping him wash and wax the car, and upon seeing their handiwork, Francis agreed to ride as a passenger, with Gio driving, in the parade. The Tucker was a huge hit, and Coppola started rethinking his position on making the movie. A short time later, he gave George Lucas a call.

3.

ALTHOUGH HE WAS COPPOLA'S benefactor in rescuing *Tucker* from the scrap heap, Lucas was by no means giving Coppola carte blanche over the film. The musical idea, no longer a priority of Coppola's, was definitely out, as were any notions Coppola might have entertained of turning the picture into an art-house film. It was going to be a strictly commercial endeavor.

Lucas's own ventures in the recent past—*Howard the Duck* and *Labyrinth*, on which he had served as executive producer—had been flops, tarnishing his reputation for picking Hollywood winners, and when he approached such studios as Universal, Disney, Tri-Star, and Paramount for backing on *Tucker*, Lucas found himself without support. The picture, budgeted at $25 million, was too expensive for studio executives, who, Lucas complained, "all wanted $15 million *Three Men and a Baby* movies or *Crocodile Dundee, Part 73* sequels." If the movie was going to be made, Lucas would have to finance it himself, at least until he was able to persuade a major studio that he had a hit on his hands.

This meant that Coppola would be making a mainstream picture, something closer to *Peggy Sue* than to *The Conversation*, perhaps the kind of movie that Frank Capra might have made. Lucas wanted something upbeat and fanciful, not unlike Tucker himself, and he agreed with Coppola's assessment that the automotive entrepreneur was not necessarily a failure just because his company had gone belly-up. Coppola's film could still show the downside of the corporate experience, but it could also present Tucker as a likable maverick. As Lucas perceived it, his role was to keep Coppola focused on these goals.

"Francis can get so esoteric it can be hard for an audience to relate to him," Lucas explained at the time of *Tucker*'s release. "He needs someone to hold him back. With *Godfather*, it was Mario Puzo; with *Tucker*, it was me."

Coppola, of course, was in no position to contest the arrangement. He didn't have the money to make the picture on his own, and, as he himself admitted, the success of *Peggy Sue Got Married* had left him doubting his own ability to gauge audiences' tastes. If people wanted a movie in the *Peggy Sue* mode, he would give it to them.

Rather than write the screenplay himself, Coppola hired Arnold Schulman, author of the script for Frank Capra's 1959 *A Hole in the Head,* as well as scripts for *Love with the Proper Stranger* and *Goodbye, Columbus,* to adapt Preston Tucker's life story for the screen. A longtime admirer of Coppola's work, Schulman had once approached Coppola on an airplane and volunteered his services, free of charge, if the director ever needed him. He would be paid handsomely for his work on *Tucker,* but Schulman would earn every penny of his fee. Beside having to please Coppola and Lucas, he had to contend with the Tucker family; quite naturally, they wanted the script to present Tucker in the best possible light, which amounted to whitewashing his extramarital dalliances, as well as some of his questionable business practices. It took several attempts, but Coppola had a complete shooting script before he led his actors through rehearsals.

As Schulman recalled, he was reluctant at first to take on the project.

"He told me all about Tucker, whom I had never heard of," Schulman said of his initial conversation with Coppola. "I told him I hated cars. 'I would like to work with you, Francis,' I said, 'but I *really* hate cars.' He said, 'Will you meet with me and George Lucas, and talk about it?'"

Lucas wound up persuading Schulman to reconsider his position.

"George said, 'This film is not about cars. It's about Francis. Why don't you go live with Francis in Napa for a few weeks and then let me know?' I did that, and then I realized of course the film was about Francis, and told them I'd love to do it."

Shooting began on April 13, 1987, with Jeff Bridges in the title role. In the past, Coppola had considered casting Burt Reynolds or Jack Nicholson as Preston Tucker, but neither was presently right for the part. Bridges had earned his chops early in his career, when he played Duane Jackson in Peter Bogdonavich's *The Last Picture Show.* His career subsequently became a hodgepodge of up-and-down roles, many in action pictures. His Oscar and Golden Globe nominations for his work in *Starman* had reaffirmed his credentials as a top-notch leading man. Bridges had the size, good looks, and winning smile necessary to any portrayal of Preston Tucker.

Joan Allen, who played Kathleen Turner's closest high school friend in *Peggy Sue Got Married,* signed on to play Tucker's wife, Vera, and Frederic Forrest was assigned the role of Eddie Dane, Tucker's top mechanic. Lloyd Bridges, Jeff's father, and a longtime movie and television star in his own right, appeared (although uncredited) as Senator Homer Ferguson. As always, Coppola had one major casting coup, this time in securing Martin Landau to play Abe Karatz, Tucker's chief financial officer. Known mostly for his starring role in television's *Mission Impossible,* Landau had rarely been given anything of substance in the movies, other than an occasional role as a heavy, and his selection for the important role in *Tucker* had been a surprise, not only to industry insiders but to Landau himself. Landau rewarded Coppola's faith by delivering a performance that would earn him a Golden Globe award, as well as an Oscar nomination for Best Supporting Actor.

Tucker was designed to be a stylish production, with the look and feel of an older picture, complete with the voice-over narration popular in older newsreels and corporate promotional films. Coppola's production team represented one of his finest crews ever, each member beautifully matched to what would be a very challenging task. Vittorio Storaro, a recent Oscar winner for his work on *The Last Emperor,* was back as the director of photography, his first feature-length assignment with Coppola since *One from the Heart,* and Milena Canonero, the costume designer for *The Cotton Club* and, more recently, *Out of Africa* and *Barfly,* was brought on board to design the late-forties costumes in *Tucker.* Dean and Alex Tavoularis returned in their customary roles in production design and art direction.

The production team came through in a big way, giving Coppola his most visually pleasing picture since *One from the Heart.*

"The late-40s world Coppola has put together for *Tucker* is an extremely stylized one," noted *Chicago Tribune* critic Dave Kehr when the movie was released in August 1988. "Vittorio Storaro's cinematography has the bright, hard, almost lacquered look of old Technicolor; Dean Tavoularis' sets, built with slanting floors and surfaces, create an imaginary, compacted space in which actors and objects seem to be thrusting out toward the camera; and the transitions between scenes, based on visual rhymes and elaborate wipes, effectively remove the movie from the orderly flow of normal film time." In an otherwise-negative review for *The New Republic,* Stanley Kauffmann wrote, "Vittorio Storaro, as usual, seems to have photographed through a paint box. Most of the film looks much too gorgeous and soft for its Yankee git-up-and-git intent."

While a handful of critics would complain that Tucker continued Coppola's style-over-substance trend in recent movies, likening the look of the film to the warm, pleasing covers of vintage *Saturday Evening Posts* or *Popular Mechanics,* the quibbles only reinforced what had been written about Coppola and his production teams since *The Godfather:* Very few directors could compete with Coppola when it came down to making a visually stunning film.

4.

ON MAY 8, LESS THAN A MONTH after Coppola began filming *Tucker,* *Gardens of Stone* premiered to a spate of negative reviews and a largely disinterested public. In the past, the release of a Francis Ford Coppola movie commanded a lot of attention—even if, in many cases, the notices were negative—but there seemed to be less interest in *Gardens of Stone* than in any Coppola picture since *Rumble Fish. Time* magazine devoted only one paragraph to a capsule review of the movie, and a *Newsweek* review used up only half a page; others ignored it entirely. There were still plenty of reviews to go around, but in far too many instances, when he wasn't being panned, Coppola was damned with faint praise, depicted as a gifted director who, for one reason or another, had lost or abandoned his muse. Pauline Kael, who seemed to have enjoyed *Gardens of Stone* more than any Coppola film in a decade, sounded downright patronizing in her review, not unlike a Little League coach patting a young kid on the back and encouraging him to do better next time. "He has gone from great director to vacuous stylist to good-and-bad director," she wrote of Coppola in her *New Yorker* review. "He seems to be fighting his way back—if not to greatness, at least to substantial, workmanlike moviemaking. In *Gardens of Stone,* he's about halfway there."

Kael was by no means alone in her assessment. Others echoed her sentiments almost to the letter. "There are remnants of a once-great director in *Gardens of Stone,*" remarked Hal Hinson for the *Washington Post.* "Here and in his last movie, *Peggy Sue Got Married,* Coppola seems to be trying to remember what it's like to build a movie on a human scale, to deal with the basics of character and story and emotion. But it's a bit like watching a gifted athlete learn to walk again after a serious injury. The moves are somewhere in his head; if only he can get to them."

These and similar notices were not the kind of reviews that Coppola could have found so much as remotely encouraging. Critics, outwardly weary or fed up with Coppola's efforts of the 1980s—yet keenly aware of the director's personal crises during that period, including the tragic loss of his son—disliked *Gardens of Stone* but seemed to be groping for something positive to say about it. Few could hide their disappointment. "The film has some fine moments," noted Tom O'Brien in *Commonweal,* "[but] it never has the sureness and tone that one hopes for from Coppola; perhaps *The Godfather* spoiled us."

Although he would have had to look carefully, Coppola could have found solace in some of the reviews. Critics singled out James Caan for his work in the film, praising his performance as one of the highlights of the movie—"Clell is the film's only fully realized character, and Mr. Caan, in his first movie in five years, plays him with humor and intensity, like the veteran he now is"—and there were, here and there, reviews touting *Gardens of Stone* as an unqualified success. Lawrence O'Toole, commenting on the picture for *Maclean's,* declared the film to be "exceptionally moving," praising it as Coppola's comeback film. "With a powerful subject to energize him," O'Toole offered, "Coppola has returned to the masterly storytelling of *The Godfather* and *The Godfather, Part II.* Like the novel from which it comes, *Gardens of Stone* stirringly acknowledges the wounds of a nation still seeking its own peace."

Gardens of Stone sank almost as quickly as *Rumble Fish.* Tri-Star, having very little confidence in the movie, offered only minimal support, distributing it to a mere sixty theaters across the country and devoting virtually nothing to advertising the picture, hoping that reviews and favorable word-of-mouth response might give the film the impetus needed to justify wider distribution at a later date. Attendance, like the reviews, was dismal. Three weeks into its release, *Gardens of Stone* had taken in $4,358,779 in gross rentals, with little indication of improvement. It quickly slid from sight.

Whether discouraged by the reception given *Gardens of Stone,* frustrated by his less-than-total control over his last three movies, fearful that he would never again make the kind of movie that he wanted to make, or weary from the crushing workload of the recent past, Coppola began to make noises about retiring from the business. It was a refrain that he had voiced in the past, but now, he informed interviewers, he had finally worked himself out of his financial hole and was in the position to choose the kind of life that he wanted to live.

His vineyard, for one, had become an unexpected source of optimism. When he purchased his Napa Valley estate in 1975, he had no intention of making a big commercial enterprise out of his vineyard. He would have been content to engage in a modest undertaking that supplemented his income and provided him with wine for gifts and table use. As much as anything else, the vineyard represented a haven during times of turmoil, and saving it had been one of the huge motivating factors in Coppola's decision to work on others' projects.

He was pleased by what his grapes yielded. People enjoyed the chardonnay and zinfandel, and he had high hopes for the Rubicon, which was being produced to the tune of three to five thousand cases per year. The Rubicon took years to age, but Coppola could afford to be patient. "I demand of my wine maker that it be full, rich, and last one hundred years," he stated.

Newspapers and magazines had posted occasional articles about Coppola's vineyard, but to most reporters, the wine making was just another of

Coppola's sidelines—a cut above his disastrous involvement in *City* magazine perhaps, but certainly nothing serious enough to take him away from making movies. In his more whimsical moments, Coppola wasn't so sure. His product was starting to gain recognition—Paris's Le Taillevent restaurant was adding his 1984 Rubicon to its wine list—and Coppola dreamed of how much more simplified his life might become if he lived at the Napa estate, produced good wine, and made small art films that didn't depend upon huge box-office figures to be considered successful.

5.

FOR THE TIME BEING, HOWEVER, he had a $25 million picture to make. To familiarize his cast and crew with the subject of the movie, Coppola had showed them the old corporate promotional films, as well as Tucker's own home movies, and, as always, there had been a two-week rehearsal period, netting a videotaped storyboard. Coppola moved quickly, feeling an urgency to get the story on film as soon as possible, not only to appease George Lucas and adhere to the budget but also to avoid any complications that might crop up if there was a Directors Guild strike, which loomed as a strong possibility later in the summer. Fortunately, the shoot went smoothly, and Coppola was able to wrap principal photography on July 17, after a mere thirteen weeks of filming.

"It was one of the most designed movies that I've ever worked on," remembered Dean Tavoularis. "Months before we were due to do it, Vittorio Storaro, my brother Alex, and I went to Napa and spent well over a week, working eight-hour days in Francis's little cottage, going over the script. We discussed different ideas about how each scene could be shot. Months later, when we were shooting, I think we shot about ninety percent of what we talked about at that cottage. It went exactly as we had discussed it."

As film biography, *Tucker* fell far short of even the loosest definition of thorough, objective reporting. Jeff Bridges turned in a commendable performance, exuding a willful optimism that defied the odds against him, yet in glossing over Tucker's less agreeable sides, Coppola risked presenting a character that was too saccharine for public tastes. Cynics argued that Coppola chose the approach because it was the way he perceived himself—which, in fact, was true enough to a certain extent—but as a filmmaker, Coppola was far more interested in presenting his fable about the American dream than in preserving historical accuracy. After all, this was the movies, and viewers were willing to concede some accuracy in exchange for entertainment.

Not that Bridges's exaggerated performance went unnoticed or unappreciated. "Could anyone else play this role with the unforced authority that

Bridges brings to it?" wondered Richard Corliss of *Time*. "The Bridges version is splendidly driven, maniacally uncomplicated. The performance is also true to the prototype." Not surprisingly, the Tucker family was thrilled with Bridges's portrayal. "He's got it all, in the mannerisms and the look," gushed John Tucker, the automaker's son. "My father was very positive, always thinking of what came next. Jeff captures that."

The family couldn't help but be pleased with Coppola's highly romanticized version of the Tucker story, from the beginning of the film, which opens in the framework of an old industrial promotional film, to the end, when Tucker, bowed but not beaten, triumphantly circles his automobiles outside the courtroom. Preston Tucker is a lovable renegade, full of the kind of delightful quirks guaranteed to make audiences smile and, ultimately, cheer. The only thing missing is canned applause at the end of the movie.

Nevertheless, the story works. We see Tucker racing around in his old armored carrier, buying ice cream for his family; hatching his plans for his new, radically different automobile; meeting with Howard Hughes, who offers his own unique take on the state of the world; and taking on the system with the kind of boyish enthusiasm that we know will not carry the day, but which will endear him to underdogs everywhere.

Tucker's singular vision for his automobile, like Coppola's vision for electronic cinema, is not immediately embraced by his contemporaries, including Abe Karatz, his financial adviser, who can see nothing but trouble ahead. Tucker disregards his advice and rents a huge government factory—on the condition that he produce $15 million in front money. Tucker, sold on his own dream, proceeds full speed ahead.

The odds are stacked against him at every turn. Not only must he act as a cheerleader with his own advisers, engineers, and builders, convincing them that his vision can be realized; he must also overcome the effects of the villainous Bennington, his chairman of the board, who betrays him and tries to sabotage his efforts. In one dazzling sequence, dancing girls stall for time, entertaining potential investors at the grand unveiling of the car, while Tucker's workers labor feverishly to repair an oil leak in the prototype car.

The problems multiply. Karatz, who, it turns out, was once jailed for bank fraud, is forced to resign. Bennington plots with Senator Ferguson, a politician in the pockets of the big three automakers, to have Tucker brought up on bogus stock-fraud charges. A hearing before a grand jury goes poorly until Tucker, in a heroic speech on his own behalf, wins over his skeptics.

Coppola might not have been able to win over his own skeptics when he attempted to launch his own studio, but his movie, when issued on

August 12, 1988, brought in a surprisingly large number of favorable reviews. There were the predictable comparisons between Coppola's new movie and the earlier films by Frank Capra, but critics were not dismissing the picture as quickly as they had waved off some of Coppola's other recent efforts; if anything, they were charmed by what was one filmmaker's homage to the American spirit, if not the American dream itself. It was an election year, and Coppola's film was released at a time when optimism from the national conventions was running at full throttle.

Coppola had to have been happy to see that reviewers shared his belief that in building fifty cars before going under, Preston Tucker had achieved a major victory.

"Preston Tucker failed to attain what we are pleased to think of as the American Dream of success," wrote Richard Schickel for *Time* magazine. "But there is another more common, more potent American Dream, which involves not the invention of products but the invention of self. And this movie, genial and fierce, is proof of Tucker's success in that more basic line. And proof of its sure grip on our imaginations."

"In the end," argued *The New Yorker*'s Terrence Rafferty, "the movie seems as if it had been made by Preston Tucker himself. His style—his 'dream,' his spirit—is all he has left after the big boys are done with him. He remains the image of the grinning American optimist, and we're not encouraged to consider him a fool for believing that the undiminished fervor of his imagination constitutes some sort of victory."

Other critics made essentially the same observation, but went one step further, making the comparison between Tucker's and Coppola's dreams.

"Tucker lost his company," noted James M. Wall in *The Christian Century*, "but not until he had made fifty cars, most of which are still around as antiques. Coppola made movies through his own company, all of which are still around, not as antiques, but as examples of innovative style. This film is a tribute to that style."

"What makes this unapologetically up movie work is Coppola's infectious idea-mongering," added Peter Travers in *People*. "No matter if Tucker the man sold only fifty cars, or if Tucker the movie sells only fifty tickets. Coppola, like his maverick mentor, has made a thing of beauty."

Unfortunately for Coppola, Travers's words carried a ring of prophecy: While *Tucker* earned Coppola some of his best reviews in recent memory, the film itself was a disaster at the box office, taking in less than $10 million in domestic rentals in its first twelve weeks.

6.

COPPOLA HAD BARELY HAD time to catch his breath from the *Tucker* experience when he agreed to contribute a segment to a movie anthology being put together by Woody Allen. The anthology, entitled *New York Stories,* would present three short films, all set in New York City, to be directed by Allen, Coppola, and Martin Scorsese. In retrospect, Coppola might have been well advised to pass on the project, but it takes no stretch of the imagination to see how the prospects of contributing to a project featuring two of America's most highly regarded film directors might have appealed to Coppola. In addition, he would be working on an extremely challenging form, trying to create a short, self-contained film that had at least a nodding relationship with the other two entries.

Coppola's involvement in the project came only after *New York Stories,* as a concept, had gone through its own evolutionary process. In the beginning, Woody Allen had hoped to offer several of his own short films in an omnibus format—similar to a collection of novellas—but his longtime producer, Robert Greenhut, countered with the suggestion that it might be "more ambitious and more fun" (not to mention more attractive to potential backers) to have different directors working on the individual segments. Allen agreed, and the search for prospective directors was on.

Allen and Greenhut were intrigued by the possibility of giving the anthology an international flavor, with contributions by such Allen favorites as Ingmar Bergman and Federico Fellini, but they dropped the idea as being impractical. Presenting an anthology in several languages would probably be too much for American audiences. Both agreed that it would be best to limit the search to American directors.

Martin Scorsese, a native New Yorker whose films were almost as closely identified with the city as Woody Allen's, was a natural choice, and he was the first to sign on. Other directors, including Bob Fosse and Mike Nichols, were discussed but ultimately crossed off the list because their approaches or styles were too similar to Allen's or Scorsese's; Steven Spielberg, although an acceptable and interested candidate, was busy with other projects. Francis Ford Coppola, Caryn James reported in a *New York Times* article announcing the movie, "seemed to occupy just the right middle ground."

Even with three of the film industry's finest directors in the fold, *New York Stories* had difficulty finding the financing for its proposed $15 million budget. Orion Pictures, Allen's regular studio, passed on the project, judging it too risky an investment. *Twilight Zone—The Movie,* a recent anthology featuring several outstanding directors and what was believed to be a can't-miss *Twilight Zone* banner, had been a disappointment at the box office, and, in all likelihood, it was more widely known for its controversial legal problems than for the excellence of its different installments. Touchstone Pictures eventually agreed to back the movie, but all parties involved recognized that the film would have to be special or face the prospects of becoming just another oddity that bombed at the box office. As critic Vincent Canby pointed out in an essay on the anthology format, audiences could be less than agreeable to the prospects of adjusting to several different and complete stories within a single film.

"The same people who will willingly sit through a double feature," wrote Canby, "appear to resent, rather than appreciate, being asked to adjust their sights to three, four, or five beginnings, middles, and ends within one film. It may be that they feel that they're not getting their money's worth, rather than getting triple, quadruple, or quintuple the value."

At first glance, Coppola's coming up with a segment for *New York Stories* appeared to be the wrong choice of project. After all, he was known for grand, operatic films, and was often hard-pressed to bring a picture in at what studio executives considered to be a reasonable running time. Just one segment of *Godfather II* ran longer than the half-hour allotment given to his *New York Stories* installment. In addition, Coppola had been grumbling about being burned-out from all the recent work, and threatening retirement to any journalist who would listen, but here he was, embarking on another new project—and one that he had serious second thoughts about, as well.

"I have no business doing this film," he confessed to one reporter, while confiding in another, "This is going to be as bad as the horse's head."

The main reason for Coppola's taking on the project was the opportunity it gave him to work with his seventeen-year-old daughter, Sofia, who not only designed the costumes and created the film's opening credits sequence but who also had a hand in the scriptwriting. Sofia showed creative potential, and Coppola was eager to help her develop it, much the way he had encouraged his sons and helped nurture their budding careers.

"My dad took me to Las Vegas," Sofia remembered, "and he got a suite. We ordered room service and worked away, writing every day. It was his scriptwriting workshop with me. He loves to go to Vegas or Reno—somewhere that you can write for hours and then go out at any hour. With the costumes, I was encouraged to do what I liked, to use my style; my dad always pushes for that, which makes something unique and personal."

However, in the case of his *New York Stories* segment, Coppola erred in favor of family over profession: If he was going to see his entry sandwiched between segments by Martin Scorsese and Woody Allen, he needed to come up with a strong script, which *Life Without Zoe* definitely was not. Scorsese was constructing an intense piece on inspiration and the relationship among art, life, and love, while Allen was skewering the Oedipus complex, as confronted by a Jewish mother and her son, in one of his funniest yarns in some time. In such company, the Coppola piece looked badly out of place.

Coppola's "horse's head" comment was a reference to his story's subject: He knew going in that he was going to be slashed by his critics for making a film about a privileged child. There was a prejudice, he claimed, against this type of story. Nevertheless, he had watched how his own children had handled wealth, and he felt that there was an important message about innocence, love, and loyalty that could be told in an entertaining way.

"I always thought my kids, when push comes to shove, are always real loyal, true blue, honest, won't let down a friend," he said. "That's much more important than whether she loves Chanel clothes."

That may very well be true, but as a story, *Life Without Zoe* is little more than a fleshed-out anecdote, a puff piece that might have been charming had Francis and Sofia Coppola been better able to anchor their tale. As it is, *Life Without Zoe* is a quick accounting of a little rich girl, left by her parents to fend for herself in New York's privileged society.

Zoe, the story's protagonist, is an eleven-year-old living in Manhattan's Sherry-Netherland Hotel. Her father, Claudio, plays the flute and is constantly traveling with an orchestra, and her mother, Charlotte, a journalist, is likewise away for long stretches of time, leaving Zoe to be raised, for all practical purposes, by Hector, the family's butler. The precocious child moves around New York City on her own, attending a private school during the day and shopping and dining afterward. She is, in almost every respect, an adult.

During the course of the story, we meet Abu, reportedly the world's richest kid, but someone who, by his own admission, has no friends; a homeless man to whom Zoe takes a liking; and an assortment of Zoe's friends. The characters are drawn in quick, broad strokes, and none are particularly memorable.

For all her worldliness, Zoe is still a child and would like to live in a more traditional family; she yearns to see her parents together. She is afforded an opportunity when she witnesses a robbery at the hotel, during which she manages to retrieve a valuable diamond earring with its own strange history, which Zoe uses to orchestrate a reconciliation between her parents. The story ends with the three in Greece, where Claudio is performing.

Coppola began production on the movie in June 1988, with newcomer
Heather McComb in the title role, and Talia Shire and Giancarlo Giannini
playing her parents. Coppola placed his father, Carmine, the inspiration for
the Claudio character, in his biggest movie role to date, as a street musician
who befriends Zoe. Don Novello, Father Guido Sarducci in the *Saturday
Night Live* skits (and a bit player in several of Coppola's earlier films), won the
role of Hector. Beside the pleasure of working with family members on
another project, Coppola was again treated to the opportunity of working
with children—a situation that might have been difficult for many directors
but which delighted Coppola, who always had a great love for youngsters.

New York Stories was released on February 26, 1989, and *Life Without Zoe*
was an unqualified disaster, easily the weakest of the anthology's three segments. Critics mercilessly pasted the brief film, the kinder reviews dismissing
it as "a mess," "self-indulgence without substance . . . a home movie by a dot-
ing godfather," or "blatantly silly." Other reviewers, weary of watching still
another disappointing offering by a director who had shown such genius
only a decade ago brought out heavier ammunition.

"Francis Ford Coppola['s] segment is so thoroughly, megalomaniacally
bad that it becomes, in a perverse way, the must-see part of this anthology,"
offered Stuart Klawans of *The Nation*. "Coppola has been a major filmmaker;
his place in Hollywood is secure. Like everyone else, I long to see him make
full use of his talent again. That's why I'm haunted by 'Life Without Zoe,'
which opens up unanticipated perspectives of egomania and self-delusion."

Stanley Kauffmann, a critic who had been especially tough on Coppola
in the past, found the segment "dull."

"Through *Apocalypse Now*, his films, whether successful or not, showed a
director with an edge, an ambition, a large-scale identity in formation,"
Kauffmann wrote of Coppola. "Since then, he has not only not developed,
he has lost identity. It's as if the strain of *Apocalypse Now* left him stranded,
grasping but not reaching."

Pauline Kael devoted only one paragraph of her lengthy *New Yorker*
review of *New York Stories* to *Life Without Zoe*, but she summarized several
other critics' sentiments when she noted that "Coppola's head doesn't seem
to be in his moviemaking."

Coppola might not have been terribly enthused about making this small
film, but he wasn't going to take a lot of criticism sitting down, either. Some
of the problems in *Life Without Zoe*, he claimed, were the results of the film's
losing some of its edge during postproduction.

"The original screenplay had a lot of dark parts about it," he explained, saying that the studio was more interested in the "Eloise at the Plaza thing" than in some of the more serious aspects of the script—particularly the relationship between the girl and her father. "In the attempt to make it delightful and charming, they were eliminated."

In all likelihood, nothing would have saved *Life Without Zoe*. Coppola had worried for some time that he had lost touch with his audiences, and if he ever needed to verify his suspicions, all he would have needed to do was study his latest thirty-four-minute effort.

7.

WITH THE COMPLETION OF *Life Without Zoe*, Coppola ended one of the most intense work periods of his career. He had never been one to sit idle or go for any length of time without a project, but in just over three years' time, he had directed three feature-length films (*Peggy Sue Got Married, Gardens of Stone*, and *Tucker*), a television movie (*Rip Van Winkle*), an amusement park video (*Captain Eo*), and a brief anthology entry. The work had produced mixed results at the box office and with critics, and if the films seemed to be a far cry from what Coppola had accomplished as a young filmmaker during the previous decade, they also served valuable purposes. Coppola needed the work—to diminish his debt and, after the death of his son, to keep him busy— and after the horrors visited upon him during and after his Zoetrope experience, he needed to prove that he was as capable as anyone of making movies the Hollywood way.

As an artist, Coppola was nearly as disappointed with some of his recent work as his critics. He continued to praise *The Rain People, The Conversation*, and *Rumble Fish* as his favorites of his own productions, and he longed to return to the kind of movies that he'd made as an ambitious young filmmaker. In his darker moods, he doubted whether he would ever again be able to pursue such projects: Movies were as formulaic as ever, and if he intended to continue working—and earning the kind of money he and his family needed—he would have little choice but to make the kind of movies that studios and distributors were willing to finance.

In January 1989, while vacationing in Italy, he found what might have been a suitable alternative. Stating that he still aspired to make a film "so big and complicated that it would seem impossible," Coppola announced that he had reached an agreement with Cinecittà, the huge Italian studio complex, and that he and his wife would be moving to Rome, where he would make two movies over the next five years. One of the films, which he was calling *Le Ribellion di Catilina*, sounded much like what he had in store for *Megalopolis*. According to an account published in *The Hollywood Reporter*, the movie would "swing from the past to the present, and the images of ancient Rome will merge and blend with the New York of today." Coppola would be bringing his electronic cinema to the homeland of his ancestors, and saying goodbye to what he called the "economic blackmail" of the American motion picture industry.

"I want to be free," he told Italy's *Grazia* magazine. "I don't want producers around me telling me what to do. The real dream of my life is a place where people can live in peace and create what they want."

Such feelings, offered in the aftermath of the battering he had taken for his recent films, were understandable. Ironically, Coppola was about to experience a rebirth as a filmmaker, at least in terms of the box-office appeal of his next four films. But the success would arrive as a result of his revisiting his past, rather than from revamping his career in a foreign country.

The Corleone family was again knocking on his door.

Chapter Sixteen

The Biggest Home Movie in History

"When I was a kid, I learned that if you didn't strike a diamond with one perfect blow, it wouldn't be perfect. I do that sixty to a thousand times a day here—and each time it costs me hundreds of thousands of dollars."

—FRANCIS FORD COPPOLA

1.

IN THE FIFTEEN YEARS that had passed since the release of *The Godfather, Part II,* there had been more rumors about a third *Godfather* installment than anyone could have possibly kept track of. All told, including television showings and video sales, the first two pictures had taken in more than $1 billion worldwide, making a cash cow out of what had originally been earmarked as a low-budget, quickie gangster flick; business and acting careers had been launched as a result of the movies' unprecedented success, and their director had used the pictures, along with *The Conversation* and *Apocalypse Now,* to launch his reputation as one of the most important directors of his time. Paramount, quite understandably, was eager to tap into the *Godfather* success as many times as the market would allow, but every time the studio approached Francis Ford Coppola with the idea of making *Godfather III,* the director refused to have anything to do with it.

Coppola was no fool. He realized that he stood to earn a huge amount of money—perhaps his biggest payday ever—by writing and directing a new *Godfather* picture, but as an artist, he had grave reservations. He had accomplished the unthinkable by winning the Best Picture Oscar, along with a slew of other awards, for the first two movies. He had redesigned the gangster film with *The Godfather,* and had redefined the movie sequel with *Godfather II.* He firmly believed that he had nothing new to offer.

"How can you top the first one?" he wondered. "It was the one that introduced the characters and the styles and the things that made *The Godfather* good. So the third film can't introduce that again; it can only try to put a new twist on it or something."

Beside this, he still harbored the familiar complaints that he had expressed when Paramount first approached him about directing *Godfather II.* He was tired of the Mafia and of depicting their violent behavior, and while he certainly didn't ever intend to dismiss all that he had achieved (and earned) in the earlier pictures, he hated the prospects of having his reputation forever chained to the *Godfather* movies. The two pictures—particularly the first—had been almost unbearably difficult to make, and with expectations raised exponentially for the third picture, Coppola dreaded the thought of the toll he might have to pay by continuing the saga. It would be best, he decided, to stand on what he had already accomplished.

This was not the response that the Paramount brass wanted to hear. After enjoying a string of major successes in the 1970s, the company's fortunes had leveled off, and officials were almost frantic for another blockbuster. In theory, a *Godfather* picture was money in the bank, but Paramount also recognized that Coppola, as a filmmaker, had set an incredibly high standard of excellence. If the new picture didn't at least approach that standard, it faced the possibility of becoming an expensive, embarrassing dud, scorned by the critics and ignored by the public. With Coppola resisting involvement in the production, Paramount considered other directors. Martin Scorsese seemed to be a natural selection, as were veteran directors Sidney Lumet (who had worked with Al Pacino on *Serpico* and *Dog Day Afternoon*), Costa-Gavras (who had turned down the director's job on the initial *Godfather*), Alan Pakula, and Robert Benton. Michael Mann, whose *Miami Vice* was one of the hippest, most popular shows on television, and Michael Cimino, still recovering from his *Heaven's Gate* fiasco, were also considered. At one point, the company even came close to signing Sylvester Stallone to direct and star in the film, but the deal fell apart.

One of the main drawbacks was the absence of an acceptable screenplay—though it wasn't for Paramount's lack of trying. Between 1974 and 1989, the studio invested nearly $800,000 on treatments and screenplays, yielding no less than a dozen finished scripts, but none met the company's approval. The list of screenwriters was impressive, including Alexander Jacobs (cowriter of *The French Connection*), Dean Reisner, and Vincent Patrick (author of *The Pope of Greenwich Village*); even Charles Bluhdorn, chairman of Gulf & Western, took a whack at writing a treatment, as did Michael Eisner and Don Simpson. In most of the scripts, Michael Corleone's son, Anthony, was the central character, with Michael either being snuffed out or relegated to a minor role, and in most cases, the story featured a lot of international intrigue, with the Corleone family locking horns with the CIA, Castro's Cuban government, or South American drug cartels. All were considered and rejected. The problem, said Paramount officials, was in the screenwriters' tendency to develop intricate, action-packed story lines at the expense of the kind of characters that made the first two *Godfather* films so appealing to viewers. "The focus has been on plotting rather than characterization," read one studio memo.

Mario Puzo, the obvious choice to write a script continuing the Corleone saga, had been involved, off and on, since June 1978, but his efforts had fared no better than the others. At first, Puzo was reluctant to work on a third *Godfather* picture. He, like Coppola, had had enough of the Corleones; he'd made his money on this particular group of characters and was ready to resume his career as a novelist. He changed his mind, however, when Paramount offered him a quarter of a million dollars for a fifty-page treatment, along with the promise of a whopping 6 percent of the gross of the eventual movie made from it. Puzo flew to the Dominican Republic and conferred with Charles Bluhdorn on what the Gulf & Western executive had in mind for the new picture, and from Bluhdorn's ideas, he put together an intricately plotted treatment involving Anthony Corleone's being recruited by the CIA to assassinate a Latin American dictator. Overflowing with foreign intrigue, double-crosses, and spectacular violence, the Puzo treatment had many of the right elements for a *Godfather* picture, but it, like the others, was turned down for being too light on characterization.

Puzo resurfaced as a screenwriter on the project eight years later, in the spring of 1986, when Paramount began mounting its strongest effort yet to see *Godfather III* into production. Paramount chairman Frank Mancuso had made the picture one of his company's top priorities, and when hiring Puzo to take another shot at the script, he advised the novelist to restore the strange balance of evil and nobility that had made the Corleone family so compelling a decade and a half earlier. Armed with these instructions, Puzo went to work, and in October 1986, he handed in a script that returned much of the story's focus to Michael Corleone. Nicholas Gage, hired by Mancuso to produce the film, subsequently revised the Puzo script, fashioning the new permutation after the dual story lines in *Godfather II*. In the Puzo/Gage script, the flashbacks dealt with Sonny Corleone's rise to prominence in the Corleone family—an interesting choice, since the script introduced Sonny's bastard son, Vincent (the product of Sonny's brief sexual encounter with Lucy Mancini during Connie's wedding in *The Godfather*), as a central character. Tracing the parallel rises of Sonny and Vincent to power not only mirrored the similar expositions involving Vito and Michael Corleone in *Godfather II* but it also filled in more of the time gap in the overall *Godfather* saga. Confident that they had finally come up with a decent, workable script, Gage announced that *Godfather III* would be going into production the following spring.

There was, however, one major roadblock: The film still had no director. Unlike some Paramount officials, who were leery of hiring Coppola, given his recent history of film flops and his long-standing reputation of being difficult to control, Frank Mancuso felt that it was imperative that Coppola be persuaded to join the *Godfather III* team. No one, with the possible exception of Mario Puzo, knew the Corleones better, and it seemed risky, if not downright bad judgment, to hire anyone but Coppola to bring the new picture to the screen.

As one might imagine, Coppola had been tracking the various developments in *Godfather III* over the years, and while he was put off by what others envisioned for a film that he admittedly wanted nothing to do with, he could not shake the residual emotions that he felt toward the characters he'd developed so many years ago. "It's a little bit like hearing that your ex-girlfriend is going out with so-and-so," he remarked at the time. "You don't care. But you *do* care."

But not enough, apparently, to change his mind. Desperate to get the picture under way, Mancuso decided to approach Coppola through intermediaries. Sid Ganis, a Coppola acquaintance dating back to the director's *Finian's Rainbow* and *Rain People* days at Warner Bros., was presently working as the head of production at Paramount, and through Ganis, Mancuso was able to convince Talia Shire to deliver the Puzo/Gage screenplay to her brother. Coppola agreed to give the script a look, but after reading through the first few pages of it, he delivered his verdict with typical hyperbolic flair.

He tossed the script into the fire.

2.

UNFORTUNATELY FOR COPPOLA, events in his past were about to force him to reconsider his position.

Jack Singer, Coppola's onetime benefactor and current nemesis, was still demanding that Coppola repay the $3 million he had loaned him to help finance *One from the Heart*. For eight years, Singer and Coppola had been engaged in a series of costly, protracted court battles over the loan, with Coppola claiming, for openers, that Singer's money had been an investment rather than a loan, and then that in selling his Zoetrope studio to Singer for well under the market value, he had fulfilled his obligations to the Canadian businessman. Singer disagreed. More importantly, the courts disagreed, and it was beginning to look as if Coppola might be forced to pay Singer the original $3 million, along with interest and perhaps even legal and court costs.

In recent months, Coppola had been boasting to the media that he had finally hacked his way out of the horrible debt that had plagued him throughout the eighties and that, in fact, his net worth could be upward of $50 million. Coppola might have been worth such money on paper, but it was very unlikely that he would have been able to come up with the actual cash to absolve his debt to Singer. With more court decisions looming in the near future, Coppola was again snagged in the position of having to drop a pet project—the ambitious *Elective Affinities*—in favor of another work-for-hire arrangement.

Under these conditions, working on another *Godfather* picture was looking more and more appealing: At least in this case, unlike some of his other work-for-hire pictures of the past, he held some significant bargaining chips. In the eyes of the public, he *was* the Godfather, and if Paramount wanted him so desperately for its new movie, he was in the position to call some of the shots, both in terms of the money he would be earning and in terms of artistic control.

When it was finally struck, the deal, like most Hollywood deals, left all parties feeling victorious. Coppola and Frank Mancuso met for dinner one evening, and afterward, as they sat in Mancuso's car and talked in Coppola's driveway, the Paramount chairman asked the filmmaker what it would take to convince him to direct the new movie. If he wanted complete control over the production, he could have it.

This was all that Coppola needed to hear. "I can assure you," he told Mancuso, "my own thing will be something coherent, and hopefully exciting. It's not going to be like an experimental movie all of a sudden."

Although Mancuso was prepared to grant Coppola his wishes, other Paramount officials were less supportive. Francis Ford Coppola films had a history of being expensive, even if the director came in on or under budget, and *Godfather III* promised to be a costly adventure, with or without Coppola at the helm. In addition, Coppola and Paramount had different ideas on what the film would be, and how long it would take to complete. Coppola, quite naturally, wanted to take his time in working on a new script and directing the film; Paramount, on the other hand, wanted the film as soon as possible—in time for the 1990 holiday season, at the very latest. With so much uncertainty about the picture, both Coppola and Paramount agreed that a feasibility study might be in order, and for a fee of forty thousand dollars, Coppola and Zoetrope were to prepare a detailed proposal on how he intended to make the movie, right down to an estimated budget and schedule.

Several months later, Coppola delivered his plans. Unlike earlier treatments and scripts that minimized the importance of—or eliminated entirely—some of the characters in the first two *Godfather* movies, the Coppola story line concentrated on the major characters in the previous films, particularly Michael Corleone. ("That's where the tragedy lies," Coppola declared.) In doing so, Coppola realized that he would also be increasing the film's budget: Al Pacino, Diane Keaton, Robert Duvall, and others had watched their careers escalate since their involvement in the 1972 *Godfather;* they would not be working for paltry salaries and the glory of appearing in a movie adaptation of the biggest best-seller of its time. This time around, there would be serious money involved. Al Pacino alone was earning in the neighborhood of $5 million per picture—a heady figure, considering that it cost a *total* of $6 million to make the original *Godfather,* and that the sequel had come in at $13 million. There was little doubt that with Coppola's writing and directing fees, Puzo's writing fee, and the actors' salaries, *Godfather III* might come close to exceeding the overall costs of the two earlier films combined.

However, the times and movie budgets had changed, and Paramount was ready to deal. Coppola could have his artistic control—along with $6 million to write and direct the picture, plus a percentage of its profits—but he would have to work quickly and on an agreed-upon budget, or risk paying the difference out of his own pocket. Furthermore, *Godfather III* was not going to be another epic-length picture: By terms of his agreement, Coppola was to deliver a film that ran no longer than two hours and twenty minutes.

With the new deal under his belt, Coppola began the task of bringing Michael Corleone and family back to life.

3.

COPPOLA HAD ALWAYS ENVISIONED Michael Corleone as a tragic figure of Shakespearean proportion, and to prepare himself for the scriptwriting of *Godfather III*, he read a number of Shakespeare's plays, including *King Lear, Titus Andronicus,* and *Romeo and Juliet.* The theme of *Godfather III,* he decided, would be very similar to the theme of *King Lear,* with Michael seen in his twilight years, and his nephew, Vincent Mancini, mirroring Edmund, the illegitimate son in *Lear.*

"The idea of the bastard, the character who is not under a good star and whose motives you are always questioning, is appealing, because in the end, the genes know who is and who is not family," Coppola said of his decision, unpopular with Paramount, to make Vincent, rather than Anthony Corleone, the heir to the Corleone family. "I could forever be rid of the idea that the movie was going to be about Michael's son becoming a gangster."

In March 1989, Coppola flew to Reno to work with Mario Puzo on a scene-by-scene outline for the screenplay. Although he was legendary for his ability to crank out scripts under extreme time constraints, Coppola preferred to devote about six months to the writing of a screenplay; for *Godfather III,* he and Puzo would have six weeks. In Reno, the two holed up in a suite in the Peppermill Hotel Casino, where they worked in creative bursts, batting ideas back and forth while Coppola's assistant, Anahid Nazarian, recorded their decisions on index cards that were carefully arranged on a bulletin board.

"We'd work for hours," Coppola remembered, "and when we ran out of ideas, we'd go down to the casino. Mario would play roulette and I'd play craps or 21. After a while we'd be embarrassed about losing so we'd go upstairs and work on the script." In a strange sense, the working/gambling situation was pure Coppola. "We're losing thousands downstairs," he joked, "but we're making millions upstairs."

After three days' time, the two had worked out an outline for the script. From there, they decided to collaborate in the fashion that had worked so successfully in the past, each writing separately and physically removed from the other. Coppola decided to write the first half of the screenplay, and Puzo took the second half. They met again at the hotel a few weeks later, during the first week of April, and they pieced the two halves into a coherent screenplay, completing their first draft on April 7—Coppola's fiftieth birthday.

Coppola was on the mark when he suggested that in making a second sequel to *The Godfather,* he would be seriously restricted by his past. Although

Godfather III is only thirty-nine minutes shorter in running time than *Godfather II*, and fourteen minutes less than the original, it has nowhere near the depth of its predecessors, nor are the new characters, with the exception of Vincent Mancini, as fully realized or interesting. To work, the film had to stand on its own, independent of the earlier pictures, yet it also had to fit into the *Godfather* saga. Asking so much might have been an impossible demand, but Coppola and Puzo came close to pulling it off.

Like the earlier films, *Godfather III* opens with a ritual. Michael Corleone is being honored with a papal award for his huge charitable donation to the Catholic Church, and if the contribution and award seem transparent to those who know the source of Michael's wealth, it is of no concern to Michael. If he must, he will pay for his redemption. He is still haunted by his role in his brother's murder—a stain that tarnishes his soul more than anything else that he has done in the past. Besides, as we will see, he has other motives for snuggling up to the Church.

After the ceremony, Michael, his family, and their friends repair to Michael's luxurious apartment for a reception. As an expository device, the party works wonderfully. We are introduced to Mary, Michael's fully grown daughter, who runs the Vito Andolini Foundation, the Corleone family's charitable organization. We also meet Anthony Corleone, Michael's son, who, like his father many years earlier, wants nothing to do with the family business. Anthony, against his father's wishes, wants to become an opera singer—an aspiration that ultimately brings Michael face-to-face with his former wife. Kay has remarried and kept her distance, but she reluctantly attends the ceremony and party, so she has occasion to ask Michael to honor his son's wishes. Michael reluctantly gives in.

Also attending the reception is Vincent Mancini, son of Sonny Corleone, who has inherited his father's strong will and nasty temper. Mary flirts with her handsome cousin, while Michael, realizing that he could use a younger and stronger person to help run the business, agrees to take Vincent under his wing. Michael understands from the onset that Vincent is not going to be an ideal pupil: At the reception, Vincent attacks Joey Zasa, one of the Corleone family's enemies, and later that same evening, while Vincent sleeps with a journalist he picked up at the reception, an attempt is made on his life. Vincent thwarts his attackers, establishing even greater tension between the Corleone family and Zasa.

Now well into his middle age, Michael is finally realizing his dream of tying all of his family's money into legitimate businesses. He is weary of the life that his father established so many years ago—a path he has followed, with grave reservations, for much of his adult life. He intends to launder his fortune by selling off the rest of the Corleone interests in the casino business and investing all of his money in Immobiliare, a multinational corporation of incredible power and wealth. To do so, however, he has to arrange an unholy alliance with the Vatican, which owns a controlling interest in the corporation.

The alliance is established through pure Corleone business savvy. The Vatican Bank, Michael learns, has run into a $769 million deficit due to corruption and poor investments, and after meeting with Archbishop Gliday, one of the bank's top officials, the deal is struck: Michael will deposit $600 million in the bank in exchange for the Vatican's interest in Immobiliare. News of the deal rocks the business world and upsets the Mafia dons who would also like a cut of the action. Don Altobello, one of Michael's father's closest friends and the godfather to Michael's sister, Connie, acts as an intermediary between the other families and Michael, but Michael insists that he wants no part of letting the underworld into his legitimate business interests. He does, however, call for a meeting between family representatives in Atlantic City.

To Michael's dismay, he faces heavy European opposition, led by a sinister Italian businessman named Lucchesi, and when he travels to Rome, expecting the Vatican to rubber-stamp its approval of his investment in the company, he is told that he doesn't have the necessary backing. To make matters worse, the Pope, who must approve the sale, is deathly ill and cannot address the issue.

Back in the United States, the heads of the different families gather in Atlantic City, where Michael announces his plans and disperses generous buyout payments to all of his casino investors. In a bold power play, Joey Zasa, now running all of the old Corleone New York business interests, challenges Michael in front of the others, hoping to gain the allegiance of the other dons. When he fails, he storms out of the meeting, publicly declaring Michael Corleone his enemy. Moments later, a helicopter appears at the side of the building. Machine-gun fire sprays the room, and all but a few dons are slaughtered. Vincent, dodging gunfire and acting as a shield, leads Michael to safety.

Michael instinctively knows what all this means: With the surviving dons fearful of Zasa and lining up behind him, Michael will inevitably be sucked back into the vortex of mob affairs. He tells Vincent, now one of his main confidants, that there has to be a connection between his Vatican dealings and the massacre in Atlantic City. Zasa, he insists, is not bright enough to plan, order, and pull off the operation on his own. "Our true enemy," he says, "has not yet shown his face."

During his meeting with Vincent, Michael suffers a diabetic stroke and is rushed to the hospital, where he lapses into a coma and nearly dies. While he is incapacitated, Vincent and Connie agree to order a hit on Joey Zasa and, in a scene mirroring the young Vito Corleone's murder of the don in *Godfather II,* Zasa is gunned down during a church festival in Little Italy. Michael, now recovering and out of immediate danger, is furious. He wants no part of the bloodshed, and he worries that the hit will drag his family back into the mob wars. Michael is aware that Vincent has been romantically involved with his daughter, and while he openly disapproves of the relationship between first cousins on moral grounds, he also fears that Vincent's role in Zasa's demise will put his daughter in danger. "When they come," he coaches Vincent, "they'll come at what you love."

Michael no longer knows who his enemies are, although he suspects Don Altobello might be involved in some of the actions against him. Altobello has been too friendly with the wrong people, including Zasa, and he has been advising Michael to retire. Altobello is only one of Michael's concerns. He is also convinced that he has powerful enemies in Europe, and to get information and advice, he travels to Sicily and confers with Don Tommasino, his old protector and benefactor in *The Godfather.* Tommasino tells Michael that in his opinion, Lucchesi is the only person with the connections to the Vatican and to mob politics capable of ordering the Atlantic City hit. He also recommends that Michael meet with Cardinal Lamberto, an influential Vatican official who might be helpful in his business dealings.

The more he becomes involved in mob activities, the more Michael is tormented by his past, but he is now convinced that he cannot escape the man he has become, or even find redemption. As advised, he meets with Cardinal Lamberto and informs him of some of the corruption at the Vatican Bank. Lamberto is now an important ally, but he can do little for Michael's soul. Michael confesses his sins—including his part in his brother's murder—but absolution is only temporary.

To confirm his suspicions about Altobello, Michael instructs Vincent to betray him to Altobello. If Vincent can gain Altobello's trust, he might be able to learn how he is connected to Michael's unknown enemy. Vincent succeeds, and Altobello meets with Lucchesi to plan a course of action. The solution, of course, is inevitable: Michael Corleone must be murdered.

Anthony is making his operatic debut in Sicily, and Kay and Michael are again reunited. Michael takes Kay on a tour of the land of his ancestors and, in a touching scene, asks her to forgive him for all he has put her through. Kay is emotionally torn: She has always loved Michael, but she also realizes that he cannot change. This much is obvious when, in the middle of their meeting, Michael is interrupted with the news that Don Tommasino has been murdered. When Michael begins speaking in Italian, Kay knows, from her previous experiences, that he is again assuming his position of leadership.

But it is a terribly reluctant position. Sitting near Don Tommasino's casket in the funeral home, Michael breaks down in tears, wondering aloud about why the old don was so loved while he, Michael, is so feared, when all he ever wanted was to preserve and protect his family. "Give me a chance to redeem myself," he prays, "and I will sin no more."

It is too late. Pope Paul VI dies and is succeeded by Cardinal Lamberto, who takes the name John Paul I. Under other circumstances, this might have been encouraging news to Michael, but when Vincent files his report about Don Altobello and the others, Michael hears that a hit man has been hired to assassinate him. Even the new Pope, as Michael's ally, might be in danger now. Vincent is prepared to take on all comers—"I want to preserve the Family"—but Michael, totally dejected, refuses to order another series of killings. Instead, he passes the torch of leadership to Vincent, on the condition that he quit seeing his daughter.

The film's climax, like those in the first two *Godfather* pictures, is revealed through montage. As Michael, Kay, and their family watch Anthony perform his first opera, the family's enemies are violently eliminated—all but the assassin, who, disguised as a priest, lurks around the opera house, awaiting his chance. When the program ends, he rushes Michael on the steps outside the opera house, firing two shots, one hitting Michael, the other hitting Mary. Michael's injury is minor. Mary, however, has been fatally wounded, and she dies while Michael, Kay, and the others look on in horror and grief. Michael's prediction has come true: When his enemy came, he destroyed the one Michael loved.

In a brief epilogue, we see flashbacks of Michael dancing with the women in his life: Mary, Apollonia, and Kay. Then he is shown as an old man, sitting in an expansive courtyard. He is utterly alone. He reaches for an orange and slumps over in his chair, a scruffy dog the only witness to his death.

4.

As soon as he had a completed script, Coppola began casting his movie. With complete control over his picture, he wouldn't be battling with Paramount over casting decisions—or so he thought—but he had plenty of challenges up the road. Securing Al Pacino's services, of course, was his number-one priority. In past interviews, Pacino had spoken favorably of his *Godfather* experiences and had indicated a desire to play Michael Corleone as an old man. Such sentiments, however, did not preclude demands for fair and proper remuneration, and Pacino reportedly asked for $7 million, plus a percentage of the movie's gross, to take up the role one more time—a figure that so enraged Coppola that he threatened to write a new script, in which the film would open with Michael Corleone's funeral. Pacino eventually settled for $5 million (and points).

Other returning key characters proved to be problematic. Diane Keaton, never satisfied with her Kay Corleone character of the earlier films, wanted $3 million to return to the part, setting off a series of delicate yet firm negotiations. In the new picture, the Kay Corleone role had been greatly expanded, but not nearly enough, in Paramount's view, to justify Keaton's salary demands. Under other circumstances, the studio might have been able to take a hard-line stance in the negotiations, but a certain diplomacy was demanded in this case, since Keaton was currently involved in a serious romantic relationship with Pacino. Keaton ultimately agreed to appear in the movie for $1.7 million.

Coppola wasn't as lucky when he and Paramount tried to bring Robert Duvall back as Tom Hagen, the Corleone family's attorney. Although he did not have Al Pacino's marquee appeal, Duvall was arguably as gifted an actor, capable of riveting an audience's attention without chewing up scenery in the process; his portrayal of Tom Hagen had been one of the highlights of the first two *Godfather* pictures. He immediately rejected Paramount's $1.5 million offer, countering with a demand for $3.5 million.

As Duvall saw it, Paramount's offer was a slap in the face, an insult to his previous contributions to the *Godfather* success story, and to his present status in the acting community.

"I did not think it was fair that they offered the lead actor four and a half to five times as much as they offered me," he complained to Cyndi Stivers, a journalist writing an account of the filming of *Godfather III* for *Premiere* magazine. "If they would have offered [Pacino] twice as much, that would have been okay—not *ideal* but okay. But the idea of four and a half to five times as much was unacceptable." He was equally adamant when he presented his case to the film's director. "Look," he told Coppola, "if I once again have to play a guy in a suit supporting the guy who's getting all the money, at least give me some money."

Duvall's main objection, Coppola felt, was not so much the size of his salary as the size of his role, and he became even more convinced of this as he tried in vain to find a way to appease the actor. In the original script, the Tom Hagen character had been pivotal to the movie's plot; when Duvall balked at the offered salary, Coppola shrunk the role until it had reached a point where Duvall would have had to work only for two or three weeks for the money

Paramount was offering. Finally, to his great dismay, Coppola had no choice but to write the Tom Hagen character out of the script and create a new Corleone confidant, a financial adviser played by George Hamilton.

Hiring Hamilton brought Coppola to loggerheads with studio officials, who believed that the actor, better known for his good looks and suntan and jetsetting lifestyle than for his acting ability, was far too lightweight for the role. Coppola saw Paramount's stance as a violation of the company's promise not to interfere with his authority, including the casting of his movie, and he made it known that he would not tolerate any further shenanigans. The company backed down.

As always, there was no lack of competition for parts in a *Godfather* movie. Robert De Niro, so brilliantly convincing in his portrayal of a young Vito Corleone in *Godfather II*, campaigned for the role of Vincent Mancini, insisting that his appearing as two different characters in the *Godfather* saga would not be too great a stretch of the imagination for filmgoers familiar with the films, since Vito Corleone and Vincent Mancini were blood relatives and, in all likelihood, would have shared a family resemblance. Intrigued, Coppola invited De Niro to the Napa Valley estate, where the actor and director tried to figure out a way to adapt the Vincent Mancini role, designed for a younger actor, to De Niro. Other candidates competing for the part included Alec Baldwin, Matt Dillon, Vincent Spano, Val Kilmer, Charlie Sheen, Billy Zane, and Nicolas Cage, with the part eventually being awarded to Andy Garcia, a young Cuban-born actor who had made his mark in *The Untouchables* and *Black Rain*.

Coppola had his heart set on casting Julia Roberts as Mary Corleone, but Roberts had other commitments that prohibited her from working on the film. Madonna, the pop singer who had established her acting credentials in *Desperately Seeking Susan*, coveted the role and she, like De Niro, met with Coppola and took a screen test. She tested well—"She was fabulous, we fell in love with her," Coppola recalled—and for a while it looked as if Coppola might actually rework the parts to accommodate the differences between De Niro's and Madonna's ages and their corresponding characters, which would have involved making Michael and Kay Corleone a little older than they were in the present script. In the end, Coppola and casting supervisor Fred Roos decided to stick to their earlier plans, and Winona Ryder, one of the most sought-after young actresses in the business, wound up winning the role.

Godfather III, like its predecessors, would become known in Hollywood circles for some of the actors who *didn't* land parts in the movie. Frank Sinatra, once an imposing vocal opponent of *The Godfather*, now decided that he wanted in on the action, and he was considered for the role of Don Altobello (played by Eli Wallach in the film), but his busy schedule would not permit him to be on location for as long as the role required. John Travolta and Sylvester Stallone, at different times prior to Coppola's involvement in the picture, were considered prime candidates to play Anthony Corleone, and Eddie Murphy expressed interest in working on the picture, if a part could be created for him.

Casting ran throughout the summer and fall of 1989, marking another hectic preproduction period for Coppola. Beside selecting his cast and crew and figuring out the logistics for a November start-up, Coppola found himself constantly revising the script. As expected, there was never a shortage of rumors about the picture, its plot, and the actors involved, but Coppola and Paramount stayed quiet, refusing to confirm the fact that the picture was being made until Pacino had signed in early August. The media blackout extended to cast and crew, who were told not to talk to journalists about the script, and who, with only a few exceptions, were not let in on how Coppola planned to end his movie. If Coppola had learned one thing from his experiences on such pictures as *Apocalypse Now* and *One from the Heart*, it was a lesson on how prerelease publicity could shape a film's image and jeopardize its chances at the box office. There would be no repeat performances with *Godfather III*.

5.

IN OCTOBER, COPPOLA DEPARTED for Italy to devote a final month to preproduction and rehearsals. In Rome, the Coppola family's escort delighted them by welcoming them to the city and recognizing Coppola as "the director of the film *Stepfather*." As he always was when engrossed in preparations for a new project, Coppola was a bundle of mixed emotions—forceful, energetic, impatient, hopeful, and anxious.

Much of the movie would be shot at Cinecittà, where production designer Dean Tavoularis had constructed intricately detailed sets, including Michael Corleone's New York apartment and an Atlantic City hotel. As of Coppola's arrival in Rome, the final shooting script had yet to be approved, and Tavoularis had to contend with an ever-changing screenplay that occasionally called for the changing or eliminating of sets. Such was life with the Godfathers—the movies and their director.

"We had one scene that was to take place in the Sistine Chapel," recalled art director Alex Tavoularis, who worked closely with his brother on the sets. "We were about five miles from the Sistine Chapel, but of course there was no way they were going to let us shoot there, so we had to find a way to duplicate at least a portion of it. We went to this company in Los Angeles, which had these canvas skins that you could put over plywood. The company had skins of the Sistine Chapel that had been used in another movie, and we had them ship them all the way from Los Angeles to Rome. I always thought it was ironic that we had go to Los Angeles to get the Sistine Chapel, even though we were only five miles away from the real one."

Coppola had much of his trusted crew working for him, including the Tavoularis brothers, costume designer Milena Canonero, and, once again, Carmine Coppola as the musical director. Coppola had been able to coax cinematographer Gordon Willis into applying his magic to his third *Godfather* production. Having these familiar people around him was crucial to Coppola, who was feeling the pressures of having to work at a faster pace than he would have preferred, in order to accommodate Paramount's insistence that the film be ready for the public in less than a year. As it was, Coppola had intentionally set much of the film's action in Italy, in order to keep studio officials from constantly watching over his shoulder.

The shoot, scheduled to last about four months, started on November 27, with a budget set at $44 million. The early stages went smoothly, on schedule and on budget, until December 28, when Coppola received jarring news that would affect not only the rest of the shoot but possibly the fate of the picture itself, as well. Winona Ryder and her boyfriend, actor Johnny Depp, had arrived in Rome the day before, but Ryder, only a couple of days removed from her work on *Mermaids,* was clearly exhausted and looking ill. On December 28, her first scheduled day on the set, Ryder was unable to get out of bed. A production physician examined her and informed Coppola that she was suffering from a nervous collapse and could break down completely if she tried to work; her involvement in the picture was over.

Coppola quickly checked off his options. Unlike Martin Sheen's heart attack during the filming of *Apocalypse Now,* which had occurred well into the production, at a point where Sheen could not have been replaced without Coppola's having to begin the shoot almost from scratch, Ryder's collapse demanded the recasting of a crucial role. Under other circumstances, this would have been exceedingly difficult, although workable; under the present circumstances, with a demanding schedule that allowed very little margin of error if he expected to meet the film's deadline, Coppola had to find an actress who was immediately available. Julia Roberts was still out of the picture, but Laura San Giacomo, an earlier candidate for the role, and Annabella Sciorra were available; there was even talk of flying in Madonna and trying to make the necessary script adjustments.

None of these options appealed to Coppola. Even if the arrangements went smoothly, he stood to lose invaluable time, not to mention the disruption it would cause the production. In a move that would stand as one of the most controversial casting decisions of his career, Coppola ordered an assistant director to call his apartment and inform his daughter, Sofia, who was on a holiday break from college and visiting her parents in Rome, that he wanted her to take over the vacated role. Sofia was just stepping into the shower when the call came through, and she thought some kind of mistake had been made.

"I could hear it was something weird, just in their voices," she recalled of the conversation between her mother and the assistant director. "And my mom hung up and said, 'Okay, Sofia, we've got to go to Cinecittà right away. You're going to be Mary.' I was like 'Excuse me? Are you sure? I just want to take a shower.'"

Eleanor Coppola had mixed emotions about seeing her daughter so suddenly thrust into such a high-pressure position.

"I told Sofia as evenly as I could," she remembered, "but tears were welling up in my eyes. She was very excited at first; then as it sank in she became anxious. I said I was sure her father would never have cast her if he didn't believe she could do it. I could see how worried she was about letting him down."

"I definitely wasn't an actress," Sofia admitted later, "but I could relate to the role of a young, awkward daughter of a powerful man. I had read the part during a read-through, when they just needed to hear it, so my dad had seen me in that role before."

Coppola, who had used Sofia as a model for Mary Corleone when he was writing the script, felt confident that his eighteen-year-old daughter could handle the role. He would rewrite the part to make Mary younger and more innocent than the older, more sexually charged character that he intended Winona Ryder to portray, but, in his opinion, Sofia brought something to the part that the others under consideration lacked: She was not a beautiful Hollywood starlet with a long résumé of acting roles; she was young and cute, and with her strong Italian features, she could have been Al Pacino's daughter. He had cast people with little or no acting experience in past movies, including the two previous *Godfathers*, and while this role was more pivotal to the plot than the others had been, he was certain that he could guide Sofia through the shoot.

"She had a big finger pointed at her, and she was tough enough. I wouldn't have subjected her to it otherwise," Coppola insisted. "I had nowhere else to turn, and I reached out for my daughter, more as I always do with members of my family, because I knew I could count on her."*

Others were not as confident. Coppola was famous for some of the chances that he'd taken in casting the first two *Godfather* pictures, but this latest decision appeared to be riskier yet, if not reckless. It was one thing for Coppola to cast his daughter or other family members in bit roles or as extras; it was an entirely different matter for him to hand over a major part in such a high-stakes production. Paramount, quite naturally, was terribly concerned—"High-anxiety time, that's what it was," remarked Sid Ganis, who flew to Rome, as did Frank Mancuso, to check out the casting move for themselves—and for nearly a week, Coppola barred the company executives from the set while he worked with Sofia.

Cast and crew members shared Paramount's apprehension, with some of the actors becoming rattled because they felt they should have been consulted before being asked to work with such an inexperienced actress. Others were concerned that Coppola was setting his daughter up for a tremendous beating by the critics and public, who were likely to judge the casting choice as a case of nepotism, and who would be brutal in their assessment of Sofia's performance.

"It was a jolt," Al Pacino allowed, conceding that "everyone was concerned about the casting at that point." Talia Shire implored her brother to reconsider; sound designer Richard Beggs, a longtime Coppola associate who had lost a daughter in an automobile accident, noticed Sofia tearfully struggling on the set and asked Coppola to find someone else. "Well-meaning people tell me I am permitting a form of child abuse, that she is not ready, not trained for what is being asked of her," Eleanor Coppola noted in a diary entry. "They also tell me that Francis can't afford to take a chance that could weaken his work at this point in his career."

Coppola, angry that Ryder's condition had not been discovered and reported prior to her arrival in Rome, and that the film's budget was getting

---

*According to Sofia Coppola, her father was probably tougher on her than he was on other cast members. "Sometimes it was hard working with him in that capacity," she told the author. "I saw it with Tally, too. He was harder on us because we're family, and you don't bullshit with family. With actors, there's so much ego to be careful of, but he'd just skip that and say, 'C'mon. . . .' He wouldn't always do the song and dance that I think actors sometimes need. It was also hard because I was eighteen, and the last thing you want to do [at that age] is listen to your parents."

out of control, lashed out at producers Fred Roos and Gray Frederickson, ultimately banishing them to the States and replacing them with Chuck Mulvehill, a veteran of seven Hal Ashby films, and, in theory, accustomed to bedlam on the set. Mulvehill, however, had barely set foot in Rome when he took one look at the mess and began to second-guess his decision to join the production. "I looked around, and I said to myself, 'This is fucking impossible,'" he recalled. "Between the language barrier and stepping into a production this big that is going full bore, I thought, 'What the fuck am I doing here?' I really thought about just going on the plane and going home."

Some of Coppola's stubborn insistence on standing behind his decision to cast his daughter in the movie could undoubtedly be attributed to principle: He was not about to let Paramount muscle any control of the film from him. He had been given complete control over production decisions—and that included the selection of his cast. He resented Paramount officials' consulting with other cast members for their input on the situation—a form of meddling that Coppola believed was a violation of his agreement with the studio.

Coppola also suspected that Paramount had more than the picture's artistic welfare in mind when fishing around for a replacement for Winona Ryder. "I think that Paramount also thought, 'God, we've got Andy Garcia, the hottest young male actor, so let's get him together with the hottest actress in an illicit cousins-in-love plot,'" he said.

Frank Mancuso wound up playing the peacemaker, meeting with Coppola and reaffirming the original agreement that the company would not interfere with the production. Coppola showed Mancuso some test footage that he'd shot of Sofia in action, and Mancuso was impressed enough to call a dinner meeting with Pacino, Keaton, and Garcia, during which he assured them that he felt everything was going to work out. "Basically what they said was, 'Frank, if you believe in it, then we feel more assured,'" Mancuso recalled. "They felt that if anybody had a lot of risk, it was certainly the studio."

Speaking with the benefit of hindsight, Talia Shire speculated that, given her brother's vulnerable state of mind, *The Godfather, Part III* might not have been made at all if Sofia had chosen not to take the role.

"Had Sofia not jumped in, I'm not so sure that the picture wouldn't have closed down," said Shire. "Francis and Mario had written a script that had a fabulous role for Bobby Duvall, and nobody wanted to lose him; it was hard for everybody because, after all these years, we were really tight, almost like family. Also, at this point, Francis had lost Gio, he was climbing out of debt, he was tired, and he was trying to find a way to do the movie that just didn't turn into a movie about drugs. When he found an eloquent hook—mixing spirituality, God, and these politics with the underworld—he had some damned interesting stuff. Then poor Winona got sick. For a moment, I wondered if the film was going to end. Francis's heart was shaky.

"Sofia wasn't angling for anything—she just happened to be there, and she would have done anything for her father. I was concerned because I didn't want to see her get trashed by the critics, which is what happened, but had she not been there . . . She gave Francis a way to structure himself, to feel justified in doing the movie. My gut feeling was, had Francis waited even one week, the whole damn thing could have just come undone. Sofia was kind of heroic, and somebody ought to remember that."

With the addition of Sofia Coppola to the cast, *Godfather III* was brimming with Coppolas and relatives on the production payroll, prompting the director to quip that the picture was "the biggest home movie in history."

6.

EVEN AS COPPOLA BATTLED to keep his film on track in Italy, another financial crisis was brewing back in the States, where, on January 25, Coppola and his film company, Zoetrope Productions, filed for protection from their creditors under Chapter 11 of the Bankruptcy Act. According to the petition, Zoetrope listed assets of $22.2 million and liabilities of $28.9 million; Coppola did not specify his personal assets or liabilities.

"The filing is intended to provide legal protection in connection with protracted legal proceedings that arose during the production of the 1981 film, *One from the Heart*," a Zoetrope statement read. "These proceedings are contested by the parties and Chapter 11 protection affords Francis Coppola and Zoetrope Productions an opportunity to resolve such disputes in an orderly fashion."

As ominous as it sounded, the Chapter 11 filing was just the latest action in a dizzying history of legal maneuverings that had transpired since the demise of Coppola's Zoetrope Studios at the old Hollywood General. For years, Jack Singer had been trying to collect the $3 million he'd lent Coppola during the making of *One from the Heart*, and for years Coppola's attorneys had successfully stalled a final court judgment. In November 1988, a superior court judge in Los Angeles ruled in Singer's favor, but Coppola appealed, setting off another series of legal encounters. In November 1989, Coppola lost again on appeal, and on January 11, 1990, he was ordered to pay the $3 million, plus interest, attorney's fees, and court costs, to Singer. Coppola's attorneys immediately contested the interest amount ($4.8 million), which had brought the total of Coppola's debt to more than $8.1 million. The Chapter 11 filing, in essence, was an attempt to stall for more time—to allow Coppola's attorneys to see if any more avenues of appeal were available, and to allow him time to finish his movie, which, if as successful as hoped, would earn him enough money to pay his debt—before he lost any of his property or other assets.

Ironically, Coppola had traveled full circle in a two-decade span: *The Godfather,* with its massive earnings, had brought him out of the debt he had accumulated during the founding of American Zoetrope; if it all went well, *Godfather III* would save him this time.

7.

DESPITE COPPOLA'S BEST EFFORTS, *Godfather III* was soon running behind schedule and over budget. Paramount was more concerned with the former than the latter, and Coppola complained, with justification, that the rush to complete the movie inevitably led to higher expenses—a fact that would become painfully clear a few months later, in postproduction, when a team of editors was employed to finish a job that could have been accomplished much less expensively by just an editor or two.

The flap over the Sofia Coppola casting had no sooner blown over than Coppola found himself up against another potential crisis, when Al Pacino and Diane Keaton decided to end their offscreen relationship. Their time in Italy had been tense to begin with, as Keaton wanted the elusive Pacino to make a solid commitment to their relationship, and while the two might have been able to parlay some of the tensions into their performances of Kay and Michael, who were at odds throughout much of *Godfather III,* the script called for a reconciliation, which could have been difficult to pull off under the circumstances. Fate intervened, however, in the form of a personal tragedy, when Pacino's grandmother died and Keaton accompanied him to New York for the funeral. The two reached an understanding during this interval from the set, and they were able to work together without any of the feared complications.

After completing the shoot in Italy—which, besides Rome, included nine weeks of location work in Sicily—the production moved to New York, where scenes were shot at the Waldorf-Astoria Hotel, a club called the Red Zone, and at Old St. Patrick's Cathedral on Mott Street in Little Italy. The film was now seven weeks behind schedule and more than 10 percent over budget—a fact that seemed to amuse the always-hungry media more than it bothered Paramount, including line producer Chuck Mulvehill, who had spent months observing Coppola at work. The additional costs, he said in defense of Coppola, "were a function of time, of the schedule.

"Every film," he explained, "has an internal rhythm, and that rhythm is set right in the beginning by the key people—the cameraman, the stars, the producer, the production designer. The rhythm was established with this film, and God Himself could have come in and it wouldn't have changed."

Frank Mancuso also sprang to Coppola's defense. "No one was more responsible about the budget than Francis himself," Mancuso stated. "He did everything possible to live up to it. I'm upset with the perception that he's irresponsible. It's absolutely untrue."

Coppola, always touchy about how his spending on films was reported by the press, again expressed his frustration with those who portrayed him as being excessive. "I've had bank executives quote stuff about me from magazines while turning down a loan application," he complained.

Coppola wrapped principal photography on *Godfather III* on May 24, 1990, leaving him only six months to bring in the completed film by the Thanksgiving deadline. As with the previous *Godfather* films, Coppola had shot more footage than he could possibly fit into the agreed-upon running time for the film—and even so, he had left out several key scenes that he wanted to shoot, including the funeral of Michael Corleone. Nevertheless, he campaigned to make the movie a little longer, more in keeping with the pacing of the other two pictures. His wishes were granted, and he wound up shooting additional scenes in New York as late as September.

For Coppola, *Godfather III* represented another balancing act between art and commerce. His debts might have been a huge determining factor when he originally overcame his reluctance to take another dip into the *Godfather* well, but as time went on, during both the production and postproduction stages of the film, he found himself becoming increasingly excited about the prospects of creating a major work that would stand with the other two pictures. The dailies had bolstered his—and Paramount's—faith, and as he, editor Barry Malkin, and others labored for long hours in postproduction, Coppola felt intense pressure—perhaps more than ever before—to deliver a film that would restore his reputation as an artist while earning him enough money to pay off his past debts and, with luck, secure the future of a project like *Megalopolis*.

Some of his immediate financial worry was put to rest in July, when he and Jack Singer were finally able to reach agreement on his debt to the Canadian developer. For years, Coppola had maintained the public stance that he believed that in selling the Zoetrope Studio in Hollywood to Singer at a bargain-basement price, he had fulfilled his obligation on the loan, and that, in his view, Singer had offered the loan with the hope that he would be able to take over the financially troubled studio; in private, however, Coppola wondered if he hadn't been getting questionable advice from his legal team—advice that wound up costing him a fortune in interest on the loan.

"It was just a lot of legalities and lawyers goofing up and missing deadlines and stuff," he told *Premiere* magazine. "I sorta just lost the case by default. I thought I was pretty much outta debt, but then I realized there was the seven million. That put me right back several years."

According to the terms of his new agreement with Singer, Coppola would pay Singer a large chunk of the sum—reportedly half of the court-ordered $8 million—in August 1990, with payments on the rest of the debt to be delivered over the next two years. To make the August payment, Coppola approached Paramount for help. To his great relief, the studio was receptive. "Paramount was very kind and advanced me money against my piece of *Godfather*," Coppola told *Variety* columnist Army Archerd.

Although it relieved some of the immediate financial pressure, the advance also reinforced Coppola's obligation to deliver the film on time. By fall, the film's release date had been postponed until Christmas Day—still in time to cash in on the holiday movie rush and guarantee consideration for the forthcoming Academy Awards nominations, but late enough to cause Paramount and theater chains concern. Paramount had what was described as an "unusually weak" holiday release schedule, and the company was counting on *Godfather III* to pick up the slack. Further complicating the issue were the stringent terms that Paramount was placing on film exhibitors: *Godfather III*, like its predecessors, was being heralded as an event, and theater owners were obliged to pay higher box-office guarantees and offer guaranteed twelve-week minimum runs on a film that could conceivably miss its delivery date. If *Godfather III* did not arrive in theaters on time, exhibitors would not only have to scurry to find a suitable substitute; they would miss out on the chance to show such holiday offerings as *Bonfire of the Vanities, Awakenings, Hamlet, Edward Scissorhands, The Sheltering Sky,* and *Dances with Wolves*—all of which were receiving plenty of advance attention.

Painfully aware of the situation, Coppola and his Zoetrope team worked virtually around the clock, pushing the limits to bring the film in on time.

"It's sort of like a hotel opening," Coppola quipped. "It's like, can we get all the showers installed and paint the trim on 1,400 windows?"

8.

THE GODFATHER, PART III OPENED on schedule, on December 25, 1990. Given the history of the two previous *Godfather* pictures, it came as no surprise to Coppola that his latest installment was scrutinized and analyzed down to the tiniest detail. He would make a point to tell anyone who would listen that far too much attention was being paid to his latest effort—"It's unfortunate that so much fuss is made over what in the end is just a movie"—although, in all probability, such statements were more of a defense mechanism than newfound modesty. *Newsweek* critic Jack Kroll pinpointed the uneasy relationship between Coppola and his *Godfather* movies when he noted that "the fear and terror that bedevil Coppola on his globe-trotting, money-gobbling, deadline-crushing Godfathering may really be the fear that this is his true work, work he has been dragooned, cajoled and forced into by the failure of his more cherished projects."

There were no surprises among the scores of reviews accompanying *Godfather III*'s release, no critics willing to gamble their professional reputations by giving the film an unqualified endorsement, let alone call it the best of the three *Godfather* films. The general attitude among those giving the film a favorable review was one of caution—"One of these has to be third best," Kroll remarked in his review—as if reviewers conceded from the outset that the new movie could not possibly measure up to its classic predecessors.

"Few sequels can match the charge of anticipation you feel before watching the third part of Francis Coppola's *Godfather* series," offered *Rolling Stone's* Peter Travers. "So when it sinks in that this nearly three-hour sequel is not up to the level of its predecessors, the disappointment runs deep. Is *Part III* worth your time? Of course. It's still *The Godfather* and some of it is deeply affecting."

Perhaps it was inevitable that *Godfather III* be so meticulously compared to the other two pictures, but in making the comparisons, the critics seemed to forget—or conveniently ignore—the fact that both *The Godfather* and *The Godfather, Part II* had received wildly mixed reviews. If anything, the release of *Godfather II* had afforded critics the opportunity to rethink their positions on the original; *Godfather III* had the same effect on the first two pictures.

As feared, Sofia Coppola's performance took some savage hits from the critics—"[her] gosling gracelessness comes close to wrecking the movie," and "almost totally lacking in charisma, not to mention acting ability"—but a number of reviewers offered sympathetic comments about the way the young actress, pressed into sudden service, had handled her part. Pauline Kael, who had run roughshod over Coppola in her *New Yorker* reviews over the past decade, was ultimately kinder to Sofia Coppola than toward her father and his movie. "It's obvious that this teen-age girl is not a trained actress," she wrote, noting that Sofia didn't seem comfortable on-screen at times, and that her voice, the object of many critics' sneers, lacked expressiveness. "But she has a lovely and unusual presence; she gives the film a breath of life, and I grew to like her."

Al Pacino was generally accorded high marks for his performance as the aging don, while many reviewers complained that Diane Keaton still had very little to do in the movie. Of all the commentary on individual performances, Andy Garcia and Talia Shire were singled out the most for praise.

"Garcia's turbulent and tender performance is the movie's freshest surprise," stated *Rolling Stone,* "and the scene in which Michael anoints him as the new don is the film's most arresting." *The New Republic*'s Stanley Kauffmann wrote, "Garcia, who first became noticeable in *The Untouchables,* had seductive strength, homicidal cool," although he was not impressed with Michael Corleone in the latest *Godfather* installment. "One reason to look forward to *Part IV* is that he'll fill the center better than Pacino does."

"Talia Shire gives the film's best performance," declared Richard Alleva in his review for *Commonweal.* "A Borgia woman transported to the twentieth century, she radiates more darkling power than any of the gun-toting males in the cast." Pauline Kael, like Alleva, found Shire to be an engaging presence in what she judged to be an otherwise-disappointing film: "The strongest performance—in terms of sheer animal strength and suggestions of emotional reserves—is given by Talia Shire, whose Connie calls up dark plotting women like Livia in 'I, Claudius,' and Lady Macbeth, and Lucrezia Borgia; she's tough. . . . Connie acts like family: when she says, 'Come *on,* Michael,' it's in a gutsy, impatient voice that only she will dare to use."

Godfather III opened strongly, taking in more than $15 million at 1,820 screens during its first three days. However, it soon became apparent that neither time nor reputation would rekindle the burning enthusiasm that had greeted the original picture. As with *Godfather II,* the film's attendance dropped off quickly, and while the movie was by no means a failure, its domestic earnings were a disappointment. A few months later, when the Golden Globe and Oscar nominations were announced, *Godfather III* received five Golden Globe and seven Academy Award nominations, including Oscar nominations for production design, editing, and score. Coppola was honored with Academy Award and Golden Globe nominations for Best Director, and *Godfather III* was chosen as a finalist for a Best Picture Oscar. Andy Garcia was similarly recognized by both awards committees for a performance in a supporting role. The awards nights, however, turned out to be depressing affairs, when *Godfather III* was shut out in both the Golden Globe and Academy Awards ceremonies.

Chapter Seventeen

Bonfire of the Vampires

"Eternal life is not what it's cracked up to be."

−JAMES V. HART, scriptwriter for
Bram Stoker's Dracula

"I am no lunatic! I'm a sane man fighting for his soul!"

−RENFIELD, in *Bram Stoker's Dracula*

*"What is there about me that invites this controversy?
Why do I have to be an oddball on the edge of extinction?
Why do people enjoy that?"*

−FRANCIS FORD COPPOLA

1.

IN LATE NOVEMBER 1990, while being interviewed by the *New York Times,* Francis Ford Coppola had spoken hopefully about *Godfather III* and its potential bearing on his money problems. "In another month, many of my problems will be over," he said. "Or they will be doubled."

Neither a blockbuster nor a bomb, *Godfather III* failed to take in sufficient money to pull Coppola from his financial doldrums, but it helped. He cringed when it was suggested that his film was a failure, and when the *Times* published an article about sequels that had flopped, he responded with an angry letter to the editor.

"How any film that has grossed more than $70 million to date and is nominated for best picture and best director can be a flop is tough for me to understand," he complained, although he acknowledged that people had expected the movie to be a blockbuster hit. "But those are tough to achieve," he continued, "and not really anyone's true expectations. Especially for a long picture with adult subject matter."

In the wake of the responses to *Tucker,* a picture he had spent so much of his career dreaming of making, and *Godfather III,* one that he had seemed pre-ordained to make, Coppola was in no frame of mind to take a lot of guff from the media. He was back in full work mode, feeling confident and ready to take on a multitude of projects, and in the months to come, Coppola and Zoetrope projects would be announced at a dizzying pace. *The Outsiders* was finally being realized as a television series. *Megalopolis,* though still lacking a finished script, was projected to be filmed sometime in the next year or so. *J. Edgar Hoover: The Man and the Secrets,* a biopic about the controversial former director of the FBI, based on the biography of the same title by *Helter Skelter* coauthor Curt Gentry, was in development for Warner Bros. In addition, Coppola would be serving as executive producer of Carroll Ballard's *Wind,* a film about the America's Cup, and he was looking into the possibilities of directing a live-action version of *Pinocchio.*

The big project, rumored for months, and agreed upon by Coppola and Columbia Pictures prior to the release of *Godfather III,* was a retelling of the Dracula story, using a script written by James V. Hart. To industry observers, Coppola's directing a horror film might have come across as another work-for-hire quickie, perhaps even a long step backward to his *Dementia-13*/Roger Corman days, but Coppola insisted that the project was close to his heart. "I've always wanted to make a Gothic romance," he said, "and the book has never been made. I want to do a science-fiction film as well in the future."

The tale of Dracula, of course, had been told many times and in many ways on film, and it had been part of the American consciousness for generations. Coppola had fond memories of those occasions when he and his brother, August, would be thrilled and terrified by boyhood screenings of *Dracula, Frankenstein,* and *The Wolfman.* He had thumbed through the *Encyclopaedia Britannica,* searching for the story of Dracula, and had been amazed to learn the story of Vlad Tepes (Vlad the Impaler), a real-life model for the Dracula character, a fierce fifteenth-century warrior who had terrified the enemy Turks by impaling their dead warriors—and even his own people—on stakes. The problem with the various movie adaptations of the Dracula story, Coppola believed, was in their deviation from the Stoker novel, and from the way Stoker had taken a historical figure—Vlad the Impaler—and made him a protagonist in his novel.

The James Hart screenplay closely resembled the 1897 Bram Stoker novel that Coppola remembered reading aloud to young campers so many years ago, when he was working as a summer-camp drama counselor. Here was the classic story, splendidly framed by the Vlad the Impaler story, revealed slowly and suspensefully in the tradition of the great gothic horror novels. Hart, who had been cowriter of the script for Steven Spielberg's *Hook*, had tried to put a little different spin on the usual horror story when he was writing his screenplay. "I wanted to make a woman's movie," he explained, "as opposed to a Victorian *guys'* movie, where the Victorian guys go out and get the bad guy."

In the Hart version of the story, Vlad the Impaler is presented as a savage romantic, unparalleled in his brutality in battle but ultimately tormented when, after defending the Church against the Muslim Turks, he returns home and finds that his wife, Elisabeta, who believed that he had been killed in battle, has committed suicide and cannot, by Church rules, be given a Christian burial. Infuriated, he rejects Christianity and is thus condemned to an eternity's dark existence. As Dracula, he is neither living nor dead, but is instead confined to a solitary limbo on earth, where he is most alive while others sleep—where pleasure, like his existence, is associated with pain, and bloodletting becomes the essence of life. Four centuries later, while trying to purchase land in London, he meets a young English solicitor, Jonathan Harker, whose fiancée, Mina Murray, happens to be the reincarnation of Elisabeta. Suddenly, Dracula is both a horrifying, menacing presence and, as he desperately attempts a reunion with his centuries-old lover, a romantic figure.

"It was a brilliant innovation of Jim Hart's to use that history of Prince Vlad to set the frame for the whole story," Coppola noted in his diary. "I felt immediately that he had written it as a story of passion and eroticism."

In London, Dracula relentlessly pursues an initially reluctant but eventually interested Mina, while three of his vampire brides hold Jonathan prisoner at the Transylvania castle. Dracula, however, has made one crucial mistake: Shortly after his arrival in London, to sate his need for blood, he brutally assaults and rapes Mina's flirtatious friend Lucy Westerna, and her subsequent illness attracts the attention of Professor Abraham Van Helsing, a Dutch physician intrigued by tales of vampirism. In time, Jonathan escapes from Dracula's castle, and he and Mina marry, although Mina, in Jonathan's absence, has become powerfully attracted to the mysterious foreign count. Van Helsing hunts and kills Dracula, but not before Dracula and his long-lost Elisabeta are spiritually and physically reunited.

Hart had originally written the script for Wilshire Court Productions, which planned to make the movie for cable television's USA Network, but he wanted to see if a major theatrical movie could be made from his script. He received permission to show the script to agents and producers, and, in a stroke of good fortune, Winona Ryder saw it and decided she wanted to star in the role of Mina Murray. Coincidentally, about the same time, unaware of the screenplay or Ryder's interest in it, Coppola contacted the young actress and asked her to meet with him, supposedly to smooth over any misunderstandings that might have arisen from her having left the *Godfather III* production. Ryder brought along the *Dracula* script and suggested that it might be a good project for the director. Coppola said he would be interested only if the screenplay was faithful to the book.

"I thought it would be great to make a *Dracula* based on the original Bram Stoker," he stated. "But I wanted something really unusual, something people had not seen before. Otherwise, you're making Dracula and people say, 'What are you making Dracula for?'"

Coppola loved the script, and within a matter of days, he and Columbia Pictures had teamed up on making a movie out of it.

"It was unbelievable," Ryder told a reporter at the time of the film's release. "There was an agent who said, 'If Francis Coppola directs this movie, I will wear a yarmulke for a year.' And I'm, like, 'You better put that thing on.'"

2.

COPPOLA PREPARED HIMSELF for making *Bram Stoker's Dracula* by watching a number of classic movies, including Eisenstein's *Ivan the Terrible* and Orson Welles's *Chimes at Midnight* and *Citizen Kane,* and taking copious notes on whatever caught his fancy, from camera angles to props; the battle scene at the beginning of *Bram Stoker's Dracula* would owe much to Welles's staging of the battle scene in *Chimes at Midnight,* and to Kurosawa's *Kagemusha.*

For Coppola, working on a script and preparing to make a movie were difficult tasks, involving a different type of thinking than he was accustomed to when not working. In a sense, it was a process of idea prospecting, or of sensory overload, in which he would pack his brain with as much information as he could hold, all with the idea of discovering what might work best in his film. "You're picking up little sensations which are not in themselves tangible information," he allowed, "but which are little radar answer-backs that let you know something is there in these areas. Upon later scrutiny you can see what it was that sent that sensation and you can go back to develop it."

Coppola had plenty of ideas for the picture. Blood—and the color red (or scarlet)—were at the visual core of the movie, symbolizing life and passion as much as the horrors that Dracula visited upon his victims. The sets were to be spacious and minimally decorated, given more to shadows and a sense of isolation and doom than might be achieved by smaller, cluttered sets. Costumes and textured fabrics would provide vital contributions to the characters and mood, as would the music, which Coppola wanted to sound "like a Prokofiev score for Eisenstein. I want it to be performed by symphonies," he wrote in his notes. "I want great music." The cinematography, he decided, should have the feel of old movies, "to approach the effects and metaphysics as if I were a nineteenth-century filmmaker, using superimpositions and double-exposures."

Many of his plans, he realized, would be further shaped or modified by the film's budget. He was still irritated by the published reports of his exceeding the budget on *Godfather III*—accounts that failed to recognize that a good number of the additional expenses came as the result of his having to work so quickly—and he was determined to prove, as he had in the past, that he could bring in a movie on budget. It would take some creative thinking and planning, but it could be done. For instance, by cutting back on expensive sets, he could afford to devote more money to costumes.

"It was clear from the beginning that Jim Hart's script was envisaged for a group of very young actors," Coppola explained. "So I said to myself, okay, if the angle is that we're going to use very beautiful young actors, let's spend our money not on the sets but on the costumes, because the costumes are the things closest to the actors."

To his chagrin, Coppola discovered that, even as he tried to put together a picture that was both innovative and cost-conscious, he was up against studio officials who wanted something more traditional in presentation and even less expensive than he had planned. Columbia wasn't interested in Coppola's idea for stripped-back sets and insisted that he shoot the film on its soundstages. Nor was the company enthralled with Coppola's ideas for the cinematography, which it deemed to be too radical. Production designer Dean Tavoularis and cinematographer Vittorio Storaro were out, victims, as Coppola described it, of the perception that they were "the kind of people that traditionally go over budget." Coppola did manage to hang on to his hopes for featuring costumes in the film, and he scored a major coup in hiring award-winning Japanese designer Eiko Ishioka, an eventual Oscar winner for her work on *Bram Stoker's Dracula*, who, years earlier, had designed the sets for the Zoetrope-produced *Mishima*.

"As it began to be clear that *Bram Stoker's Dracula* would be made," Coppola remembered, "I began to feel a bit stranded. Afraid that my collaborators were known for being really fine craftsmen and typical film artists but not wildly innovative. Afraid that money would be thrown at the project, that it would end up having great big sets and a more typical production. I started to feel desperate that my ideas were being 'practical-ized' to a point where some of the madness and irrationality that I saw in the material might be lost.

"By bringing in Eiko," he continued, "I knew I was insuring that at least one element—the costumes, which were so important in my scheme of the production—would be completely atypical, absolutely original and unique."

Casting the movie proved to be very competitive. Coppola was still considered an actor's director and, despite stumbles here and there, one of the most influential, important filmmakers of his generation, and that, along with the excitement of participating in a serious version of *Dracula,* made Coppola's film an extremely inviting project. The movie had blockbuster potential. Anne Rice's 1974 novel, *Interview with the Vampire,* had begun a string of best-selling vampire novels for Rice, and Hollywood, already in a frenzy over making the kind of horror movies that might bring teenage audiences to theaters in droves, planned no fewer than six vampire movies to be released at approximately the same time as *Bram Stoker's Dracula.*

In the early stages of the planning, Daniel Day-Lewis was rumored to be the leading candidate for the title role, but he was unavailable until he had completed his work in *The Last of the Mohicans,* the Michael Mann film that would become stiff competition for *Dracula* during the 1992 holiday season. Jeremy Irons and Eric Roberts were also mentioned in the trades as being leading candidates for the role. Antonio Banderas, Armand Assante, and Gabriel Byrne actually tested for the part, but none received the nod from Coppola. Andy Garcia was interested in what would undoubtedly be one of the most talked-about parts of the season, but he was hesitant about performing in some of the picture's more explicit sex scenes.

Coppola's choice, British actor Gary Oldman, although an outstanding actor, wound up being a questionable selection in the eyes of some critics, who felt that Oldman did not project the powerful sexuality required by the Hart script. Oldman had earned a rock-solid reputation as a character actor in his portrayal of Sex Pistols punk rocker Sid Vicious in *Sid and Nancy,* and of Lee Harvey Oswald in Oliver Stone's *JFK,* but even Coppola had to admit that Oldman did not have the romantic leading-man looks of some of the actors he had passed over for the part. Physical appearance, he insisted, was not as important as others might think.

"I remember *Sid and Nancy*, these unattractive, raunchy characters," he asserted, "but their love was so beautiful and so passionate. Even in the Joe Orton movie, *Prick Up Your Ears*. I saw him in two things where he was playing what most people think of as sort of unattractive, but having beauty and passion."

His critics saw it differently. "Few women in the audience, I'd guess, will black out with longing for Gary Oldman's Dracula," commented *The New Yorker*'s Terrence Rafferty in his review of the film. "Oldman has many gifts, but sex appeal has never been among them." Dave Kehr of the *Chicago Tribune* had essentially the same take: "He's handsome and needful enough," Kehr suggested, "though hardly the magnetic figure the part requires. Oldman doesn't possess what Andrew Sarris once memorably described as Bela Lugosi's 'demented poetry' nor the sexual threat of Christopher Lee."

What Oldman did possess was a fierce sense of perfectionism, along with an intensity that, depending upon the circumstances, could delight a director or drive him to distraction. He definitely had his own ideas about how he wanted to play a character, and he was not shy about imposing his will and vision on anyone standing in his way. "I can exhaust people sometimes," he admitted. "Because I have a hundred ideas. I'm not just a jobbing actor. You don't just employ me to learn the lines and hit the marks."

This was precisely the quality that prompted Coppola to select Oldman over others testing for the role. "Gary just seemed to be the most far-out," Coppola recalled. "I was, like, 'My God, what's he going to be like?'"

Physical appearance, on the other hand, had great bearing on Coppola's choice to play Jonathan Harker. As he explained it, Coppola wanted someone with the looks of an Errol Flynn—an actor who would appeal to the movie's teenage viewers—and he chose Keanu Reeves, who had appeared in such movies as *Dangerous Liaisons* and *Parenthood* but who was best known for his portrayal of Ted Logan in the lightweight *Bill & Ted's Excellent Adventure*.

"We tried to get some kind of matinee idol for the part of Jonathan," he said. "If we were all to go to the airport with Winona and Gary Oldman and [me] and anyone shy of Tom Cruise, Keanu is the one that the girls would just besiege."*

Anthony Hopkins, fresh from his Oscar- and Golden Globe–winning performance as Hannibal Lecter in *The Silence of the Lambs*, and Tom Waits, a Coppola favorite since Waits's composition of the songs for *One from the Heart*, became two of Coppola's more inspired casting choices. Hopkins, slated to play Van Helsing, not only added instant credibility to the picture

---

*Coppola's first choice for the part—Johnny Depp—was vetoed by Columbia.

but, as its elder statesman, commanded the kind of respect that Marlon Brando had brought to the set of *The Godfather*. Waits, cast in the role of R. M. Renfield, a solicitor driven insane from his dealings with Dracula, had seen his career develop significantly from the days when he was taking bit parts in *The Outsiders* and *Rumble Fish;* he had won critical acclaim for his appearances in *Ironweed* and *Down By Law,* and he was now almost as respected for his acting as he was for his career as a singer/songwriter.

For the role of Lucy Westenra, Coppola passed over Juliette Lewis and Ione Skye, two established actresses, in favor of Sadie Frost, an English actress who had never appeared in an American film, marking still another occasion when Coppola made a casting decision based more on instinct than the usual criteria for selection. Coppola had very specific ideas for the type of person that he wanted to cast in this important role, and he and casting director Victoria Thomas looked at more than five hundred actresses before choosing Frost for the part.

"The Lucy part is the most flamboyantly erotic, combining acting with beauty," Coppola noted in his journal. "She has to be young, no older than 22, because she'll be working opposite Mina, as her contemporary. Whoever we cast has to decide that she's prepared to do what we need. Nudity isn't the issue; it's the attitude, the intensity it takes to say, 'I'm going to do something really dazzling.' She has to be really brave."

When he first began planning the movie, Coppola envisioned a *Dracula* with sexually charged scenes with the look of "an erotic dream"—a situation that he himself was not entirely comfortable with. He had never felt at ease when directing nude scenes—even when, in his younger days, he was shooting his nudies—and *Dracula* figured to be his most erotic film to date. Realizing that his movie's success would largely ride on the emotional and sexual tensions in his two main actresses, Coppola hired acting coach Greta Seacat to work with Sadie Frost and Winona Ryder.

"I brought in Greta," he explained, "because I don't feel comfortable talking about a lot of sexual stuff to young girls. I've never been good at that in life, asking girls to take their clothes off. So I very much wanted Greta, who's a woman I feel very comfortable with, to be my go-between—to help me ask these girls to perform in more erotic ways."

3.

COPPOLA SPENT THE SUMMER of 1991 revising the *Dracula* script, working out production details, and wrestling with the self-doubt and uncertainty that seemed to turn up with each new project. Throughout his career, Coppola had spoken candidly with interviewers about the fears he encountered whenever he was directing a picture. Fear of failure . . . fear of embarrassing himself–both acted as strong motivators, although Coppola knew, when he gave the matter some thought, that he was by no means alone in confronting these demons. "These things are common to all artists: the self-doubt, the panic attacks," he wrote in his journal. "Go easy on yourself, Francis–it is not necessary to suffer in order to be an artist."

Coppola, of course, knew all about suffering for the sake of one's art, and if he needed any further reminder, he could have easily found it in *Hearts of Darkness: A Filmmaker's Apocalypse,* the intense, feature-length documentary about the making of *Apocalypse Now,* recently issued after a long, strange history that, in some respects, rivaled that of *Apocalypse Now.* What had started out as a modest proposal–Eleanor Coppola's shooting promotional footage for United Artists–wound up becoming a compelling documentary about filmmaking on (and occasionally over) the edge.

"I had sixty hours of film and forty hours of sound tape," Eleanor Coppola remembered. "When I got home, an editor and I began assembling, but as time went by, I received various directions from the publicity and marketing departments at UA. 'Just cut together all the action footage, explosions, and helicopter stuff to use as a selling tool for the European market,' they'd say. I'd do that for a while, and then I'd be told, 'No, make a personal film–one that will interest women. We'll show it at film festivals to get women interested, since women don't usually go to see war films.' By that point, my marriage was on the rocks, and I gave up on the editing and went to live in Napa.

"Every four or five years, someone would say, 'Let's get Ellie's footage out and make that documentary.' Whenever it started, Francis would say, 'Okay, as long as it's not about me. . . .' However, anyone who tried to put it together would always come to the conclusion that it *was* about him, and the project would be put back in the closet. Finally, George Zaloon came to American Zoetrope with a proposal to make a documentary. They got funding from Showtime and had a team that wanted to do it. By this time, I realized that I was never going to be the one to edit the material because I'd never be able to get the balance right: I would make Francis look too much like a genius or a jerk. American Zoetrope owned the footage, and they made a deal with the documentary that had nothing to do with me.

"I was surprised when I was invited to the editing room, and saw that the editors were using *Notes* as the foundation for the documentary. I tried to make sure that the material didn't get out of balance, one way or the other. For instance, at one point they had two actors talking about drug use during the filming. I told them that it was a subject, but that covering it twice gave too much weight to it. Things like that.

"Francis had final approval of the cut. There was stuff in the final cut that he was uncomfortable about—stuff that he thought made him look too nuts—but in the end he didn't want to tell these sincere filmmakers that they couldn't make the film the way they wanted to, because he had always fought against people telling him what *he* couldn't do."

Hearts of Darkness, a hit at the Cannes Film Festival, was unflinching in its depiction of a filmmaker under fire, struggling against powerful odds to make his movie about an unpopular topic. If, in watching the documentary so many years after the making of *Apocalypse Now,* Francis Ford Coppola felt old wounds being reopened, he could take consolation in knowing that he had survived the tumultuous decade that followed, and was presently far removed from the tortured filmmaker in the Philippines.

On the business side of moviemaking, things were looking up for Coppola. He and Columbia Pictures, pleased with their *Dracula* relationship, decided to strike up a longer-lasting arrangement, and in June, Coppola agreed to give the studio first look at his forthcoming projects over the next three years. In return, Columbia would pay Coppola a $5 million director's fee, along with about 10 percent of the gross, for any film that he made for the studio. Coppola was especially enthusiastic about the potential for Diane Johnson's *Cure,* a film about the search for a cure for AIDS, and in the months to come, he would talk about producing a film version of Frances Hodgson Burnett's *The Secret Garden.* He also optioned the rights to Norman Mailer's massive CIA novel, *Harlot's Ghost.* With all these projects in various stages of development, Coppola pushed *Megalopolis* even further into the future. By his own projections, he would now be able to pursue the project no earlier than 1996.

In early August, Coppola took a brief vacation in Mexico with his wife, children, and granddaughter. Coppola loved having his family around him. Sitting on the beach, totally content and relaxed for what would be the last time for months to come, Coppola reflected on his life and goals. In all likelihood, he concluded, he probably had about twenty years remaining in his life, and rather than spend those years fretting about the future, he might be better off living in the present; he should enjoy his family and all that his career had brought him. "Anyway," he noted in his diary, "between the Napa estate, American Zoetrope and the Blancaneaux Lodge in Belize, there are plenty of projects to work on."

The place in Belize had been a dream project since 1981, when the Central American country then known as British Honduras won its independence and changed its name. Coppola had fantasized about owning property in a tropical country since his work on *Apocalypse Now,* and after reading about Belize, he and his son Gio flew down to the country to investigate. This nation of approximately 200,000 people boasted a very high (90 percent) literacy rate, a stable parliamentary government, and a bilingual society in which a large percentage of people spoke English. Coppola, heavily into his high-tech mode at the time, believed that this country offered an ideal environment for the creation of an international telecommunications network and media center, but when he met with Prime Minister George Price and spoke of his ideas, he was greeted with a cool response: Television had yet to turn up in homes in Belize, yet here was an American film director, suggesting that the country apply for a satellite address.

While in Belize City, Coppola had spoken to Ray Lightburn, a chef at a popular local restaurant, who took him to Blancaneaux Lodge, an abandoned resort in the Mountain Pine Ridge. The property included a main lodge, seven thatched huts, and, as an added bonus, a makeshift airstrip.

"It had been built in the 1960s," Coppola said of Blancaneaux, "[at] a time when it was unbelievably remote here. It was closed, but I looked into the lodge and saw the tables and I thought, I could work here. I could write here. It was the paradise hideaway I was looking for."

Coppola purchased Blancaneaux, along with ten acres of surrounding jungle, for $65,000. The purchase, unfortunately, coincided with the dark days of *One from the Heart* and American Zoetrope, and over the ensuing years, Coppola was too financially burdened to restore the lodge, although he and his family would occasionally take vacations to Belize. The success of *Godfather III* and the likely prospects of climbing out of debt had given Coppola reason to believe that he might be able to fix up the property if *Dracula* performed well at the box office.

4.

FOR THE TIME BEING, however, he had to live in the present, and that meant returning to the States and beginning production on the new movie.

Rehearsals were conducted with typical flair and creativity, with Coppola inviting the cast members to the Napa estate (jokingly referred to as "Camp Coppola") and encouraging them to improvise until they reached the emotional center of their characters. The actors took turns reading passages from the Bram Stoker novel, and from there, the company ran through a rehearsal script of the movie. Coppola then staged a series of script readings in front of live audiences around San Francisco. The audiences were given preview cards and asked to comment on the script, characters, and action, the responses intended to help Coppola make last-minute script alterations before heading down to Los Angeles for videotaped dress rehearsals.

Coppola could not have been too happy with the reaction. In general, audiences liked the historical aspects of the screenplay but were put off by the conclusion, which came across as a contrived Hollywood ending designed to send people home in an upbeat mood. In addition, some of the respondents observed that the story seemed too predictable and familiar, and that there was no point in doing another *Dracula* if there wasn't something new and surprising about it. Coppola considered the responses and made his revisions, especially in the pursuit and battle scenes at the end of the film.

Principal photography started up on October 14, with a budget set at $40 million and what Coppola hoped would be a seventy-day shooting schedule. Almost from the beginning, Coppola had to contend with a rift that had developed between Gary Oldman and Winona Ryder. The two had worked well together during rehearsals, but for reasons that Coppola never learned, they were at odds as soon as the cameras rolled in earnest. "The issue was not only that they did not get along," Coppola explained. "They got along, and then one day they didn't—*absolutely* didn't—get along. None of us were privy to what had happened."

Nor were any explanations forthcoming, though it was speculated that Oldman's work habits were at least partially to blame. Oldman, preferring to stay in character throughout the filming, was a smoldering, brooding presence, constantly challenging the director and fellow actors. Since the shooting schedule did not call for Oldman to step before cameras during the first two weeks of filming, he had all kinds of time to consider how to deal with the many sides to his complex character. Coppola had encouraged him to go all out in his portrayal, and Oldman took him at his word, although not always with the director's approval. "He'd get together with makeup designer Greg Cannom," said Coppola, "and before I knew it, we were going to have not just one monster but five monsters in the film."

Oldman, like Brando before him, pushed Coppola to his limits. Aware that he didn't have the classic leading-man appearance, without consulting Coppola first, Oldman decided that he wanted to portray the young Dracula as a sort of sexually ambivalent character, and to achieve this effect, he had his makeup artist apply the thick white makeup to his face, much of which was then covered with bushy muttonchop sideburns. Coppola hated the look, and he and Oldman were soon going at it, Coppola insisting that Oldman remove the white makeup, Oldman battling him every step of the way. It was only the first of many clashes.

For Oldman, playing Dracula could be physically challenging. It took about four hours to apply his makeup, and at one point, he had a strong allergic reaction to the chemicals in the latex and had to be taken to the emergency room; on another occasion, he became so claustrophobic in his bat costume that he had difficulty breathing and had to have the mask cut away. He slipped on stage blood and slammed his head on the floor. He had to drop his voice an octave to achieve the deep, rich voice of the Romanian count. "You have to have a reserve of energy just to cut through all that rubber," Oldman remarked.

Winona Ryder was an entirely different kind of actor. While by no means a novice to the profession, the twenty-year-old actress was still in the process of expanding her artistic range. In her previous movies, including *Beetlejuice; Heathers; Welcome Home, Roxy Carmichael;* and *Edward Scissorhands,* she was portraying teenagers and essentially working on instinct; in *Dracula,* she was playing her first truly adult role, which required more emotional colors on her palette. Greta Seacat had been teaching her Method acting, but Ryder was finding it slow going. She had to work to dredge up some of her character's emotions, and she was not as inclined as Oldman to remain in character off the set.

Ryder was hard-pressed to provide an explanation of her strained relationship with Oldman, although she admitted that she could relate to someone like Keanu Reeves, who was a fellow American and closer to her in age, whereas she had a difficult time relating to Oldman.

"It was like I didn't know him," she said of Oldman, "because he was doing his Dracula thing. I still don't feel like I ever met Gary Oldman, but I feel like I met everyone else."

Coppola had mixed feelings about his youthful cast. As a rule, he enjoyed working with young actors, but the business had changed dramatically from the days when he was making *The Outsiders* and *Rumble Fish,* when his cast had looked up to him as a mentor The cast of *Dracula* still respected Coppola and his reputation, but in the age of big-buck contracts, they, like their other young peers in the business, realized that they had some power and control. If they didn't feel like working, Coppola complained, they would stay away from the set; if they were having affairs with others in the cast or crew, you might find yourself dealing with angry boyfriends, girlfriends, or spouses, or with depressed actors when the relationship ended. "I don't know," Coppola said at the time. "I'm a very young-at-heart type of person, but sometimes I think I'm getting too old."

As fond as he was of Gary Oldman, Coppola was annoyed by some of his drinking habits—Oldman was nailed for drunk driving after a Saturday-night bender with Kiefer Sutherland—and he felt that the actor had a habit of showing off when outsiders visited the set. "He wanted to command the set and I got really pissed off," Coppola admitted. "You gotta show off, the girl has to see that you're really dominating the set."

Coppola, who had endured the volatile temperaments of such actors as Marlon Brando, Shirley Knight, and Al Pacino, rarely let such antics get the better of him. Actors, he realized, were a strange breed, full of their own doubts and insecurities, and each had a way of preparing for a role. Oldman might be, in Coppola's words, "yet another overproducing plant"—a brilliantly gifted performer, overflowing with ideas on how a production should be done, and willing to push as many buttons as necessary to nudge it in that direction—but Coppola also recognized that Oldman was elevating his movie to a greater artistic level.

5·

COMPARED TO WHAT COPPOLA had been through on some of his previous movies, the *Dracula* shoot went smoothly. True to his vow to avoid modern special effects in his movie, Coppola bypassed such techniques as computer morphing and animation in favor of such old movie tricks as multiple exposure, variable film speed, and other optical gimmicks to create the gloomy magic associated with a character who could change shape at will. A mime was brought in to act as Dracula's shadow, which moved independently of the character. For the film's opening battle scene between the Muslim Turks and Dracula's army, Coppola shot much of the action in silhouette, using puppets and projected images in the background and middle ground and live action in the foreground, similar to the cinematography used at the turn of the century.

"We have tried for a unique, striking visual style that immediately says you are in the realm of magic," explained Coppola, who relied heavily on his son Roman, the film's second-unit director and visual effects specialist, to bring his vision to the screen. "We explored the tradition of early cinema, the era when magicians first brought cameras to the world—which was the period when Stoker wrote *Dracula*. So we have used many of those naïve effects, tricks done with the camera or with mirrors, to give the film almost a mythical soul."

Since the film was being shot on soundstages, Coppola had to rely on illusion not only to achieve the effects he wanted for filmgoers but for budgetary reasons, as well. This was especially true of the shooting of the picture's big finale, which called for a chase through the Transylvanian Alps, capped by a confrontation outside of Dracula's castle. In writing the scene, James Hart remained more faithful to the Stoker book than previous filmmakers, who came up with their own dramatic climaxes. "Nobody's ever shot that John Ford Western finale as Stoker wrote it," Hart pointed out.

Coppola, too, was enamored of the unusual ending, and he and his crew went to great lengths to assure that it would work in the movie. He had at his disposal a football field–sized soundstage, and here, production designer Tom Sanders constructed an oval track on which the chase would be staged.

"We put rock at one end of the stage to elevate the road," Sanders said, "so it looks like it's going through the mountains, and the other end we kept on ground level with lots of trees, more like the countryside. By the way they shoot and cut it, it can look like hundreds of different miles of road, because the greensmen kept moving trees around to create different backgrounds."

The set was designed in the finest detail, and real wolves and more than thirty-five horses were used. The chase, conducted during a winter snowstorm, required wind machines and a flocking machine mounted on a crane, all wreaking artificial meteorological havoc on the set while horses and wagons raced around the track at breakneck speed.

Coppola shot several scenes that did not make the final cut, mainly because, as he saw it, they were so excessive that they might have confused or been too much for viewers. In one of the excised scenes, Dracula was transformed into a gigantic blood clot; in another, originally intended for the beginning of the movie, when Vlad rejects his faith and plunges his sword into the cross in the chapel, blood was to fill the room until Elisabeta became completely submerged.

"I just thought, it's one thing to use blood as a metaphor," Coppola reflected, "but it would confuse people if, for example, I submerged Winona in blood. I would be more excessive than many people, but I [was] trying to get them into the story, rather than overwhelm them in the first two minutes."

There was also the matter of holding the movie to an R rating. When previewing the picture, Coppola kept these two scenes in—along with another, in which one of Dracula's vampire brides takes an infant down the hall, supposedly to drain its life away—partly because he wanted to see how they would play before audiences, but also, no doubt, because Coppola, the master sales-man, understood that pulling all the stops could only benefit his film's prere-lease publicity. For all his queasiness about filming sex and violence, he had been around long enough to know that both brought people to theaters, and if his movie was rumored be the sexiest, goriest *Dracula* ever, he could only gain from it. As it was, he cut the questionable scenes before showing the movie to the MPAA, and the only cut that he made as a result of the board's recommendation was the removal of some of the more sexually explicit draw-ings found in an antiquated copy of Sir Richard Burton's illustrated volume of *Arabian Nights,* which Lucy and Mina page through and giggle over early in the movie.

6.

COPPOLA WRAPPED PRINCIPAL photography—"on budget [and] ahead of schedule," he made a point of informing the press—on February 1, 1992. He felt optimistic about the film's chances. He had a good combination of attractive young stars, a respected older actor, and an excellent leading man to attract filmgoers of all ages; his story was time-honored and had been bril-liantly filmed by Michael Ballhaus. He had all kinds of time for postproduc-tion. In his interviews, he waxed enthusiastic about his latest project, rejecting some of the more salient rumors about the film's eroticism. "It's romantic, just the way the book was written," he said.

In private, however, Coppola was worried. He believed he had made a good movie, and one that did justice to the Bram Stoker novel, but he fret-ted, as he had in the past, that he might have lost touch with his audiences. Such fears appeared to be justified when Coppola previewed a rough cut of *Dracula* in San Diego, to a very negative response. "That was one of the worst previews I've ever had," he noted in his journal. "I sort of like the film myself, but now feel very insecure about it."

He reminded himself that he had scored poorly in past sneak previews of some of his successful pictures. *Peggy Sue Got Married* received the worst pre-view response that he could remember, and the film had gone on to become his biggest hit as a director for hire. He would have to rethink *Dracula,* per-haps alter some of its structure and shore up the narrative to make the picture easier to follow.

By now, Coppola's worries were as familiar as a mantra uttered repeatedly over a lifetime. Although he publicly tried to cast as good a light as possible on his movies over the past decade—and, in fact, he could find something to like in all of the films—he could admit to himself that, for one reason or another, the work-for-hire ventures had not panned out to his satisfaction. His financial turmoil, reported in intimate detail by the press, embarrassed and depressed him, forcing him to accept projects that, under other circumstances, he might have rejected as being beneath his talents and ambitions. Critics accused him of selling out, even as he labored to chip away at his enormous debts. He had lost his studio but saved his home and vineyard, and he could see better financial days up the road, but he was still in no position to pursue *Megalopolis* or any other project truly close to his heart—not yet anyway. If all this wasn't stressful enough, he felt his anxiety compounded with each new picture, when he reminded himself that he was working so close to the margin that he could not afford to fail. "If I really total out on a big-budget picture," he declared, "it's going to be difficult to get another comparably paying job for a while—maybe forever."

In an attempt to put an end to a decade's worth of financial headaches, he filed once again for protection from his creditors under Chapter 11. According to the papers filed in the Federal Bankruptcy Court in San Francisco, Coppola's total assets—which included his and Eleanor's assets, as well as those of Zoetrope Productions—were $52 million, while liabilities were listed at $98 million. As overwhelming as the figures might have appeared, Coppola saw himself in a position to put his past behind him finally, if given the chance to restructure the payment of his debts.

"The bankruptcy filing closes the book on a complicated, decade-long series of financial and legal problems arising from the making of *One from the Heart*," he offered in a statement to the press. "It will finally let us resolve all remaining debts and obligations stemming from the film and enable me to focus my attention on current projects."

It had been a long and often excruciating haul, but Coppola was finally tidying up a mess that had been created by the collision of a modest love story and a gigantic, ambitious dream. If *Dracula* turned out to be a big hit, there was no telling where his revitalized career would go.

7.

COPPOLA CONTINUED TO MAKE adjustments on *Dracula* right up to its premiere on November 13, 1992. Previews of the revised version of the film fared much better than the disaster in San Diego earlier in the year, but audiences still weren't totally sold on the movie. The review-card responses indicated that the preview audiences still strongly disliked the ending—Dracula's death, they claimed, wasn't thrilling or dramatic enough, and some viewers were uncertain about Mina's ultimate fate—and there was still a lot of confusion about the plot itself. Coppola had always appreciated the way Bram Stoker had narrated his story through the various characters' diary entries and letters, and he had attempted to use such a narrative device in his movie adaptation of the book, but after hearing from the preview attendees, he began to wonder if he would be better off having a single narrator. Preview audiences, Coppola felt, were difficult to gauge: Sometimes they didn't fully comprehend or appreciate a film until they'd had time to let it ferment in their minds. One had to be careful about making a lot of last-minute adjustments, which, in the long run, could be more harmful than what they were replacing.

After giving the matter a lot of consideration, Coppola decided to have Professor Van Helsing act as the picture's lone narrator, and he brought Anthony Hopkins to Hollywood to record the voice-over narrative, along with an additional scene. Two subsequent sneak previews in Denver in late October produced more favorable response, leading Coppola to announce that he was happy with his film, even as he expressed irritation with the critics who attended these screenings and wrote early reviews of the movie. "They killed *One from the Heart*," he said. "To what extent is a person entitled to a preview without criticism?"

Coppola needn't have been too concerned. As was the case with some of his other movies, most notably *The Outsiders* and *Peggy Sue Got Married*, all the prerelease publicity and criticism had little effect on attendance, and audiences lined up around the block to catch a glimpse of Coppola's version of the Dracula story. The opening five days produced a staggering $35,035,556 in revenue, establishing a new record for initial grosses at Columbia, and marking *Bram Stoker's Dracula* as one of the main contenders at the holiday box office. After ten days in circulation, the picture had taken in $54 million—more than all but three of Coppola's previous films.

As Coppola suspected, the movie drew a wild mixture of reviews, from critics offering glowing endorsements ("This most recent *Dracula* is scary and funny, beautiful to look at and great entertainment") to those who reviled the movie as still another example of the director's spiraling career ("Now comes *Bram Stoker's Dracula*, to confirm the vacancy of the career—no, of the man. He is not an artist who has made mistakes; he's a journeyman worker, with some skills, who has occasionally stumbled across a good project"). Most reviewers agreed that Gary Oldman had given a noteworthy performance in the title role, but they were less impressed with the rest of the cast, with the exception of Tom Waits, who drew raves, even from those reviewers who otherwise disliked the movie.

By now, Coppola was accustomed to seeing each movie inspire a number of career overviews, but *Dracula* brought out some of the most vitriolic assessments yet. In "The Fall of Francis Coppola," a lengthy essay written for *USA Today* magazine, Christopher Sharrett called *Dracula* "the last nail in the coffin (the bad pun is the only appropriate metaphor) for a director whose sagging career has been of much speculation and concern for more than a decade." The essay, an all-out assault, attacked Coppola on every front, from the professional to the personal, concluding that he had become an apt symbol for the shortcomings and failures of the New Hollywood. "The artistic and moral catastrophe of this film," Sharrett argued, "is covered over rather skillfully by the extravagant *fin de siècle* costumes, exotic musical score, special effects, and elaborate publicity effort that begs for this movie to become a 'cash machine' with its spin-off products (books, trading cards, comics, T-shirts, calendars, posters) in proper New Hollywood style."

If there was a single overriding theme running throughout the negative reviews, it concerned the complaint, registered often in reviews of other Coppola films, that the director had sacrificed substance for style, that he had created a beautiful movie at the expense of a strong story and characters.

"Coppola does deserve credit for filling each frame with magnificent costumes and mindboggling effects," wrote Gene Siskel in a review characteristic of the mixed notices received by *Dracula*, "but they overwhelm the narrative. He hasn't created a single interesting character beyond Dracula." David Ansen of *Newsweek* commented, "Coppola's remake throws so much fancy techniques at its story that the usually foolproof drama at its core gets drowned in a tide of images." And in the *New York Times*, Vincent Canby wrote, "With its gorgeous sets and mad montages that recall the original grandeur of Abel Gance's *Napoleon*, this *Dracula* transcends camp to become a testimonial to the glories of filmmaking as an end in itself."

Such observations might not have caused Coppola to jump for joy—if anything, they might have underscored his own suspicions, recorded in his diary, about the strengths and weaknesses of the movie—but they were borne out a few months later, when the Academy Award nominations were announced. David Stone would win an Oscar for his sound editing, Eiko Ishioka would take home a statuette for costume design, and Greg Cannom and his crew would earn one for makeup, while Thomas Sanders would receive a nomination for production design. The screenplay, direction, and performances, however, would be totally ignored.

Chapter Eighteen

Full Recovery

"There is ever less room for originality. If I try to make an interesting film which I have written myself and is not adapted from a bestseller, no one will let me do it."

—FRANCIS FORD COPPOLA

"All I feel is why didn't someone tell me, back in those days when I was so depressed and feeling so untalented, I wish someone had said, 'You know what, everyone's going to like you ten years from now, so go out and have dinner.'"

—FRANCIS FORD COPPOLA

1.

FRANCIS FORD COPPOLA wasn't even in the United States when the initial figures for *Bram Stoker's Dracula* were announced, and nearly a week had passed before he learned of his film's strong opening. Coppola wanted nothing to do with the rush of reviews and hubbub attendant to the release of his latest film—too much strain and anxiety, as far as he was concerned. Instead, he and Ellie flew to Guatemala, where they stopped briefly in Antigua before heading on to Panojial. Coppola was enchanted by the cobblestone streets and remnants of the Spanish colonial buildings, all reminders of the days when Antigua had been a beautiful capital during Spanish rule in Central America. In Panojial, the Coppolas stayed in a small house near a mountain lake. After the hectic final months of postproduction on *Dracula,* the vacation afforded Coppola some badly needed relaxation.

"I've run off here to Guatemala," he reported in his journal, "so I didn't have to wonder or worry about how the film opened, how it did and all that. No phone call on Saturday morning with the news, etc. because there wasn't a phone in this house. So I've been happy just relaxing here."

The Coppolas had traveled to Guatemala to shop for furnishings for their lodge in Belize. Earlier in the year, Francis had celebrated his fifty-third birthday by purchasing plane tickets for twenty family members and relatives, who were whisked down to Blancaneaux to celebrate the occasion. Surrounded by family, Coppola began to wonder what it would be like to open the place to the public. Now, in Guatemala, he and Ellie shopped for fabrics, furnishings, and artifacts to refurbish the lodge and give it a Mayan theme.

Removed from his recent pressures, Coppola felt the creative juices flowing again. He still entertained the hope of seeing Belize converted into the communications and cultural center in Central America, complete with universities, medical centers, radio and television stations, a recording studio— even a monorail. Time had not whittled away his enthusiasm for technology; if anything, some of his early ideas about the electronic cinema were beginning to look positively visionary. Television—cable and network—were on his mind, and he was considering a revival of the old *Playhouse 90* television series, along with a number of other made-for-TV projects.

For all his ambition, he was in no hurry to direct another picture. With *Dracula* faring so well at the box office, he would have career options that had been unavailable to him for many years, and he spoke, once again, of taking a sabbatical from filmmaking.

"There's no distress for me—for the first time in thirty years, no worries," he stated in a February interview in *Variety.* "It's time to rejuvenate myself. I've done one movie after another. Now, with the success of *Dracula*—even greater in Europe than in the U.S.—it has given me and my wife security. We don't have to worry about the future and I'm not worried about covering my ass anymore. I'm totally clear—debt-free and on the plus side from *Dracula.* I can have a time of repose."

Much the way he had been after the success of *The Godfather,* Coppola was now feeling every bit the mogul. As an executive producer, he could oversee the production of other filmmakers' projects. The new permutation of Zoetrope, formed when Coppola struck his deal with Columbia Pictures, was showing promise, and Coppola wanted to expand his company's horizons into a deeper involvement with television, which, he confidently announced, was "a new frontier" for cinema. He was intrigued by music videos, which, in just a few minutes, could present visual shorts that expanded the creativity already present in the songs.

Dracula had spawned at least one noteworthy new Zoetrope project. Several months earlier, while still in postproduction on *Dracula*, Coppola had agreed to coproduce, along with James V. Hart, a film adaptation of Mary Wollstonecraft Shelley's *Frankenstein*. Early rumors linked Willem Dafoe and director Roman Polanski to the project, but neither wound up having anything to do with the film, which was directed by Kenneth Branagh and starred Branagh, Robert De Niro, John Cleese, Helena Bonham Carter, and Aidan Quinn. Although he was not directing the film, Coppola took an active role in the early stages of its development, flying to New York to confer with Branagh and De Niro and seeing that the budding project received appropriate attention from the press.

"It won't be reminiscent of Boris Karloff," he announced, making certain that the press understood that this new version of *Frankenstein*, like his adaptation of *Dracula*, would be more faithful to the source material than the previous Hollywood pictures. "It's a real classic story and a good script. We go from the Arctic to England with tremendous scenes—and no super-digital filming."

With Branagh, a Shakespearean actor of great repute, playing Dr. Frankenstein, and Robert De Niro his creation, *Mary Shelley's Frankenstein* boasted of a marquee cast perhaps even more noteworthy than the names in *Bram Stoker's Dracula*, and if the new film even approached the box-office figures of *Dracula*, it might free Coppola to pursue *Megalopolis* or another pet project sometime in the near future.

A project still very much on Coppola's mind was a live-action version of *Pinocchio*. Coppola had been thinking about making a film adaptation of the popular children's book since shortly after Gio's accident, and he was enthusiastic about making what, in effect, would be a tribute to his dead son. The Coppola version would follow the book more closely than Disney's animated version.

Still, as much as he liked the project, Coppola was not about to make the picture on any terms but his own. *Pinocchio* would be an intensely personal film, and he had no intention of facing any kind of studio interference while he was making it. In his discussions with Warner Bros., he had included *Pinocchio* (along with *Hoover* and *The Secret Garden*) as part of a proposed three-film deal, but he had been dissatisfied with the money the company was offering him to make the film. Rather than take on a project under less than agreeable terms, Coppola decided to put the project aside, pending further discussion. He would cut a better deal later, either with Warner Bros. or some other studio.

Little did he know that his decision would lead to another high-profile confrontation with the old Hollywood system, and one of the landmark court cases to rise out of the motion picture industry.

2.

DESPITE ALL HIS CLAIMS ABOUT taking a breather from filmmaking, Coppola's name was never far removed from show business news in 1993. In fact, if one could judge from the reports circulating in the trade papers, he had never been busier. One day, there would be talk of his producing a miniseries about the *Titanic* for CBS television; another day, he would be rumored to be working with John Milius on a sequel to *Apocalypse Now*. He was connected with an ambitious television documentary series, *Century*, a Turner Productions enterprise examining the great events of the twentieth century, for which he would be producing a segment on Japan. He was developing *The Van Helsing Chronicles*, a *Dracula* spin-off to star Anthony Hopkins in the role he'd played in the original picture, with Van Helsing taking on evil forces all over the world; if all went according to plan, the film would be directed by Roman Coppola. In addition, Francis hoped to bring his talents and ideas about new technology to VH1 music videos. Much of the talk, of course, was pure Hollywood: If every rumor, option, or development deal blossomed into a motion picture, there never would have been time for lunches, let alone a minute's sleep.

Besides keeping an eye on the production of *Mary Shelley's Frankenstein*, Coppola spent much of the year "attend[ing] to all the things I can't do when I'm directing," enjoying his Napa Valley estate, supervising the goings-on at Zoetrope, and solidifying two nonfilm adventures: the further development of his Napa vineyard and the renovation and opening of his Blancaneaux Lodge in Belize. Both gave him not only great satisfaction but also the potential for earnings apart from the movies.

Coppola took pride in the wine his vineyard was yielding. His Edizione Pennino zinfandel, named after his maternal grandfather, was a personal favorite—"a lot like the classic big Italian reds," he boasted. Each year, Niebaum-Coppola produced five thousand cases of Rubicon, its pride and joy, and in June, the 1987 vintage was tasted during a highly publicized party at Hollywood's Chateau Marmont Hotel. "I'm lucky, in that Columbia

Pictures made me rich with *Dracula*, and I can enjoy my life in the Napa Valley," Coppola told *The Hollywood Reporter*.

The *Dracula* earnings, which would eventually top the $200 million mark worldwide, also gave Coppola the money needed to convert his Blancaneaux Lodge into a tourist hideaway. The renovation had been remarkable. The new facility, open to the public in December, still had the old thatched-roof look of the original structures, but the new villas were exquisitely furnished with items purchased in Guatemala, Mexico, Belize, the Philippines, Italy, the United States, and elsewhere, giving visitors a sampling of Coppola's eclectic multicultural tastes. Coppola even designed a small hydroelectric plant, powered by the nearby Privassion River, to provide round-the-clock electricity. "Everyone thought I was crazy," he said of the reaction to his idea of building the plant. "It's always the ideas that everyone says are crazy that turn out to be right."

Coppola had never lacked self-confidence, but the success of *Bram Stoker's Dracula* and, to a smaller extent, *Godfather III* had gone a long way in his overcoming any credibility lost with such recent flops as *Gardens of Stone, Tucker,* and *New York Stories*. The newer pictures might not have stacked up well in comparison with some of his films of the 1970s, but Coppola was at least bankable again, and in the language of Hollywood, that meant power and influence. This much was evident when, in a surprise move, Coppola was named to MGM's board of directors in late 1993, reuniting him with Frank Mancuso, an ally from his Paramount days and presently CEO of MGM. Some of Coppola's more cynical critics sneered when Mancuso announced the appointment—Coppola had proven his lack of business acumen in the failure of his Zoetrope studio and in his bankruptcies, they suggested—but for Coppola, the position was the kind of recognition that had long been denied him by the Hollywood establishment.

Not that Coppola needed any kind of pat on the back from the establishment: He had played the game his way and Hollywood's way, and he'd won and lost at both. Now, enjoying his first hiatus from filmmaking since his days at UCLA, he was back to his old self, living large and taking in every minute of it. The old Coppola swagger could still be detected in his statements to the press, but his remarks were now seasoned with a dash of humility, gained through personal and professional loss. At times, his remarks could be as self-critical as anything written about him by his detractors, but more often than not, these remarks were offered as verbal shrugs or sighs. "Lots of people have criticized my movies," he told the *New York Times* in a reflective interview published in early 1994. "But nobody has ever identified the real problem. I'm a sloppy filmmaker. Just as Alice Waters says I'm a sloppy chef."

The statement was pure Coppola. Even as he took a verbal swipe at himself, he also made it clear that he had not forgotten the slights of his past—in this case, a remark made years earlier, when his cooking had been criticized in the press. This was, perhaps, part of Coppola's charm: He had proven himself in battle and had survived setbacks that would have left others vanquished and lost, but he could still be surprisingly thin-skinned, easily annoyed by critics or angered by those who dared to disagree with him, as if he could be mortally wounded, after spending a career dodging mortar shells, by a stray dart tossed in his direction.

And in an industry so often perceived as cold and bloodless, this kind of passion, even if misguided or misdirected at times, gave people reason to applaud. It wasn't easy to be a multimillionaire *and* an underdog, but Coppola, after years of honing his pitch to a fine art, was still pulling it off.

3.

COPPOLA STARTED 1994 IN GREAT style, with the opening of Rubicon, an upscale San Francisco restaurant taking its name from Niebaum-Coppola's finest wine. Coppola has always loved to cook, particularly the kind of Italian food that he ate when he was a boy, and throughout his adult life, he has delighted in moving noisily around the kitchen, clattering pots and singing old songs while making a mess that somehow transforms into a tasty meal for guests. He hoped Rubicon would combine this type of zest with fine, atmospheric dining. Any restaurant owned by a celebrity is bound to attract attention, and Rubicon could boast having not only Coppola but also Robin Williams and Robert De Niro as high-profile investors.

De Niro, who was finishing work on *Mary Shelley's Frankenstein*, wasn't the only *Godfather* alumnus hooking up with Coppola on a new project. In February, the director announced that he would be producing *Don Juan DeMarco*, a New Line project starring Marlon Brando, Johnny Depp, and Faye Dunaway. Brando, whose intensity had challenged Coppola on the set of *Apocalypse Now*, would be playing a psychiatrist going through his own midlife crisis while examining a patient who professes to be Don Juan. Zoetrope also announced that it would be producing *Mi Familia*, a vehicle for Edward James Olmos.

Although he hoped to take another year off before directing a new picture, Coppola continued to move ahead with his plans for *Pinocchio*, which was evolving into an ambitious project, with an estimated budget running in the $40 to $50 million range. Given the popularity of the animated version of the story, Coppola's decision to make another adaptation might have seemed a strange choice, but he insisted that he would be making a different movie.

"I'd only attempt it," he said of *Pinocchio,* "because the Disney movie is different from the original story. For example, in the original, it's a giant shark, not a whale. And in the original story, Pinocchio kills the cricket and he's haunted by its ghost."

Before writing his screenplay, Coppola researched Carlo Collodi's archives in Florence, studying how the Italian author had crafted the most widely translated children's book in history. Besides adapting a script from the book, Coppola wrote a dozen songs for the movie, singing them to his assistant, Anahid Nazarian, who transcribed them on the flute before they were actually transposed. Pinocchio, Coppola told the press, would still be a puppet, but he would be "the product of a whole range of the latest (filming) technology, from puppet to live action to the computer technology started with *Jurassic Park.*" If all went well, he would begin filming early in 1995. Typically, Coppola added his own creative spin to the story, at least in a later permutation of the script.

"My friend Bill Graham, the rock impresario, had been born a German Jew in the 1930s," Coppola explained, when asked about the background of the picture. "He was in an orphanage with his sisters, and when the first Jewish policies started, it was decided to send these kids to France. Germany hadn't invaded France at that point, but they still weren't thought to be safe in the new orphanage, so they walked to Spain. One of Bill's sisters died along the way, and another got sick and had to be left behind. These little kids and some teachers walked all the way to Spain. From there, Bill was sent to live with people in New York, where he was raised and became the person we know as Bill Graham.

"He had told me all this, and I wondered, 'What if this happened, say, not in Germany, but today, in Bosnia or somewhere not really specified?' And what if all these kids had was a beat-up copy of *Pinocchio,* which the teacher would read to them when they were hiding at night? And what if, when the story began, the teacher played the role of Geppetto, and the little girl who helped him played the fairy in the story? And what if, during one of these sequences, they were strafed by planes and the little girl was wounded, which would explain why the fairy in the *Pinocchio* story was ill and dying, and could only be saved if Pinocchio was a good boy? That was my premise. If the theme of *Pinocchio* is really about how bad boys grow up to be bad men, then war and all the devastating things that people do to each other could be cured by children learning all the lessons that Pinocchio should learn."

All, however, did not go according to the plan. Warner Bros., still believing its previous discussions with Coppola precluded any arrangement that

Coppola might have with Columbia Pictures, warned Columbia that it would seek to block the production if Coppola tried to make the movie for them. The threat of a lawsuit effectively shelved the project. "You've got to clear this up," Columbia officials instructed Coppola. By the end of 1994, the project was still stuck in development, awaiting an improbable solution.

"We're trying to work it out," Coppola said. "But an individual can't compete with a whole legal department of a giant corporation."

Feeling defeated in his efforts to usher *Pinocchio* to the screen, Coppola began to consider other options.

One, a film adaptation of *On the Road*, Jack Kerouac's classic Beat novel, was much more challenging. The Kerouac book had been passed around Hollywood for nearly four decades, with a number of producers, directors, and actors, including Marlon Brando, expressing interest in making the picture, but for one reason or another, it had never found its way to the screen. Coppola had wanted to make the film for some time, but he had been too preoccupied with other projects to pursue it seriously. Now he envisioned a film that would be absolutely true to the spirit of the book, shot with period details in lavish black-and-white photography, with Michael Herr, who had written the voice-over for *Apocalypse Now* and *Gardens of Stone,* writing the screenplay.

For all his dizzying activity in 1994, Coppola's biggest and most successful move was away from the movie business. Ever since he bought the Niebaum estate in 1975, Coppola had dreamed of purchasing the adjacent Inglenook estate, which had once been part of the property owned by Gustave Niebaum in the nineteenth century. The Inglenook property included a breathtaking stone château, open to tourists for wine tastings, and eighteen acres of vineyards, although there had been no wine production on the premises for two decades. The Inglenook brand name, owned by Heublein since 1969, had been sold in June 1994 to the Canandaigua Wine Company in New York, and the estate had gone on the market a short time later. Coppola was definitely interested.

"Every time I drove through here, I wished and fantasized that one day I could buy this place," Coppola said in early December, when his bid for the estate, reportedly between $9 and $10 million, was accepted. "I didn't know for sure that I actually could," he admitted, "until a few days ago."

The media applauded the purchase, which also included a barrel-aging facility, the Gustave Niebaum Collection (fifteen thousand cases of wine first presented in 1989), and the historic Inglenook library of wines, dating back to 1886.

The reunification of the property was a major historic event in the winemaking business, and Coppola admitted that this was one of his primary reasons for purchasing the property. "It's always bugged me that this incredible chateau and this great winery were split off," he said. "The chances of bringing something like this together are slim. It was luck."

Predictably, Coppola had grand plans for the new property, beginning with an extensive restoration project intended to bring back some of the estate's historic luster. As for the wine itself, Coppola remained cautiously optimistic. "It's like a movie idea that doesn't have a script," he said. "I believe we have the potential to produce 75,000 cases of wine that will rival a major chateau in France."

Such plans demanded a substantial cash investment, and with all his recent purchases, Coppola realized that his enjoyable vacation from directing movies was coming to an end. It was time to work.

4.

FROM THE MOMENT HE HAD seen former NYU students Gary Nadeau and James DeMonaco's script, Coppola pictured *Jack* as a "warm fable," the kind of project that could be thoroughly entertaining on one level while addressing serious issues on another. This had been the way he had approached *Peggy Sue Got Married*, which had seemed like an unusual project when he agreed to direct it, and this would be the way he'd work with *Jack*.

"I've always tried different styles," he explained. "*Peggy Sue Got Married* was a kind of sweet fable, and in a way *Jack* is like that. Even though *Jack* didn't originate with me, I tried to tackle the story with as much feeling and love as I could."

Jack was the story of a boy with a fictitious disease that made him age at four times the normal rate, leaving him a child trapped in an adult's body. The movie would be another director-for-hire job, with Coppola working for Disney, and while it was a lightweight project in comparison to the type of movies most often associated with the Coppola name, the picture offered a number of appealing prospects, including the opportunity for Coppola to address some of the feelings that he had had as a child living with the loneliness of polio, and the chance to work with children.

The "feeling and love" sprang from three main sources, spanning three generations of Coppolas. The most obvious was Coppola's own childhood confrontation with polio, and his feelings of isolation, so similar to the ones felt by Jack in the movie. "I remember being pinned to this bed and being hungry, longing for friends and company," he said. "When I read *Jack*, I was moved because that was precisely his problem; there are no children in his life."

Then there was the issue of living a full, complete life in a brief period of time. If Jack physically aged four years for each calendar year that he lived, he would be lucky to live twenty years—a terribly short life span, but something that Coppola knew far too much about.

"As a kid," he reflected, "I always used to look at flies and bugs and think, 'Gee, they only live a day. Do they realize this, or does a fly think his life is a complete life.' My son Gio only lived 22 years, but it was a complete 22 years. He got to do everything—he got to be a kid, he got to be an adult, got to fall in love, got to shoot all that stuff on *Cotton Club*. And so while it's sad to think of other people or other species that don't live quite as long as us, there are people who live 80 years and are miserable the whole time. So when I saw this story in which ultimately a character with a disability doesn't live very long, I found it touching."

Finally, Coppola received an inspirational nudge from his only grandchild—Gio's daughter, Gian-Carla, born after her father's death—to whom *Jack* was eventually dedicated. The nine-year-old kept pestering her grandfather, asking, "When are you going to do a film with kids in it that I can see?" (Ironically, the only time Coppola had directed anything resembling such a picture, *New York Stories*, Gia had appeared in the movie, as the infant Zoe.)

Coppola's personal attachment to the story might have weighed heavily in his wish to become involved in the movie, but much of his decision to direct *Jack* came by default. *Pinocchio* was still hung up in legal wranglings, leading Coppola to conclude that it would be unlikely that he would be making the picture anytime in the near future. *On the Road*, despite an open casting call in New York's St. Paul the Apostle Auditorium, was, in the words of producer Fred Fuchs, in "an informal early, early phase," as a shooting script and a studio to back the film were still needed. Other projects were in even earlier stages of development. *Jack* was about all that was left.

At first, Coppola volunteered very little information about his latest project, telling the press that he was thinking about making a movie for children, or that he was interested in directing a sweet, fablelike picture. The secrecy, however, lasted only until the trades connected Robin Williams to the project.

Fresh off his work in *Aladdin*, in which his was the voice of the hyperkinetic animated genie, and *Jumanji*, in which he found himself mysteriously trapped inside a living board game, Williams was an ideal choice to play a child imprisoned in an adult's body. If anything, he was risking the accusation of playing it safe and working in an all-too-familiar role. Known for a lightning-fast mind capable of loopy free association and improvisation, Williams had applied his gifts in portraying a lovable alien in television's *Mork and Mindy* series and in playing Peter Pan in *Hook*.

Coppola had known Williams, a fellow San Franciscan, for a long time, first through mutual friends and eventually as an actor whose work he really admired. They had spoken on and off over the years about working together, but both had assumed that it would be in a dramatic role. When he saw the script for *Jack*, Coppola knew that Williams was the man to play the title character. "He's childlike, yes," he said of Williams, "but such an extraordinarily intelligent man that I knew he could pull off the illusion, and then we would be free to create the fable around that."

Ironically, this might have been the problem with the way *Jack* eventually turned out: Coppola and Williams had a compelling character to work with, even in the wake of Tom Hanks's highly acclaimed portrayal of a vaguely similar character in *Big*, but the script failed to go very far beyond the predictable—a point brought out repeatedly in the reviews of the movie. "Williams works hard at seeming to be a kid inside an adult body," noted Roger Ebert, "and some of his inspirations work well. But he has been ill-served by a screenplay that isn't curious about what his life would *really* be like."

Coppola would address such criticism with a shrug. He hadn't originated the story or written the script, he'd tell reporters, and he felt bound by the studio to honor the material.

"In the case of *Jack*, and *Peggy Sue*, I think I tried to be gentle and still do a good job at what I was hired to do, which is to realize the story," he told *Premiere* magazine's Peter Biskind. "I think what is important there in the end is to have [a] good heart and be seen to be warm and sincere. That can get you through a lot. What I did for the script for *Jack* is try to bring a little bit of my own personal feelings to it. The story begins with a woman being rushed into labor saying 'It's too soon, it's too soon, it's not even two months,' and she gives birth to this baby. Now that's a pretty serious kind of opening for such a whimsical movie, so I added a thing where the mother is at a beaux-arts ball, so that when they rush her into the hospital, everyone is in costumes to give it a little kind of, like, a Preston Sturges feeling."

After such an imaginative opening, the story jumps ahead a decade, and the whimsical part of the story begins. Jack is only ten years old, but with his adult size, receding hairline, and hairy arms, he looks like a middle-aged man. His parents, Brian and Karen Powell, show great love and patience for him, but there is something unnerving about seeing him jump into their bed at night, or teaching him how to shave. Knowing how cruel people can be to someone as different as Jack, the Powells keep him isolated from the world. He is taught at home by a kindly tutor named Lawrence Woodruff, who is his only true contact with the outside world. The kids in the neighborhood have heard stories about Jack, and

Jack can look out his window and see them playing nearby in the street, staring up in the direction of his room, but he is totally cut off from them.

Woodruff worries about the psychological effects that such isolation might be imposing on Jack, and he lobbies to have Jack placed in a regular school. The Powells finally relent, and Jack is soon in a classroom, where he towers over his fifth-grade schoolmates, barely fits into a desk, and finds himself the target of stares and jokes. He is eventually befriended by a group of boys, mainly after he poses as the principal for a meeting with the parents of one of the kids, and after the boys discover that he's the perfect center for their playground basketball team. He buys *Penthouse* for the gang, climbs up to their tree house, and engages in boyhood play that includes farting contests and eating a concoction made up of the grossest combination of ingredients imaginable.

Jack's condition causes him as much trouble in the adult world as it does among his classmates. A trip to a local watering hole finds him getting beaten up when a jealous drunk takes exception to the attention Jack is getting from an attractive young divorcée. He develops a crush on his teacher, only to suffer a heart attack after she rejects his advances. In short, he is learning cruel lessons about adulthood even as he tries to absorb the equally difficult lessons about adolescence.

After his heart attack, Jack is again removed from the outside world, but this time around, he has young allies campaigning on his behalf. Nothing will stop him from rejoining them and continuing his education—formal and otherwise—with them.

5.

FILMING ON *JACK* BEGAN IN September 1995, with Coppola at the helm for the first time in more than three years. The mood on the set was loose and relaxed, thanks largely to the presence of Robin Williams. To prepare Williams and his young cast for the production, Coppola set up his own version of a youth camp, where the kids were encouraged to adopt and treat Williams as a peer. The kids camped out in the mountains, engaged in food fights and childish pranks, went swimming and shopping, and, in general, reacquainted Williams with the life and times of ten-year-olds. In public, the young actors ran interference for Williams, waving off autograph seekers and encouraging people to call Williams Jack. "By the end of the week, he wasn't a big star to them," Coppola recalled. "He was just one of the gang. It was amazing to watch."

Williams agreed. "It was great," he said, "because you assimilate behavior without even knowing it."

As a veteran of three earlier Coppola films, Diane Lane was familiar with the director's methods of preparation, and she was happy with his latest way of getting his young actors ready for their roles.

"It was great, liberating stuff," she remembered. "Everybody got the chance to improvise, to take turns showing their ass and trying to be funny, taking liberties and playing hopscotch and being ten with ten-year-olds. It freed the kids to be as goofy as the adults would like to see children be: They weren't going to feel foolish for being childlike. And the adults set the example."

Coppola could have used a pleasant experience, if for no other reason than to take his mind off the continuing saga of *Pinocchio*, which was turning into a major source of irritation to him. Not only had he and Warner Bros. failed to find an acceptable solution to their dispute over Coppola's involvement in the project; the studio, in Coppola's mind, was determined to prevent him from ever making the film. If that wasn't bad enough, it now turned out that *The Adventures of Pinocchio* would be made as a live-action picture by another studio—without Coppola's blessing or involvement—and would be released at a time when it would be in head-to-head competition with *Jack*.

Infuriated, Coppola, along with fellow producer Fred Fuchs, filed suit against Warner Bros. in Los Angeles Superior Court. According to the suit, "This action arises from a dream of plaintiff Francis Coppola, a well-known producer and director, to bring the beloved children's story 'Pinocchio' to the screen as a live action motion picture, and from the efforts of defendant Warners first to grab Coppola's film at a bargain-basement price and then, when that failed, to ruin Coppola's efforts to bring his dream to life."

Although it outwardly appeared to be little more than a typical Hollywood squabble destined, perhaps, for an out-of-court settlement and maybe a few bruised egos, Coppola's suit, in reality, proposed a serious challenge to the way business was conducted in Tinseltown. Verbal agreements and handshake deals were a time-honored tradition in the movie business, and no one knew this better than Coppola. Nor would Coppola dispute that he and Warner Bros., despite their shaky history, had reached an understanding that, first, *Pinocchio* would be a worthy project to pursue and, second, that Coppola should be involved as a producer, director, and possibly as the screenwriter. According to Coppola, no binding agreement existed with Warner Bros., which had offered him a salary well below the fee he was accustomed to receiving for directing a feature film.

Warner Bros., on the other hand, claimed it had a binding contract with Coppola. If nothing else, the company felt it had the right to proceed with the picture—or, if it so chose, not to make the picture at all.

"To say that the case was all about agreements not being signed and baloney like that is to cover up the truth: that they had illegally and brutally stopped me from making a film that I wanted to make, just because I wouldn't bow down to them," said Coppola. "I mean, if they had any sentiment for movies at all, you'd think they'd never stop someone from making a film; in the end, they'd just say, 'Go ahead, make your film. We don't want to make it, but we're not going to prevent you because, after all, we're film people, too.' They're not film people; they're 'money and power' people."

In earlier statements to the press, Coppola had expressed doubts about whether he would be able to take on a major studio in such a dispute. What he—and Warner Bros.—seemed to overlook was the power and influence of emotion: *Pinocchio* meant much more to Coppola than its being just another project designed to fill time and earn money while Coppola the auteur tried to find the backing for the picture he really wanted to make; it was, just as Coppola stated, a dream—and one that he was willing to pursue to the bitter end, including a David versus Goliath court battle, if necessary. It was time to teach Hollywood how principles could be an ingredient in the art of the deal.

6.

COPPOLA'S AMBIVALENCE TOWARD Hollywood had never been stronger. Ever since the collapse of his Zoetrope studio after the *One from the Heart* disaster, he had worked more and more in the traditional industry framework, reluctantly abandoning his dream projects in favor of the slicker, more commercial endeavors offering the hope of ending his financial plights and reestablishing his position as a major player. He could talk up all of his director-for-hire projects, as he had done in the past and would do with *Jack*, yet one did not have to look far to find a bitter undercurrent in many of his statements to the press. You could easily take him at his word when he said he was grateful for the chance to direct a movie for a studio such as Columbia or Disney, or when he stated that his work on such projects as *Peggy Sue Got Married* or *Bram Stoker's Dracula* had been governed more by business sense than the need to create art; the operations of the new Zoetrope, however, indicated that he still wanted his independence from the Hollywood system, along with the freedom to pursue the kind of movies that he wanted to make.

He all but said as much in May 1996, while acting as president of the jury at the Cannes Film Festival, when he created a minor stir with some of his observations about the state of contemporary filmmaking.

"It's obvious that the corporations that control eighty percent of the world's culture are businesses," he said, lamenting that it had been a long time since a true classic had been made. "They would not even understand what you're talking about when you say there are other considerations," he went on, insisting that he took exception to a corporate mind-set—the same mentality that came up with the Big Mac or car designs or brands of soap— that was now being applied to the movies. In this line of thinking, people would scout around for a type of movie with mass appeal and then insist that this formula be repeated over and over, ad nauseum. But there was hope: "A new vital creative spring will well up from independent cinema"—the type of cinema, no doubt (though he did not state as much), that was being produced by Zoetrope.

Coppola was unhappy when his remarks were repeated in the trades, and he tried to apply a little damage control in a letter published in the May 21 issue of the *The Hollywood Reporter*. He had been quoted out of context, he complained, and his words had been given a tone that did not accurately reflect the mood of the press conference in which he had issued his statements. "My remarks were my opinions," he stated, "and [were] neither slamming nor lengthy. . . . I would not dream to embarrass and insult many of my friends inside the Hollywood studios, to whom I am very grateful," he wrote.

For all his protests to the contrary, Coppola apparently meant exactly what he had said—at least if one could judge from similar statements offered in months to come. In a lengthy interview with the *San Jose Mercury News*, published and nationally syndicated on the eve of the premiere of *Jack*, Coppola again blasted what he felt was a corporate mentality in the film industry. "You go to the movies today and you've already seen them," he said. "Right now the film distribution and finance world is pretty much controlled by six giant corporations—and they want you to make films similar to films that have already been made, because that's a better business bet."

Or, in an earlier interview with the *San Francisco Examiner*, published on July 31: "These days, it's very difficult to get something financed that's not basically like a film that's already been made."

Coppola, as time would show, was absolutely on the mark with some of his comments. There *was* a corporate mind-set in the film business— although, arguably, there always had been—and there *was* a sense of formula to a great number of films being produced. And, as time would also prove, the independents *would* be offering some of the most creative (and, in a few instances, most successful) films over the next few years. However, in all likelihood, Coppola's remarks were also preemptive strikes, reflective, perhaps, of his own frustrations with his recent director-for-hire efforts: *Jack* was about to be released, and it would inevitably be compared to *Big*, a film with a somewhat similar premise, or even to his own *Peggy Sue Got Married;* his next project was to be a film adaptation of John Grisham's *The Rainmaker,* a novel that had a familiar ring to it, as well.

To even the most charitable of reviewers, *Jack* turned out to be an average movie, and a disappointment when coming, as it did, from the talents of the director of *The Godfather* and *Apocalypse Now.* In all fairness, it's doubtful that any director could have done much more with the material. Robin Williams gave a strong performance, which was well supported by a cast that included Diane Lane, as Jack's mother; Bill Cosby, as Lawrence Woodruff, Jack's tutor; Jennifer Lopez, as Miss Marquez, Jack's fifth-grade teacher; and Fran Drescher, as Dolores Durante, a young divorcée who takes a romantic interest in Jack. As a rule, the performances were low-key, keeping Williams squarely in the spotlight.

The critics weren't buying. "Coppola has been expanding his California vineyard," offered Gene Siskel in a scathing review, "and the guess here is that his *Jack* fee paid for a lot of grapes. But *Jack* is anything but vintage Coppola. In fact, I would be hard pressed to point to a single image that is distinctive." Roger Ebert, who also ripped the movie, felt that the film failed both as a picture for kids and as a picture for adults. "My best guess is that the premise blinded everyone," he wrote. "Robin Williams is a 40-year-old in a 10-year-old's body. Great! When do we start shooting? If anyone dared to bring up the possibility of a better screenplay, he was probably shouted down. In the delirium of high concept, it doesn't pay to rain on the parade." *Entertainment Weekly's* Owen Gleiberman similarly assailed "the sort of 'catchy' concept that sounds like it was dreamed up during a power breakfast at Spago," calling *Jack* "a feel-good casserole that got left in the microwave too long."

A number of reviewers, including Ebert, expressed disappointment that the film failed to explore what should have been the inevitable sexual tension between the biological adult and the psychological preadolescent in Jack.

"If Jack is chronologically and emotionally ten but truly, physically forty," proposed Stephen Whitty in a syndicated review, "then he's a sexually adult male with a child's lack of inhibitions. He's a desperate and even dangerously frustrated character, and his cuddles with Mom take on a very twisted look. . . . Those issues would raise possibilities far too complex for its feel-good story. So instead, the writers sugarcoat the character and infantillize the actor playing him."

Many critics lambasted the film's sentimentality, which must have confused or rankled Coppola, who had been so highly praised for many of the same qualities in *Peggy Sue Got Married.* Once again, critics were prepared to file obituaries on Coppola's career—or, at least, declare it "in a state of arrested development." The *Chicago Tribune*'s Michael Wilmington, who liked the movie much more than the majority of his colleagues, might have summed up the general disappointment when he noted that *Jack* was "a pleasant enough picture, sunny, humane and high-spirited, done with real technical finesse. But from Francis Ford Coppola? It's like watching Rembrandt sit down to labor over an elaborate doodle for two hours."

Although less than happy that Coppola had chosen to work on a film beneath his talents, Wilmington was also astute enough to point out what Coppola (and his critics) had known all along: There was an enormous difference between giving reviewers what they wanted and audiences what they would pay to see. ("I suspect most [viewers] will respond to *Jack* with genuine pleasure. Who wants to kick an inner child?") During its first weekend in theaters, *Jack* raked in over $11 million in gate receipts, making it the top-grossing movie in the country. By year's end, it had grossed $60 million, making it one of the year's most successful films.

7·

JOHN GRISHAM, LIKE SO MANY popular novelists before him, was a good match for Hollywood. His thick, fast-paced books, although never mistaken for great literature, were staples on beaches, nightstands, and in airports across the country. More significantly, they were constant fixtures on best-seller lists. When Coppola signed to direct *The Rainmaker* in April 1996, three of Grisham's books—*The Client*, *The Firm*, and *The Pelican Brief* had already made their way to the big screen, with two more—*A Time to Kill* and *The Chamber*—already in production. Coppola had read *The Rainmaker* during one of his flights from New York to Paris, and, liking the story, he had purchased the rights to the film.

"I had never read a John Grisham book, and when I saw *The Rainmaker* on the stand, which was the No. 1 bestseller, I decided to buy it," Coppola explained, adding that he was more interested in reading the book as research, "to learn, to see what appealed to a modern audience." He found himself drawn into the story. "I became a sucker for Grisham just like everyone else," he admitted. "I couldn't put it down."

One of Grisham's strongest skills as a writer was his ability to turn dialogue-driven fiction—much of it taking place in courtrooms, in which there was very little action—into compelling reading. This was especially true in *The Rainmaker*, the story about a young law school graduate named Rudy Baylor, who, while trying to gain a foothold in the highly competitive legal community, winds up taking on a powerful law firm representing an unscrupulous insurance company.

At first, the case seems like little more than the other jobs that Baylor drums up. After graduating from law school, he finds a job with a storefront firm, operated by a sleazy lawyer appropriately named Bruiser Stone. Baylor meets Stone's paralegal, Deck Shifflet, a lawyer wanna-be who, after six attempts, still can't pass the bar exam, and together and apart, they work the ambulance-chasing scene, visiting hospitals with the hope of signing on clients. During one such visit, Rudy meets Kelly Riker, an attractive young housewife who has been admitted to the hospital after taking a terrible beating from her abusive husband. Rudy also takes on a strange inheritance case involving an eccentric elderly woman named Miss Birdie, who wants to cut her greedy family out of her will and leave what she claims is a sizable inheritance to a television preacher.

But the client who really draws Baylor's interest is a terminally ill young man named Donny Ray Black. Black, it turns out, could have been saved if he'd been given proper medical treatment, but Great Benefit, his insurance company, refused to pay for the needed bone-marrow transplant. The Black family wants to sue Great Benefit, not because a settlement will ease their grief or put money in their pockets, but to make an example of the company, which, Rudy learns, rejects virtually all claims simply because its clients are too poor to fight back. A compassionate man who will always think more with his heart than with his head, Rudy Baylor agrees to represent the Black family.

At first glance, these stories appear to offer very little, in terms of surprise, especially when one considers that they are being adapted for Hollywood. When Baylor becomes involved with Kelly Riker's problems, we correctly assume that there will be some kind of romantic interest involved, and that Rudy will successfully defend her from her brutal husband. The subplot is totally predictable. The same is true of the Miss Birdie story: After being introduced to her moneygrubbing family, we instinctively understand that there's no way that she will lose out to them.

And what of the Donny Ray Black case? Even in a David and Goliath scenario of this nature, in which an inexperienced young lawyer takes on one of the most successful and highly respected law firms in Tennessee, is there any chance that Rudy Baylor will fail? It might happen all the time in real life, but not in the movies.

Coppola, who wrote the screenplay (with help from Michael Herr, who reprised his role as author of the voice-over narrative), did a masterful job of moving the film's focus from a plot with a few twists but an inevitable conclusion to the characters themselves, which should have come as no surprise to those following the director's career. Characterization combined with technical excellence had customarily been Coppola's greatest strengths, and *The Rainmaker* was no exception. As Coppola recalled, he always liked to experiment with something different in each of his director-for-hire movies—to attempt something that he might eventually put to use in one of his more ambitious endeavors—and in this case, it was the accent on characters. "I thought I'd make my experiment on *The Rainmaker* by just focusing on the actors," he said, "and let the actors steal the show and bring the story to life."

As the story progresses, Rudy Baylor, now interested in Kelly Riker more than just as a client, tries to convince her to leave her husband before he kills her. At first, she resists both his advances and his advice, but she finally agrees to file for divorce after suffering a terrible beating with a baseball bat. As for his other case, Rudy learns that Miss Birdie has no money to speak of, but he makes a sport out of pretending that she's wealthy, just to get her family to treat her better.

Donny Ray Black passes away, setting up the confrontation between Rudy and the insurance company's lawyers, headed by a slick, eloquent attorney named Leo F. Drummond, who will use any trick in the book, including bugging his opponent's office, to gain an advantage in court. In one of the movie's many humorous moments, Rudy and Deck Shifflet foil Drummond's efforts, but they still find that they are more than matched in court. Baylor has been fortunate to have a sympathetic judge presiding over the trial, but even the judge cannot protect Rudy from the parrying and maneuvering of the more experienced and highly skilled Leo Drummond.

In one climactic scene, Rudy confronts Kelly Riker's husband, and in the inevitable brawl that follows, he knocks Cliff Riker unconscious with a baseball bat, opening a wound that may or may not be fatal. Kelly tells Rudy to leave the house, and he is no sooner outside than he hears a shot ring out, bringing an ironic conclusion to the affair: Rudy had originally been the protector, but in the end, he is saved by the victim. He will now have to use his skills to convince the district attorney that Kelly was acting in self-defense, even though he knows that, by the letter of the law, she is guilty of murder.

Meanwhile, in court, Rudy methodically wears down his opposition, exposing the insurance company and its officers as morally bankrupt businessmen preying on innocent clients. He wins the case and a stunning settlement, though his victory is only temporary. In a clever, rather cynical postscript, Great Benefit declares bankruptcy, leaving Rudy, Deck, and the

Black family with the knowledge that they had defeated the insurance company and put it out of business, but without the settlement money. This is reward enough for the Blacks, but for Rudy and Deck, the outcome is an indication of what they may expect from the justice system in the future. Deck is a survivor, well equipped for finding more work and dealing with whatever it brings him, but to the idealistic Rudy Baylor, the Donny Ray Black case is enough to convince him that he should look for another line of work. As the story ends, Rudy and a recently released Kelly Riker are leaving Memphis, ready to begin a new life elsewhere.

8.

COPPOLA'S DECISION TO MAKE characterization the focal point of *The Rainmaker* not only made the eventual movie much better than it might have been under a different director with other priorities; it also affected his actual casting decisions. Rather than pay top dollar for one or two marquee names, Coppola elected to spread the wealth among a number of players.

"It's very much economics," he explained. "If you'd paid $20 million for someone, you'd want to use them. Also you don't have any money left for anyone else. Grisham has written a lot of great characters, and that meant I could have a wonderful cast and focus on the acting."

As he had on so many other occasions, Coppola relied heavily on the recommendations of Fred Roos, who had been so brilliant in helping him assemble the casts for *The Godfather* and *The Outsiders,* among others. What they put together was a company of veteran character actors, including Jon Voight, Mickey Rourke, Virginia Madsen, Roy Scheider, Danny Glover, Mary Kay Place, and Dean Stockwell. Teresa Wright, who was nominated in 1942 for an Oscar for her work in *Pride of the Yankees* and who the same year won an Academy Award for her performance in *Mrs. Miniver,* was chosen to play Miss Birdie, while Danny DeVito, an enormously successful actor and producer, landed the role of Deck Schifflet. Claire Danes, known for her television work, but gaining a reputation as a screen actress, won the role of Kelly Riker.

For the part of Rudy Baylor, Coppola initially wanted Sean Penn, but the actor was unavailable. Coppola then considered such actors as Edward Norton, who had made a name for himself in *The People vs. Larry Flynt,* or Stephen Dorff, but he wound up casting Matt Damon, then known for his work opposite Meg Ryan in *Courage Under Fire,* but who would go on to reach new heights in *Good Will Hunting* and *Saving Private Ryan.* Within a year or two, the twenty-six-year-old would be one of Hollywood's most sought-after actors, but he admitted to being in awe of Coppola when he received the call for *The*

Rainmaker. "The whole idea of him was intimidating," Damon said. "I was so nervous that I'd let him down."

Coppola hired Greta Seacat, who had worked with Winona Ryder on *Dracula,* to coach some of the cast on *The Rainmaker,* and beside the traditional read-through of the script at his Napa estate, he took his cast through extensive acting exercises, games, and improvisation.

"Francis teaches you to be available to everything in the scene," Damon said of Coppola's method of preparing his cast for the shoot. "We never know what will happen to us in life. In a movie, it's a magic trick."

"I'll do anything I can do to make the actor not have to *act* but rather use their preparation and their talent to play the game so it will come out the way I want," Coppola explained. Too often, he believed, actors had their own defense mechanisms, devised to keep them from being overwhelmed by the sheer difficulty and uncertainty of acting. Coppola was anything but interested in seeing his cast become comfortable in their roles and performances; he preferred them a little off-guard, which made their performances seem more natural. "You do exercises to teach actors to be attentive and listen," he said. "You give them a chance to experiment. All day long we throw curves at them, sometimes very elaborate ones. The goal is to get life into the camera."

He continued to throw curves at the cast after the shooting of *The Rainmaker* began in September 1996 in Memphis. As Danny DeVito remembered, Coppola, during the filming of a scene in which Deck Schifflet is showing Rudy Baylor around his new office, stationed a beautiful young woman in the bathroom. "I opened the door of the bathroom, and I went, 'Excuse me, there's somebody on the pot,'" DeVito recalled. This went on for several takes, with the woman posing in suggestive positions and, finally, sitting there totally naked. "It was always something different," said DeVito. "It gives you a little boost, a little more zip."

Coppola used every method he could think of to get the kind of response that he wanted from his actors. Just before shooting a scene in which Rudy Baylor is fired from his job, Coppola pulled Matt Damon aside and told him that the studio had been unhappy with the early rushes of the film and was considering replacing him with Edward Norton. To get Claire Danes to shiver during a scene taking place right after she had received a savage beating from her husband, Coppola sat her on a block of ice. To prepare Virginia Madsen for a riveting scene in which she testifies against her former employer, only to have the corporate attorney humiliate her by accusing her of sleeping with several of the company's executives, Coppola had members of the cast surround her and scream insults at her until she was on the verge of tears.

The efforts did not go unnoticed. Most reviewers would comment on the strength of the film's performances, with Janet Maslin of the *New York Times* paying Coppola a typical compliment. "The filmmaker and the cast apparently put a great deal of effort into developing individual performances," she wrote, "and the result is a rich, lifelike texture for the whole film."

For Coppola, one source of dissatisfaction during the shoot was the script itself. In writing the screenplay, he had wisely trimmed the Rudy Baylor–Kelly Riker and Miss Birdie subplots, and he had tightened the main story of the struggle between Baylor and the insurance company, but he was still unhappy with the courtroom scene, which seemed to proceed too easily in Baylor's favor. What was the point of having a high-powered attorney as an adversary if he was going to be too easily beaten by his inexperienced young opponent? The courtroom scenes demanded more uncertainty, and during the Christmas break from the shooting, Coppola rewrote forty pages of script. In the revised version, Baylor made a number of mistakes that jeopardized his case, only to rally as the trial went on. Matt Damon and Jon Voight weren't pleased about having to relearn what was, in essence, about one-third of the movie, but in the end, Coppola had at least thrown some suspense into what otherwise might have been too predictable a plot.

9.

EVEN WHILE IN PREPRODUCTION for *The Rainmaker,* Coppola launched another significant project, reminiscent of his earlier endeavors with *City* magazine. *Zoetrope: Short Stories* (later retitled *Zoetrope: All Story*) was a literary magazine intended, as Coppola stated in a letter to readers, to "form a bridge to storytellers at large, encouraging them to work in the natural format of a short story."

Short story writers hardly needed such encouragement: There had always been more writers and short stories than there were magazines to publish them. Coppola's timing, however, was interesting, and his commitment to such a magazine commendable. A decade or so earlier, the short story form had enjoyed a renaissance in the United States, with such writers as Raymond Carver, Tobias Wolff, Andre Dubus, Peter Taylor, and a host of others leading the charge, many working exclusively in the short story form. New magazines such as *Granta* and *The Quarterly* presented some of the most creative short fiction available, while such established heavyweight journals as *The Paris*

Review, TriQuarterly, and *The Hudson Review* enjoyed renewed, enthusiastic readerships. Book publishers, generally reluctant to publish short story collections (which, with the exception of those written by big-name writers, never sold well), were suddenly issuing a flood of new titles.

By the early 1990s, the phenomenon had died down, and with multinational corporations snapping up publishing houses and taking a harder look at the bottom line, there were fewer and fewer titles being published during any given year. Even large, general-interest magazines like *The New Yorker,* known for being friendly to short story writers, cut back on the short fiction in each issue. The arrival of *Zoetrope* might have been suspect from a strictly business perspective, but to short story writers, it was a welcome new outlet.

Coppola had motives aside from making a profit and supporting the arts. Electronic magazines were becoming popular on the Internet, and Coppola was interested in exploring the trend with an offering of his own. *Zoetrope* could be published and sold in paper copy, but it could also be available through the Internet, where an entirely new community of artists could be established and nurtured—an idea that appealed to a man who had spent the better part of two decades heralding the marriage of electronics and the arts.

On a more practical level, as a filmmaker, Coppola recognized the value of having such a magazine at his disposal. He had grown weary of reading screenplays and treatments, most of which needed further work in terms of character development. A magazine like *Zoetrope* would encourage putative screenwriters to hone their skills in plotting, characterization, and dialogue in a form that was much more interesting to read than a screenplay.

"Most everyone agrees that a powerful form like cinema is entitled to the very best writing possible," Coppola said. "The current system doesn't really facilitate that, so our desire is an alternate method to work in the short-fiction form."

As good as that sounded, Coppola had his skeptics, who claimed that he was using the magazine as a means of saving money on the traditional way of optioning or purchasing properties for development. Writers, these skeptics noted, were not only selling print rights to Zoetrope; they also were selling film rights at a price much lower than the current rates for film treatments. In this way, *Zoetrope* was actually "a development office, and a chintzy one at that, disguised as a magazine."

Coppola was both hurt and enraged by such accusations. He was paying a six-figure sum to put out an issue of the magazine, so it was anything but a cheap endeavor. As for the writers whose works were in development for film projects, Coppola repeatedly pointed out that they would be rewarded with additional money and a percentage of the profits, if the project ever made its way to the big screen.

"I love the stories we print and the tradition we are furthering," he wrote in a letter to readers, addressing some of the criticism. "I also love the cinema—that poor shackled prisoner of Wall Street, that enslaved Prometheus who feeds all the parasites with its liver. If our magazine is able to nudge up the quality of writing that becomes the basis of the current parade of clichés and formulas, which break open each Friday like horseraces and list 'scores' each Monday, I will leap in the air with glee."

Even the naysayers had to agree that *Zoetrope,* which ran fifty thousand copies of its initial issue, offered excellent fiction. Besides a handful of quality short stories by well-knowns and unknowns alike, each issue of *Zoetrope* featured a story commissioned by Coppola himself, on a theme that Coppola presented to the commissioned writer. In addition, each issue reprinted a classic story that had eventually been adapted to film. Whatever Coppola's intentions, he was producing a quarterly magazine that rivaled the other literary magazines on the newsstands, and in its unstapled tabloid format, *Zoetrope* was as nontraditional as its flamboyant publisher.

10.

ZOETROPE, THE STUDIO, REMAINED as active as ever, developing both television and feature-film projects. The company joined forces with Jim Henson Pictures, with Coppola acting as executive producer, in putting out *Buddy,* a children's picture based on a true story about a young socialite's efforts to rescue and raise a baby gorilla. More ambitious yet was a television miniseries, *The Odyssey,* based on Homer's epic poem and starring Armand Assante, Isabella Rossellini, and Vanessa Williams, which Coppola produced for NBC. Although *The Odyssey* was by no means comparable to the grand, operatic feature films that he had directed, Coppola was pleased with the way the miniseries turned out, and since he was a man who was constantly generating ideas for new projects, he appreciated the way television worked, as opposed to the movies.

"Television," he declared, "is like cooking: Cook it, serve it, eat it and go on to the next thing. In the time we did *The Odyssey,* with a movie we'd still be trying to get people to agree on the casting. Where there is competition, they are desperate for ideas and say 'Go for it.'"

Coppola was feeling at the top of his game. The vineyard and château, beautifully renovated to include artifacts from the filmmaker's own career, had reached the point where the wine production and tourism could support the Coppola family. His last three movies had made enough money to lead him to believe that he might finally pursue the personal film he had been promising for so long.

The Rainmaker, released on November 21, 1997, continued his successful run, drawing almost universal praise. Beautifully photographed by Oscar-winning cinematographer John Toll, and filled with memorable performances both dramatic and humorous, *The Rainmaker* impressed many critics as being Coppola's best adaptation since *The Godfather.*

In the opinion of Michael Wilmington of the *Chicago Tribune,* Coppola "proves to be an ideal filmmaker for Grisham, just as he was a quarter-century ago for best-selling author Mario Puzo with *The Godfather.* Though *The Rainmaker* doesn't offer the same opportunities as Puzo's Jacobean crime-family saga, Coppola is able to preserve and enhance the book's strengths, downplay or mask most of its flaws. Working near the top of his form, he and his extraordinary cast and company turn an expert, crowd-pleasing bestseller into a film of greater warmth, humanity and humor."

"Coppola gets to show that he is still one of the most gifted moviemakers of the last 30 years," added the *San Francisco Examiner*'s Barbara Shulgasser, "even though *The Rainmaker* is meager material for Coppola to be spending his talent on. *The Godfather* wasn't exactly Dostoevski, but it offered Coppola the chance to paint a rich and textured picture of an American subculture the way no one had done it before. In this case, Coppola again shines his intelligence on this bestseller material, rather than just shoving it through the Hollywood mill unsifted."

"The good news about *John Grisham's The Rainmaker* is that Francis Ford Coppola is back," wrote Associated Press reporter Bob Thomas. "There is no bad news. The movie is brilliantly acted, well-paced, thoughtful and involving, with some of the best dramatic courtroom scenes in recent times. Coppola has served Grisham well."

And so it went: a long string of reviews, with only an occasional dissenter, offering Coppola a litany of some of the highest superlatives of his career. The notices, coming on the heels of the thrashing Coppola had taken for *Jack,* were, in a sense, only fitting. Coppola's career as a filmmaker had seen more peaks and valleys than that of any director of his generation. He had won five Academy Awards for his work—including an astonishing three Oscars for his scripts for pictures that had gone on to win Best Picture Oscars, an achievement unmatched in motion picture history. He had won the Cannes Film Festival's Golden Palm on two occasions, and, in early 1998, he would be honored with the Directors Guild's D. W. Griffith Award for Distinguished Career Achievement in Motion Picture Directing.

As monumental as some of his failures had been, Coppola was now in the position where he could be philosophical about them. "I would say, in my career, that my failures are among anyone's most interesting failures," he'd admit, knowing full well that he had given more ink to the press than just about any director in the business. He was always good copy, whether he was standing on the mountaintop, planting his flag in another successful endeavor, or jumping off the cliff, hoping that somehow, by some unforesee-able miracle, he would beat the odds and survive the fall.

It was the story of his life. Or, as he once noted, "If someone gave me $2 billion, I'd use it as leverage to borrow $30 billion and do something *really* big."

And he would have had plenty of people willing to pay to watch.

Epilogue

ON JUNE 16, 1998, IN CELEBRATION of the centenary of American filmmaking, the American Film Institute announced a list of what its voting members considered to be the one hundred greatest movies ever made in the United States. Topping the list was Orson Welles's *Citizen Kane*, easily the most time-honored and revered movie in American cinema history, and a film that stood as the model for every aspiring auteur over the next half a century. The AFI list, heavily weighted by movies made over the last four decades of the century, spawned furious debates over its inclusions and exclusions, as well as haughty overviews about the state of modern cinema and film criticism. But, then again, such lists were custom-made for arguments in taverns and restaurants, coffeehouses and classrooms; they would have no influence whatsoever on the motion picture industry itself.

Interestingly enough, Francis Ford Coppola was involved, in one capacity or another, in five of the films on the list. *The Godfather* placed third, edging out such other top-ten epics as *Gone With the Wind, Lawrence of Arabia,* and *Schindler's List. Apocalypse Now,* ranking twenty-eighth on the list, struck voters as the most essential film about Vietnam, placing higher than Oliver Stone's *Platoon* and Michael Cimino's *The Deer Hunter*, while *The Godfather, Part II* (32) was the only sequel to merit mention. Other Coppola-related films on the list were *American Graffiti* (77) and *Patton* (83).

One could debate the Coppola selections and their placement on the list—*Godfather II* is arguably a more fully realized endeavor than *Apocalypse Now*, as is *The Conversation*, which failed even to get a mention—but if nothing else, the Coppola entries spoke volumes about the filmmaker's career. Each of the movies had been made in the 1970s, during America's last true golden age of filmmaking, at a time when Coppola was young and hungry and at the pinnacle of his abilities and powers. For one glorious decade, Coppola exacted an influence on moviemaking virtually unapproached by any other filmmaker in any similar time frame.

Coppola would be the first to concede that none of his movies in the 1980s and 1990s deserved recognition on the AFI list—not by a long shot—but one cannot help but wonder (as so many critics had over the ensuing two decades), What happened to Francis Ford Coppola? Did he expend all of his artistic energy during the seventies? Was he overrated as a filmmaker? Was the failure of Zoetrope, along with his highly publicized financial problems, the driving force behind his decision to abandon his risky, yet decisively creative, auteuristic endeavors in favor of the safer and more profitable work-for-hire films? Did his son's death give him occasion to reconsider his life as a filmmaker and, in fact, guide him toward a change in priorities? Did he simply lose interest in putting himself on the line in film after film? Did he grow complacent, once he had rebuilt his personal empire?

Throughout the 1980s and 1990s, Coppola steadfastly maintained that he had lost none of the fire for making creative personal films akin to his earlier successes. Anytime one of his movies was released, he would act the role of the good company player, promoting the film and insisting that he was pleased with the picture. However, more often than not, his promotions rang hollow, and when pressed, Coppola would allow that he was still holding on to the hope for a grand finale—a film that would rival the best of his best.

"Who isn't a director-for-hire?" Coppola countered, when asked about his recent work. "Everyone needs to do it to get the resources to either make their film or make money to be in a position to write original material. I was a director-for-hire when I made *The Godfather*. I don't get why they apply this distinction to me. Is Steven Spielberg not a director-for-hire? Woody Allen may be the only director who is truly not for hire—and maybe George Lucas, since he can hire himself. I've always tried to survive, despite various setbacks, by earning money in the movie business, but perhaps not anymore. I really don't want to do things other than what I write, but then that obliges me to write something good, which I will try to do."

There were other rumors to go with his proclamations. For instance, despite his protests to the contrary, there was talk of his bringing the Corleone family to the screen for a final bow; according to reports, Mario Puzo had written a partial script for *The Godfather, Part IV.* Coppola might have been sending up a test balloon in 1997 with the national rerelease to select theaters of *The Godfather,* along with a special twenty-fifth anniversary video edition of the film, complete with interviews with Coppola and some of the picture's stars. Still, as of 1998, no announcements of a new *Godfather* picture were forthcoming, and Coppola steadfastly maintained that no such picture was in his future.

What Coppola did talk about, although in the sketchiest of terms, were two film projects—his personal film and a musical—and he spoke of making smaller-scale pictures with Zoetrope. He continued to sing the praises of the small independent companies, going so far as to predict confidently, for the umpteenth time, the demise of the big studios.

"Their days are numbered," he informed *Variety.* "Art studios will replace them. This is my dream." As for Zoetrope, Coppola dismissed the notion that the studio had been more talk than action and that it had yet to provide any solid evidence that it was going to be a threat to the Hollywood order. "We were in a cocoon," he said. "Now we're at a major moment of reconception."

Coppola could afford his optimism. His *Pinocchio* lawsuit had finally made its way to the courtroom, and by the time judge and jury had spoken, he had been awarded $80 million in compensatory and punitive damages—by far the largest judgment against a major studio in Hollywood history.

Coppola could not have scripted it better if he had been writing a sequel to *The Rainmaker.* Or, as *Variety* reported in its coverage, the courtroom drama featured all these elements: "Tales of power struggles and vendettas. Questions over when a deal is really a deal. A key witness who broke down in tears during testimony. Francis Ford Coppola's lawsuit against Warner Bros. got under way here last week with more drama than all of the summer movies combined."

To Hollywood insiders and outsiders alike, the case seemed to be a dispute over Hollywood's traditional way of conducting much of its business with a handshake, with Coppola arguing that he had no valid contract with Warner Bros. and was therefore free to pursue the *Pinocchio* project with other studios, and Warners countering that the studio had reached a binding oral agreement with Coppola—an agreement that left Warner Bros. with the rights to make the movie. Reporter Janet Shprintz, who wrote extensively about the case, thought there was much more at stake. "The real result of *Pinocchio,*" she wrote in an analytical piece published after the verdict had been delivered, "is the effect it will have on prying projects loose from development hell."

A look at the case history certainly gave credence to the argument. Neither Coppola nor Warner Bros. seemed well suited to work with each other, with bad blood between the two extending back to the early seventies, when the studio demanded that Coppola repay the money it had advanced him toward several ill-fated American Zoetrope projects. The acrimony bubbled to the surface a decade later, during Coppola's work on *The Outsiders.* Coppola and Warners had fought over creative differences during the making of the movie, which the studio almost reluctantly released, only to see it become enough of a box-office success to have its copyright revert back to Coppola and Zoetrope, as per contract. In any other business, combatants such as Coppola and Warner Bros. might have been finished with each other at this point, but in Hollywood, business often overshadows the personal. Coppola was again persuaded to work for the studio, this time by former Zoetrope executive Lucy Fisher, who had moved on to Warners, and who convinced Coppola that things had changed at the studio.

In March 1991, Coppola and his agents met with Warner Bros. officials, and *Pinocchio,* among other projects, was discussed. Both sides liked the project, and Coppola and Warners entered into negotiations that would find Coppola producing, directing, and possibly writing the script for the film. Coppola wanted the same directing deal he'd had with Columbia for *Dracula*—a $5 million fee, plus 15 percent of the film's gross—but Warners balked at the fee. While negotiations dragged on, with no signed contract, Coppola continued to develop the project, with Warners paying him $6,000 as part of its development fee.

At this point, Warner Bros. believed it had at least a producing deal with Coppola, and the company continued to sink money into the project, including the hiring of Frank Galati, whom Coppola okayed as screenwriter on the project. Warner officials disliked Galati's script, and *Pinocchio* stalled yet another time.

Believing that he would not be able to come to terms with Warner Bros., Coppola wrote his own script for *Pinocchio* and informed Warners, through his lawyers, that he felt that no deal existed between him and the studio. The studio disagreed, noting that it had a signed certificate of employment, as well as the contract that Coppola had yet to sign. According to Warner Bros., the rights to the movie were assigned in the certificate of employment.

Coppola moved ahead, showing his new screenplay to Columbia, and he and Columbia worked out an agreement in which the studio would pay $26 million of the movie's estimated $60 million budget, with the rest of the money to come, presumably, through Coppola's sale of the film's foreign rights. Warner Bros., however, informed Columbia that it owned the rights to the *Pinocchio* project, and the Coppola-Columbia deal was put on hold until such time as Coppola could work out a settlement of the issue with Warners.

That time never arrived. Coppola tried to work out an agreement with Warners, but the two sides failed to reach a compromise. Tentative foreign financing with a French company called Chargeurs fell through, as did Coppola's deal with Columbia. *Pinocchio* hung in limbo.

The lawsuit might never have occurred had New Line Cinema not released *The Adventures of Pinocchio,* starring Jonathan Taylor Thomas and Martin Landau. The existence of a recent competing film, along with its poor performance at the box office, further dampened any hopes that Coppola had of making his own version of the story. Convinced that Warner Bros.–and co-CEO Bob Daly, in particular–was blocking his movie as a kind of vendetta for its failure to reach an earlier agreement with him, Coppola sued Warner Bros., asking for $22 million in damages.

As it turned out, Coppola was still prepared to bargain. In late 1996, he instigated another lawsuit against Warner Bros.–this one involving the company's production of Carl Sagan's *Contact,* starring Jodie Foster and Matthew McConaughey. Although the timing of the filing of the lawsuit–a week after Sagan's death–was controversial, Coppola argued that he and Sagan had had a previous agreement, dating back to the 1970s, in which Sagan was to develop a story similar to the one Warner Bros. was bringing to the screen. As Coppola saw it, he would be willing to back off the *Contact* suit if Warner Bros. agreed to back off on the *Pinocchio* dispute.

The company, however, was not prepared to make any such concession, and on June 3, 1998, opening arguments in the *Pinocchio* suit were heard in the Los Angeles Superior Court. Robert Chapman, Coppola's attorney, argued that Warner Bros. had squelched the film because it wanted to teach Coppola a lesson, while J. Larson Jaenicke, the attorney for the studio, contended that a binding agreement had been reached, and that in taking

Pinocchio to Columbia after the success of *Dracula,* "Coppola was like a quar-terback who had a great season and suddenly wanted a better deal."

For all the wrangling over legal contracts, verbal commitments, and other points of the film business, the jurors were probably swayed the most by the testimony of two key witnesses: Francis Ford Coppola and Warner cochair-man Terry Semel. While detailing his hopes for the movie on the witness stand, Coppola broke down in tears—an emotional display that provoked a skeptical response from a Warner Bros. spokesperson, who claimed that Cop-pola had warned the company's attorneys in advance "that he would bring [the jurors] to tears." Coppola refuted the accusation, saying, "I was emotional because I was describing the theme of the story, and I was very much moved by this. But it wasn't a fake thing, and it wasn't manipulative."

What it was was effective, especially in comparison to the testimony of Terry Semel, who impressed several jurors as being "a rude and arrogant wit-ness." Said one of the jurors, when speaking to the press after the delivery of the verdict: "Semel disliked Francis so much it oozed out of him."

The case went to the jury on June 25, and on July 9, after first ruling in Coppola's favor on July 1 and awarding him $20 million in compensatory damages, the jury, ruling that Warner Bros. had acted with malice and fraud, awarded Coppola a staggering $60 million in punitive damages—an unprece-dented figure in a civil case against a Hollywood studio. Coppola was ecsta-tic. "Warner Bros. has traditionally not treated its creative people well," he told reporters outside the courtroom. "Hopefully, this will teach them to treat creative people as an asset, not as serfs."

Stating that Warner Bros. had "a vendetta" against his client, Robert Chapman added, "The jury is sending a message to Warner Bros. that studios have to follow the law and respect the rights of others, and that they will be held to the same standards as everyone else."

Warner Bros. deemed the award "simply ludicrous," pointing to a form that jurors had filled out during their deliberations, in which a majority responded that they felt that an agreement existed between the studio and Coppola. "Since the jury found that Warner Bros. reasonably believed it had a contract with Mr. Coppola, there is absolutely no basis for the jury's award of punitive damages," Warners contended. "Warner Bros. expects that post-judgment motions or an appeal will vindicate its position."

Warner Bros. won the first round of appeals on October 15, when Los Angeles Superior Court judge Madelein Flier, the same judge who had presided over the earlier proceedings, ruled that there was no "substantial evi-dence" that the studio had acted with "malice and fraud" in the *Pinocchio* affair. She then overturned the punitive damages and let the compensatory damages stand. Neither side was satisfied. Coppola vowed to appeal for the reinstatement of the punitive damages, while Warners said it intended to appeal the compensatory damages—a process, the *Wall Street Journal* predicted, that could drag on for up to two years, unless the two sides found a way to settle.

For Coppola, the lawsuit and its outcome underscored his career-long battle to free himself from the constrictive grip that Hollywood business practices held on creative filmmaking. That the victory came over Warner Bros.—at a time when he was as financially stable as he had ever been, and at a time when the latest version of Zoetrope was running efficiently—was especially delicious. As *Entertainment Weekly* pointed out, if the lawsuit had been a movie, "it would have been Francis Ford Coppola's third-most-profitable project to date, behind *The Godfather* ($134 million), and *Bram Stoker's Dracula* ($82 million)." And, in perhaps the greatest irony of all, if the judgment stood and punitive damages were reinstated, Coppola would be in the position to invest the money that Warner Bros. forfeited to finance the personal film of his dreams.

Michael Corleone would have loved it.

Endnotes

PROLOGUE

2. "'The most exciting . . .'": Peter Biskind, *Easy Riders, Raging Bulls: How the Sex-Drugs-and-Rock 'n' Roll Generation Saved Hollywood* (New York: Simon and Schuster, 1998), p. 141. All other quotations in this passage are from this source.

1: FROM PUPPET SHOWS TO *DEMENTIA*: A FILMMAKER'S BEGINNINGS

3. "Dear Mommy": Susan Braudy, "Francis Ford Coppola: A Profile," *The Atlantic Monthly*, August 1976.
4. "Who's this?": Michael Goodwin and Naomi Wise, *On the Edge: The Life and Times of Francis Coppola* (New York: William Morrow, 1989), p. 15.
4. "My father was very": Author interview with Talia Shire.
5. "give Daddy": David Breskin, "The Rolling Stone Interview: Francis Ford Coppola," *Rolling Stone*, February 7, 1991.
5. "We were raised": Author interview with August Coppola.
6. "My father was": Jack R. Nerad, "From the Desk of Francis Ford Coppola," *The Hollywood Reporter*, August 19, 1988.
6. "I was eight": ibid.
7. "My father was heartbroken": Author interview with Francis Ford Coppola (FFC).
7. "the tragedy of": William Murray, "The Playboy Interview: Francis Ford Coppola," *Playboy*, July 1975.
7. "It's my break!": ibid.
7. "the affectionate one," "the beautiful one," and "the brilliant one": Author interview with FFC.
8. "He was the star": David Thomson and Lucy Gray, "Idols of the King," *Film Comment*, September–October 1988.
8. "Augie was blazing": Author interview with Talia Shire.
8. "Thanks for giving": Judith Martin and Gary Arnold, "'The Godfather': A Winner the Second Time Around," *Washington Post*, April 9, 1975.
8. "After I'd spent": Braudy, "Francis Ford Coppola."
9. "I had a dream": Thomson and Gray, "Idols of the King."
9. "The hospital": Peter Cowie, *Coppola* (New York: Charles Scribner's Sons, 1990), p. 16.
9. "My parents, of course": Gay Talese, "The Conversation," *Esquire*, July 1981.
10. "I think any tough time": ibid.
10. "I lived in a bed": "'American Culture Is Controlled by Cynical Middlemen,'" *U.S. News & World Report*, April 5, 1982.
10. "I am sure": Lillian Ross, "Onward and Upward with the Arts: Some Figures on a Fantasy," *The New Yorker*, November 8, 1980.
10. "I was really": Richard Koszarski, "The Youth of F. F. Coppola," *Films in Review*, November 1968.
12. "I was to be": Author interview with August Coppola.
12. "Somewhere along the": ibid.
13. "wonderful summer": Thomson and Gray, "Idols of the King."
13. "To be honest": Author interview with August Coppola.
13. "sleeping where I could": Cowie, *Coppola*, p. 12.
13. "When I got home": Author interview with FFC.
15. "They had an eager": Author interview with Joel Oliansky.
15. "My take on him": ibid.
15. "Francis was playing": ibid.
16. "It carried a": Author interview with FFC.
17. "I wanted to experiment": Jean-Paul Chaillet and Elizabeth Vincent, *Francis Ford Coppola* (New York: St. Martin's Press, 1984), p. 2.
17. "When I was watching": Author interview with Joel Oliansky.
17. "the central figure": Chaillet and Vincent, *Francis Ford Coppola*, p. 2.
17. "Eisenstein, who was": Joseph Morgenstern, "A National Anthem," *Newsweek*, February 20, 1967.

18. "By happy coincidence": Dale Pollock, *Sky-walking: The Life and Films of George Lucas* (New York: Harmony Books, 1983; rev. ed., Hollywood: Samuel French, 1990), pp. 47–48.
18. "For a while": Paul Gardner, "Alumni of Film School Now 'Star' as Directors," *New York Times*, January 30, 1974.
18. "They provide": ibid.
19. "There was none": Chaillet and Vincent, *Francis Ford Coppola*, pp. 2–3.
19. "It was highly competitive": Author interview with Carroll Ballard.
20. "He was unbelievable": ibid.
20. "They talked a lot": John Cutts, "The Dangerous Age," *Films and Filming*, May 1969.
21. "which was the only": ibid.
21. "I have great": Jami Bernard, *First Films: Illustrious, Obscure, and Embarrassing Movie Debuts* (New York: Citadel Press, 1993), p. 251.
22. "There was a 3-D scene": ibid.
24. "At the time": Cutts, "The Dangerous Age."
24. "Monsters play well": Author interview with Roger Corman.
25. "There is a scene": Antony I. Ginnane, "Francis Ford Coppola," *Cinema Papers*, November–December 1975.
25. "I was surprised": Author interview with Roger Corman.
25. "I'd deliberately work": Stephen Farber, "Coppola and *The Godfather*," *Sight and Sound*, Autumn 1972.
25. "just exhilarating": Ginnane, "Francis Ford Coppola."
26. "I won $2000": Koszarski, "The Youth of F. F. Coppola."
27. "I knew that": Cutts, "The Dangerous Age."
27. "When we were shooting": Author interview with Roger Corman.
27. "Change the man": Cowie, *Coppola*, p. 27.
27. "We were in Ireland": Joseph Gelmis, *The Film Director as Superstar* (Garden City, New York: Doubleday and Co., 1979), p. 180.
30. "We were young": Farber, "Coppola and *The Godfather*."
30. "When I was about to film": Author interview with FFC.
31. "I was struck": Author interview with Eleanor Coppola.
31. "It was a little short": Author interview with Roger Corman.
32. "I was really a theater": Author interview with FFC.

33. "The water never": Roger Corman, with Jim Jerome, *How I Made a Hundred Movies in Hollywood and Never Lost a Dime* (New York: Random House, 1990), p. 93.
33. "I really don't remember": Author interview with FFC.
33. "Another time": ibid.
34. "Don't ask what": and "stolid": Howard Thompson, "Dementia 13," *New York Times*, October 24, 1963.
34. "At first, I thought": Author interview with FFC.
34. "*Dementia 13* is": Robert Salmaggi, "Dementia 13," *New York Herald Tribune*, October 24, 1963.

2. BIG BOY

35. "If Francis Ford Coppola": Joseph Morgenstern, "A National Anthem," *Newsweek*, February 20, 1967.
35. "I very much wanted": Author interview with FFC.
36. "I had been in": Author interview with Eleanor Coppola.
36. "They figured they'd hire": Richard Koszarski, "The Youth of F. F. Coppola," *Films in Review*, November 1968.
36. "The reaction was": Joseph Gelmis, *The Film Director as Superstar* (Garden City, New York: Doubleday and Co., 1979), p. 181.
37. "The positon of": Jean-Paul Chaillet and Elizabeth Vincent, *Francis Ford Coppola* (New York: St. Martin's Press, 1984), p. 8.
37. "It was very Alice": John Cutts, "The Dangerous Age," *Films and Filming*, May 1969.
38. "Fred Coe was": Author interview with FFC.
38. "What's a real pity": Author interview with Joel Oliansky.
39. "I decided": Gelmis, *The Film Director as Superstar*, p. 181.
40. "When the pencil" and "This nice": Antony I. Ginnane, "Francis Ford Coppola," *Cinema Papers*, November–December 1975.
40. "an insane mess": Cutts, "The Dangerous Age."
40. "Nobody would speak up": ibid.
42. "I said, 'Wait'": Stephen Farber, "Coppola and *The Godfather*," *Sight and Sound*, Autumn 1972.
42. "I wrote that first scene": Author interview with FFC.
43. "I had nothing to do": Ginnane, "Francis Ford Coppola."

44. "If there's one thing": Cutts, "The Dangerous Age."

44. "I had never": Rex Reed, "Offering the Moon to a Guy in Jeans," *New York Times*, August 7, 1966.

45. "I read the script" and "I could have": "Shy Elizabeth Hartman Gets a Brand New Look," *Life*, March 24, 1967.

45. "You should have": Reed, "Offering the Moon to a Guy in Jeans."

46. "YOU'RE SEXY, BEAUTIFUL": "Shy Elizabeth Hartman Gets a Brand New Look."

46. "The first day": Chaillet and Vincent, *Francis Ford Coppola*, p. 12.

47. "It was terrific": Michael Goodwin and Naomi Wise, *On the Edge: The Life and Times of Francis Coppola* (New York: William Morrow and Co., 1989), p. 66.

47. "one of those rare": Charles Champlin, "Big Boy: Big with Man on Campus," *Los Angeles Times*, December 12, 1966.

49. "terrific": Koszarski, "The Youth of F. F. Coppola."

50. "custard-pie plot": "Growing Up Absurd," *Time*, February 3, 1967.

50. "Francis Ford Coppola is": Howard Thompson, "Growing Pains," *New York Times*, March 21, 1967.

50. "It makes one": Richard Schickel, "Growing Up Frantic in Cloud Cuckooland," *Life*, March 24, 1967.

50. "a director's delicious": Judith Crist, "You're a Big Boy Now," *New York World-Journal Tribune*, March 21, 1967.

50. "no masterpiece": Morgenstern, "A National Anthem."

50. "I pattern my life": ibid.

51. "My allusion to Hitler": Koszarski, "The Youth of F. F. Coppola."

51. "If you were taken": William Murray, "The Playboy Interview: Francis Ford Coppola," *Playboy*, July 1975.

51. "You learn from": David Breskin, "The Rolling Stone Interview: Francis Ford Coppola," *Rolling Stone*, February 7, 1991.

52. "If I don't": Army Archerd, "Just for Variety," (Daily) *Variety*, February 1, 1967.

53. "It can only be": John Russell Taylor, "Francis Ford Coppola," *Sight and Sound*, Winter 1968–1969.

54. "The only reason": Dan Simons, " 'Rain People' by the Rule Breaker," *Los Angeles Times*, September 7, 1969.

56. "disappointing": Author interview with FFC.

56. "There was no planning": Cutts, "The Dangerous Age."

56. "Fred, go": ibid.

56. "a demonstration": Tom Milne, "Finian's Rainbow," *Sight and Sound*, Winter 1968–1969.

56. "The fact that Rainbow": "Finian's Rainbow," (Weekly) *Variety*, October 9, 1968.

57. "You always feel": Dale Pollock, *Skywalking: The Life and Films of George Lucas* (New York: Harmony Books, 1983; rev. ed., Hollywood: Samuel French, 1990), p. 72.

58. "I was in admiration": Author interview with George Lucas.

58. "I was not that interested": ibid.

58. "What do you mean": Pollock, *Skywalking*, p. 74.

59. "brother": Author interview with FFC.

60. "Everyone at Warners": Farber, "Coppola and *The Godfather*."

61. "It has been done": Judith Crist, "Finian's Rainbow," *New York*, January 6, 1969.

61. "The movie might": "Instant Old Age," *Time*, October 25, 1968.

61. "*Finian's Rainbow* is": Joseph Morgenstern, "Paradise Lost," *Newsweek*, October 21, 1968.

61. "*Finian's Rainbow* is a stunning": Milne, "Finian's Rainbow."

61. "They have kept": Arthur Knight, "The Times They Are A-Chaning," *The Saturday Review*, October 5, 1968.

3 . AMERICAN ZOETROPE

62. "In Los Angeles": "Bay Area Fetes Studio Opening," *Los Angeles Herald-Examiner*, December 15, 1969.

63. "She was crying" and "romantic preconceptions": Stephen Farber, "Coppola and *The Godfather*," *Sight and Sound*, Autumn 1972.

64. "Look, I'm starting": Joseph Gelmis, *The Film Director as Superstar* (Garden City, New York: Doubleday and Co., 1979), p. 187.

65. "We made a very creative": Author interview with FFC.

66. "I was kind of embarrassed": Author interview with James Caan.

66. "Coppola was unrecognizable": Jean-Paul Chaillet and Elizabeth Vincent, *Francis Ford Coppola* (New York: St. Martin's Press, 1984), p. 28.

66. "The crew for *The Rain People*": Author interview with George Lucas.

66. "one of the most interesting": Author interview with Barry Malkin.

67. "The system": George Lucas, *Filmmaker* (1968), a documentary written, directed, and edited by Lucas.

67. "George came up": Author interview with Mona Skager.

68. "I'm tired": ibid.

68. "If he had done": Michael Goodwin and Naomi Wise, *On the Edge: The Life and Times of Francis Coppola* (New York: William Morrow and Co., 1989), p. 88.

68. "She's very talented": Farber, "Coppola and *The Godfather*."

69. "The character that Francis": Author interview with James Caan.

69. "I chickened out": ibid.

69. "Movies are like": Marjorie Rosen, "Francis Ford Coppola," *Film Comment*, July 1974.

71. "The reason": Bill Ornstein, "Francis Coppola to Make Only Own Stories in the Future," *The Hollywood Reporter*, August 12, 1968.

72. "I'm really trying": Cathy Furniss, "Coppola Doing His 'Thing' Via Zoetrope," *Film/TV*, February 13, 1970.

72. "I remember Francis": Author interview with Carroll Ballard.

72. "We thought": Antony I. Ginnane, "Francis Ford Coppola," *Cinema Papers*, November–December 1975.

72. "Francis just didn't": Author interview with George Lucas.

75. "*The Rain People*": Gary Arnold, "*The Rain People*," *Washington Post*, October 11, 1969.

75. "*The Rain People* is": John L. Wasserman, "*The Rain People*," *San Francisco Chronicle*, September 25, 1969.

75. "It might have been": Joseph Morgenstern, "Cryin' in the Rain," *Newsweek*, September 8, 1969.

75. "It is the worst": Roger Greenspun, "*The Rain People*," *New York Times*, August 28, 1969.

75. "Coppola can't end": Arnold, "*The Rain People*."

75. "disappointing": Charles Champlin, "*The Rain People*," *Los Angeles Times*, October 21, 1969.

76. "The chance to fail": Stephen Farber, "End of the Road?" *Film Quarterly*, Winter 1969.

76. American Zoetrope: Furniss, "Coppola Doing His 'Thing' Via Zoetrope"; Dan Simons, "Cinema San Francisco Style," *Entertainment World*, March 27, 1970; Christopher Pearce, "San Francisco's Own

American Zoetrope," *American Cinematographer*, October 1971; Stephen Farber, "Coppola in Hollywood," *Los Angeles Times Magazine*, September 23, 1972; Dale Pollock, *Skywalking: The Life and Films of George Lucas* (New York: Harmony Books, 1983; rev. ed., Hollywood: Samuel French, 1990), pp. 84–87.

77. "My enthusiasm": Farber, "Coppola and *The Godfather*."

77. "I became a sort" and "You go": Simons, "Cinema San Francisco Style."

78. "One of the reasons": Pearce, "San Francisco's Own American Zoetrope."

79. "When we were working": Author interview with George Lucas.

80. "He pushed Warners": ibid.

80. "What's going on": Thomas Marema, "Celluloid Dreams, Childhood's End," *Penthouse*, May 1974.

81. "I found that": Farber, "Coppola in Hollywood."

82. "Francis would have given": Chaillet and Vincent, *Francis Ford Coppola*, p. 29.

82. "I never would have": Peter Biskind, *Easy Riders, Raging Bulls: How the Sex-Drugs-and-Rock 'n' Roll Generation Saved Hollywood* (New York: Simon and Schuster, 1998), p. 102.

82. "I was plunking": Author interview with Mona Skager.

83. "This is either": Biskind, *Easy Riders, Raging Bulls,* p. 98.

83. "the most unlikely" and "a lot of stupid": Farber, "Coppola in Hollywood."

84. "What's going on": Biskind, *Easy Riders, Raging Bulls*, p. 98.

84. "I was sort of hoping": Author interview with George Lucas.

86. "Zoetrope was down": Gerald Nachman, "Coppola of Zoetrope—Older, Wiser and Poorer," *Los Angeles Times*, November 7, 1971.

86. "Zoetrope was picked": Pollock, *Skywalking*, p. 100.

4. THE GODFATHER

87. "It was the most miserable": Peter Biskind, *The Godfather Companion* (New York: HarperPerennial, 1990), p. 29.

87. "Coppola will never": Ira Zuckerman, *The Godfather Journal* (New York: Manor Books, 1972), p. 102.

87. "*The Godfather* is a stunning": William S. Pechter, "Keeping Up with the Corleones," *Commentary*, July 1972.

88. "I had been": Mario Puzo, *The Godfather Papers & Other Confessions* (New York: G. P. Putnam's Sons, 1972), pp. 3–4.

88. "The victims": Roger Jellnick, "Just Business, Not Personal," *New York Times*, March 4, 1969.

89. "*The Godfather*": Mario Puzo on *Larry King Live*, originally broadcast on CNN on August 2, 1996, copyright 1996 Cable News Network.

89. "By the end": Mario Puzo, *The Godfather* (New York: Penguin Books, 1978), p. 211.

90. "The guy" and "He's a businessman": ibid., p. 39.

91. "the most vital": ibid., p. 21.

91. "all the quiet force": ibid., p. 17.

92. "Tell my father": ibid., p. 352.

93. "I wrote below": Puzo, *The Godfather Papers*, p. 41.

93. "Sicilian mobster films": Robert Evans, *The Kid Stays in the Picture* (New York: Hyperion, 1994), p. 218.

94. "I felt": ibid.

94. "a popular, sensational": William Murray, "The Playboy Interview: Francis Ford Coppola," *Playboy*, July 1975.

95. "Take it": Susan Braudy, "Francis Ford Coppola: A Profile," *The Atlantic Monthly*, August 1976.

95. "We're all going" and "I took four hundred": Author interview with Mona Skager.

96. "I suggested": Puzo, *The Godfather Papers*, p. 58.

96. "Usually in a film" and "I wrote": Marjorie Rosen, "Francis Ford Coppola," *Film Comment*, July 1974.

97. "He knew what made": Author interview with Mario Puzo.

98. "What happened": Author interview with Mario Puzo.

98. "If Brando plays": Evans, *The Kid Stays*, p. 216.

99. "Furthermore": Murray, "The Playboy Interview."

99. "Auguste Rodin": ibid., p. 221.

99. "I stood up": Murray, "The Playboy Interview."

100. "Why not": ibid.

100. "I made this black-and-white": Author interview with FFC.

102. "ITALIANS FOR ITALIAN ROLES" and "MORE ADVANTAGES": Gerald Gardner and Harriet Modell Gardner, *The Godfather Movies: A Pictorial History* (New York: Wings Books, 1993), p. 37.

102. "self-destructive bastard": Andrew Yule, *Life on the Wire: The Life and Art of Al Pacino* (New York: Donald I. Fine, 1991), p. 44.

102. "When I read": Chris Chase, "Will the Godfather's Son Live to Be a Godfather?," *New York Times*, May 7, 1972.

102. "I wish I could": Author interview with Fred Roos.

103. "If you could": Author interview with Mona Skager.

103. "I thought Tally" and "I figured that": Author interview with FFC.

104. "When I asked": Author interview with Talia Shire.

105. "hypocritical, craven act": "Yes, Mr. Ruddy, There Is a . . .": *New York Times*, March 23, 1971.

105. "When I made my deal": Author interview with Al Ruddy.

106. "resume his career" "Jaffee Quits as Para President": *The Hollywood Reporter*, April 2, 1971.

107. "Don't quit": Author interview with Mona Skager.

107. Pacino contract: Robert Evans offered a compelling account of the Pacino affair in his autobiography, *The Kid Stays in the Picture*. According to Evans, negotiations had reached an impasse, and Pacino was freed to work on *The Godfather* only after he (Evans) contacted Sidney Korshak to intervene on his behalf. Korshak, an attorney who had represented a number of reputed mob figures, and whom Mario Puzo supposedly used as a model for the Tom Hagen character in *The Godfather*, called Kirk Krekorian, sole owner of MGM, and asked him to see personally that Pacino was released from his contractual obligations to MGM. When Krekorian initially declined to become involved in negotiations that he always left to the company president, Korshak simply asked Krekorian "if he wanted to finish building his hotel." The MGM Grand in Las Vegas, Krekorian's pet project, was reaching completion but had run into money troubles due to large construction costs. The mention of the hotel, Evans wrote, was all it took: MGM was suddenly willing to free Pacino from *The Gang That Couldn't Shoot Straight*. Evans (pp. 222–224): "That's the inside, inside story of what actually became—mind you, against my better judgment—possibly the greatest 'sense of discovery' casting in cinema history."

107. "We were all": "The Making of The God-father," *Time*, March 13, 1972.

108. "Keep talking": Yule, *Life on the Wire*, p. 46.

108. "scared shitless": Murray, "The Playboy Interview."

108. "Diane Keaton": Lawrence Grobel, "The Playboy Interview: Al Pacino," *Playboy*, December 1979.

109. "I never felt": Chase, "Will the Godfather's Son Live to Be a Godfather?"

109. "I just wanted": Maureen Dowd, "Al Alone," *GQ*, September 1992.

109. "I created you": Grobel, "The Playboy Interview."

111. "a viciousness": Chris Chase, "Quick—What's This Man's Name?," *New York Times*, April 23, 1972.

111. "I noticed": Nicholas Pileggi, "The Making of *The Godfather*: Sort of a Home Movie," *New York Times Magazine*, August 15, 1971.

111. "They respect": Murray, "The Playboy Interview."

112. "You don't know": Zuckerman, *The Godfather Journal*, p. 92. All other quotations in this passage are from this source.

112. "a cranky, grumpy guy": Rosen, "Francis Ford Coppola."

113. "At that point": Peter Manso, *Brando* (New York: Hyperion, 1994), p. 718.

113. "He hates": Braudy, "Francis Ford Coppola."

113. "Shot by shot": Evans, *The Kid Stays in the Picture*, pp. 224–225.

114. "Here you are": Author interview with Dean Tavoularis.

114. "I had hired" and "I would have loved": Author interview with FFC.

114. "Do you still": Zuckerman, *The Godfather Journal*, p. 122.

115. "I'm gonna make him": Mario Puzo and Francis Ford Coppola, *The Godfather* screenplay.

115. "We're not murderers": ibid.

115. "powerful people": Manso, *Brando*, p. 710.

115. "I thought": Marlon Brando, with Robert Lindsey, *Brando: Songs My Mother Taught Me* (New York: Random House, 1994), p. 411.

117. "Evans and Ballard": Author interview with FFC.

117. "Everyone advised me": Paul D. Zimmerman, "'The Godfather': Triumph for Brando," *Newsweek*, March 13, 1972. Not everyone was thrilled with Brando's interpretations of his character and the film's screenplay. Mario Puzo, for one, was distressed to learn that his favorite line in the

screenplay—"A lawyer with his briefcase can steal more than a hundred men with guns"—had been dismissed by Brando as being "too preachy." According to Puzo, the line was the one most often quoted from the book. "I have had people in France, England, Germany, and Denmark quote that line to me with utmost glee, some of them lawyers," he told *Variety* ("A Novelist Is Nil in Hollywood," *Variety*, March 15, 1972).

117. "I think Marlon": Author interview with James Caan.

118. "Just once": Manso, *Brando*, p. 727.

118. "I stayed a little bit": Chase, "Will the Godfather's Son Live to Be a Godfather?"

119. "I used to walk": Groebel, "The Playboy Interview."

119. "marvelous, big": Pauline Kael, "The Current Cinema: Alchemy," *The New Yorker*, March 18, 1972.

119. "Once I got": "Heir Apparent," *Life*, March 31, 1972.

119. "I don't want": Yule, *Life on the Wire*, p. 49.

119. "*Time* magazine": Chase, "Quick—What's This Man's Name?"

120. "This film": Zuckerman, *The Godfather Journal*, p. 66.

120. "My best moon": "The Making of the Godfather" (*Time*).

122. "Francis had a": Author interview with Eleanor Coppola.

122. "You shot a good film": Evans, *The Kid Stays in the Picture*, p. 228. Al Ruddy, in an interview with the author, supported Robert Evans's story about his influence on seeing that a longer version of the film was released. "I don't care what anyone tells you," Ruddy said, "this is *exactly* what happened. When Francis brought the movie down here and we ran it in the screening room for Bob [Evans] and Peter Bart, the movie was two hours and fifty-three minutes. Bob got on the phone with Yablans and said, 'I think this movie is fantastic, but it's two-fifty-three.' Frank said, 'I don't give a fuck how good it is at two-fifty-three, I'm not putting any movie out at two-fifty-three. The guys have to cut it down to two-twenty.' So Francis went back and cut it down to two-twenty, and he came back and ran it for Bob. And Bob said, 'Jesus Christ, this movie plays longer at two-twenty. You took all the heart out.' Then he told that to Frank Yablans on the phone while we were all there. He said, 'Frank, this movie is great at two-fifty-three, and it sucks at two-twenty. We have to go with

the two-fifty-three.' And that was the end of the conversation."

123. "He wanted Henry Mancini": Author interview with FFC.

125. "one of the most brutal": Biskind, *The Godfather Companion*, p. 65.

125. "in the reverent hands": ibid.

125. "class trash": Colin L. Westerbeck, Jr., "The Screen: Life with Godfather," *Commonweal*, April 28, 1972.

125. "If it does": Author interview with FFC.

5 . R E N A I S S A N C E M A N

126. "*The Conversation*": Brian De Palma, "The Making of *The Conversation*," *Filmmaker's Newsletter*, May 1974.

126. "When Francis Ford Coppola": David Denby, "Stolen Privacy: Coppola's *The Conversation*," *Sight and Sound*, Summer 1974.

128. "youthful desire" and "I'm open": John Rockwell, "'My Own Little City, My Own Little Opera,'" *The Saturday Review*, December 2, 1972.

128. "friendship, love": Author interview with FFC.

129. "Francis has charisma": Dale Pollack, *Skywalking: The Life and Films of George Lucas* (New York: Harmony Books, 1983; rev. ed., Hollywood: Samuel French, 1990), p. 79.

129. "After the Warner Bros.": Author interview with George Lucas.

131. "I was very, very lucky": Rockwell, "'My Own Little City.'"

131. "It is as much work": Ruthe Stein, "Coppola: The Man and His Dreams," *San Francisco Chronicle*, October 22, 1995.

132. "In the novel": Author interview with FFC.

133. "It's not my place": Marjorie Rosen, "Francis Ford Coppola," *Film Comment*, July 1974.

133. "They were in trouble": Author interview with FFC.

133. Directors Company: "Paramount Forms a Directors' Unit": *New York Times*, August 22, 1972; "Directors' Company," *Washington Post*, August 22, 1972.

134. "Part of my desire": Stephen Farber, "Coppola in Hollywood," *Los Angeles Magazine*, September 23, 1972.

134. "I'm not interested": Charles Higham, "Directors Guild Winner: Francis Ford Coppola," *Action*, May/June 1973.

135. "I wasn't much": De Palma, "The Making of *The Conversation*."

135. "I thought": Rosen, "Francis Ford Coppola."

135. "I was one": De Palma, "The Making of *The Conversation*."

135. "There's no real difference": Bob Mottley, "Two 'Godfathers' Are Better Than One?," *New Times*, May 3, 1974.

136. "He put me": Author interview with Dean Tavoularis.

137. "I don't care": Francis Ford Coppola, screenplay for *The Conversation*. All other quotations from the film are from this source.

141. "running in front": Rockwell, "'My Own Little City.'" All other quotations in this passage are from this source.

143. "I tried to obtain": Mottley, "Two 'Godfathers' Are Better Than One?"

144. "It's a depressing": Michael Goodwin and Naomi Wise, *On The Edge: The Life and Times of Francis Coppola* (New York: William Morrow and Co., 1989), p. 152.

144. "San Francisco, for once": Eve Babitz, "Francis Ford Coppola and His World," *Coast*, April 1975.

144. "We had to find": Author interview with Dean Tavoularis.

145. "We did it": De Palma, "The Making of *The Conversation*."

145. "The relationship": Hal Aigner and Michael Goodwin, "The Bearded Immigrant from Tinsel Town," *City* magazine (San Francisco), June 12, 1974.

146. "You boys": Pollack, *Skywalking*, p. 119. All other quotations in this passage are from this source.

148. "Stop taking pictures": "Frisco News Lenser Files 300G Suit Against Coppola," (Daily) *Variety*, December 24, 1973. See also: "Coppola Named in Suit," *Los Angeles Herald-Examiner*, December 23, 1973.

148. "We were shooting": Author interview with FFC.

148. the motion picture event: *The Godfather* was listed in numerous year-end newspaper and magazine "Best of '72" polls, including the *New York Times*, which asked a number of celebrities to name their favorite movies of the year. Among those citing *The Godfather* were Fred Astaire, Joan Crawford, Dick Gregory, Tina Turner, and Barbara Walters. During the first week of January, *Variety* reported that *The Godfather* had become the all-time box-office champion, deposing *Gone With the Wind* in less than a year's time.

149. "You may be asking": Gene Siskel, "Indian Woman's Speech a Shocker," *Chicago Tribune*, March 28, 1973. See also Tom Shales,

"They Made Him an Offer He Refused," *Washington Post*, March 28, 1973; Michael Kerrian, "Marlon Brando: Winner with a Cause," *Washington Post*, March 28, 1973; Peter Manso, *Brando* (New York: Hyperion, 1994), p. 769; and Marlon Brando, with Robert Lindsey, *Brando: Songs My Mother Taught Me* (New York: Random House, 1994), p. 404. Ironically, Coppola knew Sacheen Littlefeather and at one time had given her Brando's address so she could contact him.

149. "because of time" and "could do more": Manso, *Brando*, p. 769.

6. THE DEATH OF MICHAEL CORLEONE

150. "When you start": Richard Albarino, "Coppola's Plans: To Lay Low in Frisco, Little Pic Project," (Weekly) *Variety*, March 27, 1974.

151. "I want to write": ibid.

151. "the Sultan": "The Final Act of a Family Epic," *Time*, December 16, 1974.

151. "baby tycoon": Jon Carroll, "Coppola: Bringing in the Next Godfather," *New York*, November 13, 1974.

153. "I told them": Author interview with Al Ruddy.

153. "never wanted to see": Peter Biskind, *The Godfather Companion* (New York: Harper-Collins, 1990), p. 81.

153. "The idea of a sequel": William Murray, "The Playboy Interview: Francis Ford Coppola," *Playboy*, July 1975.

153. "Bluhdorn was very persistent": Author interview with FFC.

154. "*You* were the star" and "Close the deal!": Biskind, *The Godfather Companion*, p. 81.

154. "I said that I wanted": Author interview with FFC.

155. "It will not be": "Paramount Plans *The Godfather, Part II*," *Washington Post*, August 1, 1972.

156. "From the very beginning": "Roundtable Discussion with Francis Ford Coppola," Paramount Pictures publicity release, 1974.

156. "I would have showed": Mario Puzo, "Dialogue on Film," *American Film*, May 1979.

160. "We were all up": Author interview with Talia Shire.

161. "When he first said": Author interview with Mario Puzo.

162. "'Francis, you have two movies'": Carroll, "Coppola."

163. "I don't know": "Roundtable Discussion with Francis Ford Coppola."

163. "I got myself": Stephen Farber, "They Made Him Two Offers He Couldn't Refuse," *New York Times*, December 22, 1974.

163. "Originally, Brando was": Author interview with FFC.

164. "There was a bottle": Lawrence Grobel, "The Playboy Interview: Al Pacino," *Playboy*, December 1979.

165. "He was so wigged": Coppola remembered the difficult negotiations to convince Pacino to become involved in *Godfather II*: "I told him that I would totally go through the script one more time, and if he'd just meet with me on Friday and tell me all his points, I would work on it day and night and give him a new script on Monday. Which I did. He then agreed to be in it. He later said that he was always going to do it, but knew I should work on it more; he just wanted to give me the motivation to do it. It was a tough session, but when the cast read that draft all together some weeks later, they gave it a hand. I don't think that's happened to me before or since."

165. "I thought he was": "Roundtable Discussion with Francis Ford Coppola." De Niro was actually assigned the role of Paulie Gatto for a brief period of time, before Coppola released him to appear in *The Gang That Couldn't Shoot Straight*.

165. "When Marty showed me": "Roundtable Discussion with Francis Ford Coppola."

165. hiring of Lee Strasberg: Coppola initially hoped to cast Elia Kazan in the role of Hyman Roth. Kazan was too busy to take the part. He did, however, have a small influence on the film. When Coppola and Fred Roos visited his office, Kazan was working without his shirt. Impressed by the sight of the bare-chested old man, Coppola made a point of writing a scene in which Hyman Roth would appear without his shirt in the movie.

166. "Ten thousand dollars": "Strasberg: Applying the Method," *Time*, December 16, 1974.

167. "Why the hell": Eve Babitz, "Francis Ford Coppola and His World," *Coast*, April 1975. *Serpico* took just over five weeks to shoot.

169. "You just have to": Harlan Lebo, *The Godfather Legacy* (New York: Fireside Books, 1997), p. 225.

169. "His assignment": "Roundtable Discussion with Francis Ford Coppola."

169. "It's like being": Lebo, *The Godfather Legacy*, p. 238.

171. "In the train station": Author interview with Gray Frederickson.

172. "Walter Murch": Brian De Palma, "The Making of *The Conversation*," *Filmmaker's Newsletter*, May 1974.

172. "Like the conversation": Colin L. Westerbeck, Jr., "The Screen," *Commonweal*, May 3, 1974.

172. "There is something": John Simon, "Films," *Esquire*, June 1974.

172. "a disappointment": John M. Dower, "*The Conversation*," *Washington Post*, April 12, 1974.

172. "a film of enormous": Jay Cocks, "Sounds of Silence," *Time*, April 15, 1974.

173. "brilliantly original": Paul D. Zimmerman, "The Bug People," *Newsweek*, May 13, 1974.

173. "This is a screenplay": Penelope Gilliatt, "The Current Cinema," *The New Yorker*, April 15, 1974.

173 " one of the darkest" and "*The Conversation*": Stephen Farber, "A Nightmare World with No Secrets," *New York Times*, May 12, 1974.

173. Cannes Film Festival: Vincent Canby, "Ins and Outs of Cannes Film Festival Competition," *New York Times*, May 18, 1974; Vincent Canby, "U.S. Film Wins Top Cannes Prize," *New York Times*, May 25, 1974; "Two Top Film Awards Go to the U.S.," *London Times*, May 25, 1974.

7. SKIRMISHES BEFORE THE WAR

175. "I'm at a Y": Maureen Orth, "Godfather of the Movies," *Newsweek*, November 25, 1974.

177. "The pressure is on": Jon Carroll, "Coppola: Bringing In the Next Godfather," *New York*, November 13, 1974.

177. "Would you believe": "The Final Act of a Family Epic," *Time*, December 16, 1974.

178. "We were working": Author interview with Barry Malkin.

178. "It's a Frankenstein's monster": Vincent Canby, "*Godfather, Part II* Is Hard to Define," *New York Times*, December 13, 1974.

178. "ambitious, imposing": Gary Arnold, "And Now Comes Son of *The Godfather*," *Washington Post*, December 18, 1974.

179. "a tall and slightly": Richard Schickel, *Time*, December 16, 1974.

179. "This is not": Stanley Kauffmann, "Stanley Kauffmann on Films," *The New Republic*, January 18, 1975.

179. "Coppola is the inheritor": Pauline Kael, "The Current Cinema: Fathers and Sons," *The New Yorker*, December 23, 1974.

180. "They've gone through": Michael Pye and Lynda Myles, *The Movie Brats* (New York: Holt, Rinehart, and Winston, 1979), p. 97. For an in-depth look at Coppola's business dealings over the years, especially from 1979 on, see Jon Lewis, *Whom God Wishes to Destroy . . . Francis Coppola and the New Hollywood* (Durham, North Carolina: Duke University Press, 1995).

181. "I thought it was like": Peter Biskind, *Easy Riders, Raging Bulls: How the Sex-Drugs-and-Rock 'n' Roll Generation Saved Hollywood* (New York: Simon and Schuster, 1998), p. 211.

181. "When are these guys": ibid., p. 212.

182. "There was disagreement": Antony I. Ginnane, "Francis Ford Coppola," *Cinema Papers*, November–December 1975.

182. a sweetheart deal: Lewis, *Whom God Wishes to Destroy*, p. 20; James Monaco, *American Film Now: The People, the Power, the Money, the Movies* (New York: Oxford University Press, 1979), p. 329; Ginnane, "Francis Ford Coppola."

183. "Ultimately, my objective" and "Coppola Cinema 7": Ginnane, "Francis Ford Coppola."

183. "I really didn't like": Author interview with Carroll Ballard.

184. "a macabre comedy": "Coppola Plans a Detroit Epic," *New York Times*, July 7, 1974.

184. "George Lucas and I": John Gallagher, "John Milius," *Films in Review*, June/July 1982.

185. "I sort of had": Author interview with George Lucas.

185. "If you want": Dale Pollack, *Skywalking: The Life and Films of George Lucas* (New York: Harmony Books, 1983; rev. ed., Hollywood: Samuel French, 1990), p. 130.

185. "about war and the human soul" and "But it's dangerous": William Murray, "The Playboy Interview: Francis Ford Coppola," *Playboy*, July 1975.

186. "to participate in certain things" and "But suffice to say": ibid.

188. "If it wasn't": Michael Goodwin and Naomi Wise, *On the Edge: The Life and Times of Francis Coppola* (New York: William Morrow and Co., 1989), p. 191. All other quotations in this passage are from this source.

188. "When Francis was": Author interview with Talia Shire.

189. "They're only alike": Orth, "Godfather of the Movies." All other quotations in this conversation are from this source.

189. "Filmmakers need ways": Jim Harwood, "'Grapes' 1st Cross-Fertilization in Coppola's Growing Media Garden," (Daily) *Variety*, August 4, 1975.

189. "A guy who could knock": Charles Champlin, "The Paper Chaser," *Los Angeles Times*, August 1, 1975.

190. "I think that *City*": Author interview with FFC.

191. "We were looking": Author interview with Eleanor Coppola.

191. rumor mill was buzzing: Addison Verrill, "Coppola Plans Self-Financing for at Least Three Pictures Under Indie Cinema-7 Banner," (Daily) *Variety*, May 29, 1975.

192. "That one movie": Gallagher, "John Milius."

192. "Basically, he wanted": Richard Thompson, "Stoked," *Film Comment*, July–August 1976.

192. "At the time": Author interview with Carroll Ballard.

192. "I have no idea": Author interview with FFC.

193. "The original script": Ginnane, "Francis Ford Coppola."

193. "To make an anti-war movie": Thompson, "Stoked."

193. first draft of *Apocalypse Now*: Brooks Riley, "'Heart' Transplant," *Film Comment*, September–October 1979.

194. "Do you know": ibid.

194. "All the great scenes": Author interview with FFC.

194. "He sees himself": Thompson, "Stoked."

196. "[If he] wants": Lawrence Suid, "*Apocalypse Now*: Francis Ford Coppola Stages His Own Vietnam War," *Cineaste*, Winter 1977–1978. All other quotations in this passage are from this source.

8. "THE MOST
IMPORTANT MOVIE
I WILL EVER MAKE"

197. "You aren't going": Gordon Hitchens, "Orson Welles' Prior Interest in Conrad's *Heart of Darkness*," (Daily) *Variety*, June 13, 1979.

199. "not a film-extra agency": Lawrence Suid, "*Apocalypse Now*: Francis Ford Coppola Stages His Own Vietnam War," *Cineaste*, Winter 1977–1978.

200. "My reality feels": Eleanor Coppola, *Notes* (New York: Simon and Schuster, 1979), p. 22.

201. "The reason for": Mary Murphy, "Movie Call Sheet," *Los Angeles Times*, March 10, 1976.

201. "It's not" and "I think it's the right": Harlan Jacobson, "Coppola's Casting Via Term-Pact Offers for *Apocalypse* Not Suspicion-Free," (Daily) *Variety*, March 10, 1976.

201. "Coppola felt abandoned": ibid.

201. "There was no choice": Author interview with Frederic Forrest.

202. "Hello, this is": Maureen Orth, "Watching the 'Apocalypse,'" *Newsweek*, June 13, 1977.

203. "Jesus, Francis": Coppola, *Notes*, p. 34.

204. "Firing my lead actor": Greil Marcus, "Journey Up the River: An Interview with Francis Ford Coppola," *Rolling Stone*, November 1, 1979.

204. "I had searched": Author interview with FFC.

204. "I think Harvey": Author interview with Gray Frederickson.

205. "I left Rome": Jean Vallely, "Martin Sheen: Heart of Darkness, Heart of Gold," *Rolling Stone*, November 1, 1979.

205. "investigating and bringing" and "terminate with extreme prejudice": Suid, "*Apocalypse Now*."

206. "I will present": ibid.

206. "When we were in": Author interview with Eleanor Coppola.

207. "The film is a $20 million": Mark Caro, "Revisiting 'Apocalypse' Now and Then," *Chicago Tribune*, January 15, 1992.

207. "With my helicopters": Orth, "Watching the 'Apocalypse.'"

207. "I hate to say it": ibid.

207. "I was a wreck": Author interview with Gray Frederickson.

208. "I had gotten": Tony Chiu, "Francis Coppola's 'Apocalypse' Is Finally at Hand," *New York Times*, August 12, 1979.

209. "on some brittle edge": Coppola, *Notes*, p. 80.

209. "I remember sheets": Author interview with Dean Tavoularis.

210. "Attila was a slob": John Gallagher, "John Milius," *Films in Review*, June/July 1982.

210. "a brilliant eccentric": Susan Braudy, "Francis Ford Coppola: A Profile," *The Atlantic Monthly*, August 1976.

211. "I got problems": ibid.

211. Concerned about the effect: Orth, "Watching the 'Apocalypse'"; Bernard Wideman, "A Vietnam Epic: Coppola's Gamble," *Washington Post*, October 14, 1976.

211. "Our people have lost": Orth, "Watching the 'Apocalypse.'"
212. "a very heavy" and "I don't know": Vallely, "Martin Sheen."
212. "He would tell Martin": ibid.
213. "Marty's character": Marcus, "Journey Up the River."
213. "Francis did a dangerous": Vallely, "Martin Sheen."
214. "the asshole of the world": Francis Ford Coppola and John Milius, screenplay for *Apocalypse Now.*
214. "The way we made it": G. Roy Levin, "Francis Coppola Discusses *Apocalypse Now*," *Millimeter*, October 1979.
214. "He went over": Author interview with Mona Skager.
215. "We were aware": Author interview with FFC. Added Coppola: "As I remember it, the sequence was fine, and I certainly liked bringing in these ghosts from the French period, as I felt the journey up the river was also a journey back in time." Coppola admitted that the budget concerns and the expensive set influenced his feelings about the scene—"I've sort of had it in for this sequence ever since"—but said it was cut because the film was running too long.
216. "I lied": Coppola, *Notes*, p. 128.
217. "I was good": Marlon Brando, with Robert Lindsey, *Brando: Songs My Mother Taught Me* (New York: Random House, 1994), p. 431.
217. "Hey, Marlon": Marcus, "Journey Up the River."
217. "He wasn't what everyone": Author interview with Gray Frederickson.
218. designing the Kurtz compound: One of the strangest rumors circulating during the filming of *Apocalypse Now* had the production crew using real corpses on the set. No one ever confirmed the rumor, though even Coppola's wife hinted, in *Notes* (p. 126), that the rumors might have been true: "I heard there are some real cadavers in body bags at the Kurtz Compound set. I asked the propman about it; he said, 'The script says, "a pile of burning bodies"; it doesn't say a pile of burning dummies.'"
218. "I was living": Orth, "Watching the 'Apocalypse.'"
218. "For the Kurtz compound": Author interview with Alex Tavoularis.
219. "The original idea": Author interview with Dean Tavoularis.
220. "There'd be long discussions": Author interview with FFC.
220. "That whole scene": Author interview with Frederic Forrest.
221. "By the time": Peter Manso, *Brando* (New York: Hyperion, 1994), p. 842.
222. "Francis, I've gone": ibid., p. 843.
222. "God! I'd go": Coppola, *Notes*, p. 147.
223. "The original idea": Ric Gentry, "A Journey into Light," in *Projections 6*, ed. John Boorman and Walter Donahue (London: Faber and Faber, 1996), p. 265.
223. "a conflict between": "The Five Best Photographed Motion Pictures of 1979: Vittorio Storaro," *American Cinematographer*, May 1980.
223. "I don't believe": ibid.
223. "I have a lot": Vallely, "Martin Sheen."
225. "an asshole": Coppola, *Notes*, p. 177.
225. "All those things": George Hickenlooper, *Reel Conversations: Candid Interviews with Film's Foremost Directors and Critics* (New York: Citadel Press, 1991), p. 45.
225. "The particular person": Davis Breskin, "The Rolling Stone Interview: Francis Ford Coppola," *Rolling Stone*, February 7, 1991.
226. "I kept waking up": Tom Buckley, "Getting Bigger Bang at the End of 'Apocalypse,'" *New York Times*, October 12, 1979.
226. "Dean Tavoularis": Vallely, "Martin Sheen."
226. "I was at": Author interview with Dean Tavoularis.
227. "I completely fell apart": Vallely, "Martin Sheen."
227. "I'll just say": Author interview with Martin Sheen. Sheen politely declined to go into detail about some of his more harrowing experiences on the film. "There are a lot of emotional memories, and they're the ones the soul hangs on to the longest," he explained. "You have to find a place to let that go, and I think that belongs to God. I wouldn't share it with others that weren't there and don't know."
228. "I sort of panicked": Hickenlooper, *Reel Conversations*, p. 45.
228. "The idea was": Chris Nashawaty, "A Coppola Things," *Entertainment Weekly*, November 21, 1997.
229. "in the running": "Coppola Coping with Bad Luck," *New York*, April 11, 1977.
229. "a fascinating view": Greg Kilday, untitled article, *Los Angeles Times*, October 26, 1977.
230. "To this end": Francis Ford Coppola, "Case

Histories of Business Management: Hollywood Artistic Division," *Esquire*, November 1977. All other quotations from this memo are from this source.

231. "a memo from": Aljean Harmetz, "Fever Dream 'Apocalypse Now' Has Coppola in Hock but Happy," *Chicago Tribune*, April 13, 1980.

9. APOCALYPSE WHEN?

233. "Even if Coppola isn't": Dale Pollock, "Apocalypse Now" (review), (Weekly) *Variety*, May 16, 1979.

233. "*Apocalypse Now* is finally": Russell Baker, "Filmmaker Shuns Hasty Judgment," *Chicago Tribune*, September 6, 1979.

234. blockbuster mentality: James Monaco's *American Film Now: The People, the Power, the Money, the Movies* (New York: Oxford University Press, 1979) was an invaluable source, particularly the chapter "Products and Profits," pp. 29–48. Miscellaneous *Variety* reports and box-office charts were also consulted, as was Jeffrey Kaye's analytical piece "Epic Pictures for Epic Price Tags," *Washington Post*, November 18, 1979.

234. "Film used to be": Monaco, *American Film Now*, p. 31.

234. "Film in America": ibid., p. 29.

235. "Everybody in the business": Kaye, "Epic Pictures for Epic Price Tags."

236. he sold his: "Coppola Sells His 72,000 Cinema 5 Shares to Rugoff," (Daily) *Variety*, May 11, 1977; "Coppola Sells Back to Cinema 5 His 70,000 Shares Bought at $2.50," (Weekly) *Variety*, May 18, 1977; Jim Harwood, "Coppola Hocks Assets to UA For 'Apocalypse' End Money," (Daily) *Variety*, June 6, 1977.

236. Coppola/UA deal: In their book, *On the Edge: The Life and Times of Francis Coppola* (New York: William Morrow and Co., 1989), Michael Goodwin and Naomi Wise disputed the degree of risk that Coppola had taken in his agreement with United Artists. The $10 million, wrote the authors, had come from Chase Manhattan Bank and had been guaranteed by United Artists, not Coppola. Coppola had indeed put up all of his personal assets in the deal, but if he defaulted on the loan, UA would be responsible for repaying Chase Manhattan and would then have the option of subsequently foreclosing on Coppola—an unlikely scenario, given the inevitable

public-relations nightmare that would follow. "It was a brilliant move," wrote Goodwin and Wise. "Announcing that he'd virtually pawned his wedding ring to pay for the film helped counteract the media image of Coppola as a self-indulgent, self-styled genius throwing money around. Instead, it made him seem like a martyr to art, risking everything for his work."

237. "I came from a family": Author interview with Eleanor Coppola.

238. "We were in": Author interview with Carroll Ballard.

238. "I listened to the person": Eleanor Coppola, *Notes* (New York: Simon and Schuster, 1979), p. 211.

238. "I have wept": David Breskin, "The Rolling Stone Interview: Francis Ford Coppola," *Rolling Stone*, February 7, 1991.

239. "nonphysical world": Coppola, *Notes*, p. 213.

239. "I didn't want": Breskin, "The Rolling Stone Interview."

239. "That was a low point": Author interview with FFC.

241. "I had worked": Author interview with Barry Malkin.

242. "I've got to do": Charles Higham, "Coppola's Vietnam Movie Is a Battle Royal," *New York Times*, May 15, 1977.

243. "You could shoot": Peter Cowie, *Coppola* (New York: Charles Scribner's Sons, 1990), p. 128.

243. "When I started": Mark Cousins, "Walter Murch: Designing Sound for *Apocalypse Now*," in *Projections 6*, ed. John Boorman and Walter Donahue (London: Faber and Faber, 1996), pp. 159–160. All quotations in this passage are from this source.

244. "We were moving": Walter Murch, "Sound Design: The Dancing Shadow," in *Projections 4*, ed. John Boorman and Walter Donahue (London: Faber and Faber, 1995), p. 246.

244. its own recent history: Steven Bach, *Final Cut* (New York: William Morrow and Co., 1985); Peter J. Schuyten, "United Artists' Script Calls for Divorce," *Fortune*, January 16, 1978.

245. "To Jim Harvey": Bach, *Final Cut*, p. 126.

246. "Francis Ford Coppola finally": Richard Cuskelly, "Francis Ford Coppola Finally Comes Out of Hiding," *Los Angeles Herald-Examiner*, April 27, 1978.

246. "The film reaches": Coppola, *Notes*, p. 266.

247. "which is more like Vietnam": Leticia Kent, "Ready for Vietnam? A Talk with Michael

Cimino," *New York Times*, December 10, 1978.

247. "When I saw": G. Roy Levin, "Francis Coppola Discusses *Apocalypse Now*," *Millimeter*, October 1979.

248. "Not until *The Deer Hunter*": Lawrence Suid, "Hollywood and Vietnam," *Film Comment*, September 1979.

248. "We were not banking": Tony Chiu, "*Apocalypse Now* Will Open, At Last," *New York Times*, January 25, 1979.

249. "very, very mixed": Author interview with FFC.

249. "the Cinematic equivalent": Dale Pollock, "'This Is My Version,' Says Coppola at 'Apocalypse' Bow," (Daily) *Variety*, May 14, 1979.

249. "to help me": David Denby, "'8 1/2' Now: Coppola's Apocalypse," *New York*, May 28, 1979.

249. "disturbed by the clear evidence": ibid.

250. "It's like watching": "Sneaking of 'Apocalypse.'"

250. "mostly stunning": Gene Siskel, "Coppola's 'Apocalypse' Excellent, Yet Confusing," *Chicago Tribune*, May 14, 1979.

250. "The film is about": ibid.

251. "*Apocalypse Now* feels": Denby, "'8 1/2' Now."

251. Coppola exploded: "Coppola and Daily Variety," (Daily) *Variety*, May 29, 1979. In defending its decision to publish a review in its daily edition, *Variety* editors pointed out that its publication, along with the *Los Angeles Times*, had adhered to Coppola's no-review request until Rona Barrett's comments, which, said *Variety*, "broke the ground rules." Coppola's anger—especially toward *Variety*, which he singled out in a later press conference—was misdirected and unwarranted. "Granted Coppola has a lot on his mind," *Variety* noted laconically, "but he also should find room to accommodate the truth."

251. "The version you just saw": Dale Pollock, "A Full Array of Never-Was-Befores," (Weekly) *Variety*, May 16, 1979.

252. "UA is in perfect" and "momentary insanity": Pollock, "'This Is My Version.'"

252. "might easily be called": "A Bet on *Apocalypse* Starts to Pay Off," *Business Week*, June 11, 1979.

252. "out-of-town tryout": Charles Michener, "Finally, *Apocalypse Now*," *Newsweek*, May 28, 1979.

252. "Ten people at United Artists": Aljean Harmetz, "Coppola: Will He Break Even?" *New York Times*, March 18, 1980. Whether Coppola was taking a serious risk, or whether he was actually reprising his role as master showman, was a topic for debate. Critic Gene Siskel, for one, believed the latter. "Showing the film unfinished was a masterstroke by Coppola," he wrote in the *Chicago Tribune*. "To give a festival jury of filmmakers and critics a chance to turn thumbs up or down on the film before it was released was to give the jury nothing less than a chance to turn thumbs up or down on Coppola's career. Just imagine if you were a member of a jury judging the work of a filmmaker who has thrilled you with *The Godfather* pictures. Would you want to cripple an unfinished film in which that filmmaker had invested his life savings and, as the story went, even mortgaged his vineyard? And if the jury didn't like the picture, well, it wasn't a finished film, was it?"

252. "I'm not afraid": Kevin Dowling, "'Apocalypse Now' Could Be Never if Francis Coppola's Go-for-Broke Gamble Fizzles," *People*, June 6, 1979.

252. Coppola was easily the center: Susan Haller Anderson, "'Apocalypse Now' Stuns Cannes," *New York Times*, May 21, 1979; Thomas Quinn Curtiss, "'Apocalypse' Unfinished," *Washington Post*, May 21, 1979; Michael Webb, "'Apocalypse Now' for Coppola and the French Press," *Los Angeles Herald-Examiner*, May 22, 1979; Sid Adilman, "Candid, Caustic, Cost-Groggy Coppola Spanks Yank Press," (Weekly) *Variety*, May 23, 1979; Gene Moskowitz, "Coppola Needs Unanimous Cannes Jury," (Weekly) *Variety*, May 23, 1979; "Americans Take Top Prizes at Cannes," *New York Times*, May 25, 1979; Michener, "Finally, *Apocalypse Now*"; Andrew Sarris, "First Assault on *Apocalypse Now*," *Village Voice*, May 28, 1979; Dowling, "'Apocalypse Now' Could Be Never."

253. "My film": Levin, "Francis Coppola Discusses *Apocalypse Now*."

253. "American journalism": Adilman, "Candid, Caustic, Cost-Groggy Coppola."

253. "the world's first": Webb, "'Apocalypse Now' for Coppola."

253. "Why is it": Curtiss, "'Apocalypse' Unfinished."

253. "Despite *The Godfather*" and "Americans are": Webb, "'Apocalypse Now' for Coppola."

254. "big, bearded bear" and "Coppola is not just": Bach, *Final Cut*, p. 249.

255. "prize in progress": Gene Siskel, "Coppola's Sales Tactics Fuel His 'Apocalypse' Launching," *Chicago Tribune*, October 14, 1979.

255. "when the celebratory mood" and "A Chianti bottle": Bach, *Final Cut*, pp. 249–250.

256. "He's in a manic": Jeanie Kasindorf, "Citizen Coppola: S.F. Expansionism," *New West*, July 2, 1979.

256. "spread out like": Tom Zito, "Shell Shock After the 'Apocalypse,'" *Washington Post*, August 13, 1979.

256. "the book [became]": Christopher Lehmann-Haupt, "Books of the Times," *New York Times*, August 7, 1979.

256. "[*Notes*] made me": ibid.

257. "Winners and losers": Aljean Harmetz, "'Rocky' Summer for Film Industry," *New York Times*, September 18, 1979.

257. "The guess here": Siskel, "Coppola's Sales Tactics."

258. "There are those" and "I've got": Dowling, "'Apocalypse Now' Could Be Never."

258. "because there is nothing": John Milius and Francis Ford Coppola, screenplay for *Apocalypse Now*.

259. "with extreme prejudice": ibid. All other quotations from the film in this section are from this source.

263. "We had to put": Samir Hachem, "Coppola Signs with Orion for 6 Films," *Hollywood Drama-Logue*, November 29–December 5, 1979.

264. Attendance figures: "Town Talk All 'Apocalypse' Pre-Opening," (Weekly) *Variety*, August 15, 1979; (chart) "50 Top-Grossing Films," (Weekly) *Variety*, August 29, 1979; "'Apocalypse' Booms Along With $1.2-Mil Posted in 20 Days," (Weekly) *Variety*, September 5, 1979; Hy Hollinger, "United Artists Now Sees 'Apocalypse' Recoupment," (Weekly) *Variety*, October 3, 1979.

264. "emotionally obtuse": Frank Rich, "The Making of a Quagmire," *Time*, August 27, 1979.

264. "a stunning and unforgettable film": Jack Kroll, "Coppola's War Epic," *Newsweek*, August 20, 1979. Kroll's piece was the kind of review that a filmmaker could only dream of receiving: "*Apocalypse Now* is the ultimate war movie, a riveting adventure story, a searching and deeply committed probing of the moral problem of the Vietnam War—and something more than all of these, transcending categories and genres in a way that only true art, and specifically true movie art, does at its best."

264. "For two-thirds": Arthur Schlesinger, Jr., "Coppola's Self-Appointed Epic," *The Saturday Review*, January 5, 1980.

264. "I assume": Vincent Canby, "The Heart of 'Apocalypse' Is 'Extremely Misty,'" *New York Times*, August 19, 1979.

264. "In dozens of scenes": Vincent Canby, "The Screen: *Apocalypse Now*," *New York Times*, August 15, 1979.

264. "a literature-lacquered version": Stanley Kauffmann, "Coppola's War," *The New Republic*, September 15, 1979.

265. "Obese and photographed": Gene Siskel, "Vietnam Film Winds Up Fighting Itself," *Chicago Tribune*, October 5, 1979.

265. "The movie peaks": Gary Arnold, "Mangled Revelations: 'Apocalypse,'" *Washington Post*, October 3, 1979.

265. "Kilgore is a vaunting": David Denby, "Hollow Movie," *New York*, August 27, 1979.

265. "baleful, explosive": Tim O'Brien, "The Violent Vet," *Esquire*, December 1979.

265. "Whether the war": Rob Edelman, "Viet Vets Talk About Nam Films," *Films in Review*, November 1979.

265. "a cartoon": ibid.

266. "Half the people": Greil Marcus, "Journey Up the River," *Rolling Stone*, November 1, 1979.

266. "Sometimes I think": Tony Chiu, "Francis Coppola's Cinematic 'Apocalypse' Is Finally at Hand," *New York Times*, April 12, 1979.

10. THE SHAPE OF THINGS TO COME

267. "The new technology": "'American Culture Is Controlled by Cynical Middlemen,'" *U.S. News & World Report*, April 5, 1982.

267. "Pretending that advanced": Peter Rainer, "Apocalypse Soon?" *Los Angeles Herald-Examiner*, March 7, 1982.

267. "moguling it up": Jeanie Kasindorf, "Citizen Coppola: S.F. Expansionism," *New West*, July 2, 1979.

267. "In the mud": Dale Pollock, "Coppola Unveils His New Studio," *Los Angeles Times*, March 21, 1980.

268. "I can see": Peter Cowie, *Coppola* (New York: Charles Scribner's Sons, 1990), p. 145.

268. The Hollywood General Studios: "Coppola Expects to Have an L.A. Studio," (Weekly) *Variety*, May 16, 1979; "H'wood Gen'l Served Notice of Foreclosure, " (Daily) *Vari-*

ety, July 17, 1979; "Coppola Interim Fees on Nassar Mortgage Generates Some Fog," (Weekly) *Variety*, July 18, 1979; "Coppola Assumes Control of Studio," *The Hollywood Reporter*, January 4, 1980; "Coppola May Not Be New Owner of Hollywood Gen'l," (Daily) *Variety*, January 31, 1980; "Coppola Fails in Bid to Stop H'w'd General Sale," (Daily) *Variety*, February 11, 1980; Coppola Loses First Round for Hywd General," *The Hollywood Reporter*, February 11, 1980; "Coppola Plan Nixed on General Studios," (Weekly) *Variety*, February 13, 1980; Gregg Kilday, "Coppola Now," *Los Angeles Herald-Examiner*, February 18, 1980; "Hollywood Gen'l Still Up For Grabs," *The Hollywood Reporter*, February 20, 1980; "Calif. Top Court Decision Due on H'wood General Case," (Daily) *Variety*, February 21, 1980; "Nassars, Coppola OK Pact for H'wood Gen'l," (Daily) *Variety*, March 5, 1980; Dale Pollock, "Has Coppola Won Battle for Studio?" *Los Angeles Times*, March 5, 1980; Dale Pollock, "Previous Attempt to Buy Studios Is Noted," *Los Angeles Times*, March 6, 1980; "Coppola May Not Get General Plant," (Weekly) *Variety*, March 6, 1980; Dale Pollock, "Coppola Unveils His New Studio"; Gregg Kilday, "Coppola Casts His Lot in Hollywood," *Los Angeles Herald-Examiner*, March 21, 1980; Aljean Harmetz, "Coppola Buys Studio for $6.7 Million," *New York Times*, March 21, 1980; Steven Ginsberg, "Coppola's Plans for Old-Line Studio," (Daily) *Variety*, March 21, 1980; "General Studios Finally Coppola's, But He Stays with 'Frisco Base," (Weekly) *Variety*, March 26, 1980.

268. "all-time favorite movie": Aaron Latham, "The Movie Man Who Plays God," *Life*, August 1981.

271. "Whether he's controlling": "After 'Apocalypse,' A Story of Love," *Newsweek*, October 24, 1979.

271. "He's a true": David Anson, with Martin Kasindorf, "Coppola's Apocalypse Again," *Newsweek*, February 16, 1981.

271. "Sure, I can": ibid.

272. "artistic director": Harmetz, "Coppola Buys Studio."

272. "I believe the most": Gene Siskel, "Director Francis Coppola Takes a New Film Gamble," *Chicago Tribune*, February 8, 1981.

272. "We must never": Samir Hachem, "Coppola Signs with Orion for Six Films," *Hollywood Drama-logue*, November 29–December 5, 1979.

273. "My idea": Michael Ventura, "Coppola's Woes and the Zoetrope Revolution," *Los Angeles Weekly*, February 19–25, 1982.

274. Brown appointed Coppola: "Brown Names Coppola to Arts Council," *Los Angeles Herald-Examiner*, March 7, 1980; "Coppola Named to Arts Council," *Los Angeles Times*, March 8, 1980; "Coppola Succeeds Miss Fonda on the Firing Line," *New York Times*, March 8, 1980.

274. "very pleased": "Brown Names Coppola to Arts Council."

274. created four television ads: "Coppola's Brown TV Spots," (Daily) *Variety*, March 20, 1980; "Coppola as a Presidential 'Star Maker'; Creates Wis. TV Spots for Gov. Brown," (Weekly) *Variety*, March 26, 1980; "Coppola Will Direct Brown Campaign Show," *Los Angeles Herald-Examiner*, March 27, 1980; "Jerry's Swan Song," (Daily) *Variety*, March 27, 1980; E. J. Dionne, Jr., "Madison, Wis., Goes Hollywood as Film Maker Plugs for Brown," *New York Times*, March 30, 1980; "Film Clips," *Los Angeles Times*, April 7, 1980; Tim Onosko, "Media Madness," *Village Voice*, April 21, 1980; Jonathan Cott, "The Rolling Stone Interview: Francis Coppola," *Rolling Stone*, March 18, 1982.

274. "Instead of spending": Cott, "The Rolling Stone Interview."

275. "If something goes wrong": Onosko, "Media Madness." All subsequent quotations in this passage are from this source.

276. "It was as spectacular": "Film Clips."

276. "The fact is": Dionne, "Madison, Wis., Goes Hollywood."

276. "It looked as if": Cott, "The Rolling Stone Interview."

276. "It was typically overambitious": Author interview with FFC.

277. "The movies I make": Marilyn Beck, "There's a Film Revolution in Director Coppola's Future," *Chicago Tribune*, December 9, 1979.

277. "I was so exhausted": Tim Hunter, "The Making of *Hammett*: How Two Directors, Three and a Half Writers, Several Studio Executives and Francis Ford Coppola Took Five Years to Make 90 Percent of What May Be a Very Good Movie," *New West*, September 22, 1980.

278. "We had a script": Author interview with FFC.

278. "It all started": Author interview with Dean Tavoularis.

278. "I didn't think": Author interview with Frederic Forrest.

279. "The real Las Vegas": Lillian Ross, "Onward and Upward with the Arts: Some Figures on a Fantasy," *The New Yorker,* November 8, 1982.

279. "I wanted to take": Scot Haller, "Francis Coppola's Biggest Gamble," *The Saturday Review*, July 1981.

280. "Of course": Jeffrey Wells, "A Film Journal Interview: Francis Ford Coppola/Part 2," *Film Journal,* September 21, 1981.

281. *Kagemusha*: Kurosawa's Latest Gets Fox Distribbing, Coppola Editing Aid," (Weekly) *Variety,* May 21, 1980; Dianna Waggoner, "Homage to the Master, George Lucas and Francis Coppola Unleash Their Clout for Kurosawa," *People,* October 27, 1980.

282. "was like telling Michelangelo": Waggoner, "Homage to the Master."

282. "I contacted Kurosawa": Author interview with George Lucas.

282. "In Japanese drama": Lee Grant, "Coppola: Dreamer . . . and Doer," *Los Angeles Times,* February 9, 1982.

283. "a little musical Valentine": Cowie, *Coppola,* p. 155.

283. "like a couple": "Coppola and Kelly Singin' in the Rain," *Los Angeles Times,* October 5, 1980.

283. "The idea was not": John Calhoun, "Dean Tavoularis: For This Celebrated Production Designer, God Is in the Details," *TCI,* October 1994.

284. bring back Vittorio Storaro: "Coppola's Hiring of Storaro Draws Ire of Film Council," *The Hollywood Reporter,* July 15, 1980.

284. "In *One From the Heart*": Ric Gentry, "A Journey Into Light," in *Projections 6,* ed. John Boorman and Walter Donahue (London: Faber and Faber, 1996), p. 267.

284. "For characters": ibid., p. 268.

285. "Something incredibly good": Ross, "Onward and Upward with the Arts."

285. "With all this": Andrew Sarris, "Riding on Coppola's Rollercoaster," *Village Voice,* January 27, 1982.

288. "technical rehearsals": Latham, "The Movie Man Who Plays God."

289. "God [was] in": Calhoun, "Dean Tavoularis."

290. *Napoleon*: "Coppola Will Present Abel Gance's *Napoleon*," *Los Angeles Times,* December 11, 1980; "Francis Coppola Brings an Epic 'Napoleon' Back from Exile," *People,* February 9, 1981; Sean French, "The

Napoleon Phenomenon," *Sight and Sound,* Spring 1982; "Napoleon," Universal City Studios press release, June 7, 1982.

11. FATAL GAMBLE

293. "It's like I'm at": Scot Haller, "Francis Coppola's Biggest Gamble," *The Saturday Review*, July 1981.

293. "Francis calls me": Mitch Tuchman and Anne Thompson, "I'm the Boss," *Film Comment,* September 1981.

294. crippling cash-flow problems: Aljean Harmetz, "Coppola Risks All on $22 Million Movie," *New York Times,* February 2, 1981; Gregg Kilday, "Coppola's Dream Postponed," *Los Angeles Herald-Examiner,* February 3, 1981; Gregg Kilday, "Coppola Explains His Big Gamble," *Los Angeles Herald-Examiner,* February 5, 1981; Todd McCarthy, "High-Roller Coppola Gambles Studio on Future of 'Electronic Cinema,'" (Daily) *Variety,* February 5, 1981; Duane Barge, "'Heart' Must Revive Zoetrope, as Story Dept. First Casualty," *The Hollywood Reporter,* February 5, 1981; Lee Grant, "The Francis Coppola Story," *Los Angeles Times,* February 6, 1981; Todd McCarthy, "Coppola's Employees Forgo Pay," (Daily) *Variety,* February 6, 1981; Ann Salisbury, "Workers Give One From Heart, Pocket to Save Coppola's Film," *Los Angeles Herald-Examiner,* February 6, 1981; Dale Pollock, "Zoetrope Workers Vote to Carry On," *Los Angeles Times,* February 7, 1981; Aljean Harmetz, "Paramount's $1 Million Saves Coppola's Studio and New Film," *New York Times,* February 10, 1981; Gregg Kilday, "Zoetrope's Survival Is Paramount," *Los Angeles Herald-Examiner,* February 10, 1981; Todd McCarthy, "Zoetrope Rejects Peranchio Offer," (Daily) *Variety,* February 11, 1981; Richard Corliss, "'I'm Always in Money Trouble,'" *Time,* February 23, 1981.

295. "a supportive act": Corliss, "'I'm Always in Money Trouble.'"

295. "Francis is": Harmetz, "Paramount's $1 Million."

295. "The mood here": Grant, "The Francis Coppola Story."

295. "A practical man": Author interview with Alex Tavoularis.

295. "I'm trying to hold": McCarthy, "High-Roller Coppola Gambles Studio."

295. "so worried": Grant, "The Francis Coppola Story."

296. "The majors don't like": Harmetz, "Coppola Risks All."

296. "It's very hard to work": Grant, "The Francis Coppola Story."

296. "the amplified power": Aaron Latham, "The Movie Man Who Plays God," *Life*, August 1981.

297. "The idea of my working": Author interview with FFC. Coppola is the first to admit that it's not a good idea for the director to be removed from the set—or even from the actor's view: "I'm always sitting next to the camera, which is where my teacher, Dorothy Arzner, told me the director should be, so the actors will see him. Ironically, now that the video system that we introduced is stock equipment on all films, many directors make the mistake of sitting way in back of the camera, behind a big monitor, and I always advise them that this is a very bad mistake. I was just the first to do many of these things, and so I made some of the first mistakes that others make to this day."

297. "some getting used to" and "It's okay": Latham, "The Movie Man Who Plays God."

297. "The way it was shot": Todd McCarthy, "Actor Forrest Gives Heart to Coppola Films," (Daily) *Variety*, February 8, 1982.

297. "in the lab" and "I think what happens": Author interview with Frederick Forrest.

297. "In interviews": Pauline Kael, "Melted Ice Cream," *The New Yorker*, February 1, 1982.

298. "This one": Judith Crist, "The Flowers and Weeds of Spring," *The Saturday Review*, March 1982.

298. "My idea for": Author interview with FFC.

299. Jack Singer: Gregg Kilday, "Coppola Gets a New Godfather," *Los Angeles Herald-Examiner*, March 1, 1981; Todd McCarthy, "$ Transfusion for Coppola's *Heart*," (Daily) *Variety*, March 2, 1981; Todd McCarthy, "Coppola Rescue Spotlights Calgary's Megabuck Clan," (Weekly) *Variety*, March 4, 1981; "From Realty to Movies," *New York Times*, April 15, 1981; Sid Adilman, "Singer's a Swinger on Can. Pic. Scene, Coppola's Bankroll," (Weekly) *Variety*, November 25, 1981.

300. "I think that people": Harmetz, "From Realty to Movies."

300. "My interest" and "At least with": McCarthy, "Coppola Rescue."

300. "What Paramount has done": "Paramount Makes Deal with Coppola," *New York Times*, March 23, 1981.

301. "Disheartened" and "It really has": Jeffrey Wells, "A Film Journal Interview: Francis Ford Coppola," *Film Journal*, September 7, 1981.

301. "a bullshit racket" and "Let me say": Gay Talese, "The Conversation," *Esquire*, July 1981.

302. "It's like the emperor's" to "I almost think": Judy Stone, "Coppola Has 'Heart' Trouble," *San Francisco Chronicle*, August 21, 1981. See also: "*Heart* Screening Doesn't Sit Well with S.F. Exhibs," (Daily) *Variety*, August 24, 1981.

302. "no-win war" and "They showed": Wells, "A Film Journal Interview."

303. "It will only take": Jeffrey Wells, "A Film Journal Interview: Francis Ford Coppola/Part 2," September 21, 1981.

303. "a nonexistent budget": Todd McCarthy, "Frederic Forrest Gives Heart to Coppola Films," (Daily) *Variety*, February 8, 1982.

303. "Orion had been": Author interview with FFC.

305. "As soon as": Richard Corliss, "Presenting Fearless Francis!" *Time*, January 18, 1982.

305. to present such a preview: Stephen Klain, "Coppola's New York Plans For 'One From the Heart' Come as Surprise to Par," (Daily) *Variety*, January 7, 1982; Janet Maslin, "Coppola Sets Up Preview, Doesn't Tell Paramount," *New York Times*, January 7, 1982; Stephen Klain, "Coppola Terminates Paramount 'Heart' Distribution Link," (Daily) *Variety*, January 18, 1982; Corliss, "Presenting Fearless Francis!"; Steven Ginsberg, "Coppola Keeps Pushing 'Heart' as Par Bows Out," (Daily) *Variety*, January 19, 1982; Stephen Klain, "Paramount-Coppola Break 'Heart' Strings Before Gotham Previews; Zoetrope Seeks New Distrib. Tie," (Weekly) *Variety*, January 20, 1982; Coppola's 'Heart' Will Not Be Released," *Chicago Tribune*, January 21, 1982; John Skow, "Going for the Cheeky Gamble," *Time*, January 23, 1982; "Coppola to Release New Film Himself," *New York Times*, January 30, 1982; Lillian Ross, "Onward and Upward with the Arts: Some Figures on a Fantasy," *The New Yorker*, November 8, 1982.

305. "I knew": Maslin, "Coppola Sets Up Preview."

305. "If the picture": ibid.

307. "Whether that happens": Ross, "Onward and Upward." All other quotations in this passage are from this source.

307. "hogwash": Rex Reed, "Here's One from the Heart: Hogwash!," *New York Daily News*, January 17, 1982.

307. "Whatever made Coppola": Andrew Sarris, "Riding on Coppola's Rollercoaster," *Village Voice*, January 27, 1982.

307. "one of those" and "The one thing": Vincent Canby, "Obsession with Technique," *New York Times*, February 21, 1982.

307. "I certainly didn't": David Denby, "Empty Calories," *New York*, February 1, 1982.

307. "Eventually the audience": Pauline Kael, "Melted Ice Cream."

308. "the film does have": "One From the Heart," (Weekly) *Variety*, January 20, 1982.

308. "It's so easy": Sheila Benson, "One From the Heart," *Los Angeles Times*, January 22, 1982.

308. "innovative and imaginative": James M. Wall, "One From the Heart," *Christian Century*, March 3, 1982.

308. "The hope and the hype": Richard Corliss, "Surrendering to the Big Dream," *Time*, January 25, 1982.

308. "They call me reckless": Jonathan Cott, "The Rolling Stone Interview: Francis Coppola," *Rolling Stone*, March 18, 1982.

309. "There are Francis": Author interview with August Coppola.

309. "so that it would": Ginsberg, "Coppola Keeps Pushing 'Heart.'"

310. "respectable and generous": Will Turner, "Coppola 'Heart' Opening Feb. 11," (Daily) *Variety*, January 29, 1982.

310. deal with Columbia: "Coppola-Columbia Pact," *New York Times*, February 2, 1982; "Col Firms Domestic Distrib Tie to Coppola's 'Heart'; Theatrical Only," (Weekly) *Variety*, February 3, 1982.

310. "less than the" and "The deal": Ross, "Onward and Upward."

312. "act more like": ibid.

312. "Everybody knows": Lee Grant, "Coppola—Dreamer and Doer," *Los Angeles Times*, February 9, 1982.

12. PALADIN
IN OKLAHOMA

315. "Francis was so far". Author interview with Diane Lane.

316. "Rather than go": David Thompson and Lucy Gray, "Idols of the King," *Film Comment*, September–October 1983.

316. Coppola's involvement with *The Outsiders*: Todd McCarthy, "WB Gets Coppola's 'Out-

siders'; Teenage Pic Eyes Fall Bow, (Weekly) *Variety*, March 17, 1982; Stephen Farber, "Directors Join the S. E. Hinton Fan Club," *New York Times*, March 20, 1983; Aljean Harmetz, "Making 'The Outsiders' a Librarian's Dream," *New York Times*, March 23, 1983.

317. "where ideals" and "So many adults": Farber, "Directors Join the S. E. Hinton Fan Club."

317. "We get tons": Harmetz, "Making 'The Outsiders.'"

318. "Check it out" and "I ended up": ibid.

318. "a *Godfather* for children": McCarthy, "WB Gets Coppola's 'Outsiders.'"

319. "I had been offered": Robert Scheer, "The Playboy Interview: Tom Cruise," *Playboy*, January 1990.

320. "We had workshops": ibid.

320. "*Gone With the Wind*" and "It's not": McCarthy, "WB Gets Coppola's 'Outsiders.'"

323. "sweet and youthful": Thompson and Gray, "Idols of the King."

323. "Who would have expected": David Ansen, "Coppola Courts the Kiddies" *Newsweek*, April 4, 1983.

323. "spectacularly out of touch": Vincent Canby, "Film: *Outsiders* Teen-Age Violence," *New York Times*, March 25, 1983.

323. "getting his credibility": Army Archerd, "Just for Variety," (Daily) *Variety*, May 10, 1982.

324. picture's scriptwriting credit: "Coppola Loses Script Credit on *Outsiders*," (Daily) *Variety*, June 25, 1982; Teri Ritzer, "Coppola: Another Defeat; WGA Says No 'Outsiders' Credit," *The Hollywood Reporter*, June 25, 1982.

324. "The woman simply did not": Author interview with FFC.

325. "antidote to the": Graham Fuller, "Francis Ford Coppola."

325. "schmaltzy classical": Thompson and Gray, "Idols of the King."

325. "I really started": Michael Covino, "The Coppola Conundrum," *Image*, May 17, 1987.

326. "Francis wanted that": Jean-Paul Chaillet and Elizabeth Vincent, *Francis Ford Coppola* (New York: St. Martin's Press, 1984), p. 104.

327. distribution deal: Steven Ginsberg, "Coppola's 'Fish' to Universal for Dom. Distribution," (Daily) *Variety*, June 30, 1982.

330. "the fight scene": Peter Cowie, *Coppola* (New York: Charles Scribner's Sons, 1990), p. 177.

332. "It's so silly": Lillian Ross, "Onward and Upward with the Arts: Some Figures on a

Fantasy," *The New Yorker,* November 8, 1982.

333. "Although I wanted": Milena Balandzich-Rimassa, "Coping with Coppola," *Performer,* September 1982.

333. *The Pope of Greenwich Village*: Army Archerd, "Just for Variety," (Daily) *Variety,* November 23, 1982; Army Archerd, "Just for Variety," (Daily) *Variety,* December 9, 1982; Thompson and Gray, "Idols of the King."

333. "I had some": Thompson and Gray, "Idols of the King." Pacino never did appear in the film. His role was eventually assumed by Eric Roberts in Stuart Rosenberg's 1984 movie.

334. "It's got to be": "Zoetrope Escapes Again; Nova Bid," (Daily) *Variety,* March 16, 1983.

334. "People expect me": Carol Rutter, "Coppola in His Own Words," *Image,* May 17, 1987.

13 . TAP DANCING THROUGH
MINEFIELDS

336. "I specialize": William Kennedy, "The Cotton Club Stomp," *Vanity Fair,* November 1984.

336. "*Godfather* with music": Robert Evans, *The Kid Stays in the Picture* (New York: Hyperion, 1994), p. 328.

337. "gangsters, music": Michael Daly, "The Making of *The Cotton Club*," *New York,* May 7, 1984. Daly's lengthy, detailed article, by far the best description of the making of the movie, was an invaluable source for this entire chapter.

337. "I've been involved": Aljean Harmetz, "Producer of *Popeye* to Try Cotton Club," *New York Times,* December 12, 1980.

339. "I have a sick": Mel Gussow, "Parting Film Shots: Coppola and Dutch," *New York Times,* March 22, 1984.

340. "Rosencrantz and Guildenstern": Evans, *The Kid Stays in the Picture,* p. 336.

340. "something of an industry yawn": "Zoetrope Up on the Block for 11th Time," (Daily) *Variety,* June 1, 1983.

340. "Just how much": David Robb, "Coppola's Zoetrope Studios Facing Foreclosure and Possible Public Auction," (Daily) *Variety,* January 6, 1983.

341. "blueprint" and "Background makes foreground": Daly, "The Making of *The Cotton Club*."

343. "I always thought": Author interview with FFC.

344. "I told Evans": ibid.

346. "Concision is the operative": Kennedy, "The Cotton Club Stomp."

346. "Francis just flails": Jack Kroll, "Harlem on My Mind," *Newsweek,* December 24, 1984.

347. "on the way": Kennedy, "The Cotton Club Stomp."

347. "I was the": ibid.

347. "Let's go out there": Daly, "The Making of *The Cotton Club*."

348. Bud Diamond: "Set Hearing on Alleged 'CC' Title Steal," (Daily) *Variety,* August 24, 1983.

348. "You sort of sit": Daly, "The Making of *The Cotton Club*."

349. "My main experience": Author interview with Diane Lane.

349. "I was very frustrated": David Sheff, "The Playboy Interview: Nicolas Cage," *Playboy,* September 1996.

350. "I tried very hard": Daly, "The Making of *The Cotton Club*."

350. Kaufman-Astoria Studios: Leslie Bennetts, "Astoria Studio Revives Film Era in New York," *New York Times,* August 3, 1983.

351. "an Ice Capades salute": "A Flashy $50 Million Gamble."

352. "I made a bargain": Jim Robbins, "Coppola Stays Away From 'Cotton Club' Lensing, Citing Lack of Pact, Pay," (Daily) *Variety,* October 3, 1983.

353. "I didn't know": Daly, "The Making of *The Cotton Club*."

354. "I didn't know what": Author interview with Diane Lane.

357. "He abnegated": Jeff Sherman, "Ego and Bile, Madness and Money: Inside *Cotton Club*," *Chicago Tribune,* March 2, 1985.

357. "I'm glad": Daly, "The Making of *The Cotton Club*."

358. "You see this": ibid.

358. "I am the producer": Frank Swertlow, "Mr. Cotton Club," *Los Angeles Herald-Examiner,* October 14, 1983.

358. "If you want": Evans, *The Kid Stays in the Picture,* p. 343.

358. "when all I do": ibid., p. 344.

359. "It was like": Daly, "The Making of *The Cotton Club*."

360. auction of Zoetrope: David Robb, "Jack Singer Forces Zoetrope Studios into Chapter 11 as Bank Finally Moves for an Auction," (Daily) *Variety,* August 3, 1983; "Zoetrope Studios Sale," (Daily) *Variety,*

September 7, 1983; David Robb, "Zoetrope Studio Saga at an End as Singer's $12-Mil Takes It All," (Daily) *Variety*, February 15, 1984; David Robb, "Coppola's General Now Singer Studio After Wrap of Sale," (Daily) *Variety*, March 7, 1984.

360. "The studio": Robb, "Zoetrope Studio Saga."

360. "There was more": David Thomson, "The Man Has Legs," *Film Comment*, April 1985.

361. "After that two-hour screening": ibid.

361. a series of nasty and complicated battles: Ray Loynd, "Evans Regains Some Control of 'CC' in Court Showdown," (Weekly) *Variety*, June 20, 1984; Sherman, "Ego and Bile"; Jon Lewis, *Whom God Wishes to Destroy: Francis Coppola and the New Hollywood* (Durham, North Carolina: Duke University Press, 1993), pp. 133–137; Michael Goodwin and Naomi Wise, *On the Edge: The Life and Times of Francis Coppola* (New York: William Morrow and Co., 1989), pp. 393–401; Evans, *The Kid Stays in the Picture*, pp. 345–346.

363. "It fills me": Goodwin and Wise, *On The Edge*, p. 397.

363. "I gave the triumvirate": Evans, *The Kid Stays in the Picture*, p. 345.

363. "Through hardship": Ray Loynd, "Doumanis Buyout of Evans Near 9 Mil; Plan More Joint Pictures," (Daily) *Variety*, August 22, 1984.

364. "The bigger the budget": Stephen Farber, "Francis Coppola Sallies into TV on a Fairy Tale," *New York Times*, December 27, 1984.

366. "I didn't want": Julie Salamon, "Budget Busters: 'The Cotton Club's' Battle of the Bulge," *Wall Street Journal*, December 13, 1984.

366. "*The Cotton Club* is" and "Coppola came in": ibid.

366. "Had they not": Sandra Salmans, "*Cotton Club* Is Neither a Smash nor a Disaster," *New York Times*, December 20, 1984.

366. "It is the sorry fate": Richard Corliss, "Once Upon a Time in Harlem," *Time*, December 17, 1984.

367. "Just as *Cleopatra*": Vincent Canby, "Screen: Coppola's *Cotton Club*," *New York Times*, December 14, 1984.

367. "In *The Cotton Club*": Stanley Kauffmann, "The Reel Thing," *The New Republic*, January 7, 1985.

367. "If a whiz-kid": Pauline Kael, "The Current Cinema," *The New Yorker*, January 7, 1985.

367. " one of the few": Kroll, "Harlem on My Mind."

367. "I love it!": Richard T. Jameson, "It Is, Too, Good," *Film Comment*, April 1985.

14. WARM NOSTALGIA, UNBEARABLE GRIEF

369. "I'm like that character": Patrick Goldstein, "If It Wasn't One Apocalypse, It Was Another," *Los Angeles Times*, August 5, 1996.

370. "*Peggy Sue*, I must say": Jeffrey Chown, *Hollywood Auteur: Francis Coppola* (New York: Praeger, 1988), p. 199.

371. "My model": Gene Siskel, "Celluloid Godfather," *Chicago Tribune*, October 5, 1986.

371. "magical, mystical element" and "I don't want": Stephen Farber, "Francis Coppola Sallies into TV on a Fairy Tale," *New York Times*, December 27, 1984.

371. "I guess the secret": "Direct Approach," *TV Guide*, March 2, 1985.

372. "I really wanted": Author interview with Kathleen Turner.

372. "an exploitation": David Sheff, "The Playboy Interview: Kathleen Turner," *Playboy*, May 1986.

372. "My agent tried": ibid.

373. "What's the most exciting": Aljean Harmetz, "Disney Gets Top Names for 3-D Film," *New York Times*, July 24, 1985.

374. "It's more exciting": Aljean Harmetz, "Movie Effects Inspire New Theme-Park Rides," *New York Times*, June 14, 1986.

374. *Captain Eo*: Harmetz, "Disney Gets Top Names"; "Michael Jackson New Drawing Card for Disney," *Chicago Tribune*, July 25, 1985; Richard Corliss, "Let's Go to the Feelies," *Time*, September 22, 1986.

374. "What can be exhilarating": Corliss, "Let's Go to the Feelies."

375. "It took a lot": Michael Goodwin and Naomi Wise, *On the Edge: The Life and Times of Francis Coppola* (New York: William Morrow and Co., 1989), p. 418.

375. "Francis had been wanting": Author interview with George Lucas.

376. "the highlight" to "He's a hands-off". James Greenburg, "Coppola-Cronenweth Union Rolling with *Stone*," (Daily) *Variety*, February 10, 1987.

377. "I started acting": David Sheff, "The Playboy Interview: Nicolas Cage," *Playboy*, September 1996.

378. "They were back to back": Author interview with Kathleen Turner.

378. "We made a deal": Fred Schruers, "Turner," *Premiere*, August 1991.

378. "His special talent": Gene Siskel, "Caring Coppola Brings Out the Best in Kathleen Turner," *Chicago Tribune*, October 5, 1986.

378. "the Lauren Bacall": Scheff, "The Playboy Interview: Kathleen Turner."

379. "The fact that I didn't": Author interview with Kathleen Turner.

381. "small story": Robert Lindsey, "Coppola Returns to the Vietnam Era, Minus Apocalypse," *New York Times*, May 3, 1987.

382. "Obviously, there is": ibid.

382. "very emotional" and "I don't know": Rita Kempley, "Francis Coppola and the Creative Bond," *Washington Post*, May 8, 1987.

382. "I find the movies": ibid.

382. "From the Army's standpoint": Lindsey, "Coppola Returns to the Vietnam Era." In *On the Edge* (p. 469), Coppola's biographers Michael Goodwin and Naomi Wise dispute some of Coppola's claims. There were, they claimed, times when the army threatened to withdraw its support unless certain scenes were cut from the movie: "One scene that had to go (which the book's author had actually witnessed) had a young widow spitting on her husband's grave at Arlington, shouting, 'At least now I know where you're spending your nights.' Another showed an angry sergeant punching out an enlisted man who had flunked inspection."

382. "enough men and material": ibid.

383. "I've always searched": Author interview with FFC.

385. Gio Coppola: "Coppola's Son Dies in Boating Accident," *Los Angeles Times*, May 28, 1986; "Coppola's Son Killed, O'Neal's Son Injured in Boating Accident," *Los Angeles Herald-Examiner*, May 28, 1986; "Francis Coppola's Son Killed in a Motorboating Accident," *New York Times*, May 28, 1986; "Coppola's Son Dies in Boating Mishap," (Weekly) *Variety*, May 28, 1986; "Maryland Jury Will Probe Death of Coppola's Son," *Los Angeles Herald-Examiner*, June 11, 1986; "Grand Jury to Look into Boating Death of Coppola," (Weekly) *Variety*, June 18, 1986; "The Nation," *Los Angeles Times*, July 29, 1986; "Maryland Jury Indicts O'Neal for Manslaughter in Coppola Son's Death," (Weekly) *Variety*, July 30, 1986; William Plummer, "Two Months After the Boating Accident, Griffin O'Neal Is Indicted in the Death of Friend Gio Coppola," *People*, August 11, 1986; "Milestones," *Time*, August 11, 1986; "Ryan O'Neal's Son Acquitted in Boat Manslaughter Case," *Los Angeles Times*, December 19, 1986; "Ryan O'Neal's Son Acquitted in Death," *Chicago Tribune*, December 19, 1986; "Ryan O'Neal's Son Guilty of Negligence in Death of Friend," *New York Times*, December 19, 1986; "Editor's Note," *New York Times*, December 25, 1986.

386. "[not] terribly excessive speed": "Ryan O'Neal's Son Guilty."

386. "I didn't want": ibid.

387. "a very, very old soul" and "There's no elaborate": Plummer, "Two Months After Boating Accident."

387. "I think there is something": Author interview with Eleanor Coppola.

387. "The best memories": Author interview with Frederic Forrest.

388. "I realized": David Breskin, "The Rolling Stone Interview: Francis Ford Coppola," *Rolling Stone*, February 7, 1991.

388. "I was in a dream": Author interview with FFC.

388. "Francis chose": Plummer, "Two Months After Boating Accident."

389. "I've often found": Gene Siskel, "Coppola Loves This Story—But It's Not Autobiographical," *Chicago Tribune*, August 7, 1988.

389. "a film about": ibid.

389. "He fainted": Author interview with Eleanor Coppola.

389. "Francis was so vulnerable": Author interview with James Caan.

390. "It's the saddest thing": ibid.

390. "Things were very hard": Walker, "Anjelica."

390. "The most important": Vincent Canby, "Film: *Gardens of Stone* Portrays Vietnam Era," *New York Times*, May 8, 1987.

390. "One is left": David Ansen, "Vietnam, Seen From the Grave," *Newsweek*, May 11, 1987.

390. "It's impossible": Dave Kehr, "Coppola's *Garden* Too Solemn to Grow on You," *Chicago Tribune*, May 6, 1987.

15. CON MAN, REFLECTED

391. "I like Tucker": Susan Braudy, "Francis Ford Coppola," *The Atlantic Monthly*, August 1976.

391. "Coppola is back": Ron Rosenbaum, "All-American Dream-Girl," *Mademoiselle*, December 1986.

392. "a classic" and "Francis Coppola's best": advertisement for New York Film Festival previews, published in *New York Times*, October 5, 1986.

392. "Who would expect": David Ansen, "Back to the Future," *Newsweek*, October 6, 1986.

392. "I came away": Pauline Kael, "Quests for America," *The New Yorker*, October 20, 1986.

392. "Mr. Coppola is": Vincent Canby, "*Peggy Sue Got Married*, Time Travel by Francis Coppola, *New York Times*, October 5, 1986.

392. "He is Coppola's": Stanley Kauffmann, "Lone Stars," *The New Republic*, November 10, 1986.

392. "With his dinky voice": Richard Corliss, "Just a Dream, Just a Dream," *Time*, October 13, 1986.

392. "You know, film": David Sheff, "The Playboy Interview: Nicolas Cage," *Playboy*, September 1996.

392. "It stuck with me": ibid.

393. "Tucker, in short": Brad Durrach, "Unlike Coppola's Movie Hero, Auto Innovator Preston Tucker Was as Daring, Lavish, and Flawed as His Car," *People*, September 19, 1988.

393. "a bewildering combination": Marcia Froelke Colburn, "Preston Tucker Set Chicago Dreaming—Until the Wheels Came Off," *Chicago Tribune*, August 7, 1988.

394. "People thought Tucker": Janet Maslin, "Two Directors Put Their Stamp on Their Dreams," *New York Times*, August 21, 1988.

394. "Nobody smokes" and "Tell that to": Durrach, "Unlike Coppola's Movie Hero."

396. "a *Citizen Kane*": Jack R. Nerab, "From the Desk of Francis Ford Coppola," *The Hollywood Reporter*, August 19, 1988.

396. "Preston Tucker dies": Jill Kearney, "The Road Warrior," *American Film*, June 1988.

396. "a dark kind of piece": Robert Lindsey, "Promises to Keep," *New York Times*, July 24, 1988.

396. "This isn't *Apocalypse*": Nerab, "From the Desk."

396. "I don't think": ibid.

397. "all wanted $15 million": Lindsey, "Promises to Keep."

397. "Francis can get": ibid.

398. "He told me" and "George said": Patrick McGilligan, "Arnold Schulman: Nothing But Regrets," published in the McGilligan-edited anthology *Backstory 3* (Berkeley: University of California Press, 1997), p. 322. In his interview with McGilligan, Schulman bitterly contested the coscreenwriting credit that he had to share with David Seidler. According to Schulman, Seidler had been hired by Coppola to research Tucker's life nearly ten years earlier. When Seidler asked Coppola if he'd mind if he worked his research into a screenplay, Coppola told him to "go ahead." Since the screenplay was a biography, Schulman said, it was only natural that there would be an overlap in material. "If ten writers wrote different scripts about Abe Lincoln," argued Schulman, "in all of them there's going to be a wife named Mary and a Civil War, and Abe's going to get shot in the end." Nevertheless, the Writers Guild decided to award Seidler with a cowriting credit—a decision that rankled Schulman over two decades later. "I'm still pissed off," he said. "That is one instance where every word of the script *is* mine."

399. "The late-40s world": Dave Kehr, "*Tucker* Has the Right Look, but Fable Runs Out of Fuel," *Chicago Tribune*, August 12, 1988.

399. "Vittorio Storaro": Stanley Kauffmann, "Late Summer Roundup," *The New Republic*, September 5, 1988.

400. "He has gone": Pauline Kael, "Nannies and Noncoms," *The New Yorker*, May 18, 1987.

400. "There are remnants": Hal Hinson, "*Gardens of Stone*: Rocky," *Washington Post*, May 8, 1987.

400. "The film has some": Tom O'Brien, "Screen," *Commonweal*, May 22, 1987.

401. "Clell is": Vincent Canby, "Film: *Gardens of Stone* Portrays Vietnam Era," *New York Times*, May 8, 1987.

401. "exceptionally moving" and "With a powerful": Lawrence O'Toole, "Fighting the War at Home," *Maclean's*, May 11, 1987.

401. "I demand": Michael Goodwin and Naomi Wise, *On the Edge: The Life and Times of Francis Coppola* (New York: William Morrow and Co., 1989), p. 418.

402. "It was one": Author interview with Dean Tavoularis.

402. "Could anyone else": Richard Corliss, "How Bridges Fights Boredom," *Time*, August 15, 1988.

403. "He's got it all": ibid.

404. "Preston Tucker failed": Richard Schickel, "On the Road to Utopia," *Time*, August 15, 1988.

404. "In the end": Terrence Rafferty, "The Current Cinema," *The New Yorker*, August 22, 1988.

404. "Tucker lost his company": James M. Wall, "Current Cinema: Tucker," *The Christian Century*, September 14, 1988.

404. "What makes this": Peter Travers, "Picks & Pans: Tucker," *People*, August 22, 1988.

405. "more ambitious": Caryn James, "Recipe for a Trilogy: Mix Carefully," *New York Times*, October 20, 1988.

405. "seemed to occupy": ibid.

406. "The same people": Vincent Canby, "Anthologies Can Be a Bargain," *New York Times*, March 12, 1989.

406. "I have no business": Goodwin and Wise, *On the Edge*, p. 456.

406. "My dad took me": Author interview with Sofia Coppola.

407. "I always thought": David Breskin, *Inner Views: Filmmakers in Conversation* (New York: De Capo Press, 1997), p. 36.

408. "a mess": Richard A. Blake, "NY, NY," *America*, April 15, 1989.

408. "self-indulgence without": Brian D. Johnson, "Manhattan Triangle," *Maclean's*, March 13, 1989.

408. "blatantly silly": Tom O'Brien, "Truth by Drollery," *Commonweal*, April 7, 1989.

408. "Francis Ford Coppola['s] segment: Stuart Klawans, "Films," *The Nation*, March 27, 1989.

408. "dull" and "Through *Apocalypse Now*": Stanley Kauffmann, "Manhattan Moods," *The New Republic*, March 27, 1989.

408. "Coppola's head doesn't": Pauline Kael, "Two-Base Hit," *The New Yorker*, March 20, 1989.

409. "The original screenplay": Breskin, *Inner Views*, p. 36.

409. "so big and complicated": "Take One," *People*, January 9, 1989.

410. "swing from the past": "Italy," *The Hollywood Reporter*, May 30, 1989.

410. "economic blackmail": Liz Smith, "Liz Smith" (syndicated newspaper column), *Los Angeles Herald-Tribune*, January 5, 1989.

410. "I want to be free": "Take One."

16. THE BIGGEST HOME MOVIE IN HISTORY

411. "When I was a kid": Barbara Grizzuti Harrison, "Godfather III," *Life*, November 1990.

412. "How can you": Cyndi Stivers, "Family Reunion," *Premiere*, January 1991.

413. "The focus": Gerald Gardner and Harriet Modell Gardner, *The Godfather Movies: A Pictorial History* (New York: Wings Books, 1993), p. 152.

414. "It's a little bit": Brian D. Johnson, "A Godfather's Christmas," *Maclean's*, December 24, 1990.

415. "I can assure you": Peter J. Boyer, "Under the Gun," *Vanity Fair*, June 1990.

416. "That's where": Peter Cowie, "Coppola Remarried to the Mob," (Weekly) *Variety*, January 3, 1990.

417. "The idea of": Larry Rohter, "Coppola: It Was an Offer He Couldn't Refuse," *New York Times*, December 23, 1990.

417. "We'd work for hours": Jack Kroll, "The Corleones Return," *Newsweek*, December 24, 1990.

417. "We're losing thousands": Stivers, "Family Reunion."

422. "I did not think": ibid.

422. "Look, if I once again": Johnson, "A Godfather's Christmas."

423. "She was fabulous": Boyer, "Under the Gun."

424. "the director of": Eleanor Coppola, "The Godfather Diary," *Vogue*, December 1990.

424. "We had one": Author interview with Alex Tavoularis.

425. "I could hear": Boyer, "Under the Gun."

425. "I told Sofia": Eleanor Coppola, "The Godfather Diary."

425. "I definitely wasn't": Author interview with Sofia Coppola.

425. "She had a big finger": David Breskin, *Inner Views: Filmmakers in Conversation* (New York: De Capo Press, 1997), p. 26.

427. "High-anxiety time": Harlan Lebo, *The Godfather Legacy* (New York: Fireside, 1997).

427. "It was a jolt": Johnson, "A Godfather's Christmas."

427. "Well-meaning people": Eleanor Coppola, "The Godfather Diary."

428. "I looked around": Peter Biskind, *The Godfather Companion* (New York: HarperPerennial, 1990), pp. 154–155.

428. "I think that Paramount": Rohter, "Coppola: It Was an Offer He Couldn't Refuse."

428. "Basically, what they said": Boyer, "Under the Gun."

428. "Had Sofia not": Author interview with Talia Shire.

429. "the biggest home movie": Kroll, "The Corleones Return."

429. another financial crisis: "Coppola Files Bankruptcy," *Long Beach Press-Telegram*, January 26, 1990; Michael Cieply, "Coppola Seeks Bankruptcy Protection," *Los Angeles Times*, January 26, 1990; "Coppola's Zoetrope Files for Chapter 11 Protection," *Wall Street Journal*, January 26, 1990; Jim Harwood, "Coppola Files for Bankruptcy,"

(Daily) *Variety*, January 26, 1990; Andrea King, "Coppola, Zoetrope Prods. File for Bankruptcy Protection," *The Hollywood Reporter*, January 26, 1990; Richard Gold, "Coppola Bankruptcy Baffles Creditors and Colleagues," (Weekly) *Variety*, January 31, 1990; John Hazelton, "Coppola Files for Bankruptcy," *Screen International*, February 3, 1990; Michael Cieply, "Coppola Ordered to Pay $4.8 Million in '81 Debt," *Los Angeles Times*, February 9, 1990; "Interest Adds to Coppola's Debt," (Daily) *Variety*, February 12, 1990; Peter Blavacek, "Apocalylpse Now, Chapter Eleven," (Weekly) *Variety*, March 10, 1990; Michael Cieply, "A Filmmaker's Finances Face a Court Assault," *Los Angeles Times*, June 3, 1990.

429. "The filing is intended": Harwood, "Coppola Files for Bankruptcy."

430. "were a function" and "Every film": Biskind, *The Godfather Companion*, p. 156.

431. "No one was more": Kroll, "The Corleones Return."

431. "I've had bank executives": Jack Kroll, "The Offer He Didn't Refuse," *Newsweek*, May 28, 1990.

432. "It was just": Stivers, "Family Reunion."

432. According to the terms: Cieply, "A Filmmaker's Finances Face a Court Assault"; Michael Cieply, "Coppola Agrees to Settle Debt with Developer," *Los Angeles Times*, July 26, 1990; "Coppola Won't Confirm Singer Settlement," (Daily) *Variety*, July 27, 1990; "Coppola Settling Debt with Canadian," *The Hollywood Reporter*, July 27, 1990; "Coppola Settles Old Debt," *Long Beach Press-Telegram*, July 29, 1990; "Coppola Near Debt Deal," (Weekly) *Variety*, August 1, 1990; "Coppola, Singer Reach Settlement," (Daily) *Variety*, August 13, 1990.

432. "Paramount was very kind": Army Archerd, "Just for Variety," (Daily) *Variety*, September 17, 1990.

432. "unusually weak": Larry Rohter, "*Godfather III* Is Producing Unrest," *New York Times*, October 27, 1990.

432. "It's sort of like": Johnson, "A Godfather's Christmas."

433. "It's unfortunate": "Francis Ford Coppola," *People*, December 31, 1990.

433. "the fear and terror": Kroll, "The Corleones Return."

433. "One of these": Jack Kroll, "Where in the Pantheon Does G3 Sit?," *Newsweek*, December 24, 1990.

433. "Few sequels can match": Peter Travers, "A Mob King Lear," *Rolling Stone*, January 24, 1991.

433. "[her] gosling gracelessness": Richard Corliss, "Schemes and Dreams for Christmas," *Time*, December 24, 1990.

433. "almost totally lacking": "Picks and Pans: *The Godfather, Part III*," *People*, January 14, 1991.

433. "It's obvious": Pauline Kael, "Vanity, Vanities," *The New Yorker*, January 14, 1991.

434. "Garcia's turbulent": Travers, "A Mob King Lear."

434. "Garcia, who first became": Stanley Kauffmann, "Blood and Thunder," *The New Republic*, January 21, 1991.

434. "Talia Shire gives": Richard Alleva, "Less than Epic," *Commonweal*, February 22, 1991.

434. "The strongest performance": Kael, "Vanity, Vanities."

17. BONFIRE OF THE VAMPIRES

435. "Eternal life is not": Gerri Hirshey, "Stand By Your Bat," *GQ*, December 1992.

435. "I am no lunatic": James V. Hart, screenplay for *Bram Stoker's Dracula*.

435. "What is there about me": Jack Kroll, "The Corleones Return," *Newsweek*, December 24, 1990.

435. "In another month": Larry Rohter, "Coppola: It Was an Offer He Couldn't Refuse," *New York Times*, December 23, 1990.

436. "How any film": Francis Coppola, "'Godfather, Part III' Anything But a Flop," *New York Times*, March 23, 1991.

436. "I've always wanted": Army Archerd, "Just for Variety," (Daily) *Variety*, March 18, 1991.

437. "I wanted to make": Hirshey, "Stand By Your Bat."

437. "It was a brilliant": Francis Ford Coppola, "Journals 1989–1993," in *Projections 3: Filmmakers on Filmmaking*, eds. John Boorman and Walter Donahue (London: Faber and Faber, 1994), p. 17.

438. "I thought it would be great": Brian D. Johnson, "The Vampire Vogue," *Maclean's*, November 16, 1992.

438. "It was unbelievable": Rachel Abramowitz, "Neck Romance," *Premiere*, December 1992.

438. "You're picking up": Coppola, "Journals 1989–1993."

439. "like a Prokofiev score": ibid.

439. "to approach the effects": Graham Fuller, "Francis Ford Coppola,"

439. "It was clear": Francis Ford Coppola and Eiko Ishioka, *Coppola and Eiko on Bram Stoker's Dracula*, ed. Susan Dworkin (San Francisco: HarperCollins, 1992), p. 19.

439. "the kind of people": Abramowitz, "Neck Romance."

441. "I remember *Sid and Nancy*": Manobla Dargis, "His Bloody Valentine," *Village Voice*, November 24, 1992.

441. "Few women": Terrence Rafferty, "The Current Cinema," *The New Yorker*, November 30, 1992.

441. "He's handsome and needful": Dave Kehr, "Long in the Tooth," *Chicago Tribune*, November 13, 1992.

441. "I can exhaust": Susan Dworkin, "A Vicious Undertaking," *New York Times Magazine*, November 8, 1992.

441. "Gary just seemed": Abramowitz, "Neck Romance."

441. "We tried to get": Janet Maslin, "Neither Dracula Nor Rumor Frightens Coppola," *New York Times*, November 15, 1992.

442. "The Lucy part": Francis Ford Coppola and James V. Hart, *Bram Stoker's Dracula: The Film and the Legend* (New York: Newmarket Press, 1992), p. 108.

442. "an erotic dream": Maslin, "Neither Dracula Nor Rumor."

442. "I brought in Greta": Trish Deitch Roher, "Coppola's Bloody Valentine," *Entertainment Weekly*, November 20, 1992.

443. "These things are common": Coppola, "Journals 1989–1993," p. 16.

443. "I had sixty hours": Author interview with Eleanor Coppola.

444. "Anyway, between the Napa estate": Coppola, "Journals 1989–1993," p. 17.

444. Blancaneaux Lodge: Lois Armstrong, "A Visit to Paradise with Francis Ford Coppola," *People*, April 4, 1994; Susan Cheever, "Francis Ford Coppola in Belize," *Architectural Digest*, September 1995.

445. "It had been built": Cheever, "Francis Ford Coppola in Belize."

446. "The issue was not": Abramowitz, "Neck Romance."

446. "He'd get together": Dworkin, "A Vicious Undertaking."

447. "You have to have": Roher, "Coppola's Bloody Valentine."

447. "It was like": ibid.

447. "I don't know": Abramowitz, "Neck Romance."

448. "He wanted to command": ibid.

448. "yet another overproducing plant": Coppola and Ishioka, *Coppola and Eiko on Bram Stoker's Dracula*, p. 93.

448. "We have tried": Coppola and Hart, *Bram Stoker's Dracula*, p. 5.

449. "Nobody's ever shot": Hirshey, "Stand By Your Bat."

449. "We put rock": Coppola and Hart, *Bram Stoker's Dracula*, p. 157.

449. "I just thought": Roher, "Coppola's Bloody Valentine."

450. "on budget": Army Archerd, "Just for Variety," (Daily) *Variety*, February 4, 1992.

450. "It's romantic": ibid.

450. "That was one": Coppola, "Journals 1989–1993," p. 24.

451. "If I really total out": ibid., p. 26.

451. he filed once again: John Lippman, "Coppola Files for Bankruptcy a Third Time, " *Los Angeles Times*, July 1, 1992; Matt Rothman, "Coppola Files for Bankruptcy," (Daily) *Variety*, July 1, 1992; Jeffrey Daniels, "Coppola Again Files Chapter 11 with Zoetrope," *The Hollywood Reporter*, July 1, 1992; "Coppola Files for Bankruptcy," *New York Times*, July 2, 1992.

451. "The bankruptcy filing": Daniels, "Coppola Again Files Chapter 11."

452. "They killed": Army Archerd, "Just for Variety," (Daily) *Variety*, October 27, 1992.

452. "This most recent": Richard A. Blake, "Blood Transfusion," *America*, January 23, 1993.

452. "Now comes *Bram Stoker's Dracula*": Stanley Kauffmann, "The Haunted and the Hunted," *The New Republic*, December 14, 1992.

453. "the last nail": Christopher Sharrett, "The Fall of Francis Coppola," *USA Today* (magazine), March 1993.

453. "Coppola does deserve": Gene Siskel, "Coppola's Sumptuous *Dracula* Needs a Little More Bite," *Chicago Tribune*, November 13, 1992.

453. "Coppola's remake": David Ansen, "L'Amour from Cradle to Coffin," *Newsweek*, November 23, 1992.

453. "With its gorgeous sets": Vincent Canby, "Coppola's Dizzying Vision of Dracula," *New York Times*, November 13, 1992.

18. FULL RECOVERY

454. "There is ever less": "Quotes of the Week," *Screen International*, May 24, 1996.

454. "All I feel": Karen Hershenson, "For Francis Ford Coppola, the Time Is Now," *Long Beach Press-Telegram*, August 4, 1996.

455. "I've run off": Francis Ford Coppola, "Journals 1989–1993," in *Projections 3: Filmmakers on Filmmakers*, eds. John Boorman and Walter Donohue (London: Faber and Faber, 1994), p. 37.

455. "There's no distress": Army Archerd, "Coppola Is 'Debt-Free,' 'Calm,'" (Weekly) *Variety*, February 22, 1993.

456. "a new frontier": Army Archerd, "Just for Variety," (Daily) *Variety*, February 10, 1993.

456. "It won't be reminiscent": Army Archerd, "Just for Variety," (Daily) *Variety*, September 1, 1993.

457. "attend[ing] to all": Army Archerd, "Just for Variety," (Daily) *Variety*, June 17, 1994.

457. "a lot like": "Hollywood and Vines: Francis Ford Coppola," *Vis a Vis*, October 1991.

457. "I'm lucky": "The Great Life," *The Hollywood Reporter*, June 23, 1993.

458. "Everyone thought": Susan Cheever, "Francis Ford Coppola in Belize," *Architectural Digest*, September 1995.

458. "Lots of people": David Rosengarten, "On Coppola's Plate, It's Food, Not Film," *New York Times*, February 16, 1994.

459. plans for *Pinocchio*: Louise Bateman, "Coppola Joins Henson's String," *Screen International*, July 15, 1994; Army Archerd, "Just for Variety," (Daily) *Variety*, August 12, 1994; Army Archerd, "Just for Variety," (Daily) *Variety*, December 22, 1994; Army Archerd, "Just for Variety," (Daily) *Variety*, January 9, 1995.

460. "I'd only attempt": Archerd, "Just for Variety," August 12, 1994.

460. "the product of": ibid.

460. "My friend Bill Graham": Author interview with FFC.

461. "You've got to": Archerd, "Just for Variety," December 22, 1994.

461. "We're trying": ibid.

461. "Every time I drove": Robyn Ballard, "Francis Ford Coppola Buys Napa Valley's Historic Inglenook Estate from Heublein," *Wine Spectator*, January 31, 1995.

461. "It's always bugged me": Florence Fabricant, "Film Director's Winery Adds Estate Next Door," *New York Times*, March 8, 1995.

462. "It's like a movie idea": ibid.

462. "warm fable": Belinda Luscombe, "Coppola's Wining Ways," *Time*, August 17, 1995.

462. "I've always tried": Martyn Palmer, "More Grapes, Less Wrath," *The Times* (London), October 9, 1996.

462. "I remember being pinned": ibid.

463. "As a kid": Peter Biskind, "Francis Ford Coppola," *Premiere*, September 1996.

463. "When are you going": Stephen Whitty, "Child's Play: Francis Ford Coppola Surveys His Career, His Future, and His Craft," *San Jose Mercury News*, August 8, 1996.

463. "too difficult": Army Archerd, "Just for Variety," (Daily) *Variety*, January 9, 1995.

463. "an informal": "Hey, Jack Kerouac: The Line Forms Here," *New York*, January 30, 1995.

464. "He's childlike": Terry Lawson, "Robin Williams Puts a Different Spin on His Man-Child Persona in *Jack*," *Detroit Free Press*, August 5, 1996.

464. "Williams works hard": Roger Ebert, "*Jack* Stunts Growth by Going for Obvious Payoffs," *Chicago Sun-Times*, August 9, 1996.

464. "In the case of": Biskind, "Francis Ford Coppola."

465. "By the end": Lawson, "Robin Williams Puts Different Spin."

465. "It was great": Palmer, "More Grapes, Less Wrath."

466. "It was great, liberating": Author interview with Diane Lane.

466. "This action arises": Stephen Galloway, "Coppola, Fuchs Sue Warners over 'Pinocchio,'" *The Hollywood Reporter*, September 14, 1995.

467. "To say": Author interview with FFC.

467. "It's obvious": Nick Vivarrelli, "Big Mac Attack on Film Bemoaned by Coppola," *The Hollywood Reporter*, May 13, 1996.

468. "My remarks": Francis Coppola, "Angry Coppola," *The Hollywood Reporter*, May 21, 1996.

468. "You go to movies": Whitty, "Child's Play."

468. "These days": Barbara Shulgasser, "A Conversation with Coppola," *San Francisco Examiner*, July 31, 1996.

469. "Coppola has been expanding": Gene Siskel, "Tiresome *Jack* Belabors a Joke That Doesn't Work," *Chicago Tribune*, August 9, 1996.

469. "My best guess": Ebert, "*Jack* Stunts Growth."

469. "the sort of 'catchy'": Owen Gleiberman, "*Jack*," *Entertainment Weekly*, August 9, 1996.

469. "If Jack is": Stephen Whitty, "In *Jack*, Robin Williams Finds His Inner Child—No, Not Again," Knight-Ridder/Tribune News Service, August 8, 1996.

470. "in a state": Gleiberman, "*Jack.*"
470. "a pleasant enough picture": Michael Wilmington, "Robin Williams, Francis Frod Coppola Are Trapped in the *Jack* Box," *Chicago Tribune*, August 9, 1996.
470. "I suspect most": ibid.
470. "I had never read": Bernard Weinraub, "Grisham's Law Attracts Coppola," *New York Times*, November 7, 1997.
472. "I thought I'd make": Mark Caro, "Coppola's Studio Work May Not Be Totally Satisfying, But It's an Offer He Can't Refuse," *Chicago Tribune*, November 20, 1997.
473. "It's very much economics": Roger Ebert, "Days of Wine and Grosses," *Chicago Sun-Times*, November 23, 1997.
474. "The whole idea": Cynthia Robins, "On the Brink of Stardom," *San Francisco Examiner*, November 18, 1997.
474. "Francis teaches you": ibid.
474. "I'll do anything": Peter Biskind, "Trial by Fire," *Premiere*, December 1997.
474. "I opened the door": ibid.
475. "The filmmaker and the cast": Janet Maslin, "A Young Legal Eagle Flies with Vultures," *New York Times*, November 21, 1997.
475. "form a bridge": Scott Collins, "Francis Ford Coppola, Magazine Publisher," *Los Angeles Times*, February 24, 1997.
476. "Most everyone agrees": Janet Allen, "Double Exposure," *New York Times*, June 22, 1997.
476. "a development office": ibid.
477. "I love the stories": Francis Coppola, "Letter to the Reader," *Zoetrope: All Story*, Winter 1998.
477. "Television is like cooking": Cynthia Robins, "Coppola: Larger than Life," *San Francisco Examiner*, November 16, 1997.
478. "proves to be": Michael Wilmington, "Courting Success," *Chicago Tribune*, November 21, 1997.
478. "Coppola gets to show": Barbara Shulgasser, "The Sun Shines on Coppola's *Rainmaker*," *San Francisco Examiner*, November 21, 1997.
478. "The good news": Bob Thomas, "*Rainmaker* Grounded in Reality," Associated Press wire review, November 21, 1997.
479. "I would say": Chris Nashawaty, "A Coppola Things," *Entertainment Weekly*, November 21, 1997.
479. "If someone gave me": Patrick Goldstein, "If It Wasn't One Apocalypse, It Was Another," *Los Angeles Times*, August 5, 1996.

EPILOGUE

481. "Who isn't a director-for-hire": Author interview with FFC.
482. "Their days are numbered": Benedict Carver, "New Dreams for Zoetrope: Coppola Refocuses Studio's Aims," (Daily) *Variety*, July 20, 1998.
482. His *Pinocchio* lawsuit: Janet Shprintz, "Coppola Challenges Studio Power in Suit," (Daily) *Variety*, January 26, 1998; Janet Shprintz, "Jiminy Cricket, Who's to Believe?," (Daily) *Variety*, June 8, 1998; Peter Bart, "The Godfather's Vendetta," (Weekly) *Variety*, June 29, 1998; "Coppola Awarded Damages in Warner Bros. Lawsuit," *Wall Street Journal*, July 6, 1998; Andrew Pollack, "Coppola Awarded $80 Million for Unmade Pinocchio Movie," *New York Times*, July 10, 1998; Janet Shprintz, "Coppola Awarded $60 Million in Damages," (Daily) *Variety*, July 11, 1998; "Winners," *Entertainment Weekly*, July 17, 1998; Janet Shprintz, "Will WB Verdict Spur Script Shakedown?," (Daily) *Variety*, July 20, 1998; "People in the News," *U.S. News & World Report*, July 20, 1998; "So Sue Me," *Time*, July 20, 1998; Judy Brennan and Chris Nashawaty, "Coppola Bucks," *Entertainment Weekly*, July 24, 1998; "Coppola's Award Is Reduced in Suit Against Warner Bros.," *Wall Street Journal*, October 16, 1998.
482. "Tales of power": Shprintz, "Jiminy Cricket."
483. "The real result": Shprintz, "Will WB Verdict Spur Script Shakedown?"
485. "Coppola was like": Shprintz, "Jiminy Cricket."
485. "that he would bring" and "I was emotional": Brennan and Nashawaty, "Coppola Bucks."
485. "a rude and arrogant": Shprintz, "Coppola Awarded $60 Million."
485. "Warner Bros. has traditionally": Pollack, "Coppola Awarded $80 Million."
485. "a vendetta": ibid.
485. "The jury is sending": Shprintz, "Coppola Awarded $60 Million."
485. "simply ludicrous": "People in the News."
485. "Since the jury found": Shprintz, "Coppola Awarded $60 Million."
485. "Warner Brothers expects": "Coppola Awarded Damages."
485. "substantial evidence" and "malice and fraud": "Coppola's Award Is Reduced."
486. "it would have been": Brennan and Nashawaty, "Coppola Bucks."

Filmography

FILMS DIRECTED BY FRANCIS FORD COPPOLA

Tonight for Sure (1961)

Screenplay: Jerry Shaffer and Francis Ford Coppola
Direction: Francis Ford Coppola
Photography (black and white) : Jack Hill
Art Direction: Albert Locatelli
Editing: Ronald Waller
Music: Carmine Coppola
Produced by Francis Ford Coppola. 75 minutes.

Dementia 13 (1963)

Screenplay: Francis Ford Coppola
Direction: Francis Ford Coppola
Photography (black and white) : Charles Hannawalt
Art Direction: Albert Locatelli
Editing: Stewart O'Brien
Music: Ronald Stein
Cast: William Campbell *(Richard Holoran)*, Luana Anders *(Louise Holoran)*, Bart Patton *(Billy Holoran)*, Mary Mitchell *(Kane)*, Patrick Magee *(Justin Caleb)*, Eithne Dunn *(Lady Holoran)*, Peter Reed *(John Holoran)*, Karl Schanzer *(Simon)*, Ron Perry *(Arthur)*, Derry O'Donovan *(Lillian)*, Barbara Dowling *(Kathleen)*
Produced by Francis Ford Coppola for Roger Corman Productions. 97 minutes.

You're a Big Boy Now (1966)

Screenplay: Francis Ford Coppola, based on the novel by David Benedictus
Direction: Francis Ford Coppola
Photography (Eastmancolor) : Andy Laszlo
Art Direction: Vassele Fotopoulos
Costumes: Theoni V. Aldredge
Choreography: Robert Tucker
Editing: Aram Avakian
Music: Bob Prince; songs by John Sebastian, performed by the Lovin' Spoonful
Editing: Melvin Shapiro
Cast: Peter Kastner *(Bernard Chanticleer)*, Elizabeth Hartman *(Barbara Darling)*, Geraldine Page *(Margery Chanticleer)*, Julie Harris *(Miss Thing)*, Rip Torn *(I. H. Chanticleer)*, Tony Bill *(Raef)*, Karen Black *(Amy)*, Michael Dunn *(Richard Mudd)*, Dolph Sweet *(Francis Graf)*, Michael O'Sullivan *(Kurt Doughty)*
Produced by Phil Feldman for Seven Arts, released by Warner Bros. 96 minutes.

Finian's Rainbow (1968)

Screenplay: E. Y. Harburg and Fred Saidy, based on the Broadway play (book by E. Y. Harburg and Fred Saidy, lyrics by E. Y. Harburg, music by Burton Lane)
Direction: Francis Ford Coppola
Photography (Technicolor, Panavision) : Philip Lathrop
Production Design: Hilyard M. Brown

Music Direction: Ray Heindorf
Associate Music Supervisor: Ken Darby
Costumes: Dorothy Jeakins
Choreography: Hermes Pan
Sound: M. A. Merrick and Dan Wallin
Editing: Melvin Shapiro
Cast: Fred Astaire *(Finian McLonergan)*, Petula Clark *(Sharon McLonergan)*, Tommy Steele *(Og)*, Don Francks *(Woody Mahoney)*, Barbara Hancock *(Susan the Silent)*, Keenan Wynn *(Senator "Billboard" Rawkins)*, Al Freeman, Jr. *(Howard)*, Ronald Colby *(Buzz Collins)*, Dolph Sweet *(Sheriff)*, Wright King *(District Attorney)*, Louil Silas *(Henry)*, Brenda Arnau *(Sharecropper)*, Avon Long, Roy Glen, Jerster Hairston *(Passion Pilgrim Gospellers)*
Produced by Joseph Landon for Warner Bros.-Seven Arts. Associate producer: Joel
    Freeman. 145 minutes.

The Rain People (1969)

Screenplay: Francis Ford Coppola
Direction: Francis Ford Coppola
Photography (Technicolor): Wilmer Butler
Art Direction: Leon Ericksen
Sound: Nathan Boxer
Sound Montage: Walter Murch
Editing: Blackie Malkin
Music: Ronald Stein
Cast: James Caan *(Kilgannon)*, Shirley Knight *(Natalie Ravenna)*, Robert Duvall *(Gordon)*, Marya Zimmet *(Rosalie)*, Tom Aldredge *(Mr. Alfred)*, Laurie Crews *(Ellen)*, Andrew Duncan *(Artie)*, Margaret Fairchild *(Marion)*, Sally Gracie *(Beth)*, Alan Manson *(Lou)*, Robert Modica *(Vinny)*
Produced by Bart Patton and Ronald Colby (American Zoetrope) for Warner Bros.–
    Seven Arts. Production associates: George Lucas and Mona Skager. 101 minutes.

The Godfather (1972)

Screenplay: Mario Puzo and Francis Ford Coppola, based on the novel by Mario Puzo
Direction: Francis Ford Coppola
Photography (Technicolor): Gordon Willis
Production Design: Dean Tavoularis
Art Direction: Warren Clymer
Costumes: Anna Hill Johnstone
Sound: Christopher Newman
Editing: William Reynolds and Peter Zinner
Music: Nino Rota, with additional music by Carmine Coppola
Cast: Marlon Brando *(Don Vito Corleone)*, Al Pacino *(Michael Corleone)*, James Caan *(Sonny Corleone)*, Richard Castellano *(Clemenza)*, Robert Duvall *(Tom Hagen)*, Sterling Hayden *(McCluskey)*, John Marley *(Jack Woltz)*, Richard Conte *(Barzini)*, Al Lettieri *(Sollozzo)*, Diane Keaton *(Kay Adams)*, Abe Vigoda *(Tessio)*, Talia Shire *(Connie)*, Gianni Russo *(Carlo Rizzi)*, John Cazale *(Fredo Corleone)*, Rudy Bond *(Cuneo)*, Al Martino *(Johnny Fontane)*, Morgana King *(Mama Corleone)*, Lenny Montanna *(Luca Brasi)*, John Martino *(Paulie Gatto)*, Salvatore Corsitto *(Bonasera)*, Richard Bright *(Neri)*, Alex Rocco *(Moe Greene)*, Tony Giorgio *(Bruno Tattaglia)*, Vito Scotti *(Nazorine)*, Tere Livrano *(Theresa Hagen)*, Victor Rendina *(Philip Tattaglia)*, Jeannie Linero *(Lucy Mancini)*, Julie Gregg *(Sandra Corleone)*, Ardell Sheidan *(Mrs. Clemenza)*, Simonetta Stefanelli *(Apollinia)*, Angelo Infanti *(Fabrizio)*, Corrado Gaipa *(Don Tommasino)*,

Franco Citti *(Calo)*, Saro Urzi *(Vitelli)*
Produced by Albert S. Ruddy (Alfran Productions) for Paramount. Associate pro-
    ducer: Gray Frederickson. 175 minutes.

The Conversation (1974)

Screenplay: Francis Ford Coppola
Direction: Francis Ford Coppola
Photography (Technicolor): Bill Butler
Production Design: Dean Tavoularis
Set Decoration: Doug von Koss
Costumes: Aggie Guerard Rodgers
Supervising Editor, Sound Montage, and Rerecording: Walter
Murch
Editing: Richard Chew
Music: David Shire
Technical Advisers: Hal Lipset, Leo Jones, and Jim Bloom
Cast: Gene Hackman *(Harry Caul)*, John Cazale *(Stan)*, Allen Garfield *(Bernie
Moran)*, Frederic Forrest *(Mark)*, Cindy Williams *(Ann)*, Michael Higgins *(Paul)*, Eliza-
beth MacRae *(Meredith)*, Harrison Ford *(Martin Stett)*, Robert Duvall *(the Director)*,
Mark Wheeler *(Receptionist)*, Teri Garr *(Amy)*, Robert Shields *(Mime)*, Phoebe Alexan-
der *(Lurleen)*
Produced by Francis Ford Coppola and Fred Roos (Coppola Company) for The
    Directors Company, released through Paramount. 113 minutes.

The Godfather, Part II (1974)

Screenplay: Francis Ford Coppola and Mario Puzo, based on events in the novel
by Mario Puzo
Direction: Francis Ford Coppola
Photography (Technicolor): Gordon Willis
Production Design: Dean Tavoularis
Art Direction: Angelo Graham
Set Decoration: George R. Neison
Costumes: Theodora van Runkle
Sound Montage and Rerecording: Walter Murch
Editing: Peter Zinner, Barry Malkin, and Richard Marks
Music: Nino Rota, conducted by Carmine Coppola
Cast: Al Pacino *(Michael Corleone)*, Robert Duvall *(Tom Hagen)*, Diane Keaton *(Kay
Adams)*, Robert De Niro *(Vito Corleone)*, John Cazale *(Fredo Corleone)*, Talia Shire *(Con-
nie Corleone)*, Lee Strasberg *(Hyman Roth)*, Michael V. Gazzo *(Frank Pentangeli)*, G. D.
Spradlin *(Senator Pat Geary)*, Richard Bright *(Al Neri)*, Gaston Moschin *(Fanucci)*, Tom
Rosqui *(Rocco Lampone)*, B. Kirby, Jr. *(Clemenza)*, Frank Sivero *(Genco)*, Francesca de
Sapio *(Young Mama Corleone)*, Morgana King *(Mama Corleone)*, Mariana Hill *(Deanna
Corleone)*, Leopoldo Trieste *(Signor Roberto)*, Dominic Chianese *(Johnny Ola)*, Amerigo
Tot *(Bodyguard)*, Troy Donahue *(Merle Johnson)*, John Aprea *(Tessio)*, Joe Spinell *(Willi
Cicci)*
Produced by Francis Ford Coppola for The Coppola Company/Paramount.
    Associate Producer: Mona Skager. Coproducers: Gray Frederickson and Fred
    Roos. 200 minutes.

Apocalypse Now (1979)

Screenplay: John Milius and Francis Ford Coppola, based on the novel *Heart of
Darkness* by Joseph Conrad

Direction: Francis Ford Coppola
Photography (Technicolor, Technovision): Vittorio Storaro
Second-Unit Photography: Stephen H. Burum
Insert Photography: Caleb Deschanel
Production Design: Dean Tavoularis
Art Direction: Angelo Graham
Costume Supervision: Charles E. James
Sound Montage/Design: Walter Murch
Supervisory Sound Editing: Richard Cirincione
Creative Consultant: Dennis Jakob
Offscreen Commentary: Michael Herr
Editing: Walter Murch, Gerald B. Greenberg, and Lisa Fruchtman
Music: Carmine Coppola and Francis Ford Coppola
Cast: Marlon Brando *(Col. Walter E. Kurtz)*, Robert Duvall *(Lt. Col. Bill Kilgore)*, Martin Sheen *(Capt. Benjamin L. Willard)*, Frederic Forrest *("Chef" Hicks)*, Albert Hall *(Chief Phillips)*, Sam Bottoms *(Lance B. Johnson)*, Larry Fishburne *("Clean")*, Dennis Hopper *(Photojournalist)*, G. D. Spradlin *(General Corman)*, Harrison Ford *(Colonel Lucas)*, Jerry Ziesmer *(Civilian)*, Scott Glenn *(Capt. Richard Colby)*
Produced by Francis Ford Coppola for Omni Zoetrope. Associate producer: Mona Skager. Coproducers: Fred Roos, Gray Frederickson, and Tom Sternberg. 153 minutes.

One from the Heart (1982)

Screenplay: Armyan Bernstein and Francis Ford Coppola, from the original screenplay by Armyan Bernstein
Direction: Francis Ford Coppola
Photography (Technicolor): Vittorio Storaro
Special Visual Effects: Robert Swarthe
Electronic Cinema: Thomas Brown, Murdo Laird, Anthony St. John, and Michael Lehmann, in cooperation with Sony Corporation
Production Design: Dean Tavoularis
Art Direction: Angelo Graham
Costumes: Ruth Morley
Choreography: Kenny Ortega
Sound Design: Richard Beggs
Editing: Anne Goursaud, with Rudi Fehr and Randy Roberts
Songs and Music: Tom Waits, sung by Tom Waits and Crystal Gayle
Cast: Frederic Forrest *(Hank)*, Teri Garr *(Frannie)*, Raul Julia *(Ray)*, Nastassia Kinski *(Leila)*, Lainie Kazan *(Maggie)*, Harry Dean Stanton *(Moe)*, Allen Goorwitz [Garfield] *(Restaurant Owner)*, Jeff Hamlin *(Airline Ticket Agent)*, Italia Coppola *(Woman in Elevator)*, Carmine Coppola *(Man in Elevator)*
Produced by Gray Frederickson and Fred Roos for Zoetrope Studios. Associate producer: Mona Skager. Executive producer: Bernard Gersten. Coproducer: Armyan Bernstein. 101 minutes.

The Outsiders (1983)

Screenplay: Kathleen Knutsen Rowell, from the novel by S. E. Hinton
Direction: Francis Ford Coppola
Photography (Technicolor, Panavision): Stephen H. Burum
Special Visual Effects: Robert Swarthe
Production Design: Dean Tavoularis
Costumes: Marge Bowers

Sound: Jim Webb
Sound Design: Richard Beggs
Editing: Anne Goursaud
Music: Carmine Coppola
Cast: Matt Dillon *(Dallas Winston),* Ralph Macchio *(Johnny Cade),* C. Thomas Howell *(Ponyboy Curtis),* Patrick Swayze *(Darrel Curtis),* Rob Lowe *(Sodapop Curtis),* Emilio Estevez *(Two-Bit Mathews),* Tom Cruise *(Steve Randle),* Glenn Withrow *(Tim Shephard),* Diane Lane *(Cherry Valance),* Leif Garrett *(Bob Sheldon),* Darren Dalton *(Randy Anderson),* Michelle Meyrink *(Marcia),* Gailard Sartain *(Jerry),* Tom Waits *(Buck Merrill),* William Smith *(Clerk)*
Produced by Fred Roos and Gray Frederickson for Zoetrope Studios/Ponyboy Productions. Associate producer: Gian-Carlo Coppola. 91 minutes.

Rumble Fish (1983)

Screenplay: S. E. Hinton and Francis Ford Coppola, based on the novel by
S. E. Hinton
Direction: Francis Ford Coppola
Photography (black and white): Stephen H. Burum
Production Design: Dean Tavoularis
Costumes: Marge Bowers
Sound: David Parker
Sound Design: Richard Beggs
Editing: Barry Malkin
Music: Stewart Copeland
Cast: Matt Dillon *(Rusty-James),* Mickey Rourke *(the Motorcycle Boy),* Diane Lane *(Patty),* Dennis Hopper *(Father),* Diana Scarwid *(Cassandra),* Vincent Spano *(Steve),* Nicolas Cage *(Smokey),* Christopher Penn *(B. J. Jackson),* Larry Fishburne *(Midget),* William Smith *(Patterson),* Michael Higgins *(Mr. Harrigan),* Glenn Withrow *(Biff Wilcox),* Tom Waits *(Benny),* Herb Rice *(Pool Player),* Maybelle Wallace *(Late Pass Clerk),* Nona Manning *(Patty's Mother),* Domino *(Patty's Sister),* Gio *(Cousin James),* S. E. Hinton *(Hooker)*
Produced by Fred Roos and Doug Claybourne for Zoetrope Studios, released through Universal. Executive producer: Francis Ford Coppola. Associate producers: Gian-Carlo Coppola and Roman Coppola. 94 minutes.

The Cotton Club (1984)

Screenplay: William Kennedy and Francis Ford Coppola, from a story by
William Kennedy, Francis Ford Coppola, and Mario Puzo, suggested by a pictorial
history by James Haskins
Direction: Francis Ford Coppola
Photography (Technicolor): Stephen Goldblatt
Production Design: Richard Sylbert
Art Direction: David Chapman and Gregory Bolton
Costumes: Milena Canonero
Principal Choreographer: Michael Smuin
Tap Choreographer: Henry LeTang
Sound Editing: Edward Beyer
Montage and Second-Unit Director: Gian-Carlo Coppola
Editing: Barry Malkin and Robert Q. Lovett
Music: John Barry and Bob Wilber
Cast: Richard Gere *(Dixie Dwyer),* Gregory Hines *(Sandman Williams),* Diane Lane *(Vera Cicero),* Lonette McKee *(Lila Rose Oliver),* Bob Hoskins *(Owney Madden),* James

Remar *(Dutch Schultz)*, Nicolas Cage *(Vincent Dwyer)*, Allen Garfield *(Abbadabba Berman)*, Fred Gwynne *(Frenchy)*, Gwen Verdon *(Tish Dwyer)*, Lisa Jane Persky *(Frances Flegenheimer)*, Maurice Hines *(Clay Williams)*, Julian Beck *(Sol Weinstein)*, Novella Nelson *(Madame St. Claire)*, Larry Fishburne *(Bumpy Rhodes)*, John Ryan *(Joe Flynn)*, Tom Waits *(Irving Stark)*
Produced by Robert Evans. Producer consultant: Milton Forman. Coproducers: Silvio Tabet and Fred Roos. Executive producer: Dyson Lovell. Line producers: Barrie M. Osborne and Joseph Cusumano. 122 minutes.

Rip Van Winkle (1985)

Screenplay: Francis Ford Coppola, from the story by Washington Irving
Direction: Francis Ford Coppola
Lighting Director: George Riesenberger
Cast: Harry Dean Stanton *(Rip Van Winkle)*, Talia Shire *(Rip's Wife)*, Sofia Coppola, Hunter Carson
Produced for HBO's *Faerie Tale Theatre* television series. 50 minutes.

Captain Eo (1986)

Direction: Francis Ford Coppola
Photography (70-mm 3-D): Vittorio Storaro
Choreography: Jeffrey Hornaday
Second-Unit Director: Gian-Carlo Coppola
Editing: Walter Murch
Music: Michael Jackson
Cast: Michael Jackson *(Captain Eo)*, Anjelica Huston *(She-Devil Supreme)*
Produced by Lucasfilm Ltd. for Disney. 17 minutes.

Peggy Sue Got Married (1986)

Screenplay: Jerry Leichtling and Arlene Sarner
Direction: Francis Ford Coppola
Photography (Deluxe): Jordan Cronenweth
Electronic Cinema: Murdo Laird, Ted Mackland, and Ron Mooreland
Production Design: Dean Tavoularis
Art Direction: Alex Tavoularis
Costumes: Theadora Van Runkle
Supervisory Sound Editing: Michael Kirchberger
Editing: Barry Malkin
Music: John Barry
Cast: Kathleen Turner *(Peggy Sue Kelcher)*, Nicolas Cage *(Charlie Bodell)*, Barry Miller *(Richard Norvik)*, Catherine Hicks *(Carol Heath)*, Joan Allen *(Maddie Nagle)*, Kevin J. O'Connor *(Michael Fitzsimmons)*, Jim Carrey *(Walter Getz)*, Lisa Jane Persky *(Dolores Dodge)*, Lucinda Jenney *(Rosalie Testa)*, Wil Shriner *(Arthur Nagle)*, Barbara Harris *(Evelyn Kelcher)*, Don Murray *(Jack Kelcher)*, Sofia Coppola *(Nancy Kelcher)*, Maureen O'Sullivan *(Elizabeth Alvorg)*, Leon Ames *(Barney Alvorg)*, with Helen Hunt and John Carradine
Produced by Paul R. Gurian for Tri-Star-Delphi IV and V, for Rastar. A Paul R. Gurian/Zoetrope Studios Production. Executive producer: Barrie M. Osborne. 104 minutes.

Gardens of Stone (1987)

Screenplay: Ronald Bass, based on the novel by Nicholas Proffitt
Direction: Francis Ford Coppola

Photography (Deluxe): Jordan Cronenweth
Production Design: Dean Tavoularis
Art Direction: Alex Tavoularis
Costumes: Will Kim and Judianna Makovsky
Sound Design: Richard Beggs
Editing: Barry Malkin
Music: Carmine Coppola
Cast: James Caan *(Clell Hazard),* Anjelica Huston *(Samantha Davis),* James Earl Jones *(Sgt. Maj. Goody Nelson),* D. B. Sweeney *(Jackie Willow),* Dean Stockwell *(Homer Thomas),* Mary Stuart Masterson *(Rachel Feld),* Dick Anthony Williams *(Slasher Williams),* Lonette McKee *(Betty Rae),* Sam Bottoms *(Lieutenant Webber),* Elias Koteas *(Pete Deveber),* Larry Fishburne *(Flanagan),* Casey Siemaszko *(Wildman),* Peter Masterson *(Colonel Feld),* Carlin Glynn *(Mrs. Feld),* Erik Holland *(Colonel Godwin),* Bill Graham *(Don Brubaker)*
Produced by Michael I. Levy and Francis Ford Coppola for Tri-Star–ML Delphi Premier Productions. Executive producers: Stan Weston, Jay Emmett, and Fred Roos. Coexecutive producer: David Valdes. 111 minutes.

Tucker: The Man and His Dream (1988)

Screenplay: Arnold Schulman and David Seidler
Direction: Francis Ford Coppola
Photography (Technicolor, Technovision): Vittorio Storaro
Production Design: Dean Tavoularis
Art Direction: Alex Tavoularis
Costumes: Milena Canonero
Sound Design: Richard Beggs
Editing: Priscilla Nedd
Music: Joe Jackson
Cast: Jeff Bridges *(Preston Tucker),* Joan Allen *(Vera),* Martin Landau *(Abe Karatz),* Frederic Forrest *(Eddie),* Mako *(Jimmy),* Elias Koteas *(Alex),* Christian Slater *(Junior),* Nina Siemaszko *(Marilyn Lee),* Anders Johnson *(Johnny),* Corky Nemec *(Noble),* Marshall Bell *(Frank),* Jay O. Sanders *(Kirby),* Peter Donat *(Kerner),* Lloyd Bridges *(Senator Ferguson),* Dean Goodman *(Bennington),* John X. Heart *(Ferguson's Aide),* Don Novello *(Stan),* Patti Austin *(Millie),* Sandy Bull *(Stan's Assistant),* Joseph Miksak *(Judge),* Scott Beach *(Floyd Cerf),* Roland Scrivner *(Oscar Beasley),* Dean Stockwell *(Howard Hughes),* Bob Safford *(Narrator),* Larry Menkin *(Doc),* Ron Close *(Fritz),* Joe Flood *(Dutch)*
Produced by Fred Roos and Fred Fuchs for Lucasfilm Ltd., released through Paramount. Executive producer: George Lucas. Associate producer: Teri Fettis. 111 minutes.

Life Without Zoe (Segment two in *New York Stories*) (1989)

Screenplay: Francis Ford Coppola and Sofia Coppola
Direction: Francis Ford Coppola
Photography (Technicolor): Vittorio Storaro
Production Design: Dean Tavoularis
Art Direction: Speed Hopkins
Costumes: Sofia Coppola
Sound Recording: Frank Graziadei
Editing: Barry Malkin
Music: Carmine Coppola
Songs: Kid Creole and the Coconuts

Cast: Heather McComb *(Zoe)*, Talia Shire *(Charlotte)*, Gia Coppola *(Baby Zoe)*, Giancarlo Giannini *(Claudio)*, Paul Herman *(Clifford)*, James Keane *(Jimmy)*, Don Novello *(Hector)*, Bill Moor *(Mr. Lilly)*, Tom Mardirosian *(Hasid)*, Jenny Bichold *(Lundy)*, Gia Scianni *(Devo)*, Diane Lin Cosman *(Margit)*, Selim Tlili *(Abu)*, Robin Wood-Chapelle *(Gel)*, Celia Nestell *(Hillary)*, Alexdra Becker *(Andrea)*, Adrien Brody *(Mel)*, Michael Higgins *(Robber)*, Chris Elliott *(Robber)*, Thelma Carpenter *(Maid)*, Carmine Coppola *(Street Musician)*, Carole Bouquet *(Princess Soroya)*, Jo Jo Starbuck *(Ice Skater)*
Segment producers: Fred Roos and Fred Fuchs for Touchstone Pictures. 34 minutes.

The Godfather, Part III (1990)

Screenplay: Mario Puzo and Francis Ford Coppola
Direction: Francis Ford Coppola
Photography (Technicolor): Gordon Willis
Production Design: Dean Tavoularis
Art Direction: Alex Tavoularis
Costumes: Milena Canonero
Sound Design: Richard Beggs
Editing: Barry Malkin, Lisa Fruchtman, and Walter Murch
Music: Carmine Coppola
Additional Music and Themes: Nino Rota
Cast: Al Pacino *(Michael Corleone)*, Diane Keaton *(Kay Adams)*, Talia Shire (Connie Corleone Rizzi), Andy Garcia *(Vincent Mancini)*, Eli Wallach *(Don Altobello)*, Joe Mantegna *(Joey Zasa)*, George Hamilton *(B. J. Harrison)*, Bridget Fonda *(Grace Hamilton)*, Sofia Coppola *(Mary Corleone)*, Raf Vallone *(Cardinal Lamberto)*, Franc D'Ambrosio *(Anthony Corleone)*, Donal Donnelly *(Archbishop Gliday)*, Richard Bright *(Al Neri)*, Helmut Berger *(Frederick Keinszig)*, Don Novello *(Dominic Abbandando)*, John Savage *(Andrew Hagen)*, Franco Citti *(Calo)*, Mario Donatone *(Mosca)*, Vittorio Duse *(Don Tommasino)*, Enzo Robutti *(Lucchesi)*, Michele Russo *(Spara)*, Al Martino *(Johnny Fontane)*, Robert Cicchini *(Lou Pennino)*, Rogerio Miranda *(Armand)*, Carlos Miranda *(Francesco)*, Jeannie Linero *(Lucy Mancini)*
Produced by Francis Ford Coppola for Zoetrope Studios, released through Paramount Pictures. Executive producers: Fred Fuchs and Nicholas Gage. Coproducers: Fred Roos, Gray Frederickson, and Charles Mulvehill. Associate producer: Marina Gefter. 161 minutes.

Bram Stoker's Dracula (1992)

Screenplay: James V. Hart
Direction: Francis Ford Coppola
Photography (Technicolor): Michael Ballhaus
Production Design: Thomas Sanders
Art Direction: Andrew Precht
Costumes: Eiko Ishioka
Visual Effects: Roman Coppola
Sound: David Stone
Editing: Nicholas C. Smith, Glenn Scantlebury, and Anne Goursaud
Music: Wojciech Kilar
Cast: Gary Oldman *(Dracula)*, Winona Ryder *(Mina/Elisabeta)*, Anthony Hopkins *(Abraham Van Helsing)*, Keanu Reeves *(Jonathan Harker)*, Sadie Frost *(Lucy Westenra)*, Richard E. Grant *(Dr. Jack Seward)*, Cary Elwes *(Arthur Holmwood)*, Bill Campbell *(Quincey Morris)*, Tom Waits *(Renfield)*, Monica Bellucci *(Dracula's Bride)*, Michaela Bercu *(Dracula's Bride)*, Florina Kendrick *(Dracula's Bride)*, Jay Robinson *(Mr.*

Hawkins), I. M. Hobson *(Hobbs)*, Laurie Frank *(Lucy's Maid)*
Produced by Francis Ford Coppola, Fred Fuchs, and Charles Mulvehill for American Zoetrope/Osiris Films, released through Columbia Pictures. Executive producers: Michael Apted and Robert O'Connor. Coproducer: James V. Hart. Associate producer: Susie Landau. 123 minutes.

Jack (1996)

Screenplay: James DeMonaco and Gary Nadeau
Direction: Francis Ford Coppola
Photography (Technicolor): John Toll
Production Design: Dean Tavoularis
Art Direction: Angelo Graham
Costumes: Aggie Guerard Rodgers
Sound: Agamemnon Andrianos
Editing: Barry Malkin
Music: Michael Kamen
Cast: Robin Williams *(Jack Powell)*, Diane Lane *(Karen Powell)*, Jennifer Lopez *(Miss Marquez)*, Brian Kerwin *(Brian Powell)*, Fran Drescher *(Dolores Durante)*, Bill Cosby *(Lawrence Woodruff)*, Michael McKean *(Paulie)*, Don Novello *(Bartender)*, Allan Rich *(Dr. Benfante)*, Adam Zolotin *(Louis Durante)*, Todd Bosley *(Edward)*, Seth Smith *(John-John)*, Mario Yedidia *(George)*, Jeremy Lelliott *(Johnny Duffer)*, Rickey O'Shon Collins *(Eric)*, Hugo Hernandez *(Victor)*
Produced by Ricardo Mestres, Fred Fuchs, and Francis Ford Coppola for American Zoetrope/Great Oaks, released through Buena Vista. Executive producer: Doug Claybourne. 113 minutes.

John Grisham's The Rainmaker (1997)

Screenplay: Francis Ford Coppola, based on the novel by John Grisham
Direction: Francis Ford Coppola
Photography (Deluxe): John Toll
Production Design: Howard Cummings
Art Direction: Robert Shaw, Jeffrey McDonald
Costumes: Aggie Guerard Rodgers
Sound: Nelson Stoll
Editing: Barry Malkin
Music: Elmer Bernstein
Cast: Matt Damon *(Rudy Baylor)*, Claire Danes *(Kelly Riker)*, Jon Voight *(Leo F. Drummond)*, Mary Kay Place *(Dot Black)*, Mickey Rourke *(Bruiser Stone)*, Danny DeVito *(Deck Shifflet)*, Dean Stockwell *(Judge Harvey Hale)*, Teresa Wright *(Miss Birdie)*, Virginia Madsen *(Jackie Lemancyzk)*, Andrew Shue *(Cliff Riker)*, Red West *(Buddy Black)*, Johnny Whitworth *(Donny Ray Black)*, Danny Glover *(Judge Tyrone Kipler)*, Wayne Emmons *(Prince Thomas)*, Adrian Roberts *(Butch)*, Roy Scheider *(Wilfred Keeley)*, Randy Travis *(Billy Porter)*, Michael Girardin *(Everett Lufkin)*, Randall King *(Jack Underhall)*, Justin Ashforth *(F. Franklin Donaldson)*, Michael Keys Hall *(B. Bobby Shaw)*
Produced by Michael Douglas, Steven Reuther, and Fred Fuchs for Constellation Films/Douglas/Reuther Productions/American Zoetrope, released through Paramount Pictures. Coproducer: Georgia Kacandes. Associate producer: Gary Scott Marcus. 135 minutes.

Selected Bibliography

Bach, Steven. *Final Cut.* New York: William Morrow, 1985.

Baker, Fred, with Ross Firestone, eds., *Movie People, At Work in the Film Industry.* London: Abelard-Schuman, 1972.

Benedictus, David. *You're a Big Boy Now.* New York: E. P. Dutton, 1964.

Bergan, Ronald. *Francis Ford Coppola.* New York: Thunder's Mouth Press, 1998.

Bernard, Jami. *First Films: Illustrious, Obscure, and Embarrassing Movie Debuts.* New York: Citadel Press, 1993.

Biskind, Peter. *Easy Riders, Raging Bulls: How the Sex-Drugs-and-Rock 'n' Roll Generation Saved Hollywood.* New York: Simon and Schuster, 1998.

——. *The Godfather Companion.* New York: HarperPerennial, 1990.

Bjorkman, Stig. *Woody Allen on Woody Allen.* New York: Grove Press, 1995.

Boorman, John, and Walter Donahue, eds., *Projections 3: Filmmakers on Filmmaking.* London: Faber and Faber, 1994.

——. *Projections 6: Filmmakers on Filmmaking.* London: Faber and Faber, 1996.

Brady, Frank. *Citizen Welles.* New York: Charles Scribner's Sons, 1989.

Brady, John. *The Craft of the Screenwriter.* New York: Simon and Schuster, 1981.

Brando, Marlon, with Robert Lindsey. *Brando: Songs My Mother Taught Me.* New York: Random House, 1994.

Breskin, David. *Inner Views: Filmmakers in Conversation.* Boston: Faber and Faber, 1992. Updated, expanded edition: New York: Da Capo Press, 1997.

Carey, Gary. *Marlon Brando: The Only Contender.* New York: St. Martin's Press, 1985.

Chaillet, Jean-Paul, and Elizabeth Vincent. *Francis Ford Coppola.* New York: St. Martin's Press, 1984.

Chase, Donald. *The Collaborative Art.* Boston: Little, Brown and Company, 1975.

Chown, Jeffrey. *Hollywood Auteur: Francis Coppola.* New York: Praeger, 1988.

Clark, Randall, ed., *American Screenwriters.* Detroit: Gale Research Company, 1986.

Conrad, Joseph. *Heart of Darkness.* New York: Signet, 1950.

Coppola, Eleanor. *Notes.* New York: Simon and Schuster, 1979.

Coppola, Francis Ford, and James V. Hart. *Bram Stoker's Dracula: The Film and the Legend.* New York: Newmarket Press, 1992,

——, and Eiko Ishioka. *Coppola and Eiko on Bram Stoker's Dracula.* Edited by Susan Dworkin, San Francisco: HarperCollins, 1992.

Corman, Roger, with Jim Jerome. *How I Made a Hundred Movies in Hollywood and Never Lost a Dime.* New York: Random House, 1990.

Cowie, Peter. *Coppola.* New York: Charles Scribner's Sons, 1989.

Evans, Robert. *The Kid Stays in the Picture.* New York: Hyperion, 1994.

Farber, Stephen, and Marc Green. *Hollywood Dynasties.* New York: Delilah, 1984.

Gardner, Gerald, and Harriet Modell Gardner, *The Godfather Movies: A Pictorial History.* New York: Wings Books, 1993,

Gelmis, Joseph. *The Film Director as Superstar.* Garden City, New York: Doubleday & Co., 1979.

Goldman, William. *Adventures in the Screen Trade.* New York: Warner Books, 1983.

Goodwin, Michael, and Naomi Wise. *On the Edge: The Life and Times of Francis Coppola.* New York: William Morrow, 1989.

Grobel, Lawrence. *Conversations with Brando.* New York: Hyperion, 1991.

Hickenlooper, George. *Reel Conversations: Candid Interviews with Film's Foremost Directors and Critics.* New York: Citadel Press, 1991.

Hinton, S. E. *The Outsiders.* New York: Dell, 1970.

——. *Rumble Fish.* New York: Dell, 1976.

Jacobs, Diane. *Hollywood Renaissance.* New Jersey: A. S. Barnes & Company, 1977.

Johnson, Robert. *Francis Ford Coppola.* Boston: Twayne Publishers, 1977.

Kennedy, William. *Riding the Yellow Trolley Car.* New York: Viking, 1993.

Kolker, Robert, *A Cinema of Loneliness.* New York: Oxford University Press, 1980.

Lebo, Harlan, *The Godfather Legacy.* New York: Fireside, 1997.

Lewis, Jon, *Whom God Wishes to Destroy . . . Francis Coppola and the New Hollywood.* Durham, North Carolina: Duke University Press, 1995.

Loeb, Anthony. *Filmmakers in Conversation.* Chicago: Columbia College, 1982.

Lourdeaux, Lee. *Italian and Irish Filmmakers in America.* Philadelphia: Temple University Press, 1990.

Lumet, Sidney. *Making Movies.* New York: Alfred A. Knopf, 1995.

Madsen, Axel. *The New Hollywood: American Movies in the '70's.* New York: Thomas Y. Crowell, 1975.

Manso, Peter. *Brando.* New York: Hyperion, 1994.

McBride, Joseph. *Steven Spielberg: A Biography.* New York: Simon and Schuster, 1997.

McGee, Mark Thomas. *Roger Corman: The Best of the Cheap Acts.* Jefferson, North Carolina: McFarland, 1988.

McGilligan, Patrick, ed. *Backstory 3.* Berkeley: University of California Press, 1997.

——. *Robert Altman: Jumping off the Cliff.* New York: St. Martin's Press, 1989.

Monaco, James. *American Film Now: The People, the Power, the Money, the Movies.* New York: Oxford University Press, 1979.

Naha, Ed. *Roger Corman: Brilliance on a Budget.* New York: Arco, 1982.

Pollack, Dale. *Skywalking: The Life and Films of George Lucas.* New York: Harmony Books, 1983. Revised edition: Hollywood: Samuel French, 1990.

Proffitt, Nicholas. *Gardens of Stone.* New York: Carroll and Graf, 1983.

Puzo, Mario. *The Godfather.* New York: G. P. Putnam's Sons, 1969.

——. *The Godfather Papers and Other Confessions.* New York: Manor Books, 1972.

Pye, Michael, and Lynda Myles. *The Movie Brats.* New York: Holt, Rinehart and Winston, 1979.

Reed, Rex. *Conversations in the Raw: Dialogues, Monologues, and Selected Short Subjects.* New York: World Publishing, 1969.

Riordan, James. *Stone.* New York: Hyperion, 1995.

Schaefer, Dennis, and Larry Salvato. *Masters of Light: Conversations with Contemporary Cinematographers.* Oakland, California: University of California Press, 1984.

Singleton, Ralph S. *Film Scheduling.* Los Angeles: Lone Eagle Publishing Co., 1984; revised edition, 1992.

Smith, Dian G., *American Filmmakers Today.* New York and Poole, Dorset, England: Blandford Press, 1983, 1984.

Travers, Peter, ed. *The Rolling Stone Film Reader.* New York: Pocket Books, 1996.

von Gunden, Kenneth. *Postmodern Auteurs.* Jefferson, North Carolina: McFarland, 1991.

Welles, Orson, and Peter Bogdanovich. *This is Orson Welles.* New York: Da Capo Press, 1992. Revised, expanded edition: New York: Da Capo Press, 1998.

Yule, Andrew. *Life on the Wire: The Life and Art of Al Pacino.* New York: Donald I. Fine, 1991.

Zuckerman, Ira. *The Godfather Journal.* New York: Manor Books, 1972.

Zuker, Joel. *Francis Ford Coppola: A Guide to the References and Resources.* Boston: G. K. Hall, 1984.

Acknowledgments

First and foremost, I wish to thank Francis Ford Coppola for his assistance in the preparation of this book. This is not an authorized biography in the traditional sense. The book was written before I had exchanged a single word with its subject, but when I contacted Coppola upon its completion, he indicated that he would appreciate the opportunity to look at the manuscript for its factual content; he promised not to challenge my judgments or interpretations, and he was good to his word. I did tell him that I would be willing to publish his side of the story whenever he contested what I or someone else had written or said about him, and there were a number of occasions when this occurred. This might not be the usual way that biographies are written, but given the incredible amount of error that I confronted during my research, and Coppola's sometimes contentious relationship with the media, I felt it fair to give him the opportunity. Not only did he not abuse the opportunity; he also answered any questions—and there were many—that I posed to him. He helped in numerous other ways, from opening doors to arranging other interviews that would have been otherwise unavailable, to supplying me with valuable source material, including the original script for *Patton*. Coppola might not agree with everything presented in this book, but I hope he finds it fair and accurate.

My thanks also to his family members, who answered my questions and offered significant contributions, often in the eleventh hour. Eleanor Coppola, a talented artist in her own right, provided me with valuable information about her husband, including details about their relationship, their family, and the tragic death of their oldest son, Gian-Carlo Coppola. Roman Coppola and Sofia Coppola, both developing successful careers in the business, offered insights into their father's life and career. August Coppola, Francis's brother, and Talia Shire, his sister, were especially helpful in offering details about their ancestry and Francis's childhood, as well as in contributing insight on Coppola's professional life.

People in the entertainment industry tend to be elusive and very busy; they may be spread out all over the world, working or promoting their latest projects, or vacationing or staying away from the public. To attain information for this book, I conducted every conceivable form of interview—including by telephone, E-mail, and fax—and I am grateful to those of Coppola's friends and colleagues, actors and actresses who worked on his films, and others who have known and dealt with him, who took the time to talk to me or supply me with needed information: Carroll Ballard, James Caan, Robert Chapman, Roger Corman, Frederic Forrest, Gray Frederickson, William Kennedy, Diane Lane, George Lucas, Tom Luddy, Barry Malkin, Walter Murch, Joel Oliansky, Mario Puzo, Fred Roos, Al Ruddy, Martin Sheen, Mona Skager, Alex Tavoularis, Dean Tavoularis, and Kathleen Turner. Thanks also to writers Peter Biskind, Harlan Lebo, Patrick McGilligan, and James Riordan, who offered valuable tips, insights, and information about the motion picture business, and to Lynne Hale and Karen Rose at Lucasfilm Ltd., who helped with my interview with George Lucas. At the Zoetrope offices, I was helped immensely by Shannon Lail, Coppola's personal assistant, and by Anahid Nazarian, his archivist.

I owe a debt of gratitude to the staff of the Margaret Herrick Library of the Academy of Motion Picture Arts and Sciences in Los Angeles, who helped immeasurably in the early research for this book. I am also grateful to the staffs at the University of Wisconsin–Parkside library and the Milwaukee Public Library for their assistance.

I have included a bibliography of the books that I found useful in my research for this volume, but I would like to make a point of singling out certain Coppola biographies and studies that were of special importance: *Coppola,* by Peter Cowie; *On the Edge: The Life and Times of Francis Coppola,* by Michael Goodwin and Naomi Wise; *Whom God Wishes to Destroy . . . Francis Coppola and the New Hollywood,* by Jon Lewis; *Francis Ford Coppola,* by Jean-Paul Chaillet and Elizabeth Vincent; *Notes,* by Eleanor Coppola; *Hollywood Auteur,* by Jeffrey Chown; and *The Godfather Legacy,* by Harlan Lebo. All of these books provided needed direction and insight when I was trying to piece together the life of the filmmaker.

Thanks to the present and former staff at Crown who helped see this book into print: Michael Denneny, who picked up the project; Karen Rinaldi, who encouraged me throughout its writing; and Bob Mecoy, who saw this biography to the finish line. Thanks also to Panio Gianopoulos and Pete Fornatale, who were occasionally caught in the crossfire, but who showed cheer and intelligence in a business often lacking in both.

Thanks Kim Witherspoon, Maria Massie, Gideon Weil, and Josh Greenhut at Witherspoon Associates for professional guidance, and for enduring my occasional bouts of frustration. I'm lucky to have them in my corner.

In knowing Carol Edwards, I am doubly blessed: Not only is she one of my most valued friends, she is also as gifted and conscientious a copy editor as I could ever hope to have work on one of my books.

A tip of the cap to those who assisted in other ways: Al and Diane Schumacher, Ken and Karen Ade, Jim Sieger, Mark Gumbinger, Amelie Littell, Glen Puterbaugh, and Simma Holt.

As always, I save the most important for last. Thanks once again, and always, to my wife, Susan, who has seen the best and worst that a writing career can visit upon a family, and to my children—Adam, Emily Joy, and Jack Henry—who always manage to keep my life in perspective.

—Michael Schumacher
May 1, 1999

Index